VISUALIZING
ELEMENTARY AND MIDDLE SCHOOL MATHEMATICS METHODS

JOAN COHEN JONES, PhD
EASTERN MICHIGAN UNIVERSITY

Visualizing Elementary & Middle School Mathematics Methods offers future teachers the opportunity to learn about teaching mathematics with real-life examples, multicultural perspectives, and powerful visuals. This dynamic approach enables students to set aside their previous beliefs about mathematics and to learn concepts and pedagogy from a new perspective.

For example, using a real-life visual like a lighthouse can help teach math in a meaningful way. Many lighthouses, like the one pictured above (an interior and an exterior photo) and on the front cover, were built with spiral staircases because they take up less floor space than traditional staircases. In addition to being used for decorative and architectural purposes, spiral curves have been studied by mathematicians since the time of the ancient Greeks. They appear in many forms—including the shell of a snail, the structure of a chambered nautilus, and the shape of a whirlpool—a reminder that math is everywhere.

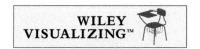

Credits

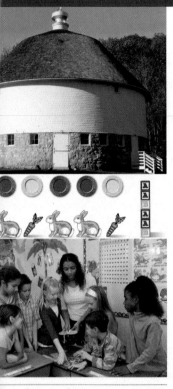

VICE PRESIDENT AND EXECUTIVE PUBLISHER   Jay O'Callaghan
EXECUTIVE EDITOR   Christopher Johnson
ACQUISITIONS EDITOR   Robert Johnston
DIRECTOR OF DEVELOPMENT   Barbara Heaney
MANAGER, PRODUCT DEVELOPMENT   Nancy Perry
WILEY VISUALIZING PROJECT EDITOR   Beth Tripmacher
WILEY VISUALIZING SENIOR EDITORIAL ASSISTANT   Tiara Kelly
PROGRAM ASSISTANT   Brittany Cheetham
EDITORIAL ASSISTANT   Mariah Maguire-Fong
ASSOCIATE DIRECTOR, MARKETING   Jeffrey Rucker
SENIOR MARKETING MANAGER   Danielle Torio Hagey
CONTENT MANAGER   Micheline Frederick
SENIOR MEDIA EDITOR   Lynn Pearlman
CREATIVE DIRECTOR   Harry Nolan
COVER DESIGN   Harry Nolan
INTERIOR DESIGN   Jim O'Shea
PHOTO MANAGER   Elle Wagner
PHOTO RESEARCHER   Teri Stratford
SENIOR ILLUSTRATION EDITOR   Sandra Rigby
PRODUCTION SERVICES   Camelot Editorial Services, LLC

COVER CREDITS: Main Image: Geri Lynn Smith/iStockphoto
Filmstrip (from left to right): Myrleen Ferguson Cate/PhotoEdit; GEORGE GRALL/
NG Image Collection; Clare Hooper/Alamy; Wealan Pollard/OJO Images/Getty Images, Inc.;
RAYMOND GEHMAN/NG Image Collection
Back Main Image: Kenneth C. Zirkel/iStock Exclusive/Getty Images, Inc.
Back Inset: Myrleen Ferguson Cate/PhotoEdit

This book was set in New Baskerville by Silver Editions, Inc. and printed and bound by Quad/
Graphics, Inc. The cover was printed by Quad/Graphics, Inc.

ISBN 13: 978-0470-450314

Printed in the United States of America
10 9 8 7 6 5 4 3 2 1

Preface

How Is Wiley Visualizing Different?

Wiley Visualizing differs from competing textbooks by uniquely combining several powerful elements: a visual pedagogy, integrated with comprehensive text; the use of authentic classroom situations and activities, actual materials from children's literature and publications such as *Mathematics Teaching Today, Teaching Children Mathematics,* and *Mathematics Teaching in the Middle School,* and the integration of *Teachscape* videos.

1. Visual Pedagogy. Wiley Visualizing is based on decades of research on the use of visuals in learning (Mayer, 2005).[1] Using the Cognitive Theory of Multimedia Learning, which is backed up by hundreds of empirical research studies, Wiley's authors select visualizations for their texts that specifically support students' thinking and learning. Visuals and text are conceived and planned together in ways that clarify and reinforce major concepts while allowing students to understand the details. This commitment to distinctive and consistent visual pedagogy sets Wiley Visualizing apart from other textbooks.

2. Authentic Classroom Situations, Activities, and Materials. Wiley Visualizing provides the pre-service teacher with an abundance of class-tested hands-on activities and full Lesson Plans based on NCTM and Common Core State Standards. *In the Classroom* features present images and research-based classroom practices, and *Multicultural Perspectives in Mathematics* features provide content-rich, culturally relevant examples of mathematics and its place in the world. Each chapter presents illustrations from children's books that contain exciting connections to mathematics content and offers detailed teaching strategies. These authentic situations and materials immerse the student in real-life issues in mathematics education, thereby enhancing motivation, learning, and retention (Donovan & Bransford, 2005).[2]

3. Teachscape Videos. Through a partnership with **Teachscape** professional development series, Wiley Visualizing provides a collection of online videocases featuring rich, authentic classroom situations, teacher reflection, and interviews. Each of the videocases is referenced within the chapters, supporting the relevant content. The combination of textbook and video provides learners with multiple entry points to the content, giving them greater opportunity to explore and apply concepts.

Wiley Visualizing is designed as a natural extension of how we learn

To understand why the visualizing approach is effective, it is first helpful to understand how we learn.

1. Our brain processes information using two main channels: visual and verbal. Our *working memory* holds information that our minds process as we learn. This "mental workbench" helps us with decisions, problem solving, and making sense of words and pictures by building verbal and visual models of the information.

2. When the verbal and visual models of corresponding information are integrated in working memory, we form more comprehensive, lasting mental models.

3. When we link these integrated mental models to our prior knowledge, which is stored in our *long-term memory*, we build even stronger mental models. When an integrated (visual plus verbal) mental model is formed and stored in long-term memory, real learning begins.

The effort our brains put forth to make sense of instructional information is called *cognitive load*. There are two kinds of cognitive load: productive cognitive load, such as when we're engaged in learning or exert positive effort to create mental models; and unproductive cognitive load, which occurs when the brain is trying to make sense of needlessly complex content or when information is not presented well. The learning process can be impaired when the information to be processed exceeds the capacity of working memory. Well-designed visuals and text with effective pedagogical guidance can reduce the unproductive cognitive load in our working memory.

Research shows that well-designed visuals, integrated with comprehensive text, can improve the efficiency with which a learner processes information. In this regard, SEG Research, an independent research firm, conducted a national, multisite study evaluating the effectiveness of Wiley Visualizing. Its findings indicate that students using Wiley Visualizing products (both print and multimedia) were more engaged in the course, exhibited greater retention throughout the course, and made significantly greater gains in content area knowledge and skills, as compared to students in similar classes that did not use Wiley Visualizing.[3]

---

[1]Mayer, R. E. (Ed.) (2005). The Cambridge Handbook of Multimedia Learning. New York: Cambridge University Press.

[2]Donovan, M. S., & Bransford, J. (Eds.) (2005). How Students Learn: Science in the Classroom. The National Academy Press. Available online at http://www.nap.edu/openbook.php?record_id=11102&page=1.

[3]SEG Research (2009). Improving Student-Learning with Graphically-Enhanced Textbooks: A Study of the Effectiveness of the Wiley Visualizing Series.

How Are the Wiley Visualizing Chapters Organized?

Student engagement requires more than just providing visuals, text, and interactivity—it entails motivating students to learn. It is easy to get bored or lose focus when presented with large amounts of information, and it is easy to lose motivation when the relevance of the information is unclear. Wiley Visualizing organizes course content into manageable learning modules and relates it to everyday life. It transforms learning into an interactive, stimulating, and outcomes-oriented experience for students.

Each learning module has a clear instructional objective, one or more examples, and an opportunity for assessment. These modules are the building blocks of Wiley Visualizing.

Each Wiley Visualizing chapter engages students from the start

Chapter opening text and visuals introduce the subject and connect the student with the material that follows.

Chapter Introductions Alongside striking photographs, narratives recount intriguing classroom experiences to evoke student interest in the chapter's central mathematics concept.

Chapter Outlines provide **Key Questions** to guide students through the chapter.

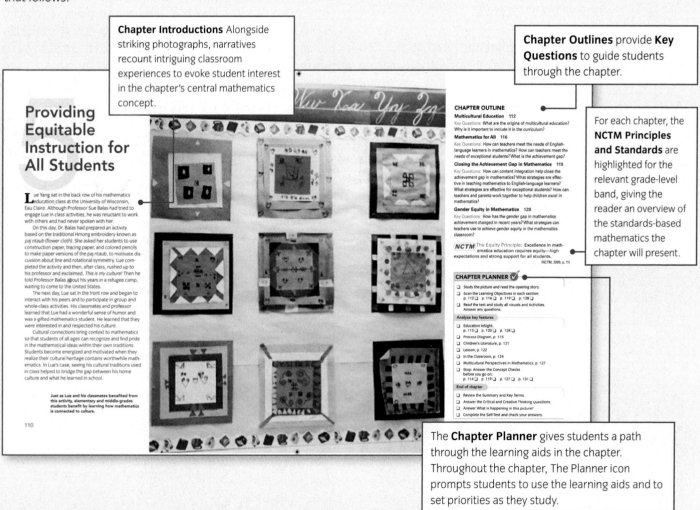

For each chapter, the **NCTM Principles and Standards** are highlighted for the relevant grade-level band, giving the reader an overview of the standards-based mathematics the chapter will present.

The **Chapter Planner** gives students a path through the learning aids in the chapter. Throughout the chapter, The Planner icon prompts students to use the learning aids and to set priorities as they study.

Wiley Visualizing guides students through the chapter

The content of Wiley Visualizing gives students a variety of approaches—visuals, words, interactions, video, and assessments—that work together to provide students with a guided path through the content.

Learning Objectives at the start of each section indicate in behavioral terms the concepts that students are expected to master while reading the section.

Teaching Mathematics with Children's Literature

LEARNING OBJECTIVES

1. **Explain** the value of teaching with children's literature.
2. **Identify** the characteristics of effective children's literature.
3. **Describe** techniques for effectively teaching with children's literature.

Storytelling is an ancient art form that originated as an oral tradition when storytellers memorized and shaped their tales to meet the needs of their audience (**Figure 3.8**). Children's literature is a modern adaptation of storytelling that has become popular in elementary education because it provides children with experiences that relate to their own lives or to situations with which they are familiar.

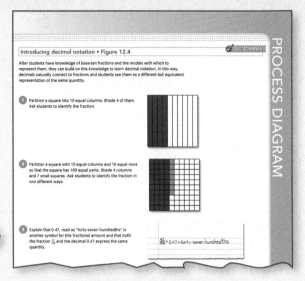

PROCESS DIAGRAM

Introducing decimal notation • Figure 12.4

After students have knowledge of base-ten fractions and the models with which to represent them, they can build on this knowledge to learn decimal notation. In this way, decimals naturally connect to fractions and students see them as a different but equivalent representation of the same quantity.

1. Partition a square into 10 equal columns. Shade 4 of them. Ask students to identify the fraction.

2. Partition a square with 10 equal columns and 10 equal rows so that the square has 100 equal parts. Shade 4 columns and 7 small squares. Ask students to identify the fraction in two different ways.

3. Explain that 0.47, read as "forty-seven hundredths" is another symbol for this fractional amount and that both the fraction $\frac{47}{100}$ and the decimal 0.47 express the same quantity.

Process Diagrams provide in-depth explanation of how to use mathematics pedagogy. Clear, step-by-step narrative enables students to grasp important topics with less effort.

Helping English-language learners with the language of mathematics • Figure 5.7

Some mathematical terms, such as *foot*, *plane*, *mean*, and *average*, have other meanings in real life. In addition, some words, such as *whole* and *sum*, sound like other words. Make sure to explain the mathematical meaning of these words to ELLs so they do not become confused about the meaning.

foot

plane

hole/whole — hole

whole

Throughout the text, visuals provide prospective teachers with samples of **tools** to use in the classroom. Several visuals offer tools for differentiating instruction to meet the needs of all learners.

Children's pre–base-ten ideas • Figure 8.2

Before learning place value and base ten, teachers should help children progress from counting by ones to counting ungrouped and pregrouped objects.

a. Children count by ones, even when they are counting large numbers of objects. They may be able to count accurately and tell you there are 38 counters on the table, say thirty-eight, and write the numeral 38, without understanding place value.

b. Give children lots of practice with counting and forming groups of different sizes by counting the objects they find in their everyday lives. Ask children to count the things they see in the classroom, such as crayons, rulers, calculators, paint brushes, chairs, and desks.

c. Provide children with opportunities to count objects that are already grouped. Help children to discover these groupings and discuss their benefits.

Other visuals support the text by providing glimpses of students using the materials and learning the concepts presented in the narrative.

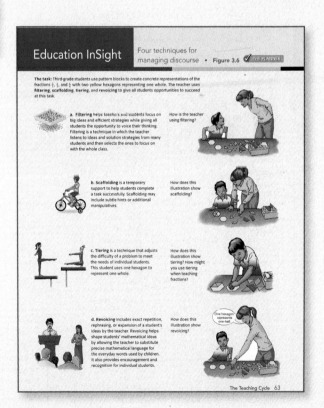

Education InSight   Four techniques for managing discourse • Figure 3.6   THE PLANNER

The task: Third-grade students use pattern blocks to create concrete representations of the fractions $\frac{1}{2}$, $\frac{1}{3}$, and $\frac{1}{6}$ with two yellow hexagons representing one whole. The teacher uses **filtering**, **scaffolding**, **tiering**, and **revoicing** to give all students opportunities to succeed at this task.

a. **Filtering** helps teachers and students focus on big ideas and efficient strategies while giving all students the opportunity to voice their thinking. Filtering is a technique in which the teacher listens to ideas and solution strategies from many students and then selects the ones to focus on with the whole class.

How is the teacher using filtering?

b. **Scaffolding** is a temporary support to help students complete a task successfully. Scaffolding may include subtle hints or additional manipulatives.

How does this illustration show scaffolding?

c. **Tiering** is a technique that adjusts the difficulty of a problem to meet the needs of individual students. This student uses one hexagon to represent one whole.

How does this illustration show tiering? How might you use tiering when teaching fractions?

d. **Revoicing** includes exact repetition, rephrasing, or expansion of a student's ideas by the teacher. Revoicing helps shape students' mathematical ideas by allowing the teacher to substitute precise mathematical language for the everyday words used by children. It also provides encouragement and recognition for individual students.

How does this illustration show revoicing?

One hexagon represents one-half.

The Teaching Cycle 63

Education InSight features are multipart visual sections that focus on a key concept or topic in the chapter, exploring it in detail or in broader context using a combination of visuals.

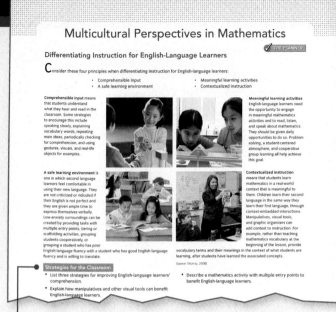

Multicultural Perspectives in Mathematics

Differentiating Instruction for English-Language Learners

Consider these four principles when differentiating instruction for English-language learners:

- Comprehensible input
- A safe learning environment
- Meaningful learning activities
- Contextualized instruction

Comprehensible input means that students understand what they hear and read in the classroom. Some strategies to encourage this include speaking slowly, explaining vocabulary words, repeating main ideas, periodically checking for comprehension, and using gestures, visuals, and real-life objects for examples.

A safe learning environment is one in which second language learners feel comfortable in using their new language. They are not criticized or ridiculed if their English is not perfect and they are given ample time to express themselves verbally. Low-anxiety surroundings can be created by providing tasks with multiple entry points, tiering or scaffolding activities, grouping students cooperatively, or grouping a student who has poor English language fluency with a student who has good English language fluency and is willing to translate.

Meaningful learning activities English-language learners need the opportunity to engage in meaningful mathematics activities and to read, listen, and speak about mathematics. Problem solving, a student-centered atmosphere, and cooperative group learning all help achieve this goal.

Contextualized instruction means that students learn mathematics in a real-world context that is meaningful to them. Children learn their second language in the same way they learn their first language, through context-embedded interactions. Manipulatives, visual tools, and graphic organizers can add context to instruction. For example, rather than teaching mathematics vocabulary at the beginning of the lesson, provide vocabulary terms and their meanings in the context of what students are learning, after students have learned the associated concepts.

(Source: Murray, 2008)

Strategies for the Classroom

- List three strategies for improving English-language learners' comprehension.
- Explain how manipulatives and other visual tools can benefit English-language learners.
- Describe a mathematics activity with multiple entry points to benefit English-language learners.

Strategies for the Classroom guide prospective teachers to analyze the material, develop insights into essential concepts, and use them in the classroom.

Multicultural Perspectives in Mathematics present content-rich, culturally relevant examples of mathematics and its place in the world.

CHILDREN'S LITERATURE

Teaching growing patterns

MITSUMASA ANNO
ANNO'S MAGIC SEEDS

Anno's Magic Seeds • Figure 14.10

Written and illustrated by Mitsumasa Anno

Jack is given two magic seeds. He eats one and plants the other. The next year, two seeds are sprouted, and he continues this pattern of eating one and planting the other. This continues for several years until he decides to plant both seeds. The next year, four seeds are sprouted. He eats one and plants the remaining three. Several events occur that change the number of seeds Jack eats and plants, and several different growing patterns can be traced.

Strategies for the Classroom

- Read the book through once with your class. Then read it again.
- Have students make a chart to keep track of the year, number of seeds eaten, planted, and produced. Ask: How many patterns can you find?

In each chapter, the **Children's Literature** feature presents illustrations from children's books that contain exciting connections to mathematics content.

Strategies for the Classroom offers detailed suggestions of how to use children's books to motivate mathematics learning.

LESSON Magic Squares

This lesson is based on an ancient Chinese legend about a turtle that was spotted on the river Lo and called Loh-Shu.

Loh-Shu

4	9	2
3	5	7
8	1	6

GRADE LEVEL
3–5

OBJECTIVES
Students will use problem-solving strategies to create magic squares.
Students will identify and create growing patterns.

STANDARDS
Grades 3–5: All students should describe, extend, and make generalizations about geometric and numeric patterns; represent and analyze patterns and functions, using words, tables, and graphs (NCTM, 2000, p. 158).

Grade 4: "Generate a number or shape pattern that follows a given rule. Identify apparent features of the pattern that were not explicit in the rule itself. For example, given the rule "Add 3" and the starting number 1, generate terms in the resulting sequence and observe that the terms appear to alternate between odd and even numbers. Explain informally why the numbers will continue to alternate in this way" (NGA Center/CCSSO, 2010).

MATERIALS
- Image of Loh-Shu
- Blank 3 x 3 grids and 4 x 4 grids for each student
- Worksheet with partially completed 3 x 3 magic squares

ASSESSMENT
Use a starting number between 1 and 5 and write a set of 9 consecutive numbers. Create a 3 x 3 magic square using the number set created.

GROUPING
Whole class, small groups, and individual

EXTENSION
Create a magic square in which the numbers in each row, column, and diagonal multiply to the same number.

Launch (5 minutes)
According to Chinese legend, more than 4000 years ago the emperor and his court were sailing on the River Loh when they spotted a turtle in the water that had had an unusual pattern on its back. Let's look at a drawing of this turtle and count the number of dots in each group (the dots in each group represent the numbers from 1 to 9).

Explore (35 to 40 minutes)
- Place the numeral that represents the number of dots in each group on the turtle's back on your 3 x 3 grid, according to its location. What do you notice? Are there any patterns? (The numbers in all rows, columns, and diagonals add up to the same number, 15.) This is called a magic square, and the sum of each row, column, and diagonal is called the magic sum. For Chinese magic squares, the magic sum is always 15.

- Next, show students a partially completed magic square grid. Have students work in groups to complete the magic square so that all the row, column, and diagonal sums equal 15 and no number is used more than once. Ask students to think about the strategies they are using.

6		8
2	9	

- As students complete their magic squares in small groups, circulate and observe or offer hints. Share results and strategies through whole-class discussion.

- Ask students to work individually to create their own magic square on a 3 x 3 grid, using the numbers from 1 to 9, with the same magic sum of 15. When students complete their squares, ask individual students to demonstrate their magic squares. Compare strategies for completing the

- Say: Now let's see whether we can create magic squares that have other magic sums. Use the numbers from 0 to 8 to make a magic square on a 3 x 3 grid. What is your magic sum? Have students share results with the class.

- Say: Work individually or in pairs, to make a new magic square with 9 consecutive numbers (such as 2 to 10 or 3 to 11) so that the sum of each row, column, and diagonal equals the same number. Have students share results with the class.

- Say: We can make magic squares on larger grids. Let's work together and use a 4 x 4 grid and the numbers 1 to 16 to create a magic square. The magic sum is 34.

Summarize (5 to 10 minutes)
- Why do you think you can make magic squares with these numbers?
- Do you notice any patterns in your magic squares? (Sample answer: You can interchange the first and third columns and still have a magic square.)
- What strategies worked best in helping you to create the magic squares?
- Magic squares can also be created on larger grids. A famous one was created by Benjamin Franklin on an 8 x 8 grid (note that this magic square does not include diagonal sums). What is the sum? (260)

52	61	4	13	20	29	36	45
4	3	62	51	46	35	30	19
53	60	5	12	21	28	37	44
11	6	59	54	43	38	27	22
55	58	7	10	23	26	39	42
9	8	57	56	41	40	25	24
50	63	2	15	18	31	34	47
16	1	64	49	48	33	32	17

Find out more about Franklin's magic square by searching the Internet.

Activity 13.12 Representing familiar percents on a 10 × 10 grid

Instructions

1. Say: For each of the 10 × 10 grids given here, identify the fractional part shaded and convert it to a decimal and to a percent.

2. Ask: How did you convert each fraction to a percent? How did the 10 × 10 grid help you make this conversion?

3. Reverse the activity by providing a percent (35%, 40%) and ask students to write it as a fraction and a decimal and illustrate on a 10 × 10 grid.

Fully-developed **Lesson Plans** model ways to make mathematics culturally relevant and reflective of students' lives outside the classroom, while fulfilling standards-based mathematics objectives.

Prospective teachers are given an abundance of hands-on **Activities,** which include illustrations of materials and complete instructions. They can be used as mini-lessons for children to practice using mathematics concepts.

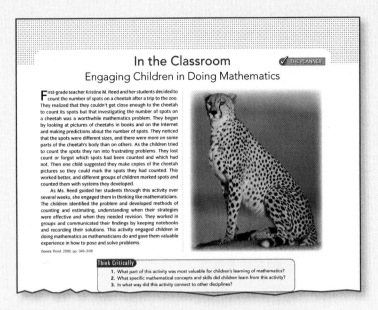

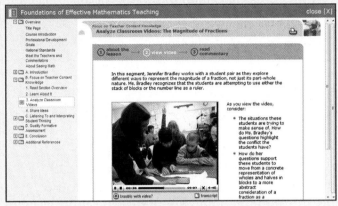

In the Classroom features provide a real-life look into a classroom and give students access to a wide range of ideas and classroom research. Many are from the pages of *Teaching Children Mathematics*.

Teaching Tip

Understanding teens numbers

When teaching place value, skip the teens numbers and come back to them later, after children understand the meaning of other two-digit numbers. Skip from 10 to 20 and make sure children understand the sequence 10, 20, 30, 40, 50, and so on. Then focus on 21, 22, 23, and so on, before tackling the numbers 11 through 19.

Teaching Tips provide applications of best practices.

Tech Tools

www.illuminations.nctm.org

Go to the *NCTM Illuminations* Web site. Select **Lessons**. The unit **All About Multiplication** consists of four lessons that model multiplication of whole numbers using different representations and introduces division as the inverse of multiplication.

Tech Tools help prospective teachers learn how to integrate technology in the classroom.

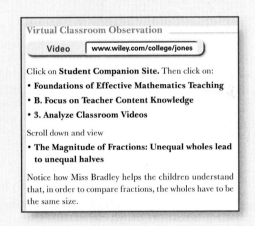

Virtual Classroom Observation

| Video | www.wiley.com/college/jones |

Click on **Student Companion Site.** Then click on:
- **Foundations of Effective Mathematics Teaching**
- **B. Focus on Teacher Content Knowledge**
- **3. Analyze Classroom Videos**

Scroll down and view
- **The Magnitude of Fractions: Unequal wholes lead to unequal halves**

Notice how Miss Bradley helps the children understand that, in order to compare fractions, the wholes have to be the same size.

Through a partnership with **Teachscape's** professional development series, a collection of videocases featuring rich, authentic classroom situations supplements the textbook's instruction. In the textbook, **Virtual Classroom Observations** highlight a videocase that corresponds to the content in the text and provides focal points for the viewer.

CONCEPT CHECK STOP

1. **What** are some benefits of teaching with children's literature?
2. **What** are some of the qualities of effective mathematics-related children's literature?
3. **How** can you best use children's literature to facilitate mathematics learning?

Concept Check questions at the end of each section allow students to test their comprehension of the learning objectives.

Student understanding is assessed at different levels

Wiley Visualizing offers students lots of practice material in several modalities for assessing their understanding of each study objective.

The **Summary** revisits each major section, with informative images taken from the chapter. These visuals reinforce important concepts.

Critical and Creative Thinking Questions challenge students to think more broadly about chapter concepts. The level of these questions ranges from simple to advanced; they encourage students to think critically and develop an analytical understanding of the ideas discussed in the chapter.

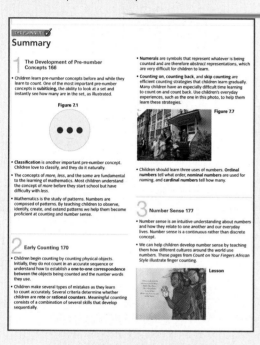

Summary

1 The Development of Pre-number Concepts 166

• Children learn pre-number concepts before and while they learn to count. One of the most important pre-number concepts is **subitizing**, the ability to look at a set and instantly see how many are in the set, as illustrated.

Figure 7.1

• Classification is another important pre-number concept. Children love to classify, and they do it naturally.

• The concepts of *more, less,* and the *same* are fundamental to the learning of mathematics. Most children understand the concept of *more* before they start school but have difficulty with *less.*

• Mathematics is the study of patterns. Numbers are composed of patterns. By teaching children to observe, identify, create, and extend patterns we help them become proficient at counting and number sense.

2 Early Counting 170

• Children begin counting by counting physical objects. Initially, they do not count in an accurate sequence or understand how to establish a **one-to-one correspondence** between the objects being counted and the number words they use.

• Children make several types of mistakes as they learn to count accurately. Several criteria determine whether children are **rote** or **rational** counters. Meaningful counting consists of a combination of several skills that develop sequentially.

• Numerals are symbols that represent whatever is being counted and are therefore *abstract* representations, which are very difficult for children to learn.

• **Counting on, counting back,** and **skip counting** are efficient counting strategies that children learn gradually. Many children have an especially difficult time learning to count on and count back. Use children's everyday experiences, such as the one in this photo, to help them learn these strategies.

Figure 7.7

• Children should learn three uses of numbers. **Ordinal numbers** tell what order, **nominal numbers** are used for naming, and **cardinal numbers** tell how many.

3 Number Sense 177

• Number sense is an intuitive understanding about numbers and how they relate to one another and our everyday lives. Number sense is a continuous rather than discrete concept.

• We can help children develop number sense by teaching them how different cultures around the world use numbers. These pages from *Count on Your Fingers African Style* illustrate finger counting.

Lesson

Critical and Creative Thinking Questions

1. Describe what is meant by algebraic reasoning. What aspects of algebraic reasoning should teachers focus on in each of the grade-level bands: pre-K–grade 2, grades 3–5, and grades 6–8?

2. What are students' misunderstandings about the equals sign? Describe an activity that can help students understand the equals sign.

3. **In the field** Interview a student in third to fifth grade about the equals sign. Present the student with a problem similar to the following: 5 + 9 = __ + 6. Ask the student to explain his or her thinking.

4. What are some advantages of using a pan balance to solve algebraic equations? Illustrate how you might use a pan balance to solve $3x + 7 = 4x - 9$.

5. Given the following table, how would you find the recursive relationship? What is it? How would you find the explicit relationship? What is it? Why is it important to be able to find explicit relationships?

2	5	8	11	14	17	20

6. How can you tell whether a function is linear without graphing it? Give examples of two linear functions and two nonlinear functions.

7. **Using visuals** This chapter illustrates repeating and growing patterns with interesting visuals. Develop a visual display that might appear on a bulletin board in your own classroom to illustrate examples of repeating and growing patterns.

In the field provides opportunities for prospective teachers to explore the concepts developed in the chapter in a variety of real-world situations, from analyzing textbooks to observing and interviewing teachers and students.

Using Visuals calls upon students to use the visuals in this textbook as a springboard for creating their own classroom materials or for understanding the concepts of the chapter.

What is happening in this picture? presents a new uncaptioned photograph or illustration, such as children's work, that is relevant to a chapter topic.

What is happening in this picture?

Think Critically

1. Does this teacher value drill and practice or conceptual learning of mathematics?
2. What can you point to in the image that tells you whether this is a drill and practice or a conceptual learning environment?

Think Critically questions ask the students to describe and explain what they can observe in the image based on what they have learned.

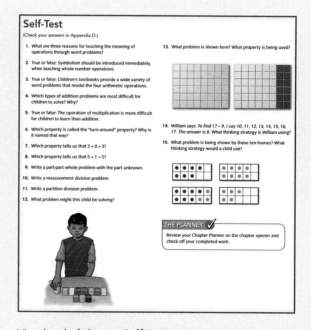

Self-Test

(Check your answers in Appendix D.)

1. What are three reasons for teaching the meaning of operations through word problems?

2. True or false: Symbolism should be introduced immediately, when teaching whole number operations.

3. True or false: Children's textbooks provide a wide variety of word problems that model the four arithmetic operations.

4. Which types of addition problems are most difficult for children to solve? Why?

5. True or false: The operation of multiplication is more difficult for children to learn than addition.

6. Which property is called the "turn-around" property? Why is it named that way?

7. Which property tells us that 3 + 0 = 3?

8. Which property tells us that 5 × 1 = 5?

9. Write a part-part whole problem with the part unknown.

10. Write a measurement division problem.

11. Write a partitive division problem.

12. What problem might this child be solving?

13. What problem is shown here? What property is being used?

14. William says: *To find 17 – 9, I say 10, 11, 12, 13, 14, 15, 16, 17. The answer is 8.* What thinking strategy is William using?

15. What problem is being shown by these ten-frames? What thinking strategy would a child use?

Review your Chapter Planner on the chapter opener and check off your completed work.

Visual end-of chapter **Self-Tests** pose review questions that ask students to demonstrate their understanding of key concepts.

Why *Visualizing Elementary and Middle School Mathematics Methods?*

The goal of *Visualizing Elementary and Middle School Mathematics Methods* is to prepare prospective elementary and middle school teachers to teach mathematics in a way that excites and motivates all children, while conveying the ideas that mathematical knowledge is necessary for full participation in society and that all students can learn mathematics. The text has an accessible format that serves as an introduction to the teaching of mathematics for those students who have little or no prior knowledge of teaching. This text is designed to help college students learn effectively by presenting mathematics content and pedagogy in a fresh new way. This unique approach, while maintaining necessary rigor, gives all students the opportunity to set aside their previous beliefs about mathematics and to learn concepts and pedagogy from a new perspective.

Representing mathematics teaching and learning with visuals

Mathematics is, of course, very visual. We use different types of visual representations to illustrate mathematics concepts all the time. This text presents some images that are familiar as well as many that are *new* and *different*. New images provide unique opportunities for learning. Specifically, the Visualizing approach offers prospective elementary and middle school teachers the opportunity to learn about mathematics and the teaching of mathematics with real-life examples of classrooms, vivid and pedagogically useful photos and illustrations, technology, video clips, multicultural perspectives, and children's literature. This approach grabs prospective teachers' attention, helps them understand the relevance of mathematics to their own lives, and gives them the necessary tools for teaching mathematics in the 21st century.

The *Visualizing Elementary and Middle School Mathematics Methods* program not only promotes better comprehension, retention, and understanding of the concepts and strategies pre-service teachers need to know about math and math education, it also shows future teachers how to use visuals well. Every page models visual learning strategies they will be able to use with the students they will soon be teaching in their own classrooms.

Differentiating instruction

Visualizing Elementary and Middle School Mathematics Methods supports The Equity Principle (NCTM, 2000) by incorporating techniques for teaching mathematics to diverse groups of students, including English language learners, students with learning disabilities, students with physical disabilities, gifted students, and students from diverse ethnic, cultural, or socioeconomic backgrounds. One chapter is entirely devoted to equity. However, instructional strategies are integrated throughout the text to help future teachers support diverse students' understanding of mathematics and facilitate their active participation in the mathematics classroom.

Correlation with standards

Visualizing Elementary and Middle School Mathematics Methods recognizes the current dynamic atmosphere of mathematics standards and the importance of preparing prospective teachers for the challenge of meeting state and local standards. The text correlates with *Principles and Standards for School Mathematics* (NCTM, 2000), *Curriculum Focal Points for Prekindergarten through Grade 8 Mathematics* (NCTM, 2006), and the *Common Core State Standards* (NGA Center/CCSSO, 2010) for mathematics.

Organization

The structure of *Visualizing Elementary and Middle School Mathematics Methods* is similar to the format of other methods texts (e.g., chapters on lesson planning, place value, problem solving). However, this text has many unique features that are designed to engage students and make the text relevant for them.

The text begins with a brief summary of the history of mathematics, just enough to pique readers' interest and motivate them to want to teach it. Diversity is integrated into the content of every chapter, through *Multicultural Perspectives in Mathematics* and related content. Lesson planning is addressed throughout the text, with 16 fully developed lesson plans. Each chapter contains explicit examples of teachers and students doing mathematics, children's literature that is integrated with mathematics content, and images of children actively learning mathematics. Each content chapter integrates technology applications to mathematics. Many chapters include Virtual Classroom Observation Videos, which are a collection of videocases from Teachscape featuring rich, authentic classroom situations keyed to the content of the text and available on the book companion site.

The written text contains just enough information for beginning teachers. It includes best practices research and enough background information without being overwhelming to the reader. Part I includes Chapters 1–5, and focuses on the foundations of teaching and learning mathematics. Part II, Chapters 6–17, addresses specific content and pedagogy. Each chapter includes the relevant *Principles, Standards, Curriculum Focal Points,* and *Common Core State Standards.*

- **Chapter 1, What Is Mathematics?**, serves as an introduction to the text. It begins by discussing the nature of mathematics, includes a timeline about the history of mathematics, and answers the question *What do mathematicians do?* This chapter illustrates how children can learn mathematics through questioning and problem solving, much like professional mathematicians. The chapter provides an overview of the evolution of school mathematics, highlighting the New Math and Back to Basics movements and discussing the origins of reform mathematics. Next, it discusses *Principles and Standards for School Mathematics* (NCTM, 2000), with a summary of each of the Principles, Content Standards, and Process Standards. The chapter concludes with a discussion of No Child Left Behind, the *Common Core State Standards* (NGA Center/CCSSO, 2010), and other issues of accountability.

- **Chapter 2, Learning Mathematics with Understanding,** discusses the importance of learning mathematics with understanding. It describes two different kinds of understanding and explains why relational understanding of mathematics is more useful for children to learn first. The chapter compares and contrasts behaviorist and constructivist learning theories, provides an overview of Piaget's theories, and provides an example of the process of equilibration. The chapter summarizes new developments in cognitive science, such as adaptive choice and cognitive variability. It discusses several factors that impact children's understanding, such as classroom culture and the selection of tasks and tools.

- **Chapter 3, Teaching Mathematics Effectively,** examines the changing role of the teacher, from telling students how to do mathematics to facilitating their sense-making. Using *Mathematics Teaching Today* (NCTM, 2007), as a guiding reference, the chapter examines the three-stage teaching cycle,

which includes knowledge, implementation, and analysis. Within the implementation stage, the chapter highlights methods of managing discourse, an important skill of effective mathematics teachers. The chapter examines teaching mathematics with children's literature and teaching mathematics with technology, providing techniques and examples for both topics. The chapter closes with a discussion of the *Common Core State Standards* (NGA Center/CCSSO, 2010) and high-stakes testing, topics that are relevant for today's teachers.

- **Chapter 4, Planning for and Assessing Mathematics Learning,** begins with a discussion of lesson planning, including yearly, unit, and daily planning. The chapter takes the reader through the process of planning a mathematics lesson, providing a template for the three-part lesson plan. It introduces the practice of Lesson Study as an alternative to individual planning. Cooperative grouping and manipulatives use are discussed. The challenge of planning for diverse groups of students is thoroughly discussed, with many examples of modifications and accommodations for mathematics lessons. The chapter compares and contrasts different types of mathematics textbooks and provides hints for using the teacher's edition of a text, with examples from actual textbooks. In the assessment portion of the chapter, different types of formative assessment are discussed, with a summary of assessment techniques.

- **Chapter 5, Providing Equitable Instruction for All Students,** begins with an examination of culture and a discussion of the origins of multicultural education The chapter examines the process of content integration, with examples from mathematics. Next, the Equity Principle and its implications are discussed. The results of the 2009 NAEP are presented with discussion of the Achievement Gap, along with effective teaching practices for overcoming this gap. Specific strategies for teaching English language learners, students with difficulty in mathematics, and gifted students are discussed. The chapter examines gender equity in mathematics, with a timeline to illustrate the evolution of gender equity in mathematics over the last 200 years.

- **Chapter 6, Problem Solving in the Mathematics Classroom**, is the first chapter in Part II. Actually, this chapter bridges the first and second parts of the text. It contains specific mathematics content but approaches problem solving as a technique that should be used when learning all mathematics content. The chapter distinguishes between routine and nonroutine problems and discusses the benefits of problem solving. With specific examples, the chapter illustrates Polya's problem-solving process. The chapter discusses how to plan for problem solving, how to organize the classroom to facilitate problem solving, and how to help students who have difficulty with problem solving. Tips for selecting problems and for problem posing are discussed. Six different problem-solving strategies are explored, with examples of each strategy.

- **Chapter 7, Counting and Number Sense,** discusses the development of counting and number sense, from pre-number concepts to counting large numbers and using estimation. Four types of pre-number concepts are discussed, including subitizing. The chapter describes the stages through which children progress as they learn to count, as well as the characteristics of a rational counter. It examines counting techniques such as counting on, counting back, and skip counting. The chapter describes the differences between cardinal, ordinal, and nominal numbers. Number sense is discussed, with emphasis on numbers from other cultures. The chapter describes how children learn numbers from 1 to 10, between 10 and 20, and numbers larger than 20. The chapter concludes with a discussion of estimation and the reasonableness of results.

- **Chapter 8, Place Value,** begins with a discussion of the characteristics of place value, with examples of ancient numeration systems and the Hindu-Arabic system. This chapter asks the question, *How do children learn place value?* Children's pre-place value and early place value ideas are explored. The chapter explains how to teach place value, with detailed explanation of proportional and nonproportional place value models. Several activities are included for learning place value, including some that use technology and some that use the hundreds chart. The chapter discusses the kinds of difficulties children often experience learning place value and how to accommodate children who are having difficulties. It discusses extending place value models to help children learn larger numbers.

- **Chapter 9, Operations with Whole Numbers,** features specific techniques for learning the four arithmetic operations. For each operation, the chapter suggests moving from the concrete to the abstract. In other words, begin instruction with word problems that have solutions children can act out using concrete manipulatives and move to symbolic representations only after children understand the meaning of the operations. For each operation, each type of problem is described with examples, strategies for teaching, and properties of the operation.

- **Chapter 10, Whole Number Computation, Mental Computation, and Estimation,** compares and contrasts these three methods of computing. The chapter begins with an overview of written computation. It compares the advantages of using traditional vs. student-created algorithms. For each of the arithmetic operations, the chapter explains specific techniques for teaching written computation, in each case beginning with student-created algorithms and introducing traditional algorithms later. The chapter discusses estimation, mental computation, and the use of calculators, providing several examples and techniques.

- **Chapter 11, Understanding Fractions and Fraction Computation,** begins with a discussion of the four meanings of fractions, with models for each of the different meanings. Children's difficulties with fractions are recognized and addressed. The chapter focuses on the meanings of partitioning and iteration. Comparison of fractions and fraction equivalence are explored informally and formally. The chapter focuses on appropriate fraction language and symbolism. The chapter concludes with a detailed discussion of fraction computation, explaining both informal, student-created algorithms and traditional algorithms.

- **Chapter 12, Decimals,** begins with a discussion of two decimal models: extending the place value system and connecting decimals to their fraction equivalents. Students' difficulties with decimals are discussed along with suggestions for overcoming their difficulties. Decimal notation is introduced as well as models and activities for learning to use decimals. The chapter discusses decimal number sense, focusing on equivalence and ordering of decimals. For decimal computation, both informal, student-created and formal algorithms are presented.

- **Chapter 13, Ratio, Proportion, and Percent,** begins with an introduction to the concept of proportional reasoning and a discussion of its importance in different areas of mathematics. The chapter discusses the concept of ratio and explains the three different types of ratios along with suggestions for teaching this topic. The chapter suggests informal methods of teaching proportions, with many examples, and activities, before formal methods are introduced. The meaning of percent is introduced along with real-world examples of percents. The use of mental computation, estimation, and informal methods are explored to solve the different types of percent problems.

- **Chapter 14, Algebraic Reasoning,** begins with a discussion of the meaning of algebraic reasoning for different grade levels, beginning concretely in the early grades and moving toward the abstract in the upper elementary grades and middle school. The chapter discusses the importance of algebraic reasoning in mathematics and the workplace. Algebraic symbols are discussed, including the equals symbol, with suggestions for teaching this difficult concept. The different meanings of variable are discussed. The chapter uses algebra to generalize the properties of arithmetic operations, odd and even numbers, and integers. The chapter concludes with a discussion of patterns and functions.

- **Chapter 15, Geometry,** begins with a discussion of the van Hiele levels and the importance of geometric thinking at all grade levels. The chapter is separated into four content areas: (1) shapes and properties, (2) location, (3) transformations, and (4) visualization. For each area, discussion and activities are based on grade level and each activity is correlated to the appropriate van Hiele level. For example, in the Shapes and Properties section, this topic is discussed for prekindergarten through grade 2, grades 3–5, and grades 6–8. Each area of discussion is organized into the same grade-level categories.

- **Chapter 16, Measurement,** begins by examining the measurement process and answers the question: *Why is measurement important?* The chapter discusses three content areas for measurement: (1) length and area; (2) volume, capacity, mass, and weight; and (3) time, money, temperature, and angle measure. Within each content area, appropriate knowledge and pedagogy are discussed for each grade level or grade-level band. For example, the length and area section begins with a discussion of nonstandard units of length and the importance of using nonstandard units before standard units are introduced. This same section also discusses customary and metric units.

- **Chapter 17, Data Analysis and Probability,** begins by explaining the difference between statistics and mathematics. The chapter continues by discussing the process of asking statistical questions, from teachers formulating questions for younger students to older students formulating their own questions. The processes used for collecting data are discussed, from the early grades to the upper elementary grades and middle school. Tools for analyzing data with graphs and descriptive statistics are discussed. The chapter concludes with a discussion of probability, its prevalence in our everyday lives, and the teaching of probability.

How Does Wiley Visualizing Support Instructors?

Wiley Visualizing Site

WILEY VISUALIZING™ The Wiley Visualizing site hosts a wealth of information for instructors using Wiley Visualizing, including ways to maximize the visual approach in the classroom and a white paper titled "How Visuals Can Help Students Learn," by Matt Leavitt, instructional design consultant. Visit Wiley Visualizing at www.wiley.com/college/visualizing.

Wiley Custom Select

WILEY *Custom* **LEARNING SOLUTIONS** Wiley Custom Select gives you the freedom to build your course materials exactly the way you want them. Offer your students a cost-efficient alternative to traditional texts. In a simple three-step process, create a solution containing the content you want, in the sequence you want, delivered how you want. Visit Wiley Custom Select at http://customselect.wiley.com.

The Wiley Resource Kit

The Wiley Resource Kit gives students access to premier, password-protected resources hosted by Wiley. Building upon what they learn in their courses, students can use interactive media, practice quizzes, videos and more at their own pace to further enhance mastery of key concepts. The Wiley Resource Kit also provides Respondus® Test Banks for many of Wiley's leading titles that instructors can assign and use for assessment through their campus learning management system. The Wiley Resource Kit and other resources can be accessed via the book companion site at www.wiley.com/college/jones.

Book Companion Site

(www.wiley.com/college/jones)

All instructor resources are housed on the book companion site.

Virtual Classroom Observation from Teachscape

(available on the book companion site)

Through a partnership with **Teachscape's** professional development series, a collection of videocases featuring rich, authentic classroom situations is keyed to the text and available to students in the Wiley Resource Kit. Instructors can access the content for classroom presentation purposes through the book companion site. To help future teachers productively learn from these visual tools, each videocase is accompanied by teacher reflections and expert interviews explaining how educational theory and research was used to guide the teacher's classroom decision. This comprehensive, virtual experience, will allow students to observe the role of the teacher for a variety of learners and classroom scenarios.

PowerPoint Presentations

(available on the book companion site)

A complete set of highly visual PowerPoint presentations— one per chapter—by Denise Collins of the University of Texas at Arlington is available online to enhance classroom presentations. Tailored to the text's topical coverage and learning objectives, these presentations are designed to convey key text concepts, illustrated by embedded text art.

Test Bank (available on the book companion site)

The visuals from the textbook are also included in the Test Bank by Verlyn Evans of Liberty University. The Test Bank has approximately 750 test items, with at least 25 percent of them incorporating visuals from the book. The test items include multiple-choice and essay questions testing a variety of comprehension levels. The test bank is available online in MS Word files.

Instructor's Manual

(available on the book companion site)

The Instructor's Manual includes creative ideas for in-class activities by Georgia Cobbs of the University of Montana, Missoula. It also includes answers to Critical and Creative Thinking questions and Concept Check questions.

Guidance is also provided on how to maximize the effectiveness of visuals in the classroom.

1. **Use visuals during class discussions or presentations.** Point out important information as the students look at the visuals, to help them integrate visual and verbal mental models.

2. **Use visuals for assignments and to assess learning.** For example, learners could be asked to identify samples of concepts portrayed in visuals or to create their own visuals.

3. **Use visuals to encourage group activities.** Students can study together, make sense of, discuss, hypothesize, or make decisions about the content. Students can work together to interpret and describe a visual or use the visual to solve problems and conduct related research.

4. **Use visuals during reviews.** Students can review key vocabulary, concepts, principles, processes, and relationships displayed visually. This recall helps link prior knowledge to new information in working memory, building integrated mental models.

5. **Use visuals for assignments and to assess learning.** For example, learners could be asked to identify samples of concepts portrayed in visuals.

6. **Use visuals to apply facts or concepts to realistic situations or examples.** For example, a familiar photograph, such as of a round barn, can illustrate key information about area and surface area, linking this new concept to prior knowledge.

Image Gallery (available on the book companion site)

All photographs, figures, maps, and other visuals from the text can be used as you wish in the classroom. These online electronic files allow you to easily incorporate images into your PowerPoint presentations as you choose, or to create your own handouts.

Wiley Faculty Network

The Wiley Faculty Network (WFN) is a global community of faculty, connected by a passion for teaching and a drive to learn, share, and collaborate. Their mission is to promote the effective use of technology and enrich the teaching experience. Connect with the Wiley Faculty Network to collaborate with your colleagues, find a mentor, attend virtual and live events, and view a wealth of resources all designed to help you grow as an educator. Visit the Wiley Faculty Network at www.wherefacultyconnect.com.

How Has Wiley Visualizing Been Shaped by Contributors?

Wiley Visualizing would not have come about without a team of people, each of whom played a part in sharing their research and contributing to this new approach.

Academic Research Consultants

Richard Mayer, Professor of Psychology, UC Santa Barbara. Mayer's *Cognitive Theory of Multimedia Learning* provided the basis on which we designed our program. He continues to provide guidance to our author and editorial teams on how to develop and implement strong, pedagogically effective visuals and use them in the classroom.

Jan L. Plass, Professor of Educational Communication and Technology in the Steinhardt School of Culture, Education, and Human Development at New York University. Plass codirects the NYU Games for Learning Institute and is the founding director of the CREATE Consortium for Research and Evaluation of Advanced Technology in Education.

Matthew Leavitt, Instructional Design Consultant, advises the Visualizing team on the effective design and use of visuals in instruction and has made virtual and live presentations to university faculty around the country regarding effective design and use of instructional visuals.

Independent Research Studies

SEG Research, an independent research and assessment firm, conducted a national, multisite effectiveness study of students enrolled in entry-level college Psychology and Geology courses. The study was designed to evaluate the effectiveness of Wiley Visualizing. You can view the full research paper at www.wiley.com/college/visualizing/efficacy.html.

Instructor and Student Contributions

Throughout the process of developing the concept of guided visual pedagogy for Wiley Visualizing, we benefited from the comments and constructive criticism provided by the instructors and colleagues listed below. We offer our sincere appreciation to these individuals for their helpful reviews and general feedback:

Visualizing Reviewers, Focus Group Participants, and Survey Respondents

James Abbott, Temple University
Melissa Acevedo, Westchester Community College
Shiva Achet, Roosevelt University
Denise Addorisio, Westchester Community College
Dave Alan, University of Phoenix
Sue Allen-Long, Indiana University – Purdue
Robert Amey, Bridgewater State College
Nancy Bain, Ohio University
Corinne Balducci, Westchester Community College
Steve Barnhart, Middlesex County Community College
Stefan Becker, University of Washington – Oshkosh
Callan Bentley, NVCC Annandale
Valerie Bergeron, Delaware Technical & Community College
Andrew Berns, Milwaukee Area Technical College
Gregory Bishop, Orange Coast College
Rebecca Boger, Brooklyn College
Scott Brame, Clemson University
Joan Brandt, Central Piedmont Community College
Richard Brinn, Florida International University
Jim Bruno, University of Phoenix
Caroline Burleigh, Baptist Bible College

William Chamberlin, Fullerton College
Oiyin Pauline Chow, Harrisburg Area Community College
Laurie Corey, Westchester Community College
Ozeas Costas, Ohio State University at Mansfield
Christopher Di Leonardo, Foothill College
Dani Ducharme, Waubonsee Community College
Mark Eastman, Diablo Valley College
Ben Elman, Baruch College
Staussa Ervin, Tarrant County College
Michael Farabee, Estrella Mountain Community College
Laurie Flaherty, Eastern Washington University
Sandra Fluck, Moravian College
Susan Fuhr, Maryville College
Peter Galvin, Indiana University at Southeast
Andrew Getzfeld, New Jersey City University
Janet Gingold, Prince George's Community College
Donald Glassman, Des Moines Area Community College
Richard Goode, Porterville College
Peggy Green, Broward Community College
Stelian Grigoras, Northwood University
Paul Grogger, University of Colorado

Michael Hackett, Westchester Community College
Duane Hampton, Western Michigan University
Thomas Hancock, Eastern Washington University
Gregory Harris, Polk State College
John Haworth, Chattanooga State Technical Community College
James Hayes-Bohanan, Bridgewater State College
Peter Ingmire, San Francisco State University
Mark Jackson, Central Connecticut State University
Heather Jennings, Mercer County Community College
Eric Jerde, Morehead State University
Jennifer Johnson, Ferris State University
Richard Kandus, Mt. San Jacinto College District
Christopher Kent, Spokane Community College
Gerald Ketterling, North Dakota State University
Lynnel Kiely, Harold Washington College
Eryn Klosko, Westchester Community College
Cary T. Komoto, University of Wisconsin – Barron County
John Kupfer, University of South Carolina
Nicole Lafleur, University of Phoenix
Arthur Lee, Roane State Community College
Mary Lynam, Margrove College
Heidi Marcum, Baylor University
Beth Marshall, Washington State University
Dr. Theresa Martin, Eastern Washington University
Charles Mason, Morehead State University
Susan Massey, Art Institute of Philadelphia
Linda McCollum, Eastern Washington University
Mary L. Meiners, San Diego Miramar College
Shawn Mikulay, Elgin Community College
Cassandra Moe, Century Community College
Lynn Hanson Mooney, Art Institute of Charlotte
Kristy Moreno, University of Phoenix
Jacob Napieralski, University of Michigan – Dearborn
Gisele Nasar, Brevard Community College, Cocoa Campus
Daria Nikitina, West Chester University
Robin O'Quinn, Eastern Washington University
Richard Orndorff, Eastern Washington University
Sharen Orndorff, Eastern Washington University
Clair Ossian, Tarrant County College
Debra Parish, North Harris Montgomery Community College District
Diana Perdue, Pride Rock Consulting

Linda Peters, Holyoke Community College
Robin Popp, Chattanooga State Technical Community College
Michael Priano, Westchester Community College
Alan "Paul" Price, University of Wisconsin – Washington County
Max Reams, Olivet Nazarene University
Mary Celeste Reese, Mississippi State University
Bruce Rengers, Metropolitan State College of Denver
Guillermo Rocha, Brooklyn College
Penny Sadler, College of William and Mary
Shamili Sandiford, College of DuPage
Thomas Sasek, University of Louisiana at Monroe
Donna Seagle, Chattanooga State Technical Community College
Diane Shakes, College of William and Mary
Jennie Silva, Louisiana State University
Michael Siola, Chicago State University
Morgan Slusher, Community College of Baltimore County
Julia Smith, Eastern Washington University
Darlene Smucny, University of Maryland University College
Jeff Snyder, Bowling Green State University
Alice Stefaniak, St. Xavier University
Alicia Steinhardt, Hartnell Community College
Kurt Stellwagen, Eastern Washington University
Charlotte Stromfors, University of Phoenix
Shane Strup, University of Phoenix
Donald Thieme, Georgia Perimeter College
Pamela Thinesen, Century Community College
Chad Thompson, SUNY Westchester Community College
Lensyl Urbano, University of Memphis
Gopal Venugopal, Roosevelt University
Daniel Vogt, University of Washington – College of Forest Resources
Dr. Laura J. Vosejpka, Northwood University
Brenda L. Walker, Kirkwood Community College
Stephen Wareham, Cal State Fullerton
Fred William Whitford, Montana State University
Katie Wiedman, University of St. Francis
Harry Williams, University of North Texas
Emily Williamson, Mississippi State University
Bridget Wyatt, San Francisco State University
Van Youngman, Art Institute of Philadelphia
Alexander Zemcov, Westchester Community College

Student Participants

Karl Beall, Eastern Washington University
Jessica Bryant, Eastern Washington University
Pia Chawla, Westchester Community College
Channel DeWitt, Eastern Washington University
Lucy DiAroscia, Westchester Community College
Heather Gregg, Eastern Washington University
Lindsey Harris, Eastern Washington University
Brenden Hayden, Eastern Washington University
Patty Hosner, Eastern Washington University

Tonya Karunartue, Eastern Washington University
Sydney Lindgren, Eastern Washington University
Michael Maczuga, Westchester Community College
Melissa Michael, Eastern Washington University
Estelle Rizzin, Westchester Community College
Andrew Rowley, Eastern Washington University
Eric Torres, Westchester Community College
Joshua Watson, Eastern Washington University

Focus Group Participants and Reviewers of *Visualizing Elementary and Middle School Mathematics Methods*

Lewis Blessing, University of Central Florida
Jane K. Bonari, California University of Pennsylvania
Dolores Burton, New York Institute of Technology
Denise Collins, University of Texas at Arlington
Sandra Cooper, Baylor University
Yolanda De La Cruz, Arizona State University
James Dogbey, University of South Florida
Verlyn Evans, Liberty University
Sandra E. Fluck, Moravian College
Christina Gawlik, Kansas State University
Gregory O. Gierhart, Murray State University
Peter Glidden, West Chester University
Sandra Green, La Sierra University
Xue Han, Dominican University
Edith Hays, Texas Woman's University
Heidi J. Higgins, University of North Carolina, Wilmington
Michele Hollingsworth Koomen, Gustavus Adolphus College
Emamuddin Hoosain, Augusta State University
Deborah Howell, Florida Atlantic University
William A. Kamm, Lee University
John Kerrigan, West Chester University

William Lacefield, Mercer University
Cheng-Yao Lin, Southern Illinois University, Carbondale
David Martin, Florida Atlantic University
Loretta Meeks, University of Illinois, Springfield
Pam Miller, Arizona State University, West
Jenifer Moore, University of Montevallo
Sarah Murray, Centre College
Diana S. Perdue, Virginia State University
Peggy Petrilli, Eastern Kentucky University
Kien T. Pham, California State University, Fresno
Edel Reilly, Indiana University of Pennsylvania
Christie Riley, Northwest Oklahoma State University
Tina Rye Sloan, Athens State University
Clyde Sawyer, Pfeiffer University
Marvin Seperson, Nova Southeastern University
Jason Silverman, Drexel University
Jane Strawhecker, University of Nebraska, Kearney
Beth McCullough Vinson, Athens State University
Maurice Wilson, Kennesaw State University
John C. Yang, Lakeland College
Dina Yankelewitz, The Richard Stockton College of New Jersey

Class Testers and Students

To make certain that *Visualizing Elementary and Middle School Mathematics Methods* met the needs of current students, we asked several instructors to class-test a chapter. The feedback that we received from students and instructors confirmed our belief that the visualizing approach taken in this book is highly effective in helping students to learn. We wish to thank the following instructors and their students who provided us with helpful feedback and suggestions:

Krista Althauser, Eastern Kentucky University
Kim Arp, Cabrini College
Gina Bittner, Peru State College
Lewis Blessing, University of Central Florida
Norma Boakes, Stockton College
Jane Bonari, California University of Pennsylvania
Delores Burton, New York Institute of Technology
Faye Bruun, Texas A&M University
Marsha D. Campbell, Jacksonville State University
Georgia Cobbs, University of Montana
Denise Collins, University of Texas – Arlington
Sandra Cooper, Baylor University
Janet Cornella, Palm Beach Atlantic University
Larry Duque, Brigham Young University – Idaho
Philip Halloran, Central Connecticut State University
Xue Han, Dominican University
Heidi Higgins, University of North Carolina – Wilmington
Gloria Johnson, Alabama State University

William Kamm, Lee University
Mary Keller, University of Louisiana at Lafayette
Chris Knoell, University of Nebraska –Kearney
John Lamb, University of Texas at Tyler
Mark Levy, St. John's University
Monica Merritt, Mount Saint Mary College
Gloria Moorer-Johnson, Alabama State University
Barbara Ridener, Florida Atlantic University
Blidi Stenm, Hofstra University
Jane Strawhecker, University of Nebraska – Kearney
Iris Striedick, Pennsylvania State University
Deb Vanoverbeke, Southwest Minnesota State University
Thomas Walsh, Kean University
Stef Bertino Wood, Rollins College
Maurice Wilson, Kennesaw State University
John Yang, Lakeland College
Sharon Young, Seattle Pacific University
Helen Zentner Levy, St. John's University

Dedication

To my husband, Steve Jones, for his ever-present support, patience, encouragement, and technical and editorial help. To the memory of my parents, Celia and Joseph Cohen, for their many sacrifices on my behalf.

JCJ

Special Thanks

A book as complex as this one is the work of many talented and dedicated people. I wish to thank the editorial and production staff at John Wiley & Sons for their expert work on this book. I am very grateful to Acquisitions Editor Robert Johnston for expertly matching my ideas with the Wiley Visualizing series, launching this process, and providing support and guidance throughout. I want to thank Nancy Perry, Manager of Product Development, who guided the entire process and worked tirelessly on the development of every detail of this book. Many thanks as well to Micheline Frederick, Senior Production Manager, and Christine Cervoni, Production Editor, for their expertise; to Elle Wagner, Senior Photo Researcher for tirelessly searching for just the right photos; to Dennis Ormond for translating my ideas into rich, clear illustrations; to Sandra Rigby for supervising the complex illustrations required; and to Jim O'Shea for creating just the right designs for the special instructional features in each chapter. Special thanks go to Anne Greenberger, Development Editor, for her many excellent ideas through several drafts. I greatly appreciate the help that editorial assistants Mariah Maguire-Fong, Brittany Cheetham, Sean Boda, and Tiara Kelly provided to this project.

I am grateful also for the support of the Wiley management team. In particular, thanks to Vice President and Publisher, Jay O'Callaghan, and Director of Development, Barbara Heaney. Special thanks go to Anne Smith, Vice President and Executive Publisher; Beth Tripmacher, Project Editor; and Jeff Rucker, Associate Marketing Director of the Wiley Visualizing Imprint; and to Senior Marketing Manager Danielle Torio for their steadfast support and efforts in preparing the way for this book.

Finally, I would like to thank my colleagues in the Department of Mathematics at Eastern Michigan University for their support, and my students, past and present, for all that they taught me and continue to teach me about what they need to learn effectively.

About the Author

Joan Cohen Jones received a Bachelor of Arts degree from Herbert Lehman College of the City University of New York, where she majored in mathematics. She received a Master of Arts in Teaching Mathematics and a doctorate in Mathematics Education from Georgia State University, where her research focused on prospective teachers' knowledge and beliefs about fractions, decimals, and percents. Dr. Jones has taught extensively at the middle school, secondary school, and university levels. While a doctoral student, she became interested in the area of multicultural mathematics and has written several articles on this topic. While teaching at the University of Wisconsin, Eau Claire, she began incorporating children's literature in her classes to facilitate students' mathematics understanding. Currently, Dr. Jones is a Professor in the Department of Mathematics at Eastern Michigan University, where she teaches undergraduate and graduate mathematics education courses for prospective and practicing teachers. Teaching has always been a priority for Dr. Jones. In 2005, she was awarded the Ronald W. Collins Distinguished Faculty Award for Teaching, a university-wide honor.

Contents

PART I: FOUNDATIONS OF TEACHING MATHEMATICS

1 What Is Mathematics?

2 Learning Mathematics with Understanding

3 Teaching Mathematics Effectively

4 Planning for and Assessing Mathematics Learning

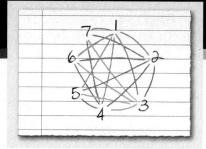

5 Providing Equitable Instruction for All Students

PART II: MATH CONCEPTS AND PEDAGOGY

6 Problem Solving in the Mathematics Classroom

7 Counting and Number Sense

8 Place Value

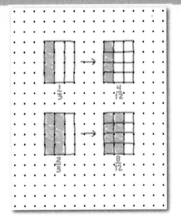

11

Understanding Fractions and Fraction Computation

12

Decimals

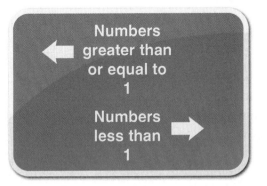

13 Ratio, Proportion, and Percent

14 Algebraic Reasoning

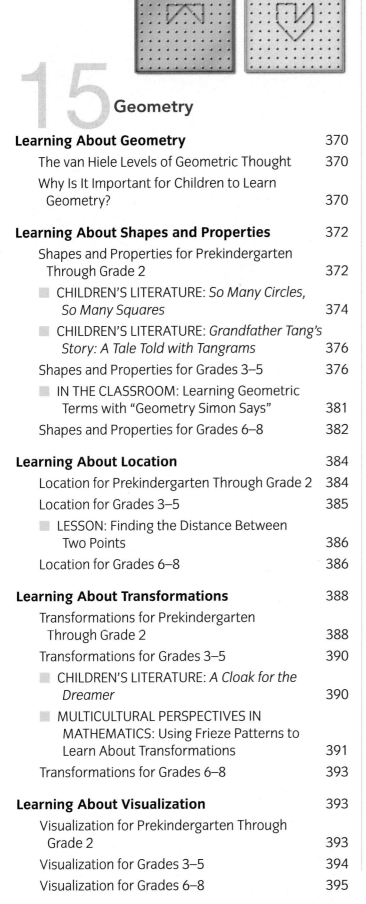

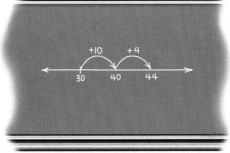

17 Data Analysis and Probability

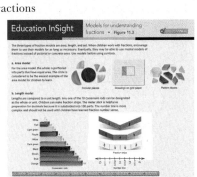
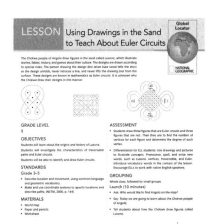

What Is Mathematics?

The first round barn in America was built at Hancock, Massachusetts, in 1824 by the Shakers, a religious community. The Shakers recognized that round barns were more efficient than square or rectangular ones because round barns used fewer building materials to enclose the same space and were structurally stronger. During this time, when labor was in short supply, a farmer with a round barn could move from one cow to another without wasted motion. Other farmers did not initially adopt the round barn because they were wary of the Shakers' beliefs. However, in the late 19th and early 20th centuries, round barns started to appear in farming communities throughout the Midwest and northern Vermont.

Children studying round barns in their elementary school classroom will probably not see an immediate connection to mathematics, because we often believe that mathematics involves numbers and rules rather than how we live our lives. The round barn is, however, an example of a real-world application of mathematics that all elementary-aged children can grasp.

Children in the primary grades can identify round, square, and rectangular shapes and describe how they are alike and different. Children in the upper grades can calculate the areas of round, square, and rectangular shapes with a fixed perimeter and determine that the round figure has the greatest area. The round barn also challenges children to think about why diverse peoples chose to live in tepees, igloos, or round huts, and how decisions that shaped people's cultures were influenced by mathematics.

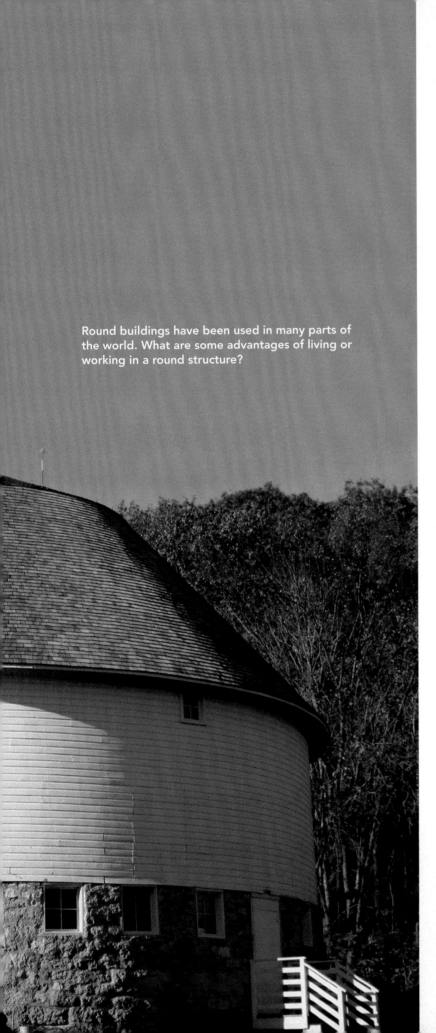

Round buildings have been used in many parts of the world. What are some advantages of living or working in a round structure?

CHAPTER OUTLINE

CHAPTER PLANNER ✓

- ❏ Study the picture and read the opening story.
- ❏ Scan the Learning Objectives in each section:
  p. 4 ❏   p. 9 ❏   p. 12 ❏   p. 15 ❏   p. 22 ❏
- ❏ Read the text and study all visuals and Activities. Answer any questions.

Analyze key features

- ❏ Multicultural Perspectives in Mathematics, p. 5
- ❏ Children's Literature, p. 6
- ❏ Process Diagram, p. 7
- ❏ In the Classroom, p. 8
- ❏ Education InSight, p. 10
- ❏ Lesson, p. 20
- ❏ Stop: Answer the Concept Checks before you go on:
  p. 8 ❏   p. 12 ❏   p. 14 ❏   p. 21 ❏   p. 23 ❏

End of chapter

- ❏ Review the Summary and Key Terms.
- ❏ Answer the Critical and Creative Thinking Questions.
- ❏ Answer What is happening in this picture?
- ❏ Complete the Self-Test and check your answers.

The Discipline of Mathematics

LEARNING OBJECTIVES

1. **Construct** a definition of mathematics.
2. **Describe** how mathematics is used in our everyday lives.
3. **Explain** what mathematicians do.
4. **Explain** how children can think like mathematicians.

If you asked elementary or middle school students to define mathematics, they might say that mathematics is about numbers, computation, and rules. Their parents would probably answer similarly because of their own experiences with mathematics. Although computation is a part of mathematics and the formulas we learn are very useful, they hardly represent the discipline. To encourage children to study mathematics, teachers must understand the discipline and then learn how to communicate this knowledge to their students through the tasks they choose and their actions as teachers.

Defining Mathematics

Some think of mathematics as a set of rules and formulas, while others view mathematics as the ability to observe and understand patterns, see connections, and use problem-solving skills. Mathematics is, foremost, a human endeavor. According to mathematician Keith Devlin (1994, p. 6), "Mathematics, the science of patterns, is a way of looking at the world, both the physical, biological, and sociological world we inhabit, and the inner world of our minds and thoughts." Mathematics is highly creative and is often likened to music or poetry. Mathematics, as a discipline, is always evolving in response to societal needs.

Mathematics is a way of thinking. Knowledge of mathematics permeates daily life. The techniques learned from doing mathematics help people make real-life decisions by teaching them how to organize and prioritize information, pose and solve problems, interpret **quantitative**, or measurable, **data**, think flexibly, analyze situations, and understand and use the technology necessary to become informed citizens. Quite simply, mathematics helps people lead their lives more successfully.

Mathematical knowledge is a tool that can be used to navigate all parts of life: personally (comparing prices at the supermarket), professionally (using a spreadsheet to identify trends), and culturally (interpreting the symbols used by ancestors). As the world we live in becomes more technological and complex, the need for mathematical competence increases.

Extending the Definition—Mathematics in Our World

Mathematical patterns abound in the natural world. For example, the Fibonacci sequence, which appears frequently in nature, sets the pattern for the number of seeds in the head of a sunflower, the number of petals on a daisy, and the family trees of bees. Other mathematical patterns can be found in the distinct markings on animals and, as illustrated in **Figure 1.1**, the structure of seashells.

> **Fibonacci sequence**
> A sequence of numbers whose first two terms are 1 and 1 and whose subsequent terms are derived from the sum of the previous two terms (1, 1, 2, 3, 5, 8, 13, . . .).

Mathematics in nature • Figure 1.1

Mathematical patterns are abundant in nature. How do each of these images illustrate mathematics?

Mathematical patterns in the real world • Figure 1.2

Throughout history, people have decorated their clothing, buildings, religious objects, and tools with interesting patterns. Navajo rugs display symmetry. Mexican weaving displays repetitive and growing patterns.

From ancient times to the present, civilizations have adapted the mathematical patterns found in nature to create decorative designs for their textiles, pottery, and dwellings (**Figure 1.2**). These patterns serve multiple purposes. Some are for embellishment only, while others have meaning. Wampum belts recorded messages, treaties, and historical events. Other designs, such as the thunderbird motif often used in American Indian rugs and blankets, reflect the maker's environment and traditions. Designs, such as those found in kente cloth, may indicate the owner's station in life. Many designs contain geometric shapes and represent sophisticated mathematical ideas through their complex repetitive patterns. Although the makers of these patterns were not aware of the formal mathematics in their designs, these patterns illustrate distinct and fascinating examples of mathematics as used in our everyday lives.

A common real-world application of mathematics is the structure of time. Different civilizations have measured time in ways to suit the needs of their societies and have created calendars and units of time that are appropriate for their needs. The manner in which we mark time evolved from mathematical decisions and cultural traditions (see *Multicultural Perspectives in Mathematics*).

Multicultural Perspectives in Mathematics

Timekeeping

THE PLANNER

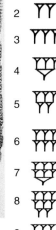

Have you ever thought about why we measure time in minutes and hours and why a week is 7 days?

Minutes and hours. Ancient Babylonians gave us the 60-second minute and the 60-minute hour. They developed a written number system around 3000 B.C.E. that used five symbols for the quantities 1, 10, 60, 600, and 3600. All other numbers were combinations of these. Anthropologist Denise Schmandt-Besserat (1999) believes the Babylonians favored the quantity 60 because it is so versatile. It can be divided by 1, 2, 3, 4, 5, 6, 10, 12, 15, 20, 30, and 60.

1	Y
2	YY
3	YYY
4	ᐺ
5	ᐺY
6	YYY
7	ᐺᐺ
8	ᐺᐺY
9	ᐺᐺᐺ
10	◁

Weeks. In some cultures, the word for *week* is the same as the word for *market day*. A market day was essential in agrarian societies when people came together to sell or barter goods. A week is now accepted as seven days, but in premodern societies, a week ranged from 3 to 10 days. The ancient Egyptian week was 10 days; the early Roman Empire designated a week as 8 days. Many experts believe that the 7-day week was established in the Roman Empire in the first century C.E. Another theory states that the 7-day week was based on the seven "planets" known in ancient times: the Sun, Moon, Mars, Mercury, Jupiter, Venus, and Saturn. No one knows why the 7-day week was established, but it was culturally determined.

Strategies for the Classroom

- Ask your students why it is important for everyone to use the same units of time, such as hour, day, and week.

- Investigate on the Internet other calendars throughout time, using the keyword "calendars."

CHILDREN'S LITERATURE

Finding mathematics problems in everyday situations  THE PLANNER

Counting on Frank • Figure 1.3

Written and illustrated by Rod Clement
Counting on Frank is a wonderful story about a young boy and his very large dog, Frank. Together they investigate mathematical problems of everyday life, much to the consternation of the boy's family. This humorous book illustrates for children how everyday situations can be the source of interesting and challenging mathematical problems. How could you use this book in your classroom to help children bridge the mathematics they learn in school with the mathematics they use in their lives outside of school?

What Do Mathematicians Do?

Mathematicians observe patterns, either in the physical world or in the world of their imaginations. They pose problems based on their observations, predict outcomes, develop strategies, collect data, and revise their strategies if necessary. They develop solutions, abstract their solutions, and share their results. Similar to musicians, mathematicians use special notation to record and communicate both their work and their results. They rarely work alone and thrive on communicating with others. Some mathematicians' work is immediately applicable to solving problems in the workplace and some is more theoretical.

To some extent, we are all mathematicians. When you throw a ball, read a map to select a route, pack a suitcase, or decide on which insurance policy to purchase, you are using mathematics. Mathematical skills, such as problem solving, are used in every type of job. Those who use mathematics intensively in their careers work in fields, such as engineering, science, statistics, and technology.

Children as Mathematicians

Teachers should help children become aware of the role that mathematics plays in their lives. When children really understand mathematics as a discipline, they can understand that mathematical knowledge is a powerful tool that can help them navigate our ever-changing world. When children understand what mathematicians do and how they think, they can learn that they, too, can think like mathematicians.

The teachers' job is to encourage children to use their natural curiosity and problem-solving abilities to ask questions, such as *why* and *how* about situations that lend themselves to mathematical inquiry. Children's literature is a great way to involve children in mathematical investigations that arise from their own experiences (see *Children's Literature*, **Figure 1.3**).

When children investigate mathematical problems, they use several steps to arrive at their conclusions (**Figure 1.4**). By completing this process, they learn to think like mathematicians.

Children as mathematicians • Figure 1.4

When children think like mathematicians, they . . .

1 . . . create or investigate problems about something they observe in mathematics or in the world around them.

I made three batches of cookies. I wonder how many cookies I made. There are four people in my family and I want to share the cookies equally. How many cookies will each person in my family get?

2 . . . connect their observations to what they already know. Do they recognize mathematical patterns in their observations? Can they create mathematical relationships from what has been observed?

If there are 12 cookies on each cookie sheet, then I can find out how many cookies there are all together and then share them equally with my family.

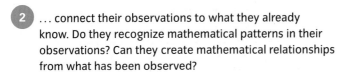

12 cookies on each cookie sheet and 3 cookie sheets

$12 + 12 + 12 = 36$

3 . . . record findings. When children record their findings with symbolic notation they find that this is the most concise way of recording their observations. The symbols become useful tools.

I know that 3 x 12 = 36 so there are 36 cookies. I can divide 36 by 4 to find the number of cookies that each person gets.

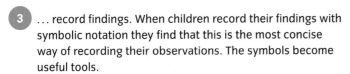

I know $3 \times 12 = 36$ and $4\overline{)36}$ ... 9

4 . . . communicate their results to others. Children communicate their results by offering oral or written explanations of what they did and why.

I know that each cookie sheet holds 12 cookies, and I have three cookie sheets, so I have 3 x 12 or 36 cookies. To share them equally I need to divide 36 by the number of people getting the cookies.

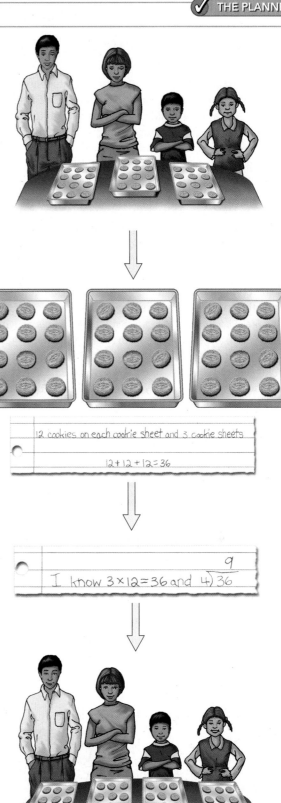

Each person gets 9 cookies.

In the Classroom

Engaging Children in Doing Mathematics

First-grade teacher Kristine M. Reed and her students decided to count the number of spots on a cheetah after a trip to the zoo. They realized that they couldn't get close enough to the cheetah to count its spots but that investigating the number of spots on a cheetah was a worthwhile mathematics problem. They began by looking at pictures of cheetahs in books and on the Internet and making predictions about the number of spots. They noticed that the spots were different sizes, and there were more on some parts of the cheetah's body than on others. As the children tried to count the spots they ran into frustrating problems. They lost count or forgot which spots had been counted and which had not. Then one child suggested they make copies of the cheetah pictures so they could mark the spots they had counted. This worked better, and different groups of children marked spots and counted them with systems they developed.

As Ms. Reed guided her students through this activity over several weeks, she engaged them in thinking like mathematicians. The children identified the problem and developed methods of counting and estimating, understanding when their strategies were effective and when they needed revision. They worked in groups and communicated their findings by keeping notebooks and recording their solutions. This activity engaged children in doing mathematics as mathematicians do and gave them valuable experience in how to pose and solve problems.

(*Source:* Reed, 2000, pp. 346–349)

Think Critically

1. What part of this activity was most valuable for children's learning of mathematics?
2. What specific mathematical concepts and skills did children learn from this activity?
3. In what way did this activity connect to other disciplines?

How can you encourage children's mathematical thinking? Classroom events, such as a field trip to the zoo, can spark mathematical thinking and problem solving and can connect mathematics to other disciplines (see *In the Classroom*).

CONCEPT CHECK

1. **Why** might we identify this photo as an example of mathematics, given the definition of mathematics in this section?

2. **How** does the definition of mathematics in this section conflict with your own beliefs about the nature of mathematics and how it is used in everyday life?
3. **What** kinds of tasks do mathematicians perform?
4. **How** can teachers help children think like mathematicians?

How Is Mathematics Used?

LEARNING OBJECTIVES

1. **Explain** the development of mathematics in history, including the contributions of non-Europeans to the development of mathematics.
2. **Discuss** developments in the field of mathematics.

Mathematics is as old as civilization. The development of mathematics originates from (1) the social and economic needs of society and (2) the curiosity of the intellect. The earliest developments in mathematics arose from the everyday needs of society. Where did mathematics begin? How did it evolve? This section examines the earliest contributions to mathematics from around the world and highlights the development of mathematical ideas over time.

Mathematics in History

Many people think that modern mathematics was developed in western Europe, citing, for example, the mathematics of ancient Greece or the much later discovery of calculus. Although European contributions are significant, developments from many cultures, in particular those of China, India, pre-Columbian America, and the Arabic countries, played an important role in the growth of mathematics. Until recently, these non-European contributions to the development of mathematics were largely ignored by mathematics historians and completely absent from the mathematics curriculum. When we teach children that mathematics has been used by virtually every society and that important mathematical discoveries originated all over the world, they will learn to value the contributions of diverse cultures to mathematical thinking.

The first mathematics was the study of numbers (**Figure 1.5**). Because the Nile River flooded annually, the ancient Egyptians had to learn about surveying to reestablish land boundaries. They needed to learn geometry and measurement to build tombs for their dead pharaohs. The Babylonians developed a number system because they had to give specific amounts of oil or livestock each month, as a tax to their ruler. More than 3000 years ago, the Egyptians developed a symbolic numeration system that was based on powers of 10. As early as 3500 B.C.E. they extended their number system to include hundreds of thousands and millions. They

> **symbolic numeration system** An abstract system in which symbols represent quantities.

also developed an accurate approximation of **pi**, the constant whose value is about 3.14 and represents the ratio of the circumference of a circle to its diameter. At about the same time, the Babylonians also developed a numeration system, multiplication tables for squares and square roots, and an approximation for pi.

Ancient counting systems • Figure 1.5

a. The Ishango bone was found in Zaire and dates to between 25,000 and 18,000 B.C.E. Some researchers believe it reveals an ancient counting system, while others believe its patterns show a lunar calendar.

b. Of the many versions of the abacus developed in ancient times, one of the most popular is the Chinese abacus. It is still used in many parts of the world for arithmetic calculations and can be faster than a calculator. The abacus is used in modern elementary school classrooms as a model of place value for whole numbers and decimals.

c. The Egyptian numeration system was a sophisticated system of counting. Trained scribes used it to solve problems relating to taxes, surveying, and astronomy.

Mathematics as a discipline has evolved over thousands of years. At first, mathematics was used for counting, navigation, and astronomy. Later, its study became more abstract in nature.

Egyptian hieroglyphics

Pythagorean theorem

500 B.C.E.–300 C.E.
Greeks use proofs to justify their thinking.

Mayan depiction of zero

250–900 C.E.
Maya discover and use the symbol for zero.

3500 B.C.E.
Egyptians and Babylonians discover squares and square roots.

Mathematics became an intellectual pursuit in the Greek era from 500 B.C.E. to 300 C.E. Greek mathematicians pioneered the study of geometry by formalizing the **Pythagorean theorem** and developing much of the geometry we study today.

During the Dark Ages or early Middle Ages, from 476 to 1000 C.E., no mathematical discoveries occurred in western Europe. In the late Middle Ages, Europe was devastated by the bubonic plague, and half of its population was destroyed. During this time Greek mathematics was kept alive and further developed by Arabic scholars. At the same time, mathematics continued to flourish in China and India. The Renaissance, which began in about 1450

> **Pythagorean theorem** This theorem states that the sum of the squares of the sides of a right triangle is equal to the square of the hypotenuse of the right triangle (the side opposite the right angle).

C.E., signaled the renewal of western Europeans' interest in and contributions to mathematics. The societal needs of the time (navigation tools for seafaring and cannon trajectories for warfare) motivated the development of mathematics, such as logarithms and trigonometry.

Modern mathematics occurred after 1600 C.E. with the development of calculus. The invention of calculus allowed mathematicians to study the nature of change and motion for the first time. Mathematicians were often considered physicists as well and concerned themselves with solving the mysteries of the physical world. From the middle of the 18th century, mathematics came to be studied as a discipline in its own right and was studied in universities. Mathematicians became interested in developing new knowledge, both theoretical and for application to real life. The development of mathematics throughout history can be viewed in **Figure 1.6**.

Indian mathematician/ astronomer Aryabhata

Leonardo's Vitruvian Man

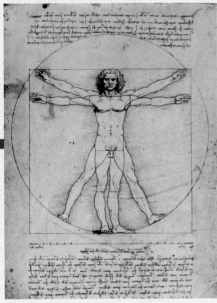

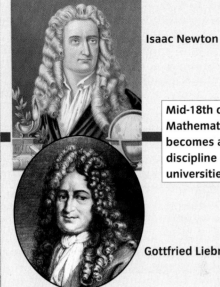

Isaac Newton

Mid-18th century Mathematics becomes a discipline studied in universities.

Gottfried Liebniz

476–1000 C.E.
Mathematics flourishes in Baghdad, China, and India.

1450 C.E.
Mathematics and science are once again studied in western Europe.

1670–1690 C.E.
Newton and Leibniz simultaneously develop calculus.

Mathematics Today

More than half of all mathematics has been invented in the last 60 years. Mathematical knowledge grew dramatically in the 20th century and continues to do so in the 21st century. Fractal geometry was first invented in the 20th century and is used today to model everything from the growth of epidemics to the ups and downs of the stock market (**Figure 1.7**). Much of this explosion of knowledge

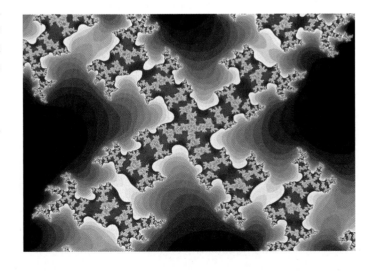

Fractal geometry • Figure 1.7

Fractal geometry is a branch of mathematics that developed in the 20th century and received recognition because of the beautiful computer images that can be created using fractals. Children can begin to explore the characteristics of fractals by studying the patterns in ferns, broccoli, and coastlines.

The growth of mathematical knowledge • Figure 1.8

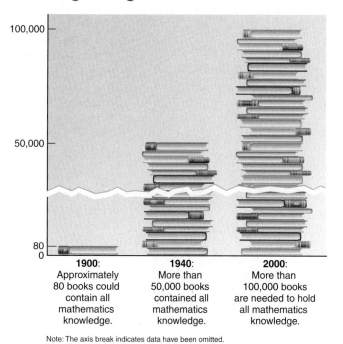

1900:	1940:	2000:
Approximately 80 books could contain all mathematics knowledge.	More than 50,000 books contained all mathematics knowledge.	More than 100,000 books are needed to hold all mathematics knowledge.

Note: The axis break indicates data have been omitted.

is due to the use of computer technology. Computers both facilitate mathematics and provide additional purposes for mathematics. About one hundred years ago, all the mathematical knowledge of the time could be compiled in about 80 books. Today, more than 100,000 books would be necessary to contain the present mathematical knowledge (**Figure 1.8**).

CONCEPT CHECK STOP

1. **How** might a teacher use this picture to help children understand non-western contributions to the development of mathematics?

2. **Why** has mathematics as a discipline experienced unprecedented growth in the last 60 years?

Mathematics as a School Subject

LEARNING OBJECTIVES

1. **Describe** the evolution of the mathematics curriculum from 1900 to 1980.

2. **Explain** the reform movement in mathematics education from 1980 to the present.

The mathematics we need to know changes over time and is a response to the immediate and perceived needs of our society. For example, in 1900 there were no computers; today mathematics education incorporates computer technology because students need these skills to function in today's world. The mathematics we need to know today is different from what it was just ten years ago. Social networking systems, including Facebook and Twitter, have challenged mathematicians' ability to organize and regulate very large quantities of data.

Mathematics in the Schools: 1900–1980

From about 1900 to the early 1950s, the mathematics curriculum was organized around the needs of the industrial age (**Figure 1.9**) with emphasis on learning basic skills. Throughout this period, educators evaluated topics in the mathematics curriculum and eliminated those that did not seem useful in the workplace or in people's everyday lives. Although the curriculum underwent some changes, students continued to learn **algorithms**, which were practiced repeatedly with the goal of achieving speed and accuracy. Students demonstrated proficiency in mathematics by completing timed pencil-and-paper tests. Students worked individually in classrooms and learned mathematics by copying down the methods demonstrated by their teachers.

> **algorithm** A procedure or formula for solving a mathematical problem.

Mathematics in the industrial age • Figure 1.9

In the industrial age, the needs of society and the expectations of workers determined the mathematics that was taught in school. What mathematics skills do you think were needed to perform the tasks shown in this photo?

New Math "New Math was really born in 1951 with the creation of the University of Illinois Committee on School Mathematics (UICSM), but only after 1957 did the federal government provide substantial support for mathematics and science education" (Willoughby, 2000, p. 4). Why did it take seven years for the United States to implement the New Math? In 1957, the Soviet Union launched *Sputnik*, the first artificial satellite to successfully orbit Earth. This marked the beginning of the race to conquer space. The cold war with the Soviet Union and its advances in science and technology were perceived as threatening to the security of the United States. At a time when science and technology were gaining new respect, enrollment in college-level mathematics courses was dropping because students entering college were not prepared for the more abstract thinking that college mathematics demanded.

> **New Math** A mathematics curriculum that emphasized understanding of mathematical concepts through inquiry and discovery.

As a response, curriculum reform efforts were implemented that became known as the New Math. These reform efforts were funded by the newly formed National Science Foundation (created in 1950).

The New Math was implemented into the curriculum about 1960. It focused on learning mathematics through learning abstract concepts, such as **set theory**. Critics felt that the New Math demanded a level of abstraction that children were not ready for, such as emphasis on learning different **number bases** in addition to base ten. Unfortunately, teachers who were not trained to teach this new curriculum felt uncomfortable with it. Children who were taught the New Math often did not learn basic facts as quickly as their parents wanted them to, which led to parents' frustration and confusion. The New Math may have seemed like a failure at the time, but as we look back on it with a fresh perspective, many positive ideas emerged from this period, including an emphasis on conceptual learning and the use of concrete manipulatives to aid in learning.

> **set theory** A branch of mathematics that studies collections of objects known as sets.
>
> **number base** A number base tells you how many digits you have. Base ten uses the digits 0 through 9. Computers often use base two, called binary systems.

Back to Basics In the early 1970s, parents, educators, and policy makers revolted against the New Math and ushered in the Back to Basics movement. This again brought traditional mathematics and the learning of algorithms to the forefront of the mathematics curriculum. With the implementation of this new curriculum, U.S. children once again learned basic facts but were not well prepared for college-level mathematics courses. Children schooled in the United States continued to perform poorly on international tests that compared their mathematical competence with those of students from other industrialized nations.

Reform Mathematics: 1980 to Present

In 1980, The National Council of Teachers of Mathematics (NCTM) assumed the leadership in curriculum reform with the publication of *An Agenda for Action*, which brought a new focus for reform of school mathematics. With this document, educators sought to emphasize mathematical problem solving and to use **cognitive psychology** and **constructivism** as a framework for understanding how children learn mathematics. These efforts culminated in 1989 with the publication of the *Curriculum and Evaluation Standards for School Mathematics*, followed closely by *The Professional Standards for Teaching Mathematics* (1992) and *The Assessment Standards for School Mathematics* (1995), all published by NCTM. These standards provided a vision for what mathematics education should look like and articulated what students should learn at each grade level. They were updated and expanded with *Principles and Standards for School Mathematics* (NCTM, 2000) and *Mathematics Teaching Today* (NCTM, 2007), which emphasize learning mathematics through problem solving, conceptual understanding, and necessary mastery of algorithms. Theories about how children learn mathematics are fully integrated into these texts.

> **cognitive psychology** A branch of psychology that examines internal processes, such as problem solving, memory, and the acquisition of language.
>
> **constructivism** A theory of learning that asserts that humans construct their own knowledge.

Tech Tools

www.nctm.org

The National Council of Mathematics has an excellent Web site with links to activities, lessons, journals, and news in mathematics education. The Web site also provides a link to *Principles and Standards for School Mathematics*. You can also access the standards directly at http://standards.nctm.org.

In 2006, NCTM published *Curriculum Focal Points for Prekindergarten through Grade 8 Mathematics*, which identifies three important mathematical concepts, skills, or understandings that students should know or be able to do for each grade level (access these from Appendix B). In contrast to *Principles and Standards* (NCTM, 2000), which provides guidelines for mathematics learning across grade-level bands, *Curriculum Focal Points* provides focused goals for each grade level along with a coherent curriculum model. Some critics believe that these focal points represent a return to the Back to Basics movement. However, NCTM maintains that *Curriculum Focal Points* was designed to help state and local school districts create mathematics curricula that highlight the most important mathematical ideas for each grade level. The United States does not have a national curriculum for mathematics. Individual states determine what mathematics children learn. However, *Principles and Standards for School Mathematics* and *Curriculum Focal Points* strongly influence the development of state and local mathematics curricula and mathematics textbooks and software in this country and worldwide.

CONCEPT CHECK

1. **How** have earlier reform movements, such as the New Math, influenced today's mathematics education reform?

2. **What** are some factors that influenced the development of mathematics education in the last 30 years?

Principles and Standards for School Mathematics

LEARNING OBJECTIVES

1. **Describe** the six principles from *Principles and Standards for School Mathematics*.

2. **Describe** the five content standards.

3. **Explain** the five process standards.

Principles and Standards for School Mathematics (NCTM, 2000) includes six principles, five **content standards**, and five **process standards** that apply to all grades pre-K through 12. Together they communicate a vision of mathematics instruction in the 21st century (**Figure 1.10**). The ten standards are separated into four grade-level bands that discuss the specific mathematics content students should know and the processes they should be able to use.

A vision of mathematics instruction • Figure 1.10_____

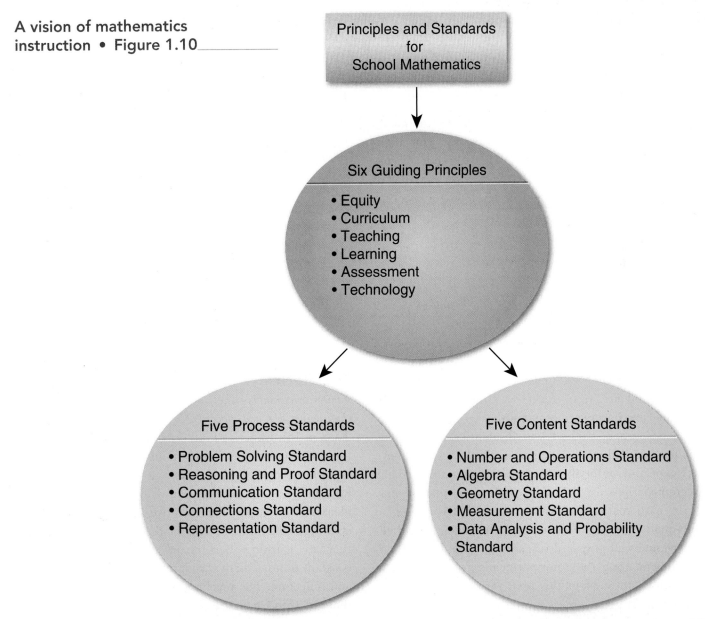

Principles and Standards for School Mathematics

Six Guiding Principles

- Equity
- Curriculum
- Teaching
- Learning
- Assessment
- Technology

Five Process Standards

- Problem Solving Standard
- Reasoning and Proof Standard
- Communication Standard
- Connections Standard
- Representation Standard

Five Content Standards

- Number and Operations Standard
- Algebra Standard
- Geometry Standard
- Measurement Standard
- Data Analysis and Probability Standard

Diversity in the mathematics classroom • Figure 1.11

Equity means providing all children with the opportunity to learn mathematics.

The Six Principles

The six principles for school mathematics are statements that clarify the underlying ideals necessary for high-quality mathematics education. They do not discuss specific mathematics content but convey an overview of the guiding principles inherent in developing a coherent mathematics curriculum that will serve every child equally. Each principle is described in more detail in subsequent chapters.

The Equity Principle *"Excellence in mathematics education requires equity—high expectations and strong support for all students"* (NCTM, 2000, p. 12). Mathematics competency is necessary for full participation in society. Mathematics must be accessible to all students, including those who traditionally have been underserved by the education system: students from diverse cultural backgrounds, students from lower socioeconomic backgrounds, English-language learners, students with disabilities, and students who have difficulty in mathematics. Teachers should have high expectations for all students and be prepared to make accommodations for individual students so that all may thrive mathematically. All students should have access to high-quality mathematics materials, technology, and well-trained and well-prepared teachers (**Figure 1.11**). Ideas for implementing the equity principle are explained in more detail throughout this text, with special emphasis in Chapter 5.

The Curriculum Principle *"A curriculum is more than a collection of activities: it must be coherent, focused on important mathematics, and well articulated across the grades"* (NCTM, 2000, p. 14). A coherent mathematics curriculum must make sense and hold together. Major topics, minor topics, and daily activities need to be connected so that students can understand the big ideas across grade levels. In the past, the mathematics curriculum often consisted of isolated topics. The mathematics curriculum described in *Principles and Standards for School Mathematics* (NCTM, 2000) connects topics to one another within and across grade levels. The theories represented by the curriculum principle are discussed throughout this book.

The Teaching Principle *"Effective mathematics teaching requires understanding what students know and need to learn and then challenging them and supporting them to learn it well"* (NCTM, 2000, p. 16). Effective mathematics teachers understand the mathematics they are planning to teach as well as the importance of designing tasks that elicit students' **prior knowledge** and using that knowledge as a bridge to new ideas and concepts. The effective teacher is capable of creating tasks that challenge and support students while they are learning. Further, effective teaching requires constant improvement through professional development and reflection. The teaching principle is explained more thoroughly in Chapter 3.

The Learning Principle *"Students must learn mathematics with understanding, actively building new knowledge from experience and prior knowledge"* (NCTM, 2000, p. 20). Learning is not a passive experience. Learners construct mathematical knowledge by actively doing mathematics through a process that connects what they already know to new knowledge. Students benefit from the kinds of tasks their teachers provide. Tasks that include classroom **discourse** or discussion, conjecturing, problem solving, and reasoning encourage students to develop mathematical reasoning skills. The learning principle is explained more thoroughly in Chapter 2.

The Assessment Principle *"Assessment should support the learning of important mathematics and furnish useful information to both teachers and students"* (NCTM, 2000, p. 22). Assessment can help teachers improve instruction. Teachers often think of assessment in terms of written tests, but mathematics teachers have many assessment options available to them, including interviews, portfolios, self-assessment, and rubrics. When assessment is an integral part of the mathematics curriculum, students' learning is enhanced. The assessment principle is explained more thoroughly in Chapter 4.

The Technology Principle *"Technology is essential in teaching and learning mathematics; it influences the mathematics that is taught and enhances students' learning"* (NCTM, 2000, p. 24).

Students should have access to up-to-date technology as part of their mathematics education. Technology has fundamentally changed how students learn mathematics, what mathematics they learn, and how teachers teach mathematics. Technology enhances students' learning and offers teachers many options for teaching mathematics. Technology also is helpful for adapting instruction to students with special needs. The technology principle is addressed throughout this book.

The Content Standards

The content standards discuss exactly what content is to be learned in each of the four grade-level bands. Each of the content standards applies across all grade levels; however, individual standards "receive different emphases across the grade bands" (NCTM, 2000, p. 30). This is illustrated in **Figure 1.12**. As students progress through the curriculum, the individual goals described within each standard become more sophisticated and complex. The five content standards are

- Number and operations
- Algebra
- Geometry
- Measurement
- Data analysis and probability

The content standards across the grade-level bands • Figure 1.12

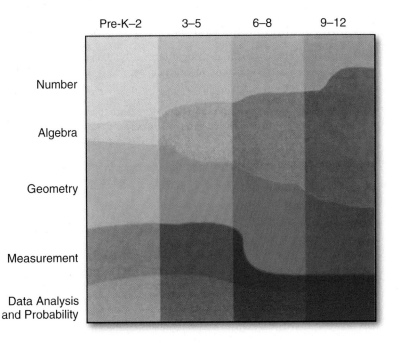

The content standards (**Table 1.1**) are described in detail in Appendix A and frame the content of Chapters 7 through 17.

The Process Standards

The five process standards highlight how students should acquire and use mathematical content knowledge. They are

- Problem solving
- Reasoning and proof
- Communication
- Connections
- Representation

This section examines the process standards and their implications for the mathematics curriculum.

The Problem Solving Standard emphasizes the importance of problem solving as the main process through which students learn mathematics. This represents a major shift in how we view mathematics teaching and learning. The goal of this standard is that students learn how to formulate problems and use a variety of strategies with which to solve problems. The teacher's role in a problem-solving classroom is quite different from his or her role in a traditional mathematics classroom and includes the selection of problems that will advance students' mathematical development. The problem solving standard is explained thoroughly in Chapter 6.

The content standards Table 1.1	
Each of the five content standards has several expectations. For each standard, this table illustrates an expectation in three different grade-level bands.	
Content Standards	**Grade-Level Examples**
Number and operations	In grades pre-K through 2, students learn to count how many are in a set of objects. In grades 3–5, students learn several meanings of multiplication and division. In grades 6–8, students learn about factors, multiples, and prime factorization.
Algebra	In grades pre-K through 2, students learn to analyze and create both repeating and growing patterns. In grades 3–5, students use tables, graphs, and words to describe and analyze functions. In grades 6–8, students learn to differentiate between linear and nonlinear functions.
Geometry	In grades pre-K through 2, students learn to name and draw two-dimensional shapes, such as circles, squares, and rectangles. In grades 3–5, students learn to classify two- and three-dimensional shapes. In grades 6–8, students learn to use the defining properties of two- and three-dimensional shapes to describe and classify them.
Measurement	In grades pre-K through 2, students learn about both nonstandard and standard units of measure. In grades 3–5, students learn the importance of standard units of measure. In grades 6–8, students learn the customary and metric systems.
Data analysis and probability	In grades pre-K through 2, students collect data about their environment and themselves. In grades 3–5, students gather and evaluate data, using different representations of the same data. In grades 6–8, students gather and evaluate data about shared characteristics in more than one population.

Using analytical reasoning in the primary grades • Figure 1.13

Keisha has just made a repeating pattern using pattern blocks. Her teacher, Mr. Murray, asks her, *What do you notice about the pattern? How many different kinds of blocks did you use? What block comes next?* By asking these questions, Mr. Murray is engaging Keisha in reasoning and proof.

The Reasoning and Proof Standard emphasizes the need for students' use of reasoning through logical arguments in their solutions throughout the grade levels. The term **proof**, as used in this standard, can be misleading at first. It does not imply the two-column formal proofs of high school geometry but rather the inclusion of logical reasoning, appropriate for the grade level. For example, when a second-grader knows that 34 is larger than 25 because 34 has three 10s and 25 has two 10s, this is considered reasoning and proof for that grade level. Reasoning and proof also includes making conjectures or reasoned guesses and then using **analytical,** or logical, **reasoning** to determine whether conjectures are valid. This can occur throughout schooling, beginning in the primary grades and encouraged with questions, such as *What do you notice? Why did that happen?* and *What do you think is next?* This process is illustrated in **Figure 1.13**.

The Communication Standard emphasizes communication between students and between teachers and students as a necessary component of learning mathematics. By communicating their ideas with others, students learn to reflect and refine their arguments and to strengthen and clarify their understanding of mathematics. Communicating about mathematics is important because mathematics uses so many symbols. Teachers can discuss the ideas that these symbols represent and foster communication by creating a classroom atmosphere that encourages questions and discussions.

The Connections Standard describes the importance of recognizing connections among mathematical topics as well as connections to topics outside of mathematics. Mathematics is not a collection of isolated facts or topics, even though it has often been represented this way in the curriculum. When teachers help students connect mathematics to other topics within mathematics and to areas outside of mathematics, they provide students with contexts for learning. This helps students remember what they have learned. The teacher can focus on connections with questions, such as *How is this similar to something we have done before?*

The Representation Standard explains how **representations** in mathematics can take different forms and serve multiple purposes. A representation is a graph, equation, chart, table, diagram, symbol, or picture that helps you visualize and understand mathematics more thoroughly. Notice how representations are used to make sense of the mathematics illustrated in the lesson in this chapter. The choices students use for representing ideas affect how well they understand those ideas. Sometimes, multiple representations of the same problem are helpful. Representations can be invented by students or presented by teachers. They can help students organize and clarify their thinking.

In the following *Lesson*, children create representations in the form of graphs or charts to help them understand the patterns in the story.

LESSON | Using Children's Literature to Identify and Extend Growing Patterns

The classic children's book, *A Grain of Rice,* written and illustrated by Helena Clare Pittman, takes place in ancient China and tells of a humble servant named Pong Lo who outsmarts the emperor by using mathematics. The standards are from the *Operations and Algebraic Thinking* domain for grade 4 of the *Common Core State Standards* (NGA Center/CCSSO, 2010). The lesson can be adapted for the primary grades by using *The King's Chessboard* by David Birch, which tells a similar story at a lower reading level and uses smaller numbers.

GRADE LEVEL

4

OBJECTIVES

Students will identify, describe, and represent growing patterns.
Students will learn the result of doubling a number repeatedly.
Students will learn about exponential growth.

STANDARDS

Grade 4

Generate a number or shape pattern that follows a given rule. Identify apparent features of the pattern that were not explicit in the rule itself. (NGA Center/CCSSO, 2010)

MATERIALS

- *A Grain of Rice* by Helena Clare Pittman, one copy
- Small colored chips or counters, about 100 for each group of three students
- Paper and pencils
- Calculators

ASSESSMENT

Students write a paragraph describing how to find the number of grains of rice Pong Lo collects on day 15, as well as his total amount of rice for day 15.

GROUPING

Whole class followed by small groups.

EXTENSION

Ask students to explore the patterns that would emerge if the number of grains of rice were tripled each day instead of doubled.

Launch (5 minutes)

Ask: *How would you buy things if money had not been invented?* After a short discussion, introduce the term *bartering,* a system of paying for something without using money.

Instruct (35 to 40 minutes)

- Read *A Grain of Rice* to the class. As you read, students work in pairs to model and record how many grains of rice Pong Lo receives each day, using counters. (This can only be modeled for the first few days because the amount of rice grows so quickly.)

- After the story is read, ask the following questions: *How can you describe how Pong Lo's supply of rice grew? Were you surprised?* (The number of grains of rice started off small and then grew rapidly. This is an example of an exponential function, but it is not necessary to use that term.)

- Ask students to develop a chart or graph that shows how much rice Pong Lo receives for the first 6 days and the totals he accumulates for the first 6 days.

Day	Number of Grains of Rice	Total
1		
2		
3		
4		
5		
6		

- Ask: *What if I wanted to find out how much rice Pong Lo receives on the tenth day, without extending the chart? Do you see a pattern that could help you find the answer? What is the pattern?*

- Ask: *What if I wanted to find out Pong Lo's total of rice on the tenth day without extending the chart? Do you see a pattern that could help you find this out? What is the pattern?*

- The students should discuss these questions in small groups. As they are searching for the patterns, the teacher listens to students in their groups and provides hints, if necessary.

- Students should realize that to find the number of grains of rice Pong Lo receives on the tenth day, they have to find the value of 2^9. To find the total number of grains of rice received by day 10, they have to calculate $2^{10} - 1$. A student might express this as follows: *Find the number of days, subtract 1, and find 2 to that power.*

Summarize (5 to 10 minutes)

- Ask: *Who can explain how to find the number of grains of rice on any given day?*

- Say: *In the story, rice was used as a kind of currency. It was bartered for servants, clothing, homes, and other fine possessions. There are many instances in history where material things were traded because money did not exist or was unavailable. Some common items used for barter were gold, cows, and cowry shells.* Ask students to discuss the advantages and disadvantages of bartering in general and using rice in particular.

CONCEPT CHECK STOP

1. **Which** of the six principles discussed in this section are illustrated in the *Lesson*?

2. **Which** one of the content standards is the *Lesson* based on?

3. **Which** process standards are demonstrated in the *Lesson*?

Accountability

LEARNING OBJECTIVES

1. **Explain** the impact of the NCLB legislation on state standards, curriculum, teaching, and learning.

2. **Describe** both the advantages and disadvantages of grade-level expectations.

The legislation known as No Child Left Behind (NCLB) was signed into law in 2002. This law represents an effort to hold schools accountable for what their students learn. NCLB mandates that children be tested periodically in academic subjects, including mathematics (**Figure 1.14**). The law stipulates that all children become proficient in mathematics but does not dictate national standards for proficiency. Each state develops its own definition of proficiency in mathematics and then tests its students. Schools that perform poorly over a period of years are denied federal funding.

State Standards

Most states have developed **grade-level learning expectations (GLEs)** or *benchmarks* in mathematics for students in all grades as a response to the NCLB legislation. Compliance

> **grade-level learning expectations (GLEs)** Specific academic content standards for mathematics, developed at the state level in response to NCLB.

with these expectations is assessed through standardized tests. Because these GLEs are based on the NCTM standards, we would expect to see consistency across the states in what elementary and middle grades students are expected to know and be able to do in mathematics.

Unfortunately, this is often not the case. Grade-level expectations in mathematics vary quite a bit from state to state. Although all expectations reflect the NCTM standards, individual states have standards that are very specific or that are not commonly found in other states. This means that textbooks may not meet all the GLEs or benchmarks in a given state and may include some that are not part of the state's curriculum. This lack of consistency creates a dilemma for the elementary or middle-grades teacher, who must be aware of the state standards and be able to supplement the textbook where it is lacking, or delete material from the text, while maintaining continuity of content. To address this lack of consistency, the National Governors Association Center for Best Practices and the Council of Chief State School Officers released the *Common Core State Standards Initiative for Mathematics* in June 2010

Standardized testing in mathematics • Figure 1.14

These children are taking a standardized test in mathematics to assess their knowledge and skills. What are some advantages and disadvantages of standardized tests?

(available at www.corestandards.org). See Appendix C. These standards are meant to replace or supplement states' existing GLEs or benchmarks. While compliance is voluntary, states who choose to adopt the core standards may adopt them in their entirety or augment them with up to 15% additional content.

Benefits and Drawbacks

Some educators find that No Child Left Behind has been beneficial for mathematics education, while others disagree. On the positive side, NCLB focuses on mathematics proficiency and mandates that all students have an equal opportunity to learn mathematics. It is also true that high-stakes testing can affect curriculum development because of conflicting goals. Should teachers try to teach conceptually and ensure long-term understanding but teach fewer topics? Or should teachers include as many topics as possible and teach algorithms to ensure success on high-stakes tests? Conceptual learning takes more time, and students may not learn as many rules as they would if they were learning algorithms. However, when students learn mathematics conceptually,

they understand and retain what they learn, develop problem-solving skills, and are able to connect what they have learned to other topics. In some sense, this struggle is always present when curriculum is developed and goals are established. Do teachers want to demonstrate that their students have met the numerous goals of a broader curriculum and sacrifice depth? Or is it more important for teachers to focus on depth even though fewer topics are covered? Finding the balance between depth and breadth is a continuing dilemma, one that the NCTM standards hope to address with their *Curriculum Focal Points*.

CONCEPT CHECK

1. **What** role has the federal government played in developing mathematics standards for schools through NCLB?

2. **How** might grade-level expectations or common core standards affect your ability to offer high-quality mathematics instruction for your students?

Summary

THE PLANNER ✓

1 The Discipline of Mathematics 4

- Mathematics is the study of patterns: patterns that arise in the natural world, as depicted here, and patterns that inhabit the world of our thoughts and imaginations.

Figure 1.1

- Mathematical patterns found in nature have been adapted by civilizations all over the world to create decorative designs for their textiles, pottery, dwellings, and other structures.

- Mathematicians observe patterns, pose problems, predict results, develop strategies for solving problems, develop solutions, abstract their solutions, and share their results.

- We can encourage children to succeed in mathematics by connecting school mathematics with the mathematics used in the world outside the classroom.

2 How Is Mathematics Used? 9

- The earliest developments in mathematics arose from the practical needs of counting, measuring, and keeping records. Although many of us believe that mathematics developments occurred mainly in western Europe, the roots of mathematics are actually quite diverse.

- The field of mathematics has grown tremendously in the 20th and 21st centuries, as shown in this chart, due in large part to advances in computer technology.

Figure 1.8

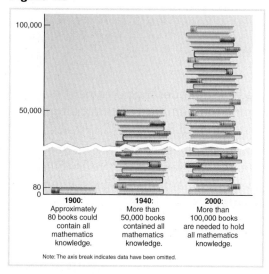

100,000		
50,000		
80 0		
1900: Approximately 80 books could contain all mathematics knowledge.	**1940:** More than 50,000 books contained all mathematics knowledge.	**2000:** More than 100,000 books are needed to hold all mathematics knowledge.

Note: The axis break indicates data have been omitted.

3 Mathematics as a School Subject 12

- In the early- to mid-20th century, the mathematics that was taught and how it was taught were influenced by factors, such as the industrial age (shown here), the Cold War, and the launch of *Sputnik*. The **New Math**, with its focus on **set theory** and **number bases**, was launched to encourage more students to understand mathematics concepts.

Figure 1.9

- In the late 20th century and early 21st century, mathematics teaching has been influenced by developments in computer technology and **cognitive psychology**.

4 Principles and Standards for School Mathematics 15

- *Principles and Standards for School Mathematics* (2000) is the authoritative source for mathematics teaching and learning. The six principles are statements that clarify the underlying ideals necessary for a high-quality mathematics education.

- The five content standards articulate the content to be learned in each of the four grade level bands: pre-K–2, 3–5, 6–8, and 9–12. Each of these standards applies across all grade levels, although the emphasis placed on each standard varies with the grade-level band, as illustrated here.

Figure 1.12

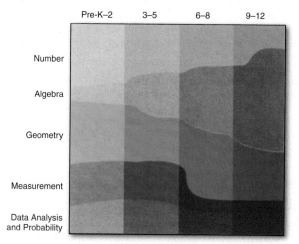

- The five process standards highlight how students should acquire and use mathematics content knowledge.

5 Accountability 22

- In the early 21st century, accountability became an important issue in school mathematics. Many states developed specific **grade-level learning expectations** for mathematics along with standardized tests to comply with the No Child Left Behind (NCLB) legislation. The children in this photo are taking a standardized test.

- NCLB has both benefits and drawbacks that have been debated since its passage.

Figure 1.14

Key Terms

- algorithm 12
- analytical reasoning 19
- cognitive psychology 14
- constructivism 14
- content standards 15
- discourse 17
- Fibonacci sequence 4

- grade-level learning expectations (GLEs) 22
- New Math 13
- number base 13
- pi 9
- prior knowledge 16
- process standards 15

- proof 19
- Pythagorean theorem 10
- quantitative data 4
- representation 19
- set theory 13
- symbolic numeration system 9

Additional Children's Literature

- *The King's Chessboard,* written by David Birch and illustrated by Devis Grebu
  After a wise man performs a service for the king, the man accepts as his reward a grain of rice doubled each day for 64 days, based on the 64 squares of a chessboard. Appropriate for all elementary grades.

- *The History of Counting,* written by Denise Schmandt-Besserat and illustrated by Michael Hays
  This book depicts the history of counting, from Egyptian and Babylonian numerals to the present time. Appropriate for upper-elementary or middle-grades students.

Online Resources

- **No Child Left Behind**
  www2.ed.gov/nclb/
  This is the official government Web site for the NCLB legislation. It provides an overview of the law and suggested resources for implementation.

- **National Council of Teachers of Mathematics**
  www.nctm.org
  This is the official Web site for the NCTM. It provides links to principles and standards, curriculum focal points, and other resources including lessons, Web links, and publications.

Critical and Creative Thinking Questions

1. Look at the photo and answer these questions:

   a. How does knowledge of the history of mathematics enhance children's learning experience of mathematics?
   b. Why are historical and cultural examples central to the mission expressed by Principles and Standards for School Mathematics?
   c. How can historical and cultural examples of mathematics be employed to offer diverse approaches that benefit children?

2. How is mathematics used in the real world? Give an example that is not used in this chapter.

3. In your own words, explain each of the five process standards.

4. **In the field** Select one of the process standards and find three examples of how it is used in an elementary or middle-grades mathematics text. Choose a textbook that was published after 2000. Include the grade level in your response.

5. **In the field** Ask a teacher you know how his or her practice has changed since the passage of NCLB.

6. Select a topic in elementary or middle-grades mathematics (i.e., multiplication of 2-digit whole numbers, addition of fractions, the Pythagorean Theorem). Compare how *Curriculum Focal Points* and the *Common Core State Standards* address this topic. Do they stipulate teaching the topic at the same grade level? Do they require the same depth of knowledge? Explain the similarities and differences in how both documents address this topic.

What is happening in this picture?

Think Critically

1. How does this picture illustrate NCTM's *Principles and Standards for School Mathematics*?
2. Identify one principle and one process standard that are being used.

Self-Test

(Check your answers in Appendix D.)

1. Describe three examples from nature that exhibit mathematical patterns.

2. Describe three examples from our everyday lives that incorporate mathematical thinking.

3. What view of mathematics teaching and learning is illustrated by this photo?

4. State one advantage and one drawback each for the New Math and the Back to Basics movements.

5. How are changes in society reflected in the mathematics that is taught? Consider the following photo as you answer this question.

6. What are the five content standards described in *Principles and Standards for School Mathematics*?

7. The National Council of Teachers of Mathematics standards documents were developed at the _____ level.
   a. national
   b. state
   c. local

8. Grade-level expectations for mathematics were developed at the _____ level.
   a. national
   b. state
   c. local

9. The NCTM's *Curriculum Focal Points* were developed at the _____ level.
   a. national
   b. state
   c. local

10. The National Council of Teachers of Mathematics' *Principles and Standards for School Mathematics* was written in _____.
    a. 1960
    b. 2000
    c. 1989

11. Which legislation prompted the development of grade-level expectations?

12. What are representations in mathematics? Why are they important? Provide an example of the representations used in the *Lesson* in this chapter.

13. What are the purposes of assessment?

14. List two types of assessment.

15. Describe two advantages and two difficulties of grade-level expectations in mathematics.

THE PLANNER ✓

Review your Chapter Planner on the chapter opener and check off your completed work.

Learning Mathematics with Understanding

Laquita Williams is a college junior taking a mathematics methods class. Her professor gave an in-class assignment on fractions, decimals, percents, and the relationships among them. To provide context for this topic, Laquita's professor passed out 10 x 10 grid paper to each student, distributed crayons, read the book *Sweet Clara and the Freedom Quilt*, and asked each student to design a quilt square with exactly three colors that fit on the 100-block grid. Students were asked to describe the fraction, decimal, and percent of each color that was used in their quilt squares.

Laquita enjoyed listening to the story and the book's detailed depiction of how slaves escaped to freedom before the Civil War. She concentrated on designing her quilt square, recalling the tradition of quilting in her own family. She was a little anxious, however, about using fractions. Even so, Laquita had so much fun choosing the quilt colors and creating her design that she forgot her anxiety about fractions. Spontaneously, Laquita shouted out, "I get it! I finally get it! I never understood fractions before, but now I get it!"

Laquita's experience is not unique. The quilt square provided a concrete representation of fractions as well as a context that made sense to her. Unfortunately, many of us learned mathematics by memorizing rules and procedures rather than understanding the concepts they were based on. When we learn mathematics through understanding, our knowledge is connected and more easily remembered.

Shapes and patterns in quilt squares offer concrete examples of fractional parts of a whole that students at various grade levels can readily understand.

28

CHAPTER OUTLINE

What Do We Mean by Learning with Understanding? 30

Key Questions: How is relational understanding different from instrumental understanding? Why is it important to learn mathematics with relational understanding?

How Do Children Learn Mathematics? 34

Key Question: How do behaviorist learning theories differ from constructivist learning theories?

Fostering Mathematical Understanding Through the Culture of the Classroom 37

Key Questions: What are the characteristics of a classroom culture that fosters understanding? What are some techniques for collaboration and communication in the mathematics classroom?

Fostering Mathematical Understanding Through the Selection of Tasks and Tools 43

Key Questions: What are the best kinds of tasks to give children? What are manipulatives? How can they be used to foster children's understanding of mathematics?

NCTM The Learning Principle: Students must learn mathematics with understanding, actively building new knowledge from experience and prior knowledge. (NCTM, 2000, p. 20)

CHAPTER PLANNER ✓

- ❏ Study the picture and read the opening story.
- ❏ Scan the Learning Objectives in each section:
  p. 30 ❏ p. 34 ❏ p. 37 ❏ p. 43 ❏
- ❏ Read the text and study all visuals and Activities. Answer any questions.

Analyze key features

- ❏ Process Diagram, p. 35
- ❏ Multicultural Perspectives in Mathematics, p. 36
- ❏ In the Classroom, p. 43
- ❏ Children's Literature, p. 45
- ❏ Education InSight, p. 46
- ❏ Stop: Answer the Concept Checks before you go on:
  p. 33 ❏ p. 37 ❏ p. 43 ❏ p. 47 ❏

End of chapter

- ❏ Review the Summary and Key Terms.
- ❏ Answer the Critical and Creative Thinking Questions.
- ❏ Answer What is happening in this picture?
- ❏ Complete the Self-Test and check your answers.

What Do We Mean by Learning with Understanding?

LEARNING OBJECTIVES

1. **Compare** and **contrast** relational and instrumental understanding.

2. **Describe** why it is important to learn mathematics with relational understanding.

3. **Distinguish** between conceptual and procedural knowledge in mathematics.

Many of us learned mathematics without understanding. "Learning with understanding is essential to enable students to solve the new kinds of problems they will inevitably face in the future" (NCTM, 2000, p. 21). In recent decades, research in psychology and education has clarified and emphasized the importance of different types of mathematical understanding.

What Is Mathematical Understanding?

Learning mathematics with understanding is something most teachers strive to achieve. However, not everyone agrees on what it means to learn mathematics with understanding. "We understand something if we see how it is related or connected to other things that we know" (Hiebert et al., 1997, p. 4). In other words, something in mathematics is understood if it is part of a network or web of connected ideas, facts, and procedures. Understanding is not an all-or-nothing idea. Understanding grows as new connections among ideas are built over time.

Ideas can be richly connected to one another, somewhat connected, or not at all connected. At opposite ends of this range of connection are **relational understanding** and **instrumental understanding**. Someone who has relational understanding of mathematics has the flexibility to make several possible plans for performing a mathematical task. Someone who has instrumental understanding must follow a fixed, step-by-step procedure to perform

> **relational understanding** Type of understanding that is characterized by knowing what to do and why.
>
> **instrumental understanding** Type of understanding that is characterized by the possession of a rule and the ability to use it.

a mathematical task (Skemp, 2006). In many ways, instrumental understanding of mathematics is easier to teach and easier to understand because it asks less of both the learner and the teacher. Instrumental understanding allows us to obtain the right answer with less knowledge. Our goal as educators is to help our students achieve relational understanding of mathematics because of its many benefits.

Look at a nonmathematical and a mathematical example of learning with understanding (**Figure 2.1**).

The Importance of Learning Mathematics with Understanding

Learning mathematics with relational understanding supports students' autonomy and confidence while defeating **math anxiety**, or fear of mathematics, and lack of interest in mathematics. Students become anxious when they memorize procedures without understanding the reasons for their actions. Students who learn mathematics with understanding are more likely to figure things out on their own, tackle new problems, and gain satisfaction from taking on challenging tasks. Learning mathematics with understanding promotes flexibility in thinking and the development of problem-solving skills, which are necessary for success in our highly technological and rapidly changing society.

There are several more advantages to learning mathematics with understanding.

- **"Understanding is generative"** (Hiebert and Carpenter, 1992, p. 74).

  When children understand mathematics, they are more likely to invent strategies and procedures to enhance their current understanding and generate new knowledge. *Example*: If children understand the result of multiplying any number by 10, they can extend this pattern to multiplication by 100 or 1000, thus generating new knowledge of multiplying by multiples of 10.

- **"Understanding promotes remembering"** (Hiebert and Carpenter, 1992, p. 74).

  When children understand what they have learned,

Learning with understanding • Figure 2.1

a. Problem: Finding alternative routes between home and school

You may know one route between your home and school, but the more you know about the locations of your home and school, the deeper your understanding and the greater your flexibility will be. If you explore several routes, you develop a connected network of knowledge relating these two locations. This gives you more choices, so that if one route is blocked by construction, you can take another one.

b. Problem: *53 – 28*

1.

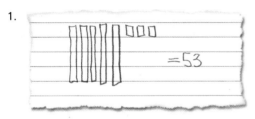

Keenan says,

> *I know that 53 means 5 tens and 3 ones and 28 means 2 tens and 8 ones. Subtracting 28 from 53 means I have to change 53 into 4 tens and 13 ones.*

Does Keenan's work demonstrate understanding of 2-digit subtraction?

2.

Mia solves the problem by changing it to addition and says,

> *28 plus what number equals 53? I know that 28 plus 2 equals 30 and 23 more equals 53.*

Does Mia's work demonstrate understanding of two-digit subtraction?

Both Keenan and Mia understand how to subtract 28 from 53 because they can connect these quantities to concepts, such as place value, relative size of numbers, and the **inverse relationship** between addition and subtraction even though they approach the problem very differently. Merely producing the correct answer is not enough to claim full understanding.

they are more likely to remember it when it is applied to something else. *Example*: If children understand that a parallelogram can be converted to a rectangle by slicing off a right triangle on one end of the parallelogram and reattaching it on the other end, they are more likely to remember the formula for the area of a parallelogram.

- **"Understanding reduces the amount that must be remembered"** (Hiebert and Carpenter, 1992, p. 75). If something is understood, it is connected to other facts and concepts. *Example*: If when children learn multiplication facts they understand the **commutative property**, they will only have to learn half of the multiplication facts.

- **"Understanding enhances transfer"** (Hiebert and Carpenter, 1992, p. 75).

  When children understand mathematics, they can identify the similarities that new ideas have to previously learned mathematics and can transfer previously learned knowledge to new tasks. *Example:* If children understand whole number computation, they can transfer much of what they know to computation with decimals.

- **"Understanding influences beliefs"** (Hiebert and Carpenter, 1992, p. 77).

  Children's beliefs about mathematics are influenced by their experiences with it. *Example:* If children are asked to memorize facts and step-by-step rules, then they tend to believe that mathematics consists of facts and rules. If their experience of mathematics involves building connections, then they tend to believe that mathematics is a connected body of knowledge.

Conceptual and Procedural Knowledge

Within the framework of mathematical understanding, *The Learning Principle* (NCTM, 2000) identifies three types of mathematical knowledge:

- **Factual knowledge** includes knowledge of unchanging facts in mathematics, such as the number of hours in a day or the number of minutes in an hour.

- **Conceptual knowledge** is knowledge that is richly connected to other ideas and stored as part of a network.

- **Procedural knowledge** includes knowledge of the rules and procedures necessary to carry out mathematical tasks.

Together these constitute important and necessary mathematical knowledge (**Figure 2.2**). Conceptual knowledge is closely related to relational understanding, whereas procedural knowledge is related to instrumental understanding.

The importance of factual knowledge in mathematics is taken for granted. However, there has been much debate over the importance of procedural versus conceptual knowledge and how to determine the appropriate balance between the two for instruction. For much of the 20th century, procedural knowledge received priority. With the advent of cognitive psychology in the 1960s, psychologists and educational researchers became more interested in the value of conceptual knowledge. By the late 20th century, the importance of both procedural and conceptual knowledge was understood, but researchers questioned which type of knowledge to teach first.

Researchers now understand that conceptual knowledge should be taught before procedural knowledge. When procedures are stored in the brain, each step is at first stored separately, but later, all the steps may be merged together. If procedures are taught first and then practiced, it is difficult to **retrieve**, or remember, the individual steps and connect them to the concepts on which they are based.

The three types of mathematical knowledge • Figure 2.2

Three types of mathematical knowledge can be identified for a circle.

factual: pi = 3.14159 . . .

conceptual: A circle is the set of points that are a fixed distance from a given point.

procedural: To find the circumference of a circle use the formula $C = 2(pi)r$.

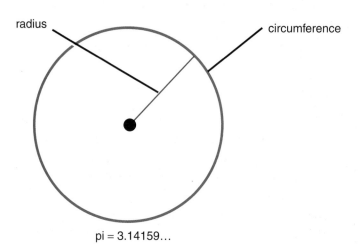

radius   circumference

pi = 3.14159...

Children using procedural and conceptual knowledge • Figure 2.3 _____

Problem: *There are 176 students in the second grade and 215 students in the third grade. How many students are there in all in the second and third grade?*

Kiera, Justin, and Samir all solve this addition problem correctly. Which of the children's work demonstrates conceptual knowledge? Kiera and Justin's work both seem to indicate conceptual knowledge. What about Samir? His work may indicate conceptual knowledge or he may be following established rules. To find out, you would have to ask him why he regrouped.

a. Kiera solves 176 + 215 by adding 5 + 6 = 11, 70 + 10 = 80, 100 + 200 = 300, then 300 + 80 + 11 = 391.

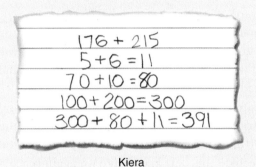

Kiera

b. Justin solves 176 + 215 by saying 176 + 200 = 376, 376 + 4 more = 380, then 11 more = 391.

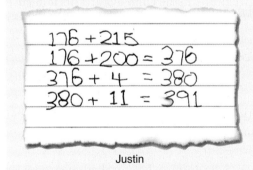

Justin

c. Samir solves 176 + 215 by listing 176 below 215, regrouping 11 ones into 1 ten and 1 one and adding.

Samir

Conceptual knowledge and procedural knowledge are usually highly correlated. In other words, children who demonstrate a high level of conceptual knowledge typically demonstrate a high level of procedural knowledge. Conceptual knowledge actually enhances the ability to recall and use skills. When teachers devote a substantial portion of the lesson to concept development, students' performance on skill-based tests improves (Hiebert, 2003). These results have been demonstrated in recent studies of second and third graders in Korea and first through fifth graders in Japan and China (Siegler, 2003), which showed that students solving two- and three-digit addition and subtraction problems with regrouping or trading demonstrated a high degree of both procedural and conceptual knowledge. In contrast, children in the United States in grades two to five frequently lack both kinds of knowledge. Let's take a look at how conceptual knowledge can help children solve a word problem (**Figure 2.3**).

Virtual Classroom Observation _____

Video	www.wiley.com/college/jones

Click on **Student Companion Site.** Then click on:
- **Foundations of Effective Mathematics Teaching**
- **A. Introduction**
- **3. Diving in Activity**

View:
- **2. Teaching Example** and
  3. Commentary

In these video clips, students work with a "broken calculator" activity. To use a calculator on which keys have been disabled, students use both conceptual and procedural knowledge of computation and learn to distinguish between the two. The commentator clarifies the mistakes the children have made in computation.

CONCEPT CHECK 🛑 STOP

1. **Why** is it important for children to have both relational and instrumental understanding of mathematics?

2. **What** is an example of relational understanding in mathematics? What is an example of instrumental understanding?

3. **What** is an example of a mathematics procedure? What is an example of a mathematics concept?

How Do Children Learn Mathematics?

LEARNING OBJECTIVES

1. **Compare** and **contrast** the behaviorist and constructivist theories of learning.

2. **Describe** Piaget's theory of equilibration.

3. **Identify** characteristics of a constructivist-oriented mathematics class.

4. **Describe** cognitive variability and explain its relevance to the learning of mathematics.

How do children learn mathematics? In the 20th century, two major psychological learning theories emerged and dominated the research in this area—behaviorism and constructivism. Both of these theories have been applied to the learning of mathematics and have significantly influenced what mathematics is taught and how it is taught.

Behaviorism

In the early 20th century, Edward Thorndike proposed the **S-R bond theory** of learning, also called **behaviorism**, connectionism, and associationism. Thorndike applied his theory to the teaching of arithmetic. His belief that arithmetic should consist of memorization of facts and rules has influenced the teaching of mathematics for the past 80 years. Behaviorism provided the foundation for the Back to Basics movement of the 1970s. Educators who teach with a behaviorist perspective believe that teachers transmit knowledge and learners absorb it.

> **behaviorism** A theory of learning that asserts that learning occurs when bonds are created between stimuli (events in the environment) and responses (reactions to the stimuli).

The behaviorist approach is still popular today, probably because it meets the needs of the current educational atmosphere, with its focus on high-stakes tests and accountability. Behaviorism provides clear, well-structured objectives and learning outcomes, which can easily conform to the grade-level expectations or benchmarks that most states have developed and thus can be very attractive to educators and curriculum developers.

Constructivism

The development of cognitive psychology in the 1960s ushered in a new psychology of learning, called **constructivism**. This theory was based initially on the work of Jean Piaget and Lev Vygotsky. Other contributors include Jerome Bruner, Howard Gardner, and Nelson Goodman. Piaget believed that humans are always developing cognitively. When we are presented with something that we do not understand or that contradicts what we think we already know, we are thrown into a state of **disequilibrium**, or mental confusion. During this time of disequilibrium, we have the greatest opportunity to learn. As we reorganize our mental networks to include this new knowledge we again reach a state of **equilibrium**, or balance. The process of resolving disequilibrium is called **equilibration** (**Figure 2.4**).

> **constructivism** A theory of learning that asserts that humans construct their own knowledge.

Teaching based on constructivist learning theory is fairly recent in Western culture. In the United States, its influence is apparent in *The Curriculum and Evaluation Standards for School Mathematics* (NCTM, 1989), *Principles and Standards for School Mathematics* (NCTM, 2000), and *Curriculum Focal Points for Prekindergarten through Grade 8 Mathematics* (NCTM, 2006). Other cultures have used constructivist learning practices for quite some time. One example comes from traditional American Indian classrooms (see *Multicultural Perspectives in Mathematics*, on page 36).

Mathematics educators who apply constructivist theory believe that the role of the teacher is one of facilitator rather than transmitter of knowledge. They believe that children learn most effectively in a problem-solving environment, where they are presented with opportunities to investigate new concepts, raise questions, develop **hypotheses** (theories about what is true) and test their hypotheses. They also believe that **communication** (learning through interaction with others) and **reflection** (thinking about what we have learned and relating it back to what we already know) are essential components of learning. These ideas are discussed later in the chapter.

The process of equilibration • Figure 2.4

When children learn about fractions, their new knowledge often contradicts what they know about whole numbers.

1 Ethan thinks that when you multiply two fractions your answer should be larger than the numbers being multiplied, because he knows this is true when he multiplies two whole numbers. His incorrect assumption has caused what Piaget terms *disequilibrium*.

How can $\frac{1}{6}$ be the answer? It's smaller than $\frac{1}{2}$ and smaller than $\frac{1}{3}$.

$\frac{1}{3} \times \frac{1}{2} = \frac{1}{6}$

2 Rachel uses a candy bar as a concrete model to represent $\frac{1}{3} \times \frac{1}{2}$, first breaking the bar into two equal pieces and then breaking half of the bar into three equal pieces. Rachel gives Ethan a small piece of the candy bar, which represents $\frac{1}{6}$ of the whole bar.

3 Moving away from the concrete model of the candy bar, Mr. Fennel shows Ethan and his classmates how to represent $\frac{1}{3} \times \frac{1}{2}$ with a picture. He shows them that $\frac{1}{3} \times \frac{1}{2}$ means one of the three equal parts of one half. First, Mr. Fennel shades one half of the whole. Then he shades one third of one half of the whole with a different color. The area that is shaded with both colors represents $\frac{1}{6}$ of the whole, or $\frac{1}{3}$ of $\frac{1}{2}$.

4 Ethan now has a new understanding of the meaning of multiplication of fractions and how it differs from the multiplication of whole numbers. This new understanding brings him back to a state of equilibrium.

Multicultural Perspectives in Mathematics

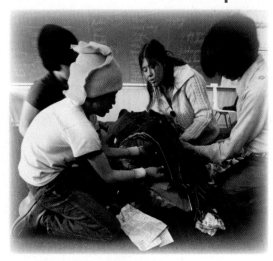

American Indian Classrooms

Classrooms in which the teacher and the students are American Indians share some surprising characteristics. Children are encouraged to work together, help each other, respect each other, and cooperate. Group learning is valued over individual achievement, although each student is viewed as capable of learning. The teacher facilitates learning rather than imposing it. Curriculum and instruction are structured around real problems that the students may have in their lives, such as an art lesson that simulates the stretching of a bearskin in a Yup'ik classroom, or mathematics lessons that incorporate the weighing of corn, or the study of symmetry as it applies to weaving and jewelry making in Navajo classrooms.

American Indian classrooms are not time-driven. There is no predetermined schedule for the completion of tasks. Instead, class members undertake new assignments only after previous ones are completed and fully understood by everyone. These classrooms emphasize harmony, balance, and holistic thinking. The patterns of interaction, role of the teacher, attitude toward time, selection of learning tasks, and emphasis on group learning and cohesiveness are congruent with American Indian cultural values.

There are similarities between American Indian classrooms and classrooms that apply constructivist learning theory. Both value the input of the learner, view students as capable of learning complex tasks, focus on problem solving, view the teacher as a facilitator, encourage group cooperation rather than individual competitiveness, and value the interactions of students to the learning process.

Strategies for the Classroom

- Why is it important to consider children's cultural heritage when planning for instruction?

- What characteristics of American Indian classrooms would you like to adopt in your own classroom?

New Developments in Cognitive Science

According to the theory of **cognitive variability**, children switch back and forth between less and more advanced strategies for many years (**Figure 2.5**). Even if you try to discourage children from using less advanced strategies, they will continue to do so. This kind of cognitive variability is to be expected, and "children actually learn better . . . when they are allowed to choose the strategy they wish to use" (Siegler, 2003, p. 294). Immature strategies, such as finger counting, will drop away naturally as students substitute more advanced strategies and techniques. However, it is important for students to develop **adaptive choice**. Research has shown that most children from second grade onward are capable of doing this. Children from low-income groups show no disadvantage in adaptive choice, at least with arithmetic tasks.

> **cognitive variability**
> The use of multiple strategies when solving the same type of problem.

> **adaptive choice**
> Selecting or adjusting the choice of strategy based on the characteristics of the problem.

Cognitive variability • Figure 2.5

Children will often count on their fingers long after they have learned basic facts, even if they are told not to. It is not uncommon to observe children holding their hands behind their backs or sitting on their hands so they can continue to count on their fingers without the teacher seeing them.

As early as first grade we note differences in cognitive variability among students. These individual differences are not influenced by variables such as gender, location (suburban, urban, rural), or income. Some students will become gifted in mathematics, others will be proficient, and some will develop learning difficulties in mathematics.

Why do some students have difficulty learning arithmetic? Children who have had limited exposure to numbers before school are already behind when they enter school. Also, some children have limited **working memory capacity**. That is, they cannot hold the original problem in memory while they are computing the answer. Also, some children have a poor conceptual understanding of arithmetic. It is important that teachers help students who fall behind as early as possible.

CONCEPT CHECK STOP

1. **What** are three characteristics of a mathematics classroom that apply behaviorist learning theory?
2. **What** is meant by Piaget's theory of equilibration? How is it applied in the mathematics classroom?
3. **What** are three characteristics of a mathematics classroom that apply constructivist learning theory?
4. **How** is finger counting an example of cognitive variability?

Fostering Mathematical Understanding Through the Culture of the Classroom

LEARNING OBJECTIVES
1. **Identify** the four characteristics of a classroom that is a community of learners.
2. **Identify** different methods for collaboration in the mathematics classroom.
3. **Explain** the importance of communication.

Children will learn what they have the opportunity to learn. An important factor influencing children's opportunity to learn mathematics is the **culture of the classroom,** or the learning environment. According to *Principles and Standards for School Mathematics,* "The classroom environment communicates subtle messages about what is valued in learning and doing mathematics" (NCTM, 2000, p. 18).

The Classroom Environment

In order for children to learn mathematics effectively, they must be part of a community of learners. That is, they must be part of a cohesive group of people who share common goals. As in any other community, a community of learners establishes rules and expectations that guide its interactions. Researchers (Hiebert et al., 1997) list four characteristics of a classroom culture that fosters learning and understanding in mathematics:

1. **Ideas are important.** They can be expressed by anyone and should be appreciated, respected, and examined. The teacher is not the only originator and transmitter of ideas about mathematics. All students have ideas and should feel comfortable expressing them.

2. **The autonomy of the student.** Each student is entitled to his or her own methods for learning and doing mathematics. A variety of methods are accepted, and students respect each others' methodology and thinking even if it is different from their own.

3. **Mistakes are learning opportunities.** Mistakes are wonderful learning opportunities. Some amazing discoveries originated from mistakes (**Figure 2.6**). If we are given opportunities to investigate our own and others' mistakes, we can develop new understanding.

4. **The correctness of an argument is based on its logic.** We are accustomed to the teacher deciding whether an answer is right or wrong. In a community of learners, the logic of the argument decides whether it is right or wrong, independent of who offers the answer.

In the traditional mathematics classroom, the teacher is the sole authority on what is right or wrong, and the teacher's method of doing mathematics is considered the only acceptable method. The stereotypical mathematics classroom is rigid and teacher-centered with no time permitted for discussion, collaboration, or mistakes.

Today, we understand that learning can only flourish in an environment where children feel that their thinking, strategies, and mistakes are respected and heard. They need to feel comfortable exploring ideas, inventing methods and strategies, and expanding their understanding. When students are encouraged to think about their results, they realize they are competent thinkers. In a community of learners students develop self-esteem and confidence in their ability to do mathematics.

Collaboration in the Mathematics Classroom

Have you ever collaborated with someone else? Perhaps you and a friend repaired a car, studied for a test, or cooked a meal together (**Figure 2.7**). What benefits did you gain from collaboration? Were there any drawbacks? Did you find that you were saddled with most of the work or that expectations were not clearly defined before you started? Collaboration can be a positive experience when it is carefully structured, especially for learning mathematics.

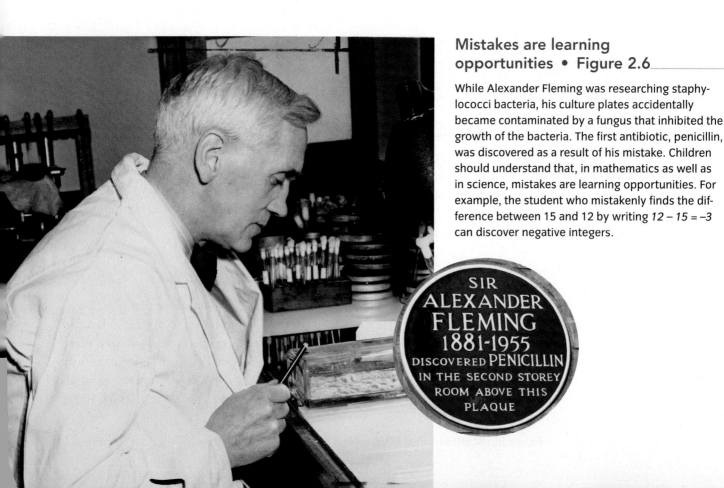

Mistakes are learning opportunities • Figure 2.6

While Alexander Fleming was researching staphylococci bacteria, his culture plates accidentally became contaminated by a fungus that inhibited the growth of the bacteria. The first antibiotic, penicillin, was discovered as a result of his mistake. Children should understand that, in mathematics as well as in science, mistakes are learning opportunities. For example, the student who mistakenly finds the difference between 15 and 12 by writing *12 − 15 = −3* can discover negative integers.

SIR ALEXANDER FLEMING 1881-1955 DISCOVERED PENICILLIN IN THE SECOND STOREY ROOM ABOVE THIS PLAQUE

Collaboration and helping others • Figure 2.7

In projects such as Habitat for Humanity, everyone pitches in and works together to get the job done. Collaboration encourages people to share the work, learn new skills, and build on individual strengths. Collaboration in the mathematics classroom has similar results.

The traditional mathematics classroom does not encourage collaboration and often forbids it. Somehow, we have passed down the tradition that working alone is the only way to achieve mathematics proficiency and that working with others is not as good. It is part of our American history and culture to explore new frontiers and admire self-reliance. We have revered heroes who accomplished great things while "going it alone." Consider frontiersman Daniel Boone or aviator Charles Lindbergh as examples. Although this is an admirable trait in some situations, it is not the best way to learn mathematics. The greatest mathematicians have learned through collaborating with others, sometimes writing to colleagues they would never meet (**Figure 2.8**). When we collaborate, we learn how others think, get the opportunity to share how we think about a problem, refine our thinking, and gain new insights.

There are many ways for students to collaborate in the mathematics classroom. **Think-pair-share** is one collaborative technique. Each student thinks about the solution to a problem independently and then is paired with a partner to talk about their solutions. Finally, they share their thinking in a whole-class discussion.

Peer tutoring pairs a student who is more knowledgeable about a topic with a student who is less knowledgeable about that topic. **Peer collaboration** involves pairing students to work together to solve a problem that separately they cannot solve on their own. Students engaged in peer collaboration learn more when working with a partner than when working alone.

Mathematicians who collaborated • Figure 2.8

The Hungarian mathematician Paul Erdos (1913–1996) founded the field of discrete mathematics, which provided the foundation for computer science. Erdos authored over 1500 papers with approximately 500 collaborators worldwide.

Cooperative learning, a technique that has become very popular in the last two decades, involves small groups of equally knowledgeable students working together to solve mathematics problems.

Cooperative learning needs to be carefully structured and monitored to be effective. Classrooms that use cooperative groups successfully share several characteristics (**Figure 2.9**).

Characteristics of successful cooperative groups • Figure 2.9

1. Norms are clearly established. Children understand that everyone in the group must be given a chance and will be expected to participate. Members of the group may disagree but should respect others' views and work to reach consensus.

2. Before students begin work, the teacher carefully launches the activity by explaining what is expected. Students are given time to read directions and ask questions before beginning work in their groups.

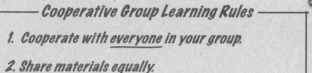

Cooperative Group Learning Rules

1. Cooperate with *everyone* in your group.

2. Share materials equally.

3. Listen to others.

4. Find a group solution to the task.

5. Make sure everyone understands the solution.

6. Share leadership among all members of the group.

3. Tasks are carefully selected so that they are interesting, challenging, and encourage group discussion. The teacher provides tasks that require brainstorming, interdependence, and interaction, rather than tasks that can be broken into parts with each student taking one part.

4. Individual accountability is stressed. Each student in the group understands that she or he may be called upon to explain the group's method or solutions to the rest of the class.

Communication in the Mathematics Classroom

Have you ever explained something complicated to someone and found that, afterward, you understood it better because you had to explain it to someone else? The process of communicating, in the real world and in the mathematics classroom, helps us clarify our understanding. By communicating we mean talking, listening, watching, writing, and demonstrating (Hiebert, 2003). Communication through peer interaction is beneficial in many ways. When students work alone, they tend to get "locked into" a particular way of thinking. However, when they communicate with others, they can expand their thinking and free up their thought patterns so they can look at alternative ways of solving a problem. Communicating about mathematics allows students to solve problems that might otherwise be beyond their grasp, helps them to share their individual expertise, and helps them determine the validity of their intuitive ideas (Hiebert, 2003).

Another benefit of communication is **cognitive conflict**, the internal conflict we sense when our ideas are challenged. Such conflict is very productive in mathematics class. It helps students to question their own ideas as well as the ideas of others, resolve questions they may have, clarify solution methods, and reorganize their thinking. For example, when a student learns multiplication basic facts and understands she can find the answer to 7×12 if she already knows the value of 5×12 and 2×12, this can help reorganize how the student thinks about multiplication of whole numbers.

Another kind of communication is the talk that occurs between teachers and students or students and students in whole class discussions. Chapin and O'Connor (2007) suggest five specific strategies for using classroom talk to help students learn mathematics (**Table 2.1**).

Regarding classroom talk, Chapin and O'Connor (2007) note that wait time has long been an issue when discussing equitable learning environments for female students and English-language learners. Educators have recognized that both of these groups of students need additional wait time. Now we understand that all students need additional time to formulate their responses in subjects such as mathematics because of the complexity of the concepts. In their work with teachers, Chapin and O'Connor observed wait times as long as 8 seconds with positive results.

Strategies for learning mathematics with classroom talk   Table 2.1

1. **Restate a student's statement** and then ask the student whether the restatement is completely accurate. This helps students clarify their thinking.

2. **Ask students to repeat what another student has just said.** This strategy broadens the discussion by including more students and also motivates students to pay attention so that they can answer correctly if they are called on.

3. **Ask questions, such as "Do you agree or disagree and why?"** (Chapin and O'Connor, 2007, p. 122) This encourages students to use reasoning to evaluate other students' statements and analyze other students' mistakes.

4. **Ask simple questions.** Pose questions such as, *Can anyone tell us more about this?* or *What can you add to this discussion?* This elicits comments from students who had not previously contributed.

5. **Increase wait time. Wait time** is the time a teacher waits after asking a question before calling on students. Often, teachers become uncomfortable after about three seconds of silence and either call on someone before students have a chance to volunteer, call on a different student than the one to whom the question was originally addressed, or give the answer themselves. Three seconds is not enough time for students to think about a question and compose an answer.

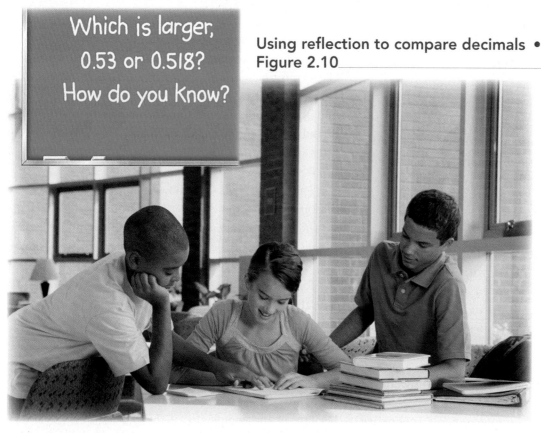

Using reflection to compare decimals •
Figure 2.10

Which is larger,
0.53 or 0.518?
How do you know?

When a class of fifth-grade students was given the task of comparing two decimals, 0.518 and 0.53, some students at first said that 0.518 was larger. (Miguel said that the more numbers there are, the larger the number has to be, right?) Other students compared the decimals by lining up the digits according to their place value. Still other students converted the decimals to fractions. After reflection on all of these ideas, the students decided that 0.53 is the larger number.

Reflection is another kind of communication. It is a process of self-evaluation and self-observation and is an integral part of constructivist learning theory. Students can reflect by thinking, talking, or writing. Reflection is the process of figuring something out or thinking about what we learned and how it connects to something else (**Figure 2.10**).

Teaching Tip

Asking questions to encourage reflection

Ask questions such as:

- *Why do you think that is true?*
- *Have you ever seen something like this before?*
- *How does this remind you about something else you learned?*
- *Did anyone get the same answer in a different way?*
- *What would happen if . . . ?*

After the activity shown in Figure 2.10, the teacher asked whether there was something the class had learned

previously that might have led Miguel to conclude that 0.518 was larger. Students realized that when they compare whole numbers, the numbers with more digits are always larger. Through classroom discussion and the reflection of other students, Miguel came to understand that this rule does not transfer to decimals because decimals are fractions, not whole numbers.

Writing in the mathematics classroom is an excellent way to develop both reflection and written communication skills. One technique is to ask students to write their answer along with two or three reasons why they know their answer is correct. Another technique is to create a learning log in which students record what they learned each day in their own words. These types of activities encourage both reflection and **metacognition**, our understanding of how we learn. Writing also encourages student learning in mathematics because it helps students internalize what they are learning and develop self-confidence in their ability to do mathematics (see *In the Classroom*).

In the Classroom
Writing in the Mathematics Class

A team of elementary school teachers in the Prince George's County public schools partnered with researchers from the University of Maryland. They discovered that when children engage in writing about mathematics and read other children's writing, their problem-solving abilities improve. The team developed an instructional program that assigned students writing tasks during problem solving. Some students struggled to communicate their mathematical thinking through writing because they had never learned how to do this.

The team developed strategies to help students become more effective writers in mathematics. Teachers demonstrated techniques for writing in mathematics and helped students organize their thoughts before writing. Here are some of the techniques the teachers used:

- A fourth-grade teacher demonstrated how students could use a graphic organizer to write down their steps during problem solving.
- A second-grade teacher used sentence starters, such as: *I know this is the answer because* . . . . This added support was so helpful that students were able to write without supports later in the year.
- Some students did not understand what was being asked of them. The teachers developed a rubric to which students could refer as they wrote their responses.

When the teachers reflected on the entire project, they understood that writing helped their students focus on understanding and connecting mathematics to their own lives.

(*Source*: S.R. O'Connell et al., 2005)

Think Critically

1. How can writing help children understand problem solving?
2. Why is it crucial to guide children in writing about mathematics?

CONCEPT CHECK

1. **What** are four characteristics of a community of learners?

2. **What** are three ways that children can collaborate in the mathematics classroom?

3. **How** can we facilitate children's communication about mathematics?

Fostering Mathematical Understanding Through the Selection of Tasks and Tools

LEARNING OBJECTIVES

1. **Describe** how to select learning tasks for children.

2. **Identify** characteristics of meaningful tasks.

3. **Describe** the importance of learning tools.

"The kinds of experiences teachers provide clearly play a major role in determining the extent and quality of students' learning" (NCTM, 2000, p. 21). In other words, the tasks we choose for students and the tools that they have available to them dramatically influence the type of learning that occurs.

Choosing Classroom Tasks

Children develop their understanding of mathematics from the tasks they are given. If they are asked to complete worksheet after worksheet to practice a certain skill or technique, they will learn how to perform that skill better, but they may not be able to remember or apply that skill to other situations. If children spend their time watching their teacher do mathematics and then mimic their teacher by using the same techniques, they will learn those techniques. However, if children are given tasks in which they are asked to think, explore, write, and reflect on the meaning of the task and how it connects to other things they know, they will most probably build new understandings and connect them to their existing framework of knowledge.

What are the best kinds of tasks to give children? Children learn mathematics most effectively when tasks are designed to move from the concrete to the abstract. For example, in **Activity 2.1** children build rectangular shapes (which are concrete) to understand the concepts of prime and square numbers (which are abstract concepts). Sometimes it is difficult to recognize what children regard as concrete or abstract. Adults tend to think of numerals, such as 1, 2, or 3, as concrete, but to children they are often viewed as symbolic or abstract representations of quantities.

Similarly, what is concrete for one child may not be concrete for another one. For one child, the decimal 0.25 is a concrete representation, but for another child, a grid with 100 boxes, 25 of which are shaded, is the concrete representation (**Figure 2.11**). To build understanding, it is important that we help children understand concrete representations of concepts before they move on to symbolic or abstract representations.

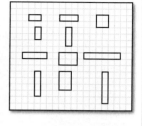

Activity 2.1 Using multiplication facts to learn about prime and square numbers

INSTRUCTIONS

1. Ask students to build rectangles on grid paper to represent multiplication facts.

2. Say: *List all the ways that the numbers 2, 3, 4, 5, 6, 7, 8, 9, 10 can be arranged when their factors are the length and width of rectangles.*

3. Ask: *How many rectangles do you have for each of the numbers?*

4. Ask: *Do you notice any patterns?*

5. Ask: *Which numbers have only two rectangles?* (2, 3, 5, 7) *What do we call these numbers?* (prime numbers)

6. Ask: *Which numbers have an odd number of rectangles?* (4, 9) *Why? What do we call these numbers?* (perfect squares)

Some researchers believe that children learn mathematics best by solving word problems that have real-world **contexts**, or situations. Such problems should genuinely interest children and must include the opportunity to explore, reflect, and communicate about mathematics with others. These are not the typical word problems we are all familiar with. These are problems that have many solution paths and are designed to help children construct knowledge rather than to practice skills already learned.

Children's literature provides a fun and effective way to facilitate conceptual learning in mathematics. Children's books promote active involvement of the learner. They are, by their very nature, contextual and are an excellent source for contextual problems. Several possible problems are provided in *Math Curse* (see *Children's Literature*, **Figure 2.12**).

Concrete representations of 0.25
• Figure 2.11 _____

These all can be considered to be concrete representations of twenty-five hundredths. What is concrete for one student may not be concrete for another one.

a.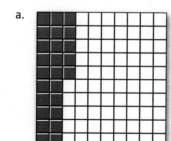

b.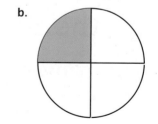

c.

$$\frac{25}{100}$$

We can tell whether problem situations are authentic and meaningful for children by how the children respond to them. When a problem is meaningful, the words children use to describe their thinking remain within the context of the problem. Fosnot and Dolk (2001) identify three components that should be present when selecting word problems.

1. The problem should contain a real-world situation that can be **modeled**, or represented with mathematics.

2. The situation should allow children to picture or imagine something concretely.

CHILDREN'S LITERATURE

Finding mathematics in familiar contexts

THE PLANNER

Math Curse • Figure 2.12

Written by Jon Scieszka and illustrated by Lane Smith

A young girl goes through an entire day in which everything she encounters becomes a mathematics problem. As she recounts these problems, she communicates situation after situation that provide opportunities for mathematical exploration. In one example, five children get on the school bus at each stop. You might ask: *If the school bus has 32 seats and 5 students get on at each stop, how many times will the bus stop to pick up passengers?* What are some other problems that can be created from this book?

3. The situation should encourage children to ask questions and identify patterns. Growth potential should be built into the problem situation so that it can be used as a springboard to new ideas and explorations.

For example, Fosnot and Dolk (2001) discuss a problem presented to kindergarten and first-grade children. The children are asked to make necklaces by stringing together five beads of one color, five beads of a second color, and then repeating the pattern. The children are planning on selling their necklaces, which are many different lengths (but all multiples of five), for a penny a bead. They discuss how to price the necklaces by making charts that relate the number of beads to the cost of the necklaces. Because the cost is five cents for five beads and one dime for ten beads, some of the children discover and explore ideas about place value within the context of pricing the necklaces. Throughout the discussion, student comments relate to the prices of the necklaces rather than to abstract mathematical ideas.

Other researchers agree that mathematics tasks should encourage children to reflect and communicate and that for tasks to be effective children must make the tasks their own. Not all researchers, however, believe that all mathematics problems must be situated in real-world contexts. Sometimes the intellectual challenge of solving a mathematical problem can be motivation for children. Hiebert et al., (1997) present the task of asking children to develop a method of adding $\frac{1}{3} + \frac{1}{4}$ before they have learned about common denominators. To solve this problem, children would need to rely on what they already know about fractions, to construct representations using drawings or fraction manipulatives such as pattern blocks or fraction strips, and to think about whether the methods they are using produce reasonable results. They would certainly be reflecting, and if they worked on this task in small groups or peer partnerships, they would be communicating as well. The process of finding a solution would engender learning.

The types of tasks described here, whether they are embedded in real-world contexts or not, are very different from the tasks typical of traditional mathematics classrooms. These new types of tasks ask children to apply what they already know to solve new mathematical problems, learn new concepts, and create reasonable procedures. When children learn in a meaningful way, their learning creates **residue**. In other words, they tend to take with them what they have learned.

Manipulatives are concrete objects that children use to discover and make sense of mathematics. There are many kinds of concrete tools that are available to children: commercially made materials, such as pattern blocks, tangrams, Cuisenaire rods, base-ten blocks, snap-together cubes, and geoboards, as well as handmade materials, such as five and ten frames, spinners, charts, and popsicle sticks. Four different manipulatives are described here.

a. Base-ten blocks can be used to model whole numbers and decimal fractions. They help children learn place value and operations with whole numbers and decimals. Sample problem:

Use base-ten blocks to find three equivalent representations for the number 49.

b. Cuisenaire rods can be used to model whole numbers or fractions. They can also be used for measurement or for building geometric shapes. Sample problem:

If the brown rod represents one whole, which rod represents $\frac{1}{2}$?

c. Pattern blocks provide a concrete model for fractions. They can also be used for creating repeating patterns, or tesselations. Sample problem:

How many greens make a yellow?

d. Geoboards can be used to model geometric shapes to find area, perimeter, or symmetry. They can also be used to model fractional parts. Sample problem:

Find the area of the given irregular shape.

Using Tools for Learning Mathematics

Learning tools are defined as things that children know, plus strategies and concrete or virtual materials they can use to solve problems. These include verbal language, writing, mathematical symbols, skills, and physical or virtual **manipulatives**. Manipulatives help children model problems with physical or virtual tools (**Figure 2.13**).

Tech Tools

http://nlvm.usu.edu

The **National Library of Virtual Manipulatives** contains many types of virtual manipulatives, including pattern blocks, base-ten blocks, and geoboards. Activities with these manipulatives are organized by topic and grade-level band.

The use of tools for learning mathematics helps children build mental and physical models of mathematical situations that represent complex tasks in ways that are meaningful for the learner. The tools shape the way children think and the understandings they gain from completing tasks (Hiebert et al., 1997).

Tasks and tools go hand in hand. When selecting tasks for children to complete, make sure that they have the tools they need to be successful (**Figure 2.14**). For example, to add fractions, the tools children need include an understanding of the meaning of unit fractions, an understanding of the process of addition, and recognition that adding these fractions presents a new challenge because they have different denominators.

Tools for addition of fractions • Figure 2.14

To solve this problem, children may require tools, such as the ability to represent fractions with drawings or the knowledge of how to use pattern blocks. With these tools, children can construct the knowledge of how to add these fractions. Here are four approaches to adding $\frac{1}{3} + \frac{1}{2}$. For each approach, the child demonstrates that he or she has the appropriate tools for figuring out how to add fractions with different denominators.

a.

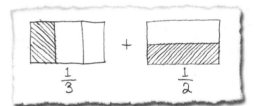

John partitioned each rectangular whole into equal parts.

b.

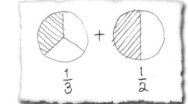

Christina used fraction circles that are partitioned into two or three equal parts.

c.

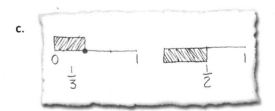

Keisha used the number line to represent $\frac{1}{2}$ and $\frac{1}{3}$ as distances.

d.

Juan used pattern blocks to represent $\frac{1}{3}$ and $\frac{1}{2}$, where one hexagon represents one whole.

CONCEPT CHECK **STOP**

1. **What** is meant by context in the selection of tasks?

2. **What** characteristics do good mathematics problems share?

3. **How** do teachers communicate their beliefs about mathematics through their selection of tools?

Summary

 What Do We Mean by Learning with Understanding? 30

• There are two types of mathematical understanding: **relational understanding** and **instrumental understanding**. Relational understanding is related to **conceptual knowledge** and instrumental understanding is related to **procedural knowledge**. Although both types of knowledge are important, we learn mathematics more effectively if we learn concepts before we learn procedures.

• Learning mathematics with understanding has many advantages. When you understand something, you have less to memorize and you can transfer your knowledge to new situations, as illustrated in the figure.

Figure 2.1

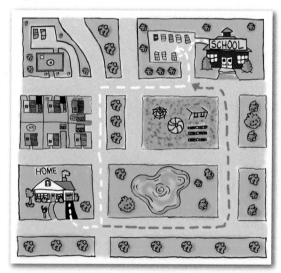

• There are three types of mathematical knowledge: **factual**, **conceptual**, and **procedural**. Although the importance of factual knowledge has not been debated, there has been some disagreement over whether conceptual or procedural knowledge should be taught first.

 How Do Children Learn Mathematics? 34

• **Behaviorism** is one of the two major learning theories that emerged in the 20th century and still influences how mathematics is taught and what mathematics is taught. It is characterized by clear learning objectives, with the teacher transmitting knowledge and the learner receiving it.

Procedures are emphasized over concepts and are broken down into a series of logical steps.

• **Constructivism** emerged in the second half of the 20th century. It is characterized by the belief that learners construct their own knowledge through reflection and communication with others and based in part on the works of Piaget, who developed the theory of equilibration, as illustrated in the figure. This theory is related to the reform mathematics movement of the late 20th and early 21st centuries.

Figure 2.4

• The theory of **cognitive variability** states that children use a variety of strategies while solving mathematics problems, and switch back and forth between less and more advanced strategies for many years. Although this is normal and to be expected, it is still advantageous for students to develop **adaptive choice**, the ability to shift their methods to meet the needs of the problem at hand.

Fostering Mathematical Understanding Through the Culture of the Classroom 37

• The classroom environment is a powerful influence on the learning that takes place. Classrooms that foster learning share a number of characteristics. They create warm and caring atmospheres where ideas are important and everyone has a voice, where correctness is based on the logic of the discipline, and where mistakes are viewed as opportunities for learning.

- Collaboration is a necessary component of learning. There are many ways to achieve collaboration, as shown in the photo, including **cooperative learning**, **think-pair-share**, **peer tutoring**, and **peer collaboration**.

Figure 2.7

- When students communicate with others, they have the opportunity to expand their thinking and find alternative ways of looking at a problem. Communicating also helps children share their individual ideas and be exposed to the ideas of others, as shown here.

Figure 2.9

4 Fostering Mathematical Understanding Through the Selection of Tasks and Tools 43

- The mathematics students learn is very much a product of the tasks they are given to complete. Effective learning tasks should have challenging mathematics and encourage reflection and communication. Mathematical tasks that arise from contextual situations can be very effective.

Figure 2.13

- When children investigate mathematical tasks, they should have all the tools they need, from skills to concrete or virtual manipulatives. The tools students use shape the way they think and the understandings they gain from completing tasks. In this photo, the student is using concrete pattern blocks to build and investigate patterns.

Key Terms

- adaptive choice 36
- behaviorism 34
- cognitive conflict 41
- cognitive variability 36
- communication 34
- commutative property 31
- conceptual knowledge 32
- constructivism 34
- contexts 44
- cooperative learning 40
- culture of the classroom 37
- disequilibrium 34

- equilibration 34
- equilibrium 34
- factual knowledge 32
- hypotheses 34
- instrumental understanding 30
- inverse relationship 31
- learning tools 47
- manipulatives 47
- math anxiety 30
- metacognition 42
- modeled 45

- peer collaboration 39
- peer tutoring 39
- procedural knowledge 32
- reflection 34
- relational understanding 30
- residue 45
- retrieve 32
- S-R bond theory 34
- think-pair-share 39
- wait time 41
- working memory capacity 37

Online Resources

- **Math Forum**
  http://mathforum.org/mathed/constructivism

  This site explains constructivism in easy-to-understand terms and provides links to other valuable sites.

- **Southwest Educational Development Laboratory**
  http://www.sedl.org.scimath/compass

  This site explains constructivism and compares the work of Dewey, Piaget, and Vygotsky.

Critical and Creative Thinking Questions

1. How can you shape the classroom climate to benefit children's learning of mathematics? Provide three examples.

2. **In the field**   Examine an elementary mathematics textbook. Find two mathematics tasks and explain why these tasks provide students with the opportunity to learn mathematics. Revise these tasks to make them more meaningful to students.

3. What are manipulatives? What is their purpose? How do concrete manipulatives connect to the work of Piaget?

4. **In the field**   Read the children's book *Math Curse*. Using a situation described in the book, write a meaningful problem for children to investigate, including the grade level of the

intended audience. Read the book to a child at that grade level, and give the child the problem to solve. Describe your experience.

5. **In the field**   What are virtual manipulatives? Investigate the National Library of Virtual Manipulatives Web site and investigate at least three learning tools that are available through this resource. Write a one-paragraph summary of each learning tool.

6. **Using visuals**   Pick a topic (e.g., measurement, geometry, or fraction computation). Create a scrapbook of at least five different tools that can be used for learning this topic. Use screenshots for virtual manipulatives.

What is happening in this picture?

Think Critically

1. Based on the content of this chapter, what does this picture tell you about the kind of mathematics learning that is occurring in this classroom?
2. What ideas about learning mathematics are reflected in the activities of the children in this picture?

Self-Test

(Check your answers in Appendix D.)

1. Explain relational understanding and instrumental understanding with regard to mathematics.

2. Give two examples of factual knowledge in mathematics.

3. Give one example of procedural knowledge and one example of conceptual knowledge of mathematics for each of the following topics: (a) whole numbers; (b) fractions, decimals, and percents; (c) geometry; (d) measurement.

4. Why is it important to learn mathematics with understanding? Provide at least five reasons.

5. Explain at least three differences between the behaviorist and the constructivist approaches to learning.

6. What is the child in this photo doing? How is this an example of cognitive variability?

7. What do we mean by adaptive choice? Give an example in mathematics.

8. Are timed tests consistent with a supportive learning environment? Discuss in terms of the characteristics of a community of learners.

9. List three ways to facilitate communication in the mathematics classroom.

10. What is wait time and why is it important?

11. How does reflection help these students understand comparison of decimals? What are three questions that can be used to foster reflection?

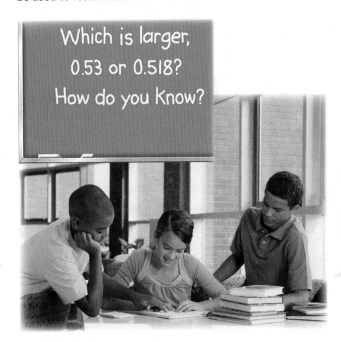

12. Discuss three techniques for making cooperative group learning successful.

13. Discuss at least three additional techniques for peer collaboration.

14. What are three components that should be present when selecting word problems?

15. Identify at least three examples of concrete learning tools for mathematics.

THE PLANNER ✓

Review your Chapter Planner on the chapter opener and check off your completed work.

Teaching Mathematics Effectively

One-room schoolhouses developed from the needs of people living in rural parts of America in the early 19th and 20th centuries. When people first settled in sparsely populated areas, they taught their children at home. As farmers became more prosperous and the population grew, one-room schoolhouses were built. Typically, one teacher was employed to teach students every subject in every grade.

Rebecca Freeman attended Iron Hill School, a one-room African American school constructed in 1923 in northern Delaware. Ms. Freeman remembers how the teacher added wood to the fire to keep the students warm and worked with one group of children to get them going on a project, and then moved on to another group, and then another, teaching children of many different ages and skills in the same day. She said, "I wonder how she did it. Looking back, I really do."

Today, we might look back at the era of the one-room schoolhouse with awe. How did one teacher do all that? In reality, though, the challenges faced by today's teachers are much more complex than those of the past. Although modern elementary and middle school teachers do not teach multiple age groups, they are often responsible for teaching curriculum in several subjects, managing the classroom, meeting the needs of diverse students, complying with closely regulated grade-level standards, and preparing students for success on high-stakes tests. From this perspective, the demands placed on the teacher in the one-room schoolhouse seem nostalgically simple.

Teaching mathematics to students in a one-room schoolhouse was challenging. The skills and knowledge needed by today's teachers are different but no less challenging.

CHAPTER OUTLINE

The Changing Role of the Teacher   54

Key Questions: How has the role of the mathematics teacher changed in recent years? What are the eight areas of proficiency for teachers of mathematics?

The Teaching Cycle   58

Key Questions: What are the three components of the teaching cycle? Why is each of them important?

Teaching Mathematics with Children's Literature   66

Key Questions: What are five benefits of teaching with children's literature? What are six guidelines for choosing effective children's literature?

Teaching Mathematics with Technology   69

Key Questions: What are two benefits of using calculators in the mathematics classroom? What types of software and computer applets are available? How should teachers supervise computer use in the classroom?

Teaching Mathematics in the Era of Standards and Accountability   73

Key Questions: How will the No Child Left Behind Act influence your own teaching? Why is it important for standardized tests to have validity and reliability?

(NCTM) The Teaching Principle: Effective mathematics teaching requires understanding what students know and need to learn and then challenging and supporting them to learn it well.   (NCTM, 2000, p. 16)

The Changing Role of the Teacher

LEARNING OBJECTIVES

1. **Compare** and **contrast** the teacher's role in the traditional vs. reform mathematics classroom.
2. **Describe** the shifting emphasis in the role of the elementary and middle school mathematics teacher.
3. **Describe** eight areas of proficiency for teaching mathematics.

"Students learn mathematics through the experiences that teachers provide" (NCTM, 2000, p. 16). Teachers are the key players in improving how mathematics is taught in school. If we are to improve mathematics learning and meet the goals set forth in *Principles and Standards for School Mathematics*, we must change teaching itself. This section discusses the role of the teacher and how it has changed and continues to change.

Shifting Emphasis

The teacher in a typical U.S. mathematics classroom spends a great deal of the mathematics lesson checking homework, demonstrating procedures, and asking questions that reinforce those procedures. Next, students do seatwork using those same procedures. The class ends with a homework assignment that is meant to provide additional practice. Students often work in pairs or cooperative groups as they complete their seatwork and have calculators and manipulatives available for reinforcement or to check work. Does the mathematics taught in the typical classroom correspond to the Teaching Principle? Today's teaching methods differ from how many of us were taught mathematics—using rules and doing problems and worksheets on our own. But are these changes enough to help children meet today's challenges?

Even though many of us were taught with rules, today we need to do substantially more as teachers. Here's what we know about teaching mathematics effectively (**Figure 3.1**).

This type of shift in perspective is very difficult to make. It cannot be accomplished in a day, a week, or even a semester. It is a lifetime objective that requires a great deal of work. You are being asked to teach mathematics in a way that is different from how you were taught. Moreover, the way you teach is deeply ingrained in your cultural values, beliefs, and expectations—which makes it even more difficult to change. Still, as teachers, you can shift your perspective and actions by taking small steps that will incrementally change your role from transmitters of knowledge to facilitators of learning.

Research studies have shown that Japanese mathematics classrooms demonstrate many of the goals set forth in *Principles and Standards for School Mathematics* (NCTM, 2000). Specifically, Japanese teachers encourage

Students actively making sense of mathematics • Figure 3.1

Teachers must change their perspective from delivering information to facilitating students' understanding and sense-making. What appears to be happening in this classroom? How does this photograph illustrate this change in perspective?

Multicultural Perspectives in Mathematics

A Japanese Primary Classroom

At Green Leaf School, one of the learning objectives in grade one is for children to learn to add 9 + another number, 8 + another number, 7 + another number, and so on as a way of learning to group numbers by tens. Weeks are spent on this one concept, with group work, individual work, and whole-class practice.

The teacher starts with the example of 9 + 4, by placing nine counters of one color and four counters of another color on a magnetic board. Children immediately call out 13, but the teacher asks them to explain their thinking. Each child explains his or her strategy, accompanied by visual representations.

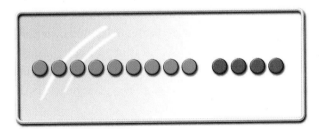

With guidance from the teacher, the class votes to use the strategy of decomposing the second addend into 1 + 3, since 9 + 1 = 10. This strategy can be applied to adding 9 + any other one-digit number (e.g., 9 + 5 = 9 + 1 + 4 = 10 + 4 = 14). This same strategy is applied to adding 8 + another number.

Initially, the teacher uses counters, diagrams, and gestures to help children practice the strategies. Gradually, the teacher withdraws these supports as students learn to perform the operations without them. Whenever a student gives an answer, the teacher asks the class whether it is correct, and the class responds. When a mistake is made, the teacher asks questions to find out where the student went wrong.

In this mathematics class, children's diverse ideas are valued and recognized. Children are encouraged to use counters and diagrams. They also feel safe making mistakes because of the supportive classroom environment.

(*Source:* Murata, Otani, Hattori, and Fuson, 2004)

Strategies for the Classroom

- What strategies does the teacher in this classroom use to get everyone involved?

- How does the teacher help students of varying ability levels succeed?

- How could the strategies used by this teacher work in your own classroom to meet the needs of children from different cultures?

students to share their thinking, provide visual representations for learners, accommodate differences in learners by asking questions with differing levels of difficulty, and provide whole-class practice for slower learners (Murata, Otani, Hattori, and Fuson, 2004).

Green Leaf School is a Japanese school in the suburbs of Chicago (see *Multicultural Perspectives in Mathematics*). It is operated by the Japanese Ministry of Education to educate the children of Japanese families whose fathers are temporarily working in the United States.

Jaime Escalante • Figure 3.2

Jaime Escalante's dream was to educate Latino youth. To accomplish this, he taught mathematics at Garfield High School in East Los Angeles. He helped Latino students realize their mathematical potential by teaching them calculus and preparing them for the Advanced Placement Examination in calculus, a stepping stone to college. Escalante's methods were sometimes criticized as unorthodox. His story was dramatized in the movie *Stand and Deliver*.

Shifting your conceptions of what it means to teach mathematics takes courage and commitment (**Figure 3.2**). To make this shift, you must first reflect on your beliefs and knowledge about how children learn and then be willing to act on this knowledge by developing new methods and skills for teaching mathematics. This includes learning how to design challenging tasks and manage **classroom discourse**. These shifts require taking chances, trying new ideas and strategies, learning or relearning some mathematics, and being willing to reflect on what you already know and what you still need to learn about mathematics teaching and learning. This is especially difficult for those teachers who do not like mathematics or do not understand it well. It is easier to stick with what you already know because it feels safe. As a future elementary teacher, you may not even see yourself as a mathematics teacher, because you will be teaching all subjects. However, it will be your job to teach mathematics and support your students as they are learning new concepts and strategies. Are you ready?

> **classroom discourse**
> The language that teachers and students use to communicate with each other in the classroom.

The Teaching Standards

Mathematics Teaching Today (NCTM, 2007), the second edition of the *Professional Standards for Teaching Mathematics* (NCTM, 1991), was written to complement *Principles and Standards for School Mathematics* (NCTM, 2000). *Mathematics Teaching Today* clearly articulates the changing role of the teacher by describing eight areas of proficiency for teachers of mathematics (**Table 3.1**).

Seven standards that represent the core features of mathematics teaching are conceptualized by a teaching cycle that consists of three categories: knowledge, implementation, and analysis (**Figure 3.3**). These standards clearly delineate the changing role of the mathematics teacher. Each of these categories will be explored in subsequent sections.

Eight areas of proficiency for teachers of mathematics   Table 3.1

Teachers will be competent in

1. "designing and implementing mathematical experiences that stimulate students' interests and intellect;

2. orchestrating classroom discourse in ways that promote the exploration and growth of mathematical ideas;

3. using, and helping students use, technology and other tools to pursue mathematical investigations;

4. assessing students' existing mathematical knowledge and challenging students to extend that knowledge;

5. fostering positive attitudes about the aesthetic and utilitarian values of mathematics;

6. engaging in opportunities to deepen their own understanding of the mathematics being studied and its applications;

7. reflecting on the value of classroom encounters and taking action to improve their practice; and

8. fostering professional and collegial relationships to enhance their own teaching performance."

(*Source:* NCTM, 2007, pp. 5–6)

The teaching cycle • Figure 3.3

The teaching cycle consists of three interdependent stages: knowledge, implementation, and analysis. Each stage benefits from and informs the others in the cycle.

1 Knowledge
Knowledge of Mathematics and General Pedagogy
Knowledge of Student Mathematical Learning   (NCTM, 2007, p. 15)

A first-grade teacher understands the importance of using nonstandard units of measurement when teaching this topic to children. The teacher knows that in the early years of school, linear measurement should be emphasized.

2 Implementation
Worthwhile Mathematical Tasks
Learning Environment Discourse   (NCTM, 2007, p. 15)

The teacher gives the children a variety of tasks, such as measuring the length of the classroom with footprints, the height of the desk with their palms, and the length of their desk with pencils.

3 Analysis
Reflection on Student Learning
Reflection on Teaching Practice   (NCTM, 2007, p. 15)

As students complete their measurement tasks, the teacher reflects on what they have learned about nonstandard units of measure, what they still need to learn, and what the next lesson should cover.

CONCEPT CHECK   STOP

1. **What** do you see the teacher in this photo doing to promote mathematical understanding?

2. **What** does it mean for a teacher to be a facilitator of learning?

3. Select three of the eight areas of proficiency listed in Table 3.1. **Why** are they important? How might you implement them in your classroom?

The Teaching Cycle

LEARNING OBJECTIVES

1. **Describe** the importance of teachers' knowledge of their students and of mathematics content and pedagogy.

2. **Explain** the importance of choosing challenging tasks.

3. **Identify** methods for choosing challenging tasks, facilitating discourse, and influencing the learning environment.

4. **Distinguish** between reflection on practice and reflection on student learning.

The teaching cycle is a process consisting of three main components. Teachers need knowledge of mathematics, the teaching of mathematics, and students as learners of mathematics. Teachers must be able to select and implement worthwhile mathematical tasks and create active yet nurturing classroom environments. Teachers must also be able to analyze and assess their students' learning and their own practice.

The Teaching Cycle: Teachers' Knowledge

Effective teachers of mathematics need knowledge of mathematics content, knowledge of how students learn mathematics, specific knowledge of what their students already know, and knowledge of **pedagogy**. Teachers use this knowledge to craft lessons that engage and challenge learners.

> **pedagogy** Strategies or methodologies for teaching.

Why is it important for teachers to understand mathematics content and pedagogy? Teachers who are secure in their understanding of mathematics tend to be more flexible in their choice of content, pedagogy, and assessment. They are willing to focus on conceptual understanding by encouraging students to explore, investigate, predict, describe, and discuss mathematical ideas. They have a repertoire of representations from which to choose. At the same time, they can identify and help children focus on important mathematical concepts and skills.

For example, in **Activity 3.1** students in a third-grade class are asked to make fraction strips to learn about equivalent fractions. Rather than showing the children how to fold each strip into the correct number of equal parts, their teacher, Ms. Greene, encourages the children to discover this on their own and asks them to justify their methods. Her questions also press her students to generalize their results. Ms. Greene's questions derive from her sound knowledge of mathematics and her understanding of the big ideas within this activity and how to draw them out. By letting the children investigate how to fold the strips on their own, they will learn about partitioning into equal parts, factors of numbers, and the Commutative Property of Multiplication. More importantly, they will learn that they can make sense of mathematics themselves, without having to rely on their teacher for the correct answer.

What can you do if your knowledge of mathematics is weak in an area you will be teaching? Ask yourself: *What mathematics do I need to know in order to present this material well?* Next, honestly reflect on your strengths and weaknesses. Find resources and activities from journals such as *Teaching Children Mathematics*, from reliable Internet sites, and through professional development. Do not hesitate to ask for help from colleagues. Always work through activities yourself before asking your students to do them. It can be helpful to keep a journal that describes your lessons. Then next year, when you teach the same topic again, you will have gained both knowledge and experience.

Activity 3.1 Using fraction strips to compare fractions

Instructions

Children make fraction strips to represent the fractions $\frac{1}{2}, \frac{1}{3}, \frac{1}{4}, \frac{1}{6}, \frac{1}{8}$.

1. Cut six strips of paper for each student, each about 2 inches wide and 6 inches long.

2. Ask students to fold one strip of paper into two equal parts, a second strip into three equal parts, and a third strip into four equal parts.

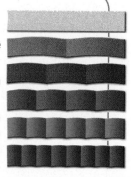

3. Ask students to fold the next strip of paper into six equal parts. After children have folded their strips of paper, Say: *I noticed that you did this in different ways. Does it matter whether you fold your paper first into thirds and then into two equal parts or the other way around? Will both ways work? Why or why not?* (It works both ways because $\frac{1}{2} \times \frac{1}{3} = \frac{1}{3} \times \frac{1}{2}$.)

4. Ask: *In how many ways can you fold a strip of paper into eighths?*

5. Ask: *What if you wanted to fold a strip into twelve equal parts? Can you predict in how many ways you can do this? What knowledge helps you predict the answer?* (You can fold a strip into twelve equal parts four ways because 2 x 6, 6 x 2, 3 x 4, and 4 x 3 are the factors of 12.)

6. Compare the fraction strips by placing one above the other horizontally.

7. Ask: *What patterns do you notice?* (All the strips of paper are the same length; the length of $\frac{1}{2}$ is the same as the length of $\frac{3}{6}$.)

Virtual Classroom Observation

Video www.wiley.com/college/jones

Click on **Student Companion Site.** Then click on:

Foundations of Effective Mathematics Teaching

• **A. Introduction**

View:

• **Watch Video Introduction** and read the commentary.

In this video clip and discussion, you learn about the importance of teacher content knowledge and how this knowledge is essential to teaching mathematics today.

Next, click on:

• **B. Focus on Teacher Content Knowledge**

• **2. Learn About It**

View:

• **2. Hear From Commentator**

This explains how deep content knowledge can help you differentiate instruction.

Knowledge of student learning In Activity 3.1, Ms. Greene demonstrated knowledge of her students' prior knowledge, what they were capable of learning, and how to challenge and motivate them. Ms. Greene understood that students learn best when they have the opportunity to investigate ideas, experiment, and move from concrete to abstract representations. Therefore, she began the study of equivalent fractions by asking students to create a concrete representation of fractions with fraction strips. This gave students the opportunity to develop their own mathematical understandings of equivalence. She guided students through their observations and questions rather than telling them the answers.

The Teaching Cycle: Implementation

"Teachers must implement their knowledge about the teaching of mathematics by choosing challenging tasks and facilitating mathematical discourse within a healthy and supportive learning environment" (NCTM, 2007, p. 32). This section discusses how to choose challenging tasks and how to orchestrate classroom discourse. A sample lesson is provided as an example (see the *Lesson* on the next page). The standards are from *Curriculum Focal Points for Prekindergarten through Grade 8 Mathematics* (NCTM, 2006). A more detailed discussion of lesson planning, an important component of implementation, can be found in Chapter 4.

Choosing challenging tasks Chapter 2 discussed the importance of choosing intellectually challenging tasks for children and provided guidelines as well as examples of effective tasks. This issue will be revisited in later chapters. Let's focus now on what you need to consider when choosing tasks for your students. First, keep in mind how the tasks you give your students fit with your overall curricular scheme. In other words, when you choose problems, games, children's literature, and software, consider how that task fits with your objectives. Ask questions such as:

● *What will my students learn from this task?*

● *How can I tailor this task to meet my students' abilities?*

● *How can I connect this task to key objectives my students need to learn?*

● *How will this task add to students' cumulative understanding?*

Asking questions such as these will help you choose worthwhile and challenging tasks for your students and still maintain "a curricular perspective" (NCTM, 2007, p. 33).

LESSON Finding Prime Numbers

Hundreds Chart

1	2	3	4	5	6	7	8	9	10
11	12	13	14	15	16	17	18	19	20
21	22	23	24	25	26	27	28	29	30
31	32	33	34	35	36	37	38	39	40
41	42	43	44	45	46	47	48	49	50
51	52	53	54	55	56	57	58	59	60
61	62	63	64	65	66	67	68	69	70
71	72	73	74	75	76	77	78	79	80
81	82	83	84	85	86	87	88	89	90
91	92	93	94	95	96	97	98	99	100

GRADE LEVEL

6–7

OBJECTIVES

Students will learn the meaning of prime numbers.
Students will learn to identify prime and composite numbers.
Students will learn how prime numbers are used in the real world.

STANDARDS

Grade 7

Students continue to develop their understanding of multiplication and division and the structure of numbers by determining if a counting number greater than 1 is prime, and if it is not, by factoring it into a product of primes. (NCTM, 2006, p.19)

MATERIALS

- Hundreds chart for each student
- Crayons or colored pencils for each student

ASSESSMENT

- Write a journal entry that explains the meaning of prime and composite numbers and provide three examples of each type of number.

- Do an Internet search for the Sieve of Eratosthenes and write a summary of what you found.

The learning environment Effective teachers share the belief that all students are capable of learning mathematics, respect and value their students, and encourage them to participate in class. They choose challenging tasks and ask questions that elicit individual students' ideas and thoughts (**Figure 3.4**). When students believe they are valued members of the classroom community, they are more likely to contribute to class discussions and benefit from the opportunity to share and refine their thinking. Teachers' expectations directly influence students' opportunities to learn mathematics.

Setting and meeting high expectations •
Figure 3.4

A coach sets high expectations for athletes, pushing them to succeed. What similarities do you find between a coach and a teacher of mathematics?

GROUPING

Whole class followed by pairs.

EXTENSION

1. After completing the lesson, find all the numbers that have both a blue and a red mark. What is the smallest such number? (6) This is called the **least common multiple of 2 and 3.**

2. Use the Sieve to find the least common multiple of 3 and 4, 4 and 5, and 5 and 6.

3. **Twin primes** are numbers that differ by 2, such as 3 and 5. Find three other pairs of twin primes.

Launch (5 minutes)

• Ask students to name numbers between 1 and 10. Write the numbers on the board in three columns:

1	2	4
	3	6
	5	8
	7	9
		10

• Ask: *Why do you think the numbers are arranged in this way? What do all the numbers in the second column have in common?* (They are prime numbers.)

• Ask: *What does it mean for a number to be prime?* (Its only factors are itself and 1.)

• Ask: *What do the numbers in the third column have in common?* (They are not prime.)

• Ask: *Does anyone know what these kinds of numbers are called?* (composite)

• Say: *Notice that 1 is neither prime nor composite.*

• Say: *Prime numbers are very important. They are used today to create encryption codes to keep Internet information secure.*

Instruct (25 minutes)

• Working with a partner, use a hundreds chart. Cross out 1 because it is neither prime nor composite. Select a blue crayon or colored pencil, circle 2 in blue, and put a mark in all the numbers that are multiples of 2.

• Choose a red crayon or colored pencil, circle 3, and put a mark in all the numbers that are multiples of 3.

• Continue in this way. The number 4 already has a mark through it, so go to the next number. Circle 5 in green, and put a mark in all the multiples of 5. Continue in this way until you have identified all the prime numbers between 1 and 100. This method is called the Sieve of Eratosthenes because it was discovered by the Greek mathematician Eratosthenes (275–194 B.C.E.). This method acts like a strainer that separates prime and composite numbers.

• Although this method works well for small prime numbers, it does not work for very large prime numbers. However, mathematicians have discovered ways of testing large numbers to see whether they are prime.

Summarize (5 minutes)

• Ask: *Is 15 a prime number? Why or why not? Is 17 prime? How can you tell whether a number is prime?*

• Ask: *How does the Sieve of Eratosthenes work?*

Effective teachers model positive attitudes about mathematics. As the teacher, you are the only mathematician your students will meet for an entire year. Your beliefs and attitudes about mathematics will influence your students' beliefs and attitudes. If you are enthusiastic about mathematics and believe it is interesting and worthwhile, your students will too. On the other hand, if you fear or dislike mathematics, your students will realize this and will be more likely to fear and dislike mathematics as well.

Teachers demonstrate their attitudes about mathematics through their day-to-day actions in the classroom. The total time you spend on mathematics during the day, as well as the time you spend on concepts as compared to drill and practice, communicates how much you value mathematics and what kind of mathematics you value. Despite what you might say to students, they will learn what you really believe about mathematics from your actions as a teacher.

Managing discourse "Shaping mathematical discourse is a significant aspect of a teacher's work" (Franke, Kazemi, and Battey, 2007, p. 230). The manner in which teachers and students talk to each other in the classroom shapes what students learn about mathematics and what it means to do mathematics (**Figure 3.5**).

In the traditional mathematics classroom, the teacher does most of the talking by explaining procedures, giving directions, interpreting students' responses, and explaining students' mistakes. Even when the teacher emphasizes understanding, the pattern remains the same.

In reform classrooms, the discourse is more complex even though the teacher talks less. Teachers must continually monitor who is participating in class discussions, how they are participating, what mathematical ideas are expressed, and whether students are making progress toward the objectives. The teacher makes on-the-spot judgment calls on questions such as these:

- *How much time should I devote to this activity?*
- *Should the pace be quicker to keep students engaged or slower so that more students can complete the task?*
- *What representations should I use to model this concept?*
- *Which strategies and ideas should I avoid?*
- *What should I focus on?*
- *Should I call on someone who knows the answer or someone who does not?*

A teacher may need to make all these decisions within a single class period. These decisions determine how much mathematics students learn and the type of understanding they gain. Several techniques have been identified for managing discourse (**Figure 3.6**).

The conductor of a symphony orchestra • Figure 3.5

The conductor is the most important person in an orchestra. The conductor is responsible for making decisions about the pace, volume, softness, or aggressiveness of individual sections and interpreting the music to create a unified whole from the different sounds produced by various instruments. In what ways is the teacher's role similar to that of a conductor?

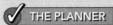
The task: Third-grade students use pattern blocks to create concrete representations of the fractions $\frac{1}{2}$, $\frac{1}{3}$, and $\frac{1}{6}$ with two yellow hexagons representing one whole. The teacher uses **filtering**, **scaffolding**, **tiering**, and **revoicing** to give all students opportunities to succeed at this task.

a. Filtering helps teachers and students focus on big ideas and efficient strategies while giving all students the opportunity to voice their thinking. Filtering is a technique in which the teacher listens to ideas and solution strategies from many students and then selects the ones to focus on with the whole class.

How is the teacher using filtering?

b. Scaffolding is a temporary support to help students complete a task successfully. Scaffolding may include subtle hints or additional manipulatives.

How does this illustration show scaffolding?

c. Tiering is a technique that adjusts the difficulty of a problem to meet the needs of individual students. This student uses one hexagon to represent one whole.

How does this illustration show tiering? How might you use tiering when teaching fractions?

d. Revoicing includes exact repetition, rephrasing, or expansion of a student's ideas by the teacher. Revoicing helps shape students' mathematical ideas by allowing the teacher to substitute precise mathematical language for the everyday words used by children. It also provides encouragement and recognition for individual students.

How does this illustration show revoicing?

One hexagon represents one-half.

In the Classroom
Learning How to Ask Questions

Ms. Tyler, a third-grade, first-year teacher, participated in a research study called Project IMPACT (Increasing the Mathematical Power of All Children and Teachers). She used math centers, children's literature, hands-on materials, and journals to teach mathematics. She often gave her students worksheets to complete, but she also asked open-ended questions (those with more than one possible answer). On the surface, she seemed to be following the recommendations found in *Principles and Standards for School Mathematics* (NCTM, 2000).

The mathematics specialist from Project IMPACT noticed that Ms. Tyler's questioning skills needed improvement. Ms. Tyler did not ask students to explain correct answers and sometimes misinterpreted students' reasoning. When students answered incorrectly, she led them to the correct answer through her questioning.

After attending a summer in-service program with Project IMPACT, Ms. Tyler gradually learned to change her practice. During her second year of teaching, she focused on asking students questions, listening to their responses, and pressing them to explain their thinking, whether their answers were correct or incorrect. She learned that it is just as important to press students for explanations when they give correct answers because their reasoning may be wrong. Ms. Tyler also learned that by listening carefully to her students' responses, she could learn to understand their thinking about mathematics and modify her lessons accordingly.

(*Source:* Adapted from White, 2000)

Think Critically

1. Why are questioning skills so important for a teacher?
2. Why do teachers tend to accept correct answers and move on?
3. What are three questions you could ask to probe students' understanding?

Teaching Tip

Managing discourse

Managing discourse helps English-language learners or students with low self-esteem in mathematics to succeed. For example, the recognition students receive when the teacher revoices their ideas can be a turning point that leads to personal success in mathematics.

Good teachers ask questions that shape classroom discourse by motivating students to think about and explore mathematical ideas. Always ask questions that require students to explain their thinking, not only the procedures they used. To understand how children think, spend more time listening to them rather than having them listen to you. Listening to children has many benefits. All children need the opportunity to share their ideas. When teachers listen to children's thoughts, they are better able to understand their strengths and weaknesses and modify instruction to meet their needs. When teachers listen to students, they demonstrate how much they value student ideas.

Whether children give correct or incorrect answers, teachers should always press them for justification. When students give correct answers, it is tempting to move on rather than ask them to explain their thinking. This practice can inadvertently reinforce incorrect reasoning. One young teacher learned this lesson during her first year of teaching (see *In the Classroom*).

Lesson Study • Figure 3.7

In *Lesson Study*, a group of teachers works together to create a lesson. They observe one of their colleagues teach the lesson and then debrief together after the lesson has been taught. They may rewrite the lesson, based on their experience with it. How is *Lesson Study* an example of reflecting on practice?

Virtual Classroom Observation

Video — www.wiley.com/college/jones

Click on **Student Companion Site.** Then click on:

• **Foundations of Effective Mathematics Teaching**
• **B. Focus on Teacher Content Knowledge**
• **3. Analyze Classroom Videos**

Scroll down and view:

• **Patterns and Functions: Piles of tiles**

Note how Ms. von Rotz encourages her students to share their ideas and even names methods after the students who contributed them. The teacher is using *revoicing* to encourage her students and manage discourse.

The Teaching Cycle: Analysis

As a teacher you must be prepared to evaluate your effectiveness and your students' understanding. This can be especially challenging for new teachers who are facing the realities of teaching for the first time. **Reflection** plays a crucial role in teacher effectiveness. It allows you to analyze both your teaching and your students' learning so that you can make positive changes.

Reflection on practice When you reflect on your practice, you analyze what you see and hear in your classroom and interpret that information to improve your

teaching. In general, you might think about what went well, what you would like to do differently, and how you can implement changes to improve your practice. More specifically, you might focus on the classroom environment, the discourse, the questions you ask, and the tasks you select for students (**Figure 3.7**). New teachers may find it helpful to keep a daily journal that they can refer to later.

Reflection on student learning When you reflect on student learning you analyze what students know and how they know it. This type of reflection happens both during and after teaching. During teaching, you have to be ready to scrap your entire lesson plan or use different representations, examples, and strategies, if the ones you planned to use are not working. After teaching, you can use reflection to guide your instructional planning for the future. In this sense, reflection is a valuable form of assessment.

CONCEPT CHECK

1. **Why** is it important for teachers to have content knowledge about mathematics?

2. **What** must teachers consider when selecting classroom tasks?

3. **What** are four ways of managing discourse?

4. **What** are the two types of reflection? Why is reflection an important part of the teaching cycle?

Teaching Mathematics with Children's Literature

LEARNING OBJECTIVES

1. **Explain** the value of teaching with children's literature.

2. **Identify** the characteristics of effective children's literature.

3. **Describe** techniques for effectively teaching with children's literature.

Storytelling is an ancient art form that originated as an oral tradition when storytellers memorized and shaped their tales to meet the needs of their audience (**Figure 3.8**). Children's literature is a modern adaptation of storytelling that has become popular in elementary education because it provides children with experiences that relate to their own lives or to situations with which they are familiar.

The Benefits of Teaching Mathematics with Children's Literature

Children's literature that is related to mathematics has been available for years. However, it was not until the late 1980s that the movement to integrate children's literature with mathematics instruction gained momentum, due in large part to the publication of *Curriculum and Evaluation Standards for School Mathematics* (1989) and, later, *Principles and Standards for School Mathematics* (2000). Children's literature helps to accomplish the goals for teaching and learning mathematics set forth in these documents by:

- providing rich contexts for understanding mathematical ideas,

- showing children how to view the world from a mathematical perspective,

- illustrating how mathematics has been used throughout history by all people to make sense of their lives,

- illustrating interdisciplinary connections to mathematics and sparking children's imagination and curiosity.

Let us look at some specific children's books that effectively demonstrate these goals (see *Children's Literature*, **Figure 3.9**).

The titles in Figure 3.9 are just a few examples of the hundreds of fine children's literature books that can be used to enrich students' understanding of mathematics. Throughout this text, you will have the opportunity to explore many children's literature books in detail.

A storyteller working with children • Figure 3.8

Storytelling can be used to provide real-life contexts for mathematics, so that children can connect mathematics to their lives. Storytelling can engage children in exciting adventures that use mathematics and can teach children the importance of learning mathematics.

CHILDREN'S LITERATURE

Using children's literature to teach mathematics

✓ THE PLANNER

On Beyond a Million • Figure 3.9a

Written by David M. Schwartz
Illustrated by Paul Meisel
The school's popcorn machine is producing so much popcorn that students are unable to count the number of kernels. Professor X shows the students how to count in powers of 10, such as 10, 100, 1000, 10,000, and 1,000,000. How might you use the illustrations and examples in this book to teach children about very large numbers, the powers of 10, and exponents?

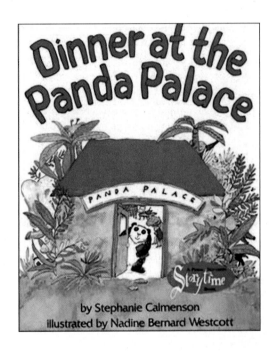

Dinner at the Panda Palace • Figure 3.9b

Written by Stephanie Calmenson
Illustrated by Nadine Bernard Westcott
Animals arrive at a restaurant for dinner—first, one elephant, next two lions, and then three pigs. Each group has one more animal than the group before. When all the seats are taken, a mouse arrives and asks to be seated. They find there is always room for one more. This counting book examines the sum of $1 + 2 + 3 + \cdots + 10$ as well as the concept that there is no largest number. Ask your own students to name the largest number they know and then find one more than that.

The Doorbell Rang • Figure 3.9c

Written and illustrated by Pat Hutchins
Ma has made a dozen cookies for Sam and Victoria, so each child's equal share is six cookies. Then two neighbors arrive, so each child's share is three cookies. More and more people arrive until there is only one cookie for each child. Then Grandma arrives with a big batch of cookies. How can you use this story to teach children about multiplication, division, and fractions?

How to Choose Mathematics-Related Children's Literature

As the benefits of linking mathematics and literature have become well known, publishers and authors have produced hundreds of new children's books every year, creating an abundance of children's literature from which to choose. With so many choices, how do you decide which books will serve students best? **Table 3.2** illustrates guidelines to consider when choosing children's literature for your mathematics class.

Guidelines for choosing children's literature for the mathematics classroom   Table 3.2
Select children's books that
• Use the mathematics correctly, are set in reasonable contexts, and are expressed in an easily understandable manner
• Are aesthetic as well as functional; they unleash imagination and curiosity through their stories and rich illustrations
• Appeal to multiple grade levels and provoke thinking and learning for a wide range of ages
• Invite active participation and investigation on the part of the reader
• Are gripping to both adults and children and hook the reader with a "hard to put down" quality
• Use inclusive language, avoid stereotypes, and promote cultural, racial, and gender equity
(*Source:* Adapted from Whitin and Whitin, 2004)

How to Teach Mathematics with Children's Literature

Once you have selected mathematics-related children's books, how can you use them effectively in your classroom? First, when introducing a new book, read the entire story to the class without pausing to emphasize the mathematics. You may want to read the story a second time to make sure that children have heard the story and understood it.

After you are sure that children are familiar with the story, begin to focus on the mathematics. Ask children what they liked best about the story, whether they have any questions about it, or whether they have a favorite character or picture. Next, pose problems based on the story and encourage children to pose their own mathematics problems as well.

Encourage children to talk about the book by using the same words that were used in the story to foster the development of effective communication skills. You might suggest that children act out the story, modify it with different numbers or situations, or write their own story. Finally, refer to the story often and connect it to the mathematics concepts that are being studied. These guidelines are illustrated in **Activity 3.2**.

Activity 3.2 Modeling eleven

Instructions

Read *12 Ways to Get to 11*, written by Eve Merriam and illustrated by Bernie Karlin, to children in grades K–2, showing the pictures for each page and showing how the items add up to 11. Read the book to children a second time.

1. Ask: *What is your favorite example of 11?*
2. Provide each pair of children with about 20 counters or snap-together cubes in four different colors.
3. Say: *Let's make each 11 in the story using your counters. First, let's show nine pinecones and two acorns, using one color for the pinecones and another color for the acorns.* Continue for each number combination, using a different color counter for each category (i.e., red for pinecones and blue for acorns).
4. Say: *Draw a picture that makes 11 with three types of objects.*
5. Say: *How many different ways can you make 11? Show with your counters.*
6. As a class, make a list of all the ways you can make 11.

Teaching Tip

Beginning a new topic with children's literature

Children's literature is a great way to introduce a new topic. As you read the book, write any new vocabulary on the board, and read and pronounce the new words with children so they will learn and understand them. Make the book available for children to look at individually, as some will want to read it again.

CONCEPT CHECK

1. **What** are some benefits of teaching with children's literature?
2. **What** are some of the qualities of effective mathematics-related children's literature?
3. **How** can you best use children's literature to facilitate mathematics learning?

Teaching Mathematics with Technology

LEARNING OBJECTIVES

1. **Explain** the value of teaching with technology.
2. **Describe** types of computer software and how they are used.
3. **Identify** criteria for choosing high-quality software.
4. **Identify** techniques for using technology effectively.

NCTM has recognized the impact of **technology** on mathematics education and created The Technology Principle, which states, "Technology is essential in teaching and learning mathematics; it influences the mathematics that is taught and enhances students' learning" (NCTM, 2000, p. 24). Technology changes the way children learn mathematics and how teachers and schools view mathematics by increasing the range of mathematics content that is taught, supporting student learning, and making mathematics more accessible to a broader population of students (Flores, 2002). This section examines the importance of technology in teaching mathematics and ways to use technology effectively in your mathematics classroom.

The Impact of Technology on the Teaching and Learning of Mathematics

Technology use in schools can enhance students' learning of mathematics by providing opportunities for creativity and experimentation. Although educators express different opinions on the amount and type of technology that should be used, most agree that technology, when used appropriately, can make a positive impact on school children's ability to learn mathematics. There are many choices available for technology. Most schools have four-function calculators for elementary school students, and some have fraction calculators as well. Many middle schools have graphing calculators available. Many elementary and middle schools also have computers in every classroom. Calculators and computers "furnish visual images of mathematical ideas, they facilitate organizing and analyzing data, and they compute efficiently and accurately" (NCTM, 2000, p. 24).

Calculators Even though hand-held four-function calculators have been available and affordable for more than three decades, their use in the classroom was slow to gain acceptance until the 1990s. Some critics fear that calculators prevent students from learning basic facts and computation skills. Most educators agree that although calculators should not be used as a substitute for learning basic skills, they can alleviate tedious computations that have few educational gains.

Calculators can also facilitate concept development for children of all ages. Consider a first-grade class that is learning the concept of number. Children can investigate a variety of topics using the automatic constant feature (which keeps adding the same number if you press the number, the plus sign, and then the equals sign repeatedly), including counting by ones, counting by twos, pattern recognition, and number magnitude. In **Activity 3.3**, adapted from Huinker (2002), the calculator supports students' ability to count back by ones, something that is very difficult for children. If children continue to count back, they will go beyond zero and encounter negative numbers.

> ### Activity 3.3 Using a calculator to learn the concept of number
>
> **Instructions**
>
> 1. Enter your age into the calculator and then press $+$ 1 $=$ $=$ $=$. This will give your age next year, the year after, and the year after that. This is the automatic constant feature.
>
> 2. Clear the calculator and enter the last number the calculator showed. Now press $-$ 1 $=$ $=$ $=$.
>
> 3. What will happen if you keep going?
>
> Most four-function calculators have the automatic constant feature.

Computer software Personal computers can be used with software or the Internet to facilitate mathematics learning. There are hundreds of programs available today from software publishers. With so many choices and the limited financial resources of most schools, how do you decide which software to purchase (**Table 3.3**)?

Choosing mathematics software   Table 3.3

Ask the following questions when evaluating software:

- Look at the mathematics. Is it correct?
- Will children be able to make sense of the activities?
- Is the program easy to use?
- Does the software do what it says it will do?
- Are the mathematics, attention span, and reading level appropriate for the grade level?

(*Source:* Kerrigan, 2002)

Software for mathematics has several different purposes. It can promote higher-order thinking through problem solving; teach children to collect, analyze, and display data with spreadsheets; provide drill and practice; introduce new concepts, and develop algebraic and geometric thinking. Computer applications are helpful to visual learners and should be accessible to English-language learners because of their visual approach. If your schools' computers have Internet access, you will be able to download and use smaller applications called *applets* for free.

Specific software programs and Internet sites will be highlighted as **Tech Tools** throughout this text in the appropriate content areas. **Figure 3.10** provides an example of an applet game from the NCTM Illuminations Web site.

Tech Tools

illuminations.nctm.org

The *NCTM Illuminations* Web site offers more than 100 applets activities sorted by grade level.

You can also access **virtual manipulatives** on the Internet. These are virtual shapes and objects that children manipulate on the computer (**Figure 3.11**). They are as effective as the physical manipulatives that children use in the classroom. Virtual manipulatives often look exactly like concrete manipulatives (such as pattern blocks, base-ten blocks, geometric solids, Cuisenaire rods, and geoboards). They can be moved around, rotated, shaded, and colored and are therefore considered interactive.

virtual manipulatives Web-based representations of physical objects that are stand-alone applications on the Internet and can be manipulated by children using a computer mouse.

Virtual manipulatives encourage students to be creative and explore new ideas. Researchers found that when kindergarten children were asked to make repeating patterns with wooden pattern blocks, virtual pattern blocks, and construction paper pattern blocks, the

The Factor Game

Using computer software to practice multiplication: The Factor Game Applet • Figure 3.10

Students in grades 3–5 can use this applet to practice multiplication in a fun way.

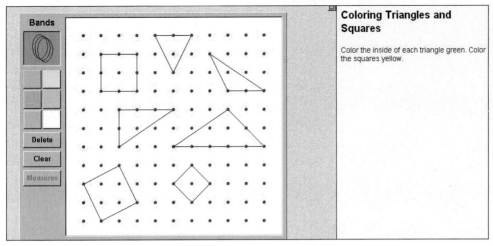

Coloring Triangles and Squares

Color the inside of each triangle green. Color the squares yellow.

Encouraging creativity with virtual manipulatives • Figure 3.11

What are some advantages and disadvantages of using virtual geoboards as opposed to concrete ones?

children were more creative with the virtual pattern blocks (Moyer, Niezgoda, and Stanley, 2005). Some teachers use concrete manipulatives first and then repeat the same activity with virtual manipulatives to connect concrete, visual, and abstract ideas. Virtual manipulatives serve as a bridge between concrete representations and abstract or symbolic notation.

Tech Tools

http://nlvm.usu.edu

The National Library of Virtual Manipulatives has a large collection that is free to anyone with Internet access. The virtual manipulatives are organized by grade-level band and content area.

Computers promote positive communication. Children tend to talk more with their peers when working on the computer than when working on written tasks. When children use a computer with their peers, they have to learn to negotiate and share. The computer also helps children with disabilities have more interactions with their peers, rather than being isolated.

Effective Ways to Use Technology in the Classroom

Like any other tool, technology is not effective for every problem. It is important that you teach children to make thoughtful choices about when to use technology and when to use written mathematical notation or mental mathematics. Consider the following problem:

There were 30,000 fans in the football stadium. Each person paid $20 for a ticket. How much money was collected for the tickets?

This is a problem for which students might use calculators because the numbers are large, but it can probably be solved with mental mathematics faster than with a calculator. Students can also learn some valuable mathematical ideas by solving this mentally.

Students who use technology well understand that the decision to use technology must be made on a case-by-case basis. You can promote judicious technology use by discussing the choices with students and deciding together whether to use technology to solve a given problem. You can also encourage students to reflect on and monitor their own use of technology.

Classroom computers should be centrally located so that computer users are not isolated and other children can pass by and interact with them. Clements and Sarama (2005) recommend there be fewer than 10 children per computer, so a classroom with 25 children would have at least three computers. Each computer station should have two seats in front of it to encourage social interaction and to teach children the meaning of taking turns. It is also important to place print material and physical manipulatives next to the computer so that children waiting for their turn on the computer can have something to do.

Effective use of technology in the classroom • Figure 3.12

This photo demonstrates how to use computers effectively. What do you notice about how the computer is used and how the children are organized?

This practice also emphasizes the connection between the mathematics experienced on the computer and the mathematics experienced off the computer (**Figure 3.12**).

Before students ever use a computer in your classroom, discuss proper computer etiquette. Explain that they may have to share a computer with a partner and, if so, they will have to take turns operating the mouse and making choices or selections. Sitting at a computer does not excuse students from listening in class. If the teacher or another student is speaking to the entire class, computer usage should stop and students at the computer should focus their attention on the speaker.

In classrooms with just a few computers, the computer can be used as a learning station, just one of the activities that children complete to learn a particular concept. Those children not working at the computer will be involved in other meaningful activities on the same concept. After everyone has completed activities at various learning stations, the class may come together to describe and summarize what they learned.

In classrooms with enough computers for every child or every pair of children, an entire lesson may focus on computer activities. In this case, the teacher should introduce the activity before students go to the computer stations and explain clearly what children are expected to do at the computer.

Computers place additional demands on teachers. Even though it is tempting to leave children on their own

when they are working on the computer, this may result in off-task behavior. When introducing computer activities, demonstrate one or two activities at a time, offer a lot of support and guidance at the beginning, and then gradually withdraw the support so that children can operate the software themselves or with a peer.

Teaching Tip

Guiding students' computer use

Guide students' learning by making the mathematical objectives clear. Do not assume that students will recognize the purpose of computer activities on their own. Use questioning, modeling, peer tutoring, and class discussion to make sure that everyone understands and benefits from the opportunities provided by computer activities.

CONCEPT CHECK

1. **How** do students benefit from using calculators in the mathematics classroom?

2. **What** are three types of computer software programs?

3. **What** are five criteria for selecting and evaluating technology for classroom use?

4. **What** are three techniques for effectively using technology in the classroom?

Teaching Mathematics in the Era of Standards and Accountability

LEARNING OBJECTIVES

1. **Explain** the effects of the No Child Left Behind Act on mathematics teaching and learning.

2. **Compare** *Common Core State Standards* from three different grade levels.

3. **Describe** the effects of high-stakes testing on mathematics teaching and learning.

tandards and accountability in public education will continue to have a powerful influence on educational practice in the 21st century. This focus will drive the mathematics curriculum you will be expected to teach and influence the decisions you make as a teacher. This section discusses state and local standards and how they will affect you as a teacher.

The Challenge of State and Local Standards

Beginning in the late 1980s, the national spotlight has focused on weaknesses in our public education system. Former U.S. presidents William J. Clinton and George H. W. Bush both called for reform in education and greater achievement in mathematics and science through national standards and national testing, culminating in 2002 with the passage of the No Child Left Behind Act (NCLB). This legislation mandates the development of statewide content standards in mathematics (known as Grade-Level Learning Expectations [GLEs] or benchmarks) and the creation and administration of statewide tests.

In 2010, the *Common Core State Standards* Initiative released uniform standards to replace individual states' GLEs. More than 40 states immediately adopted these standards, as discussed in Chapter 1 and described in Appendix C.

As a new teacher, it will be your job to interpret the standards for your grade level and teach your students the mathematics that is described within them. How do these standards affect you as a teacher? Do they specify how you should teach? Let us answer these questions by looking at specific common core standards for three different grade levels (**Table 3.4**).

***Common Core State Standards* for mathematics Table 3.4**

There are three levels of organization. Clusters are groups of related standards. Domains are larger groups of related standards and clusters.

Grade Level	Domain	Cluster Title	Sample Standard
1	Measurement and Data	Measure lengths indirectly and by iterating unit lengths	Order three objects by length; compare the lengths of two objects indirectly by using a third object.
3	Number and Operations in Base Ten	Use Place Value Understanding and properties of operations to perform multi-digit arithmetic	Multiply one-digit whole numbers by multiples of 10 in the range 10–90 (e.g. 9 x 80, 5 x 60) using strategies based on place value and properties of operations.
5	Operations and Algebraic Thinking	Write and interpret numerical expressions	Use parentheses, brackets, or braces in numerical expressions and evaluate expressions with these symbols.

(*Source: Common Core State Standards* (NGA Center/CCSSO, 2010).)

Although standards describe specific content, none of them dictates how the mathematics content should be taught or in what order. It is possible for teachers to meet grade-level expectations and still teach mathematics with understanding. For example, if you teach students the meaning of place value and multiplication, they will necessarily meet the standards associated with multiplication as a by-product of the learning process. If you look at standards as individual skills to be learned, they seem overwhelming. However, if you look at them as representative of a connected body of knowledge, then the standards can be met as part of the learning process.

High-Stakes Testing

Although **high-stakes tests** are an accepted part of our culture, high-stakes testing for assessment of students and schools has become a "hot" topic in education since the passage of the No Child Left Behind Act in 2002. This law mandates that all children in U.S. public schools be tested in

> **high-stakes tests**
> Tests characterized by a single standardized assessment.

reading and mathematics every year in grades 3–8 and once in high school through statewide, standardized, high-stakes tests. These tests are used to make decisions about whether students may progress to the next grade and whether schools are functioning properly. Some criticisms of these tests are as follows:

1. They are one-time measures or "snapshots" and may not accurately represent what students know or how well schools are performing.

2. They may not be accurate for students with disabilities or students who are English-language learners (ELLs) because it is more difficult to measure "adequate yearly progress" for such students.

The two sources of potential errors in high-stakes tests are **validity** and **reliability**. Validity is essential for high-stakes tests. To examine the validity of a test,

> **validity** The meaningfulness, usefulness, and appropriateness of the data collected from the test.
>
> **reliability** The extent to which the data are free of errors.

you must ask whether the test actually measures what students know and whether students are likely to score well on the test without understanding the content being tested. Reliability is a characteristic of both the test and the test takers and can differ for different populations

Reliability and validity on a high-stakes test • Figure 3.13

How does a driver's test show validity and reliability?

(**Figure 3.13**). There are three potential sources of reliability errors in all tests: the test, the test takers, and the scoring process. In high-stakes tests we are most concerned with user reliability, or whether different users across the state come to the same conclusions when faced with identical data.

How has the high-stakes testing required by NCLB affected mathematics education? How will it affect you as a teacher of mathematics? Because state-level test scores are publicly reported, school systems feel enormous pressure to demonstrate success. This pressure filters down from the superintendent to the principal and then to the teacher. As a result of high-stakes testing, many teachers are "teaching to the test." In other words, they teach content topics that are on the test and remove topics that are not on the test; spend a great deal of time on review, drill, and practice tests; and structure their own tests to have the same format as the standardized tests their students will be taking. In many cases, this means that teachers are giving multiple-choice tests and eliminating problem solving, writing, and open-ended questions from their classroom practice. A recent study of elementary teachers in Massachusetts, Kansas, and

Michigan found that "testing programs in their state have led them to teach in ways that contradicted their ideas of sound instructional practices" (Wilson, 2007, p. 1107). In other words, high-stakes tests have a very strong influence on educational practice and will likely influence your practice as well.

1. **How** will NCLB affect what and how you teach mathematics?

2. **What** do you notice about the mathematics standards in the three grades described?

3. **How** has high-stakes testing changed the learning environment in mathematics?

Summary

 THE PLANNER

1 The Changing Role of the Teacher 54

- Teachers need to shift their perspective from delivering information to facilitating students' understanding and sense-making, as shown here.

Figure 3.1

- *Mathematics Teaching Today* details eight areas of proficiency for teachers of mathematics.

2 The Teaching Cycle 58

- Effective teachers have knowledge of the big ideas in mathematics and the ways those ideas connect to one another. This knowledge influences their choice of content, **pedagogy**, and assessment.

- Effective teachers choose classroom tasks that challenge students to struggle and grow mathematically. They create classroom environments where students are respected and valued. They manage **classroom discourse** by using tools such as **filtering**, **scaffolding**, **tiering**, and **revoicing**. Effective teachers can be compared to musical conductors, as illustrated in these images.

Figure 3.5

- Part of your role as a teacher is to evaluate your own effectiveness and your students' understanding. This may be more challenging for new teachers who are used to the camaraderie of college classes. **Reflection** plays a crucial role in teacher effectiveness. It allows you to analyze both your teaching and your students' learning so that you can make positive changes.

3 Teaching Mathematics with Children's Literature 66

- Mathematics-related children's literature helps to accomplish the goals for teaching and learning mathematics set forth in *Principles and Standards for School Mathematics.*

- When choosing children's literature for the mathematics class, make sure to choose books, such as the one shown here, that are mathematically correct, aesthetically pleasing, and interesting to multiple grade-levels.

Figure 3.9

- When teaching mathematics with children's literature, read the book in its entirety; then go back and read it again, emphasizing different parts.

4 Teaching Mathematics with Technology 69

- **Technology** increases the range of mathematics content that is taught, supports student learning, and makes mathematics more accessible to a broader population of students. There are many technology choices for the elementary classroom. The four-function calculator has been available for more than 30 years but has just become a mainstay of the elementary classroom in the last 10 to 15 years. Many classrooms now have computers. These can be used in a variety of ways, from using purchased software to accessing applets and **virtual manipulatives** on the Internet, such as the one shown here.

Figure 3.10

- Like any other tool, technology should be used wisely. Arrange computers in a central location, give children meaningful tasks while they are waiting to use the computer, and make sure that no more than two children work at the same computer station at one time. Introduce computer tasks one or two at a time, and initially provide guidance so children benefit from the activities.

5 Teaching Mathematics in the Era of Standards and Accountability 73

- Standards and accountability in public education have a powerful influence on educational practice. The No Child Left Behind Act mandates the development of statewide content standards in mathematics (known as grade-level learning expectations, or GLEs) and the creation and administration of statewide **high-stakes tests** based on those standards.

- There are many types of high-stakes tests, as shown here. In all high-stakes tests, the two sources of potential errors in high-stakes tests are **validity** and **reliability**. Validity refers to the meaningfulness of the data collected by the test, and reliability refers to the extent to which the test is free of random errors.

Figure 3.13

Key Terms

- classroom discourse 56
- filtering 63
- high-stakes tests 74
- pedagogy 58
- reflection 65
- reliability 74
- revoicing 63
- scaffolding 63
- technology 69
- tiering 63
- validity 74
- virtual manipulatives 70

Additional Children's Literature

- *Rooster's Off to See the World,* **written and illustrated by Eric Carle**
  When a rooster goes off to see the world, other animals want to go along with him, including two cats, three frogs, four turtles, and five fish. As the sun sets, the animals decide to return to their homes.

- *The History of Counting,* **written by Denise Schmandt-Besserat and illustrated by Michael Hays**
  In this book, appropriate for upper elementary or middle school children, the development of counting is told, from societies that do not use numbers to the origin of numerals and up to Hindu-Arabic numerals.

- *The Great Graph Contest,* **written and illustrated by Loreen Leedy**
  Three friends have a contest to see who can make the best

  graph. In the process, many different kinds of graphs are illustrated in a way that children will enjoy.

- *The Village of Round and Square Houses,* **written and illustrated by Ann Grifalconi**
  This story, set in West Africa, tells the story of why the women in a village live in round houses while the men live in square houses. The book is a great way to introduce shapes and classification to children.

- *Just a Little Bit,* **written by Ann Tompert and illustrated by Lynn Munsinger**
  An elephant and a mouse are playing on a seesaw. To get the mouse's side to go down, more and more animals come to help. This provides an excellent introduction to size and weight for young children.

Online Resources

- **The Math Forum**
  http://mathforum.org

  This site has excellent resources, including Ask Dr. Math, a resource for both students and teachers. You can search their archives for previously asked questions or ask new ones. The Math Forum also contains problems of the week and resources for English-language learners.

- **Number Time**
  http://www.bbc.co.uk/schools/numbertime/

  This is a site for both teachers and students that contains worksheets, and songs that link mathematics and real-world contexts.

- **PBS TeacherSource: Math**
  http://www.pbs.org/teachers.html

  This site is for both teachers and students, pre-kindergarten through grade 12. It contains content, games, and links to other sites.

- **Funbrain**
  http://www.funbrain.com

  This site is for elementary and middle school students and their teachers. It contains both content and interactive games. When students play the games, they receive feedback on their answers. The site has a feature for creating quizzes online.

- **MathPlayground**
  http://www.mathplayground.com

  This is a site of word problems, logic puzzles, and math videos that integrate mathematics and technology for students in elementary and middle grades.

Critical and Creative Thinking Questions

1. One of the most famous lines from Shakespeare's *Hamlet* is "To thine own self be true," spoken by Polonius to his son Laertes before Laertes goes off on a voyage. How does this statement apply to teaching? How does it apply to the current atmosphere of accountability through high-stakes testing?

2. Select a children's literature book for mathematics that is not discussed in this chapter. Evaluate the book using the criteria established in this chapter, and write a short summary that describes how you would use this book in the classroom.

3. Select some educational software or an interactive Web site for elementary or middle grades mathematics. Evaluate the technology, using the criteria established in this chapter, and write a short summary that describes the strengths and weaknesses of this technology.

4. **In the field** When should elementary school children use four-function calculators in the mathematics classroom? Describe two activities in which calculators can help children develop conceptual understanding, and try one of the activities with a child you know. Describe the results.

5. Table 3.1, which you saw earlier in the chapter, describes eight shifts in the role of the teacher. Select one of these shifts, and describe how it differs from your beliefs about the nature of teaching. How can you change your practice to incorporate this shift?

Eight areas of proficiency for teachers of mathematics Table 3.1
Teachers will be competent in

1. "designing and implementing mathematical experiences that stimulate students' interests and intellect;	5. fostering positive attitudes about the aesthetic and utilitarian values of mathematics;
2. orchestrating classroom discourse in ways that promote the exploration and growth of mathematical ideas;	6. engaging in opportunities to deepen their own understanding of the mathematics being studied and its applications;
3. using, and helping students use, technology and other tools to pursue mathematical investigations;	7. reflecting on the value of classroom encounters and taking action to improve their practice; and
4. assessing students' existing mathematical knowledge and challenging students to extend that knowledge;	8. fostering professional and collegial relationships to enhance their own teaching performance."

(*Source:* NCTM, 2007, pp. 5–6)

What is happening in this picture?

Think Critically

1. Does this teacher value drill and practice or conceptual learning of mathematics?
2. What can you point to in the image that tells you whether this is a drill and practice or a conceptual learning environment?

Self-Test

(Check your answers in Appendix D.)

1. Describe two of each of the following types of standards from *Mathematics Teaching Today*. Explain what they mean and why they are important.
   a. Knowledge Standards
   b. Implementation Standards
   c. Analysis Standards

For questions 2–5, choose from the following to fill in the blank:

a. filtering   c. scaffolding
b. revoicing   d. tiering

2. Ms. Carrero has observed that some of her fourth-grade students have more difficulty with spatial skills than others. She anticipates that the students weak in spatial skills will have difficulty identifying figures with rotational symmetry. Therefore, she plans two sets of activities. In the first set, students determine line symmetry for a number of plane figures. In the second set, they determine both line and rotational symmetry. Ms. Carrero is using _____.

3. Mr. Hernandez gives his students the following word problem and instructions.

Seventy-five children are going on a field trip. If each bus holds 32 students, how many buses will be needed to take all the children on the field trip? Please be prepared to explain your answer.

Mr. Hernandez notices that Kea has his hand raised and calls on him.

Kea says, "Three, because I added one more."

Mr. Hernandez replies, "That's exactly right, Kea! 75 divided by 32 equals 2 with a remainder of 11. In this problem, the remainder means we have to round up the answer to one more than 2, or 3."

Mr. Hernandez is using _____.

4. In her second-grade class, Ms. Tyler is helping her students learn to read and write numbers to 1000 in numerals and words. She is playing a game in which she pulls a number out of a hat, reads the number, and asks students to write it with numerals. She notices that Kevin has difficulty with this task. For example, when asked to write *three hundred forty-five*, Kevin writes 30045. Ms. Tyler helps Kevin by giving him a place value mat with hundreds, tens, and ones, and helps

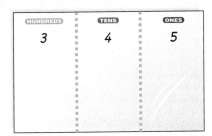

Kevin write the numbers in the correct columns of the mat. Ms. Tyler is using _____.

5. Mr. Arroyo posed a problem for his second-grade class. He listened to many students' suggested solutions, and then decided to follow one student's suggestion. Mr. Arroyo is demonstrating _____.

6. Ms. Carson's second-grade class is learning about place value. Because Ms. Carson knows this is often a difficult topic for students, she begins by having her students count and group objects found in the classroom. Ms. Carson is demonstrating _____.
   a. knowledge of mathematics
   b. knowledge of student learning
   c. both of the above

7. Describe three benefits of using children's literature in the elementary mathematics classroom.

8. Describe three guidelines for choosing effective children's literature.

9. Student teacher Mike Frees lets his fourth-grade students use the computer when they finish their assigned work. Because his classroom has only three computers, this means that some students get more time on the computer than others. True or false: Mike is effectively managing technology in his classroom.
   a. True   b. False

10. Describe three types of technology that can be used in the classroom.

11. What are three rules that need to be established for computer usage in the classroom?

12. Why does a driver's test have validity? Why is it important for high-stakes tests to have validity?

13. What does it mean for a test to have reliability? Why is it important for high-stakes tests to have reliability?

14. Student teacher Marc Spiegel has just taught a geometry lesson to his fourth-grade students. After the lesson he emails his cooperating teacher to discuss the strengths and weaknesses of his lesson. Marc's actions demonstrate _____.
   a. reflection on practice
   b. reflection on student learning

15. Ina Jacoby is tutoring a third-grade student as part of her pre-student teaching practicum experiences. She is supposed to work with the student on subtraction of three-digit numbers with regrouping but notices that the student is making a lot of errors. When Ina asks the student to solve 346 − 129, the student answers 123. Ina realizes that the student does not understand regrouping and probably has a weak understanding of place value. She decides instead to work with the student on place value, composing, and decomposing numbers. Ina's actions demonstrate _____.
   a. reflection on practice
   b. reflection on student learning

Review your Chapter Planner on the chapter opener and check off your completed work.

Planning for and Assessing Mathematics Learning

Student teacher Tara Wrenn had carefully planned a lesson for her fourth graders about subtraction of decimals. Tara's school was located in an urban Atlanta neighborhood and her students were avid Atlanta Braves fans, so Tara decided to ask her students to compare the batting averages of several Braves players.

Tara explained to students that the batting average is the ratio of hits to official at-bats, and she showed her students a chart she prepared that listed players alphabetically in one column and their batting averages for the season in the next column. Then she asked students to compute the difference between the batting averages of two specific players. The students, who previously were excited and interested in the lesson, suddenly became silent. Finally, one child said that he did not know which batting average was higher. Tara now understood what was wrong. She had mistakenly assumed that her students understood how to identify the larger decimal from a pair of decimal fractions. Tara immediately scrapped her subtraction lesson in order to teach her students how to compare decimals.

Tara's experience illustrates two important principles. First, when planning a mathematics lesson, check that students have the understanding necessary to learn the new concepts and skills you intend to teach them. Second, if your lesson is not going well, just stop it. Take a deep breath, and go on to your next scheduled activity for the day. Later, think back to what went wrong and what you want to change to make your lesson more effective.

Baseball provides many statistics to motivate mathematics learning, but teachers need to check students' prior knowledge before teaching any topic.

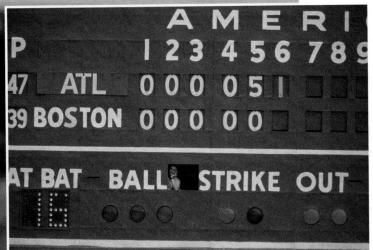

CHAPTER OUTLINE

Why Planning Is Important 82

Key Questions: Why is planning important? How do yearly plans, unit plans, and daily plans differ?

Planning a Mathematics Lesson 84

Key Questions: What are the components of a daily lesson plan? What are the two types of daily lesson plans?

Planning for Diversity 90

Key Question: How can teachers differentiate instruction to meet the needs of all students?

Using Mathematics Textbooks 94

Key Questions: What types of textbooks are available for mathematics instruction? How should teachers use the mathematics textbook to facilitate students' learning?

What Is Assessment? 97

Key Question: What are the three types of assessment?

Assessment Tools 100

Key Questions: What are the different kinds of tools that teachers can use for formative assessment? How do these assessment tools inform teachers about instruction?

NCTM The Assessment Principle: Assessment should support the learning of important mathematics and furnish useful information to both teachers and students.   (NCTM, 2000, p. 22)

CHAPTER PLANNER ✓

- ❑ Study the picture and read the opening story.
- ❑ Scan the Learning Objectives in each section:
    p. 82 ❑   p. 84 ❑   p. 90 ❑
    p. 94 ❑   p. 97 ❑   p. 100 ❑
- ❑ Read the text and study all visuals and Activities. Answer any questions.

Analyze key features

- ❑ In the Classroom, p. 83
- ❑ Process Diagram, p. 85
- ❑ Lesson, p. 86
- ❑ Multicultural Perspectives in Mathematics, p. 93
- ❑ Education InSight, p. 98
- ❑ Stop: Answer the Concept Checks before you go on:
    p. 83 ❑   p. 90 ❑   p. 93 ❑
    p. 96 ❑   p. 99 ❑   p. 105 ❑

End of chapter

- ❑ Review the Summary and Key Terms.
- ❑ Answer the Critical and Creative Thinking Questions.
- ❑ Answer What is happening in this picture?
- ❑ Complete the Self-Test and check your answers.

Why Planning Is Important

LEARNING OBJECTIVES

1. **Explain** why planning is important.
2. **Describe** yearly planning.
3. **Describe** what is included in a unit plan.
4. **Explain** the importance of daily lesson plans.

Most of us use a day planner, PDA, or BlackBerry to plan our time because planning makes us more efficient and more organized and helps us to set and meet important goals. In education, planning helps to establish priorities, set educational goals, determine how to meet these goals, assess our actions, and keep a record of what we accomplished.

Yearly Planning

Because of the No Child Left Behind legislation, most states have detailed standards that include specific learning goals for each grade level. Individual school systems provide **scope and sequence charts** or curriculum guides based on these standards. Even though yearly plans may be provided for you, it is important to read, evaluate, and annotate them to make them your own so that when you begin the school year you understand how topics and units connect to one another (**Figure 4.1**).

When making yearly plans, consider what your students learned the previous year and what they are going to learn the following year. Consider how you want

Making yearly plans • Figure 4.1

Before the school year begins, work with your colleagues to decide what you want your students to learn. Consider your goals in the context of your state's standards, *Principles and Standards for School Mathematics* (NCTM, 2000), your textbook, the *Common Core State Standards* (NGA Center/CCSSO, 2010), and *Curriculum Focal Points for Prekindergarten through Grade 8 Mathematics* (NCTM, 2006).

them to think about mathematics and their roles in doing mathematics and the actions you can take to encourage that view. Finally, think about how you can effectively assess what your students have learned.

As a new teacher, investigate how flexible your school and school system are in terms of making individual changes to yearly plans. If you have a great deal of flexibility, it is still a good idea to follow the established curriculum guides for the first year and make a few small changes as needed, carefully noting the changes you made and how well they worked. If you have little flexibility, it is possible to provide meaningful instruction within strict guidelines. In either situation, think about the plans for the entire school year before addressing unit and daily plans.

Unit Planning

Unit planning involves one curriculum topic and may include lesson plans for several days or several weeks, depending on the grade level and the complexity of the topic. Add your own annotations to the guide provided by your school. For each unit plan, consider the following:

- **Curriculum goals**
- **Prior knowledge needed by students**
- **New concepts and skills to be introduced**
- **Vocabulary students will need to know**
- **Activities you will provide to encourage students to learn, practice, and apply the new concepts and skills**
- **Materials you will use, including manipulatives, technology, and children's literature**
- **Ancillary or supplementary materials provided by your textbook for this unit**
- **The needs of your students and how you will** differentiate instruction **to accommodate diverse learners**
- **How you can relate the topic to real-world contexts and other subject areas**
- **How you will incorporate problem solving**
- **How you will pace the lessons**
- **How and when you will assess what your students have learned**

> **differentiate instruction** Create different but equal methods of teaching students based on their individual preferences, abilities, and learning styles.

In the Classroom

Lesson Study

Lesson study is a locally initiated, teacher-driven, grassroots effort to improve mathematics education. It shows teachers what to improve and how to improve; it helps teachers make sense of reform curriculum and promotes a collaborative atmosphere.

In New Jersey, 10 teachers and the principal of Paterson Public School No. 2 began a lesson study group after viewing a video about Japanese teaching. With help from lesson study researchers, they developed research lessons across grade levels. In one session, teachers and mathematics tutors sat around a "child-size table, rolling a die, laughing, and filling in empty circles with little quarter-circles of colored construction paper" (Viadero, 2004).

By trying this mathematics game about fractions, they learned about how children might respond to the game in the classroom.

Lesson study is a form of professional development that has been used successfully in Japan for many years. It includes a four-phase cycle:

1. A group of teachers meets to identify specific goals for student learning and plans a research lesson to meet those goals.
2. One member of the team teaches the research lesson while the other members observe and collect data on student learning.
3. The team shares their data and insights.
4. The team decides whether or not to revise and reteach the lesson, based on their data and observations.

After completing the cycle, the teachers write a report explaining the purpose of the lesson and documenting its effectiveness. Finally, they disseminate the lesson informally to teachers and schools.

(*Source*: Lewis, 2002)

Think Critically

1. "Lesson study recognizes the central importance and difficulty of teaching—of actually bringing to life standards, frameworks, and 'best practices'" (Mills, 2002, p. 12). What is meant by this quotation?
2. What aspects of lesson study would be most helpful to you as a new teacher?

Daily Planning

Daily lesson plans break down unit plans into smaller, more manageable parts. Even though you make detailed daily plans, you may not be able to follow them exactly. In fact, you need to be prepared to stop, regroup, and scrap a plan in progress if it is not working, as illustrated in the opening story of this chapter. Yet, it is still important to prepare detailed lesson plans because they focus attention on the children in your class: what they already know, how they learn, what they need to learn, how you can facilitate their learning, and how you can assess what they have learned. Lesson plans provide a permanent record of your actions that you can learn from later when you reflect on your teaching. Unexpectedly, writing daily plans also helps teachers learn to plan "in their heads," which can be enormously helpful when you have to change a plan in the middle of a lesson.

As a new teacher, you will probably be asked to submit your lesson plans to a supervisor. The degree of detail and the format of these plans vary widely by school system.

You may receive little or no feedback on your plans or you may be asked to revise them. Your lesson plans will be evaluated based on their written content, not how well they worked in the classroom.

In the United States, teachers traditionally write and revise lesson plans alone. In recent years, reform efforts in mathematics education have introduced a new practice called *lesson study*, which involves teacher collaboration for lesson planning (see *In the Classroom*).

CONCEPT CHECK

1. **How** would you explain to a friend why planning is important?
2. **Why** are yearly plans important?
3. **How** might you benefit from preparing unit plans?
4. **Why** is it important for you to write daily lesson plans?

Planning a Mathematics Lesson

LEARNING OBJECTIVES

1. **Describe** the components of a daily lesson plan.
2. **Distinguish** between teacher-directed and student-centered lesson plans.
3. **Explain** how to use grouping for instruction.
4. **Describe** how to use manipulatives effectively.

I n mathematics education, careful planning is essential because of the nature of the discipline. We cannot teach our students new concepts and skills without anchoring the new learning to concepts and skills that they already know. Lesson planning uses sequential steps to bridge the concepts and procedures students already understand to what you want them to learn.

Components of Every Lesson

Lesson plans are like stories (**Figure 4.2**). They have a beginning, middle, and end. Although there are a variety of names used for each of these parts, we will use the following terminology:

- *Launch* (the task is introduced)
- *Explore or instruct* (detailed instructions are given about the activity and what students will be doing)
- *Summarize* (questions are asked or activities are presented that summarize what was learned)

All lesson plans are organized with these three parts. Daily lesson plans have additional components that are placed in an introductory section, which may include categories for grade level, topic, objectives, materials, standards, grouping choices, differentiation, assessment, and extensions (ways to make the lesson more complex or connect it to other areas).

Lesson plans can be written in paragraph form, in outline form, or as a combination of the two. In this chapter the lesson plan is written as an expanded outline. The *Lesson* on page 86 is based on an activity in *About Teaching Mathematics* (Burns, 2000). The standards are from the *Operations and Algebraic Thinking* domain for grade 4 of the *Common Core State Standards* (NGA Center/CCSSO, 2010).

Types of Lesson Plans

There are two types of lessons: **teacher-directed lessons** and **student-centered lessons**. Most lessons have elements of each type of instruction. For example, the teacher might spend part of the lesson explaining and asking questions of the whole class and spend another part of the lesson engaging students in individual or group explorations. In the palindromes *Lesson*, the first part of the lesson is teacher-directed, with the teacher closely structuring the experiences through questioning. The second part of the lesson is student-centered, with students working in small groups to investigate a problem and discover patterns. Effective lessons often involve both types of experiences and flow easily from one to the other.

How do you decide which lesson format to use? Teacher-directed lessons are appropriate for introducing new ideas, procedures, or vocabulary to the whole class. They are most effective when all students are on the same level and possess the prior knowledge necessary to learn the new material. The teacher does most of the talking and controls the development of the lesson more closely than in student-centered lessons. As a new teacher, you will probably be more comfortable with teacher-directed lessons because they more closely resemble the lessons you experienced when you were a student.

Student-centered lessons provide opportunities for students to explore patterns, investigate new ideas, practice skills, and gain experience with problem solving while working individually or in small groups. In student-centered lessons, the teacher's role is to support students' learning through observations, questions, and strategically placed comments. When using this type of format, it is important to give clear instructions and communicate your expectations before students

> **teacher-directed lessons** Lessons in which the teacher plays a central role in disseminating information, communicating ideas, and asking questions. Also called *direct instruction*.
>
> **student-centered lessons** Lessons that involve students in inquiry-based explorations and practice.

The three-part lesson plan • Figure 4.2

In a lesson plan, the time designated for each part of the lesson will vary according to the grade level. In lower elementary grades, a lesson may take 20 to 30 minutes. In the upper elementary and middle grades, a lesson may take between 30 and 60 minutes. The times given here are approximate, based on a 45-minute class period.

1 Launch (5 to 10 minutes)
Introduce the task and check for prior knowledge. Whenever possible, the launch also should be an attention grabber. Just as the first sentence in a novel pulls the reader in, the launch should pique students' interest and focus their attention.

2 Instruct (25 to 30 minutes)
Describe the actual instruction that will take place. Write detailed, sequenced instructions for the development of the lesson. Include specific descriptions of what the students and teacher will be doing and saying, such as examples, statements, questions, tasks, and investigations.

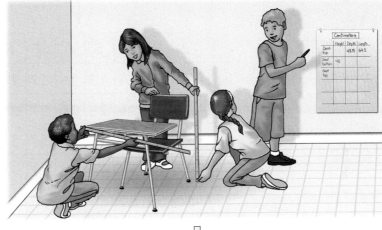

3 Summarize (10 minutes)
Create questions and activities that summarize what was learned and encourage students to share and reflect. This section brings closure to the lesson.

LESSON Palindromes

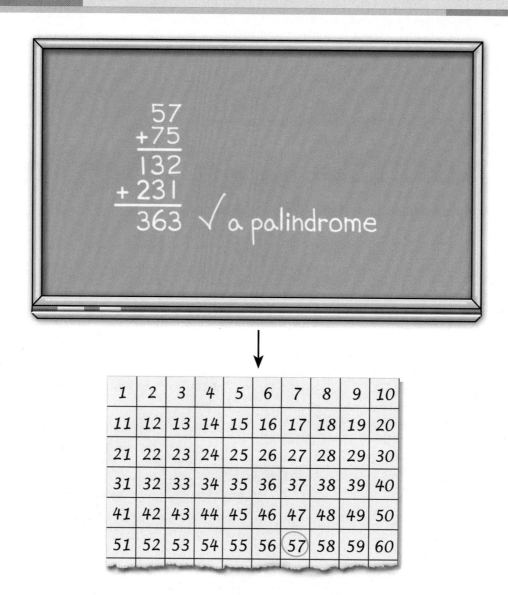

GRADE LEVEL
4

OBJECTIVE
The students will convert numbers to palindromes to look for visual and numeric patterns.

STANDARDS
Grade 4

Generate a number or shape pattern that follows a given rule. (NGA Center/CCSSO, 2010)

MATERIALS
• Crayons, three or four for each student

• 0–99 chart, one for each student, and transparency and pens if the teacher is using an overhead projector, or a teacher copy if the teacher is using another projection device.

ASSESSMENT

- Observe the students as they work in groups. Have the students put their results on the chalkboard or overhead, in table and chart format, and allow them to check their work. During the Summarize portion of the lesson, ask questions about the patterns that result.

- Differentiation for ELL students: Elicit definitions of each of the words used in the lesson, such as *Dad, Mom, Pop*.

GROUPING

Whole class, followed by cooperative groups of three or four students each.

EXTENSION

Find numbers that are more than three-step palindromes.

Launch (10 minutes)

- Write words such as *MOM, POP, DAD, KOOK* on the chalkboard or overhead. Say: *Can anyone think of another word that goes with these? What do these words all have in common?* (They are spelled the same backward and forward. Other examples are *TOT* and *DEED*.) Make sure students understand the meaning of each word.

- *Can you think of numbers that are the same backward and forward?* (44, 77, 33)

- *Find each of these numbers on your 0–99 chart. What do you notice about them?* (They are all multiples of 11.)

- *What does it mean when we say that 44 is a multiple of 11?* (that 11 is a factor of 44, because 4 x 11 = 44 and 44 ÷ 11 = 4)

- *Numbers such as 44, 77, and 33, which are the same forward and backward, are called palindromes.* (Write, spell, and pronounce the word palindrome slowly for ELL students.)

- *Using the 0–99 chart and your crayons, let's select a color to designate all numbers that are palindromes. Which color would you like to use?* (blue) *Okay, now circle all the palindromes on your chart with a blue crayon.*

Instruct (30 minutes)

- *Today we are going to learn how to change numbers that are not palindromes into palindromes.*

- *For example, is 15 a palindrome? Why not? But if we reverse the digits and add the new number (51) to 15, we get 66, which is a palindrome. Since it took only one step to convert 15 to a palindrome, 15 is called a one-step palindrome. What color should we use to designate one-step palindromes?* (red) *Okay, circle the number 15 box on your chart in red.*

- *Do you think that all numbers are either palindromes or one-step palindromes? How can we find out? Let's check another number together—for example, 57. 57 + 75 = 132, which is not a palindrome. What should we do now?* (Try the process again.) *132 + 231 = 363, which is a palindrome. So 57 is a two-step palindrome. What color should we use for this?* (green) *Circle the number 57 in green.*

- *As you can see, some numbers take more than one step to convert to palindromes. Some even take more than two steps.*

- *Now, get into groups of four. Together, find palindromes for the numbers 0–50 on the chart. For each number, make a list of the steps you used, identify how many steps it took to convert each number to a palindrome, and the resulting number. Each time you convert a number to a palindrome, use the same color code that we discussed to color your chart (red for one step, green for two steps, etc.). As you complete your work, look for patterns. How can you know whether a number is going to be a one-step palindrome just by looking at it? What characteristic do all palindromes have in common?*

Summarize (5 to 10 minutes)

- Say: *Let's color in the overhead chart together.*

- Ask: *What patterns do you notice? How many of the numbers are one-step palindromes? How can you predict whether a number is going to be a one-step palindrome?* (When the sum of the digits is less than 10, the number is always a one-step palindrome.)

- Ask: *Do you notice anything else?* (All palindromes are multiples of 11.)

Mini-lessons with resource boxes • Figure 4.3

Some educators set up mini-lessons in cardboard or plastic shoeboxes, as seen in this classroom photo. These can be stacked on shelves for children to retrieve or set up at desks around the classroom. Each box contains a selection of hands-on activities, games, manipulatives, and word problems to practice a particular skill or concept.

begin working and to provide closure for the lesson by bringing students together as a class to share results and observations.

Student-centered lessons vary in length. Some can take an entire class period, whereas others may take 10 or 15 minutes. Students may work in pairs, in small groups, or individually, depending on the activities in the lesson. Short lessons, or **mini-lessons**, are especially effective with young children because of their shorter attention span (**Figure 4.3**). Teachers often conduct mini-lessons with resource boxes that have self-contained manipulatives, worksheets, and activities for students.

Mini-lessons can be set up at learning stations throughout the classroom, with tasks, directions, and materials needed for each mini-lesson inserted in a folder or container and placed at the station ahead of time or retrieved by students individually from a central location. Plan on four to eight stations per topic and let students progress through the various learning stations during the class period. Technology can be integrated into the lesson when computers are used at one or more learning stations. Learning stations can be very effective for differentiating instruction because children can be given specific tasks to meet their individual needs.

Even though mini-lessons are short in length, they should be planned with the three-part lesson format. For mini-lessons:

- The Launch is used for explaining instructions.
- The Explore portion occurs at the learning stations.
- The Summarize step takes place through whole class discussion toward the end of the class period or at individual learning stations where the teacher sits with each individual, pair, or group of students and discusses what they did and what they learned.

Grouping for Instruction

Many mathematics lessons use small-group instruction because of its effectiveness. Here are some questions to consider when planning for small-group instruction:

- How should I select groups?
- What size groups should I use?
- How often should I change groups?
- How should I assess groups to build individual accountability?
- Should I grade each student's work or the group's work?

There are many ways to group children. Before selecting a grouping method, think about the activities you planned and the strengths and challenges of your students. You may want to select groups randomly or select groups so that each one is composed of students with particular strengths. Once students are placed in groups, make sure to monitor their progress and provide helpful hints if a particular group is struggling.

For children in kindergarten through second grade, pairs work best, but three children per group is fine for some activities. For older children, group size should be limited to three or four children. Groups that are any larger than four children lose cohesiveness. For one activity children might work in groups of four, and for another activity they might work in pairs. Let the needs of the activity guide your choice of group size.

There is no set rule for how often to change groups. Some teachers change groups every week. Others change groups at the end of a unit or topic. Students should be allowed to work in the same group long enough to form solid, helpful relationships with one another. However, groups should be changed often enough so that students have the opportunity to work with many of their peers and experience different ways of thinking.

As you plan to incorporate cooperative group learning into your classroom, plan to build **individual accountability** into group work. In other words, each person in the group should understand the task, take part in and understand its completion, and be capable of communicating the solution to the rest of the class. This can be accomplished by asking questions of individual group members, collecting written answers from each person in the group, or having students write journal entries. It is also important to build **group accountability (Figure 4.4)**, where group members learn to work together toward a common goal and to rely on one another. You can build group accountability by clearly stating your expectations for group interactions and assessing students' compliance through observation.

Teaching Tip

Learning the rules

Before directing students to form cooperative groups, spend time talking to your class about your expectations for their behavior. Develop a list of rules with your class and post them for everyone to see. Here is a possible list of cooperative group rules:

- Every group member has a chance to talk and be listened to.
- Group members can disagree with one another but should do so politely.
- Each group member works with others.

Using Manipulatives

As an elementary or middle-grades mathematics teacher, you will probably use manipulatives for some of your lessons. Manipulatives help students move from concrete to symbolic or abstract representations of numbers and concepts. Some students use manipulatives longer than others, so it is important to keep them available for students' use. How you arrange for their storage,

Building group accountability • Figure 4.4

How does this swim team demonstrate both individual and group accountability?
For effective small-group instruction in mathematics, teachers need to build both individual and group accountability into their expectations. How can this be accomplished?

distribution, use, collection, and return is an important part of the planning process. Here are some tips:

- Develop an organized method for storing manipulatives. Many teachers organize them into bags with enough pieces in each bag for small-group or partner activities. The bags are then stored in clear plastic bins that are shelved at a level most students can reach.

- Assign one member of each group to distribute manipulatives and another member to collect and return them.

- During some nonstructured time, allow students to explore the manipulatives. They will do this anyway,

so it is best if they do it before they are using them for a task.

- Try the manipulatives yourself first so that you understand how they work and can offer hints, if necessary, during an activity.

Tech Tools

`http://nlvm.usu.edu`

The **National Library of Virtual Manipulatives** offers many different kinds of virtual manipulatives. They are free to anyone with an Internet connection.

CONCEPT CHECK 🛑 STOP

1. **What** components of the daily lesson plan are illustrated by the *Lesson* in this section?

2. **How** does this photo exhibit student-centered instruction? What are the benefits of student-centered instruction?

3. **How** can you organize and select groups to benefit students' learning in mathematics?

4. **What** steps can you take to plan for manipulative use in your classroom?

Planning for Diversity

LEARNING OBJECTIVES

1. **Identify** the importance of differentiated instruction.

2. **Describe** how to plan instruction for students with special needs.

3. **Explain** how to plan instruction for students who are English-language learners.

P*rinciples and Standards for School Mathematics* (2000) made a commitment to providing all students with equal opportunity to learn mathematics. Included are students with special needs, gifted students, students who are English-

language learners, and populations that have traditionally been underserved. Diverse learners require specific strategies to support their learning. This section discusses how to plan effectively for diversity.

Planning Mathematics Instruction for Students with Special Needs

The Individuals with Disabilities Education Act (IDEA), reauthorized in 2004, mandates that students with disabilities are educated in the least restrictive way possible. In many cases, this means **inclusion**, where special-needs students are placed in the general classroom and the responsibility for their education rests mainly with the classroom teacher. In order to design activities in which special-needs children can be successful, consider the following three questions when planning instruction (Karp and Howell, 2004, p. 119).

- "What organizational, behavioral, and cognitive skills are necessary for students with special needs to derive meaning from this activity?
- Which students have important challenges in any of these skills?
- How can I provide additional support in these areas of weakness so that students with special needs can focus on the conceptual task in the activity?"

To help children with special needs achieve success in mathematics, teachers need to differentiate instruction to meet their individual needs. This often means that teachers must make specific **accommodations** and **modifications** to their lessons.

Specific accommodations and modifications for mathematics are described in **Table 4.1** and **Table 4.2**.

accommodation A different environment or circumstance made with a particular student or students in mind.

modification A change in the task or problem.

Accommodations for mathematics lessons   Table 4.1

- Ask students who have difficulty with written expression to audiotape their assignments or give oral reports.
- Give extra time for students who work more slowly, and provide extra wait time when they answer questions in class.
- Redesign charts and tables to make them more accessible to students with organizational problems.
- Provide enlarged charts and diagrams for students with visual disabilities.
- Create charts and templates for tasks that would otherwise not have them.
- Provide both written and auditory instructions for tasks, or ask students to paraphrase instructions to make sure they understand what is being asked of them.

Modifications for mathematics lessons   Table 4.2

- Create tasks with multiple entry points. In other words, provide tasks that can be approached in different ways. For example, consider the following problem:

  Find the length of your desk using two different units of measure.

- Create multiple versions of the same activity with different levels of difficulty and place them at various learning stations. In the following word problem, there are three choices of number combinations, each representing a different level of difficulty: one-digit multiplication, multiplication of a one-digit number by 10, and one-digit by two-digit multiplication.

  Martin brought (3, 6, 8) cookies to school for each of the (5, 10, 16) students in his class. How many cookies did he bring to school?

- Use heterogeneous grouping, or group students who have specific weaknesses with stronger students who are willing to help.

- Break complex problems into smaller parts. Consider how this is done in the following example:

  How can we estimate the surface area of this rectangular prism? Let's look at its net or two-dimensional representation first. How many rectangles are in the net? What is the dimension of each rectangle?

heterogeneous grouping A relatively even distribution of students with different abilities, backgrounds, and cultural experiences.

In U.S. classrooms, students with special needs receive accommodations and modifications that allow them to participate fully in the classroom. What accommodations have been made in this classroom?

> Please make a journal entry now.
> Pick two different multiplication facts.
> Explain three ways of finding each of those facts.

Specific accommodations for mathematics are illustrated in **Figure 4.5**.

Planning Mathematics Instruction for Gifted Students

Within a typical classroom, you may have one or more students who are gifted. Even in school districts that offer special programs for gifted learners, the primary responsibility for gifted students' education falls on the classroom teacher. In teaching gifted students, differentiation is the key to success. Use preassessments

English-language learners in mathematics classrooms • Figure 4.6

A common myth is that students can learn mathematics even if they cannot speak English because mathematics is about numbers, not words. In fact, students who are not native English speakers may need special help in mathematics because of the emphasis on communication in the mathematics classroom.

and a variety of lessons that stress both verbal and written expression. Kindergarten teacher Rebecca Leff (2004) recommends preassessing students before the beginning of a unit and using the results to plan instruction. With a co-teacher, she plans and implements more than one lesson on each topic, depending on students' prior knowledge. Although this may not be possible in the typical classroom, teachers can differentiate students' experiences by stocking learning centers with more advanced materials for gifted students. Remember, too, that students may be gifted in mathematics but still need to develop social skills.

Planning Mathematics Instruction for English-Language Learners

There are now more than five million English-language learners (ELL) in K–12 schools (**Figure 4.6**). These students may have additional difficulties learning mathematics because they are trying to learn a second language at the same time. Despite common beliefs, mathematics is not language-free. Mathematical tasks are becoming increasingly verbal and contextualized. When students learn mathematics, they are expected to reason, explore, and justify their solutions with words. English-language learners may need additional support to be successful in mathematics. This topic is discussed in detail in Chapter 5.

Teachers can help English-language learners acquire academic English and help them improve their ability to learn mathematics by differentiating instruction using the guidelines given in *Multicultural Perspectives in Mathematics*.

Multicultural Perspectives in Mathematics

Differentiating Instruction for English-Language Learners

Consider these four principles when differentiating instruction for English-language learners:

- Comprehensible input
- A safe learning environment
- Meaningful learning activities
- Contextualized instruction

Comprehensible input means that students understand what they hear and read in the classroom. Some strategies to encourage this include speaking slowly, explaining vocabulary words, repeating main ideas, periodically checking for comprehension, and using gestures, visuals, and real-life objects for examples.

Meaningful learning activities English-language learners need the opportunity to engage in meaningful mathematics activities and to read, listen, and speak about mathematics. They should be given daily opportunities to do so. Problem solving, a student-centered atmosphere, and cooperative group learning all help achieve this goal.

A safe learning environment is one in which second language learners feel comfortable in using their new language. They are not criticized or ridiculed if their English is not perfect and they are given ample time to express themselves verbally. Low-anxiety surroundings can be created by providing tasks with multiple entry points, tiering or scaffolding activities, grouping students cooperatively, or grouping a student who has poor English language fluency with a student who has good English language fluency and is willing to translate.

Contextualized instruction means that students learn mathematics in a real-world context that is meaningful to them. Children learn their second language in the same way they learn their first language, through context-embedded interactions. Manipulatives, visual tools, and graphic organizers can add context to instruction. For example, rather than teaching mathematics vocabulary at the beginning of the lesson, provide vocabulary terms and their meanings in the context of what students are learning, after students have learned the associated concepts.

(*Source*: Murrey, 2008)

Strategies for the Classroom

- List three strategies for improving English-language learners' comprehension.
- Explain how manipulatives and other visual tools can benefit English-language learners.

- Describe a mathematics activity with multiple entry points to benefit English-language learners.

CONCEPT CHECK

1. **What** is meant by inclusion? Why is it important?
2. **How** do accommodations and modifications differ? Give two examples of each.
3. **What** steps might a teacher take to help ELLs become confident and successful in mathematics?

Using Mathematics Textbooks

LEARNING OBJECTIVES

1. **Compare** and **contrast** the different kinds of elementary and middle-grades mathematics textbooks.

2. **Explain** the benefits of using a textbook for mathematics learning.

3. **Describe** the characteristics and benefits of teachers' guides and teachers' editions.

Y ou will probably be required to use a textbook that has been selected by your state or local school system. All textbooks have advantages and disadvantages. However, they can help new teachers see the big picture. Textbooks help with sequencing topics and activities, and they offer **ancillary**, or supplementary, materials plus teachers' guides. Textbooks also provide unit and daily lesson plans and assessment options that can lighten your load during the first few years of teaching.

Elementary and Middle-Grades Mathematics Textbooks

Elementary and middle-grades mathematics textbooks cover a broad spectrum, from traditional textbooks to National Science Foundation–funded reform curricular projects and almost everything in between. Most textbooks claim to be standards based, but there are significant differences in how closely individual textbooks adhere to *Principles and Standards for School Mathematics* (NCTM, 2000).

Most traditional textbooks have similar formats. Textbooks in the lower elementary grades often follow a two-page format with the concept or topic introduced with pictures and an example on the left page, with carefully developed examples. The right page has practice exercises.

Textbooks for the upper elementary and middle grades follow a similar format but may have fewer examples and more practice. Many textbook series contain problem solving, writing, real-world examples, technology applications, and children's literature. Traditional textbooks follow the same format for each

lesson. Students may become bored with this and skip the pictures and examples to get to the practice problems. In other words, they skip over the conceptual development to learn the procedures.

Over the last 20 years, researchers have developed standards-based elementary and middle-grades curricula that use a problem-solving approach to teach mathematics (**Figure 4.7**). Three examples for elementary school are: *Math Trailblazers*, *Investigations in Number, Data, and Space*, and *Everyday Mathematics*. For middle school, *Connected Mathematics 2* is a standards-based textbook series. These series consist of separate activity books for each unit rather than one large textbook. They promote student-centered instruction with hands-on investigations that lead to students' conceptual knowledge of mathematics. Each lesson and unit uses a unique format. Reform materials have their critics as well. Some educators believe that reform materials do not contain enough skill practice and that they require supplementation.

Whether you use a traditional or reform textbook, think of the textbook as an anchor to provide you with the big ideas and concepts, as well as examples of how to sequence lessons around those ideas. Be willing to supplement the text when it does not provide exactly what your students need.

The Teachers' Edition of Your Textbook

Teachers' editions or teachers' guides suggest alternative activities and approaches that are not presented in the textbook. Most teachers' editions include an overview of each unit, the pacing of individual lessons, the mathematical emphasis, correlation with *Principles and Standards for School Mathematics* (NCTM, 2000), *Curriculum Focal Points* (NCTM, 2007), the *Common Core State Standards* (NGA Center/CCSSO, 2010), and assessment options. Teachers' guides include a list of materials you will need, how to incorporate technology, questions to ask, and in some instances, they offer a scripted dialogue with sample responses from students. Some teachers' editions include interdisciplinary connections such as children's literature.

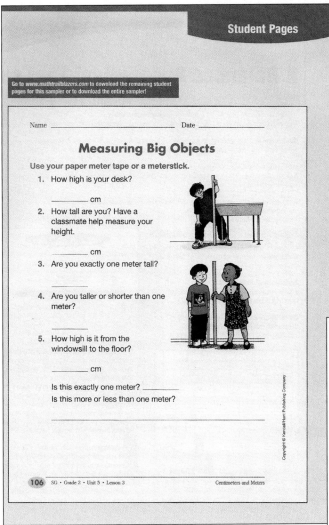

a. *Math Trailblazers* (Kendall Hunt, 2008)

Note how the activity described on this page engages children in hands-on investigations.
(From *Math Trailblazers*, 3rd Edition by the TIMS PROJECT. Copyright © 2008 by Kendall Hunt Publishing Company. Reprinted with permission.)

b. *Investigations in Number, Data, and Space* (Pearson Scott Foresman, 2008)

Note how the activity described provides an open-ended task.
(From INVESTIGATIONS STUDENT ACTIVITY BOOK GRADE 3 © 2008 Pearson Education, Inc., or its affiliates. Used by permission. All rights reserved.)

Name _____ Date _____

Trading Stickers, Combining Coins

Daily Practice

Dimes and Pennies

NOTE Students practice breaking up 2-digit numbers into 10s and 1s as they find combinations of dimes and pennies that equal a given amount.

SMH 9, 37–38

1. Show three ways to make 41¢, using dimes and pennies.

2. Show three ways to make 87¢, using dimes and pennies.

20 Unit 1

Session 1.5

© Pearson Education 3

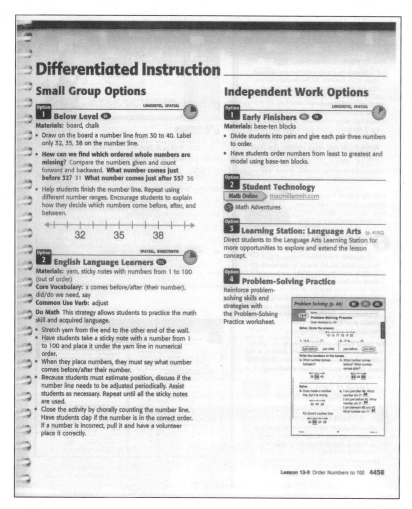

Differentiating instruction in the teachers' edition of *Math Connects* • Figure 4.8

This page from the teachers' edition of the first-grade book for *Math Connects* shows options for differentiating instruction for a lesson on ordering numbers to 100. Note the options for small groups for students that are below level or for English-language learners. Also note the options for independent work. What strategies would you add?

(From *MathConnects 1*, © 2009 MacMillan/McGraw Hill. Used by permission of The McGraw-Hill Companies.)

Many teachers' editions emphasize the importance of differentiation, especially for English-language learners, and include specific suggestions. Unfortunately, suggestions for special needs students may not be as extensive as needed. Some series anticipate the difficulties students may have and provide suggestions for how to respond. Other series include tiered activities that have different levels of difficulty, learning station activity cards in English and Spanish, and **enrichment** worksheets to provide background information or greater depth for advanced students (**Figure 4.8**).

Consider teachers' editions as helpful resources rather than something you have to follow word for word. Take what you can from the teachers' edition—from its organization and connections to standards—but pace your lessons according to your own students' needs and be ready to supplement, adapt, and modify the content for your students.

CONCEPT CHECK **STOP**

1. **How** do traditional mathematics textbooks and standards-based curricular materials differ? How are they similar?

2. **What** are some benefits of using a mathematics textbook?

3. **How** do you think you will benefit from the teachers' edition of your textbook?

What Is Assessment?

LEARNING OBJECTIVES

1. **Explain** the four purposes of assessment.
2. **Distinguish** between the three types of assessment.
3. **Describe** what should be assessed.

Assessment is an important component of planning and instruction and should contribute to the development of students' mathematical knowledge (NCTM, 2000). Although many adults think of assessments as testing, this is just one purpose of assessment. Assessment should inform planning and teaching so that each student learns mathematics to the best of her or his ability. This section discusses the purposes of assessment, the types of assessment, and what to assess.

What Are the Purposes of Assessment?

It is difficult to separate classroom assessment from planning. In order to provide all students with high-quality mathematics education, teachers need to understand the purposes of assessment. Assessment helps teachers determine what students know, how they think, and what they are able to do. It is crucial to understand how students think so that they can be effectively instructed. The *Assessment Standards for School Mathematics* (NCTM, 1995) lists four purposes of assessment (**Figure 4.9**).

The four purposes of assessment • Figure 4.9

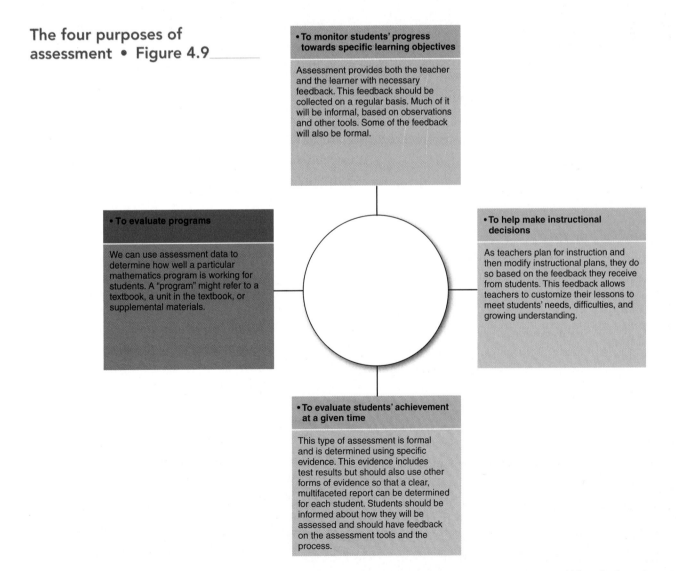

• To monitor students' progress towards specific learning objectives

Assessment provides both the teacher and the learner with necessary feedback. This feedback should be collected on a regular basis. Much of it will be informal, based on observations and other tools. Some of the feedback will also be formal.

• To evaluate programs

We can use assessment data to determine how well a particular mathematics program is working for students. A "program" might refer to a textbook, a unit in the textbook, or supplemental materials.

• To help make instructional decisions

As teachers plan for instruction and then modify instructional plans, they do so based on the feedback they receive from students. This feedback allows teachers to customize their lessons to meet students' needs, difficulties, and growing understanding.

• To evaluate students' achievement at a given time

This type of assessment is formal and is determined using specific evidence. This evidence includes test results but should also use other forms of evidence so that a clear, multifaceted report can be determined for each student. Students should be informed about how they will be assessed and should have feedback on the assessment tools and the process.

When we think of assessment, we often think of tests. However, tests are only one type of assessment. In teaching children, you will be using three types of assessment.

Geometric Solid Facts

What we know	What we want to know	What we learned
Cube	Cylinder	
Rectangular prism	Pyramid	
Octagonal prism	Cone	
Hexagonal prism		

a. Diagnostic assessment: What do your students know now? Teachers use diagnostic assessment to figure out what students know and what they need to learn. Here, a third-grade teacher and her students constructed a KWL chart.

Types of Assessment

Three types of assessment are used in the classroom: **diagnostic assessment**, **formative assessment**, and **summative assessment** (**Figure 4.10**).

> **diagnostic assessment** Informs teachers about what students already know, what they need to learn, and what misconceptions they may have.
>
> **formative assessment** Tells teachers what students are learning during a lesson or activity.
>
> **summative assessment** Tells teachers what students have learned.

Diagnostic assessment, also called *preassessment*, occurs before teaching. Its purpose is to help the teacher understand and connect with students' prior knowledge. Some textbooks offer pretests for this purpose, but questioning, problem solving, or using concept maps or **KWL charts** are often more effective, informal methods for diagnostic assessment.

Formative assessment occurs during a learning activity and provides information about what students are learning. It provides important feedback for both the teacher and the learner. This is the most important type of assessment used in the classroom because it allows teachers to adjust learning tasks and plan interventions that give all students opportunities to be successful. Formative assessment provides important feedback for students as well. It helps students become more responsible for their own learning.

> **KWL chart** Chart that determines what students know, what they want to know, and what they learned.

Summative assessment is a high-stakes assessment that judges students' attainment of specific learning goals. It occurs at the end of a chapter, unit, school year, or other defined learning experience and often results in a numerical or letter grade. In mathematics, tests are often used for summative assessment. Other options include presentations, research papers, portfolios, and projects. Summative assessments that include problem solving take more time, but they help teachers to evaluate students' learning on multiple levels.

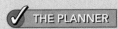

b. Formative assessment: How are your students progressing?
Mathematics teachers use formative assessment by talking with students, listening to them, and reading their written work to assess student progress and make decisions on what to teach next.

c. Summative assessment: What have your students learned?
Mathematics teachers use summative assessment to find out what students have learned at the end of a chapter, unit, or semester. A final examination is an example of summative assessment.

Virtual Classroom Observation

Video | **www.wiley.com/college/jones**

Click on **Student Companion Site**. Then click on:

• **Foundations of Effective Mathematics Teaching**

• **C. Listening To and Interpreting Student Thinking**

• **3. Analyze Classroom Videos**

View:

• **Area of a Triangle: Fernando wants a better method**

Note how Ms. Winningham questions students to find out what they already know about area, focusing on vocabulary and conceptual knowledge.

What Should Be Assessed?

Students learn to value what teachers assess. It is important that your curriculum, goals, mathematics instruction, and assessments be closely aligned. Choose assessment tasks that reflect what actually happens in the classroom and focus on what you think is important for students to learn. If you only assess students' ability to perform procedures, they will learn to value these. However, if you assess students' ability to think about problems, devise solutions, and communicate their thinking through discussion and writing as well as the ability to perform procedures, then students will learn to value all of these abilities.

CONCEPT CHECK STOP

1. **What** are the purposes of assessment?

2. **What** are the differences between diagnostic, formative, and summative assessment?

3. **Why** should assessment and curriculum be closely aligned?

Assessment Tools

LEARNING OBJECTIVES

1. **Describe** observation, interviewing, and writing as tools for formative assessment.

2. **Consider** the importance of homework.

3. **Distinguish** between holistic and analytic rubrics for assessment.

The many choices available for formative assessment include observation, interviewing, portfolios, projects, and journals. These tools provide multidimensional feedback on students' learning and can be easily integrated into the classroom routine. As a new teacher, choose one or two assessment tools to focus on. Then the following year you can incorporate additional innovative assessment tools.

Observation

Observation is a powerful tool for formative assessment. You can observe students informally as you walk around the classroom, while they are working in groups, individually, or in pairs. Before beginning your observation, think about the characteristics, knowledge, or skills that you want to observe and how you plan to record your observations. For example, if students are problem solving in small groups or pairs, you might observe their specific mathematical understandings. As an example, for the lesson plan described earlier in this chapter, you might observe how students carry out the addition necessary to form palindromes, how often they use calculators to add the numbers, and how often they use mental mathematics. Observe how the students discover the patterns associated with palindromes and whether the color-coded charts facilitate their thinking.

It is impossible to observe every student in your class in a single class session. Try to observe no more than five students per day. Then, as soon as possible after class, record your observations in an organized manner. Some

Using a checklist for student observations • Figure 4.12 _____

Checklists provide a quick way to record observations. Some teachers have checklists for individual students as well as checklists for small-group assessment.

Gemma S.   October 2

Gemma easily counts to 100 and shows understanding of one-to-one correspondence of objects to numerals.

She can count on by ones but has some difficulty counting back.

She understands "more than," "less than," and "the same as."

Using index cards for student observations • Figure 4.11 _____

By writing your observations on an index card, you will be able to assess how each student's knowledge changes over time.

teachers create an index card for each student and pull out the cards for the students they intend to observe that day (**Figure 4.11**). Other teachers develop a checklist of skills and behaviors they are planning to observe, make a copy of the checklist to record observations for each student in the class, and place their checklist on a clipboard (**Figure 4.12**).

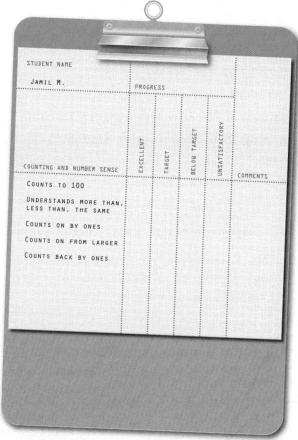

Sample assessment interview for geometry • Figure 4.13 _____

OBJECTIVE
To determine students' knowledge of angles and triangles

GRADE LEVEL
3–4

MATERIALS
Geoboards and rubber bands, paper and pencil, ruler

QUESTIONS

1. Ask: *Can you make a triangle on your geoboard? How many sides does it have? How many angles?* (Begin with whatever triangle the student has made.)

2. Ask: *Can you compare the lengths of the sides? Are they all the same length, all different, or are two the same length? How can you tell?*

3. Ask: *What about the angles? Are they all the same size? If not, which angle is the largest? Which is the smallest? How can you tell?*

4. Say: *Here is another triangle.* (Teacher draws a right triangle on paper or makes it on the geoboard.)

5. Ask: *What is the name of this kind of triangle? What is this angle called?* (Teacher points to the right angle.) *Can you make another angle this size on your geoboard?*

6. Ask: *What can you tell me about the size of the other angles in this triangle? How do you know? What is the special name for these kinds of angles?*

7. Ask: *Can you draw a triangle with two right angles? Why or why not?*

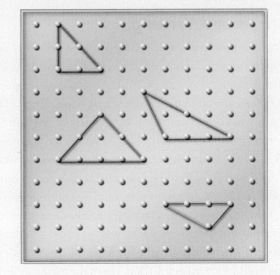

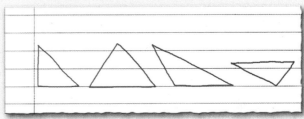

8. Ask: *What does it mean for an angle to be obtuse? Can you draw an obtuse angle? How do you know this angle is obtuse?*

9. Ask: *Can you draw a triangle with an obtuse angle?*

10. Ask: *Can you draw a triangle with more than one obtuse angle? Why or why not?*

Interviews

Interviewing provides you with the opportunity for a one-on-one experience with each of your students. It can be time consuming but very worthwhile, especially at the beginning of the school year. Interviewing allows you to develop rapport with your students, to demonstrate that you value their thinking, and to get to know how they think. Before you interview a child, think about how you can create a supportive environment for talking about mathematics.

1. Find a quiet place and a quiet time for the interview, and put the child at ease through informal conversation.

2. Ask questions that require more than yes or no answers, and be prepared to sequence your questions from easy to hard.

3. Use observations to effectively assess the child's understandings and misunderstandings.

4. Ask the child to explain his or her thinking with questions such as: *How did you get that answer? Why do you think that answer is right?*

Remember that an interview is for gathering assessment data and not for instruction. Resist the urge to explain and teach. Interviews should take between 10 and 30 minutes for each student, depending on the age and the individual needs of the student (**Figure 4.13**).

By administering the assessment interview in Figure 4.13, you can learn what students understand about angles and triangles. If the questions are answered correctly, you will know that you can proceed to more complicated geometric figures and concepts. If students try to make a triangle with two right angles or with two obtuse angles, they should realize that this is impossible. If they articulate their reasoning clearly, you can learn about their understanding of geometric relationships.

Journals and Writing

Writing is a powerful tool for formative assessment. When students write regularly, they come to value writing as a tool that helps them reflect on what they learned and connect it to what they already know (Lester and Kroll, 1996). There are many ways to use writing in the classroom. We will focus on journals or learning logs, where students write entries in notebooks and make written responses to specific writing prompts. Journals should be read and responded to but not graded. Grading a journal entry implies there is only one correct way to respond to a writing prompt or an exercise.

Journal entries are a great way to open or conclude lessons. After children have written in their journals, ask for volunteers to read their journal entries or collect them and read them for formative assessment purposes. Following are some examples of journal prompts.

At the conclusion of a lesson on perimeter and area, you might ask students to respond to open-ended questions such as:

- *What did you learn about perimeter and area today?*
- *What do you still have questions about?*

At the end of a problem-solving session, you might ask students:

- *Which was the hardest problem you solved today? Explain how you solved it.*
- *How do you know that your answer is correct?*

Virtual Classroom Observation

Video	www.wiley.com/college/jones

Click on **Student Companion Site**. Then click on:

- **Foundations of Effective Mathematics Teaching**
- **D. Quality Formative Assessment**
- **3. Analyze Classroom Videos**

Scroll down and view:

- **Calculating the Area of a Triangle: Journaling**

Ms. Winningham plans to use "on-the-fly assessments." What formative assessment tools does Ms. Winningham use with her fifth-grade class? How does Ms. Winningham use writing for formative assessment?

For children who are too young to write, drawings or pictures pasted on a page can take the place of words. For example, you might ask a kindergartener or first grader to show *five* in three different ways (**Figure 4.14**). The journal entry becomes a written record of what the student knows and understands.

A young child's mathematics journal entry • Figure 4.14

For a young child, a journal entry may consist of pictures pasted into a book or a combination of words, pictures, and numerals.

What to include in a mathematics portfolio for the middle grades • Figure 4.15

This is one possibility of what to include in a mathematics portfolio. Before deciding on the requirements, discuss with your class and develop a list together.

This is a collection of your work in mathematics for this semester. Include each of the following components.

I.   Cover letter:
Include a letter that tells a little bit about you, describes the contents of your portfolio, and describes how you have improved in mathematics this semester.

II. Portfolio selections:
- A sample of your best work. Explain why it is your best.
- A sample of something you don't completely understand yet.
- A sample that shows how your understanding has grown mathematically.
- A sample that shows flexible thinking and problem solving.

III. Organization:
Put your portfolio in a folder or binder, decorate the cover, and place the cover letter first, followed by portfolio selections.

Self-Assessment

When students assess themselves, they find out what they know, what they learned, and what they still need to learn. In this way, self-assessment can be a powerful learning tool because it helps provide specific learning goals for students. Self-assessment can also boost students' confidence in mathematics, a subject that may seem frightening. Students' ability to recognize what they have accomplished can raise their morale and encourage them to become more involved in mathematics activities.

How can you incorporate self-assessment in your own classroom? One way to begin is to provide a questionnaire to which students can answer "Yes" or "No." This is a great way to help students think about what they have learned as well as to get information about their attitudes toward mathematics. Another technique is to ask students to fill out an index card, weekly, with two items: (1) something they learned in mathematics that they are proud of and (2) something they still are not sure of and want to ask questions about. This technique helps focus students' attention on what they have learned and instills pride in their accomplishments. It also supports communication between you and your students. If a student is shy about asking a question in class, by having the student put the question on the card and you answering it on the card, you are communicating to the student that you value him or her while also providing an answer to the question.

Another self-assessment tool is the portfolio. Portfolios are used for other types of assessment, such as journals or research projects, and they are also very well suited to self-assessment. Even though they are collected by the teacher and may be graded using a rubric, portfolios really provide a means for students to assess themselves. Provide criteria for what students should include in their portfolio (**Figure 4.15**).

Homework

Homework provides students with an important opportunity to apply what they learned to new problems and situations. Show students that you value homework assignments by referring to the homework during class, collecting it, grading it, and expecting students to be responsible for learning from it. Assign homework that gives students the opportunity to practice new skills and to solve problems that may take some time to think about. It does not make sense to give students pages of exercises. If they are making mistakes, the repetition will only reinforce their errors. Also, let parents know that you will be giving homework so that they can be prepared to monitor its completion. Many schools offer online newsletters that help parents keep up with their children's assignments. If the homework involves a special project or something that may be unfamiliar to parents, send a letter home that describes the purpose of the assignment and clarifies vocabulary or instructions. If you demonstrate that you value homework, then students will value it as well.

A four-point rubric allows the teacher to quickly sort papers. Those needing little revision can be put in one pile and those needing more extensive revision in a second pile. This is a rubric for grading a problem-solving activity.

4 Excellent — Full accomplishment

The task is completed and correct. The student demonstrates in-depth understanding of the problem. The student used an appropriate strategy or multiple strategies to solve the problem. If there is more than one solution, this is noted and other solutions are demonstrated.

3 Proficient — Substantial accomplishment

The task is completed but may have minor errors. Or, there may be no errors but the explanation is not entirely clear. The student demonstrates understanding of the major concepts in the problem but misses some minor components or details. The student used an appropriate strategy.

2 Marginal — Partial accomplishment

The task was started but is not completed or was completed incorrectly because of some misunderstandings. The student may have been able to generate a strategy and use it to partially complete the problem but the strategy did not lead to a correct answer or there may be no answer at all.

1 Unsatisfactory — Little accomplishment

The student has major misunderstandings and did not select a strategy or start the problem in a meaningful way. The answer is missing or incorrect and does not connect to the problem.

Rubrics

Rubrics are used to assess open-ended tasks such as those found in problem solving. Problem solving lends itself to formative assessment because it often encompasses several skills in one activity. Through problem-solving tasks, teachers learn about students' reasoning, communicating, and thinking. This provides a lot of data for the teacher but also raises questions. How can you grade problem-solving tasks effectively in a reasonable amount of time and also provide meaningful feedback for students? One solution is to use rubrics. They are efficient for the teacher and can give students meaningful feedback by

> rubric A scoring tool that allows for standardized evaluation according to specified criteria.

helping them understand what a correct and complete response looks like.

There are two kinds of rubrics. **Analytic rubrics** involve "the use of a scale to assign points to certain phases of the mathematical problem-solving process" (Lester and Kroll, 1996, p. 5). They provide insight into students' thinking but are very time consuming. **Holistic rubrics** are efficient and consistent. They focus on the entire solution as a whole and provide a single number for evaluation. Of the different ways to create holistic rubrics, the four-point rubric is one of the most commonly used. There are many ways to create the four-point rubric. One method is illustrated in **Figure 4.16**.

One of the benefits of a four-point rubric is that it allows you to quickly sort your papers into two piles. The papers that will get a three or four can be placed in one pile and the papers that will get a two or one can be placed in a second pile. Grading a series of papers that have similar mistakes or features can save you time and increase the consistency of your feedback.

Holistic rubrics that are used in the classroom may have more detail than the one illustrated here and may have different numbers of points. Five- and six-point rubrics are also commonly used. Before creating a rubric, ask for feedback from students. Ask them what they think is important about the assignment and what the rubric should include. After the rubric is complete, make sure that students understand it, know what is expected of them, and have a copy of the rubric before they begin the task for which it will be used.

CONCEPT CHECK   STOP

1. **What** are some benefits and drawbacks of observation, journals, and interviews?

2. **Why** is it important to assign and grade homework?

3. **How** do rubrics help to make grading more efficient and fair? How do holistic and analytic rubrics differ?

THE PLANNER ✓

Summary

1 Why Planning Is Important 82

- Planning helps to establish priorities, set educational goals, determine how to meet the goals we set, and keep a record of our actions so that we can look back and reflect on what happened, what went well, and what we would like to change next time.

- There are three types of planning in elementary education: yearly planning, unit planning, and daily planning.

  Yearly plans are usually prepared by the school system and consist of an overview of the learning objectives for the entire year. Unit plans provide an overview of each unit and include vocabulary, objectives, materials, pacing, and formative and summative assessments for each unit.

- Daily plans describe what will happen on a day-by-day basis. They break tasks down into more manageable goals. Although lesson planning is usually done alone, a new practice, called lesson study, has recently made inroads into U.S. schools, as shown in this photo.

Figure 4.1

2 Planning a Mathematics Lesson 84

- There are three main sections of a daily lesson plan: launch, instruct or explore, and summarize. Each plan should also list grade level, objectives, materials, assessment, grouping, possible extensions, and adaptations.

- There are two types of lesson plans, teacher-directed and student-centered. **Teacher-directed lessons** are appropriate when you want to introduce new ideas, procedures, or vocabulary to the whole class. **Student-centered lessons** provide opportunities for students to explore patterns, investigate new ideas, practice skills, and gain experience with problem solving while working individually or in small groups.

- When using small groups, make sure that the groups are no larger than three or four students, and build in both individual and **group accountability.** A small group of middle-school students is shown in this photo.

Figure 4.4

- Effective use of manipulatives entails understanding how to use the manipulatives and developing a plan for their storage, distribution, and collection. When using a new manipulative, first become familiar with it yourself, and then build some unstructured time for children to explore it.

3 Planning for Diversity 90

- Teachers need to carefully plan to **differentiate instruction** in order to meet the diverse needs of students. This challenge has intensified in the 21st century as our classrooms are becoming even more diverse.

- Students with special needs are included in regular classrooms and may require **accommodations** and **modifications** to maximize their success in mathematics, as shown here.

Figure 4.5

- English-language learners need extra support to learn mathematics and English at the same time. Help them to learn mathematics by providing real-world examples of mathematics as well as visual learning tools such as graphic organizers, charts, and concrete manipulatives.

4 Using Mathematics Textbooks 94

- Textbooks help you see the big picture, sequence lessons, offer **ancillary** or supplementary materials, and provide unit and daily lesson plans and assessment. Elementary and middle-grades mathematics textbooks cover a broad spectrum, from traditional textbooks to National Science Foundation–funded reform curricular projects and almost everything in between.

- Teachers' guides or instructors' editions can help new teachers by providing assessments, extension activities, and ideas for differentiating instruction. They show the teacher how to sequence lessons and often offer alternative assignments and explanations, activity by activity.

5 What Is Assessment? 97

- Assessment has four purposes: to monitor students' progress, make instructional decisions, evaluate student achievement, and evaluate programs.

- There are three different types of assessment: **diagnostic**, **formative**, and **summative**.

- **Diagnostic assessment** informs the teacher about what students already know. It is often informal and can be done through questioning, concept maps, or by using **KWL charts**, as shown in the figure. **Formative assessment** provides feedback to both teachers and students to assess how well students are learning material. **Summative assessment** evaluates student knowledge at the end of a unit or lesson, often with a high-stakes test.

Figure 4.10

Geometric Solid Facts		
What we know	What we want to know	What we learned
Cube	Cylinder	
Rectangular prism	Pyramid	
Octagonal prism	Cone	
Hexagonal prism		

- Students learn to value what teachers assess. It is important that our curriculum, goals, mathematics instruction, and assessments be closely aligned so that assessment tasks reflect what actually happens in the classroom. If we assess students' ability to reason, problem solve, and communicate about mathematics through writing and discussion, as well as to perform procedures, then students will learn to value all of these abilities.

6 **Assessment Tools 100**

- Tools for formative assessment include observations, interviews, self-assessment, writing, and journals. Each of these assessments takes time, but such assessment of students' progress enables teachers to make modifications in instruction that benefit students' learning of mathematics. This figure illustrates how you might record your observations.

- Homework is an important part of planning and assessment. Show students that you value homework by collecting it, referring to it, and holding them responsible for learning the content in the homework assignment. Make sure to communicate with parents so they know what kind of homework to expect and when.

- There are two kinds of rubrics: **analytic rubrics** and **holistic rubrics**. Analytic rubrics assign points to key portions of an assignment. They are helpful but time consuming. Holistic rubrics evaluate the assignment as a whole. They are easier to use and can help teachers manage their workload.

Figure 4.11

> Gemma S.   October 2
>
> Gemma easily counts to 100 and shows understanding of one-to-one correspondence of objects to numerals.
>
> She can count on by ones but has some difficulty counting back.
>
> She understands "more than," "less than," and "the same as."

Key Terms

- ancillary 94
- analytic rubric 104
- accommodation 91
- diagnostic assessment 98
- differentiate instruction 82
- formative assessment 98
- enrichment 96

- group accountability 89
- heterogeneous grouping 91
- holistic rubric 104
- inclusion 90
- individual accountability 89
- KWL chart 98
- mini-lesson 88

- modification 91
- rubric 104
- scope and sequence charts 82
- student-centered lesson 84
- summative assessment 98
- teacher-directed lesson 84

Online Resources

- **The Chicago Public Schools**
  http://research.cps.k12.il.us

  This site provides a collection of rubric resources that includes both analytic and holistic scoring rubrics for mathematics. There are examples from several states as well as rubrics used by mathematics education research projects.

- **NCTM Illuminations**
  illuminations.nctm.org/Lessons

  This site has hundreds of lessons in different areas of mathematics. Lessons are organized by grade-level band and content standard.

Critical and Creative Thinking Questions

1. Select the teacher's edition of a recent elementary or middle-grades mathematics text. These are often available in university or public libraries. Evaluate the teachers' edition for a particular grade level by answering the following questions:

   • How detailed and useful are the suggestions?
   • Does the teachers' edition set pacing? Does the pacing seem realistic?
   • Does the teachers' edition include technology applications?
   • Does it differentiate instruction for special-needs students, ELLs, and gifted students?

2. Select a lesson from the teacher's edition you used in item 1. Design an assessment for the lesson that includes some self-assessment options and some writing.

3. Why is planning crucial in education and especially in mathematics education? What benefits do you, the teacher, receive from planning? What benefits do your students receive?

4. **In the field** Interview a student about a mathematics concept. Select the student, write a set of interview questions or use the one in this chapter (for a student in grades 3 or 4), and interview the student. Begin by taking a few minutes to get to know the student. Explain that this is an assignment for your college course. After the interview, reflect on how it went. Did you learn what the student already knows and needs to learn about the topic of your interview? How would you revise the interview in the future to make it better? If you were to construct a lesson based on this interview, what specific content would your lesson contain?

5. What are the differences between diagnostic, formative, and summative assessment? Give examples of each for a particular topic.

What is happening in this picture?

Think Critically

Look closely at this picture.
1. What can you tell about the goals of this lesson from the type of grouping the teacher used?
2. What type of formative assessment would be appropriate here?

Self-Test

(Check your answers in Appendix D.)

1. Describe the three levels of planning.

2. List at least five components that should be present in every unit plan. Why are they important?

3. A student in your class is working on a division word problem. What prior knowledge should you check for?

4. Describe the three parts of a lesson plan. Given a 45-minute period, about how many minutes should be spent for each part of the lesson plan?

5. How can the resource boxes in this photo be used to facilitate mini-lessons? What are the advantages of mini-lessons?

6. What is differentiated instruction? Why is it important?

7. What is the difference between a modification and an accommodation? List three examples of each.

8. What accommodations or modifications are indicated by this image?

> Please make a journal entry now.
> Pick two different multiplication facts.
> Explain three ways of finding each of those facts.

9. The *Lesson* on palindromes might provide difficulties for students with certain learning disabilities, who tend to reverse digits and letters. What accommodations could you make to the lesson to help those students?

10. The *Lesson* on palindromes might also be difficult for ELLs. How did the lesson plan address these potential difficulties? Describe the modifications made in the palindrome *Lesson* to meet the needs of ELLs.

11. Of the three kinds of assessment, which should you use every day?

12. What is a rubric? Describe the difference between an analytic rubric and a holistic rubric.

13. Ms. Antunez notices that Cleon can identify three-dimensional figures but has difficulty drawing their nets. What kind of assessment is Ms. Antunez using?

14. Mr. Blakita assigns students to write about what they learned today during mathematics time. What kind of assessment is Mr. Blakita using?

15. Why is it important for you to assign and grade homework?

THE PLANNER ✓

Review your Chapter Planner on the chapter opener and check off your completed work.

Providing Equitable Instruction for All Students

Lue Yang sat in the back row of his mathematics education class at the University of Wisconsin, Eau Claire. Although Professor Sue Balas had tried to engage Lue in class activities, he was reluctant to work with others and had never spoken with her.

On this day, Dr. Balas had prepared an activity based on the traditional Hmong embroidery known as *paj ntaub* (flower cloth). She asked her students to use construction paper, tracing paper, and colored pencils to make paper versions of the paj ntaub, to motivate discussion about line and rotational symmetry. Lue completed the activity and then, after class, rushed up to his professor and exclaimed, "This is my culture!" Then he told Professor Balas about his years in a refugee camp, waiting to come to the United States.

The next day, Lue sat in the front row and began to interact with his peers and to participate in group and whole-class activities. His classmates and professor learned that Lue had a wonderful sense of humor and was a gifted mathematics student. He learned that they were interested in and respected his culture.

Cultural connections bring context to mathematics so that students of all ages can recognize and find pride in the mathematical ideas within their own traditions. Students become energized and motivated when they realize their cultural heritage contains worthwhile mathematics. In Lue's case, seeing his cultural traditions used in class helped to bridge the gap between his home culture and what he learned in school.

Just as Lue and his classmates benefited from this activity, elementary and middle-grades students benefit by learning how mathematics is connected to culture.

CHAPTER OUTLINE

Multicultural Education 112

Key Questions: What are the origins of multicultural education? Why is it important to include it in the curriculum?

Mathematics for All 116

Key Questions: How can teachers meet the needs of English-language learners in mathematics? How can teachers meet the needs of exceptional students? What is the achievement gap?

Closing the Achievement Gap in Mathematics 119

Key Questions: How can content integration help close the achievement gap in mathematics? What strategies are effective in teaching mathematics to English-language learners? What strategies are effective for exceptional students? How can teachers and parents work together to help children excel in mathematics?

Gender Equity in Mathematics 128

Key Questions: How has the gender gap in mathematics achievement changed in recent years? What strategies can teachers use to achieve gender equity in the mathematics classroom?

NCTM The Equity Principle: Excellence in mathematics education requires equity—high expectations and strong support for all students.

(NCTM, 2000, p. 11)

CHAPTER PLANNER ✓

- ☐ Study the picture and read the opening story.
- ☐ Scan the Learning Objectives in each section:
  p. 112 ☐   p. 116 ☐   p. 119 ☐   p. 128 ☐
- ☐ Read the text and study all visuals and Activities. Answer any questions.

Analyze key features

- ☐ Education InSight,
  p. 113 ☐   p. 120 ☐   p. 128 ☐
- ☐ Process Diagram, p. 115
- ☐ Children's Literature, p. 121
- ☐ Lesson, p. 122
- ☐ In the Classroom, p. 124
- ☐ Multicultural Perspectives in Mathematics, p. 127
- ☐ Stop: Answer the Concept Checks
  before you go on:
  p. 114 ☐   p. 119 ☐   p. 127 ☐   p. 131 ☐

End of chapter

- ☐ Review the Summary and Key Terms.
- ☐ Answer the Critical and Creative Thinking Questions.
- ☐ Answer What is happening in this picture?
- ☐ Complete the Self-Test and check your answers.

Multicultural Education

LEARNING OBJECTIVES

1. **Explain** the meaning of culture and America's core cultural characteristics.

2. **Describe** cultural values of ethnically and culturally diverse students.

3. **Discuss** the origins and goals of multicultural education.

4. **Explain** the four levels of content integration.

"**M**ulticultural education incorporates the idea that all students—regardless of their gender and social class, their ethnic, racial, or cultural characteristics—should have an equal opportunity to learn in school" (Banks, 2007a, p. 3). Some students today have a better opportunity to learn than others. The goal of multicultural education is to effect change in schools so that all students have an equal opportunity to learn.

What Is Culture?

culture The values or beliefs we think are important, what we think is true, and the way we believe things are done.

Culture is an important variable that influences teaching and learning. It includes beliefs, traditions, practices, habits, symbols, ceremonies, and history, some of which we are aware of and some of which we are not. In the United States it is not uncommon to find many types of cultural festivals and a wide variety of ethnic foods because our population represents people from many parts of the world (**Figure 5.1**).

We tend not to think about our behaviors as cultural practices. Rather than thinking about these behaviors as culture, we just assume, "It's the way things are done around here" (Kilmann, 1985, p. 5). This can be a dangerous assumption. If we believe that our own cultural values are the "right" way of doing things, then other people's values may be viewed as "wrong." The first step in providing equitable learning opportunities for all students is to become aware of our own cultural roots. This knowledge empowers us to recognize and respect the cultural values of our students and use this information to improve instruction.

It can be easier to recognize the cultural traditions of other groups than to recognize our own. Some might even ask, *Do I have culture?* or, more generally, *Do Americans*

Cultural practices in the United States • Figure 5.1

What do these images have in common? Which of these images illustrate obvious cultural practices that we take for granted? Which of these images illustrates practices that are fairly invisible?

The United States has often been viewed as a melting pot because its citizens originally came from all over the world and brought with them varied cultural traditions. Even so, three basic values permeate U.S. core culture.

a. Americans believe in equality. The Declaration of Independence says that *All men are created equal.* This idea was considered radical for its time. In 1776 it was not generally believed that human beings were born with equal rights. Since then, our understanding of equality has undergone significant change but still maintains a powerful place in our culture. In what ways has our understanding of equality changed in recent years?

b. Americans are highly individualistic. In U.S. mainstream culture, individual success is considered more important than commitments to family or community. Children grow up and sometimes move thousands of miles from their parents to attend college or find employment.

c. Americans believe that anyone can begin life in meager circumstances and grow up to become successful. We believe that America is a place where anything is possible if we work hard. Justice Sonia Sotomayor, the first Hispanic justice of the Supreme Court, was raised by a single, working mother in public housing. She attended college and law school on scholarships.

have culture? Yes, absolutely! Every person and every social group is cultural. Let's look at a typical situation. Suppose a distant relative calls unexpectedly and says he will be in town overnight. Do you feel obligated to invite your relative to stay at your home or do you suggest that he stay at a hotel? How you answer this question tells something about the expectations that you learned from your family and reflects the cultural values that were transmitted to you.

The United States is a multicultural society with a large, shared culture and many smaller cultures. Banks (2007a) describes three

individualism A social outlook that stresses independence and self-reliance.

individual opportunity The idea that each person has the opportunity to achieve success through hard work and that failure to achieve success is the person's own fault.

basic values that permeate United States core culture: equality, individualism, and individual opportunity (**Figure 5.2**). These cultural themes are very different from the expectations in countries such as China and Japan, where people are committed first to their family, second to their group, and third to themselves.

Individualism and individual achievement are not shared by all cultures in the United States. For example, African Americans, Hispanics, and American Indians tend to be more **field dependent** or group oriented than mainstream Americans. In these cultural groups, harmony within the community, cooperation, and interdependence appear to be crucial. Students from these cultures may experience problems in traditional school settings, where individual achievement is often emphasized. Students who are group oriented usually learn more effectively in cooperative groups because they reflect the values of their culture.

You can gain important clues about your students' learning preferences when you have knowledge of the cultural groups to which they belong. Remember, though, that every person is a member of several different groups at the same time and will be influenced to various degrees by the values of those groups. In other words, don't automatically assume that all members of a particular group act in a certain way. Learn about the cultural and ethnic groups that are represented in your classroom, but also learn about the backgrounds and learning styles of individual students.

The Origins of Multicultural Education

Multicultural education evolved out of the political unrest and social change of the 1960s and early 1970s (Sleeter and Grant, 2009). The civil rights and women's rights movements motivated the creation of Black Studies and Women's Studies programs at the university level. In turn, this focused attention on the exclusion of diverse groups' contributions from K–12 curriculum and texts and the lack of culturally and ethnically diverse teachers and administrators. Multicultural education is a response to these issues. Multicultural education is also seen as a solution to the well-documented differences in academic achievement between ethnically and culturally diverse students and their dominant-culture peers. Changing demographics has also fueled the movement for multicultural education. It is estimated that by 2040 the percentage of children and youth who are Latino or Asian will exceed 50%. If schools are to meet the needs of these students and train them as the workforce of the future, the need to engage and empower all students in school learning is urgent.

The Meaning of Multicultural Education

Multicultural education is also known as **culturally relevant** or **culturally responsive** pedagogy. Simply stated, the goal of multicultural education is to provide an equitable, empowering learning environment for all students. Such an environment celebrates the richness of cultural diversity while recognizing its importance in learning. Multicultural education benefits all students by expanding the knowledge base, providing students with accurate information, encouraging them to understand diversity, providing students with interesting, interactive topics and methods of learning, and preparing students to be responsible citizens. Multicultural education also empowers parents, teachers, and school administrators by fostering clear communication, community cohesiveness, and understanding and respect for diverse cultural traditions.

Content integration is "the extent to which teachers use examples and content from a variety of cultures and groups to illustrate key concepts, principles, generalizations, and theories in their subject area" (Banks, 2007a, p. 20). History, social studies, and language arts are obvious choices for multicultural topics; however, both science and mathematics also provide excellent opportunities for content integration. Banks (2007b) describes approaches to content integration in terms of four levels (**Figure 5.3**). Most schools probably meet the descriptions of the first or second levels, although they should aim for the third or fourth level.

CONCEPT CHECK   STOP

1. **What** American cultural themes are depicted in this image?

2. **How** might the American tradition of individualism be defeating for culturally and ethnically diverse students?

3. **What** social and political undercurrents preceded the development of multicultural education?

4. **What** are the four levels of content integration? Which levels should schools strive to achieve?

The four levels of content integration • Figure 5.3

These levels can be viewed as a hierarchy. Schools usually enter the hierarchy at the contributions level because multicultural content can be integrated quickly at this level, although it is somewhat superficial. The goal is to work up to level four.

4 The social action approach

Classroom learning is used to foster social action. It is based on the belief that schools should prepare students to be responsible citizens by encouraging them to work collectively to solve societal problems. An example from mathematics is a class that collects and analyzes data on the number of hungry people in their community and then sponsors a food drive to provide resources for a community food bank.

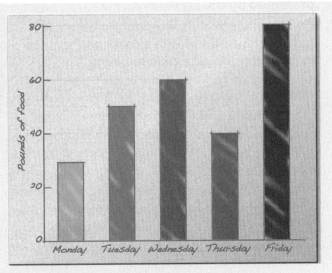

3 The transformational approach

Multicultural topics become part of the regular curriculum, are connected to other topics, and carry equal weight. This approach enables students to view content from several perspectives. An example from mathematics includes comparing the surface area of round and rectangular houses and analyzing why round houses are used in parts of Africa.

2 The additive approach

The inclusion of multicultural topics in the curriculum, such as the contributions of a female scientist or an African American mathematician. The topic is labeled as "special" and is used as enrichment, but it is not part of the regular curriculum. An example from mathematics is the biography of African American mathematician Benjamin Banneker.

1 The contributions approach

Focuses on ethnic festivals and holidays, ethnic foods, signs in different languages, and posters of ethnically diverse people. At this level, the curriculum remains unchanged. An example from mathematics is the inclusion of words for numbers in different languages.

(*Source*: Adapted from Banks 2007b, p. 251)

	1	2	3	4	5	6	7	8	9	10
English	one	two	three	four	five	six	seven	eight	nine	ten
German	eins	zwei	drei	vier	fünf	sechs	sieben	acht	neun	zehn
Spanish	uno	dos	tres	cuatro	cinco	seis	siete	ocho	nueve	diez
Swahili	moja	mbili	tatu	nne	tano	sita	saba	nane	tisa	kumi

Mathematics for All

LEARNING OBJECTIVES

1. **Describe** the vision of mathematics education presented by the Equity Principle.
2. **Explain** the achievement gap in mathematics between average white students and their culturally and ethnically diverse peers.
3. **Describe** the needs of exceptional learners in mathematics.

Principles and Standards for School Mathematics (NCTM, 2000) describes a vision of mathematics in which all students have access to high-quality mathematics instruction provided by effective teachers who have adequate resources as well as access to ongoing professional development. This vision, although very ambitious, is within our reach.

It means that all students—regardless of their race, gender, socioeconomic class, physical challenges, or exceptionality—should have the opportunity to learn mathematics. Equity does not mean that all students should have identical instruction but that reasonable accommodations and modifications are made so that all students have the opportunity to learn challenging mathematics.

The Disparity in Mathematics Achievement

achievement gap
The observed disparity on a number of educational assessments between the performance of certain groups, especially groups defined by gender, race/ethnicity, and socioeconomic status.

The **achievement gap** in mathematics between white students and black, Hispanic, and American Indian/Alaska Native students has been documented for many years. The National Assessment of Educational Progress (NAEP) is often called The Nation's Report Card. The NAEP is an assessment that has been administered to hundreds of thousands of students in grades 4 and 8 for more than 30 years.

- In 2009 NAEP collected data from approximately 168,800 fourth-grade students in 9510 schools and 161,700 eighth graders in 7030 schools (**Figure 5.4**).

- Average scores on the NAEP fourth-grade mathematics assessment did not increase from 2007 to 2009; however, average scores on the eighth-grade assessment did increase by 2% from 2007 to 2009.

- For fourth grade, white, black, Hispanic, and Asian/Pacific Islander students did not show gains from 2007 to 2009 but maintained the gains they had achieved in assessments prior to 2007.

- For fourth grade, on average, white and Asian/Pacific Islander students scored higher than black, Hispanic, and American Indian/Alaska Native students.

- For fourth grade, on average, Asian/Pacific Islander students scored higher than white students.

- For fourth grade, on average, white students scored higher than black students.

- For fourth grade, on average, white students scored higher than Hispanic and American Indian/Alaska Native students.

- For eighth grade, on average, Asian/Pacific Islander students scored higher than black, Hispanic, and American Indian/Alaska Native students.

- For eighth grade, on average, Asian/Pacific Islander students also scored higher than white students.

- For eighth grade, on average, white students scored higher than black, Hispanic, and American Indian/Alaska Native students.

Why does this disparity in mathematics achievement exist? Researchers attribute a number of factors to the differential achievement of culturally and ethnically diverse students in mathematics, including curriculum, instruction, student perceptions, assessment, classroom culture, and teacher expectations.

- **Curriculum** If students feel that the mathematics they are taught is irrelevant to their cultural backgrounds and their lives outside of school, they may "feel invisible and unconnected with the content" (Davidson and Kramer, 1997, p. 139) and literally "turn off" school.

Trends in fourth-grade NAEP: mathematics average scores and score gaps by selected racial-ethnic groups • Figure 5.4

The 2009 National Assessment for Educational Progress shows a 26-point score gap in mathematics between white fourth graders and black fourth graders. These test results show no significant differences from 2007 to 2009.

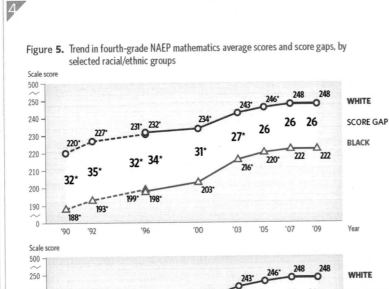

Figure 5. Trend in fourth-grade NAEP mathematics average scores and score gaps, by selected racial/ethnic groups

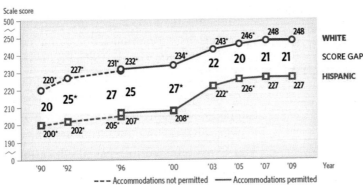

--- Accommodations not permitted   ——— Accommodations permitted

* Significantly different (p < .05) from 2009.
NOTE: Black includes African American, and Hispanic includes Latino. Race categories exclude Hispanic origin. Score gaps are calculated based on differences between unrounded average scores.

Racial/ethnic gaps persist

The 26-point score gap in mathematics scores between White and Black students in 2009 was not significantly different from the gap in 2007, but was narrower than in 1990 (figure 5). The 21-point score gap between White and Hispanic students in 2009 was not found to be significantly different from the gaps in either 2007 or 1990.

Table 1. Percentage of students assessed in fourth-grade NAEP mathematics, by race/ethnicity: Various years, 1990-2009

Race/ethnicity	1990[1]	1992[1]	1996	2000	2003	2005	2007	2009
White	75*	73*	66*	64*	60*	58*	57*	56
Black	18*	17*	16	16	17	16	16	16
Hispanic	6*	6*	11*	15*	18*	19*	20	21
Asian/Pacific Islander	1*	2*	5	‡	4*	4	5	5
American Indian/ Alaska Native	1*	1*	1	1	1	1	1	1

‡ Reporting standards not met. Special analysis raised concerns about the accuracy and precision of the results for Asian/Pacific Islander students in 2000; therefore, they are omitted from this table.
* Significantly different (p < .05) from 2009.
[1] Accommodations were not permitted in this assessment year.
NOTE: Black includes African American, Hispanic includes Latino, and Pacific Islander includes Native Hawaiian. Race categories exclude Hispanic origin. Detail may not sum to totals because results are not shown for students whose race/ethnicity was unclassified.

The proportion of fourth-graders in each of the five racial/ethnic groups NAEP reports on has remained relatively stable since 2007 (table 1). However, in comparison to the first assessment in 1990, the percentage of White students decreased from 75 to 56 percent, the percentage of Hispanic students increased from 6 to 21 percent, and the percentage of Asian/Pacific Islander students increased from 1 to 5 percent.

SOURCE: U.S. Department of Education, Institute of Education Sciences, National Center for Education Statistics, National Assessment of Educational Progress (NAEP), various years, 1990-2009 Mathematics Assessments.

- **Instruction** In the traditional mathematics classroom, where speed and procedural knowledge are stressed, students are expected to keep up with the pace of the teacher and do mathematics the way their teacher does. This can be alienating and defeating for ethnically and culturally diverse students whose learning styles may not correspond with the methods used by their teacher.

- **Student perceptions** Research has shown that culturally and ethnically diverse students sometimes silence themselves in mathematics classes because they are afraid to be wrong, they think they are the only person in class who doesn't understand, or they are afraid of being made fun of for speaking imperfect English or "Black English."

- **Assessment** Timed, skills-oriented tests often focus on what students do not know and are unfair to all students. This type of assessment creates additional problems for culturally and ethnically diverse students. For example, ELLs who are required to take mathematics tests in English may not understand the directions or the technical mathematical language and may need more time to think in one language and to write in another.

- **Classroom culture** Culturally and ethnically diverse students need a classroom atmosphere that is challenging and exciting, yet caring and safe. Researchers have found that culturally and ethnically diverse students who have good personal relationships with their teachers feel more confident in class and are more engaged in learning.

- **Teacher expectations** Teachers' beliefs about who can learn mathematics affect how they teach it. Unfortunately, culturally and ethnically diverse students have often been tracked into low-achieving groups where rote algorithms are emphasized over problem solving, because of teachers' preconceived ideas about how their diverse students learn and what they are capable of learning.

Meeting the Needs of Exceptional Students

"Students with disabilities as well as gifted students are considered exceptional. Exceptional students are those who have learning or behavioral characteristics that differ substantially from most other students and that require special attention in instruction" (Banks and Banks, 2007, p. 327).

Students with learning difficulties in mathematics

The *Individuals with Disabilities Education Act* (IDEA), reauthorized in 2004, guarantees that students with disabilities have access to the regular mathematics curriculum whenever possible. In recent years, a new approach, called **Response to Intervention (RTI)**, has been used to identify and instruct students who are disabled in mathematics. Rather than rely on testing alone to identify children with disabilities, RTI uses early interventions to adjust instruction to the needs of the individual student. RTI is based on a three-tier approach. Students placed in Tier 1 are provided with the same high-quality instruction as other students. Those who do not achieve at a level similar to their peers are evaluated and may be placed in Tier 2. Students in Tier 2 are individually evaluated, and interventions, accommodations, and modifications are designed, implemented, and closely monitored. Tier 2 students may receive additional support in the form of after-school tutoring, peer tutoring, and extra time to complete assignments. Teachers use explicit, targeted instructional techniques. Students who do not achieve in Tier 2 are referred for special education services, which are part of Tier 3.

Gifted students

"Gifted mathematics students need accommodation in the mathematics curriculum but frequently they are not appropriately challenged" (Wilkins, Wilkins, and Oliver, 2006, p. 6). When gifted students finish their work early, they are often given more worksheets on the same topic or asked to sit quietly. These actions encourage gifted students to work more slowly. Instead, you can create tasks that will challenge gifted students. One possibility is to set up a series of investigations for each unit of study that are generally related to the unit of study but also connected to new ideas. Mathematics history is a great source for such investigations. Place these enrichment activities in a folder or a computer file. When the gifted students finish their work, they can access the investigations while the rest of the class is working on the assignment.

Gifted students learn differently. They usually learn new material very quickly and need to learn to pace themselves. They may also approach a given task differently than their peers. They can learn with more independence than their peers but still need help from teachers, who can challenge them to look at concepts differently or make connections to new ideas.

Gifted students may appreciate being praised privately (Barger, 2009). If you announce to the whole class that a particular student has produced yet another perfect paper, this may give unwanted attention to a student who just wants to fit in. Everyone needs praise, but sometimes public praise can be embarrassing if it exceeds the praise given to other students.

CONCEPT CHECK   STOP

1. **What** are the ideals set forth in the Equity Principle?
2. **What** is the achievement gap in mathematics?
3. **Who** are exceptional students? How is RTI designed to help students with learning disabilities in mathematics?

Closing the Achievement Gap in Mathematics

LEARNING OBJECTIVES

1. **Describe** content integration in mathematics.
2. **Explain** how children's literature can facilitate content integration in mathematics.
3. **Describe** effective teaching practices for multicultural mathematics education.
4. **Describe** the role of the family in multicultural mathematics education.

ulticultural mathematics education or ethnomathematics is often viewed as a means of overcoming the achievement gap between white students and their ethnically and culturally diverse peers. In the multicultural mathematics classroom, content, effective teaching, a nurturing classroom environment, parental involvement, and a supportive school structure work together to create equitable learning opportunities for all students.

ethnomathematics
The study of the mathematics of different cultural groups.

Content Integration

Mathematics was once thought to be culture-free and therefore not a candidate for content integration. We tend to think of mathematics as purely factual and objective and therefore not culturally determined. Actually, mathematics does vary from culture to culture. Many examples of mathematics, such as counting, measuring, locating, creating calendars, inventing, and engaging in games, are found in every cultural group throughout history and vary according

✓ THE PLANNER

Every culture imprints its symbolism and its history on its textiles, pottery, or dwellings, which illustrate important aspects of geometry that can be applied to the classroom.

b. Patterns in Hmong needlework help students understand the concept of line and rotational symmetry in geometry.

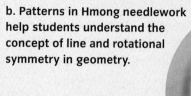

a. Repeated geometric patterns are seen in Maori art.

Multicultural topics for content integration

Multicultural Topics	Content Area
Egyptian and Mayan numerals	Counting, place value
The Yoruba number system	Counting, subtraction
Egyptian multiplication	Whole number operations
Egyptian unit fractions	Rational numbers
Lusona sand drawings	Geometry
Chinese and Russian abacus	Whole number operations
Mayan calendar round	Greatest common factor
Inca quipu	Counting, place value
Mankala and other games	Probability, logical thinking

c. In African architecture, buildings are often added on to the main building, using the same shape but a different scale, clearly showing *fractal* relationships. Fractal patterns are also found in African carvings and traditional hair braiding designs.

to the needs of the culture (Weinglass, 2000). There are many opportunities for integrating multicultural mathematics content at the elementary or middle school levels (**Figure 5.5**).

Teaching Tip

Finding multicultural activities

An increasing number of elementary mathematics textbooks and resources include multicultural activities, and a number of educators' Web sites also address multicultural mathematics topics.

Tech Tools

http://mathforum.org/library/ed_topics/multiculturalism/

The Math Forum is a wonderful resource for multicultural activities in both English and Spanish, with links to articles and activities, including a site that explains the Mayan number system.

In recent years, many children's books have been published with multicultural themes. Many of these books lend themselves to mathematical exploration (see *Children's Literature*, **Figure 5.6**).

CHILDREN'S LITERATURE

Choosing children's books with multicultural themes

THE PLANNER

The Black Snowman • Figure 5.6a

Written by Phil Mendez
Illustrated by Carole Byard

The Black Snowman is the story of a boy who hates everything about himself until he finds a scrap of cloth that connects him to a magical snowman who teaches the boy about the glorious history of his African ancestors. The story provides opportunities for mathematics learning, including addition, subtraction, money, and percents.

Moja Means One • Figure 5.6b

Written by Muriel Feelings
Illustrated by Tom Feelings

This is a counting book for primary-grades children. The book teaches children to count in English and Swahili while learning about East African life. The number 2 appears with the Swahili word for 2 (*mbili*) next to it. On the next page, two children are shown playing Mankala, a board game that uses counting, estimating, and logic.

Everybody Bakes Bread • Figure 5.6c

Written by Norah Dooley
Illustrated by Peter J. Thornton

A young girl visits her neighbors to find out if any of them have a rolling pin her mother can borrow and in the process finds out about the breads of many different cultures. Recipes are included for seven different types of bread. Use the book to study measurement or ratio and proportion by adapting the recipes to different servings.

LESSON Using Drawings in the Sand to Teach About Euler Circuits

The Chokwe people of Angola draw figures in the sand called *Lusona*, which illustrate stories, fables, history, and games about their culture. The designs are drawn according to special rules: The person drawing the design (the *akwa kuta sona*) tells the story as the design unfolds, never retraces a line, and never lifts the drawing tool from the surface. These designs are known in mathematics as Euler circuits. It is unknown why the Chokwe draw their designs in this manner.

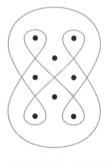
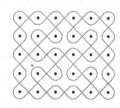
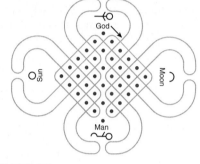

GRADE LEVEL

5

OBJECTIVES

Students will learn about the origins and history of Lusona.

Students will investigate the characteristics of traversable paths and Euler circuits.

Students will be able to identify and draw Euler circuits.

STANDARDS

Grades 3–5

All students should

- Describe location and movement, using common language and geometric vocabulary.
- Make and use coordinate systems to specify locations and describe paths. (NCTM, 2000, p. 164)

MATERIALS

- World map
- Paper and pencils
- Worksheet

ASSESSMENT

- Students draw three figures that are Euler circuits and three figures that are not. Then they are to find the number of vertices for each figure and determine the degree of each vertex.

- Differentiation for ELL students: Use drawings and pictures to illustrate concepts. Pronounce, spell, and write new words, such as *Lusona, vertices, traversable,* and *Euler*. Introduce vocabulary words in the context of the lesson. Encourage ELLs to work with native English speakers.

GROUPING

Whole class, followed by small groups

Launch (10 minutes)

- Ask: *Who would like to find Angola on the map?*

- Say: *Today we are going to learn about the Chokwe people of Angola.*

- Tell students about how the Chokwe draw figures called *Lusona*.

The *Lesson* illustrates how to effectively integrate multicultural topics with mathematics, in this case, geometry. The standards are from the *Geometry Standard* for grades 3–5 from *Principles and Standards for School Mathematics* (NCTM, 2000).

As you select multicultural content for your classroom, there are several factors to keep in mind.

- The content should have clear learning objectives that have clear connections to the curriculum. If an activity

Instruct (30 minutes)

- Show students a square. Ask: *Can this figure be drawn without lifting your pencil and without retracing over any lines? Try it.* (Yes, it can.)

- Show the following figure. Ask: *Can this figure be drawn without lifting your pencil and without retracing over any lines?* (Yes.)

- Say: *Figures that can be drawn without lifting your pencil or retracing any lines are called* traversable.

- Draw the following figure.

- Ask: *Is this figure traversable?* (Yes.)

- Provide several designs and ask students to work in small groups to classify whether each design is traversable. Bring the class together to discuss the results and reach consensus.

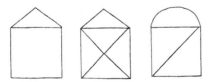

- Say: *Let us return to the square. The corners of the square are called* **vertices**. *How many vertices does the square have?*

(four) *The lines connecting the vertices are called* edges. *Edges can be made with curves, as in the Lusona. The point at which two or more edges meet is called a* vertex.

- Say: *How many edges meet at each vertex of the square?* (two) *Since two is an even number, each of these vertices is called* **even**, *and this vertex is* **second degree**.

- Say: *Look at the figure with squares side by side. How many vertices does this figure have?* (six) *Are all the vertices even? Do some vertices have more than two edges?* (There are four even, two odd vertices.)

- Say: *Look at the square with one diagonal drawn. How many vertices are there? Are all the vertices even?* (The vertices of the diagonal are odd and the others are even.)

- Say: *In your groups, look at the designs we have discussed. Classify the vertices for each figure as odd or even and note the degree of the vertex. Can you find any relationship between whether a design is traversable and its number of odd or even vertices?* (A figure is traversable if all vertices are even or if all but two are even. In the latter case, one of the odd vertices must be the starting point and the other odd vertex is the ending point.)

Summarize (5 to 10 minutes)

- Ask: *What does it mean for a figure to be traversable?*

- Ask: *What does it mean for a vertex to be even or odd?*

- Say: *When we draw a design without lifting our pencils or retracing, we are creating an Euler path. An Euler path travels along every edge in the graph exactly once. An Euler circuit is an Euler path that ends where it begins.*

- Ask: *How can Euler paths and Euler circuits make us more efficient? What are the advantages of living in a home that is traversable? How can this theory be applied to train routes or telephone networks?*

is selected for enrichment only, without clear objectives and with no assessment of learning, students may view the activity as unimportant.

- The multicultural topic should be connected to other

units of study to reinforce the importance and relevance of the topic for students.

- The topic should help students to become critical thinkers.

In the Classroom
Using Fabrics from Many Cultures to Explore Mathematics

 THE PLANNER

University professor Dorothy Y. White used the fabric designs of different cultures to build bridges to mathematical concepts for first graders. First, the children looked at a map of the world and identified each continent. Next, they explored sample fabrics

from each continent and discussed with their teacher how clothing can reflect peoples' cultural heritage. For Africa, they looked at kente cloth and identified the colors, shapes, and patterns used to make this vibrant fabric. Children also examined tartan scarves from Europe and silk scarves from Korea, India, Japan, and Singapore.

Next, the children used hexagonal patches to make "faces" that told something about themselves. Girls used yellow hexagons and boys used green ones. Using a key prepared by the teacher, the children placed shapes on their hexagons to represent their eyes, nose, hair, and mouth. For example, a child who was six years old placed a triangle on the hexagon for her nose while a child who was seven used a square.

After each child assembled a hexagonal "face," they looked at the similarities and differences of their hexagons. They put all "boy" hexagons inside a large hoop and noticed that all the hexagons were green. Next, they put all the "girl" hexagons made by six-year-olds inside the hoop. They noticed that all the noses were triangles.

The fabric examples motivated students to discuss the characteristics of shape and color. The hexagonal faces activity reinforced this knowledge and facilitated the children's understanding of classification by shape or color.

(*Source*: White, 2001)

Think Critically

1. How does this activity make use of cultural artifacts to teach first-grade mathematics?
2. How do you think children benefit when teachers integrate cultural examples such as these into mathematics instruction?

Strategies for Teaching Culturally or Ethnically Diverse Students

Effective multicultural mathematics teachers are, first of all, effective teachers. They have sound knowledge of subject matter and pedagogy, the ability to listen to and question students effectively, the skill to build on students' prior knowledge, and the ability to reflect on their own teaching. Effective multicultural teachers also understand how to use cultural knowledge to build bridges to new knowledge, have a sense of their own **efficacy**, show respect for students' ability and competence, and demonstrate respect for students' cultural beliefs and values. They understand that students learn best in a warm, supportive atmosphere where interdependence and cooperation are fostered.

efficacy The ability to produce a desired effect.

Some teachers share the same culture with their students, and many do not. In the United States, most elementary teachers are white females, but increasingly, more and more children are from diverse backgrounds.

If you do not share the same culture as your students, here are some suggestions for connecting with your students and their cultures:

- Recognize what you know and what is unfamiliar to you about your students' cultures and learn to value both the commonalities and the differences. For example, you both value family get-togethers but you do not celebrate the same holidays.

- Bridge the cultural gap by spending time in the community, shopping, talking with parents, and attending community celebrations.

- Seek out ways to incorporate students' culture into your mathematics teaching (see *In the Classroom*).

Strategies for Teaching English-Language Learners

How can teachers help **English-language learners (ELLs)** learn mathematics? ELLs develop reading, speaking, and writing skills concurrently. You can encourage language

Helping English-language learners with the language of mathematics • Figure 5.7

Some mathematical terms, such as *foot*, *plane*, *mean*, and *average*, have other meanings in real life. In addition, some words, such as *whole* and *sum*, sound like other words. Make sure to explain the mathematical meaning of these words to ELLs so they do not become confused about the meaning.

acquisition by teaching students new vocabulary words within the context of the lesson.

Researchers make the distinction between spoken English (day-to-day casual conversations) and academic English (mostly used in the classroom). Students may appear fluent in English but may lack academic fluency. For example, ELLs may be able to converse with their peers or order lunch in the cafeteria but may have serious deficits in the English language as it is used in the classroom. It takes about two years for students to master the English needed for day-to-day conversations but five to seven years to achieve the same level of academic English as their native English-speaking peers. The vocabulary of mathematics can be especially problematic to ELLs (**Figure 5.7**).

Here are several specific strategies that can help ELLs learn both mathematics and language skills:

- Arrange small groups so that ELLs have a peer who speaks the same language in their group, if possible. Use small-group instruction before whole-group instruction so that students can talk about the mathematics in their native language and practice talking about it in English.

- Encourage students to use all of their resources to communicate mathematical ideas, including mixed English-native language talk, diagrams, pictures, and gestures.

- "Push for details" (Maldonado et al., 2009, p. 12). Ask questions that encourage students to explain their thinking more thoroughly, or ask two students to discuss a problem or solution together.

- Engage children in problem solving using stories that are set in familiar contexts (Turner et al., 2009).

A number of instructional programs are available to help educators teach ELLs effectively. One of these is the

Sheltered Instruction Observation Protocol (SIOP), a research-based program that helps teachers increase their ELLs' language proficiency and content knowledge. SIOP has lesson plan templates online (www.siopinstitute.net) that help teachers focus on both content and language objectives. Many other types of materials are available. SIOP is used in hundreds of schools all over the United States and abroad.

Virtual Classroom Observation

Video — www.wiley.com/college/jones

Click on **Student Companion Site**. Then click on:

- **Foundations of Effective Mathematics Teaching**
- **D. Quality Formative Assessment**
- **3. Analyze Classroom Videos**

View:

- **Measures of center: What is data collection?**

In this video, Ms. Sahakian teaches an ESL class about data analysis. In this class, more than five native languages are spoken. What techniques does the teacher use to make sure the vocabulary words are learned by the students?

Tech Tools

www.nctm.org

Read NCTM's Position Statement on equity. This statement discusses the issue of teaching mathematics to ELLs and stresses the importance of creating a welcoming and warm instructional setting.

Strategies for Teaching Students with Difficulties in Mathematics

NCTM has reviewed strategies for teaching students who are learning disabled in mathematics (NCTM, 2007) and would be categorized as Tier 2 by RTI. The strategies suggested include **systemic and explicit instruction** and **think-alouds**. In systematic and explicit instruction the teacher models how to do the problem for the student in a detailed, step-by-step scripted manner, giving instructions for each step as well as the decision-making process for each step, and the student uses the same procedure. In think-alouds, students verbalize their thinking through each step of a problem. This method has proven to be very successful, perhaps because students with difficulties in mathematics often rush through problems, and verbalizing their thinking slows them down.

Many students with learning disabilities also have difficulty with memorization. It is best to limit the content they need to memorize by helping them learn alternative strategies such as problem solving. These students also need more repetition and practice than their peers. An effective way of providing additional practice for children with learning disabilities is to provide the practice "in small doses, throughout the day and week as the opportunity arises" (Karp and Howell, 2004, p. 122). Learning stations and computer activities provide excellent options for extra practice.

Students with learning disabilities often have difficulty when presented with too many choices and too many stimuli competing for their attention (**Figure 5.8**). It is important to provide explicit guidance about which manipulatives, procedures, or representations are best suited to specific tasks. At the same time, think about the physical arrangement of the classroom, and choose a quiet area in which students with learning disabilities can work.

Students with learning disabilities need strong, at-home support through homework and parental involvement. When planning homework, make sure the directions and the problems are clear, adjust the length of the assignment so that it is presented in smaller units, provide manipulatives and calculators (do not assume that students have these at home), and partner with parents to promote students' success.

Engaging Parents and Family Members in Mathematics Education

When parents and other family members are involved in their children's mathematical learning, everyone benefits. Children whose family members are involved in school have increased achievement, fewer days absent, and better social behavior. When parents help their children with homework, the children get to spend time with their parents, realize that adults can make mistakes in mathematics, and believe that mathematics is worthwhile because their parents are spending time on it. Parents benefit too because they learn what their children are doing in school and feel that they are valued by the teacher and school system. The teacher benefits because communication with parents becomes easier and students' learning improves.

To help parents get involved in the homework process, many teachers send newsletters and email updates home to parents, in which they offer suggestions for helping children with their homework while stressing the importance of not doing the homework for their children.

Creating a classroom with minimal distractions • Figure 5.8

Think carefully about the visual displays, classroom noise and movement, and manipulatives used in lessons to make sure they are not distracting for students with learning disabilities.

Multicultural Perspectives in Mathematics

The Literature/Mathematics Program

The literature/mathematics program, developed by the Baltimore city public school system, familiarizes parents with current reforms in mathematics education. Parents and children are invited to attend six weekly sessions that focus on mathematics and multicultural children's literature.

At each session:

- A facilitator reads a book to the parents and children.
- A facilitator gives the parents and children a series of problems based on the book.
- Parents and children present their solutions.
- The facilitator responds with probing questions that model for parents how their children learn mathematics in school while exposing parents to questions they can ask at home to help their children with mathematics.

One of the books used in this program is *Sadako and the Thousand Paper Cranes* (Coerr, 1993), the story of a young girl who developed leukemia as a result of the atomic bombing of Hiroshima in 1945. Sadako and her family are struggling to make 1000 paper cranes, which according to Japanese legend will make her well. As the story is read, the facilitator asks parents and children to reflect on their own customs and beliefs and compare

them to those of Sadako's family. The mathematics problems from this story focus on *average*: "Sadako became sick in February and died in October. By the time of her death, Sadako, her family, and friends had folded 644 cranes. What was the average [number] of cranes folded per day from the time Sadako became ill until her death?" (Strutchens, 2002, p. 452) To solve this problem, families discuss the meaning of *average* and estimate how many days to count.

(*Source*: Strutchens, 2002)

Strategies for the Classroom

- How can instructional programs such as this one benefit children's mathematical knowledge?
- How do programs such as this one bring the children, parents, teachers, and school system together with a common goal?

Family involvement is especially important for children from ethnically and culturally diverse backgrounds. In these families, parents may be reluctant to contact schools because it is not done in their culture, they do not feel comfortable speaking English, or they work during hours that school is in session. When schools and teachers make efforts to engage diverse families in the education of their children, they demonstrate respect for the values and beliefs held by these families.

There are several steps that you can take as a teacher to involve families in their children's mathematics education.

- Learn about the cultures and backgrounds of your students. Learn about how they use mathematics in their culture.

- Find out whether your students speak English at home. If not, get help and prepare materials to send home in the languages that your students speak with their parents. Some teachers send letters home to describe what their child will be learning in mathematics.

- Host in-school mathematics activities for parents during school conferences, school events, or on weekends. Some

teachers develop activity folders that are sent home to parents once a week. These folders may contain mathematics activities and manipulatives, along with instructions for completion. Teachers who use activity packets have found them to be very successful.

- Involve parents and children in learning mathematics together through children's literature (see *Multicultural Perspectives in Mathematics*).

CONCEPT CHECK

1. **How** can the inclusion of multicultural content in the mathematics curriculum benefit all students?
2. **How** can children's literature support multicultural mathematics learning?
3. **What** are three methods of connecting students and their cultures to mathematics?
4. **What** are the benefits of involving parents in their children's mathematics learning?

Gender Equity in Mathematics

LEARNING OBJECTIVES

1. **Describe** the evolution of schooling for girls in the United States.

2. **Compare** and **contrast** the gender gap in mathematics achievement from the 1970s and 1980s until the present time.

3. **Identify** the social and psychological factors that play a crucial role in career choice.

4. **Identify** strategies for creating gender-fair mathematics classrooms.

Education InSight

The evolution of gender equity in U.S. education • Figure 5.9

This timeline details the evolution of gender equity in education for girls in America, from the end of the Revolutionary War to the beginning of the 21st century.

1800. Financially well-off families sometimes sent their daughters to female seminaries, where they learned both religious and academic lessons. After completing their seminary studies, girls were sometimes allowed to be teachers until they married.

1865. By the end of the Civil War, the casualties on both sides resulted in a shortage of male students. Public colleges and universities began to admit women out of financial necessity.

1800

1783. After the Revolutionary War, schools were open to both males and females.

1821. Emma Hart Willard opened the Troy Academy in Troy, New York, which offered education for girls that was equivalent to the college-preparatory courses taken by boys at that time. She dedicated her life to providing educational opportunities to women.

1873. Even though women were allowed to attend college, they were often tracked into vocational coursework. Dr. Edward Clarke, a member of the Harvard University medical faculty, argued that women were too frail to attend high school and college. Dr. Clarke believed that if women studied challenging subjects such as mathematics, it could be dangerous to their health.

In history and in the not-so-distant past, women have been seen as "lesser than" in mathematics. In colonial America, less than one third of the female population could sign their name (Sadker and Zittleman, 2007). Young males and a few lucky females attended school but were taught different subjects. Males were taught reading and writing in preparation for more formal studies while females were taught cooking and sewing, with enough reading to enable them to read the Bible. After the Revolutionary War, it took more than 200 years for females to achieve equity in education (**Figure 5.9**).

Many changes have occurred in the last 30 years. Women are no longer underrepresented in high school and undergraduate mathematics classes, they perform better on high school mathematics testing, and the gender gap in mathematics has significantly narrowed. However, many challenges remain.

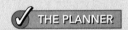

1900. In the 20th century, women gained greater access to educational programs than ever before, but gender bias remained a serious problem. In 1900, approximately half of the students enrolled in commercial or business courses in high school were women.

1980s. Researchers began studying the achievement gap between white males and females in mathematics and science. It was noted that girls stopped taking mathematics courses somewhere around middle school, often being silent and "playing dumb" to be socially acceptable. Females also performed more poorly on standardized tests such as the Scholastic Achievement Test.

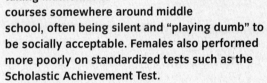

 1900

2000

1972. The passage of the Title IX Educational Amendments Act of 1972 guaranteed that females were afforded equal opportunities in education. Most of us are familiar with Title IX because of its impact on school sports programs, but it also prohibits discrimination in school admissions and allows access to programs and courses.

2000. Over the last 30 years, researchers have noted significant narrowing of the gender gap in mathematics and science.

Gender Equity in Mathematics   129

Closing the gender gap   Table 5.1

Areas of Progress	Areas Still Needing Attention
1. Young girls outperform boys in verbal skills, equal them in science, and almost equal them in mathematics.	1. NAEP data still indicates that fourth-grade boys outperform fourth-grade girls in mathematics.
2. Half of bachelor's degrees in mathematics are awarded to women.	2. White males still outperform other racial and ethnic groups on the mathematics portion of the SAT.
3. Women receive twice as many master's degrees in mathematics and four times as many doctorates than they did 30 years ago.	3. In 2003, only 13% of the science faculty at the Massachusetts Institute of Technology were women—up from 8% in 1993.
4. Women have achieved **parity** or equal participation in medicine and law.	4. Women are far from achieving parity in the fields of science and engineering.
	5. Only 22% of the doctoral degrees in science and engineering are earned by women.
	6. Less than one quarter of women work in science or engineering.

Gender Equity in Mathematics in the Twenty-First Century

A great deal of progress has been made in closing the gender gap in achievement in mathematics and science (Table 5.1).

Why is there still a substantial gender gap in careers that use mathematics? This is very much a cultural issue. Researchers (Fox and Soller, 2001) have identified four social and psychological factors that play a crucial role in determining career choices: attitudes, support from significant others, classroom atmosphere, and out-of-school learning (Table 5.2).

Strategies for Achieving Gender Equity in the Elementary and Middle-Grades Mathematics Classroom

Even though the gender gap in mathematics achievement has significantly narrowed, there is still work to be done. What can you as a teacher do to make sure that both boys

Factors that affect choosing mathematics as a career   Table 5.2

1. **Attitudinal differences** Researchers have consistently noted attitudinal differences in males and females toward mathematics. Males seem to like mathematics more and feel more self-confident about their ability to learn mathematics. Males perceive mathematics to be more useful to their future careers than females, and the perception remains that males are better in mathematics.

2. **Support from significant others** Parents and teachers influence students' career choices and, although they are now less likely to stereotype mathematics as a male domain, they may subtly or unconsciously discourage girls from pursuing careers involving mathematics.

3. **Classroom atmosphere** The classroom atmosphere is influential in determining career choices. Until recently, many textbooks and computer software depicted stereotypical versions of male and female roles. Males were seen as active and adventurous while girls were depicted as passive. Textbooks had few if any examples of women mathematicians to serve as role models. Because boys are often more verbal and aggressive during class, they received more attention. When boys and girls are seated separately, girls often feel invisible when teachers talk to the boys' side of the room. Traditional instructional strategies also favor boys. Girls are thought to learn better by constructing knowledge through hands-on activities in cooperative groups. However, such strategies also benefit boys.

4. **Gifted students and out-of-school learning** One difference between boys and girls is how they spend their leisure time. Researchers found that boys who are gifted are more likely to spend their free time playing computer games than girls who are gifted. Girls who are gifted are less likely to do projects in physical or earth science or to participate in accelerated courses or programs. This is particularly true for gifted African American and Hispanic girls.

and girls have equal opportunities to learn mathematics? Here are several strategies for creating gender-fair mathematics classrooms that encourage all students to consider careers that involve mathematics, adapted from Sadker and Zittleman (2007).

- **Check textbooks and computer software** for bias and stereotypes. Find supplementary materials if your required ones are biased, and discuss the stereotypes with students in an age-appropriate manner.

- **Analyze the seating chart** and look for areas of class, race, or gender segregation. Change seating so that boys, girls, and students from diverse cultural and ethnic backgrounds work together. Monitor your own teaching so that you are teaching to everyone and not just talking to one part of the room.

- **Use cooperative group learning** and monitor group work to ensure that all students are treated fairly within their groups and have equal opportunities to express their ideas. Use positive reinforcement to encourage appropriate behavior.

- **Develop a schedule and sign-up procedure** for computer time so that all students have equal access to technology.

- **Invite guests** to your class who challenge stereotypes and serve as role models for your students. Ask guests to talk about how they use mathematics in their jobs.

- **Talk with students about careers** that use mathematics. A great resource is *101 Careers in Mathematics*, published by The Mathematics Association of America (1996).

- **Track your questioning patterns** or ask someone to do it for you. Pay attention to how many times you call on boys versus girls, how often you praise boys versus girls, how long you wait for answers from boys versus girls, and how often you give constructive feedback to boys versus girls.

- **Stay up to date on issues of gender equity** in mathematics. This is a quickly changing field, so attend conferences and read journals that address these issues.

CONCEPT CHECK

1. **How** would you describe the evolution of schooling for girls in the United States?

2. **How** has the gender gap in mathematics changed from the 1970s and 1980s to the present time?

3. **How** can you encourage females to consider careers in science and mathematics?

4. **What** are the four crucial social and psychological factors that influence girls' selection of careers in science and mathematics?

THE PLANNER ✓

Summary

1 Multicultural Education 112

- The United States is a multicultural society with a large, shared culture and many smaller cultures. Three basic values permeate United States core culture: equality, **individualism**, and **individual opportunity**. This image of the Jefferson Memorial illustrates equality.

- Multicultural education originated in the political unrest of the 1960s. The purpose of multicultural education is to change schools so that all students have an equal opportunity to learn. The first step in providing equitable instruction is to become aware of our own cultural roots.

Figure 5.2

2 Mathematics for All 116

- The Equity Principle presents a vision of equity in mathematics education. Although ambitious, it is within our reach. Equity requires that all students have up-to-date textbooks, access to manipulatives and technology, and effective teachers who treat all students as capable of learning.

- Equity in mathematics means that teachers need to meet the needs of exceptional students—those who have difficulty in mathematics as well as those who are gifted in mathematics.

- In the 21st century a significant **achievement gap** in mathematics still exists between white students and all other students. Results from the 2009 NAEP illustrate this trend.

Figure 5.4

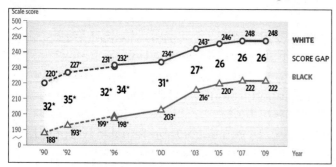

3 Closing the Achievement Gap in Mathematics 119

- Multicultural mathematics education is often viewed as a way of overcoming the **achievement gap**. When integrating content, be sure to integrate content that has clear learning objectives and is connected to the regular curriculum. This image features real-world use of geometry that can be used to motivate students.

Figure 5.5

- ELLs are learning English at the same time that they are learning mathematics. Many strategies are effective, such as using small-group instruction, having students speak in their native language and/or use gestures and pictures to explain their thinking, and using stories as contexts for mathematics.

- Strategies for learning-disabled students include **think-alouds** and **systemic and explicit instruction**.

- Family involvement is important for all children but especially for children from culturally or ethnically diverse backgrounds, whose families may be reluctant to contact the teacher. Everyone benefits when the family is involved in their children's mathematics education.

4 Gender Equity in Mathematics 128

- In the 20th century, women gained greater access to educational programs than ever before, in part due to the Title IX Education Amendments Act of 1972. Women's increased participation in upper-level science and mathematics courses is illustrated in this photo.

Figure 5.9

- In the 21st century, women have achieved parity in the fields of law and medicine. Today, half of the bachelor's degrees in mathematics are earned by women, but they are still underrepresented in science and engineering. Although progress had been made in the last 30 years to close the gender gap in achievement in mathematics and science, males still outperform females on high-profile standardized tests.

- To help close the **achievement gap,** ensure that your classroom is gender-fair by taking note of how many times you call on boys versus girls, the amount of wait time you give, and the types of questions you ask. Provide equal opportunities for technology by providing sign-up sheets at computers. Bring speakers who challenge stereotypes, and make students aware of the many interesting careers available to females and males in mathematics and science.

Key Terms

- achievement gap 116
- content integration 114
- culturally relevant 114
- culturally responsive 114
- culture 112
- English-language learners (ELLs) 124
- efficacy 124
- ethnomathematics 119
- field dependent 113
- individual opportunity 113
- individualism 113
- Response to Intervention (RTI) 118
- systemic and explicit instruction 126
- think-alouds 126

Additional Children's Literature

- *Her Seven Brothers,* **written and illustrated by Paul Goble**
  In this mythical tale, a young Indian woman finds her brothers and takes care of them by cooking for them and making their clothes. Although the book is not specifically about mathematics, the designs in the illustrations can be used to learn symmetry.

- *Girls Think of Everything,* **written by Catherine Thimmesh and illustrated by Melissa Sweet**
  This nonfiction book details many inventions by women.

- *Amelia's Road,* **written by Linda Jacobs Altman and illustrated by Enrique Sanchez**

Amelia is the daughter of migrant farm workers and must move from harvest to harvest. Although the book is not about mathematics, it can provide contexts for learning measurement, distances, and location.

- *Hello Amigos!* **written by Tricia Brown and illustrated by Fran Ortiz**
  This story tells about a day in the life of a Mexican American child through black-and-white photographs. Although not mathematical, it can provide contexts for sequencing or time activities.

Online Resources

- **Working to Improve Schools and Education (WISE)**
  www.ithaca.edu/wise/topics/

  This site provides links to articles for teachers on multicultural education.

- **The National Research Center for Learning Disabilities**
  www.nrcld.org

  Sponsored by Vanderbilt University and the University of Kansas, this site provides information about response to intervention (RTI) at this site.

- **LDOnline**
  www.ldonline.org

  Use this site to find resources and articles for the parents and teachers of children with learning disabilities.

- **Colorado Department of Education: Cognitive Academic Language Learning Approach (CALLA)**
  www.cde.state.co.us

  This site provides an overview of the CALLA approach to instruction for ELLs.

- **National Association for Gifted Children (NAGC)**
  www.nagc.org

  This site provides a number of resources and links for parents and teachers of gifted children.

- **National Association for Multicultural Education**
  www.nameorg.org

  This site provides resources, publications, and links for multicultural education.

Critical and Creative Thinking Questions

In this chapter we highlighted some children's books that could be used to integrate multicultural content into the elementary mathematics curriculum. Questions 1–3 refer to this discussion.

1. **Using visuals** Use two of the children's books discussed in this chapter. Read the books and summarize the content of each book, identify the intended grade level, and explain the multicultural features. How might you ask children to learn

from the visuals in each story? Create a list of questions to help children focus on and understand the visuals.

2. For each book, explain how the book can connect to specific mathematics content and identify that content in your state's standards document.

3. **In the field** Create a mathematics activity for each of the books that correlates with your state's mathematics content standards. Identify the grade level for your activity. Teach one of the activities to a child at the appropriate grade level and write a summary that describes your activity and how it went. In your summary answer the following questions:

   • Did the child understand the mathematics?
   • How did the children's literature help the child connect to the mathematics?

4. Why do you think that, in the past, mathematics has often been regarded as culturally neutral?

5. Select a grade level and topic, and develop an activity that can help children understand that mathematics is mediated by cultural events.

What is happening in this picture?

Think Critically

This is the crew of NASA space shuttle mission STS-116 in 2006.

1. How can this photo break down stereotypes about who is capable of doing mathematics and science?
2. How can photos such as this one help motivate children to excel in mathematics and science?

Self-Test

(Check your answers in Appendix D.)

1. What is culture? Identify three examples of cultural practices that are fairly obvious and three examples of cultural practices that are not obvious.

2. Which core theme in U.S. culture is illustrated by this photograph? Give two other real-life examples of this theme.

3. This chapter examined two additional core themes in U.S. culture. What are they? Give two real-life examples of each theme.

4. What is meant by the term field-dependent? Why might students who are field-dependent have difficulty in a traditional classroom?

5. Which level of content integration does teaching about Benjamin Banneker represent? What are the other three levels? Give an example of each one.

6. What do these graphs tell us about the achievement gap in mathematics?

7. Identify three strategies for teaching ELLs.

8. What is RTI? What does it mean for a student to be in Tier 2?

9. Identify two strategies for teaching learning-disabled students in mathematics.

10. What legislation during the 20th century guaranteed equal access to programs for students with disabilities?

11. What are some ways you can involve parents and families in their children's mathematics education?

12. What is the gender gap? How has the gender gap changed in the last 30 years?

13. What are the four social and psychological factors that influence career choice in women?

14. In which careers have women reached parity? In which careers are they underrepresented?

15. Identify some strategies for achieving gender-fair classrooms.

THE PLANNER ✓

Review your Chapter Planner on the chapter opener and check off your completed work.

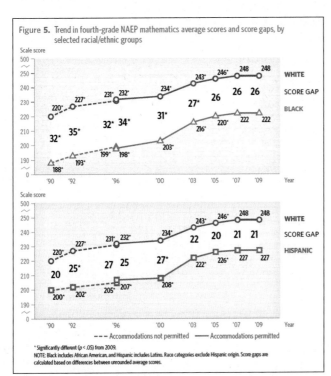

Figure 5. Trend in fourth-grade NAEP mathematics average scores and score gaps, by selected racial/ethnic groups

--- Accommodations not permitted — Accommodations permitted

* Significantly different (p < .05) from 2009.
NOTE: Black includes African American, and Hispanic includes Latino. Race categories exclude Hispanic origin. Score gaps are calculated based on differences between unrounded average scores.

Problem Solving in the Mathematics Classroom

The story of *Apollo 13* is just one example of how people solve problems. As we teach children about problem solving in mathematics, it is important to include examples with real-life contexts that make sense to children.

Apollo 13 was the third lunar-landing mission launched by NASA. Two days after the launch, an explosion on board crippled the astronauts' service module, forcing them to seek shelter in the lunar module. This smaller craft, designed for landing on the moon, was equipped to support two humans for three days but instead had to serve as a "lifeboat" in space and support three astronauts for four days on their trip back to Earth.

As Americans watched this real-life drama unfold, the *Apollo 13* crew and mission control staff demonstrated considerable problem-solving ability to overcome the many life-threatening situations that developed as a result of the explosion. One problem involved the canisters of lithium hydroxide that were used to remove carbon dioxide from the air in the module. Although the service module had sufficient canisters for a four-day journey, the lunar module did not, and the canisters could not be interchanged because they were different shapes (one was a cylinder, the other a cube). Flight controllers designed a jury-rigged tool to scrub carbon dioxide from the air, using only the materials the astronauts already had on board: plastic bags, cardboard, and tape. This tool, dubbed "the mailbox," allowed the astronauts to fit the cubical canisters from the service module into the space designed for the cylindrical canisters in the lunar module, ultimately saving the astronauts' lives.

The flight controllers, when faced with a situation for which they had no solution, used ingenuity, tenacity, and trial and error to find a solution. This is the essence of problem solving.

CHAPTER OUTLINE

What Is Problem Solving? 138

Key Questions: What are the differences between routine and nonroutine problems? Why should children learn to solve both kinds of problems?

Teaching Mathematics Through Problem Solving 141

Key Questions: How is teaching mathematics through problem solving different from the traditional approach to teaching mathematics? How can effective problems be found?

Helping All Children with Problem Solving 150

Key Question: What factors influence children's success as problem solvers?

Problem-Solving Strategies 154

Key Question: What problem-solving strategies are effective for elementary and middle-grades students?

(NCTM) Problem solving is one of the five process standards described in NCTM's *Principles and Standards for School Mathematics* (2000). This standard states:

Instructional programs from prekindergarten through grade 12 should enable all students to

- build new mathematical knowledge through problem solving;
- solve problems that arise in mathematics and in other contexts;
- apply and adapt a variety of appropriate strategies to solve problems;
- monitor and reflect on the process of mathematical problem solving. (NCTM, 2000, p. 52)

What Is Problem Solving?

LEARNING OBJECTIVES

1. **Describe** the characteristics of a problem.
2. **Distinguish** between routine and nonroutine problems.
3. **Explain** the benefits of children engaging in problem solving as a way to learn.

roblem solving is a process and a way of thinking. "Problem solving is an integral part of all mathematics learning and it should not be an isolated part of the mathematics program" (NCTM, 2000, p. 52). Problem solving in mathematics should be integrated into all content areas.

What Is a Problem?

Problems and figuring out how to solve them are part of our everyday life. How much does it cost to take care of your dog in its lifetime—from puppyhood through age 12? By how many miles do you need to increase your running every month

> **problems** Tasks or activities for which the solution method is not immediately obvious.

Problem solving in the real world • Figure 6.1

Whenever we face new situations, choose strategies, make decisions, and evaluate our choices, we use problem solving.

a. The farmer just purchased another acre of land, and he plans which varieties of pumpkins to plant and how many he will need in order to earn maximum profit. At the end of the season, he evaluates his decisions.

b. The architect is designing a new building and needs to make decisions about the placement of windows to achieve maximum light and energy efficiency.

c. A child is counting her money to decide whether she has enough to buy something at the vending machine.

Multicultural Perspectives in Mathematics

Oware

Oware, a game of strategy and problem solving, is one of the world's oldest games. It has hundreds of names, dozens of versions of play, and is popular throughout Africa and in many other parts of the world (Zaslavsky, 1999). In the United States, this game is called *Mancala*.

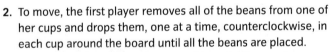

In Ghana, Africa, Oware is played on a board with two rows of six cups, an "endpot" at either end of the board, and 48 seeds. To create your own game, use an egg carton, small bowls, and beans.

Each player's territory consists of the six cups on one side of the board and the endpot to the right of the player.

1. To start, each player places four beans in each of the six cups.

2. To move, the first player removes all of the beans from one of her cups and drops them, one at a time, counterclockwise, in each cup around the board until all the beans are placed.
3. The second player does the same thing, starting on the opposite side of the board.
4. When the last bean dropped into a cup on the opponent's side of the board brings the total to two or three beans in that cup, those beans are captured along with the beans in the cups that came before that one, on the opponent's side.
5. The player who has captured the most beans is the winner.

Strategies for the Classroom

- How could you use Oware in the classroom to teach problem solving?
- What kinds of questions could you ask students as they play the game, to encourage their problem solving?

---

to train for a marathon? We know we are faced with a problem when we are unable to apply our previously learned repertoire of strategies to a new situation. (You've never owned a dog before, or run a marathon!) At first, we don't know how to proceed. Often, problem solving is personal. In other words, what is a problem for one person is not necessarily a problem for someone else.

Problem solving is used by people with highly technical jobs such as scientists or engineers, but problem solving is also a daily activity for people from all walks of life (**Figure 6.1**). It is used for everyday activities such as recreation, gardening, and eating out at a restaurant. Even games and puzzles involve problem solving (see *Multicultural Perspectives in Mathematics*).

In elementary mathematics we use problem-solving strategies to find solutions to word problems. There are two kinds of word problems: routine and nonroutine problems. **Routine problems**, also called **story problems**, are often found in elementary mathematics textbooks on the same page or the page after exercises. Story problems use words to build stories around computation practice and can have one or more steps. Here is an example of a story problem:

> *I have 22 pennies and 13 nickels. How many coins do I have in all?*

To solve these types of problems successfully, children need to understand how arithmetic operations are described in the real world and be able to translate those descriptions into number sentences such as $22 + 13 = 35$. Routine problems have one correct answer and often have only one way of obtaining the correct answer.

Nonroutine problems are more like the mathematical problems we face in the real world. They are more challenging for children because they may have extraneous information, there are usually several approaches to solving them, and there often can be more than one correct answer. In fact, we may not know whether we chose the best strategy or the best answer until we have completed the problem.

Some of the best nonroutine problems come from everyday activities. Here is one example:

> *Kevin found some change in his pocket. If he had nickels, dimes, and quarters, and took out three coins, how much money could he have taken out?*

To solve this problem, students need knowledge of addition and knowledge of the value of nickels, dimes, and quarters. There are many ways to go about solving this problem and several answers. You might think about the largest amount of money Kevin could have taken out of his pocket (75 cents or 3 quarters), the smallest amount (15 cents or 3 nickels), or different combinations of these three types of coins.

What Does Teaching Mathematics Through Problem Solving Mean?

Teaching mathematics through problem solving is much more than selecting from a menu of fun, real-world problems (Lambdin et al., 2003). It is fundamentally a new pedagogical approach to the teaching of mathematics that transforms the nature of the subject, the learner, and the teacher. Teaching and learning mathematics through problem solving means that teachers engage students in tasks that are problematic for them—tasks in which they must connect what they already know to solve new problems. Teachers can structure the curriculum so that students struggle to figure out problems that are within their reach, which helps them to develop a deep understanding of mathematical concepts and procedures (Hiebert, 2003).

Problem solving requires students to develop a unique solution plan for each problem. Although we teach heuristics to draw from, these strategies are general rather than step-by-step algorithms. In problem solving, students invent a strategy or choose one with which they are already familiar and apply that strategy to a specific situation. Problem solving should be included in all areas of the mathematics curriculum.

> **heuristics** Methods of problem solving that involve trial and error.

The Benefits of Teaching Mathematics Through Problem Solving

In this era of high-stakes testing, you may be reluctant to teach mathematics through problem solving. Because of pressure from school systems, administrators, and parents to raise test scores, you may believe that all your time should be spent helping children learn the procedures on which they will be tested.

Although your reluctance is understandable, it should not outweigh the many benefits of teaching mathematics through problem solving. As you may know, you cannot make your students understand mathematics by explaining or re-explaining it. Understanding is a process that takes place in students' minds. It occurs "as a by-product of solving problems and reflecting on the thinking that went into those solutions" (Lambdin, 2003, p. 11). In other words, students learn mathematics by analyzing solutions to problems, both correct and incorrect. Analyzing their own and other students' methods encourages students to construct mathematical relationships. This is "at the heart of understanding" (Hiebert, 2003, p. 56). When students learn mathematics

Using problem solving
in learning geometry
• Figure 6.2 _____

Children use problem solving to learn how to find the perimeter, area, and volume of geometric shapes.

through problem solving, they make connections between mathematical ideas and develop concepts, strategies, and procedures in the process. Problem solving facilitates skill development, enhances students' beliefs in their ability to do mathematics, and reinforces the notion that mathematics makes sense (**Figure 6.2**).

CONCEPT CHECK   **STOP**

1. **What** are some examples of problem solving in everyday life?
2. **Why** is it important for children to have experience with both routine and nonroutine word problems?
3. **How** do children benefit from learning mathematics through problem solving?

Teaching Mathematics Through Problem Solving

LEARNING OBJECTIVES

1. **Explain** the problem-solving process.
2. **Describe** the characteristics of a problem-solving classroom.
3. **Describe** how to choose effective tasks.
4. **Explain** the benefits of problem posing.
5. **Discuss** the importance of technology in problem solving.
6. **Explain** how to decide what to tell students about the problems they are solving.

Teaching mathematics through problem solving requires changing what you teach and how you teach. "Solving problems is not only a goal of learning mathematics but also a major means of doing so" (NCTM, 2000, p. 52). The primary focus becomes the students and their thought processes. It will be your job to

- structure the classroom atmosphere so that it is conducive to problem solving,
- select appropriate problems, and
- decide what to tell and what to withhold.

The problem-solving process • Figure 6.3

Good problem solvers cycle through all four stages but often cycle through the same stage more than once before completing a problem.

PROBLEM-SOLVING STAGE	SAMPLE PROBLEM

1 Understanding the problem

a. Read the problem aloud.
b. Ask students to rephrase the problem in their own words. (This is more effective than the teacher rereading the problem.)
c. Ask whether there are any words in the problem that students do not understand. If so, define them.

Are girls taller than boys? Ms. Rossini's class wants to find out.

2 Devising a plan

a. Planning works best in small groups.
b. Children should have knowledge of several problem-solving strategies but should also have the option to create their own.
c. Beginning problem solvers often rush through this stage or skip it entirely, whereas experienced problem solvers understand its value and spend more time planning.

Children decide to stand against a wall and have a partner draw a mark at the height of their heads.

3 Carrying out the plan

a. This is a time when children often get stuck. Your role is to observe, question, and provide hints.
b. Remind children that there are other strategies to choose from. Beginning problem solvers tend to stick with their original plan, whereas experienced problem solvers are often more willing to revise their plan and try again.

Children measure their heights using yardsticks, rulers, and measuring tapes.

4 Looking back

Unfortunately, this stage is often de-emphasized in the United States.

a. Looking back gives students the opportunity to reflect on their answers and methods and those of other students.
b. This stage also provides opportunities to look forward and solve the same problem with a different strategy or extend the problem in some way.

Children discuss their results. They cannot find a definite pattern. How else can you compare children and their heights?

(*Source*: Problem–solving steps based on Polya 1948.)

The Problem-Solving Process

Most educators look to George Polya's (1948, p. 5) research as a framework for problem-solving instruction in mathematics. Polya's four phases of problem solving are described in **Figure 6.3**. Remember that good problem solvers often cycle through the same stage more than once.

Planning for Problem Solving

When you teach mathematics through problem solving, show students that you value problem-solving behaviors. Demonstrate confidence, perseverance, the flexibility to try different strategies, and a willingness to be wrong. Successful problem solving often involves making mistakes, getting stuck, struggling, and starting over (**Figure 6.4**). Through your own actions, you can help children understand "the difference between not knowing the answer and not having found it yet" (Burns, 2000, p. 29).

How will you group your students for problem-solving activities? Cooperative groups or pairs work well because they encourage students to collaborate. Many teachers use whole-group instruction for introducing problems and for looking back. In stages two and three of the problem-solving process, students can work in small groups, pairs, or individually, depending on the complexity of the problem and the experience of the students.

What does it mean to create a classroom culture that encourages problem solving? Students collaborate with one another, respect each others' thinking, and listen to each other so that they can understand and evaluate their classmates' ideas while giving everyone a chance to participate. Listening is an often overlooked skill, and the listening skills needed by students in a problem-solving classroom are very different from those needed in a traditional mathematics classroom. In the problem-solving classroom, students need to listen to one another carefully, trying to understand their classmates' mathematical ideas (Sweeney, 2003).

The Wright brothers • Figure 6.4

The Wright brothers were credited with inventing and building the world's first self-powered, heavier-than-air flying vehicle. Before their successful flight on December 17, 1903, they spent years building many prototypes for gliders and planes that failed to fly.

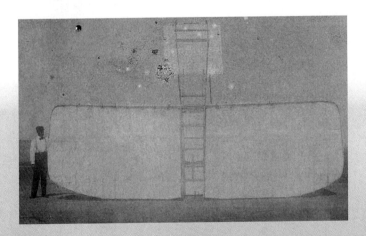

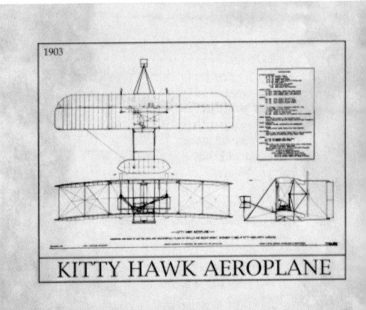

Choosing Effective Problems

Present children with a variety of problems that are motivating, have contexts that are meaningful to them, and offer a range of solution strategies. Include some problems that have missing or extraneous information and some that encourage the use of technology. See **Figure 6.5** for some options for creating effective problems.

Finding effective, challenging problems for students is not an easy task. When you find good problems, add them to a resource file so that you have access to them as needed. If your textbook does not offer nonroutine problems, many other sources are available. Look for effective problems on the Internet, from colleagues, through professional development, and in educational journals. The journal *Teaching Children Mathematics* has a Problem Solvers section in each issue and the journal *Mathematics Teaching in the Middle School* has a problem-solving section called Mathematical Explorations. Teachers can find a large variety of word problems on the National Council of Teachers of Mathematics Web site (http://www.nctm.org/).

Problem Posing

Problem posing is another way to create effective problems. Problem posing is beneficial for students of all ages because it motivates students to ask questions when they do not immediately know the answer. Children enjoy problem posing because it makes them

> **problem posing**
> A strategy in which a learner looks at an existing mathematical problem and either extends or modifies it.

Creating effective mathematics problems • Figure 6.5

a. Teachers create problems for students to solve.
You can create problems from everyday situations, such as attendance, school lunch, and school or community activities:

1. *Today's lunch is chicken tenders or a combo sub for the main entree, fresh fruit or fruit cocktail for dessert, and white or chocolate milk for a beverage. How many different lunch combinations can be ordered today?*

> ∘ **Today's Lunch** ∘
>
> Chicken Tenders or Combo Sub with Fresh Fruit or Fruit Cocktail $2.40
>
> White or Chocolate Milk   50¢

2. *At the school store, pencils cost 10 cents each and erasers cost 45 cents each. Mr. Benuto's class spent $5.90 on pencils and erasers. How many pencils and how many erasers did they buy?*

c. Children create problems from everyday situations.
Challenge children to create meaningful problems from everyday situations. Provide newspaper advertisements, menus, team schedules, and ticket prices. Ask children to write problems using these data. One example is:

Suppose you are going to the movies with your brother and sister. You buy three tickets with a 20-dollar bill. How much change should you get?

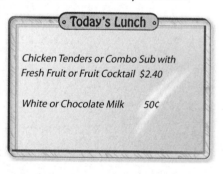

Clague Middle School
**** 4:00 PM ****
Jazz Band CONCERT
$10.00 **Admit One** $10.00
Sunday 9/13/10   Sunday 9/13/10

CT1009   CHILD
$6.50 $6.50
C 39812   CINEMA METROPLEX
HARRY POTTER
CL   3X   AND
THE HALF-BLOOD PRINCE
CTG8991   AUDITORIUM 4
10OCT10   SUN 10 OCT 2010 1:45PM

b. Children create problems to solve.
Other sources of good problems are the ones children write themselves. Give children a number sentence or mathematical situation and ask them to write a word problem with it. Here are some examples:

1. *Write a story problem that you would answer with the number sentence 14 − 5 = 9.*
2. *Write a story problem that you would answer with the number sentence 5 × 24 = 96.*
3. *Write a two-step story problem that requires you to multiply and then add.*
4. *Write a story problem that requires division of a whole number by a fraction.*

"We have already collected 20 cans for a food drive. Mr. Chin asked us to each bring in 5 more cans. If 24 students each bring in 5 more cans for the food drive, how many more cans will we have?"

Child's solution to the problem

3 × $6.50 = $19.50

$20 − 19.50 = .50

Answer: You get back 50 cents

CHILDREN'S LITERATURE

Using children's literature for problem posing

Math for All Seasons • Figure 6.6a

Written by Greg Tang
Illustrated by Harry Briggs
This bright and colorful book presents various pattern problems with one or more pieces missing. Readers are asked to count "how many" using the hints given on the opposite page. The book teaches children to problem solve by looking for patterns and being open to new ideas.

Strategies for the Classroom

- After reading each rhyming clue in the book, ask students: *How did you figure out the pattern?*
- Ask: *What if we changed the number of objects in the pattern?*
- Ask: *How can you change the clue to fit the new pattern?*

The Great Divide: A Mathematical Marathon • Figure 6.6b

Written by Dayle Ann Dodds
Illustrated by Tracy Mitchell
In this story, 80 racers line up for a cross-country race. They travel by bike, boat, and hot-air balloon. First, the Grand Canyon claims half of the racers. As the other half continue on, their numbers continue to be divided by one catastrophe after another.

Strategies for the Classroom

- After reading the book with children ask: *Why did the author start with the number 80? What other numbers would work well in this story?*
- Ask students to retell the story using their own starting numbers and see whether these numbers work as well.

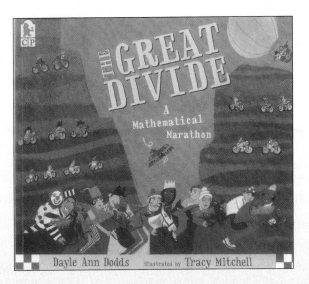

feel like they are in charge. Problem posing encourages "risk-taking, perseverance, curiosity, skepticism, and the postponement of judgment" (Whitin, 2004, p. 139). In other words, problem posing encourages children to think like mathematicians.

One way to encourage students to develop their problem-posing skills is through books (see *Children's Literature*, **Figure 6.6**). Children can create their own patterns and rhyming clues to share, as in *Math for All Seasons*, or they can question the author's intention, as in *The Great Divide*.

Developing Problem-Solving Lessons

See the *Lesson* on the next page for a problem-solving activity based on a mathematics problem presented in *Teaching Children Mathematics* (NCTM, February 2007). The problems described in the *Lesson* offer more than one possible solution and can be approached with more than one strategy. The standards used in this lesson are from the Algebra Standard from Principles and Standards for School Mathematics (NCTM, 2000) and the *Operations and Algebraic Thinking* domain of the *Common Core State Standards* (NGA Center/CCSSO, 2010).

This lesson is based on an ancient Chinese legend about a turtle that was spotted on the river Lo and called Loh-Shu.

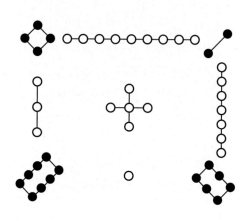

GRADE LEVEL

3–5

OBJECTIVES

Students will use problem-solving strategies to create magic squares.

Students will identify and create growing patterns.

STANDARDS

Grades 3–5

All students should describe, extend, and make generalizations about geometric and numeric patterns; represent and analyze patterns and functions, using words, tables, and graphs. (NCTM, 2000, p. 158)

Grade 4

Generate a number or shape pattern that follows a given rule. Identify apparent features of the pattern that were not explicit in the rule itself. *For example, given the rule "Add 3" and the starting number 1, generate terms in the resulting sequence and observe that the terms appear to alternate between odd and even numbers. Explain informally why the numbers will continue to alternate in this way.* (NGA Center/ CCSSO, 2010)

MATERIALS

- Image of Loh-Shu

- Blank 3 x 3 grids and 4 x 4 grids for each student

- Worksheet with partially completed 3 x 3 magic squares

ASSESSMENT

Use a starting number between 1 and 5 and write a set of 9 consecutive numbers. Create a 3 x 3 magic square using the number set created.

GROUPING

Whole class, small groups, and individual

EXTENSION

Create a magic square in which the numbers in each row, column, and diagonal multiply to the same number.

Launch (5 minutes)

According to Chinese legend, more than 4000 years ago the emperor and his court were sailing on the River Loh when they spotted a turtle in the water that had an unusual pattern on its back. Let's look at a drawing of this turtle, called Loh-Shu, and count the number of dots in each group. (The dots in each group represent the numbers from 1 to 9.)

Explore (35 to 40 minutes)

- *Place the numeral that represents the number of dots in each group on the turtle's back on your 3 × 3 grid, according to its location. What do you notice? Are there any patterns?* (The numbers in all rows, columns, and diagonals add up to the same number, 15.) *This is called a magic square, and the sum of each row, column, and diagonal is called the magic sum. For Chinese magic squares, the magic sum is always 15.*

4	9	2
3	5	7
8	1	6

- Next, show students a partially completed magic square grid. Have students work in groups to complete the magic square so that all the row, column, and diagonal sums equal 15 and no number is used more than once. Ask students to think about the strategies they are using.

6		8
2	9	

- As students complete their magic squares in small groups, circulate and observe or offer hints. Share results and strategies through whole-class discussion.

- Ask students to work individually to create their own magic square on a 3 × 3 grid, using the numbers from 1 to 9, with the same magic sum of 15. When students complete their squares, ask individual students to demonstrate their magic squares. Compare strategies for completing the magic squares.

- Say: *Now let's see whether we can create magic squares that have other magic sums. Use the numbers from 0 to 8 to make a magic square on a 3 x 3 grid. What is your magic sum?* Have students share results with the class.

- Say: *Work individually or in pairs, to make a new magic square with 9 consecutive numbers (such as 2 to 10 or 3 to 11) so that the sum of each row, column, and diagonal equals the same number.* Have students share results with the class.

- Say: *We can make magic squares on larger grids. Let's work together and use a 4 x 4 grid and the numbers 1 to 16 to create a magic square. The magic sum is 34.*

Summarize (5 to 10 minutes)

- Ask: *Why do you think you can make magic squares with these numbers?*

- Ask: *Do you notice any patterns in your magic squares?* (Sample answer: You can interchange the first and third columns and still have a magic square.)

- Ask: *What strategies worked best in helping you to create the magic squares?*

- Say: *Magic squares can also be created on larger grids. A famous one was created by Benjamin Franklin on an 8 x 8 grid (note that this magic square does not include diagonal sums). What is the sum?* (260)

52	61	4	13	20	29	36	45
4	3	62	51	46	35	30	19
53	60	5	12	21	28	37	44
11	6	59	54	43	38	27	22
55	58	7	10	23	26	39	42
9	8	57	56	41	40	25	24
50	63	2	15	18	31	34	47
16	1	64	49	48	33	32	17

Find out more about Franklin's magic square by searching the Internet.

Sample Problem: Using calculators in problem solving • Figure 6.7

"If 1 BILLION children climbed onto one another's shoulders to form a tower, how many times would that tower reach to the moon and back to Earth? (Figure an average of four feet for the height of the children because they are standing on shoulders, not heads. There are 5,280 feet in a mile. The moon is approximately 239,000 miles from Earth.)"
(Kempf, 1997, p. 25)

Using Technology in Problem Solving

When children are asked to solve problems that have difficult numbers but are otherwise reasonable, calculators, spreadsheets, and computer software can enhance the problem-solving experience.

Calculators Consider the problem in **Figure 6.7**, which is appropriate for fourth or fifth graders if they use calculators for the computations.

Calculators also help children understand mathematical operations, identify patterns, and learn concepts through problem solving. Broken-key activities (**Activity 6.1**) are popular with younger children and require children to focus on number operations and their meanings.

Activity 6.1 The broken calculator key

Instructions

1. Say: *Suppose you are using a four-function calculator to compute 1097 − 399 and the "3" key is broken.* Then ask: *How can you use the calculator to evaluate this expression?*

2. Ask: *What numbers can you use to estimate this result and then calculate it, without using the "3" key?* (A child might understand that 399 is one less than 400, so if you subtract 400 from 1097, you have to add 1 to the answer to get the correct result. Another approach is to use the distributive property: 1097 − 399 = 1097 − (400 − 1) = 1097 − 400 + 1.)

Activity 6.2 illustrates another way that calculators enhance problem solving. In this activity, calculators refine children's understanding of decimal size by using the Guess and Check strategy to estimate the answer (Crown, 2003). This activity uses the ⊠ and ⊟ keys in succession to help children compare decimals and learn about square roots. On most four-function calculators, when you input a number and then press ⊠ followed by ⊟, the starting number will be multiplied by itself. Thus, 6 × = yields 36.

> ### Activity 6.2 Using the calculator to estimate square roots
>
> **Instructions**
>
> 1. Enter 5 followed by the ⊠ and ⊟ keys in succession. You should see 25 displayed on your calculator. Next, enter 6 followed by the ⊠ and ⊟ keys in succession. You should see 36.
>
> 2. Say: *Suppose you entered a starting number, followed by the* ⊠ *and* ⊟ *keys, and got 34 as an answer. What kind of number is the starting number?* (A fraction or decimal between 5 and 6.) *How can you use the calculator to estimate your starting number?*
>
> 3. Ask: *In other words, what number did you multiply by itself to get 34? How can you use the calculator to estimate your answer?* (This helps students estimate square roots.)

Software Computers offer numerous options for problem solving, including Web sites with downloadable sets of word problems, applets with virtual manipulatives that require the user to use logic and problem solving, geometry drawing programs, and videos (Crown, 2003). More details are found in the *Online Resources* section at the end of this chapter. When using computer games in the classroom, discuss strategies and best moves with students to make the game an object of study rather than a reward for finishing work early.

Tech Tools _____

> http://peabody.vanderbilt.edu/projects/funded/jasper

The Adventures of Jasper Woodbury is a 12-video series designed for students in grades 5 and up that takes students through fictional scenarios where they engage in critical thinking and problem solving about mathematics at several points in the adventure.

_____

Spreadsheets Spreadsheets can be used to represent data and identify trends. *Tinkerplots: Dynamic Data Exploration* (Key Curriculum Press, 2005) provides easily accessible spreadsheets for students in grades 4–8 and is an excellent vehicle for studying data analysis and measures of central tendency (mean, mode, median) (**Figure 6.8**).

Spreadsheets in problem solving • Figure 6.8 _____

In this graph, created using the Tinkerplots software, students investigate whether there is a mathematical relationship between their grade level and the weight of their backpack with the help of a spreadsheet.

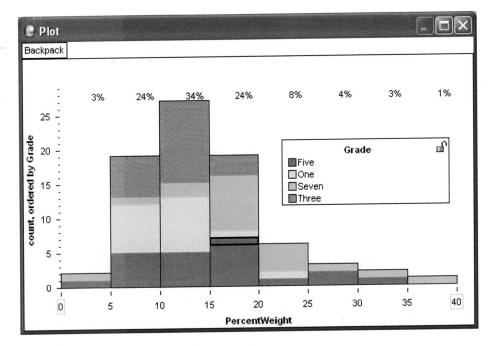

Deciding What to Tell

When teaching mathematics through problem solving, how do you decide what and how much to tell? Sometimes teachers are afraid to tell anything because they do not want to interfere with their students' thought processes. On the other hand, as teachers, we find it very difficult to let our students struggle. However, students who struggle with mathematics problems that are reasonable but whose solutions are not immediately apparent attain deeper understanding.

How much should you explain to students about a problem? Here are some guidelines (Hiebert, 2003):

1. Explain words, symbols, and notation. Students cannot be expected to figure these out on their own. For example, if the topic is money, explain the value and names of the different coins. If the topic is percents, introduce the percent notation (%) and the meaning of *percent* (hundredths).

2. Present methods that have not already been suggested by students. Offer your method as an alternative, not as the method of choice. Students should feel comfortable using their own methods too. Always highlight the mathematical ideas in students' methods because students may not be able to do this on their own. Notice that in the *Lesson*, the questions in the Summarize section help students focus on mathematical ideas they might otherwise have overlooked, such as patterns in the magic squares.

CONCEPT CHECK

1. **How** can you encourage students to use the problem-solving process?
2. **What** type of classroom culture encourages problem-solving?
3. **How** can you find effective problems if the textbook you use does not provide them?
4. **What** are the benefits of problem posing? How can you facilitate this in your classroom?
5. **How** can technology help with problem solving?
6. **How** can you decide how much to tell students about the problems they are solving?

Helping All Children with Problem Solving

LEARNING OBJECTIVES

1. **Identify** factors that influence children's success in problem solving.
2. **Distinguish** among three ways to change the difficulty of problems.
3. **Describe** effective strategies for helping English-language learners with problem solving.

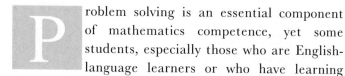roblem solving is an essential component of mathematics competence, yet some students, especially those who are English-language learners or who have learning disabilities, find problem solving especially challenging. How can you help all children learn to become proficient problem solvers? Several factors influence students' ability in problem solving.

Factors that Influence Children's Problem-Solving Success

Children are natural problem solvers. They come to school with an informal ability to solve problems and should be given this opportunity at every grade level, beginning in kindergarten. Children can solve word problems before they learn to read and before they learn written computation. For example, a young child can probably solve the following:

> *I have 4 balloons and my friend gave me 3 more. How many balloons do I have now?*

Expand on children's natural ability by providing them with word problems that

- build on what they already know,
- are based on their developmental levels,
- spark their imagination, and
- are based on their interests and experiences.

Researchers have identified four broad categories that affect children's problem-solving success: prior knowledge, beliefs and affect, self-regulation (control), and sociocultural factors.

Prior knowledge
Good problem solvers pay attention to the underlying structure of problems rather than to their surface features. Children need sufficient practice with problem solving to understand how a given problem is similar in structure to others they have solved. You can facilitate students' understanding of problem structure by helping them to compare new problems with ones they have already solved and guiding them to make wise choices about which strategies to use. Ask questions such as:

- *Where have you seen this before?*
- *What does this remind you of?*
- *How is this similar to the problem we just solved?*
- *How is it different?*

Beliefs and affect
Children's self-confidence and beliefs about themselves as problem solvers critically influence their performance (either positively or negatively).

Teachers who exhibit beliefs, such as *there is only one way to solve a problem, mathematics must be memorized,* or *mathematics should be done alone,* can hamper their students' problem-solving confidence and ability. Help your students gain confidence by making time for problem solving, praising their efforts, listening to their ideas, and selecting tasks at which they can succeed.

Self-regulation
Self-regulation is the process by which children **monitor** and **control** their thinking during problem solving. Good problem solvers do this consciously on a regular basis. They think about what they are doing and why they are doing it, as well as how much time they are spending during each phase of problem solving. This is called **resource allocation.**

> **self-regulation**
> Resource allocation during problem-solving activity.
>
> **monitor** In self-regulation, to keep track of one's own thinking.
>
> **control** In self-regulation, to be able to make changes in strategies and approaches.

Teaching Tip

Developing self-regulation

Encourage the development of students' self-regulation with questions such as

- *What did you do first? Why?*
- *What did you do next?*
- *How did you decide which strategy to use?*
- *Why did you decide to change strategies?*
- *Why do you think your answer is right (wrong)?*

Sociocultural factors
Problem solving can only flourish when teacher and students create a risk-free environment that values students' reasoning rather than their answers (Stephan and Whitenack, 2003). In such classrooms, students are encouraged to explain their thinking, explore and invent new strategies, ask questions of one another, and collaborate with their peers. Create a risk-free environment by stating your expectations for problem solving at the beginning of the year. Let students know that you value problem-solving behaviors.

Addressing Children's Difficulties with Problem Solving

Help children become better problem solvers by changing the difficulty of problems (Jacobs and Ambrose, 2008). This can be done by changing the problem **context**, the problem structure, or the mathematics.

The context of a problem refers to its nonmathematical setting. Children may have difficulty with contexts or situations with which they are unfamiliar. Change the context by elaborating on it, simplifying the situation, breaking it down into additional steps, or substituting familiar names and places.

Original problem

A box of 12 pencils costs $1.08. At that rate, how much would 15 pencils cost?

New context

I went to the school store today. I noticed that they were selling 12 pencils for $1.08. I thought that was a pretty good price but I really needed 15 pencils so I could give one to each of my students. How much would I pay for each pencil at that rate? How much would I pay for 15 pencils?

Some problem types are more difficult for children than others. Longer, multipart problems or problems with extraneous information can be challenging. Problems that have no "action" also tend to be more difficult because children are not sure what to do. Change the structure of the problem so that it matches children's understanding. In the following problem, the words were changed to indicate the action of moving from outside to inside.

Original problem

Twelve grandchildren are visiting Grandma. Five are outside playing ball and the rest are inside watching TV. How many children are watching TV?

Revised structure

Twelve children are visiting Grandma. They were all outside playing ball, but then five stayed outside and the rest came inside to watch TV. How many children are watching TV?

Sometimes it is necessary to change the mathematics in a problem. Children may understand the structure of a problem and what it is asking them to do but have difficulty completing it because of the numbers used. To help children overcome these difficulties, allow them to use calculators or change the numbers to make them easier to work with.

Original problem

Marcy was picking apples. She had 6 barrels and put 18 apples into each barrel. How many apples did she pick?

Revised numbers

Marcy was picking apples. She had 5 barrels and put 10 apples into each barrel. How many apples did she pick?

Problem solving can be especially challenging for English-language learners (ELLs) because so many problems are contextualized and, therefore, involve verbal skills as well as mathematical ones. We can support students whose first language is not English by employing specific strategies that are designed to increase both English language proficiency and problem-solving competency (see *In the Classroom*).

CONCEPT CHECK

1. **What** actions can you take as a teacher to support students' problem-solving success?

2. **What** are three ways you can change the difficulty of problems?

3. **What** are some techniques you can use to help English-language learners with problem solving?

In the Classroom
Problem-Solving Support for English-Language Learners

Chickens   Barn   Pigs

Chickens and Pigs Problem

"Brandon and Vanessa went to their grandfather's barn. When they got back to the house, their mom asked what they had seen. Brandon said they saw some chickens and pigs. Vanessa agreed and said that she had counted 18 animals. Brandon hadn't noticed that, but he had counted 52 legs. If Brandon and Vanessa are correct, how many chickens and pigs were there?" (Wiest, 2008, p. 480)

One half of the students in Mrs. Higgins' fourth-grade class are English-language learners (ELLs). When she gave her students the chickens and pigs problem, she used specific strategies to support her ELL students.

- She reworded the problem to include names of children in her class.
- She asked a volunteer to read the problem aloud.

- She separated students into groups of four with two native English speakers and two ELLs in each group. Whenever possible, she paired a "lower-proficiency ELL" (Wiest, 2008, p. 480) with a "more advanced ELL" (p. 480) who spoke the same language.

Before students began to solve the problem, Mrs. Higgins wrote the word *barn* on the board, pointed to a picture of a barn, and asked: *What is a barn?* Mrs. Higgins followed the same procedure to elicit the meanings of *chickens* and *pigs*. Finally, Mrs. Higgins asked her class to explain what the problem asked them to do.

After students completed the problem, Mrs. Higgins asked them to explain their reasoning. Next, instead of giving students a completely different kind of problem to solve, she chose another problem with a similar context, because she believes that it is helpful for English-language learners to solve several problems within a single context so that the context does not prevent students from successfully solving word problems.

(*Source*: Wiest, 2008)

> ### Think Critically
> 1. What are the benefits of grouping ELLs with advanced English language skills with ELLs with poorer English language skills?
> 2. What other techniques can you use to help ELLs become good problem solvers?
> 3. How do the techniques used by Mrs. Higgins benefit all students' problem-solving abilities?

Problem-Solving Strategies

LEARNING OBJECTIVES

1. **Describe** seven problem-solving strategies.
2. **Identify** problems that lend themselves to particular strategies.
3. **Identify** strategies and problem types that are more suitable for younger children.
4. **Identify** strategies and problem types that are more suitable for older children.

As you gain more experience solving problems you may notice that certain strategies crop up again and again. Naming and identifying these strategies helps students remember and access them. Although it is fine to suggest a particular strategy to students, do not dictate the use of one strategy over another. As you consider the following problems, notice that many of them can be solved with more than one strategy.

Strategy: Act It Out

The Act It Out strategy helps children visualize what the problem is asking. It is helpful for younger children, who can act out simple real-life situations themselves or with manipulatives, as illustrated by the first three problems. In the later grades, children can act out a simpler version of a problem to gain insight into solving the problem.

Problems to solve using the Act It Out strategy

Erin brought 15 muffins to school to share for her birthday, but there were 20 students in her class. How many students did not get a muffin?

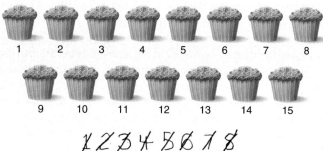

Maria has 7 chocolate chip cookies. She gives 4 away. How many does she have left?

Five children were sitting at computer stations. Then 7 more children joined them. How many children were sitting at computer stations?

Strategy: Guess and Check

Guess and Check is an often misunderstood strategy. It does not mean randomized guessing. What it does mean is guessing a solution, checking to see whether that solution is accurate, and then picking the next guess based on the results of the previous one. You can help students use this strategy successfully by requiring them to evaluate and discuss each guess before choosing their next guess. Here are two problems that can be solved with this strategy. Note that the second problem has several correct answers.

Problems to solve using the Guess and Check strategy

Ellie had two cousins. The sum of their ages is 19, and one cousin is five years older than the other. How old are the cousins?

Cousin 1	Cousin 2	Sum	
13	6	19	no
12	7	19	yes

Juan is two years older than twice his brother's age. Both Juan and his brother are younger than 15. How old is Juan?

Strategy: Solve a Simpler Problem

The purpose of the Solve a Simpler Problem strategy is to modify an existing problem so that it is easier to work with. Modifications are often made to the size of the quantities to make them easier for computation. Smaller numbers also make it easier to identify patterns. When students solve an easier problem, they gain insight into the problem structure that can be transferred to more difficult problems. **Activity 6.3** shows how to use this strategy.

An additional problem to solve with the Solve a Simpler Problem strategy

The next problem can also be solved with this strategy. This problem presents two challenges. First, finding the day of the week for the 100th day of school seems daunting because 100 is a big number. Second, if you try to use the strategy of counting by sevens because there are seven days in a week, you obtain an incorrect answer because there are only five school days per week. To solve this problem, children have to realize that they are counting by fives. This problem can be made simpler by finding the day of the week after just five days, then 10, 15, and 20 days.

School started on a Wednesday this year. What day of the week is the 100th day of school?

Wednesday is the first day of school. Thursday is the second day. Friday is the third day. Monday is the fourth day. Tuesday is the fifth day. Next Tuesday is the 10th day of school. In 100 school days it will be Tuesday.

> **Activity 6.3 Using a simpler problem to find sums of consecutive whole numbers**
>
> **Instructions**
>
> 1. Provide students with the following problem:
>   *Find the sum of the whole numbers from 1 to 100. That is, find 1 + 2 + 3 + . . . + 100.*
>
> 2. Ask: *Is there a simpler problem you can consider first?* (Find the sum of the first 10 whole numbers: 1 + 2 + 3 + 4 + 5 + 6 + 7 + 8 + 9 + 10 = 55.)
>
> 3. Ask: *What is special about 55?* (It is an odd number and its factors are 5 and 11.)
>
> 4. Ask: *What is special about 11? Where do you notice 11 in this problem?* (1 + 10 = 11; 2 + 9 = 11; 3 + 8 = 11; 4 + 7 = 11; 5 + 6 = 11. Working with the first and last number, the second and next to last, etc., each pair of numbers adds to 11 and there are 5 pairs.)
>
> 5. Ask: *How can we apply this strategy to the original problem?* (The sum of the numbers from 1 to 100 have 50 pairs and each pair sums to 101. 50 x 101 =5050.)

Strategy: Make a Table

The Make a Table strategy is helpful for organizing information and identifying function relationships. When information is organized it is easier to solve problems and recognize patterns. This strategy is often taught by giving children tables that are partially filled in, with columns labeled. Later, children can make tables from scratch and decide on column headings and how many rows and columns are needed to represent the information. This strategy works well with spreadsheets.

Problems to solve with the Make a Table strategy

Claire had some coins in her pocket for ice cream. On the way to the store she found a nickel and put it in her pocket with the other coins. When she got to the store she counted the money in her pocket and found that she had 85 cents. What coins might have been in her pocket before she found the nickel?

A rectangular yard has an area measuring 100 square feet. Its length and width are measured in whole feet. What combinations of length and width are possible for this yard? Which combination gives the smallest perimeter?

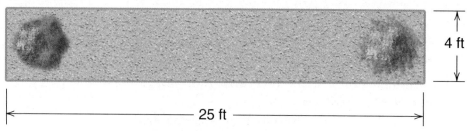

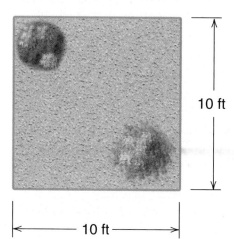

Strategy: Work Backwards

The Work Backwards strategy helps develop logical reasoning. It is effective when a problem includes the result and children have to figure out the beginning.

Problems to solve using the Work Backwards strategy

"Ted gave half of his baseball cards to Bob. Then he gave 5 cards to Dan. Now Ted has 6 cards. How many cards did he have to start with?" (Hartweg and Heisler, 2007, p. 364)

Aunt Betts baked gingerbread cookies and gave half of the cookies to her three nieces. Then she gave half of the remaining cookies to her two nephews. She had three cookies left. How many cookies did Aunt Betts bake?

Maya and some friends watched DVDs at two o'clock. One friend's Mom picked her up at three o'clock. Two more friends left one hour later. At five o'clock, three friends were still there. How many friends were at Maya's house at two o'clock?

Strategy: Draw a Diagram

The Draw a Diagram strategy is used frequently in everyday life. You might draw a map to show a friend which bicycle paths to take when visiting your house, or you might draw a diagram of how you want to plant your vegetable garden. This strategy is especially beneficial for visual learners. It allows the learner to visually see the problem and identify or organize the data with a picture or diagram. When teaching this strategy, children sometimes get lost in the details of their drawings and miss the problem-solving opportunities. Explain to children that the diagrams do not have to be detailed.

Problems to solve using the Draw a Diagram strategy

Tina wanted to cut a 36-inch-long ribbon into 4 equal pieces. How many cuts does she have to make in the ribbon?

How many people can be seated at 12 square tables lined up end to end if each table individually holds four persons?

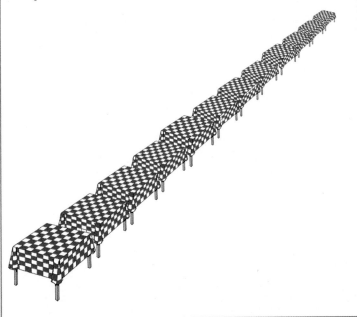

Strategy: Look for a Pattern

The Look for a Pattern strategy promotes algebraic thinking. This strategy helps young children recognize visual patterns that are either repeating or growing. Older children use this strategy to identify numerical relationships in conjunction with other problem-solving strategies. With this strategy, list several examples and then find the pattern that links the examples together.

Problems to solve using the Look for a Pattern strategy

Find the next two elements of the pattern.

Extend the following pattern:

This pattern of numbers is called Pascal's triangle. Find the next row. Identify two patterns in Pascal's triangle.

```
            1
          1   1
        1   2   1
      1   3   3   1
    1   4   6   4   1
```

This sequence is called the Fibonacci sequence. What is the pattern? Find the next three entries.

1, 1, 2, 3, 5, 8, 13, . . .

Provide children with problems that can be solved with several solution strategies and give them the opportunity to share their thinking with classmates. The following problem can be solved using a variety of strategies. Let us take a look at how three children solved it.

Problem

The seven members of the Abbott School girls' gymnastics team have a tradition. Before each match each team member high-fives each of the other team members. How many high-fives does that make?

a. Solve a simpler problem.

Jason solves this problem first with simpler numbers. He asks: *How many high-fives with three people? How many with four people?* Jason discovers a pattern and applies that to the original problem. Can you identify the pattern he found?

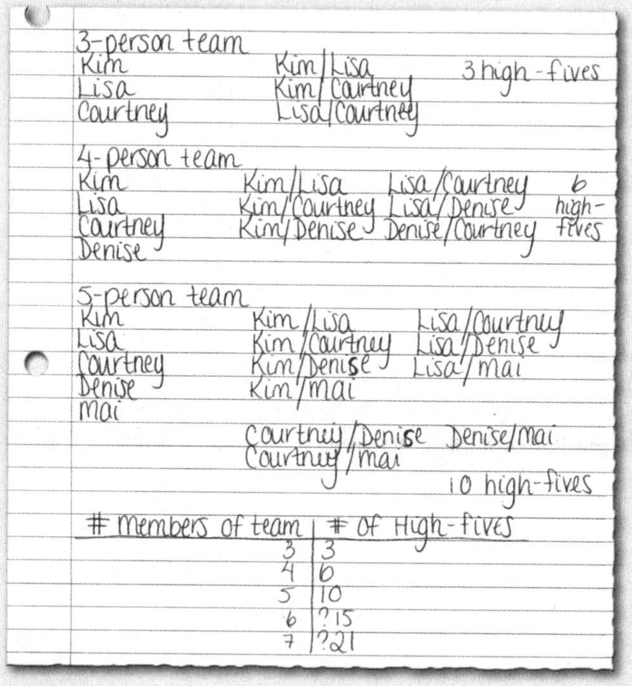

(handwritten notes:)

3-person team
Kim
Lisa
Courtney

Kim/Lisa
Kim/Courtney
Lisa/Courtney   3 high-fives

4-person team
Kim
Lisa
Courtney
Denise

Kim/Lisa   Lisa/Courtney   6
Kim/Courtney Lisa/Denise   high-
Kim/Denise   Denise/Courtney fives

5-person team
Kim
Lisa
Courtney
Denise
Mai

Kim/Lisa   Lisa/Courtney
Kim/Courtney Lisa/Denise
Kim/Denise   Lisa/Mai
Kim/Mai

Courtney/Denise Denise/Mai
Courtney/Mai
                10 high-fives

# members of team	# of High-fives
3	3
4	6
5	10
6	?15
7	?21

b. Draw a diagram.

Anika draws a diagram to show all of the high-fives, first labeling the team members by the numbers 1, 2, 3, 4, 5, 6, 7. She uses a different color for each team member to help keep track of their high-fives. Before she finishes, she notices a pattern. Can you describe the pattern Anika found?

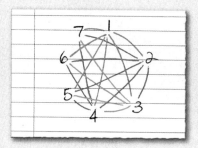

c. Make a table.

Carmen uses a strategy similar to Anika's but also makes a table to count the number of high-fives. Before she finishes the table, she notices a pattern and fills in the rest of the table. Can you find the pattern?

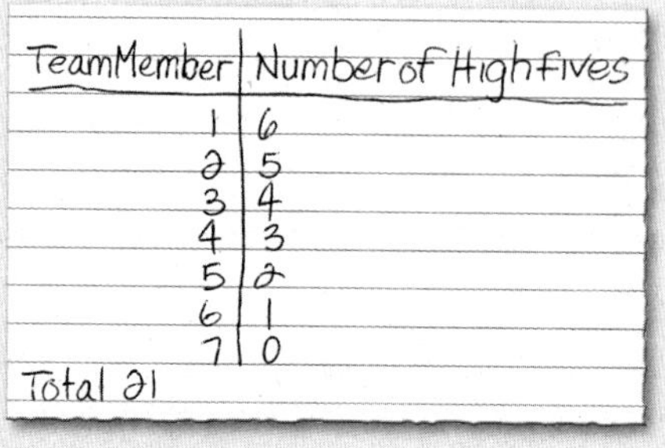

Team Member	Number of High fives
1	6
2	5
3	4
4	3
5	2
6	1
7	0

Total 21

Using Multiple Strategies

When children solve problems, they often approach the same problem differently, based on their prior knowledge and learning preferences. It can be very helpful for children to see how others approach the same problem. **Figure 6.9** examines how three different children might solve the same problem using three different strategies.

CONCEPT CHECK STOP

1. **What** are seven problem-solving strategies?
2. **How** can solving the same problem with multiple strategies be beneficial to students?
3. **What** strategies are effective with younger children?
4. **What** strategies are effective with older children?

THE PLANNER ✓

Summary

1 What Is Problem Solving? 138

- A **problem** is a task or activity for which we have no immediate solution. We know we are faced with a problem when we are faced with a situation and do not at first know how to proceed. Problem solving is part of everyday life, as shown in the photo.

Figure 6.1

- In mathematics, there are two types of word problems, **routine** and **nonroutine** problems.

- Problem solving is a new approach to the teaching and learning of mathematics that engages students in tasks that are problematic for them. In solving problems, students either invent a strategy or choose one that they are familiar with and apply that strategy to a specific situation. When teaching problem solving, we teach **heuristics** that students can use again and again.

- There are many benefits to learning mathematics through problem solving. When students learn mathematics through problem solving, they make connections between mathematical ideas and develop concepts, strategies, and procedures in the process.

2 Teaching Mathematics Through Problem Solving 141

- Polya's problem-solving process includes four phases: understanding the problem, devising a plan, carrying out the plan, and looking back. Good problem solvers often cycle back through one or more phases before reaching a satisfactory solution.

- Planning for problem solving includes deciding how to group students, how to create a classroom atmosphere conducive to problem solving, and how to model appropriate problem-solving behaviors for children.

- There are many options for finding effective problem-solving tasks. One option is to create them yourself from the everyday activities of the classroom, as illustrated.

Figure 6.5

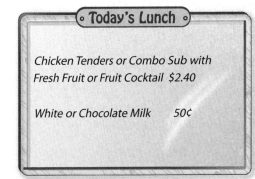

⊙ Today's Lunch ⊙

Chicken Tenders or Combo Sub with Fresh Fruit or Fruit Cocktail $2.40

White or Chocolate Milk   50¢

- **Problem posing** is a technique by which students modify or extend existing problems. It can be very beneficial to students because it builds confidence and ownership in the problem-solving process. Children's literature can be an effective aid to problem posing.

- There are many ways to use technology to support problem solving. Calculators, computer software, and spreadsheets can all be helpful.

- It is often difficult for teachers to decide what and how much to tell while their students are engaged in problem solving. You want to be helpful, but you don't want to take away students' initiative or sense of discovery. There are specific guidelines to help you decide how much to tell.

3 Helping All Children with Problem Solving 150

- There are four factors that influence students' success with problem solving: knowledge, beliefs and affect, sociocultural factors, and **self-regulation**. Teachers can take specific actions to help students in each of these areas.

- Problem solving can be challenging for ELL students. There are many ways to help these students be successful, as illustrated in the photo.

In the Classroom

- You can help children who struggle with problem solving by changing the difficulty of the problem. There are three ways to do this: change the **context**, change the structure, or change the mathematics in the problem.

4 Problem-Solving Strategies 154

- **Act It Out** is a strategy that helps children visualize what the problem is asking. It is helpful for younger children who can act out simple real-life situations in the classroom.

- **Solve a Simpler Problem** is a strategy that helps children gain insight into a problem's structure that can then be transferred to more difficult problems with similar structure.

- The **Guess and Check** strategy is often misunderstood. It does not suggest or recommend random guessing but encourages guessing a solution, checking to see whether that solution is accurate, and then picking the next guess based on the results of the previous one.

- The **Make a Table** strategy is effective for organizing information, identifying patterns, and identifying function relationships. Children should be able to make tables and label column heads from scratch.

- The **Draw a Diagram or Picture** strategy is especially effective for visual learners. It allows the learner to see the problem and identify or organize the data with a diagram. When using this strategy, explain to children that it is not necessary to have detailed drawings.

- **Look for a Pattern** is a strategy that promotes algebraic thinking. Use this strategy to help younger children recognize visual patterns. With older children, the strategy can be used to identify numerical relationships.

- The **Work Backwards** strategy is effective when a problem includes the result and children have to figure out the beginning. It helps develop logical reasoning.

- Solving the same problem with multiple strategies can help children learn about other ways of thinking about the same problem. This diagram illustrates one way of solving a problem.

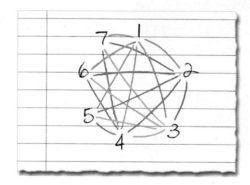

Figure 6.9

Key Terms

- context 152
- control 151
- heuristics 140
- monitor 151

- nonroutine problems 140
- problem posing 144
- problems 138
- resource allocation 151

- routine problems 140
- self-regulation 151
- story problems 140

Additional Children's Literature

- *Counting on Frank*, written and illustrated by Rod Clement
  A young boy and his very large dog, Frank, investigate many different kinds of problems from real life, much to the amazement of his parents. This book helps children realize that problem solving is a part of everyday life. Find more details about this book in Chapter 1.

- *How Much Is a Million?*, written by David M. Schwartz and illustrated by Steven Kellogg
  The values of large numbers, such as one million and one billion, are explored in this book. Many problems are posed and answered, such as how long it would take to count from one to one million.

- *Math Curse*, written by John Scieszka and illustrated by Lane Smith
  This classic book tells the story of a little girl who is told that everything can be thought of as a math problem. For the next 24 hours, everything in her life becomes a math problem.

- *The Grapes of Math*, written by Greg Tang and illustrated by Harry Briggs
  This clever book uses rhyming clues and pictures in clusters to develop mental mathematics and spatial skills.

Online Resources

- **Math Playground**
  www.mathplayground.com

  1. *Word Problems*—Select from a huge selection of word problems. You can choose problems using all arithmetic operation, fractions, decimals, ratios, percents, or geometry. You can also choose problems with extraneous information.

  2. *Logic Problems*—Select from a large selection of virtual board games and games such as **The Tower of Hanoi**.

- **Math Forum**
  www.mathforum.org/

  Offers a collection of problems including a problem of the week.

- **Megamath**
  www.c3lanl.gov/megamath

  Focuses on discrete mathematics topics such as map coloring.

- **National Council of Teachers of Mathematics**
  www.nctm.org/

  Has downloadable sets of word problems for members.

- **National Library of Virtual Manipulatives**
  http://nlvm.usu.edu/

  1. *Number and Operations (3–5)*: Choose from several magic square–type problems.

  2. *Number and Operations (6 –8)*: Play virtual logic games based on "Mastermind" or the classic game **Peg Puzzle**.

Critical and Creative Thinking Questions

1. **In the field** Find two routine story problems from an elementary mathematics textbook. Change the problems from routine to nonroutine, and explain how you changed them and why they are now considered nonroutine.

2. Solve each of the problems you created in question 1 with at least two different strategies. Explain each strategy that you used. Which strategy is a better fit for the problem? If your problems have more than one possible answer, explain all possible answers and identify whether one is more appropriate than the other(s).

3. Analyze what difficulties students might have understanding and solving your problems. Explain how you might modify the word problems so that students can be more successful with them.

4. Find a children's literature book with a mathematical theme. What problems can be posed from the content of this book?

5. **In the field** Choose one of the problems from this chapter. Ask two different children (at the same grade level) to solve it. Observe their solutions and identify the strategies they used. What did you learn about the children's problem-solving strengths and weaknesses from their solutions?

6. Choose one of the children's solutions from question 5. If you were to teach a lesson on problem solving, based on this child's solution, what strategies would you focus on? How would you help the child improve his or her problem-solving abilities?

7. **Using visuals** Consider Figure 6.1. Notice how this figure places problem solving in a real-world context. Choose a grade level and create a bulletin board or visual display that you could use in your own classroom to convey problem solving in real-world situations.

What is happening in this picture?

Going grocery shopping with mom or dad is a familiar and fun experience for many children. Grocery shopping also provides a rich context for problem solving for children of all ages. The many opportunities for problem solving at the grocery store include money, time, capacity, patterns, measurement, or the route you take through the store.

Think Critically

1. Why is it important for children to solve problems that have a familiar context?
2. How does a trip to the grocery store serve as an example of problem solving in daily life?
3. Why is it important for children to recognize that people in all walks of life use problem solving to complete their daily activities?
4. Write a problem based on one of the topics described in the caption and using this photo of a grocery store.

Self-Test

(Check your answers in Appendix D.)

1. Differentiate between routine and nonroutine problems.

2. Identify Polya's four phases of problem solving.

3. What are two advantages of teaching mathematics through problem solving?

4. What problem-solving behaviors should teachers model for students?

5. What are the characteristics of a classroom culture that encourages problem solving?

6. How should children be grouped for problem solving?

7. How might you use a calculator to solve this problem?

   "If 1 BILLION children climbed onto one another's shoulders to form a tower, how many times would that tower reach to the moon and back to Earth? (Figure an average of four feet for the height of the children because they are standing on shoulders, not heads. There are 5,280 feet in a mile. The moon is approximately 239,000 miles from Earth.)"
   (Kempf, 1997, p. 25)

8. How does problem posing differ from students writing their own problems?

9. What does this histogram tell you about the relationship of a student's grade level to the weight of his or her backpack? Why is a visual representation a good way to solve this problem?

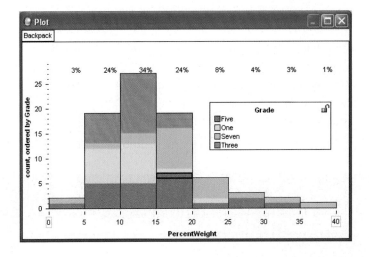

10. What are the four factors that determine success in problem solving?

11. Identify three ways to change the difficulty of a problem.

12. Solve the following problem:

    Ann bought a purse on e-Bay for $60, sold it to a friend for $70, bought it back for $80, and then sold the purse again for $90. How much money did Ann earn or lose after the final transaction?

13. What strategy did you use to solve the problem in question 12?

14. Give an example of a problem that can be solved with the Act It Out strategy. Solve the problem and explain your solution.

15. What are three techniques that can be used to help English-language learners with problem solving?

THE PLANNER ✓

Review your Chapter Planner on the chapter opener and check off your completed work.

Counting and Number Sense

In celebration of his birthday, student teacher Todd Bayles brought cupcakes to share with his first-grade class. Before he handed out the cupcakes, he asked his students to guess his age. Children shouted out numbers, "Fifteen!" "Sixty-two!" and "Eighty-five!" Todd was surprised by the range of guesses but then realized that his question was too open-ended for first graders.

To guide his students to reasonable guesses and encourage their number sense, Todd altered the activity by offering extra clues and requiring students to explain their thinking. Todd explained to the class that he is one of three children. His older sister is 32 and his younger brother is 21. After hearing Todd's clues, children called out new guesses and explained why they made sense in relation to the new information Todd had provided.

As each student guessed his age, Todd responded so that students could refine their thinking. For example, when one student guessed "twenty-five," Todd said that 25 was a reasonable guess, but that he was older than 25. Finally, someone guessed Todd's correct age of 27, and this student was given the privilege of passing out the cupcakes.

This birthday activity helped Todd's students broaden their knowledge of numbers and learn estimation skills by developing intuition about which numbers were reasonable guesses. The students also practiced the concepts *more than, less than,* and *the same as* in a real-world context.

CHAPTER OUTLINE

NCTM The NCTM Number and Operations Standard is the first of the content standards described in *Principles and Standards for School Mathematics* (2000). Its placement emphasizes the importance of counting and numbers. The expectations for grades pre-K to 2 that relate to this chapter are the following:

In pre-kindergarten through grade 2, all students should

- count with understanding and recognize "how many" in sets of objects;

- develop understanding of the relative position and magnitude of whole numbers and of ordinal and cardinal numbers and their connections;

- develop a sense of whole numbers and represent and use them in flexible ways, including relating, composing, and decomposing numbers;

- connect number words and numerals to the quantities they represent, using various physical models and representations (NCTM, 2000, p. 78).

Children develop informal concepts of number sense through their everyday activities. Can you think of another number sense activity that can be done with the number of cupcakes the children have?

The Development of Pre-Number Concepts

LEARNING OBJECTIVES

1. **Distinguish** between the two meanings of subitizing.

2. **Describe** the role of classification activities.

3. **Describe** the concepts of *more, less,* and *the same.*

4. **Recognize** the importance of patterns.

Early experiences that lead to the development of counting skills are known as **pre-number experiences**. They do not necessarily use numbers and can occur concurrently with the development of counting. Children's acquisition of pre-number concepts is essential to their complete understanding of the meaning of numbers, place value, and whole number operations.

Subitizing

> **subitizing** Looking at a set and instantly seeing how many objects are in the set, without counting.

Subitizing is one of the most important pre-number concepts for children to learn. Educators are not sure whether subitizing develops before or after counting. In the first half of the 20th century, educators believed that subitizing was a prerequisite to counting. In the second half of the 20th century, some educators questioned this and theorized that subitizing develops after counting and is used as a shortcut to counting. Although this debate has not been settled, subitizing is recognized as an important skill and a prerequisite to developing strategies for whole number operations such as adding and subtracting.

There are two types of subitizing. The first, **perceptual subitizing**, is the recognition of a small number of objects without the use of mathematical processes. Two-year-old children and some animals can do this (Clements, 1999). For example, young children can look at a picture of three teddy bears and instantly know how many there are. The second type, **conceptual subitizing**, involves seeing the whole and recognizing it as a sum of its parts. For example, when a child sees a pattern such as six dots on a domino and just knows how many dots there are because of their arrangement, the child is using conceptual subitizing (**Figure 7.1**).

Although children begin school with some ability to subitize, teachers can enhance their skills with specific activities that promote subitizing. Such activities should show simple forms, such as squares or circles, symmetric arrangements, and clear images that are not embedded in a pictorial context (**Activity 7.1**).

Activity 7.1 How many?

Instructions

1. Decorate paper plates with peel-off circular labels available at the grocery store. Create different spatial arrangements to represent the numbers from 1 to 10.

Two types of subitizing • Figure 7.1

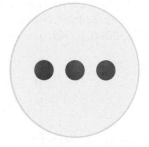

a. How many dots are in this circle? How does this image represent perceptual subitizing?

b. How many bowling pins are in this picture? How does this image represent conceptual subitizing?

Classification in everyday life • Figure 7.2

There are many opportunities for classification in the classroom and in children's lives outside of school. In your own classroom, what kinds of objects can you use for classification activities?

2. Pick a paper plate. Show the image quickly to the class. Ask: *How many?*

3. Do this several times with different paper plates.

4. Then show several paper plates quickly, all with different arrangements of the same number, such as six dots. Ask: *What number is displayed on each plate?*

5. Next show several paper plates quickly, all but one having different arrangements of six dots. Ask: *Which one doesn't fit?*

6. Repeat with different numbers.

Classification

Classification is the process of sorting with regard to a particular attribute or characteristic. Young children love to sort and classify objects according to categories and have many opportunities to do so in their everyday lives (**Figure 7.2**). As children begin classifying, it is easier for them to sort by one category. For example, they can sort a box of candy into chocolate or not chocolate, a bag of marbles into red or not red, or a group of pebbles into smooth or not smooth. In all of these examples, children are sorting things that are alike from things that are different.

You can create additional classification activities to stimulate children's thinking by arranging a collection of objects into two groups, secretly selecting the attribute they are sorted by and then asking children to guess that attribute (**Activity 7.2**). This activity requires children to **hypothesize** about the attribute that objects have in common. This can be a lot of fun for children, while also fostering concept formation.

hypothesize To suggest an explanation for facts or observations.

Activity 7.2 Hoop game

Instructions

1. Select an attribute. Instruct the class not to discuss their guesses.

2. Place two large hoops on the floor.

3. Designate one hoop as a "yes" for objects that have the attribute and the other as a "no."

4. Select objects to put into a bag: toy cars, shells, leaves, seeds, chalk, erasers, and pencils.

5. Remove objects from the bag, one at a time. For the first several draws, tell children whether the object is a "yes" or a "no" and put the object inside the appropriate hoop.

6. Remove the rest of the objects from the bag, one at a time, and ask "yes" or "no," to determine where the object should be placed.

7. At any time during the game, children can guess the attribute that you have selected.

The attribute here is "things with wheels." Can you think of another way to sort these objects?

Developing children's concepts of less • Figure 7.3

How can these photographs help children develop the concept of *less*? What questions could you ask children to emphasize this concept?

As children become more practiced at classification they can sort by two attributes. For a classroom activity, you might select the attributes of "walking to school" and "taking the school bus" and sort the children in the class according to these two attributes. It is possible that some children will fall into neither category, since some children may ride their bikes to school or be driven by a parent. It is important to discuss this issue and decide how to handle it, perhaps by creating a third category for children who do not take the bus or walk to school.

More, Less, and the Same

The concepts of *more, less,* and *the same* are fundamental to the learning of mathematics. Most children understand the concept of *more* before they start school because of their real-world experiences. They may have asked for more cookies, more television time, or more toys. Children have greater difficulty with the concept of *less*. We can help children understand *less* by doing comparison activities, such as showing two unequal collections of objects and asking, *Which has less?* whenever we ask, *Which has more?* (**Figure 7.3**).

Children should experience activities that make comparisons between sets by using all three concepts. In **Activity 7.3**, when the teacher asks the class to *Show me more* or *Show me less*, there can be more than one correct response. For example, if the teacher holds up a dot card with 6 dots, students can hold up dot cards with 7 or 8 dots to show more or with 5, 4, 3, 2, or 1 dot to show less. However, when the teacher asks the class to *Show me the same* there is only one correct response.

Numbers are composed of patterns. Some examples are: every number has a double; *one more than* always produces the next counting number; and *one less than* always produces the previous counting number. By teaching children to observe, identify, create, and extend patterns, teachers can help them become proficient at counting and number sense and develop the skills necessary for abstract thinking.

For young children, begin patterning activities in which they can actively participate (**Activity 7.4**). This type of activity can be done several times a week with variations. Let each child take turns starting a new pattern. Make sure to talk about the pattern in words.

Activity 7.3 Show me

Instructions

1. Create sets of dot cards that show the numbers 1, 2, 3, 4, 5, 6, 7, 8 with peel-off paper labels.

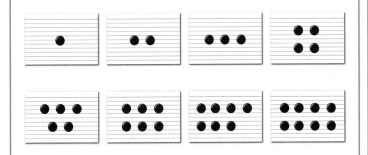

2. The teacher holds up a dot card and says, *Show me more.*

3. Students respond by holding up appropriate dot cards.

4. As there can be more than one correct answer, student responses are discussed.

5. Next, holding up the same dot card, the teacher says, *Show me less.*

6. Again, students hold up appropriate dot cards, followed by class discussion.

7. Finally, the teacher says, *Show me the same,* and children again respond by holding up the appropriate card.

8. This activity can also be done in small groups where one child assumes the role of the leader.

Activity 7.4 Make a pattern with children

Instructions

1. Ask children to stand in a circle.

2. Begin a pattern for the group by doing and saying the pattern, such as: *Clap, hands over head, clap, hands over head.* Circulate behind the group to make sure everyone is following the pattern.

3. Continue the pattern a few times and then change it to something new, such as: *clap-clap, turn around, clap-clap, turn around.*

4. As children become familiar with the patterns, add another element or ask one class member to make a new pattern.

5. Develop a signal that means the pattern will be changing. You might snap your fingers twice to indicate that the next round will have a new pattern.

Young children should also have the opportunity to extend patterns. Show an initial pattern with colored beads, chips, or pattern blocks and ask children to extend it. This activity can be done with physical or virtual manipulatives.

Tech Tools

http://nlvm.usu.edu

The National Library of Virtual Manipulatives **Color Pattern** activity shows colored beads in a pattern, with several beads that are left uncolored. The user decides how to color the uncolored beads to extend the pattern and then selects a new problem.

Patterns

Patterns are everywhere around us (September follows August, Tuesday follows Monday). Mathematics is, foremost, the study of patterns, both numerical and nonnumerical. Children should have the opportunity to explore both types of patterns.

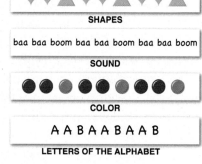
In **Activity 7.5**, children create their own nonnumerical patterns and translate them from one medium to another. The completion of activities such as this one helps children to generalize and recognize patterns in contexts other than mathematics.

CONCEPT CHECK

1. **How** do you use subitizing when counting?
2. **What** kinds of classification activities are important for children to experience?
3. **Why** is it important for children to learn *more, less,* and *the same* before they learn to count?
4. **How** can pattern recognition improve children's number sense?

Early Counting

LEARNING OBJECTIVES

1. **Describe** the criteria that determine meaningful counting.
2. **Explain** the importance of connecting physical quantities with the number names and numerals that represent them.
3. **Distinguish** between counting on, counting back, and skip counting.
4. **Distinguish** between cardinal, ordinal, and nominal uses of number.

Counting is the process of establishing a **one-to-one correspondence** between objects and the number words that represent them. Children develop informal concepts of number and counting long before they begin school. From the age of 2 most children can verbally tell you their age and show it by holding out the appropriate number of fingers. They may be able to tell you the number of people in their family, how many pets they have, or other information that involves numbers. Most middle-class children younger than $3\frac{1}{2}$, learn to count sequentially from 1 to 10, and most children who are between the ages of $3\frac{1}{2}$ and $4\frac{1}{2}$ learn to count from 10 to 20 (Fuson, 1988).

When children begin to count, they count physical objects. Counting is one of the best ways for children to develop number sense and efficient counting strategies, but research indicates that teachers do not do enough of it in their classrooms (Fuson, 1988). Teachers can engage children in counting activities with anything readily available, such as desks, chairs, erasers, or computers.

> **one-to-one correspondence**
> A unique matching of pairs of items from two sets where each item from one set is paired with one and only one item from the other set.

Teaching Tip

Engaging children in counting activities

Keep buckets of countable objects, such as buttons, bottle tops, and popsicle sticks, available. Ask children to count them and observe how they are counting. Have children who can count by ones, count prepackaged items, such as boxes of paper clips or index cards.

Conservation of number • Figure 7.4

Would a child who is a conserver of numbers say that there are the same number of white counters as red counters in drawings **a** and **b**? How might a child who is not a conserver of numbers interpret these images?

a.

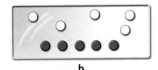

b.

Meaningful Counting

Numbers and counting are the foundations of mathematics. However, children cannot learn to count meaningfully unless they understand **conservation** of number (**Figure 7.4**). The theory of conservation is based on the work of Jean Piaget, who proposed that children develop conservation of number when they reach the **concrete operational stage of development**. Children younger than 6 years old are often not conservers, but by the age of 7 most children are conservers.

Meaningful counting consists of a combination of four skills that develop sequentially (**Figure 7.5**).

conservation of number A principle that states that the number of objects remains the same even when they are rearranged.

concrete operational stage of development The stage in which children gain the ability to think logically about concrete concepts such as mathematics.

✓ THE PLANNER

Counting stages • Figure 7.5

Children become meaningful counters when they can recite the counting words in their proper order, understand and demonstrate one-to-one correspondence, understand not to recount objects, and understand the concept of **cardinality**.

1 Counting in the proper sequence

When children first learn to count, they may count in the wrong sequence.

2 Using one-to-one correspondence

Children need to develop the concept of one-to-one correspondence between the number name and the object being counted. Before learning this concept, they may name one object with more than one number.

3 Not recounting the same number twice

Children need to count in such a way as to not recount objects. They may point to the object being counted, move it, or mark it to recognize that it has already been counted.

4 Cardinality

Children need to develop cardinality, the understanding that the last number counted always gives the cardinality or number of objects in the group.

A child who cannot consistently meet these criteria is a **rote counter**. A child who is a rote counter may say the names of numbers in sequence but not be able to make a one-to-one correspondence or meet the other criteria. A child who can count in the proper order, who understands the one-to-one correspondence between number names and the objects being counted, who understands how to remember what has already been counted, and who understands that the last number counted tells how many is a **rational counter**. By the age of 5, most children in the United States can count rationally to 10 or 20. By the end of first grade, most children can rationally count to 100.

Cardinality is not an easy concept for children to understand. Young children will learn how to count before they develop the cardinality principle, although most children will develop the principle by age 4. We can help children develop cardinality by giving them many experiences in counting collections of objects and asking questions such as *How many are there in all?* For the children who are having difficulty understanding the concept *how many*, demonstrating and stating cardinality for them can be an effective teaching tool.

Numeral Recognition

When children first learn to count, they use number words such as *one, two, three*. They also may use **concrete** or physical representations for numbers: dots, popsicle sticks, cubes, chips, or other counters. In kindergarten, children learn that **numerals** are a third way to represent numbers. They learn to write numerals by tracing over enlarged examples.

Connecting numerals to the quantities they represent is a complex process and something we often take for granted. Numerals

> **numerals** Mathematical notations for representing numbers of a given set by symbols in some sort of consistent manner.

Multicultural Perspectives in Mathematics

 THE PLANNER

Positive numbers			Negtive numbers		
	Vertical	Horizontal		Vertical	Horizontal
0			0		
1	I	—	−1	I	—
2	II	=	−2	II	=
3	III	≡	−3	III	≡
4	IIII	≣	−4	IIII	≣
5	IIIII	≣	−5	IIIII	≣
6	T	⊥	−6	T	⊥
7	TT	⊥	−7	TT	⊥
8	TTT	⊥	−8	TTT	⊥
9	TTTT	⊥	−9	TTTT	⊥

are used to represent units, hundreds, tens of thousands, and so on. When using vertical rods, the inclusion of a horizontal rod represents the quantity five. Horizontal rods are called *Hengs* and are used to represent tens, thousands, hundreds of thousands, and so on. When using horizontal rods, the inclusion of a vertical rod represents the quantity five.

Rod numerals are a base-ten system and can be used for calculations with all the whole number operations. Rod numerals in red or black represent positive and negative numbers. They are also an intuitive system, since it is easy to connect the appearance of the rod numeral with the quantity it represents. They can be useful as a transitional tool to help young children bridge the gap between concrete or physical representations of number and their abstract representation with numerals.

Chinese Counting Rods

Counting rod numerals have been used in China since at least the second century C.E. These numerals are derived from the bamboo sticks that were used on counting boards. The rods are either horizontal or vertical, and the number of rods represents the quantity being counted. Vertical rods are called *Tsungs*, and

Strategies for the Classroom

- How would you use vertical and horizontal rods in the classroom to teach number concepts?

- How can learning about Chinese counting rods help children transition from concrete representations of number to abstract representations?

CHILDREN'S LITERATURE

Matching numbers and quantities

Anno's Counting Book • Figure 7.6

Written and illustrated by Mitsumasa Anno

Each page shows one number as a numeral and with illustrations. For example, on the facing pages that represent the number 1, children should see one tree, one truck, one building, one child, one shaded counting block, one o'clock, and other examples of one. Subsequent pages provide similar illustrations for the numbers 2 through 12. The illustrations challenge children to find examples of each number while showing the relationship between concrete objects and the numerals that represent them. The numbers are also correlated with the months of the year.

Strategy for the Classroom

- Read the book with children, one page at a time. Ask children to find examples of the number represented on each page.

---

are symbols that represent whatever is being counted and are therefore **abstract** or symbolic representations, which are very difficult for children to learn. For children who are having difficulty understanding numerals, show them many examples of object, number, and related numerals. Many counting books do this.

Most cultures throughout history have expressed numerical quantities with oral names as well as with written symbols. When children are first learning numerals, it can be helpful for them to learn about the numerals used by other cultures. One example comes from ancient China. Although the Chinese had four different ways of representing numerals, they are best known for their counting rod numerals, which look very much like the tally marks made by young children (see *Multicultural Perspectives in Mathematics*).

Kindergarten children should be able to write numerals from 1 to 10 and connect the numerals with oral names for numbers and physical quantities (**Activity 7.6**). First-graders should be able to do this for numbers from 1 to 100. Teachers need to reinforce these connections by asking children to represent quantities in three ways: by number name, physical representation, and numeral. The children's book *Anno's Counting Book* (see *Children's Literature*, **Figure 7.6**) accomplishes this in an entertaining and clever way.

Activity 7.6 The matching game

Instructions

1. Prepare three sets of index cards in three categories.

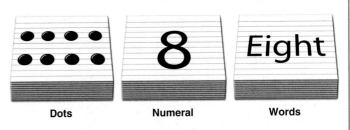

| Dots | Numeral | Words |

2. Set up three stations in the classroom, one for each category, and have a stack of index cards that demonstrate the category at each station.

3. Ask children to pick an index card from one station and match it up with the appropriate index card from the other two stations.

4. Have children paste their three representations of a given number on a piece of paper and mount this on the wall.

Counting On, Counting Back, and Skip Counting

Children in kindergarten practice combining two small collections as a precursor to addition. Suppose a child is

Education InSight

Counting on and counting back • Figure 7.7

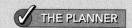

The daily activities of the classroom provide many opportunities to develop counting on and counting back. As children discover these strategies, you can encourage their mathematical understanding by asking questions about routine occurrences.

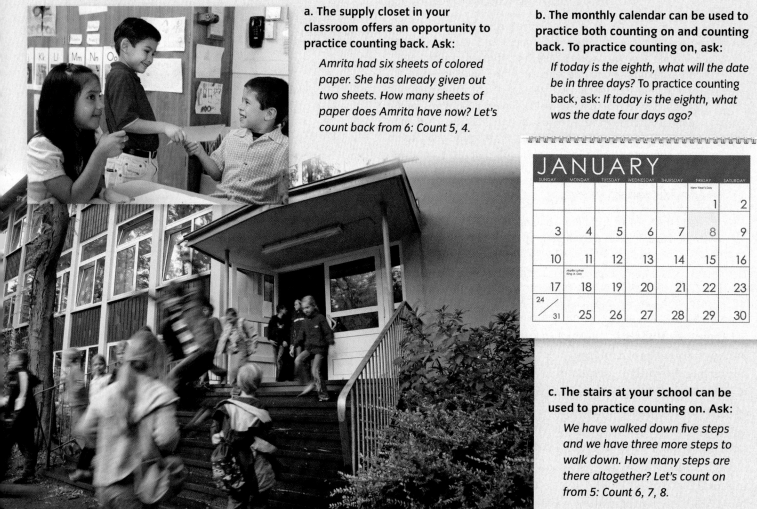

a. The supply closet in your classroom offers an opportunity to practice counting back. Ask:

Amrita had six sheets of colored paper. She has already given out two sheets. How many sheets of paper does Amrita have now? Let's count back from 6: Count 5, 4.

b. The monthly calendar can be used to practice both counting on and counting back. To practice counting on, ask:

If today is the eighth, what will the date be in three days? To practice counting back, ask: If today is the eighth, what was the date four days ago?

c. The stairs at your school can be used to practice counting on. Ask:

We have walked down five steps and we have three more steps to walk down. How many steps are there altogether? Let's count on from 5: Count 6, 7, 8.

combining a collection of four crayons with a collection of three crayons. One way to find *How many?* is to count the first collection of four crayons, count the second collection of three crayons, then put the collections together and count the total collection of seven crayons.

A more efficient method of finding out *How many?* is to use the **counting on** strategy, where counting can start at either number and proceed by counting forward by ones. To solve the crayon problem by counting on, a child would think or say, *I start with 4 and counting on from the 4, I count 5, 6, 7.* Children discover this strategy from their experiences with counting in school and in their everyday lives. Fosnot and Dolk (2001) have called this a "landmark" strategy for children to learn because it is a precursor to addition and place value.

In **counting back**, the child starts at a number and counts back by ones. Instead of teaching these as rote procedures, teachers should provide activities that help children discover these strategies on their own. Some examples from the classroom are illustrated in **Figure 7.7**.

There are many children's books that can also provide experiences in counting on and counting back (see *Children's Literature*, **Figure 7.8**).

Skip counting, the process of starting at any point and counting by twos, fives, tens, or some other number, is an important strategy that increases efficiency in counting and helps develop skills that will be useful in learning addition and multiplication. Children can practice skip counting by using the automatic-constant feature on a calculator (**Activity 7.7**). As children skip count with the calculator, ask them to count out loud while they watch the display on the calculator change. Children also enjoy skip counting to books, songs, rhymes, and hand-clapping (see *Children's Literature*, **Figure 7.9**). A clock is a useful real-life tool for skip counting. You can use it to count in groups of 5, 10, or 15 minutes. Money is another helpful tool. To count a collection of nickels, count by fives, and to count a collection of dimes, count by tens.

> ### Activity 7.7 Patterns with numbers
>
> **Instructions**
>
> 1. Ask children to clear their calculators and press ⊞ 5 ⊟. The number 5 should appear.
> 2. Ask them to press the equal key three more times. What numbers appear?
> 3. Clear the calculators and try again with other numbers.

CHILDREN'S LITERATURE

Practicing the counting back strategy

Five Little Monkeys Jumping on the Bed • Figure 7.8

Written and illustrated by Eileen Christelow
Five Little Monkeys Jumping on the Bed is a silly and entertaining tale of five monkeys who jump on their bed and, one by one, hurt their heads. Through its rhyming verse, this book shows counting back to young children in an understandable and easily accessible manner.

Strategies for the Classroom

- As you read the book with children, practice counting back to find out how many monkeys are on the bed.
- After reading the book, change the numbers and tell the story again with new numbers, again practicing counting back.

Practicing skip counting

Two Ways to Count to Ten • Figure 7.9

Written by Ruby Dee
Illustrated by Susan Meddaugh
In this retelling of a Liberian legend, King Leopard looks for a successor to his throne and a husband for his daughter. To find the best candidate, he challenges the animals of the forest to throw up his spear and count to 10 before the spear drops to the ground. Many animals try and fail, but the antelope throws up the spear and counts 2, 4, 6, 8, 10, thus winning the contest. What mathematics concepts are illustrated by this story?

Strategy for the Classroom

- Tell the story again with different numbers such as 6, 8, 12, and 15. Ask children how many ways there are to count to each of these numbers.

www.mathwire.com

The **Snowman Skip Counting** activity provides students with practice in skip counting by fives. Students fill in the missing multiples of 5 on Frosty's path to the igloo.

Cardinal, Ordinal, and Nominal Numbers

Adults understand the different meanings of number words and can shift between them as needed. As children become more familiar with numbers and counting in their everyday lives, they gradually recognize three uses of numbers: **cardinal**, **ordinal**, and **nominal numbers**. Children who are meaningful counters will already be familiar with cardinal numbers, which answer the question, *how many?* A cardinal number is the last number counted in a collection of objects.

Children also have many opportunities to use ordinal numbers, which answer the question, *which one?* and indicate the relative position of one member of a collection in relation to other members. As an example, if children are lined up to go to lunch and the teacher asks the first person in line to open the door and the tenth person to close the door, this is an ordinal use of numbers (*first, tenth*). Ordinal numbers can be emphasized by using rhymes and children's literature. The children's story described in **Activity 7.8** encourages children to explore words such as *first, second,* and *third*.

By the time children begin school, they have already been exposed to nominal numbers, which are numbers used for identification. Phone numbers, room numbers, and addresses all represent nominal numbers.

You can encourage children to explore these three meanings of number words by using them in contexts that are familiar to them. For example, you might create groups of three children each, note that the library is in room number 22, or ask the fourth person in each row to distribute the morning snacks. Although it is not necessary or recommended that children learn the terms *cardinal, ordinal,* and *nominal,* it is important for them to be familiar with and have extensive practice with the different uses of numbers.

Activity 7.8 Learning ordinal numbers with children's literature

Instructions

Read the book *Make Way for Ducklings* (McCloskey, 1941) with your class. After you read the book, ask questions such as:

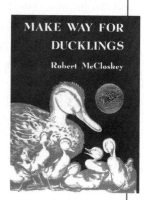

1. *What happened first in the story?*
2. *Which duckling hatched first?*
3. *Who hatches next after the second duckling?*
4. *Which duckling hatched third?* If necessary, reread passages of the story when students are answering the questions.

(*Source*: Adapted from Cavanaugh et al., 2004)

CONCEPT CHECK STOP

1. **What** are the four characteristics of meaningful counting?

2. **Why** is it important for children to have many opportunities to count things?

3. **Which** children's books that you read about in this section can help children learn how to skip count and count back?

4. **What** types of activities can help children understand the difference between cardinal, ordinal, and nominal numbers?

Number Sense

LEARNING OBJECTIVES

1. **Construct** a definition of number sense in the early grades.
2. **Identify** ways to help children find meaning for numbers.
3. **Describe** how knowledge of number systems from other cultures can enhance children's number sense.

What do we mean by number sense? Number sense is really an intuitive sense about numbers and their relationships to each other and the real world that develops gradually over time. The concept of number sense is fluid rather than static. It is something we refine throughout our lives, as our experiences with numbers in different contexts grow. We will revisit this topic in future chapters as we discuss other kinds of numbers.

Early Number Sense

In the primary grades, children with number sense understand the size of numbers, how numbers relate to one another, and how numbers provide us with meaningful information about the world outside the classroom. Children should have multiple experiences modeling the numbers 1 through 10, so that they develop meaning for these quantities, learn to decompose them into parts, and construct meaning for specific quantities (see *In the Classroom*).

In the Classroom
Developing "Five-Ness" in the Classroom  THE PLANNER

At the beginning of the school year, kindergarten teacher Janice Novakowski asked her students to tell her everything they knew about five. Many of them knew that they were five years old. Thus began her students' semester-long investigation of "five-ness." Ms. Novakowski next asked her students to make five in as many ways as possible with snap cubes and to read their combinations aloud. Some students modeled five as *3 and 2, 2 and 2 and 1*, or *1 and 2 and 2*. They put the snap cubes on their fingers or made towers out of them and compared the patterns. The children also made combinations of five with popsicle sticks. Each time they created combinations of five with cubes or sticks, they discussed whether the patterns were unique or the same. Their investigation of five was enriched with songs, stories, and children's literature such as *Five Little Monkeys Jumping on the Bed*.

The children benefited a great deal from the ongoing investigation of "five-ness." They discovered that they could imagine five mentally and decompose it into parts (such as *3 and 2* or *3 and 1 and 1*). Ms. Novakowski also discovered other benefits from her students' investigations. They were better able to subitize small groups within a set of five objects, rather than counting them individually. As students became more familiar with five, they increased their number sense about an important benchmark in mathematics.

(*Source*: Novakowski, 2007, pp. 228–230)

Think Critically
1. Why do you think Ms. Novakowski selected the number five for her activity?
2. Why is five an important number for children to understand?
3. Why is it important for children to learn to mentally decompose five into parts?

All these people live in the same country in East Africa— Kamba, Taita, Maasai. They all live in Kenya. Yet they all have different ways of showing eight on their fingers.

Count on Your Fingers African Style, written by Claudia Zaslavsky and illustrated by Wangechi Mutu

GRADE LEVEL
Pre-K–2

OBJECTIVES

Students will learn finger counting techniques from Africa.

Students will enhance their number sense about the meaning of numbers.

Students will learn pattern recognition using finger counting.

Students will enhance their knowledge of the number benchmarks of 5 and 10.

Students will learn about the mathematics of cultures.

Finger counting flourished in many civilizations around the world and was particularly useful when groups of people who spoke different languages interacted with one another or when people did not have written symbols in their language for numerical quantities.

STANDARDS

Instructional programs from prekindergarten through grade 12 should enable all students to understand numbers, ways of representing numbers, relationships among numbers, and number systems. (NCTM, 2000 p. 78)

Kindergarten

Understand the relationship between numbers and quantities; connect counting to cardinality.

- When counting objects, say the number names in the standard order, pairing each object with one and only one number name and each number name with one and only one object. (NGA Center/CCSSO, 2010)

MATERIALS

- *Count on Your Fingers African Style,* written by Claudia Zaslavsky and illustrated by Wangechi Mutu

- (Optional) Blackline master with sketches of finger counting techniques for the Indians of the Great Plains, one copy of each per student

- Paper and pencils

Learning Number Sense from Other Cultures

Teachers can help children enhance their number sense by teaching them how different cultures express and communicate numerical quantities. As children learn how people of diverse cultures have used numbers in their daily lives, they understand how numbers facilitate communication and how numbers can be used to make sense of their own lives outside the classroom.

When children use all of their senses to learn about numbers, they can learn more effectively (Zaslavsky, 2001). For example, when children practice different methods of finger counting from African and American Indian traditions, they use their kinesthetic sense to gain tactile experiences by actually feeling the quantities their

ASSESSMENT

- Observe children as they make the finger gestures to represent the numbers in the book.

- Observe whether children can extend the finger counting patterns to numbers not described in the book.

- When children create their own systems, notice whether finger counting systems demonstrate consistent patterns and make sense.

GROUPING

Whole class, then pairs

Launch (5 to 10 minutes)

Ask:

- *Have you ever gone to a farmer's market with your parents? What kinds of things can you buy there?*

- *What do you think would happen if you went to a farmer's market where no one spoke English? How could you get what you wanted?*

There are many cultures around the world where people speak different languages but still trade with one another. They use a system of finger counting to show how many they want. The American Indians of the Great Plains invented a system of finger counting. Many cultures in Africa invented finger counting too.

Instruct (30 to 35 minutes)

- Say: *We are going to read the book* Count on Your Fingers African Style. *The book tells the story of a young girl in a marketplace in East Africa who wants to buy three oranges.*

She speaks only English and does not know how to communicate to the vendor. She signals that she wants "three" by holding up three fingers and then points to the oranges. She then watches other people use their own forms of finger gestures to indicate the numbers of fruit they want to buy.

- Next, read the book *Count on Your Fingers African Style* with the class. As you read the book, show the illustrations of finger counting and ask the class to model the finger gestures illustrated in the book while describing them verbally and stating the number they represent.

- Ask questions as you read, such as *Let's make the Kamba gesture for three. What is another way to show three? How do you think the Kamba people would show four? Now let's make the Kamba gesture for eight. What is another way to show eight? How do you think the Kamba people would show nine?*

- Ask children to work in pairs and invent their own finger counting system for the numbers 1 through 10 and record their gestures by making drawings.

- Bring the class together again and ask children to show how individual numbers, such as 3, 4, 5, or 6, were represented by different children.

Summarize (5 to 10 minutes)

- Ask: *What do you like best about finger counting? What part is hard?*

- Ask: *Would it be hard to use finger counting all the time instead of writing numbers?*

- Ask: *Who has the best finger counting system? Why do you think that?*

---

fingers represent. The *Lesson* employs the art of counting on one's fingers. The standards used in this lesson are from the Number and Operations Standard from *Principles and Standards for School Mathematics* (2000, p. 78) and from the *Counting and Cardinality* domain of the *Common Core State Standards* (NGA Center/CCSSO, 2010).

| CONCEPT CHECK | STOP |

1. **What** are three characteristics of children's early number sense?

2. **How** might you help children find meaning for the number 4?

3. **How** can knowledge of the ways in which other cultures use numbers improve children's number sense?

Numbers 1 Through 10

LEARNING OBJECTIVES

1. **Describe** the importance of ordering relationships.
2. **Explain** why the numbers 5 and 10 are important benchmarks for children.

Once children are considered rational counters and have developed meanings for the numbers from 1 to 10, it is time for them to develop relationships between the numbers from 1 to 10 to encourage the development of children's number sense. This includes focusing on ordering numbers and using benchmarks with which to compare numbers. These two ideas are developed in this section.

Ordering Relationships

Given a number, children should understand how to relate that number to others between 1 and 10. Focus attention on the *one more than, two more than, one less than,* and *two less than* relationships. Children should be able to express these relationships both orally and visually (**Activity 7.9**).

Activity 7.9 Tell me all about it

Instructions

1. Place slips of paper marked with the numerals 1 to 10 in a paper bag.

2. As children select a number from the bag, prompt them to "tell me all about it." For example, if a child selects 4, he might say, *one more than four is five, two more than four is six, one less than four is three,* and *two less than four is two.*

3. After children finish their turn, ask: *Is that all you know about it? Can anyone tell us more?*

The Benchmarks of 5 and 10

By the time children begin school, they usually understand that 10 is an important number. In our number system, 5 and 10 are special numbers because two 5s are 10 and our place value system is based on powers of 10. It is important for children to recognize how other numbers relate to 5 and 10 so that these numbers can provide **benchmarks** or anchors. Children can represent numbers 5 and under with a five-frame, which is a 1 × 5 array (**Activity 7.10**).

Activity 7.10 Guess my number

Instructions

1. Show students several examples of numbers on five-frames, either on cardboard, large index cards, or the overhead projector.

2. Ask students to guess the number and describe as many ordering relationships as possible for the numbers from 1 to 5. For example, when 3 is shown, a child might answer, *Three and two more make five, Three is one more than two,* or *Three and one make four.*

Students can use the numbers represented on these five-frames to describe ordering relationships. Can you describe an ordering relationship for each of these examples?

Numbers greater than 5 can be represented with a ten-frame, which is a 2 × 5 array. By representing numbers in such a way, children can understand how individual numbers compare to 10. For example, children should be able to express 8 on a ten-frame and understand that 8 is 2 less than 10 or that 8 and 2 more is 10 (**Activity 7.11**).

Activity 7.11 Make your own

Instructions

1. Call out a number from 1 to 10 or show the number written as a numeral.

2. Ask children to represent that number on a ten-frame in as many ways as possible.

3. Compare results with others in the class and encourage children to explain their thinking.

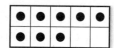 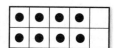

Two ways of displaying 8 on a ten-frame.

Teaching Tip

Displaying numbers on five-frames and ten-frames

Give students lots of practice displaying numbers on five-frames and ten-frames. This practice will help them understand how to decompose numbers, which will be necessary for addition and subtraction later on.

Tech Tools

illuminations.nctm.org

The *NCTM Illuminations* Web site has a virtual **Five-Frame** activity in which the user plays games, including identify-ing how many colored circles are on a five-frame, building a certain number of circles on the five-frame, and finding out how many more circles are needed to fill the five-frame.

CONCEPT CHECK STOP

1. **How** can we help children learn the ordering relationships of *more than* and *less than* for the numbers from 1 to 10?
2. **How** can we teach children to relate other numbers to 5 and 10?

Numbers 10 Through 20 and Beyond

LEARNING OBJECTIVES

1. **Identify** the difficulties children have in learning number names for numbers from 10 to 20.
2. **Identify** the difficulties children have in learning decade names.
3. **Explain** how we can help first graders understand the concept of 100.

C hildren in the early grades will have some exposure in their daily lives to numbers between 10 and 20 and beyond (**Figure 7.10**). These numbers also appear naturally in counting activities as children count on or find *one more than* or *two more than*. Even though children are familiar with these numbers, they cannot easily extend the number

Numbers between 10 and 20 in our daily experiences • Figure 7.10

Young children have many experiences with numbers between 10 and 20 and beyond in their daily lives. Look around your classroom and see examples of objects that, when counted, are between 10 and 20. Ask students to count these and also to bring in examples from home.

sense they gained about numbers from 1 to 10 to numbers from 10 to 20 and beyond. It is premature, at this stage, to expect children to understand **place value** (the concept of one 10 representing 10 ones, and so on).

Number Names for Numbers from 10 to 20

The English-language names for numbers from 10 to 20 are difficult for children to learn. One reason may be the incongruity between the number name and the quantity it represents. For example, the number name *eleven* does not reflect its meaning of 10 and 1, does not use either the word *ten* or the word *one*, and does not sound like *10 and 1*. Similarly, the number name *thirteen* does not reflect its meaning of 10 and 3. In fact, none of the names from 10 to 20 do this. American children have to learn new words for these quantities, words that have no similarity to the number words they learned previously. This is also true for languages such as Spanish, French, and Italian.

In contrast, in Asian languages, specifically Chinese, Japanese, and Korean, the number names for numbers from 10 to 20 precisely describe the quantity that the number name represents and use the same words that were used for the numbers from 1 to 10 (Miura and Okamoto, 1999). For example, the Chinese word for 11 is *shi-yi*, which literally means "ten and one" or "ten one." Each of the number names through 19 follow this same pattern.

The number 20 is literally "two ten." The Japanese and Korean languages have similar patterns. Number words for different languages are compared in **Table 7.1**. Notice how the number words in Chinese for numbers greater than 10 are created. What would the word for 11 be in English if the same pattern were followed?

Research shows that American preschoolers make more errors in number naming than their Chinese counterparts. By recognizing the problem, teachers can help children develop meaning for these number names through activities with ten-frames (**Activity 7.12**). To increase children's number sense of the numbers from 10 to 20, have them practice the same types of comparison activities they did with numbers from 1 to 10. For example, they can find *one more than, two more than, one less than*, and *two less than* relationships with these numbers.

Activity 7.12 Tweens time

Instructions

1. Provide each child with two ten-frames and a pile of counters.
2. Choose a number between 10 and 20—say, 14.
3. Ask children to count out 14 counters.
4. Next ask children to put their counters on their ten-frames, first filling up one ten-frame and putting the excess counters on the second ten-frame.
5. Ask how many counters are on the first ten-frame (10) and how many counters are on the second ten-frame (4).

Number words	Table 7.1		
Number	**English Name**	**Spanish Name**	**Chinese Name**
1	one	uno	yi
2	two	dos	er
3	three	tres	san
4	four	cuatro	si
5	five	cinco	zwu
6	six	seis	liu
7	seven	siete	qu
8	eight	ocho	ba
9	nine	nueve	jiu
10	ten	diez	shi
11	eleven	once	shi-yi
12	twelve	doce	shi-er
20	twenty	veinte	er-shi

6. Ask how many counters there are in all. Children may have to recount all the counters before answering (14).

7. Finally, say as a group, *Ten and four is fourteen*. Repeat with other numbers between 10 and 20.

Two ten-frames show 10 and 4.

Numbers Beyond 20

By the end of second grade, children are expected to count meaningfully to 100. To focus importance on the quantity 100, many schools have begun to celebrate the 100th day of school with activities for all grade levels. Although conceptualizing 100 is very difficult for pre-kindergarten and kindergarten children, first graders can participate in activities that celebrate 100. You might ask children to bring in 100 of something to share with the class or 100 items of food to eat. They can also visualize 100 of something by taking 100 steps or modeling how far a distance 100 children would cover if they were lying down end to end. An effective strategy is to pair first graders with older children who can help keep track of their counting (Thomas, 2000).

Children often have difficulty learning number names for the decade numbers from 20 to 100 because the number names do not sound like the quantities they represent or follow an easily identifiable pattern. For example, *thirty* does not sound like *three tens* and *fifty* does not sound like *five tens*. An added difficulty is that decade names and teen names sometimes sound alike to children (Fuson, 2003). For example, they may have difficulty hearing the difference between *thirteen* and *thirty* or *fourteen* and *forty*. This is especially problematic for ELLs. One way to help children learn the words for decades is to link decade names to the numbers that come before them. That is, link 29 to 30 and 39 to 40. Another way to help children learn these words is to find visual cues with which they are familiar (**Figure 7.11**).

Teaching Tip

Understanding decade names

Help children understand decades by identifying a pattern in the names. Link two with twenty, three with thirty, and four with forty, then ask children to identify patterns for the remaining decade names. Children tend to learn the decade names one or two at a time, rather than learning them all together.

| CONCEPT CHECK | |

1. **Why** do children have difficulty learning the words for number names between 10 and 20?

2. **Why** is it difficult for children to learn the number words for decades?

3. **What** activities can help children understand the concept of 100?

Learning the decade names • Figure 7.11

Seeing examples of the decade names in real life can help children remember them and understand the quantities they represent.

Estimating and the Reasonableness of Results

LEARNING OBJECTIVES

1. **Explain** how to help young children to develop estimation skills.

2. **Describe** how to help young children develop intuitive ideas about what is reasonable regarding numbers.

As you saw in the opening page of this chapter, young children have a difficult time estimating quantities and understanding when their results are reasonable. Estimation is a very important skill to learn. It is used in arithmetic, in problem solving, when using technology, and in many types of real-world situations. It is important that teachers work with children to improve their understanding of estimation.

Estimation in the Early Grades

Children in grades pre-K through 2 do not really understand the concept of estimation. Teachers can help them develop estimation skills by providing structured activities that focus on the concept *about*. Instead of asking children to provide a numerical estimate, begin by asking them to provide an estimate within a given range. Use the terms *more or less than, closer to*, and *about* to frame estimation questions for young children (**Figure 7.12**). For example, ask whether there are *more or less* than 10 blocks in a bucket or whether the squirrel in the tree weighs *more or less* than the bird. Using the same example, you might ask, *Is it closer to five or ten steps from the squirrel to the bird?* Show children a jar filled with snap-together cubes and ask, *Using the numbers 10, 20, or 30, about how many cubes are in this jar?* With all these activities, use numbers that make sense to children. For example, do not use numbers that are too large for children.

What Is Reasonable?

When a first-grade teacher held up a peanut butter jar filled with plastic cubes and asked her students *How many?* their responses ranged from five hundred to one million (Auriemma, 1999). These kinds of responses are typical for young children. The teacher's job is to help students understand which numbers represent reasonable

Early estimation experiences • Figure 7.12

To promote the development of estimation skills in the early grades, ask children questions such as, *About how many jelly beans are in the jar? Is it closer to 50 or closer to 100?*

What is reasonable? • Figure 7.13

Is it reasonable for this person to be 10 feet tall? Why do you think it is reasonable or unreasonable? Do you know anyone who is 10 feet tall? How tall are you? How tall is an adult you know? Is it reasonable for this house to be 5 feet wide? Is it reasonable for this car to weigh 20 pounds?

estimates of real-world situations. You can help students develop the idea of reasonable results through a number of activities, many of which have to do with measurement (**Figure 7.13**).

As children gain more experience in understanding what is reasonable, you can develop this concept further with additional activities. For example, you might provide a number, such as *20 feet*, and brainstorm with children to name as many objects as possible that are about 20 feet long. This kind of activity will provoke much discussion, as some children will immediately offer reasonable examples and some will not. Rather than telling them whether they are correct or not, help children develop number sense by asking questions such as *How can we find out whether that is reasonable?* and discussing options as a class, such as using a scale to see how much something weighs or a ruler to measure its length.

CONCEPT CHECK **STOP**

1. **Why** is it important for children to learn estimation skills?

2. **How** can teachers help children develop reasonable estimates?

Summary

 The Development of Pre-Number Concepts 166

- Children learn pre-number concepts before and while they learn to count. One of the most important pre-number concepts is **subitizing,** the ability to look at a set and instantly see how many are in the set, as illustrated.

Figure 7.1

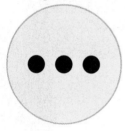

- **Classification** is another important pre-number concept. Children love to classify, and they do it naturally.

- The concepts of *more, less*, and the *same* are fundamental to the learning of mathematics. Most children understand the concept of *more* before they start school but have difficulty with *less*.

- Mathematics is the study of patterns. Numbers are composed of patterns. By teaching children to observe, identify, create, and extend patterns we help them become proficient at counting and number sense.

 Early Counting 170

- Children begin counting by counting physical objects. Initially, they do not count in an accurate sequence or understand how to establish a **one-to-one correspondence** between the objects being counted and the number words they use.

- Children make several types of mistakes as they learn to count accurately. Several criteria determine whether children are **rote** or **rational counters.** Meaningful counting consists of a combination of several skills that develop sequentially.

- **Numerals** are symbols that represent whatever is being counted and are therefore *abstract* representations, which are very difficult for children to learn.

- **Counting on**, **counting back**, and **skip counting** are efficient counting strategies that children learn gradually. Many children have an especially difficult time learning to count on and count back. Use children's everyday experiences, such as the one in this photo, to help them learn these strategies.

Figure 7.7

- Children should learn three uses of numbers. **Ordinal numbers** tell what order, **nominal numbers** are used for naming, and **cardinal numbers** tell how many.

 Number Sense 177

- Number sense is an intuitive understanding about numbers and how they relate to one another and our everyday lives. Number sense is a continuous rather than discrete concept.

- We can help children develop number sense by teaching them how different cultures around the world use numbers. This page from *Count on Your Fingers African Style* illustrates finger counting.

Lesson

4 Numbers 1 Through 10 180

- Once children are meaningful counters, it is important that they learn about the numbers 1 through 10 and how these numbers relate to one another. For example, they should learn ordering relationships and understand that 4 is 1 more than 3, 5 is 2 more than 3, 2 is 1 less than 3, and 1 is 2 less than 3. Five-frames, illustrated here, are very helpful.

Activity 7.10

  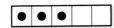

- Children should also understand that 10 is a special number in our number system and that 5 and 10 are important benchmarks that we can use for comparing other numbers to them.

5 Numbers 10 Through 20 and Beyond 181

- Although children have experience with the numbers 10 through 20 in their everyday lives, they have difficulty learning the number words for these numbers because of the words used in the English language for these quantities. The number names for numbers between 10 and 20 do not reflect the meaning of these numbers. This is not so in some other languages, especially those languages derived from Chinese.

- Children also have difficulty learning the decade names for similar reasons. Help children learn decade names with real-world examples, as shown here. We can expect children in the first grade to understand the meaning of 100 and children in the second grade to count meaningfully to 100.

Figure 7.11

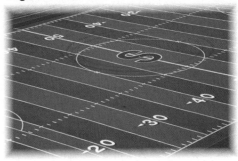

6 Estimating and the Reasonableness of Results 184

- Young children in grades pre-K through 2 do not understand the concept of estimation. We can help them develop estimation skills by teaching them to understand the concept *about*.

- We can also help students learn which numbers are reasonable for different real-world situations by providing children with numerous structured activities, for example, whether it is reasonable for this house to be 5 feet wide.

Figure 7.13

Key Terms

Additional Children's Literature

- *Sea Squares*, written by Joy N. Hulme and illustrated by Carol Schwartz.
  This counting book is about sea creatures. It not only counts from 1 to 10 but also counts the squares of each of the numbers.

- *Uno, Dos, Tres: One, Two, Three*, written by Pat Mora and illustrated by Barbara Lavalee.
  A young girl goes to the market to shop for Moma's birthday. Includes wonderful illustrations of the folk art of Mexico as well as bilingual counting.

- *Moja Means One*, written by Muriel Feelings and illustrated by Tom Feelings.
  The numbers from one to ten are written and pronounced in English and Swahili with illustrations from Africa that represent the value of each numeral.

- *Rooster's Off to See the World*, written and illustrated by Eric Carle.
  A rooster sets off to see the world. On his way, he meets other animals that want to go along, including two cats, three frogs, four turtles, and five fish. As night falls, the animals want to go home.

- *Anno's Counting House*, written and illustrated by Mitsumasa Anno.
  Ten children move from one house to another, one at a time. As the children move, they bring their possessions along with them. This is a wonderful way to illustrate counting back or counting on by ones.

Online Resources

- **NCTM Illuminations**
  illuminations.nctm.org/

  1. Select **Activities** and grade range **K–2**. The **Ten-frame** applet contains activities that use the ten-frame to learn number facts. The user identifies how many squares of the ten-frame are empty, builds a ten-frame with a certain number of items, and finds out how many more items are needed to complete the ten-frame.

  2. Select **Activities** and grade range **K–2**. The **Bobbie Bear** applet lets children use counting strategies to make outfits for Bobbie Bear.

  3. Select **Lessons, Number and Operations Standard**, and grade range **K–2**. The **Let's Count to 10** unit consists of eight lessons that help students make groups of objects and use both numerals and number names to connect to the group of objects. The **Here's a Handful** lesson asks students to build sets of five objects and identify the set with a numeral and the word *five*.

- **ABC Count Us In**
  www.abc.net.au/countusin/

  This site contains 15 interactive games and activities designed to develop the concept of number. For each game, the user can choose an easy game or a hard one. For example, in one game the user drags items in a room from a bookshelf to make patterns. The easy game has only a few items on the bookshelf, whereas the hard game has lots of items from which to choose.

- **MathWire**
  www.mathwire.com

  This is an easy-to-navigate site with interactive and downloadable activities on standards-based mathematics topics. It has many fun activities for counting and number sense. Some activities related to counting are based on children's literature.

Critical and Creative Thinking Questions

1. How can teachers of kindergarten through second grade emphasize the importance of counting to students, parents, and administrators?

2. What is number sense? How does it change as children mature?

3. **In the field**   During a classroom observation or with young children that you know, observe how they count. What strategies do they use? What errors do they make?

4. Describe an activity you could develop to help children refine their counting skills.

5. **Using visuals**   Describe an activity that can help children learn to connect number words with numerals and physical representations of number.

6. Find a children's book that will help teach children to estimate what is reasonable. What are two or three questions you can ask about the content of this book that will help children to develop estimation skills?

What is happening in this picture?

Seeing a movie at a multiple-screen theater is a common experience for most children. This experience offers opportunities for children to experience pre-number concepts and counting.

Think Critically

1. What questions can you ask about the movie theater and classification?
2. How can the movie theatre offer children opportunities to count meaningfully?
3. What are some examples of one-to-one correspondence?
4. How can the movie theater help children with estimation and finding out what is reasonable?

Self-Test

(Check your answers in Appendix D.)

1. Which of the following is not a pre-number concept?
   a. subitizing
   b. classification
   c. patterns
   d. counting on

2. Which type of subitizing is represented by this figure? Briefly explain why subitizing is an important skill for children to learn.

3. Briefly explain what is meant by one-to-one correspondence with regard to counting.

4. Explain the difference between rote counting and rational counting.

5. Give an example of a cardinal number, an ordinal number, and a nominal number.

6. Explain how counting on and counting back prepare children to learn whole number addition and subtraction.

7. What relationships can students learn from this five-frame example? Describe how students can use five-frames and ten-frames to develop relationships between the numbers from 1 to 10.

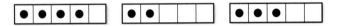

8. How do the English and Chinese number words for numbers between 10 and 20 differ?

9. How can children learn decade names meaningfully?

10. Explain how examples of numbers from other cultures can help children gain number sense.

11. Describe an activity that can help children learn the decade names.

12. Describe an activity that can help young children develop estimation skills.

13. Demonstrate how the Kamba would finger count the number six.

14. Write the numbers 437 and 2309 each as Chinese rod numerals.

15. If you show young children a box of 25 calculators, what questions can you ask to help them develop early estimation skills without asking them to give a numerical estimate?

Place Value

Both the ancient Mayans and the first computers built in the 1940s harnessed the power of place value to meet their needs.

What does ancient Mayan civilization have in common with modern computers? The Mayans, whose civilization flourished from about 250 C.E. to 900 C.E., lived in what is now Guatemala and Mexico. They developed a complex numeration system capable of writing very large numbers with just three different symbols. The Mayans used their number system to create calendars and make astronomical predictions that have proved accurate even today. Descendants of the ancient Mayans still live in Central America and use the calendars first developed by their ancestors.

The first programmable, digital, electronic computers, built in the 1940s to decode encrypted messages during World War II, used binary (base-two) systems. These early computers were programmed by turning on and off a series of switches (inset). Since the switches could only be flipped to the on or off positions, only two digits (0 and 1) were required to record the series of steps needed to program the computers.

Both the Mayan numeration system and modern computers illustrate the use of place value with different number bases. When we first teach children about place value, it is best to begin with base ten because place value is such a difficult concept for children to learn. Once children fully understand place value, it can be interesting for them to explore other number bases to reinforce the meaning and structure of our own number system and arouse their curiosity about mathematics and its place in the world.

CHAPTER OUTLINE

What Is Place Value?   192

Key Question: What are the characteristics of place value systems?

How Do Children Learn Place Value?   194

Key Question: Why is it important for children to find equivalent representations by composing and decomposing numbers when learning place value?

Teaching Place Value Concepts   198

Key Question: How can models and technology facilitate children's understanding of place value?

Extending Place Value   206

Key Question: How can we help children understand very large numbers?

NCTM The NCTM Number and Operations Standard includes several expectations for place value. In prekindergarten through grade 2 all students should

- use multiple models to develop initial understandings of place value and the base-ten number system;

- develop a sense of whole numbers and represent and use them in flexible ways, including relating, composing, and decomposing numbers;

- connect number words and numerals to the quantities they represent using various models and representations.   (NCTM, 2000, p. 78)

In grades 3–5 all students should

- recognize equivalent representations for the same number and generate them by decomposing and composing numbers.   (NCTM, 2000, p. 148)

What Is Place Value?

LEARNING OBJECTIVES

1. **Describe** the characteristics shared by all place value systems.
2. **Identify** the characteristics of the Hindu-Arabic numeration system.

An understanding of **place value** is fundamental for children. In the primary grades, children need knowledge of place value to understand the relative size of numbers and to learn **computational algorithms,** or procedures, for addition, subtraction, multiplication, and division of whole numbers. In the later elementary grades, children apply their understanding of place value to learn about decimal fractions.

> **place value** The position of a digit to represent its value.

Characteristics of Place Value Systems

> **base** The size of the group being counted.

Every place value system has a **base** and grouping rules that are unique to that system. Place value permits us to express very large quantities with a limited number of symbols. For example, in the Mayan system discussed in the opening of this chapter, place value is illustrated by vertical levels, with most levels representing groups of 20 (**Figure 8.1**). The binary system, often used in computer technology, uses groups of two. One of the earliest place value systems in recorded history was developed by the Sumerians, who lived about 5,000 years ago in what is now Iraq. Their numeration system used groups of 10 and 60. Whatever place value system you use, two rules seem to be universal. Let's illustrate them with base ten.

1. Once you acquire 10 ones you trade them for one ten. This is known as **explicit trading**. When you acquire 10 tens, you trade them for one hundred, and so on. You can trade in either direction, and it is a good idea to practice this, because trading in both directions is necessary for many arithmetic computations.

2. The position of the digit indicates the number being represented. For example, although the numbers 317 and 731 use the same digits, these numbers have different values based on the position of their digits.

The Hindu-Arabic System

Although we consider the **Hindu-Arabic numeration system** to be "our" number system, it was probably developed in India as early as 900 C.E., then modified and

> **Hindu-Arabic numeration system** A positional decimal numeral system.

The Mayan system of counting • Figure 8.1

The Mayans used three symbols: a dot, a horizontal line, and a symbol for zero, often referred to as an eye. These symbols were assembled in vertical levels. The Mayan place value system used a base of 20, with one exception. At the third level, which should have represented groups of 20 x 20 or 400, they used 20 x 18, possibly because they considered 360 to be a special number.

Multicultural Perspectives in Mathematics

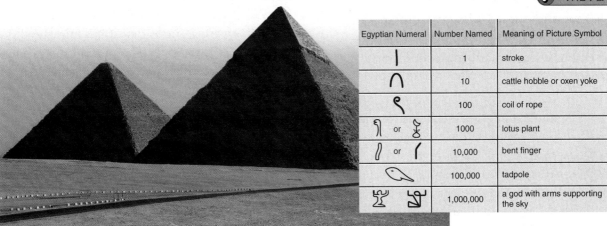

Egyptian Numeral	Number Named	Meaning of Picture Symbol
I	1	stroke
∩	10	cattle hobble or oxen yoke
?	100	coil of rope
? or ?	1000	lotus plant
? or ?	10,000	bent finger
?	100,000	tadpole
? ?	1,000,000	a god with arms supporting the sky

The Egyptian Numeration System

About 5000 years ago, Egypt became a powerful empire. The Ancient Egyptians carved their history on the walls of their temples and the tombs of their kings or pharaohs, using picture symbols known as hieroglyphs. These hieroglyphs also illustrated their numeration system. The Egyptian numeration system was an additive system that used a base of 10. It had individual symbols for 1 and the multiples of 10 up to 1,000,000. This system was very advanced for its time, but it was cumbersome to use because it had no mechanism for place value. For example, to express the quantity 70 or 7 tens you would have to write the symbol for 10 seven times. To express the quantity 973 you would have to write the symbol for 100 nine times, the symbol for 10 seven times, and the symbol for 1 three times.

Another problem with this system was that no order was specified for writing the numbers. In our system, we write our numerals left to right, with the digit representing the largest place to the left and the smallest to the right. However, no such ordering convention existed for Egyptian numerals, which easily could have led to confusion.

70 = ∩∩∩∩∩∩∩

973 = III∩∩∩∩∩∩∩?????????

Strategies for the Classroom

• How can learning about the Egyptian numeration system help your students appreciate the characteristics of the Hindu-Arabic system?

• How can learning about the Egyptian numeration system help your students learn place value?

---

spread to the Western world by Arabic mathematicians. This numeration system is used throughout the United States, Europe, and parts of Asia and Africa. The Hindu-Arabic system has four characteristics:

1. It is a decimal system that uses the ten digits 0, 1, 2, 3, 4, 5, 6, 7, 8, 9.

2. It has place value with a base of 10 (called a **base-ten** system).

3. It is an additive system. In other words, the total value represented by a number is determined by adding the sum of the digits with respect to their place value. For example, 263 is a symbol that represents the value $200 + 60 + 3$.

4. The symbol for zero serves as a placeholder and means the absence of something.

Place value provides the Hindu-Arabic system with incredible versatility that ancient numeration systems did not have (see *Multicultural Perspectives in Mathematics*).

CONCEPT CHECK	

1. **Why** is place value an important characteristic of all numeration systems?

2. **What** are the four characteristics of the Hindu-Arabic numeration system?

How Do Children Learn Place Value?

LEARNING OBJECTIVES

1. **Compare** and **contrast** how children count before and after learning place value.

2. **Identify** how equivalent representations of numbers help develop place value knowledge.

C hildren acquire some number sense before starting school, but they do not acquire the concept of place value on their own because this concept represents an imposed organization of numbers, not a natural one. Research (Kamii and Joseph, 1988) indicates that many third and fourth graders do not understand place value even though it has been taught to them in earlier grades. "Place value instruction cannot be hurried" (Payne, 2002, p. 106). Place value can be learned by children as early as first grade if it is introduced slowly and thoughtfully. By the end of second grade all students should understand place value for two-digit numbers.

Children's Pre–Base-Ten Ideas

Before learning place value, children naturally count by ones. They may be very capable of counting objects up to 100, but conceptually they are still counting them one at a time. Teachers can help children gradually make the transition from counting by ones to counting by grouping objects (**Figure 8.2**).

Children's pre–base-ten ideas • Figure 8.2

Before learning place value and base ten, teachers should help children progress from counting by ones to counting ungrouped and pregrouped objects.

a. Children count by ones, even when they are counting large numbers of objects. They may be able to count accurately and tell you there are 38 counters on the table, say *thirty-eight*, and write the numeral 38, without understanding place value.

b. Give children lots of practice with counting and forming groups of different sizes by counting the objects they find in their everyday lives. Ask children to count the things they see in the classroom, such as crayons, rulers, calculators, paint brushes, chairs, and desks.

c. Provide children with opportunities to count objects that are already grouped. Help children to discover these groupings and discuss their benefits.

CHILDREN'S LITERATURE

Grouping numbers by tens

"At last, we're at the picnic!
A hey and a hi dee ho!"

One Hundred Hungry Ants •
Figure 8.3

Written by Elinor Pinczes
Illustrated by Bonnie MacKain

In this charming tale, 100 hungry ants are on their way to a picnic. Because they are trying to get there before the food disappears, they try to arrange themselves in efficient groups. They find that 2 rows of 50 does not work very well. Neither does 5 rows of 20 or 4 rows of 25. Eventually they discover that 10 rows of 10 ants each is a very efficient way to travel.

Strategy for the Classroom

• Read the book with your class. *Ask: Why did the ants decide to travel in 10 rows of 10?* Explain to children that there are many ways to group numbers, but in the Hindu-Arabic system we group by 10s.

Children's literature is an effective tool for helping children learn about the importance of grouping and how to group (see *Children's Literature*, **Figure 8.3**).

You can informally assess children's initial understanding of place value with classroom activities, such as the one illustrated in **Activity 8.1**. The answers children provide can help you determine whether they have developed the concept of grouping by tens. For example, when children are asked how many chips there would be if 10 more chips are added or subtracted, if they need to recount to determine their answer, they do not understand place value.

Activity 8.1 Ten more or less

Instructions

1. Place an equal bunch of chips (between 20 and 50) on each child's desk. Ask: *How many chips are there?*

2. Give children time to count the chips, and observe whether children are grouping first and then counting the groups or counting one at a time.

3. Write each child's answer on the chalkboard. Discuss their answers and reach consensus on the number of chips.

4. Ask: *How many would there be if there were 10 more chips? How many would there be if there were 10 fewer chips?*

Children's Early Place Value Ideas

When children first learn place value they need to learn how to connect counting by ones and counting by tens. They need to realize that they will get the same answer both ways. Children should have many opportunities to practice how to find **equivalent representations** for the same

> **equivalent representations**
> A method of grouping that uses fewer than the maximum number of tens.

group of objects. The importance of these ideas cannot be overstated. Children will encounter equivalent representations again and again when they regroup for arithmetic operations. Teachers can encourage children's ability to develop equivalent representations of numbers by giving them many opportunities to **decompose** or separate numbers into component parts and **compose** or put them back together again using models (**Figure 8.4**).

Decomposing and composing numbers using models • Figure 8.4

a. Using five-frames and ten-frames
Children can use five-frames and ten-frames, which are familiar to them from counting, to compose and decompose numbers. Here the number 17 is first shown on five-frames as 5 + 5 + 5 + 2 and then shown on ten-frames as 10 + 7.

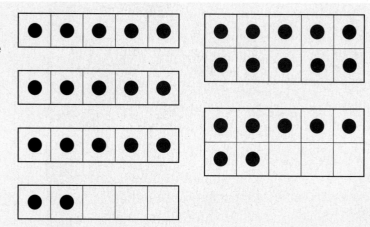

b. Using base-ten blocks
Children can practice composing and decomposing numbers with base-ten blocks. Here the number 26 is shown with base-ten blocks in three different ways: as 2 tens and 6 ones, as 1 ten and 16 ones, and as 26 ones.

c. Using metric measurement
Metric measurement lends itself to decomposing and composing numbers because it is based on groups of ten. Representing 1 meter as 100 centimeters is similar to decomposing numbers. Representing 400 centimeters as 4 meters is similar to composing numbers.

Meters	Centimeters
1	100
2	200
3	300
4	400

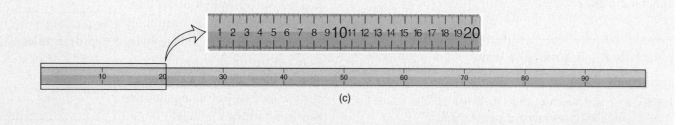

(c)

You can assess children's growing understanding of place value with activities that ask them to find equivalent representations of numbers using tens and ones. In **Activity 8.2** some children will be able to count 27 pennies in group A but not understand that the same number of pennies is represented in groups B and C without counting them individually. These children have not yet learned place value. Some children, who are making the transition to place value understanding, may be able to count two stacks of 10 pennies and 7 left over in group B but may not know the total number of pennies in group B. When children understand that groups A and B contain the same number of pennies without actually counting each penny in group B, they are developing the concept of place value. When they understand that groups B and C also contain the same number of pennies, they are demonstrating the ability to identify equivalent representations of the same quantity. This concept is very important because it is often used in computation where **regrouping** or **trading** one ten for 10 ones and one hundred for 10 tens is common.

Activity 8.2 More than one way

A   B   C

Instructions

1. Ask: *How many pennies are in group A? How do you know?*

2. Ask: *How many stacks of pennies are in group B? How many are left over? How many pennies are in group B? How can you find the answer without counting each penny? Did you get the same answer as for group A?*

3. Ask: *How many stacks of pennies are in group C? How many are left over? How can you find out without counting each penny? How can you tell this is the same number of pennies as in group B?*

Counting the days of school is an excellent way to practice decomposing numbers (see *In the Classroom*).

In the Classroom
Counting School Days

 THE PLANNER

Kasia Kidd teaches second grade at Lincoln Central Elementary School in Lincoln, Rhode Island. Each day she asks her students to count the number of days they have been in school to strengthen their place value understanding. On the seventieth day of school, her students wrote number sentences in their journals that equaled seventy. One student said "one hundred minus thirty equals seventy." Another student offered "1 + 2 + 3 + 4 + 5 + 6 + 7 + 8 + 9 + 10 + 20 − 10 + 10 − 1 − 1 − 1 − 1 − 1" as an equivalent representation for seventy. When one student suggested fifty-seven plus thirteen, Ms. Kidd focused on this representation and asked her students to explain why

| 57 | 58 |
| 67 | 68 |

fifty-seven plus thirteen equals seventy. In particular, she asked students to explain where the seven tens were. Several students explained their reasoning but seemed to stumble. Ms. Kidd supported her students' explanations by writing the numbers 57 and 67, as they would appear in the hundreds chart. This helped students verbalize that 57 plus 10 is 67 and 3 more is 70.

Activities such as this one offer children opportunities to compose and decompose numbers into component parts, and they help set the foundation for learning about place value and the base-ten structure of our number system.

(*Source*: Goodrow and Kidd, 2008)

Think Critically

1. Why did Ms. Kidd focus on the example 57 + 13 = 70?
2. How did writing the numbers as they would appear in the hundreds chart help Ms. Kidd's students understand that 57 + 13 = 70?

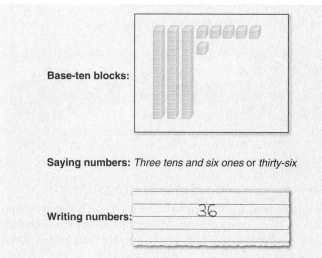

Base-ten blocks:

Saying numbers: *Three tens and six ones* or *thirty-six*

Writing numbers: 36

Saying and writing numbers using base-ten language • Figure 8.5

These types of representations help children make the transition from knowing how many groups of ten and how many ones to writing numbers in standard form with an understanding of what the number represents. When you represent groups of tens and ones with pictures or symbols, be consistent with the way you write numbers symbolically in standard form: ones to the right, tens to the left, and so on.

You can help children develop place value concepts through the language you use when saying numbers. When you say the number 36, for example, encourage children to say *three tens and six ones*, *three tens and six singles*, *three groups of ten and six ones*, or *three tens and six left over*. Use this type of oral language to name numbers throughout the second grade. It can help connect number names with the quantities they represent and solidify students' understanding of place value. In addition to saying numbers to emphasize place value, students should be aware of how to write numbers. These ideas are modeled in **Figure 8.5**.

CONCEPT CHECK	

1. **How** do children count before and after they learn place value? How can you observe children's counting and determine their place value knowledge?

2. **Why** is it important for children to understand equivalent representations of the same number and how to decompose and compose numbers?

Teaching Place Value Concepts

LEARNING OBJECTIVES

1. **Distinguish** between the two different types of place value models.
2. **Identify** the three stages of place value development.
3. **Describe** the benefits of using the hundreds chart to facilitate place value understanding.
4. **Describe** three types of difficulties that children typically face when learning place value.

The Hindu-Arabic number system, with its underlying place value structure, is so pervasive in our culture that, as adults, we take place value for granted. For children, however, place value is a new and difficult idea. It is not a developmental step that they reach. To help children understand place value, teachers use models and carefully sequenced instruction.

Models for Place Value

When teachers begin teaching children about place value they use **concrete models,** or physical models, to help them understand the connection between counting by ones and counting and grouping by tens. There are two kinds of models, **proportional models** and **nonproportional models** (**Figure 8.6**). In most cases it is best to begin with proportional models.

proportional models Models in which ten is represented as ten times as large as one, and so on.

nonproportional models Models in which there is no size relationship between the representation for one and the representation for ten.

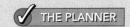
There are many concrete models for learning about place value. Some of the models shown can be handmade, and others are commercially available. All of the models fall into one of two categories.

a. PROPORTIONAL MODELS

Proportional models for place value help children understand that each ten, while an entity all by itself, is also a representation of ten units. The size of the ten is 10 times as large as the size of the one, and so on.

1. One easily constructed example of a proportional model uses straws to count ones and bundles of ten straws each to count groups of tens.

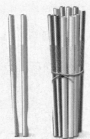

2. Another handmade model uses individual beans to count ones and beans glued to popsicle sticks, 10 to a stick, to count groups of 10.

3. Base-ten blocks are commercially available. The smallest piece, called a *unit,* represents 1. The piece that is made up of 10 units, called a *long,* represents 10, and the piece that is made of 10 longs, called a *flat,* represents 100. The piece that is made of 10 flats, called a *cube,* represents 1000.

4. *Digi-Blocks* are another commercially available proportional model. The ones, which are rectangular, pack into a holder that holds exactly 10 ones. The holder looks identical to the ones rectangular pieces but is 10 times as large. Ten of these larger rectangles pack into another rectangle, which is 10 times its size and represents 100.

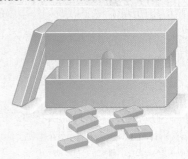

b. NONPROPORTIONAL MODELS

Nonproportional models for place value are usually employed after children have developed the basic concepts. In these models, no size relationship exists between the pieces that represent ones and the pieces that represent tens.

1. The abacus is still used in many parts of the world for calculations. The arrangement and color of the beads illustrate place value.

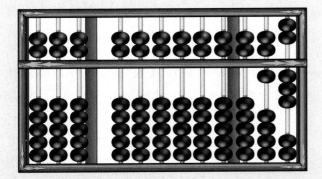

2. Money is a typical example of a nonproportional place value model. Although a quarter has the same value as 25 pennies, its size is not 25 times the size of a penny.

3. Different colored chips can also be used for place value. Here, the red chips are ones and the blue chips are tens. What number is represented by the chips?

Groupable and pregrouped base-ten models • Figure 8.7

a. Groupable models

With groupable models, children actually have the experience of making 10 from 10 ones. These models require children to think about and make sense of what they are doing.

1. The beans-and-cups model is probably the cheapest and easiest to use groupable model. Ten single beans placed in a cup represent 10. Ten cups with 10 beans in each cup placed in a box represents 100.

2. Snap-together cubes are a popular commercially available groupable model. A tower of 10 snap-together cubes represents 10. Ten towers of 10 snap-together cubes represent 100.

There are two types of proportional models, **groupable** and **pregrouped** (**Figure 8.7**).

Technology Calculators are an excellent tool for learning about place value (**Activities 8.3** and **8.4**).

Activity 8.3 Using the calculator to reinforce place value ideas

Instructions

1. Provide students with a start number and an end number. For example: Start number 45. End number 75.

2. Ask: *Use the calculator to add or subtract just one number to go from the start number to the end number. What number and operation did you use?* (Add 30.)

3. Repeat with other start and end numbers that require adding or subtracting 10 or multiples of 10.

4. Provide start and end numbers that require adding or subtracting 100 or multiples of 100. For example: Start number 56. End number 156.

5. Repeat with the same start number (56) and end numbers of 166, 256, 356, 366, and 367.

Activity 8.4 Make it zero

Instructions

1. Provide each student with a calculator. Write a number on the board—for example, 830.

2. Ask: *What can I add or subtract to this number to make the tens place zero?* (Add 70 or subtract 30.)

3. Continue with other numbers that are a bit more difficult.

4. Ask: *What can I add or subtract to 645 to make the tens place zero?* (Add 55 or subtract 45.)

Virtual manipulatives have become increasingly popular models for learning about place value. These are easy to use, especially if you can project the image on the computer monitor for the entire class to see. If you have access to several computers in your classroom, students can use these individually or in pairs.

b. Pregrouped models

With pregrouped models, children cannot take the pieces apart or put them together. Pieces are traded after 10 of one size have been accumulated. Pregrouped models are easy to use, but children may use them without really understanding what they are doing.

1. Base-ten blocks are a popular type of pregrouped model. They use units, longs, flats, and cubes to represent ones, tens, hundreds, and thousands.

2. Ten-frame cards are easily made and have many advantages. Children can visually identify how numbers are configured and the distance to 10.

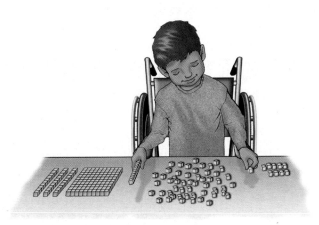

Tech Tools

> http://nlvm.usu.edu

The National Library of Virtual Manipulatives **Base Blocks** applet has the user represent numbers using base-ten blocks by clicking and dragging the blocks with a mouse.

Teaching place value to students with special needs

For children with special needs, extra care needs to be taken when selecting place value models. Proportional models such as snap-together cubes or base-ten blocks may be too abstract because they require proportional reasoning (Losq, 2005).

- Children with auditory processing difficulties may have difficulty learning the terms *units*, *longs*, and *flats* that are used with base-ten materials.

- Children with visual processing difficulties may have trouble seeing the subtle scoring on the tens and hundreds pieces of base-ten blocks.

For some children, especially those with special needs, ten-frame cards may be the best choice. This model "helps students connect each number name and the quantity it represents" (Losq, 2005, p. 310) by showing unique configurations for the numbers between 0 and 10. Ten-frame cards also help students form mental images of the numbers so that they understand, for each number, how many more are needed to get to 10.

Technology is an excellent tool for teaching place value to students with special needs. Students who are not able to physically use manipulatives may be able to use virtual manipulatives. Students who have difficulty verbalizing their answers can show them on the computer screen. Also, students who have difficulty working with others in a group may do well with computer technology.

From concrete to abstract: Teaching the three stages of place value development • Figure 8.8

To teach place value, move children through three types of representations of quantities: from concrete, to semiconcrete, and finally to symbolic or abstract. The goal is for children to ultimately use only symbolic representations, which are considered abstract. To accomplish this, switch back and forth many times between the different representations to help solidify the concept of place value. As you use each model, also use language appropriate for that model.

1 Concrete representations

Twenty-four lunch trays can be represented concretely with unifix cubes, bundled sticks, or chips. Children should understand equivalent representations (i.e., 24 can be represented by 2 tens and 4 ones or 1 ten and 14 ones). They should also understand that the most meaningful concrete representation uses the fewest number of pieces to represent each quantity. Here you might say, *two tens and four*.

3 Abstract or symbolic representations

Twenty-four lunch trays can be represented symbolically by writing the number 24. This is considered symbolic or abstract because it uses symbols or digits and place value to represent the quantity. Here you have the option of saying *two tens and four, twenty and four, or twenty-four*.

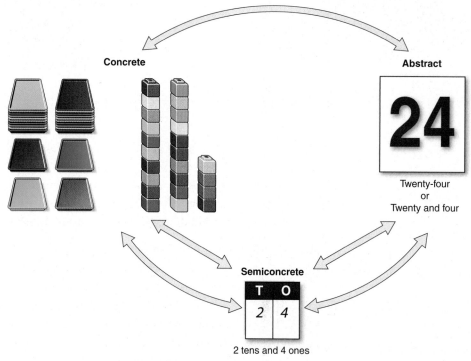

Concrete

Abstract

24

Twenty-four
or
Twenty and four

Semiconcrete

T	O
2	4

2 tens and 4 ones

2 Semiconcrete representations

Twenty-four lunch trays can be represented semiconcretely by a chart with two columns, titled tens/ones. This is known as a place value mat. In the tens column, write 2 and in the ones column write 4. Here you might say, *two tens and four ones*.

Teaching Place Value

Let's look at the step-by-step techniques with which to teach children place value. When teachers teach children place value, they carefully sequence activities so that children move from concrete representations to semiconcrete representations and finally to abstract or symbolic representations (**Figure 8.8**).

Some educators like children to organize their concrete models on **place value mats**, which are simply charts with columns. When using place value mats for this purpose, it is not necessary to use column titles (**Activity 8.5**).

Activity 8.5 Using place value mats

Instructions

1. Provide each student with a place value mat. This can be a large piece of paper with three columns. Provide each student with a set of base-ten blocks.

2. Say: *Use your base-ten blocks to represent the number 35. Use the fewest number of blocks possible.*

3. Repeat with other two-digit and three-digit numbers, making sure to ask how students know they have used the fewest blocks possible.

4. Reverse the activity by providing the base-ten blocks for a number and asking students what number is represented. For example, display two flats, three longs, and five units. Ask: *What number is this?*

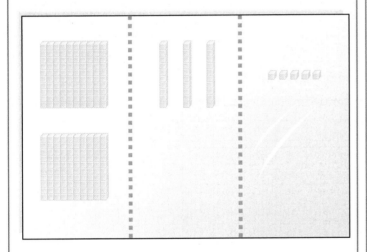

Place value mats can be used to organize concrete materials and display them in the same order as numbers, with the largest quantity to the left, and so on. What are the advantages of using a place value mat in this manner?

When children are learning place value, one of the most important skills for them to learn is how to compose and decompose numbers, especially during regrouping, the process that moves the number to the next tens or the next hundreds. Use word problems to provide children with practice in regrouping (**Activity 8.6**).

Activity 8.6 Using word problems to practice regrouping

Instructions

1. Say: *Use base-ten blocks to solve the following problem. Explain your thinking.*
   If you counted 29 paintbrushes and then found one more, how many paintbrushes would you have?

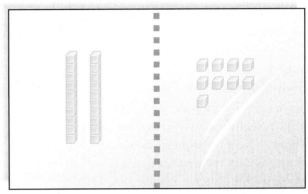

"First, I counted 2 groups of 10 and 9 ones."

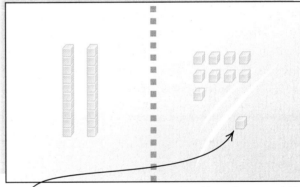

"Then I found one more paintbrush. Now I have 2 groups of 10 and 10 ones."

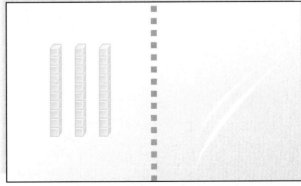

"I regrouped 10 ones into 1 ten. Now I have 3 groups of 10."

2. Next, give students the following to solve with base-ten blocks.
   If your school has 499 students and one more student enrolls, how many students are enrolled in your school?

The Hundreds Chart

The hundreds chart is a wonderful tool for examining place value. Make sure to have at least one large hundreds chart prominently placed in your classroom. It is helpful to use transparencies of the hundreds chart for whole class activities. Whenever you do so, also provide individual copies for children.

Several activities using the hundreds chart are illustrated. In **Activity 8.7**, children discover column patterns in the hundreds chart. They should recognize that each number is 10 more than the number above it and 10 less than the number below it. In **Activity 8.8**, children discover row patterns in the hundreds chart. That is, they discover that all the numbers in a given row have the same tens digit and that the number to the right of a given number is 1 more, and the number to the left of a given number is 1 less. In **Activity 8.9**, children use the patterns they learned in the previous activities to place numbers on the hundreds chart.

Activity 8.7 Patterns on the hundreds chart

1	2	3	4	5	6	7	8	9	10
11	12	13	14	15	16	17	18	19	20
21	22	23	24	25	26	27	28	29	30
31	32	33	34	35	36	37	38	39	40
41	42	43	44	45	46	47	48	49	50
51	52	53	54	55	56	57	58	59	60
61	62	63	64	65	66	67	68	69	70
71	72	73	74	75	76	77	78	79	80
81	82	83	84	85	86	87	88	89	90
91	92	93	94	95	96	97	98	99	100

Instructions

1. Distribute this hundreds chart to each student. This is the typical hundreds chart with 10 rows of 10 numbers each, counting from 1 to 100.

2. Ask students to pick any number in the first row of the hundreds chart. Starting from that number, count down the numbers in that column, until you reach the end of the chart. For example, if you selected 3, you would count down 3, 13, 23, 33, 43, 53, and so on.

3. Ask: *What do you notice? What patterns do you see?* (Children should notice that all the numbers in a particular column have the same units digit and that the tens digit changes from 1 to 9. Each number is 10 more than the one directly above it.)

Activity 8.8 More patterns on the hundreds chart

0	1	2	3	4	5	6	7	8	9
10	11	12	13	14	15	16	17	18	19
20	21	22	23	24	25	26	27	28	29
30	31	32	33	34	35	36	37	38	39
40	41	42	43	44	45	46	47	48	49
50	51	52	53	54	55	56	57	58	59
60	61	62	63	64	65	66	67	68	69
70	71	72	73	74	75	76	77	78	79
80	81	82	83	84	85	86	87	88	89
90	91	92	93	94	95	96	97	98	99

Instructions

1. Distribute this 0–99 chart to students. This is an alternative hundreds chart. The tens digit in each row remains the same. This can be helpful for certain applications.

2. Ask students to select any two columns (for example, the second and seventh columns).

3. Say: *Look at the third row for both of these columns. What is alike and what is different?* (Students should notice that in the third row, the entry in the second column is 21 and the entry in the seventh column is 26. Both entries have the same tens digit; 26 is to the right of 21, and it is 5 more than 21.)

4. Say: *Now look at the sixth row for both of these columns. What is alike and what is different? What patterns do you see?*

When looking for patterns on the hundreds chart, use different-colored crayons to highlight patterns. For example, color all the numbers with a tens digit of 2 in blue. This can help this column stand out and make patterns more evident.

Activity 8.9 More patterns on the hundreds chart

1	2	3	4	5	6	7	8	9	10
11	12	13	14	15	16	17	18	19	20
21	22	23	24		26	27	28	29	30
31	32	33				37	38	39	40
41	42	43				47	48	49	50
51	52	53	54			57	58	59	60
61	62	63	64	65	66	67	68	69	70
71	72	73	74	75	76	77	78	79	80
81	82	83	84	85	86	87	88	89	90
91	92	93	94	95	96	97	98	99	100

Instructions

1. Give each child a hundreds chart with several boxes blank.

2. Use a transparency of this same hundreds chart for the overhead projector. Select one of the blank boxes.

3. Ask: *What number goes here? Why? What number goes above it? What number goes below it? What number is to its left? What number is to its right?*

Children's Difficulties with Place Value

A common mistake made by children when learning place value is to reverse the digits of numbers. For example, a child might write the quantity forty-two as *24*. This is often a careless error; however, it can also be an indication of dyslexia. We can help children overcome this error by using models to visualize the original quantity and the quantity with digits reversed. By examining both quantities, children can see the effect of reversing digits. Ten-frame cards are especially effective for this, as illustrated by **Activity 8.10**.

Activity 8.10 Using models to help children who reverse digits

42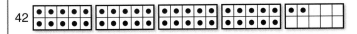

24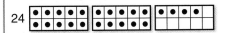

Instructions

1. Ask children to use ten-frame cards to represent the number 42. They can color dots on their ten-frame cards or place chips on them.

2. Ask: *How many tens are there in 42? How many ones?*

   Keep the cards. Do not discard them or remove the chips.

3. Next, ask children to use different ten-frame cards to represent the number 24. Again, color dots or use chips.

4. Ask: *How many tens are there in 24? How many ones?*

5. Ask: *Which number is larger, 24 or 42? How can you tell?*

6. Ask: *Who can explain what happens when we reverse the digits?*

7. Ask: *Who can think of a number that has the same value when its digits are reversed?*

When children are learning place value, they often have difficulty with the teens numbers, those numbers from 11 to 19, because they do not follow the typical naming pattern. In Chapter 7, we discussed how in many other languages, the names for the numerals from 11 to 19 quite literally reflect their meaning. For example, 11 actually means *ten and one*, or *ten one*; 12 means *ten and two* or *ten two*; and so on. However, in English this is not the case. Children also have a lot of difficulty understanding the two 1s in 11, misinterpreting them to mean 2 tens or 2 ones, with a value of 20 or 2.

Teaching Tip

Understanding teens numbers

When teaching place value, skip the teens numbers and come back to them later, after children understand the meaning of other two-digit numbers. Skip from 10 to 20 and make sure children understand the sequence 10, 20, 30, 40, 50, and so on. Then focus on 21, 22, 23, and so on, before tackling the numbers 11 through 19.

In the Hindu-Arabic system, zero is used as a placeholder and a symbol for the absence of something. Having a zero makes our system very easy to use; however, it is a complex idea that can be confusing for children who are learning place value. When children first learn about zero, they learn its use as a placeholder. Even so, this may present difficulties. For example, if you ask children to write seven hundred four, they may write 7004 instead of 704. Make sure to give children many opportunities

to practice saying and writing numbers that have zero in them (**Activity 8.11**).

Activity 8.11 Say it / Write it

Instructions

1. Say: *I have three tens. What's my number?*

2. Ask children to write this number and show their results.

3. Next, say: *I have two hundreds and three tens. What's my number?*

4. Ask children to write the number and show their results. If children have difficulty writing this number you might ask questions such as: *How do you write two hundreds? How do you write three tens? How do you write two hundreds and three tens?*

5. Repeat with other numbers that use zero as a placeholder, such as *six hundred seven, five hundred eighty,* or *three hundred eight.*

CONCEPT CHECK

1. **Which** models are most appropriate for introducing place value?

2. **What** are the three stages of place value development, and how do they help solidify students' ideas of place value?

3. **What** activities using the hundreds chart can be used to improve students' understanding of place value?

4. **How** can place value models help children overcome typical misunderstandings of place value?

Extending Place Value

LEARNING OBJECTIVES

1. **Consider** how to teach children the meaning of larger numbers.

2. **Describe** how to use models to represent large numbers.

3. **Explain** the characteristics of rounding numbers.

Accarding to *Curriculum Focal Points* (NCTM, 2006, p. 14), by the end of second grade "children develop an understanding of base-ten concepts (at least to 1000)." They learn to count in ones, tens, and hundreds. In grade 3 they extend their place value knowledge to numbers up to 10,000. By grade 4 they learn place value for numbers up to 100,000. By grade 5 they learn about numbers in the millions. This

Modeling large numbers • Figure 8.9

A concrete model of the number 1234.

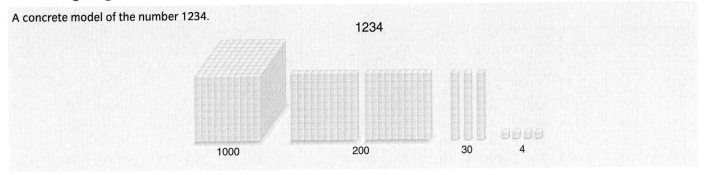

1234

1000   200   30   4

can be very challenging, because teachers are asking children to understand something they probably have not experienced in their lives: very large quantities. To facilitate their understanding, provide children with as many concrete experiences with large numbers as are reasonable and teach them how to write, say, represent, and compare the magnitude of large numbers.

Learning About Thousands

Base-ten blocks provide concrete representations for large numbers, with the cube representing 1000 and the flat representing 100 (**Figure 8.9**).

Place value mats are also helpful for organizing and modeling larger numbers. To model numbers in the thousands, use two place value mats, side by side (**Figure 8.10**).

Place value mats can help children express numbers symbolically, in **expanded notation**, which highlights the value of each place. For example:

$$4132 = 4 \times 1000 + 1 \times 100 + 3 \times 10 + 2 \times 1$$
$$2134 = 2 \times 1000 + 1 \times 100 + 3 \times 10 + 4 \times 1$$

Teaching Tip
Comparing the magnitude of numbers

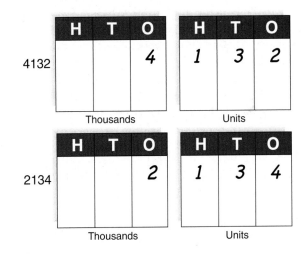

Use place value mats to compare the **magnitude** of two numbers. For example, the numbers 4132 and 2134 have the same digits in different places. To compare the size of these numbers, put each number in its own set of place value mats, one set above the other, and then compare place by place, starting from the left.

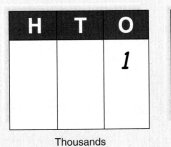

Using place value mats to model larger numbers • Figure 8.10

How many thousands are in this number? How many hundreds? How many tens? How many ones? Can you say this number?

Activity 8.12 The thousands chart

10	20	30	40	50	60	70	80	90	100
110	120	130	140	150	160	170	180	190	200
210	220	230	240	250	260	270	280	290	300
310	320	330	340	350	360	370	380	390	400
410	420	430	440	450	460	470	480	490	500
510	520	530	540	550	560	570	580	590	600
610	620	630	640	650	660	670	680	690	700
710	720	730	740	750	760	770	780	790	800
810	820	830	840	850	860	870	880	890	900
910	920	930	940	950	960	970	980	990	1000

Instructions

1. Say: *Start on any number. Count forward four boxes. Where did you stop? Count forward six boxes. Where did you stop? What do you notice?* (Numbers are increasing by 10 with each box. First move increased the number by 40, second move increased the number by 60.)

2. Say: *Start on any number in the first row. Count down that column until you get to the end of the chart. What do you notice?* (Numbers are increasing by 100 with each count down the column.)

3. Ask: *How can we use the chart to skip count by tens?* (Go across rows.)

4. Ask: *How can we use the chart to skip count by hundreds?* (Go down columns.)

Just as hundreds charts help children identify numbers between 1 and 100, a thousands chart can help children identify patterns for numbers between 10 and 1000 (**Activity 8.12**).

Learning About Millions and Billions

When modeling numbers in the millions, use three place value mats side by side. This representation helps children understand the meaning of larger numbers while also emphasizing the additive property of the Hindu-Arabic numeration system. Extend the place value mat to organize, represent, read, and make sense of numbers to one million and beyond by creating a place value mat for each triple of digits. For example, numbers in the millions require three place value mats side by side. Numbers in the billions require four place value mats, side by side (**Activity 8.13**).

Activity 8.13 Writing numbers in the millions and billions

Instructions

1. Ask: *What number is represented by these place value mats?* (624,278,351)

Millions   Thousands   Units

2. Ask: *How would you say this number?* (Six hundred twenty-four million, two hundred seventy-eight thousand, three hundred fifty-one.)

3. Repeat with other numbers.

4. Say: *We can represent numbers in the billions using place value mats. It takes 14,286,000,000 fireflies to generate the brightness of the sun. How would you write this number on the place value mats? How would you say this number?*

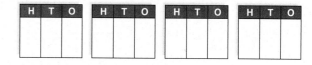

Rounding

Rounding numbers makes them easier to work with. Rounding combines knowledge of place value with knowledge of how to find a "nice number" for computation.

There are many ways to round numbers. In elementary school, children are taught to round numbers to a particular place value by finding the digit for that place value and looking at the digit to its immediate right. If the digit is 5 or greater, round up. If it is lower than 5, round down (**Table 8.1**).

Rounding numbers using place value		Table 8.1
Place Value	**Number**	**Rounded Number**
To nearest 10	342	340
To nearest 10	437	440
To nearest 100	437	400
To nearest 100	3482	3500
To nearest 1000	3482	3000

Base-ten blocks can help children learn how to round numbers to the nearest 10, nearest 100, or nearest 1000 (**Activity 8.14** and **Activity 8.15**).

Activity 8.14 Using base-ten blocks to round numbers to the nearest 10

Instructions

1. Distribute base-ten blocks to each child or pair of children.
2. Say: *Represent the number 246 with base-ten blocks. We are going to round this number to the nearest 10.*
3. Ask: *What multiples of 10 are closest to 246? (240 and 250) Represent each of those numbers with base-ten blocks.*
4. *Which of these numbers is 246 closer to?*

Activity 8.15 Using base-ten blocks to round numbers to the nearest 100 and nearest 1000

Instructions

1. Distribute base-ten blocks to each child or pair of children.
2. Say: *Represent the number 678 with base-ten blocks. We are going to round this number to the nearest 100.*
3. Ask: *What multiples of 100 are closest to 678? (600 and 700) Represent each of those numbers with base-ten blocks.*
4. *Which of these numbers is closer to 678? (700)*
5. *Represent the number 3240 with base-ten blocks. We are going to round this number to the nearest 1000. Which multiples of 1000 are closest to 3240? (3000 and 4000) Represent each of those numbers with base-ten blocks.*
6. *Which of these numbers is closer to 3240? (3000)*

When using the rounding rules taught in elementary school, cumulative rounding errors can occur, especially when a large quantity of numbers are rounded for arithmetic operations. Computers avoid these rounding errors by using the following rule:

1. When the digit to be rounded ends in 5, if it is preceded by an odd number, round up.
2. When the digit to be rounded ends in 5, if it is preceded by an even number, round down.

This rule is used by scientists and statisticians to avoid substantial rounding errors.

How can teachers provide children with concrete experiences of very large numbers? The *Lesson* on the next page engages students in grades 3–5 in learning about large numbers while also introducing rounding, estimation, and area. In the *Lesson*, children use rounding to find the number of stars that can fit in a three-inch square of paper and to find out how many classroom floors are needed to hold one million stars. The standards are from the *Common Core State Standards* (NGA Center/CCSSO, 2010) for grades 3, 4, and 5.

IF A GOLDFISH BOWL WERE BIG ENOUGH
FOR A MILLION GOLDFISH…

How Much Is a Million? by David M. Schwartz

GRADE LEVEL

3–5 (Intermediate)

OBJECTIVES

Students learn to estimate quantities up to one million.

Students learn to round numbers to the nearest ten.

Students learn about units of area.

Students learn an appropriate use of calculators.

STANDARDS

Grade 3

Recognize area as an attribute of plane figures and understand concepts of area measurement. (NGA Center/CCSSO, 2010)

Grade 4

Use place value understanding to round multi-digit whole numbers to any place. (NGA Center/CCSSO, 2010)

Grade 5

Fluently multiply multi-digit whole numbers using the standard algorithm. (NGA Center/CCSSO, 2010)

MATERIALS

- *How Much Is a Million?* by David M. Schwartz, one copy

- Rulers

- 12-inch square of cardboard or construction paper, one per group

- Paper, one sheet per student

- Scissors

- Two packages of star labels, 440 to a package

- Four-function calculators, one for each student

ASSESSMENT

- Observe how children use their rulers. Do they understand area? Can they mark off 3-square-inch units? Do they know how many 3-inch squares fit in a 12-inch square without measuring?

- Observe how children place and count the stars. Are their estimates close to the estimates of other members of the class?

- Observe how students use calculators. Can they use either repeated addition or multiplication to compute the necessary calculations?

- Observe how students write and say large numbers.

GROUPING

Small groups of three or four students each

Launch (10 minutes)

- Read portions of the book *How Much Is a Million?* Focus on representations of one million.

- Ask: *Have you ever seen one million of anything?* Possible answers might be one million snowflakes or one million stars in the sky.

- Say: *We can't count the stars in the sky but we can find out whether one million star labels will fit on the ceiling of our classroom.*

- Ask: *How can we find this out?* Discuss possible strategies with children. Be ready to suggest a method that will be explored in the next section.

Instruct (30 minutes)

- Say: *We are going to investigate how many stars we can place on the ceiling of our classroom by using the floor, which is the same size. First, let's find out how many stars can fit on one small square. Use rulers and scissors to cut a piece of paper three inches square. Place as many stars as you can on that piece of paper so that the stars are as close as possible without overlapping.*

- Children cut out paper squares and place star stickers on them. When they report the number of stickers on each square, results are close to 40 stars.

- Say: *All of you placed about the same number of stars on your square. Let's round that number to 40 stars, since this is close to all the answers and an easy number to work with.*

- Say: *Working in small groups, measure the size of one of the tiles on the floor.* (12 inches square)

- *How many of the small paper squares fit on each of the large floor tiles? Look up when you have an answer.* (Sixteen 3-inch squares fit in each 12-inch square.)

- *Calculate how many stars would fit on one floor tile.* (16 x 40 = 640)

- *Our classroom is 30 feet by 20 feet. What is the area of the room? How many floor tiles are on the floor?* (The floor area is 30 x 20 = 600 square feet, so there are 600 tiles on the floor.)

- *How many stars will fit on our classroom floor?* (600 x 640 = 384,000)

- *How many classrooms will be needed for one million stars to fit on their floors? How can we figure that out?*

- As children discuss this, help them understand that 384,000 is close to 400,000. So two classrooms the same size can hold 800,000 stars and three classrooms the same size can hold 1,200,000 stars.

Summarize (10 minutes)

- Ask: *Can the ceiling of our classroom hold one million stars that do not overlap? How can you tell?*

- Ask: *Does anything else at school contain one million?* (Possible answers: storage containers of rice, nuts, chocolate chips; grass on field outside school.)

- Ask: *If we wanted to count the number of chocolate chips in the storage container in the kitchen, how could we do this without counting each one?*

CONCEPT CHECK STOP

1. **What** models work best for teaching children the meaning of large numbers?

2. **How** can we provide children with real-world examples of larger numbers?

3. **How** can rounding help children work with larger numbers?

Summary

1 What Is Place Value? 192

- All place value systems share two characteristics. Each has **bases** and grouping rules that are unique to that system. Place value permits us to express very large quantities with a limited number of symbols. We can do this because the position of the digit denotes the value of the digit.

- The **Hindu-Arabic numeration system** has four properties: place value, zero, additive property, and base of 10. The Hindu-Arabic system was first developed in India and then adapted by Arabic mathematicians. It came into wide usage in the Western world after about 1500.

2 How Do Children Learn Place Value? 194

- Before children learn place value, they count by ones. Counting through grouping is not a naturally acquired skill. We need to give children multiple opportunities to group collections of objects before teaching them base-ten place value concepts, as shown in the photo.

Figure 8.2

- When children first learn place value, they need to be given tasks in which they find **equivalent representations** of numbers using tens and ones, and **compose** and **decompose** numbers.

3 Teaching Place Value Concepts 198

- There are two types of place value models: **proportional models**, as shown here, and **nonproportional models**. Within the proportional models, there are **groupable** and **pregrouped models**. In most cases, it is best to begin place value instruction with proportional groupable models.

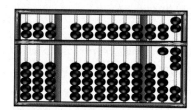

Figure 8.6

- As we teach place value, it is important to give students three types of experiences. They should use **concrete**, semiconcrete, and symbolic representations of numbers to help them develop place value understanding.

- The hundreds chart is an excellent tool for learning place value. Several activities with this tool can help children learn to count by tens and to recognize the meaning of the ones place and the tens place.

- Children have various difficulties in learning place value. One of the most common is the reversal of the digits in the tens and ones places. Children with learning disabilities are especially prone to this error.

4 Extending Place Value 206

- By the end of second grade and into third grade, children study three-digit numbers, from 100 to 999. To facilitate their understanding, we provide children with many concrete experiences with large numbers, such as the base-ten blocks illustrated here. We can help children become familiar with large numbers through activities that involve counting and estimating very large numbers.

- We teach children how to write, say, represent, and compare the magnitude of large numbers. **Place value mats** are an excellent tool for this.

- When teaching place value, we can also teach **rounding** and estimating. As children learn about rounding, they learn that rounding rules are not universal. They change depending on the numbers we are rounding and for what purpose.

Figure 8.9

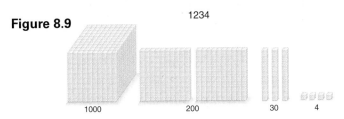

1234

1000   200   30   4

Key Terms

- base 192
- base-ten 193
- compose 196
- computational algorithms 192
- concrete models 198
- decompose 196
- equivalent representations 195
- expanded notation 207
- explicit trading 192
- groupable 200
- Hindu-Arabic numeration system 192
- magnitude 207
- nonproportional models 198
- place value 192
- place value mats 203
- pregrouped 200
- proportional models 198
- regrouping 197
- rounding 209
- trading 197

Additional Children's Literature

- *The King's Commissioners*, **written by Aileen Friedman and illustrated by Susan Guevara**
  When the king wants to know how many royal commissioners there are, he asks the royal advisors to count them. One counts by twos and the other counts by fives. The king doesn't understand until his daughter explains, using place value.

- *12 Ways to Get to 11*, **written by Eve Merriam and illustrated by Bernie Karlin**
  This book illustrates 12 fun, imaginative, and real-world examples of decomposing 11.

- *A Million Fish . . . More or Less*, **written by Patricia C. McKissack and illustrated by Dena Schutzer**
  When young Hugh Thomas went fishing in the bayou, he caught 1 million fish. Then on the way home he lost all his fish except for three of them.

- *On Beyond a Million: An Amazing Math Journey*, **written by David M. Schwartz and illustrated by Paul Meisel**
  Very large numbers such as millions, billions, and trillions are described with colorful and interesting illustrations.

Online Resources

- **MathWire**
  www.mathwire.com

  Contains interactive and downloadable activities on standards-based mathematics topics. This site has excellent place value resources for the teacher, including games and lessons.

- **National Council of Teachers of Mathematics**
  www.nctm.org

  Select **Standards and Focal Points** and then **e-examples**. **E-example 4.5.2** uses a virtual calculator and hundreds chart to explore patterns.

- **National Library of Virtual Manipulatives**
  http://nlvm.usu.edu

  Select the **Chip Abacus** activity. This applet allows children to work with base ten, five, or two and exchange chips between the hundreds, tens, and ones place.

- **Digi-blocks**
  www.digi-block.com

  The Web site for this commercial product contains download-able lessons for pre-K through grade 5 using digi-blocks for learning place value.

Critical and Creative Thinking Questions

1. **In the field** Create an activity that will assess a child's place value knowledge. Try out the activity with a child in first or second grade and summarize your findings.

2. How can concrete models help children to understand place value ideas?

3. Using one of the concrete models described in this chapter or a different model that you develop:
   a. Suggest an activity that includes trading, composing, and decomposing.
   b. Explain how your model can be used to compare the relative size of two numbers.
   c. Describe the advantages and drawbacks of your model.

4. Describe an activity that will help children understand numbers larger than 100.

5. Should you use the hundreds chart before children experience concrete models of place value or after? Why? Describe patterns on the hundreds chart.

What is happening in this picture?

Look closely at this picture. It is estimated that one million eight hundred thousand people attended President Barack Obama's inauguration on January 20, 2009.

Think Critically

1. What is one activity about large numbers that you could create with this image?
2. Can you think of similar images to teach the meaning of larger numbers?
3. What are other real-world examples that can motivate children's understanding of large numbers from 100 to one million?

Self-Test

(Check your answers in Appendix D.)

1. Illustrate the number 375 with Egyptian numerals.

2. Identify two difficulties with the Egyptian numeration system.

3. Illustrate the number 90 with Mayan numerals.

4. What are the two characteristics shared by all place value systems? Why are they important?

5. Identify the four characteristics of our number system.

6. Show how you would represent the numbers 325 and 253 with two different place value models.

7. Explain the difference between proportional and nonproportional models. Which of these images is proportional? Why? Which of these images is nonproportional? Why?

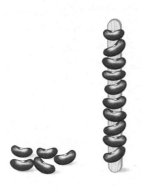

8. Explain the difference between groupable and pregrouped models. Which of these images is groupable? Which of these images is pregrouped?

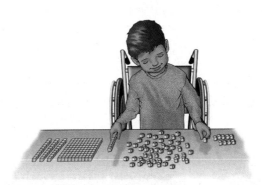

9. Why is it important for children to learn how to compose and decompose numbers? How does trading give them opportunities to practice these skills?

10. What types of difficulties might children have when learning about zero as a placeholder?

11. Why is it difficult for children to learn the meaning of the numbers from 11 to 19?

12. How can we help children who reverse the digits when learning place value?

13. Draw a picture to illustrate how you can use place value mats to compare the size of the numbers 5632 and 5432.

14. Draw pictures to illustrate how you can express the number 21,689,234 with place value mats.

15. Round each of the following numbers.
    a. 829 to the nearest 10
    b. 829 to the nearest 100
    c. 3572 to the nearest 100
    d. 3572 to the nearest 1000

THE PLANNER ✓

Review your Chapter Planner on the chapter opener and check off your completed work.

Operations with Whole Numbers

Lewis Montoya had established a daily routine with his first-grade class. As soon as he said *math time*, children brought crayons, paper, and counting blocks to the large rug under the windows of his classroom and sat down together, ready for problem solving.

On this day, Lewis sat among the children and asked the following problem: *Valentina had 5 stickers. Her brother gave her some more stickers. Now she has 12. How many stickers did Valentina's brother give her?* Then all the children went to work. Sheletha counted out 12 blocks and placed them in a row. Then she counted out 5 more blocks and placed them in a second row beneath the first. Sheletha then paired a block from the top row with a block from the bottom row and pushed them aside. She did this until she had moved aside all the blocks from the bottom row. Then Sheletha counted the remaining blocks.

Michael drew a picture with 12 circles, stopping now and then to count how many circles he had drawn, crossed out 5 of them, and counted the remaining circles by ones. Other children in the class used similar methods. After a few minutes, Mr. Montoya asked children to show their work and give their answers.

Mr. Montoya understood the importance of connecting word problems and whole number operations. He encouraged his students to use whatever methods made sense to them in solving the problem and then to share their strategies with others.

Children come to school with some knowledge of whole number operations. Their understanding is strengthened by focusing on word problems and children's informal or invented strategies.

CHAPTER OUTLINE

Whole Number Operations: An Overview   218

Key Question: Why is it important to begin teaching whole number operations with word problems and concrete manipulatives?

Teaching Addition and Subtraction   220

Key Questions: What are the four types of addition and subtraction problems? Through what stages do students progress as they learn the meanings of these operations?

Teaching Multiplication and Division   225

Key Questions: What are the four types of multiplication and division problems? Through what stages do students progress as they learn the meanings of these operations?

Learning the Basic Facts   233

Key Question: What thinking strategies do children use in learning the basic facts for addition, subtraction, multiplication, and division?

NCTM The NCTM Number and Operations Standard includes several expectations for whole number operations.

Instructional programs from prekindergarten through grade 12 should enable all students to

- understand meanings of operations and how they relate to one another.   (NCTM, 2000, p. 78)

In prekindergarten through grade 2, all students should

- understand various meanings of addition and subtraction of whole numbers and the relationship between the two operations;
- understand the effects of adding and subtracting whole numbers;
- understand situations that entail multiplication and division, such as equal groupings of objects and sharing equally.   (NCTM, 2000, p. 78)

In grades 3–5, all students should

- understand various meanings of multiplication and division;
- understand the effects of multiplying and dividing whole numbers;
- identify and use relationships between operations, such as division as the inverse of multiplication, to solve problems.   (NCTM, 2000, p. 148)

Whole Number Operations: An Overview

LEARNING OBJECTIVES

1. **Explain** the importance of teaching whole number operations through problem solving.

2. **Describe** when and how symbolic notation should be introduced.

In the United States and Canada, children often learn computation with whole numbers first and apply these skills to problem situations later. This is not the best way to teach children whole number computation. According to Fuson (2003),

- Children who have difficulty learning the operations may spend all their time learning isolated skills that have no application to real life.

- In traditional textbooks, word problems are often placed at the end of a section, so children already know which operation to use when solving problems. They miss out on the opportunity of selecting the correct operation for modeling the problem.

- When operations are taught first, teachers sometimes focus on key words in problems (*is* means *equals, and* means *add, of* means *multiply,* and *how many more* means *subtract*) to help children decide which operation is called for. This can be misleading.

- When children see word problems after they learn the mathematical operations, they have difficulty connecting the operations to the contexts illustrated in the word problems.

Start with Word Problems

Children come to school with some understanding of whole number operations. You can build on what children already know by giving them many opportunities to use the operations in problems that build on their everyday experiences. Use numbers that are appropriate to the grade level (up to 10 or 12 for prekindergarten to kindergarten, one- and two-digit numbers for first graders, and two-digit numbers for second graders). Encourage children to model and explain their solutions (**Figure 9.1**).

Selecting word problems and modeling their solutions
• Figure 9.1

a. *Lisa has five silver stars. Her teacher gave her three more silver stars. How many stars does Lisa have altogether?*

This child acts out the problem situation by using the actual objects from the problem. She counts five stars, then counts three more stars, and then puts together all the stars and counts eight stars.

b. *Turner has five pieces of candy. Whitney has three times as many pieces of candy as Turner. How many pieces of candy does Whitney have?*

This child models the problem by counting on the number line. First, he jumps five places and then jumps two more lengths of five on the number line.

c. *Masoud brings 12 dog biscuits to the park. If there are three dogs at the park, how many biscuits will each dog get?*

This child draws 12 marks, one for each dog biscuit, and three circles, one for each dog. She gives a "biscuit" to each dog by placing marks in the circles and then counts the number of biscuits in one circle after all the biscuits are used.

Writing problems from number sentences • Figure 9.2

Ms. Morris wrote the number sentence 8 – 6 = 2 on the chalk-board for her second-grade class and asked each student to write a word problem that would be solved with this number sentence. Here are examples of two children's work:

a. Mollie wrote

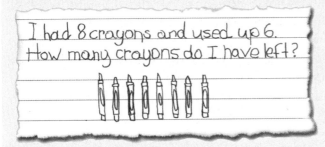

In what way are the problems written by Mollie and Antonio different? In what way are they similar?

b. Antonio wrote

I saw some little birds at the feeder. Then 6 flew away and now 2 are left. How many birds were at the feeder to start with?

Experience solving word problems helps children understand the meanings of the operations and may actually help their computation skills. As they gain understanding, children will progress to more advanced strategies. "The goal is for children to generalize themselves—from many, many experiences—how the arithmetic operations are described in the language of the real world" (Burns, 2000, p. 13).

Bring in Symbolism Later

Chapter 8 discussed teaching place value with concrete, then semiconcrete, and finally abstract representations of numbers. The process is similar when teaching whole number operations. Children's experiences progress through the following stages:

1. Children model their solutions concretely, using the objects in the problem or counters to represent those objects.

2. Children use semiconcrete representations by drawing pictures to represent the quantities and objects in the problem.

3. After children have had many opportunities to use the operations in word problems, introduce mathematical **symbols** and **number sentences**, such as 3 + 5 = 8.

When you think children understand an operation, introduce symbols for that operation. For example, when children are ready to learn symbols and number sentences

for addition, ask them to solve a word problem, such as:

Inez had five quarters and her mother gave her seven more.
How many quarters does she have now?

After children have explained their solutions, say: *Here is a way you can write this: 5 + 7 = 12.* Offer the symbols as an alternative, but do not force children to use them until they are ready. Introduce the symbols for subtract, multiply, and divide similarly. Read the subtraction symbol as *subtract* or *minus.* Avoid using the phrase *take away,* since this implies one limited meaning of subtraction. When reading number sentences to the class, say *is the same as* for the equals sign and encourage children to say it. Throughout elementary school, children often misinterpret the meaning of the equals sign. They think it means "the answer is" because we press the equals sign on calculators to get the answer.

Once symbols have been introduced and understood, give children word problems and ask them to represent the problems in number sentences with symbols. Reverse the process by giving them number sentences and asking them to write problems that can be solved with those number sentences. This process is illustrated in **Figure 9.2**.

CONCEPT CHECK

1. **What** are three advantages of teaching whole number operations with word problems?

2. **How** can you tell when it is time to introduce symbolism?

Teaching Addition and Subtraction

LEARNING OBJECTIVES

1. **Identify** the four types of addition and subtraction word problems.
2. **Explain** the three stages through which children progress in solving addition and subtraction problems.
3. **Describe** the properties of addition.
4. **Describe** the inverse relationship between addition and subtraction.

When teachers teach children in grades K–2 the whole number operations of addition and subtraction, they need to understand the structures of the different types of addition and subtraction problems, know which tend to be more difficult for children, understand how to help children achieve success with the more challenging types of problems, and be able to express all four types through word problems and number sentences. Teachers also

Education InSight   The four types of addition and subtraction problems • Figure 9.3

There are four types of addition and subtraction problems (Carpenter et al., 1999; Gutstein and Romberg, 1995): join, separate, part-part-whole, and compare. It is important for you to identify them so that you can supplement the problems found in your students' textbook. Textbooks often include only the easiest of the problem types (join/result unknown and separate/result unknown).

a. JOIN

Join problems demonstrate action and are among the easiest to solve. They involve joining two sets of objects together. All problems have three quantities: the **start**, the **change**, and the **result**. The start and change quantities are known as **addends** in addition problems. There are three types of join problems.

Result unknown: *Chris had 5 wristbands. Antonio gave her 4 more. How many wristbands does Chris have now?*

Change unknown: *Chris had 5 wristbands. Antonio gave her some more wristbands. Now Chris has 9 wristbands. How many wristbands did Antonio give Chris?*

Start unknown: *Chris had some wristbands. Antonio gave her 4 more wristbands Now Chris has 9 wristbands. How many wristbands did Chris have to start with?*

b. SEPARATE

Separate problems are usually easy to solve because they demonstrate the action of removing objects from a set. All problems have three quantities: the **start**, the **change**, and the **result**. There are three types of separate problems.

Result unknown: *Saaman had 9 wristbands. She gave 4 wristbands to Hiraldo. How many wristbands does Saaman have now?*

Change unknown: *Saaman had 9 wristbands. She gave some wristbands to Hiraldo. Now she has 4 wristbands. How many wristbands did Saaman give to Hiraldo?*

Start unknown: *Saaman had some wristbands. She gave 5 to Hiraldo. Now she has 4 wristbands. How many wristbands did Saaman have to start with?*

A child's solution to the change unknown problem

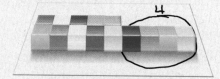

Crystal counted out 5 blocks. Then she counted out 9 blocks. She paired blocks from the first row with blocks from the second row and found that she had 4 more blocks in the second row.

A child's solution to the start unknown problem

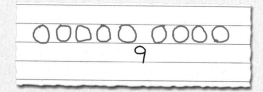

Jarrod drew 5 circles in a row. Then he drew 4 more circles. He counted all the circles and saw that his answer was 9.

need to address the special properties of addition as well as the relationship between addition and subtraction.

Types of Addition and Subtraction Problems

Researchers (Carpenter et al., 1999; Gutstein and Romberg, 1995) have categorized addition and subtraction problems by how children actually understand and solve them (**Figure 9.3**). Children do not need to identify the different types of problems.

Teachers are sometimes confused if children do not solve word problems in the same way that adults solve them. Consider again the problem Mr. Montoya gave his class at the opening of this chapter:

> *Valentina had 5 stickers. Her brother gave her some more stickers. Now she has 12. How many stickers did Valentina's brother give her?*

Many adults would consider this a subtraction problem and write *12 – 5 = 7*. Children often see this as a join problem because the action involves putting stickers together, and think of it as *5 + some number = 12*. First-graders Michael

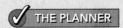

c. PART-PART-WHOLE

Part-part-whole problems are often more difficult for children to solve because no action takes place. They relate the parts of a set of objects to the set as a whole. They have three quantities: the **two parts of the set** and the **whole**. There are two types of part-part-whole problems.

Whole unknown: *Jung has some wristbands: 5 are red, and 4 are yellow. How many wristbands does Jung have?*

Part unknown: *Jung has 9 wristbands: 4 are yellow, and the rest are red. How many red wristbands does Jung have?*

d. COMPARE

Compare problems are also difficult for children to solve because no action takes place. They compare two different sets of objects. They have three quantities: the **two sets** and the **difference**. There are three types of compare problems.

Difference unknown: *Andre has 9 wristbands, and Brenda has 4 wristbands. How many more wristbands does Andre have than Brenda?*

Larger unknown: *Andre has 4 wristbands. Brenda has 5 more wristbands than Andre. How many wristbands does Brenda have?*

Smaller unknown: *Brenda has 9 wristbands. She has 4 more wristbands than Andre. How many wristbands does Andre have?*

A child's solution to the part unknown problem

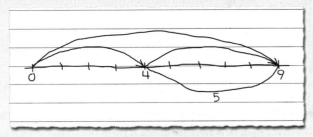

Casey drew a number line and made a loop from 0 to 9. Then he made another loop from 0 to 4 and counted how many more from 4 to 9.

A child's solution to the difference unknown problem

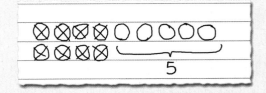

Taik drew 9 circles in a row. Then he drew 4 more circles in a second row. He paired a circle from the top row with a circle from the bottom row, marking them with Xs, until there were no more circles in the bottom row.

Children's learning of addition • Figure 9.4

When children first learn addition, they rely totally on counting techniques, using their knowledge of counting words such as *one, two, three, four, . . .* and their understanding of one-to-one correspondence. Gradually children develop more efficient strategies that rely less on counting and more on their growing understanding of addition.

These steps are illustrated with three solutions to the problem:

Nora had 8 crayons. Serita gave her 6 more crayons. How many crayons does Nora have now?

1 Counting all

Children represent the quantities in the problem with objects and count all. De Lynn counted eight crayons by using the counting words *one, two, three, . . . eight* and moved each crayon as she counted it. Next, she counted six additional crayons in the same way. Then she put the two groups of crayons together and counted them again.

2 Counting on

When children begin counting on, they use objects. Later, they count on with words and keep track with their fingers. Ascencio noticed that he did not have to count the first eight crayons. He began counting from eight. He said, *9, 10, 11, 12, 13, 14,* and kept track of how many he had counted by pointing to the blocks as he counted. After he had pointed to six blocks, he knew he was finished.

3 Thinking strategies

Children use thinking strategies such as doubling, adding one, and making 10 to solve addition problems. De Lynn remembered that 8 and 2 more make 10. She also knew that 2 and 4 are 6. So she counted on her fingers from 10. She said: *Eight and two more are 10. To add four more I can count 11, 12, 13, 14.*

and Sheletha, whose solutions were highlighted in the opening of this chapter, did not use subtraction to solve this problem. Sheletha created a one-to-one correspondence by counting out a set of 12, then counting out a set of 5, matching up pairs, and essentially finding *5 and how many more make 12*. Michael's solution was similar, but his counting method was more efficient. Rather than impose a solution structure on children, allow them to solve word problems in ways that make sense to them.

Helping Children Learn Addition and Subtraction

When children initially learn addition and subtraction of whole numbers, they use counting techniques. Let us take a closer look at the main steps through which children progress as they learn to understand addition (Fuson, 2003) (**Figure 9.4**).

Children go through a similar process when they learn subtraction, moving from counting all to thinking strategies. In the second step, instead of counting on, they may **count down** or **count up to**.

> *Manuel had 15 cookies. He gave 7 to Carson. How many cookies did Manuel have left?*

To solve this problem by counting down, a child might say *15* and then count down *14, 13, 12, 11, 10, 9, 8,* keeping track of how many numbers were counted by using fingers or counters. To solve the problem by counting up to, the child might say *7*, and then count *8, 9, 10, 11, 12, 13, 14, 15,* again keeping track of how many have been counted with fingers or counters. Children understandably have a lot of difficulty with counting down. We learn to count forward and not backward. The strategy of counting up to is more natural and easier for children to learn (Fuson, 2003).

Children initially find it easier to solve join and separate problems, because these problems show action and are easier to model. Within these categories, children have the most difficulty with start unknown problems, because they do not know how many counters to put down or what to draw. Help children model start unknown problems by giving them guidance in setting up the problem (**Activity 9.1**). Activities such as this one can help children successfully solve start unknown problems.

As children gain experience solving many examples of the four types of addition and subtraction word

Activity 9.1 Where do I start?

Instructions

1. Give students the problem:

Devon had some cookies. She gave four to her brother. Now she has six cookies. How many cookies did Devon have to start with?

2. Ask: *How many cookies did Devon give to her brother?* (4)

3. Say: *Please count out four blocks.*

4. Ask: *How many cookies does Devon have now?* (6)

5. Say: *Please count out six blocks.*

6. Ask: *How many blocks are there in all?* (10)

7. Ask: *How many cookies did Devon have to start with?*

problems, they come to understand the connection between counting and addition and subtraction. Support children's understanding through the use of concrete and semiconcrete models and eventually symbols.

Tech Tools

> illuminations.nctm.org

Go to the *NCTM Illuminations* Web site. Select **Lessons**. The unit **Comparing Connecting Cubes** consists of six lessons that model addition and subtraction of whole numbers using problem solving.

Properties of Addition and Subtraction

Children should understand that addition and subtraction are **inverse** operations. That is, they undo, or reverse, one another. If I have five marbles and then get three more marbles, I have eight marbles. However, if I then give away three marbles, I now have five marbles again. Adding the three marbles and then subtracting them again returns the number of marbles to the original amount of five marbles. It is important for children to understand this relationship, because they will be using it when they learn the basic facts, in whole number computation and, later, in algebra.

Addition has three important properties that help children learn the basic facts and are used throughout the K–12 curriculum for written computation, mental mathematics, and algebra. The *Curriculum Focal Points* (2006) for grade 1 specify that children "use properties of addition (commutativity and associativity) to add whole numbers" (NCTM, 2006, p. 13). The *Common Core State Standards* also specify that children learn these properties in grade 1 (NGA Center/CCSSO, 2010).

The commutative property for addition This is often called the "turn-around" property. It means that the order in which two numbers are added does not affect the answer. When teaching this property, explain to children that a commuter goes back and forth to work or school. Similarly, in addition, numbers can go back and forth or turn-around the + symbol without affecting the answer. Research (Schifter, 2001) has found that children use this property but may not be sure what it really means or whether it works all the time. Help children understand this property with activities such as the following (**Activity 9.2**).

Activity 9.2 The turn-around property

Instructions

1. Give children two addition word problems that are the same type of problem, describe different situations, and use the same two numbers, in reverse order. Two sample problems are illustrated.

   Nicole helped her mom plant 20 bulbs. Tomorrow she is going to help her plant 36 more bulbs. How many bulbs will Nicole help her mom plant altogether?

   All the second-grade classes at Jared's school went on a field trip. There were 36 children on one school bus and 20 children on the other school bus. How many children in the second grade went on the field trip?

2. Ask: *What do you notice about these two problems? How are they alike?* (Some children will notice that they use the same numbers and that, by solving one of the problems, they also find the answer to the other problem.)

The associative property for addition The associative property states that when adding three or more numbers, you can associate, or group, the numbers however you like, without affecting the answer. In other words, $3 + 5 + 8$ is equal to $(3 + 5) + 8$ or $3 + (5 + 8)$. The associative property is especially helpful with mental mathematics, where you might want to group together numbers that are **compatible**, or easy to add. In **Activity 9.3**, children can use both the commutative and associative properties.

Activity 9.3 Find a partner: Addition

Instructions

1. Provide children with several sets of numbers to add, where each set has three or more numbers and within each set, one pair of numbers adds to 10 or is a double.

2. Ask children to add each set of numbers in at least two ways by pairing each of the numbers with a different "partner" number. After they add the numbers, ask: *What did you notice? What did you do to make the numbers easier to add?*

3. Sample number sets are given here.

   $6 + 8 + 4 = ?$

   $5 + 9 + 5 = ?$

   $3 + 6 + 7 + 9 = ?$

The zero property Teachers can help children become familiar with zero through activities that ask children to read street addresses and phone numbers that contain zero. Make sure that children read zero as "zero," not as "oh." Children should understand that zero is the **additive identity** for addition and subtraction. This can be confusing for children because they often see addition as making something larger and subtraction as making something smaller, and this is not true when adding or subtracting zero. "Zero difficulties permeate whole-number computation" (Wheeler, 2002, p. 29). It is important to clear up any difficulties at this stage, because children will encounter zero again when they learn multiplication and division (**Activity 9.4**).

> **additive identity**
> A number that, when added to or subtracted from another number, does not change its value.

Activity 9.4 Plate cover-up

Instructions

1. For pairs of children, give each pair two paper plates and a set of counters.

2. Children will turn their paper plates face down.

3. One child places a given number of counters under one plate (6, 7, or 8 counters) and no counters under the second plate.

4. The other child uncovers both paper plates.

5. Ask: *How many counters are under the first plate?* (6) *How many counters are under the second plate?* (0) *How many counters are there in all?*

6. Ask: *Can you write addition and subtraction sentences to show this?* (6 + 0 = 6; 6 − 0 = 6)

7. The children reverse roles. Continue the activity with other quantities of counters.

CONCEPT CHECK

1. **Why** is it important for teachers to understand and identify the four types of addition and subtraction problems?

2. **What** are the stages through which children progress as they learn the operations of addition and subtraction?

3. **What** are the properties of addition? Why is it important for children to learn them?

4. **Why** is it important for children to learn the inverse relationship between addition and subtraction?

Teaching Multiplication and Division

LEARNING OBJECTIVES

1. **Identify** the four types of multiplication and division word problems.

2. **Explain** the three stages through which children progress in solving multiplication and division problems.

3. **Describe** the properties of multiplication.

4. **Describe** the inverse relationship between multiplication and division.

Teach third-grade children multiplication and division of whole numbers by offering many experiences in solving word problems. It is important that teachers understand the structures of the different types of multiplication and division problems, know which problems tend to be more difficult for children, and develop strategies to help them overcome these challenges. Teachers also need to understand the special properties of multiplication and the inverse relationship between multiplication and division.

Types of Multiplication and Division Problems

Multiplication and division problems are categorized by how children actually solve them (**Figure 9.5** on the next page). Notice that, within the equal groups category, there are two types of division problems. In **measurement division**, the total is known and the number of objects in each group is known, but the number of groups is unknown. In **partitive division**, the total is known and the number of groups is known, but the number of objects in each group is unknown.

Equal groups measurement and partitive division problems may seem similar at first. However, when you try to solve them with models, as children would solve

There are four types of multiplication and division problems. It is important for you to identify them so that you can supplement the problems found in your children's textbook. Textbooks often include only the easiest of the problem types (equal groups/product unknown or equal groups/factor unknown).

a. EQUAL GROUPS

Equal groups problems have three numbers. One **factor**, or number, tells how many sets, or groups, of equal size there are. The other factor tells how many objects are in each set, or group, and the third number, the **product**, tells how many objects there are in all. Depending on which of the numbers is unknown, equal groups problems can be solved by either multiplication or division.

Multiplication

Maleka has 3 cups and each cup has 6 jellybeans in it. How many jellybeans does Maleka have in all?

b. COMPARISON

Comparison problems involve comparing one quantity in relation to another quantity and reasoning about them multiplicatively.

Multiplication

Garth made $6 selling lemonade. Aisha made three times as much money as Garth selling lemonade. How much money did Aisha make?

c. COMBINATIONS

Combination problems are somewhat harder than the other types because they are more difficult to model. They involve finding out how many different combinations can be made from a given set of objects.

Multiplication

The school cafeteria is having a make-your-own-pizza day. There are 3 kinds of crusts: thick, herb, and thin. There are 6 kinds of toppings: pineapple, veggie, sausage, ground beef, green peppers, and pepperoni. If you have to pick one topping and one crust, how many different kinds of pizza can you make?

d. AREA AND ARRAY

Area problems involve completely covering an area with equal-sized square units and counting the number of squares. Array problems involve placing objects in a rectangular array, with rows and columns. The number of rows is the first factor and the number of columns is the second factor.

Area multiplication

Caron's grandmother is tiling her bathroom. She has laid 3 rows of 6 tiles each. How many tiles has Caron's grandmother put in her bathroom?

Measurement division

Maleka has 18 jellybeans. She wants to put them in cups so that each cup has 6 jellybeans. How many cups does Maleka use?

Partitive division

Maleka has 18 jellybeans, and she wants to put an equal amount in 3 cups. How many jellybeans will be in each cup?

Division

Aisha made $18 selling lemonade. She made three times as much money as Garth made. How much money did Garth make selling lemonade?

Aisha   Garth

Division

Anina can make 18 different types of ice-cream sundaes. If she has 6 different toppings to choose from, how many flavors of ice cream does she have?

Division

Renau's dad stored 18 jars of homemade tomato sauce on 3 shelves in their pantry. How many jars were on each shelf?

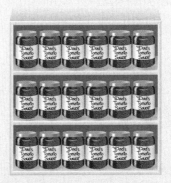

them, their differences become easier to understand. Consider the following measurement problem, which is illustrated in **Figure 9.6**.

> *Jenna has 24 pennies that she wants to put in some piggy banks. She wants to put 8 pennies in each piggy bank. How many piggy banks will she need?*

Now let's change the problem structure to partitive (**Figure 9.7**).

> *Jenna has 24 pennies that she wants to put into 3 piggy banks. How many pennies will she put in each piggy bank if she puts the same number of pennies into each one?*

Helping Children Learn Multiplication and Division

Multiplication and division of whole numbers are very different in structure from addition and subtraction. Multiplicative reasoning is more complex than additive reasoning. When children add or subtract, they may be adding or subtracting cookies, stickers, or toys, but they are always working with the same units. However, when children multiply, they are almost always using more than one unit. One factor refers to one unit and the other factor refers to the other unit. For example, consider the following equal groups multiplication problem. It has two different units: bags and oranges.

> *Eric has four bags of oranges with three oranges in each bag. How many oranges does Eric have altogether?*

When teaching children multiplication and division, help them transition from thinking additively to thinking multiplicatively. Children do not initially realize that multiplication is a new and different operation. They conceptualize multiplication as repeated addition: four groups of six is $6 + 6 + 6 + 6$. This is fine as a first step but does not indicate understanding of the operation of multiplication.

Measuring equal sets • Figure 9.6

This child counts out 24 pennies and then measures off groups of 8 pennies each. After counting out one set of 8 pennies, the child sets this to the side, counts out the next set, and so on, until no pennies are left. This process is sometimes called repeated subtraction. Some children keep track of how many times they are subtracting with counters. Other children keep track by counting on their fingers.

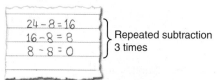

$$24 - 8 = 16$$
$$16 - 8 = 8$$
$$8 - 8 = 0$$

} Repeated subtraction 3 times

Sharing equally • Figure 9.7

The child counts out 24 pennies and then "deals out" the pennies one by one to each of three piggy banks until all the pennies are used up. This process of dealing out equally is a characteristic of partitive division. It is the process of partitioning the whole into a known number of fair shares.

Children's learning of multiplication • Figure 9.8

When children learn multiplication, they initially rely on counting by ones, as they did with addition. Children gradually learn to use more efficient strategies as they develop the meaning of multiplication and find that they can use composite wholes. This process is illustrated with three solutions to the following problem:

Han has four boxes of cupcakes. There are six cupcakes in each box. How many cupcakes does Han have?

1 **Counting all**

Ian made a tower of six snap-together cubes, counting *one, two, three, four, five, six* as he put the cubes together. He repeated this process as he made a second, third, and fourth tower. Then Han counted all the cubes. In all, Han counted five different times.

2 **Skip counting**

Haley skip counted to find the total number of cupcakes, using her fingers to keep track. She said: *Six, twelve, eighteen, twenty-four.* Haley is using a combination of counting and composite wholes. She is still counting all the cupcakes, but she is working toward an understanding of multiplication.

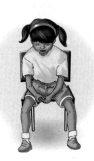

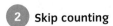

3 **Using composite wholes**

Desi says: *If I take one cupcake from each box, that leaves five in each box. Four times five is twenty and four times one is four. Twenty plus four is twenty-four.* Desi is using composite wholes and is focused on the multiplication. He understands that he does not have to count every cupcake in each box to find the total number of cupcakes.

"Children's ability to understand multiplication depends on their ability to understand and work with what are called **composite wholes**" (Killion and Steffe, 2002, p. 90). In other words, children should understand that when they count groups of objects, each group is made up of objects, but it is not necessary to count each individual object in a group to find the total amount. Children should be able to view 6 items as one group of 6 and to understand that 4×6 means four groups of 6 objects without having to count each 6. As children solve multiplicative contexts, they gradually construct this process (Fosnot and Dolk, 2001) (**Figure 9.8**).

> **composite wholes**
> A group of objects, such as oranges in a bag, keys on a key ring, or houses on a street.

Teaching Tip

Developing a rich understanding of multiplication and division through language

Encourage children to use phrases such as *groups of* instead of "times" when they first learn multiplication. When children first learn division, use phrases that are commonly heard, such as *sharing equally* and *equal groups* rather than "divided by." Save more formal language for later.

CHILDREN'S LITERATURE

Understanding multiplication

THE PLANNER

Amanda Bean's Amazing Dream: A Mathematical Story • Figure 9.9

Written by Cindy Neuschwander
Illustrated by Liza Woodruff

Amanda Bean loves to count but does not want to learn multiplication facts. At home she sees 12 rows of 12 tiles. Instead of multiplying 12 x 12, she counts 144 tiles. At the library she sees a bookcase with 7 shelves and 9 books on each shelf. Instead of multiplying 7 x 9, Amanda counts the books. Then she has a dream that convinces her that multiplying is a much faster way of counting. This is a great book to help children transition from counting and additive thinking to multiplicative thinking. The illustrations show different groups of objects that can be counted.

Strategy for the Classroom

- After reading the book, ask children questions about the illustrations in the book, such as *How many jars of pickles are on the shelf? How many pickles are in each jar? How many pickles are there in all? How does this picture remind you of multiplication?*

Learning about remainders

Five lines of soldiers with five in each row . . . perfect at last—and that's *counting* Joe.

A Remainder of One • Figure 9.10

Written by Elinor Pinczes
Illustrated by Bonnie MacKain

The 25-bug squadron marched for their queen. When they tried marching by twos, there were 2 rows of 12 soldiers, each with soldier Joe left out. Then they tried to march in 3 rows of 8 soldiers each and 4 rows of 6 soldiers each, but each time Joe was left out. Finally, they marched in 5 rows of 5 soldiers each.

Strategies for the Classroom

- Have children act out the story with counters or fake bugs.
- Ask children to write division number sentences for each part of the story.
- Ask: *Why is the book called* A Remainder of One?
- Ask: *Why do you think the author decided to have 25 bugs in the story?* (25 has few factors and is one number away from 24, which has many factors.)

Children's literature is a wonderful way to help children understand the meaning of multiplication and division (see *Children's Literature*, **Figure 9.9**).

In the real world, division problems often have **remainders**. When children learn multiplication and division, they should become familiar with remainders and learn that when you have a remainder, there are three options:

> **remainders** The amounts left over in division problems.

1. To discard the remainder
2. To change the answer to the next highest whole number
3. To round the answer to the nearest whole number for estimation

The children's book in *Children's Literature*, **Figure 9.10** provides an excellent introduction to remainders.

Virtual Classroom Observation

Video | www.wiley.com/college/jones

Click on **Student Companion Site**. Then click on:

- **Foundations of Effective Mathematics Teaching**
- **B. Focus on Teacher Content Knowledge**
- **3. Analyze Classroom Videos**

Scroll down and view:

- **Division with Remainders: The van problem**

Notice how Ms. Horowitz uses a contextual problem to help her students decide what to do with the remainder in the problem $36 \div 8$. She points out to her students that in real life, there are often remainders. She also stresses the connection between multiplication and division.

Tech Tools

illuminations.nctm.org

Go to the *NCTM Illuminations* Web site. Select **Lessons**. The unit **All About Multiplication** consists of four lessons that model multiplication of whole numbers using different representations and introduces division as the inverse of multiplication.

Properties of Multiplication and Division

Multiplication and division are inverse operations. In other words, they reverse one another. For example, 3 groups of 8 apples is equal to 24 apples. 24 apples divided into 3 equal groups equals 8 apples in each group, which is the original amount. It is important for children to understand the relationship between multiplication and division.

Multiplication has five important properties that are helpful for learning the basic facts, written computation, mental mathematics, and algebra. The *Curriculum Focal Points* for grade 3 specify that children "use properties of addition and multiplication (e.g., commutativity, associativity, and the distributive property) to multiply whole numbers" (NCTM, 2006, p 15). The *Common Core State Standards* also specify that children learn these properties in grade 3 (NGA Center/CCSSO, 2010).

The commutative property of multiplication

This property states that order is not important in multiplication. Three groups of 8 has the same answer as 8 groups of 3. This property is demonstrated with array and area models (**Figure 9.11**).

The commutative property of multiplication • Figure 9.11

Both the array and area models of multiplication demonstrate the commutative property of multiplication.

3×8 8×3

The associative property of multiplication This property states that when multiplying three or more numbers, you can associate the numbers however you like without affecting the answer. In other words, $3 \times 5 \times 8 = (3 \times 5) \times 8 = 3 \times (5 \times 8)$. The associative property is helpful with mental mathematics (**Activity 9.5**).

Activity 9.5 Find a partner: Multiplication

Instructions

1. Provide children with several sets of numbers to multiply, where each set has three or more numbers and within each set, one pair multiplies to a multiple of 10.

2. Ask children to multiply each set of numbers in at least two ways by pairing each of the numbers with a different "partner" number. After they multiply the numbers, ask: *What did you notice? What did you do to make the numbers easier to multiply?*

3. Here are some sample number sets:

   $5 \times 8 \times 7 = ?$

   $4 \times 6 \times 5 = ?$

   $4 \times 7 \times 5 \times 3 = ?$

The distributive property of multiplication over addition This property states that, when multiplying two numbers, one of the numbers can be split into two or more parts, and each of those parts is multiplied by the other number with the results added together. For example, $3 \times 13 = 3 \times (10 + 3) = 3 \times 10 + 3 \times 3 = 30 + 9 = 39$. The distributive property is helpful when learning basic facts and two-digit computation. In **Activity 9.6**, children are encouraged to discover the distributive property.

Activity 9.6 Splitting up

Instructions

1. Draw a 5 x 6 grid.

2. Ask the children to write the product represented on the grid.

3. Ask the children to split the grid into two unequal parts by making vertical slices so the number of rows remains the same and to write the product represented by each part.

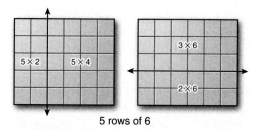

5 rows of 6

4. Repeat, finding as many ways of splitting up this grid as possible using vertical or horizontal slices.

5. Repeat with other grids.

The zero property for multiplication How can teachers help children understand that zero times any number is equal to zero? Children often mix up the rules for addition with zero and multiplication by zero. Help children understand the rule through solving word problems. Consider the following problem:

> *Keeley had three bags with zero oranges in each bag. How many oranges did Keeley have in her bags?*

Ask children to model the problem with a drawing. Then ask how many oranges are in each bag and how many in all the bags. Give children opportunities to solve many problems with zero groups or zero objects in each group, using familiar contexts.

Division by zero causes more difficulties for children than any other computation with zero. For example, they find it difficult to understand why 0 divided by 5 equals zero, but 5 divided by 0 is undefined. Many adults cannot explain this either but have just accepted the answer they learned as children. How can teachers explain why division by zero is impossible? Consider the following word problems:

> *Jonathon has 16 chocolate candies that he wants to put in groups of zero candies each. How many groups can he make?*

> *Mary Alice has 10 cookies that she wants to divide into zero equal groups. How many cookies are in each group?*

Discuss these problems with students and model their solutions. In each of these problems, there is no possible answer, and this is not the same as an answer of zero.

The identity property The number 1 is known as the **multiplicative identity**. Children often confuse multiplication by zero and multiplication by one, so it is important to give them several opportunities to solve both types of problems. Offer children interesting problems in familiar contexts that use the quantity one, and give them opportunities to model their solutions.

> **multiplicative identity** A number whose product when multiplied with any other number is the other number.

Matt has one bag of eight candies. How many candies does Matt have?

James has three bags with one plum in each bag. How many plums does James have?

CONCEPT CHECK

1. **Why** is it important for teachers to understand and identify the different types of multiplication and division problems?

2. **What** are the stages through which children progress as they learn the operations of multiplication and division?

3. **What** are the properties of multiplication? How can the distributive property help children multiply one-digit numbers by two-digit numbers?

4. **What** is the relationship between multiplication and division?

Learning the Basic Facts

LEARNING OBJECTIVES

1. **Describe** basic facts and basic fact mastery.

2. **Explain** the three-step process for fact mastery.

3. **Identify** six thinking strategies for learning addition and subtraction basic facts.

4. **Identify** six thinking strategies for learning multiplication and division basic facts.

According to *Curriculum Focal Points* (NCTM, 2006), in grade 2 "children should use their understanding of addition to develop quick recall of basic addition facts and related subtraction facts" (p. 14). In grade 4, children "use understandings of multiplication to develop quick recall of the basic multiplication facts and related division facts" (NCTM, 2006, p. 16). This section discusses the definition of basic facts, the reasons it is important for children to learn them, and the best approaches for mastery.

What Are the Basic Facts?

The basic facts for addition and multiplication refer to all possible combinations of single-digit addends and factors. There are 100 basic facts for addition and 100 basic facts for multiplication. When a child demonstrates **mastery of a basic fact**, this means that the child can recall the fact in about three seconds. Given the number of basic facts to learn, this can be a daunting task for elementary school children.

Educators agree that children should learn the basic facts because computational fluency is an important component of overall mathematical proficiency. However, there are different opinions about how basic facts should be taught (Baroody, 2006). Some educators still favor rote memorization of individual facts. Educators who support Standards-based reforms understand the difference between rote memorization of isolated facts and **automaticity**: "A child who thinks of 9×6 as $(10 \times 6) - 6$ produces the answer of 54 quickly, but thinking not memorization is at the core" (Fosnot and Dolk, 2001, pp. 85–86). When children learn basic facts by using thinking strategies, they will remember the facts over time and be able to connect them to other facts and concepts.

> **automaticity** The use of thinking strategies to retrieve the basic facts.

In the Classroom
Parents and Children Working Together to Master the Basic Facts

Fourth-grade teacher Emily Calais's believed that it was important for children to use thinking strategies to master the basic facts, but she understood that some parents favored rote memorization. This year, Emily hatched a plan to win parents over. During parents' visitation night, she invited children and parents to work together to find multiplication facts. For each fact, she asked: *What are two strategies you can use to find this fact?* For example, when she asked for 8 x 7, the parents looked baffled. One parent said: *I just know that 8 x 7 = 56.* Then one child raised her hand and said, *I know 7 x 7 is 49 and one more 7 is 56.* Another child skip counted and said, *7, 14, 21, 28, 35, 42, 49, 56,* while he counted the number of skips on his fingers and stopped when he reached eight.

The parents in Ms. Calais's class were so impressed that they applauded the children's answers. Many parents commented, "I wish I had been taught that way when I was in school." Then Ms. Calais told the parents, "Your children are learning to reason their way to the facts. By learning them in this way they have a much better chance of remembering their facts in the future."

Think Critically

1. Why is it important to have parental support for your mathematics program?
2. Why is it important for children to learn basic facts with thinking strategies?

Multicultural Perspectives in Mathematics

Learning Number Facts in Other Cultures

In countries whose written number system is based on Chinese, children learn the make ten strategy to learn basic addition facts. This strategy may have evolved because the Chinese number system emphasizes grouping by tens. For example, the word for eleven translates to ten-one, the word for twelve translates to ten-two, and so on. This pattern continues with the decade numbers.

To learn addition facts, Chinese children learn to decompose numbers into tens and ones. For example, to add 8 + 7, they learn that 8 + 2 = 10 and 2 + 5 = 7, so 8 + 7 = 8 + 2 + 5 = 10 + 5 = 15.

In American textbooks, children learn all the sums of a particular number. For example, they learn all the pairs of numbers that add to 8: 1 + 7, 2 + 6, 3 + 5, 4 + 4. In contrast, Chinese textbooks arrange the basic facts as fact tables. Rather than learning all the facts that sum to the number 8, children learn 8 + 1, 8 + 2, 8 + 3, 8 + 4, and so on, and use the make ten strategy to find the sums. The result is fewer facts to learn. When

they make use of the commutative property, Chinese children only have 45 addition facts to learn.

(*Sources*: Fuson, 2003, pp. 68–94; Sun and Zhang, 2001, pp. 28–31)

Strategies for the Classroom

- Why is the make ten strategy important?
- How can you use it in your classroom?

Parents are sometimes very concerned about their children's learning of the basic facts. Here is how one teacher handled parental concerns (see *In the Classroom*).

Before you learn about how basic facts are taught in the United States, take a look at basic fact instruction in other cultures (see *Multicultural Perspectives in Mathematics*).

Helping Children Master the Basic Facts

Children will not learn the basic facts and remember them through practice alone. A three-step process is effective for mastering the basic facts (**Figure 9.12**).

A three-step process to mastering the basic facts • Figure 9.12

THE PLANNER

The three steps for mastering the basic facts are "Counting strategies"; "Reasoning strategies"; and "Mastery" (Baroody, 2006, p. 22). Children find it easier to learn basic facts for addition than for multiplication. This process works for both addition and multiplication facts but will be illustrated with multiplication because it is more complex.

1 Counting strategies

Children understand when each operation is called for, based on the meaning of the operation, and can successfully apply that operation to the problem, finding the answer in whatever informal ways they understand. This usually involves counting.

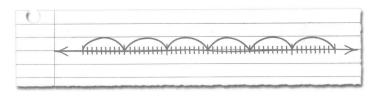

2 Reasoning strategies

Children use reasoning strategies and use facts that they know to find facts that they do not know. For example, to find 6 x 9, a child might find 5 x 9 and then add one more 9. Through practice, they begin to recall facts more quickly.

3 Mastery

Children practice the facts they are learning in step 2 through games, songs, and other activities so that the facts are recalled with automaticity.

100 addition facts   Table 9.1

+	0	1	2	3	4	5	6	7	8	9
0	0	1	2	3	4	5	6	7	8	9
1	1	2	3	4	5	6	7	8	9	10
2	2	3	4	5	6	7	8	9	10	11
3	3	4	5	6	7	8	9	10	11	12
4	4	5	6	7	8	9	10	11	12	13
5	5	6	7	8	9	10	11	12	13	14
6	6	7	8	9	10	11	12	13	14	15
7	7	8	9	10	11	12	13	14	15	16
8	8	9	10	11	12	13	14	15	16	17
9	9	10	11	12	13	14	15	16	17	18

What can you do when children have trouble remembering the basic facts?

1. Assess their prior knowledge of mathematics. Find out whether they can count meaningfully.

2. Find out whether they understand the meaning of the four operations.

3. Find out which facts they already know.

4. Help them practice basic facts in a fun, nonthreatening way.

5. Encourage them to look for patterns.

6. Keep practice sessions short (about 10 minutes each) and upbeat.

7. Be positive and encouraging.

Teaching Tip

Remediating basic fact instruction

By the fifth or sixth grade, if students do not already know their facts, more drill is not the solution. In this case, work with students individually to diagnose their difficulties and find out which facts they know, focus on reasoning strategies rather than memorization, and create activities that begin with easy facts to build students' confidence.

Mastering Addition and Subtraction Facts

The 100 addition facts are illustrated in **Table 9.1**.

To find 6 + 7, go down the first column on the left to 6, then across that row until you find the column headed by the number 7. The number in the box, 13, is the sum of 6 + 7. You could also do the reverse. That is, go down the left-most column to 7, then across that row until you find

the column headed by the number 6. The number in the box is again 13 and is the sum of 7 + 6. You have just used the commutative property. This cuts the number of sums to learn almost in half.

The subtraction facts can also be found by using this table. One of the best strategies for subtraction is to think addition. If you are asked to find 12 − 5, think: *What number do I add to 5 to get 12?* Start in the left-most column and go down to 5, then across that row until you find the box with 12 in it. Look at the top number in that column and you will find 7. 12 − 5 = 7, because 5 + 7 = 12. Here you are using the inverse relationship of addition and subtraction.

Next, we examine several strategies that can facilitate learning the basic facts for addition and subtraction.

Counting on When children use counting on, they begin with one addend and then count on to the other addend. When children begin using this strategy, they may use objects for counting on and later use their fingers. After they are more practiced with the strategy, they notice that they can count on from the larger addend. In other words, if asked to add 3 + 8, instead of counting on from 3, they start at 8 and count on 3 more numbers. This is a result of the commutative property. Children can practice this strategy through a number of activities (see **Activity 9.7**).

Activity 9.7 Numbers in a bag

Instructions

1. Give each pair of students a small bag containing slips of paper with the numbers 0 through 9 written on them. Each bag should have two slips of paper for each number.

2. Ask one student to select two numbers from the bag and the other student to find the sum of the numbers using counting on.

3. Reverse roles and play again.

Learning the doubles strategy for addition facts • Figure 9.13

Which doubles facts are illustrated by these examples?

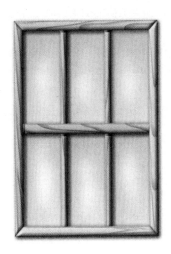

Counting back This is a more difficult strategy and can be used in subtraction problems. For example, to find 15 − 7, start at 15 and count back by ones 7 times. Children have a lot of difficulty learning to count back. A better choice is to change the problem to addition and find 7 plus what number equals 15 by counting on to 15.

Doubles Look back at the addition facts in Table 9.1. All of the double facts are along a diagonal line from the top left to the bottom right of the table. Children learn the doubles facts very easily. You can facilitate their memory of doubles with real-world examples (**Figure 9.13** and *Children's Literature*, **Figure 9.14**).

CHILDREN'S LITERATURE

Using the doubling strategy

Two of Everything •
Figure 9.14

Written and illustrated by Lily Toy Hong
This Chinese folktale tells the story of an elderly couple who find a magic pot. Everything that is put into the pot doubles, with some unexpected humorous results. This book is a great way to teach children doubles facts.

Strategies for the Classroom

- Read the book with children.
- Make a T-chart on the overhead or board with titles "In the magic pot" and "Out of the magic pot."
- Read the book again, this time filling in the T-chart with numbers and words.
- Ask children to describe the pattern they see.

One more than or one less than This is a wonderful strategy to use when children know some facts and want to expand their knowledge. It is a great strategy to combine with the doubles strategy. Doubles facts are usually the first ones children commit to memory. If you ask children what 6 + 7 is, they can recall that 6 + 6 is double 6, or 12, and then 6 + 7 is one more than 12, or 13. As an alternative, a child might recall that double 7 is 14, so 6 + 7 is one less than 14, or 13.

Making 10 and up over 10 This is the strategy that is used in China, Japan, and Korea. It can also be used very successfully with American children. When given an addition fact such as 8 + 5, you find that 8 + 2 = 10, and then decompose 5 into 2 + 3 and write 8 + 5 = 8 + 2 + 3 = 10 + 3 = 13.

Learning fact families As children learn addition and subtraction facts, it is helpful for them to learn **fact families**, or the entire group of facts that use the same three numbers. When learning 8 + 5 = 13, you can also recognize that 5 + 8 = 13, 13 − 5 = 8, and 13 − 8 = 5. Learning fact families helps children connect their knowledge of basic facts to the properties of addition and subtraction.

Mastering Multiplication and Division Facts

The 100 multiplication facts are illustrated in **Table 9.2**.

To find 4 × 8, go down the left-most column to 4 and across that row until you reach the column that is headed by 8. The number in the box is 32. You can also go down the left-most column to 8 and across that row to the column headed by 4. The number in the box is again 32, because of the commutative property.

Division facts can also be found using this table. For example, to find 32 ÷ 4, go down the left-most column to 4 and across that row until you find the box with 32 in it. Then look to the top of the column with 32, and you will see 8.

There are several strategies that can facilitate learning the basic facts for multiplication and division.

Repeated addition This is the strategy that children use when they are first learning to multiply. A child using this strategy might find 4 groups of 6 by saying or writing

$$6 + 6 + 6 + 6$$

Skip counting This is another beginning strategy. Children often skip count by counting out loud and keeping track of the number of skips by using counters or counting on their fingers. To solve 4 × 6 by skip counting, a child might say, *6, 12, 18, 24.* A clock is a great tool for learning skip counting by fives and 5 facts

100 multiplication facts		**Table 9.2**								
×	**0**	**1**	**2**	**3**	**4**	**5**	**6**	**7**	**8**	**9**
0	0	0	0	0	0	0	0	0	0	0
1	0	1	2	3	4	5	6	7	8	9
2	0	2	4	6	8	10	12	14	16	18
3	0	3	6	9	12	15	18	21	24	27
4	0	4	8	12	16	20	24	28	32	36
5	0	5	10	15	20	25	30	35	40	45
6	0	6	12	18	24	30	36	42	48	54
7	0	7	14	21	28	35	42	49	56	63
8	0	8	16	24	32	40	48	56	64	72
9	0	9	18	27	36	45	54	63	72	81

(**Activity 9.8**). Activities such as this one can reinforce that one 5 is 5, two 5s are 10, three 5s are 15, and so on.

Activity 9.8 Using the clock to learn 5 facts

Instructions

1. Use a large clock or make a clock using a paper plate on which you affix two stick hands. Position the minute and hour hands so the clock is pointing to 7 o'clock.

2. Say: *What time is it now?* (7)

   Ask (as you move the minute hand to 1): *How many minutes past seven is it now?*

3. Continue in this manner as you move the minute hand in 5-minute intervals around the clock. Do not accept answers such as, *A quarter to 8.* The answer should always reflect how many minutes past the hour it is.

Doubles This is another easy strategy for children to learn and is a natural extension of repeated addition when both factors are the same. For example, 2 groups of three is the same as $3 + 3$ or 2×3. Children already know the doubles facts as addition. Help them understand that addition doubles facts are the same as multiplying by 2. Remind children of the commutative property so they understand that $2 \times 3 = 3 \times 2$.

Using known facts A powerful strategy for learning multiplication facts is to split one of the factors into two smaller parts, both of which have known facts. For example, if children are asked to find 3×8 and do not know this fact, they can split 3 into $2 + 1$, writing $3 \times 8 = (2 + 1) \times 8 = 2 \times 8 + 1 \times 8$. This changes the fact to an easily retrievable one, double 8 along with adding one more 8. Notice that this strategy depends on the distributive property of multiplication over addition.

Here is another application of this strategy: Suppose you are asked to find 6×8. Once you know that $3 \times 8 = 24$, 6 is twice 3, so 6×8 is twice 3×8. Therefore, $3 \times 8 = 24$ and 6×8 is 2×24, or 48.

Patterns The 9 facts are often difficult for children, but with the use of patterns, they are accessible (see the *Lesson* on the next page). The standards in this *Lesson* are from Curriculum Focal Points for grades 2 and 4 (NCTM, 2006) and the *Operations and Algebraic Thinking* domain of the *Common Core State Standards* (NGA Center/CCSSO, 2010).

Learning fact families As children learn multiplication and division facts, have them learn fact families for these operations as well. This helps connect the operations of multiplication and division and reinforces the commutative property. For example, when learning $3 \times 4 = 12$, children should also know that $4 \times 3 = 12$, $12 \div 4 = 3$, and $12 \div 3 = 4$.

CONCEPT CHECK   **STOP**

1. **Why** is it important for children to learn basic facts?

2. **What** is the difference between automaticity and rote memorization?

3. **Suppose** one child adds 5 and 7 by counting on and another child adds $5 + 7$ by decomposing 7 into 5 and 2 and then making 10. Is one strategy better than the other?

4. **Suppose** one child multiplies 6 x 5 by skip counting five times 5 and then adds one more 5, and a second child uses repeated addition to add six 5s. Is one strategy better than the other?

LESSON Finding 9 Facts

9
Nine

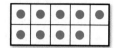

GRADE LEVEL
2–4

OBJECTIVE

Students identify patterns in addition facts where 9 is an addend.

Students identify patterns in multiplication facts where 9 is a factor.

STANDARDS

Grade 2

Developing quick recall of addition facts and related subtraction facts and fluency with multi-digit addition and subtraction. (NCTM, 2006, p. 14)

Fluently add and subtract within 20 using mental strategies. By end of grade 2, know from memory all sums of two one-digit numbers. (NGA Center/CCSSO, 2010)

Grade 4

Developing quick recall of multiplication and related division facts and fluency with whole number multiplication. (NCTM, 2006, p. 16)

MATERIALS

- 100 addition facts table for each child
- 100 multiplication facts table for each child
- Colored highlighter for each child

ASSESSMENT

- Observe students as they work in pairs. Can they find the 9 patterns for addition and multiplication? Can they apply the patterns to problems where one addend or factor is unknown? Can they apply the patterns to problems when the 9 addend or factor is second?

- Do children recognize how the commutative property is used in the patterns when 9 is the second addend or factor?

GROUPING

Whole class followed by pairs

Launch (5 to 10 minutes)

- Write the number 9 on the board. Show a ten-frame with 9 dots on it. Write "nine" and show 9 o'clock on a clock.

- Ask: *What can you tell me about the number 9?* (Children give various replies, such as *9 is one less than 10.*)

- Ask: *What comes in 9s?* (There will be various answers. If no one says this, tell children that there are nine players on a baseball team.)

- Say: *9 is a very important number. Today we are going to learn about some patterns with 9.*

Instruct (25 to 30 minutes)

- Say: *Working in pairs, look at your addition facts table. Highlight the row and column that has 9.*

- Say: *Make a table that lists the 9 facts for addition. What pattern do you notice?*

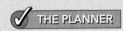
9 Facts for Addition
1 + 9 = 10
2 + 9 = 11
3 + 9 = 12
4 + 9 = 13
5 + 9 = 14
6 + 9 = 15
7 + 9 = 16
8 + 9 = 17
9 + 9 = 18

- If no one identifies the pattern, ask children to look at the sum of the digits in the answer. Ask: *What is the sum of the digits in the answer? What is 1 + 0? What is 1 + 1?*

- Elicit from children the idea that the sum of the digits of the answer is always equal to the first addend, so 6 + 9 = 15 and 1 + 5 = 6.

- Ask: *Will this pattern still work if we use the turn-around property? Find 9 + 6.* (Yes, it still works, but now the sum of the digits of the answer is equal to the second addend.)

- Say: *Now put away your addition facts table. Solve the following addition sentences from the pattern we learned.*

    ? + 9 = 14   Find *?*
    ? + 9 = 12   Find *?*
    9 + ? = 13   Find *?*

- Say: *Now still working in pairs, I would like you to look at your multiplication facts table. Highlight the row and column that has 9.*

- Say: *Make a table that lists the 9 facts for multiplication. What patterns do you notice?*

9 Facts for Multiplication
1 × 9 = 9
2 × 9 = 18

3 × 9 = 27
4 × 9 = 36
5 × 9 = 45
6 × 9 = 54
7 × 9 = 63
8 × 9 = 72
9 × 9 = 81

- Circulate as children work in pairs. Suggest that they look at the product to find the pattern. Ask: *What is 1 + 8? What is 2 + 7?*

- Children should notice that the numbers in the product always add to 9. If they do not see another pattern, continue as follows:

- Say: *There is another pattern too. Look at the factor and the product to find this pattern.*

- Children should notice that the first factor is always one more than the tens digit of the product. So for 2 × 9, the product is 18 and the 2 is one more than 1. For 5 × 9, the product is 45 and 5 is one more than 4.

- Ask: *Will this pattern work if we reverse the digits? Try 9 × 5.* (The pattern still works but now the second factor is one more than the tens digit of the product.)

- Say: *Now put away your multiplication facts table. See if you can solve the following multiplication sentences from the patterns you learned. Make sure to explain your reasoning.*

    ? × 9 = 72   Find *?*
    ? × 9 = 81   Find *?*
    9 × ? = 27   Find *?*

Summarize (5 minutes)

- Ask: *What patterns did you learn about the 9 facts for addition and multiplication?*

- Ask: *Will these patterns always work when one of the addends or factors is a 9?*

Summary

1 Whole Number Operations: An Overview 218

- Whole number operations are best taught through word problems that provide familiar contexts for children, as illustrated. Children come to school with some knowledge of the operations, especially addition and subtraction and informal strategies for adding and subtracting. Capitalize on what children know by encouraging them to use their invented and informal strategies as they learn the operations.

Figure 9.1

- Do not rush symbolism. Make sure children understand each operation before introducing **symbols** and **number sentences.** When you do introduce symbolism, do it for one operation at a time.

2 Teaching Addition and Subtraction 220

- Join problems are one type of addition and subtraction problem. There are three other types. You should understand the different types of problems so you can make sure that children have the opportunity to solve a variety of problems with different strategies. In this picture, the child uses the counting all strategy. Textbooks usually give only the easiest types of problems.

Figure 9.4

- Children progress through three stages as they learn addition: counting all, counting on, and using thinking strategies.

- It is important that children learn the properties of addition: the zero property (zero is the **additive identity**), the commutative property, and the associative property. Children need to understand the inverse relationship between addition and subtraction. In other words, addition and subtraction reverse each other.

3 Teaching Multiplication and Division 225

- There are four types of multiplication and division problems, although textbooks usually present only the easiest. Become familiar with these different types of problems so your students will understand them. Multiplication is a much harder concept for children to learn than addition. To understand multiplication, children must understand the concept of **composite wholes**. Children progress through three stages as they learn multiplication: counting all, a combination of counting and composite wholes, and recognizing composite wholes. This picture illustrates an array of 4 sets of 6 cupcakes each.

Figure 9.8

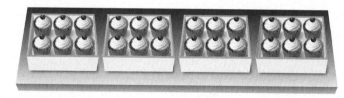

- Children need to learn the properties of multiplication: the distributive property, the commutative property, and associative property, and the **multiplicative identity.** Children should also learn that multiplication and division are opposites—that is, they reverse one another.

- Children should learn the meaning and use of **remainders** in division. Most real-world problems that use division involve remainders. The context of the problem determines how to handle remainders.

4 Learning the Basic Facts 233

- When children learn the basic facts, they are becoming proficient in mathematics. There are two philosophies of how to teach the basic facts. One philosophy calls for rote memorization of random facts. The other, standards-based philosophy, calls for **automaticity**, which is learning the basic facts through thinking strategies.

- A three-step process is effective for learning basic facts: understand the operations, use thinking strategies, and get lots of practice so that facts can be recalled quickly.

- There are a number of strategies for learning basic addition facts. The doubles strategy is one of the easiest, as illustrated here. It is important to use the commutative property and the **additive identity** to reduce the number of facts that children need to learn. When practicing facts, keep sessions short and keep a positive atmosphere.

Figure 9.13

- There are a number of strategies for learning basic multiplication facts. Use the commutative property and the **multiplicative identity** to reduce the number of facts that children need to learn. Multiplication facts seem to be more difficult for children than addition. Keep practice sessions short and maintain an upbeat atmosphere.

Key Terms

- addends 220
- additive identity 224
- automaticity 233
- compatible 224
- composite wholes 229
- count down 223

- count up to 223
- fact families 238
- factor 226
- inverse 223
- mastery of a basic fact 233
- measurement division 225

- multiplicative identity 233
- number sentences 219
- partitive division 225
- product 226
- remainders 231
- symbols 219

Additional Children's Literature

- *The Doorbell Rang,* written and illustrated by Pat Hutchins
  This book tells the story of Sam and Victoria, whose Mom made 12 cookies for them. Before they can eat their cookies, more and more visitors arrive, creating division situations and illustrating the relationship between multiplication and division.

- *Each Orange Had 8 Slices,* written by Paul Giganti Jr. and illustrated by Donald Crews
  This book presents a number of questions that involve counting, multiplication, and addition with clever illustrations.

- *Anno's Magic Seeds* written and illustrated by Mitsumasa Anno
  This is the story of Jack, who received two magic seeds. He baked one seed and ate it. He planted the other seed. The next year he planted both seeds. As the years go by, many different patterns emerge for multiplication.

Online Resources

Critical and Creative Thinking Questions

1. **In the field** Interview a first- or second-grade child. The interview should take about 30 minutes.
   - Prepare five or six addition and subtraction problems that represent all four types explained in this chapter.
   - Write the problems out clearly, and be prepared to read the problems to the child you are interviewing.
   - Bring along counters, blocks, large sheets of paper, crayons, and markers.
   - Find a quiet spot for the interview.
   - Do not teach the child how to do the problems. Simply provide the problems and materials and observe how the child solves them.
   - What did you notice? What problems was the child able to solve? What difficulties did the child have? Was there anything that surprised you?

2. What are some advantages to learning the basic facts through thinking strategies?

3. In this chapter, you read about the Chinese strategy of making 10 and learning all the facts for a single number. What are some advantages of this strategy? Would it work well in American classrooms? Why or why not?

4. Describe three strategies that could be used to learn the fact $8 + 7$.

5. Describe three strategies that could be used to learn the fact 4×5.

6. **Using visuals** Figure 9.5 illustrates the four types of multiplication and division problems with rich illustrations. How do these illustrations help you to understand the different types of problems? What illustrations would you use if you were teaching this topic to your own students? Develop your own illustrations to represent each of the four types of multiplication and division problems.

What is happening in this picture?

Visiting a garden center or farmer's market is a familiar activity in the spring in many parts of the United States.

Think Critically

1. What is one activity about the meaning of multiplication that you could create with this image?
2. Can you think of similar images that relate to children's lives outside of school that can help teach the meaning of multiplication?

Self-Test

(Check your answers in Appendix D.)

1. What are three reasons for teaching the meaning of operations through word problems?

2. True or false: Symbolism should be introduced immediately, when teaching whole number operations.

3. True or false: Children's textbooks provide a wide variety of word problems that model the four arithmetic operations.

4. Which types of addition problems are most difficult for children to solve? Why?

5. True or false: The operation of multiplication is more difficult for children to learn than addition.

6. Which property is called the "turn-around" property? Why is it named that way?

7. Which property tells us that $3 + 0 = 3$?

8. Which property tells us that $5 \times 1 = 5$?

9. Write a part-part-whole problem with the part unknown.

10. Write a measurement division problem.

11. Write a partitive division problem.

12. What problem might this child be solving?

13. What problem is shown here? What property is being used?

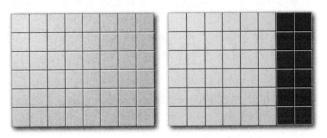

14. William says: *To find 17 – 9, I say 10, 11, 12, 13, 14, 15, 16, 17. The answer is 8.* What thinking strategy is William using?

15. What problem is being shown by these ten-frames? What thinking strategy would a child use?

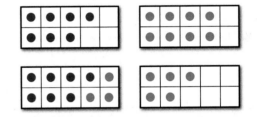

THE PLANNER ✓

Review your Chapter Planner on the chapter opener and check off your completed work.

Whole Number Computation, Mental Computation, and Estimation

The first-, second-, and third-grade classes at Bach Elementary School in Ann Arbor, Michigan, recently returned from a trip to their state's capital in Lansing. Third-grade teacher Marla Johnston used the experience to provide her children with a real-world example of multiplication. She said to her class, *Yesterday, five buses went to Lansing. There were 36 children and adults on each bus. How many people went on our trip to Lansing?* Ms. Johnston noticed that some students used base-ten blocks or drew arrays while other children solved the problem with mental computation.

Jayonne volunteered her solution. She said, *I doubled 36 to 72. Then I doubled it again to 144. That's*
4 × 36. Then I added another 36. I know 144 + 6 = 150, plus another 30 = 180. Tyler said, *I split up 36 into 30 and 6. I know 5 × 3 = 15, so 5 × 30 = 150 and 5 × 6 = 30, so the answer is 150 + 30 = 180.* Many of the solutions offered by the students were similar to those presented by Jayonne and Tyler.

Ms. Johnston was pleased that students in her class used a variety of strategies to solve the problem and were able to explain their thinking to the class. She also knew that research strongly suggests that children develop their own strategies for arithmetic operations with a focus on mental computation and written computation that is efficient and easy to understand.

CHAPTER OUTLINE

Whole Number Computation in the Elementary Grades: An Overview 248

Key Question: What are the goals of whole number computation?

Strategies for Whole Number Addition and Subtraction Computation 252

Key Question: How should we teach whole number addition and subtraction?

Strategies for Whole Number Multiplication and Division Computation 258

Key Question: How should we teach whole number multiplication and division?

Computational Estimation, Mental Computation, and Calculators 267

Key Question: What role do computational estimation, mental computation, and calculators play in computation?

NCTM The NCTM Number and Operations Standard from *Principles and Standards for School Mathematics* (2000) includes several expectations for whole number computation.

In prekindergarten through grade 2, all students should

- develop and use strategies for whole number computations, with a focus on addition and subtraction;
- use a variety of methods and tools to compute, including objects, mental computation, estimation, paper and pencil, and calculators.   (NCTM, 2000, p. 78)

In grades 3–5, all students should

- develop fluency with basic number combinations for multiplication and division and use these combinations to mentally compute related problems, such as 30×50;
- develop fluency in adding, subtracting, multiplying, and dividing whole numbers;
- develop and use strategies to estimate the results of whole number computations and to judge the reasonableness of such results.   (NCTM, 2000, p. 148)

Using real-world examples, such as a field trip, can help children develop a better understanding of mathematics.

Whole Number Computation in the Elementary Grades: An Overview

LEARNING OBJECTIVES

1. **Describe** the history of algorithms.
2. **Explain** the characteristics of computational fluency.
3. **Identify** children's developmental steps in learning computation.
4. **Describe** how to help children who have difficulties with computation.

Traditionally, computation has meant written computation (as opposed to mental computation) and the use of **algorithms** to obtain results. This is a fairly narrow view of computation. There are many ways to approach whole number computation. Many calculations can be done mentally, with calculators, or by using paper-and-pencil algorithms that are more accessible to children than traditional algorithms. In the opening story of this chapter, neither Jayonne nor Tyler used the traditional multiplication algorithm to find the answer to the bus problem. In fact, not every calculation requires an exact answer. In some cases, estimated results are more appropriate. This chapter will examine strategies for paper-and-pencil computation, mental computation, and computation with calculators.

> **algorithm** A procedure or formula for solving a mathematical problem.

A Brief History of Algorithms

The algorithms that we use for whole number computation were invented by Persian mathematician Muhammad ibn Musa al-Khwarizmi in the ninth century (Fosnot and Dolk, 2001a). Before that time, computations were done with the abacus by people who were specially trained to use it for calculations related to commerce, trade, and taxation. The development of algorithms standardized mathematics computation, made it possible to keep written records so that computations could be checked, and allowed more people to learn how to compute with numbers. Although algorithms were a very important development in mathematics, it is time to broaden our view of algorithms and learn about new ways to compute with whole numbers.

Computational Fluency

Your goal as a teacher is to help children develop **computational fluency**, which "requires a balance and connection between conceptual understanding and computational proficiency" (NCTM, 2000, p. 35). In the past, computational fluency meant that children learned one algorithm for each class of problems and practiced those algorithms throughout the elementary grades with increasingly more difficult computations. Often, algorithms were learned as rote methods without understanding the steps involved.

Now a new view of computational fluency is evolving. "Computational fluency is rooted in an understanding of arithmetic operations, the base-ten number system, and number relationships" (Bresser, 2003, p. 294). Educators recognize the importance of learning algorithms, but also understand that many algorithms are available for whole number computation and that learning just one algorithm for each type of problem may be a disadvantage rather than an advantage. Children benefit from learning to use algorithms that they understand and that are efficient, easy to use, and will apply to all problems of a given class.

Before reading any further, try solving the following task: 3007 − 88. Now read three solutions to this problem, illustrated in **Figure 10.1**.

Which method did you use? You probably used the traditional algorithm (**Figure 10.1a**) because this is how you were taught subtraction in school. Now imagine for a moment that you are a child first learning a subtraction algorithm. Compare the three methods. What are the advantages and disadvantages of each method? Can you explain your steps for each method? Which methods are more likely to lead to errors? Which methods rely on an understanding of place value and number sense?

a. In this solution, the traditional subtraction algorithm is used: 1000 is traded for 10 hundreds. Then 1 hundred is traded for 10 tens, and 1 ten is traded for 10 ones. The 10 ones are combined with 7 ones to make 17 ones. Here, after regrouping, or trading, we are subtracting from right to left, from the smallest values (the ones) to the largest values (the thousands).

$$
\begin{array}{r}
3007 \\
-88 \\
\hline
\end{array}
\qquad
\begin{array}{r}
{\scriptstyle 9\ \ 9} \\[-2pt]
{\scriptstyle 2\,10\,10\,17} \\[-2pt]
3007 \\
-88 \\
\hline
2919
\end{array}
$$

b. In this solution, 12 is added to the top number and the bottom number, making it much easier to subtract 100 from 3019. There is still one trade, but it is much less complex than in the original problem. Here, we again work from right to left, although the numbers are easier to work with than in the previous solution.

$$
\begin{array}{r}
3007 \\
-88 \\
\hline
\end{array}
\qquad
\begin{array}{r}
3007 + 12 \\
-88 + 12 \\
\hline
\end{array}
\qquad
\begin{array}{r}
{\scriptstyle 2\ 10} \\[-2pt]
3019 \\
-100 \\
\hline
2919
\end{array}
$$

c. This solution is worked from left to right, counting up from 88 to 100, then to 1000, then to 3000, then by ones to 3007.

$$
\begin{array}{r}
3007 \\
-88 \\
\hline
\end{array}
\qquad
\begin{aligned}
88 + 12 &= 100 \\
100 + 900 &= 1000 \\
1000 + 2000 &= 3000 \\
3000 + 7 &= 3007 \\
12 + 900 + 2000 + 7 &= 2919
\end{aligned}
$$

Teaching Whole Number Computation

Most elementary mathematics textbooks teach the traditional algorithms for addition, subtraction, multiplication, and division. As a new teacher, you may feel pressured to comply because the traditional algorithms are part of your curriculum and you may be uncomfortable with alternative algorithms. Consider teaching the traditional algorithms after children have had many opportunities to create, refine, and share their own algorithms. Work with your class to analyze each of their created algorithms. Some student-created algorithms are just as efficient as the traditional algorithms because children make fewer mistakes using them.

As a class, choose a few algorithms for each operation. Make a list of the algorithms you like, name them, and post them in prominent places in your classroom. Then introduce the traditional algorithm and some accessible alternatives. If you introduce the traditional algorithm first, children will feel they have to use it. However, if you introduce it later, they have a better opportunity to understand it and recognize that it provides a choice rather than an obligation. "As students move from third to fifth grade, they should consolidate and practice a small number of computational algorithms for addition, subtraction, multiplication, and division that they understand well and can use routinely" (NCTM, 2000, p. 155).

Comparing Traditional and Student-Created Algorithms

There are a number of differences between traditional and student-created algorithms.

- **Most traditional algorithms are right to left**. That is, they begin with the smallest part of the number and move to the largest part of the number (division is an exception). Student-created algorithms are often left to right, which is consistent with students' preferred way of working. After all, you read and write from left to right, and it seems more natural to compute that way as well.

- **Traditional algorithms often focus on the digit rather than the number, while student-created algorithms focus on the value of the digit**. Consider the problem 8×24. In using the traditional algorithm, you would multiply the digits 8×2, and ignore that the 2 is really 2 tens or 20. In the student-created algorithm, you would recognize that you are multiplying 8×20.

- **Traditional algorithms lack flexibility**. They do not adapt to different problem conditions as well as student-created algorithms do. For example, if given the problem 19×23, with a student-created algorithm you might calculate $(20 - 1) \times 23 = (20 \times 23) - (1 \times 23)$. This can make the problem a lot less complicated, and some students might solve it mentally. With the traditional algorithm, this becomes a longer, more difficult calculation and more prone to error.

In this chapter, you will learn how to teach computation strategies for the four whole number operations. Although the operations are very different, the approach to teaching whole number computation is similar for all four operations (**Figure 10.2**).

Children's Difficulties with Whole Number Computation

Children make many kinds of errors with computation, especially when regrouping or trading is involved. Diverse learners are at risk for making more regrouping or trading errors. **Table 10.1** provides strategies for helping children who have difficulty learning algorithms for whole number computation.

Strategies for helping children learn algorithms   Table 10.1

- Make sure children possess the prerequisite knowledge: counting, place value, and meanings of the operations.

- Model solutions for children and give them practice problems often.

- Correct errors early so error patterns do not become routine.

- Use visual cues to help students who have trouble remembering procedures (for example, an array model for multiplication).

- Give students opportunities to practice more student-created algorithms if the traditional algorithms are too difficult for them. The traditional algorithms depend on proportional reasoning (i.e., trading 1 ten for 10 ones) and may be challenging for some children with learning disabilities.

- For English-language learners, connect symbols (+, −, ×, ÷) with words by pointing to the symbols as you are reading the words of a problem. (For example, as you point to the plus sign, say the word "plus.") Pair ELL students with other students who speak their own language but have greater fluency in English.

CONCEPT CHECK

1. **How** did algorithms develop?
2. **What** is computational fluency?
3. **Through which** three developmental stages should children progress as they learn whole number computation?
4. **What** are four strategies for helping children who have difficulty learning whole number computation?

Learning whole number computation • Figure 10.2

When children learn whole number computation, they should progress through three stages. First, they count with concrete objects. Next, they create their own strategies and develop and learn a few reliable algorithms. Finally, they learn the traditional algorithms, which students can use if they can explain why they work. These are the preferred stages of development when student learning is supported by teaching strategies.

These three steps are modeled with the solution to the following problem:

Sam and his dad cooked 8 packages of sausages for their scout troop's breakfast. If there are 24 sausages in each package, how many sausages did they cook?

1 Counting

Children use concrete materials or drawings to model the problem. Here, base-ten blocks are used to model each group of 24. Children should record the method they used, using their own words, to connect the concrete to the abstract. Here, a child might say, *I made 8 groups of 24 and then put them all together*.

2 Student-created strategies

Children create strategies for whole number computation. In this strategy, the distributive property is used to decompose 24 into easier parts. This is a very common student-created strategy. Note that this strategy involves left to right computation: finding 8 groups of the bigger number, 20, and then 8 groups of the smaller number, 4, using knowledge of place value. Children should record their methods to connect the algorithm and the symbolism. Here, a child might say: *I split 24 into 20 and 4. I know that 8 × 20 = 160 and 8 × 4 = 32, so I added 160 and 32.*

$$8 \times 24 = 8 \times (20 + 4) = 8 \times 20 + 8 \times 4$$
$$= 160 + 32$$
$$= 192$$

3 Traditional algorithm or efficient alternative algorithms

After children have had lots of practice creating, using, sharing, and evaluating their created algorithms, they will narrow down their choices to a few reliable algorithms, with teacher support. At this time, the teacher can introduce the traditional algorithm or another, more accessible algorithm.

Strategies for Whole Number Addition and Subtraction Computation

LEARNING OBJECTIVES

1. **Explain** the importance of student-created strategies for addition and subtraction.

2. **Describe** student-created strategies for addition and subtraction.

3. **Identify** the steps in teaching the traditional algorithms for addition and subtraction.

4. **Compare** and **contrast** traditional and alternative algorithms for addition and subtraction.

When children begin adding and subtracting numbers, they initially count. Although this is fairly efficient for one-digit numbers, it is not very efficient for two- and three-digit addition and subtraction. The strategies that children create for adding and subtracting one- and two-digit numbers are somewhat similar. In this section several of these strategies are investigated. Traditional algorithms and student-created algorithms are described.

Student-Created Strategies for Addition and Subtraction

Children create many strategies for addition and subtraction (Fuson, 2003). Examples of children's addition strategies are illustrated in **Figure 10.3**. Notice that two of the strategies use an **open number line**, which is a number line that does not have any units or numbers on it (Fosnot and Dolk, 2001a). Children will not invent this model on their own, but once they are shown the open number line, they can use it to create their own strategies and record their work.

Tech Tools

http://nlvm.usu.edu

Go to the National Library of Virtual Manipulatives Web site and select the **Number Line Bounce** applet. This applet uses an open number line and arrows that move in both directions to model addition and subtraction problems.

Student-created strategies for addition • Figure 10.3

Give children time to explore their strategies so they understand them well. Encourage them to discuss their strategies and record their work. Children's solutions to the following story problem are illustrated:

Jackson and his family drove in their car to visit his grandmother. First they drove 36 miles and stopped for lunch. Then they drove 27 more miles. How many miles did Jackson's family drive?

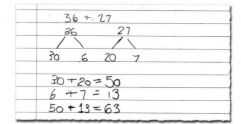

a. Splitting each number into tens and ones

Nathan solved this problem by adding the tens, adding the ones, and then combining them to get the answer.

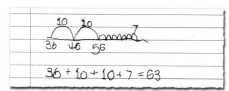

b. Starting at one number and adding on tens and then adding ones

Keisha used an open number line, started at 36, and then made two leaps of 10 and one leap of 7. When children have more practice with this strategy, they make one leap of 20 instead of two leaps of 10.

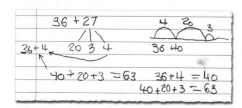

c. Making a nicer number

Terry wrote an equivalent representation for 27: 27 = 20 + 3 + 4 and added 4 and 36 because 36 + 4 = 40. Then she added 40 + 20 + 3. She illustrated her thinking with an open number line.

Student-created strategies for subtraction • Figure 10.4

Give children time to explore the strategies so that they understand them well. Encourage children to discuss their strategies and record their work. Children's solutions to the following story problem are illustrated:

Kim counted 54 dog biscuits in the treat jar. She gave away 22 biscuits to the dogs at the shelter. How many biscuits were left?

a. Counting down by tens and then by ones

Kelsey drew an open number line, started at 54, and then counted down 4 to 50, then down 10 to 40, then 10 again to 30, then down 4, and then down another 4. Even though Kelsey is counting down, she still adds 4 + 10 + 10 + 4 + 4 to get the answer.

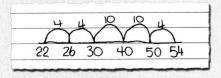

b. Counting up by tens and overshooting the number, then backing up by ones

Jaime drew an open number line, started at 22, and then added 40 to get to 62. He knew that he had gone over 54, so he counted back by ones, first to 60 and then to 54.

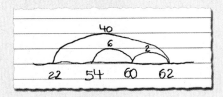

c. Making ten

Mario added 8 to 22 to get a nice number, then added 20 to get 50. He then added by ones to get 54 and found the answer by adding 8 + 20 + 4.

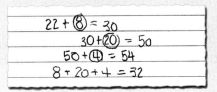

Children also create strategies for subtraction. When numbers are close together, some of the best strategies use the relationship between addition and subtraction. Instead of actually subtracting, children change the subtraction problem to addition and count up. For example, if asked to find 88 – 53, a child might say, *What number must I add to 53 to get 88?* This strategy is not very efficient when numbers are far apart. For example, if asked to find 53 – 5, counting up is not the best strategy to use. Counting down is another effective subtraction strategy. Some student-created subtraction strategies are illustrated in **Figure 10.4**.

For both of the problems illustrated in Figures 10.3 and 10.4, the children needed to **bridge** or cross from one decade to another. This can be challenging, even with student-created strategies and, if done with the traditional algorithms, would have required regrouping and trading. Give children lots of practice adding and subtracting numbers that do not need bridging and then, when they feel confident about their strategies, include problems with bridging (**Activity 10.1**).

Activity 10.1 Solving addition and subtraction problems with and without bridging

Instructions

1. Ask students to solve each of the following problems using any strategies they want.

16 – 4	27 – 3	46 – 2	38 – 3
22 + 3	12 + 4	65 + 4	45 + 2

2. Ask: *What do all these problems have in common?* (They can be solved without bridging or crossing decades—for example, 46 – 2 = 44, still in the 40s.)

3. Ask students to solve each of the following problems using any strategies they want.

16 – 9	27 – 8	46 – 7	38 – 9
22 + 9	12 + 8	65 + 7	45 + 6

4. Ask: *What do all these problems have in common?* (They require crossing decades or bridging—for example, 65 + 7 = 72, moving from 60s to 70s.)

In the Classroom

Using Tens to Add One- and Two-Digit Numbers

Second-grade teacher Jennifer DiBrienza taught a mini-lesson to help her students use tens when they add one- and two-digit numbers. Ms. DiBrienza created the following string of problems:

15 + 10
15 + 9
15 + 19
28 + 19
28 + 32
39 + 21

(*Source*: Fosnot and Dolk, 2001a, p. 128)

She wrote one problem at a time on the board. After children discussed their strategies she wrote the next one. Ms. DiBrienza began with 15 + 10 because it clearly shows a leap of 10. She hoped children would use the same idea when adding 15 + 9, and make a leap of 10 and then go back one. To solve 15 + 9, one child decomposed 15 into 10 + 4 + 1, added 9 + 1 and then 10 + 4.

Another child used the hundreds chart, started at 15, went down one row to 25 and back one. Even though these were not the strategies Ms. DiBrienza hoped her children would use, she discussed the strategies, modeled her students' thinking, and paraphrased their solution strategies so that everyone would understand. Then she suggested the more efficient strategy of using tens, which can be done mentally.

(*Source*: Fosnot and Dolk, 2001)

Think Critically

1. Why did Ms. DiBrienza write problems on the board one at a time in a particular order?
2. How can these strategies help children solve addition and subtraction problems that cross decades?
3. How can these strategies help children when they use the traditional addition algorithm?

Student-created strategies are very useful, and children should be strongly encouraged to create and practice them. However, there are important strategies that they will not create on their own. Help children recognize patterns and develop these strategies through structured activities that you prepare. In the *Mathematics in the City* program developed by Fosnot and Dolk (2001a), teachers create mini-lessons to encourage strategy development. See *In the Classroom* for a lesson that helps children bridge decades by using ten facts.

Teaching the Traditional Algorithms for Addition and Subtraction

After children have created strategies for addition and subtraction and have narrowed down the ones they use to a few reliable strategies, they are ready for the next step. This is the time for them to learn the traditional algorithms and some alternative algorithms that may be more accessible. The traditional algorithms for addition and subtraction are illustrated in **Figure 10.5**.

When teaching traditional algorithms, begin with word problems in familiar contexts, use base-ten blocks, and place value mats to reinforce the idea of regrouping, to encourage children to record their work, and to help children understand each step. These algorithms work from right to left.

a. The traditional addition algorithm

Chris had 34 baseball cards. His cousin gave him 58 more. How many baseball cards does Chris have?

1. Represent both addends with base-ten blocks and write both numbers on the place value mat.

2. *Group the ones. How many ones are there altogether?* (12)

3. *Do you need to make a trade? (Yes) Trade 1 ten for 10 ones.*

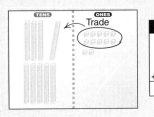 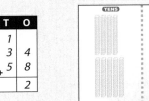

4. *Group the tens. How many tens are there altogether?* (9)

5. *Do you need to make a trade? (No)*

b. The traditional subtraction algorithm

Marie is having a party. She has invited 31 of her classmates, but 12 cannot come. How many classmates are coming to Marie's party?

1. Represent only the top or larger number with base-ten blocks. Write both numbers on the place value mat.

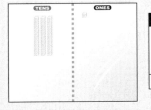 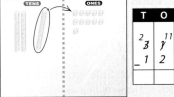

2. *Can you remove two ones? (No) Make a trade. Trade 1 ten for 10 ones.*

3. *Remove 2 ones. How many ones remain?* (9)

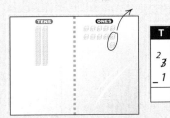 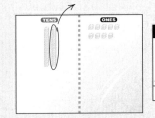

4. *Can you remove 1 ten? (Yes) How many tens remain?* (1)

The partial sums algorithm for addition • Figure 10.6

```
   34              3 tens + 4 ones
 + 78              7 tens + 8 ones
   12   4+8=12   or   10 tens + 12 ones
  100  30+70=100    1 hundred + 1 ten + 2 ones
  112
```

The partial sums algorithm helps children maintain their focus on the value of the digits. It can be worked either from the left or the right.

The traditional algorithms for addition and subtraction can be difficult to learn. Children like to work from larger numbers to smaller numbers, and the traditional algorithms do the opposite. Children also have difficulty with trading and regrouping. If they do not understand when to trade or regroup, they may either do it all the time or not at all.

Teaching Tip

Helping children who have difficulties with the traditional algorithms

Provide a variety of practice problems, some of which require regrouping and some of which do not. Carefully monitor when students are regrouping and trading and ask them to explain each step. Use base-ten blocks and place value mats until students demonstrate complete understanding of the steps of the algorithms.

Tech Tools

http://nlvm.usu.edu

Go to the National Library of Virtual Manipulatives Web site and select the **Base Blocks Addition** applet. This allows students to practice addition using both base-ten blocks and the symbolic representation of the numbers. A variety of problems are provided, including those that require regrouping.

To minimize difficulties with the addition algorithm, try teaching the **partial sums algorithm**. Teachers often refer to the process of grouping together numbers in the same place, (such as 8 + 4) as **chunking**. This algorithm is similar to the traditional algorithm but tends to be easier for children if they understand place value (**Figure 10.6**).

> **partial sums algorithm** A strategy that adds the digits in each place separately.

Lattice addition is another popular alternative to the traditional addition algorithm (**Figure 10.7**).

Lattice addition • Figure 10.7

To use the lattice addition method, insert the numbers in the boxes shown. To find the answer, first add down each column and place the sum of each column in the lattice, then add along the diagonals.

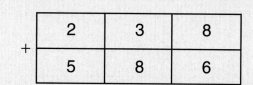
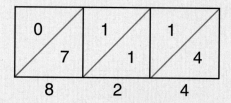

Children's errors when subtracting with zeros • Figure 10.8

Can you identify the errors these children made? What misunderstandings do they have about subtraction with zeros?

		25
250	536	3̶6̶0
-137	-205	-125
127	301	130

Children have many difficulties with the traditional subtraction algorithm, especially when zeros are involved (**Figure 10.8**). When the number of regroupings and trades increases, so does the number of errors. If children are making errors when subtracting numbers with zeros, make sure they use base-ten blocks to make the actual trades, and then record their trades on a place value mat. Model double trades for children and give them plenty of practice. Encourage them to talk through and record their solutions as they model them.

Alternative algorithms for subtraction are often easier to understand (**Figure 10.9**). Introduce the **partial differences algorithm** and the **equal additions algorithm** as alternatives to the traditional algorithm.

> **partial differences algorithm** A strategy that subtracts the bottom digit from the top digit in each place, regardless of size, and requires no trades.
>
> **equal additions algorithm** A strategy that adds 1 ten, 1 hundred, or 1 thousand to the top and bottom numbers so that trading is not necessary.

Two alternative subtraction algorithms • Figure 10.9

a. The partial differences algorithm

With this algorithm, computations will sometimes result in negative numbers in one or more of the computations. Even though students have not been formally introduced to negative numbers, they seem to know how to compute with them. In this problem, $5 - 7 = -2$, $80 - 90 = -10$, and $300 - 200 = 100$. To obtain the final answer, subtract 2 and 10 from 100 ($100 - 10 = 90$ and $90 - 2 = 88$).

385
-297
-2
-10
100
88

b. The equal sums algorithm

Rather than regrouping, add 10 to the top number and the bottom number. In the top number, add the 10 as 10 ones. In the bottom number, add the 10 as 1 ten. Use expanded notation to illustrate the algorithm.

```
  482 = 4 hundreds + 8 tens + 2 ones (add 10 ones)
- 235 - 2 hundreds + 3 tens + 5 ones (add 1 ten)

    = 4 hundreds + 8 tens + 12 ones
    - 2 hundreds + 4 tens + 5 ones
      2 hundreds + 4 tens + 7 ones = 247
```

Rather than regrouping, add 10 tens to the top number and 1 hundred to the bottom number. Use expanded notation to illustrate the algorithm.

```
  325 = 3 hundreds + 2 tens + 5 ones (add 10 tens)
- 134 - 1 hundred + 3 tens + 4 ones (add 1 hundred)

    = 3 hundreds + 12 tens + 5 ones
    - 2 hundreds + 3 tens + 4 ones
      1 hundred + 9 tens + 1 one = 191
```

CONCEPT CHECK STOP

1. **Why** is it important for children to create their own algorithms for addition and subtraction?

2. **What** are some advantages of using an open number line for addition and subtraction computation?

3. **How** do concrete manipulatives and place value mats help children learn the traditional addition and subtraction algorithms?

4. **How** can the equal additions algorithm help children who have difficulty subtracting when zero is one of the top numbers?

Strategies for Whole Number Multiplication and Division Computation

LEARNING OBJECTIVES

1. **Describe** the importance of student-created strategies for multiplication and division.

2. **Describe** student-created strategies for multiplication and division.

3. **Identify** the steps in teaching traditional algorithms for multiplication and division.

4. **Compare** and **contrast** traditional and alternative algorithms for multiplication and division.

W hen children begin multiplying numbers, they often use counting strategies such as repeated addition. Division problems can be turned into multiplication using the inverse relationship between multiplication and division (i.e., 24 ÷ 6 means 6 × what number = 24). Although this is efficient for one-digit numbers, it is not efficient for two- or three-digit problems. When children create strategies for multiplication, their strategies rely on their ability to split numbers into parts and use the distributive property. This section describes student-created strategies, traditional algorithms, and accessible alternatives.

Student-created strategies for multiplication • Figure 10.10

Children create various algorithms for multiplication. Give them time to deeply understand their methods and encourage them to record their work and discuss their solution strategies. Children's solutions to the following story problem are illustrated.

Tamika has 12 bags of cookies. Each bag has 24 cookies. How many cookies does Tamika have?

a. Using the distributive property

1. William split the second factor into 20 + 4 and then used the distributive property. He knew that 12 x 2 = 24 and therefore 12 x 20 = 240. He also knew that 12 x 4 = 48. He added 240 + 48 for an answer of 288.

$$12 \times 24 =$$

$$12 \times (20 + 4) = 12 \times 20 + 12 \times 4$$
$$= 240 + 48$$
$$12 \times 24 = = 288$$

2. Lin split the second factor in a different way. He decided that, since 24 + 6 = 30, he would multiply 12 x 30 = 360 and subtract 12 x 6 = 72. To reach his final answer, he found 360 – 72 = 288.

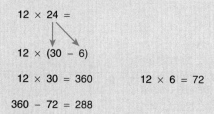

$$12 \times 24 =$$

$$12 \times (30 - 6)$$

$$12 \times 30 = 360 \qquad 12 \times 6 = 72$$

$$360 - 72 = 288$$

b. Drawing an open array

Kathy used a rectangular array. She marked one side of the array with 10 and 2 and the other side with 20 and 4. She found partial products by finding the area of each rectangular section within the array and added all the partial products to get a total of 288.

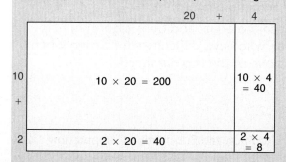

c. Using number sense

John knew that double 3 is 6 and double 6 is 12. He knew that 3 x 24 = 72, so he doubled 72 and got 144, then doubled 144 and got 288.

$$2 \times 3 = 6 \qquad 2 \times 6 = 12$$

$$3 \times 24 = 72$$

Double 72 = 144

Double 144 = 288

$$12 \times 24 = 288$$

Here the open array is demonstrated with one-digit by two-digit multiplication tasks and two-digit by two-digit tasks.

a. **3 × 20**

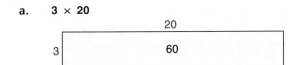

b. **3 × 24**

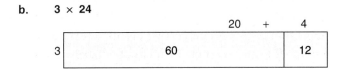

c. **30 × 24**

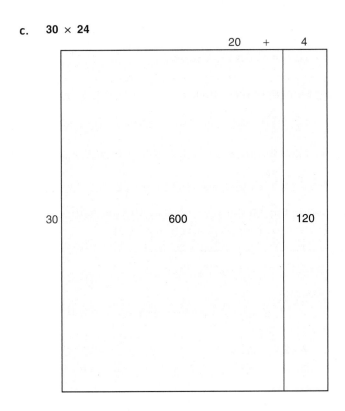

d. **36 × 24**

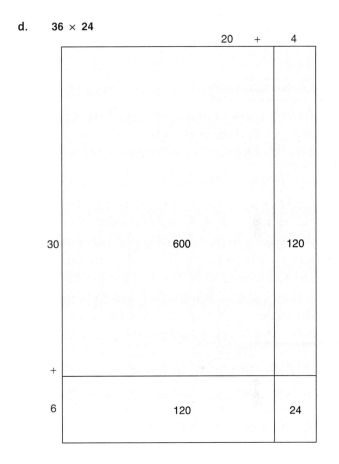

Student-Created Strategies for Multiplication and Division

Children create many strategies for multiplication and division (Fuson, 2003). Examples of children's multiplication strategies are illustrated in **Figure 10.10**. Notice that one strategy uses the **open array**, an array with no numbers on it. "While it initially is used as a model of children's strategies, it eventually becomes a powerful tool to think with" (Fosnot and Dolk, 2001b, p. 86). Children will not think of the open array themselves, but will make use of it when it is introduced to them. To use the open array for two-digit multiplication, children will need to understand that $10 \times 10 = 100$. To use an open array, prepare large rectangles for children to use and help them divide the rectangle into smaller rectangles to illustrate partial products.

The open array illustrated in Figure 10.10 is a very helpful model for multiplication and division. It is a flexible model to learn as it can later be applied to fraction concepts. Let's look at some additional examples of how this array can be used to model multiplication, beginning with one-digit by two-digit multiplication and progressing to two-digit by two-digit multiplication. Children decompose numbers into tens and ones, place numbers on the open array, and find partial products. When using the open array, emphasize place value language. For example, say: *3 ones times 2 tens and 4 ones*. This model fosters the development of multiplication and division strategies as well as the development of spatial understanding. The open array also serves as an excellent transitional model to the traditional algorithms (**Figure 10.11**).

Teaching Tip

Using an open array

For students who have difficulty using the open array, construct rectangles that will exactly fit base-ten blocks. For example, to model the problem 12 × 34, create a rectangle that is 12 centimeters by 34 centimeters. Ask students to fill this rectangle with base-ten blocks and to find the area of the rectangle with dimensions 12 cm by 34 cm.

Tech Tools

[http://nlvm.usu.edu]

Go to the National Library of Virtual Manipulatives and select the **Rectangle Division** applet. The user can practice both multiplication and division using arrays.

As children gain more experience with multiplication and move from one-digit to two-digit multiplication, the patterns resulting from multiplying by 10 or multiples of 10 gain importance. In Figure 10.10, William split 24 into 20 + 4 and knew that 24 × 20 = 240 because 24 × 20 = 24 × 2 × 10. Lin split 24 into 30 − 6 and knew that 12 × 30 = 360 because 12 × 30 = 12 × 3 × 10. When children can split a factor so that it becomes the sum or difference of a multiple of 10 and another number, it simplifies their work. **Activity 10.2** illustrates how teachers can help children learn about the multiples of 10. **Activity 10.3** illustrates how to extend this knowledge to hundreds and parts of a hundred.

Activity 10.2 Tens and more tens

Instructions

1. Say: *Find the following products on your calculator.*

    2 × 4

    2 × 40

    20 × 4

    2 × 400

    2 × 4000

2. Ask: *What pattern do you notice?*

3. Say: *Now find the following product:*

    20 × 4000

4. Ask: *What pattern do you notice now? Has the pattern changed?*

5. Say: *Use this pattern to find 23 × 4, 23 × 40, and 23 × 400 without using a calculator.*

Activity 10.3 Hundreds are helpful

Instructions

1. Say: *Find the following products on your calculator.*

    100 x 36

    50 x 36

    25 x 36

    75 x 36

2. Ask: *What patterns do you notice?* (Children should notice that 50 × 36 is one half of 100 × 36, etc.)

3. Say: *Now find the following products without your calculator, using the pattern you learned.*

    100 × 24

    50 × 24

    25 × 24

    75 × 24

Another technique for solving multidigit multiplication problems is to group facts (**Activity 10.4**).

Activity 10.4 Grouping facts

Instructions

1. Ask students to solve the following collection of multiplication problems, in order:

    7 × 5

    7 × 3

    7 × 10

2. Ask: *How can you use these facts to solve 7 × 35?*

3. Ask students to solve the following collection of multiplication problems:

    2 × 6

    2 × 10

    2 × 7

    4 × 6

    4 × 10

    4 × 7

4. Ask: *How can you use these facts to solve 24 × 76?*

Throughout history, different cultures have invented unique multiplication algorithms (see *Multicultural Perspectives in Mathematics*).

Chapter 9 examined two meanings of division: measurement and partitive. When children create division strategies, their strategies and models are based on the type of division problems they are asked to solve (**Figure 10.12**).

Multicultural Perspectives in Mathematics

Multiplying Like an Egyptian

In ancient Egypt, scribes recorded their work on thin material made from the papyrus plant. The Rhind Papyrus, which dates to about 1650 B.C.E., contains the solutions to 84 mathematics problems, including the Egyptians' method for multiplication, which consisted of doubling numbers to find products and obtaining the final answer by using the distributive property. We'll demonstrate with 12 × 14.

$$1 \times 14 = 14$$
$$2 \times 14 = 28$$
$$4 \times 14 = 56$$
$$8 \times 14 = 112$$

We continue until the multiplier is greater than the first factor in the original number. Since the next multiplier would be double 8 or 16, and this is greater than 12, we stop here. Next, we go back and find factors that add up to 12. We place slash marks next to those factors.

$$1 \times 14 = 14$$
$$2 \times 14 = 28$$
$$/4 \times 14 = 56$$
$$/8 \times 14 = 112$$

We obtain the answer by adding the numbers in the right column that corresponded with the slashed multipliers. In this case, 56 + 112 = 168.

(*Source*: Bazin, Tamez, and The Exploratorium Teacher Institute, 2002)

Strategies for the Classroom

- How might you use the Egyptian method of multiplication to teach children about the distributive property?

- How could you use this method to motivate children to develop their own multiplication algorithms?

Student-created strategies for division • Figure 10.12

Children may find it easier to create strategies for division problems than for multiplication tasks. It is much easier to model partitive division with concrete objects because partitive division represents fair sharing. Children often use repeated subtraction to model measurement division. Encourage children to discuss their strategies and record their work.

a. Measurement division

Tanya had 100 strawberries. She put them in bags containing 12 strawberries each. How many bags of strawberries were there?

To solve this problem, Barbara subtracted 12 from 100 until she got to zero or a number smaller than 12.

Ron used the missing factor strategy. He thought of this as a multiplication problem and guessed and checked what number times 12 comes closest to 100. Which strategy do you think is more efficient?

Barbara
100 − 12 = 88
88 − 12 = 76
76 − 12 = 64
64 − 12 = 52
52 − 12 = 40
40 − 12 = 28
28 − 12 = 16
16 − 12 = 4
8 groups of 12 with 4 left
100 ÷ 12 = 8 with 4 left

Ron
100 ÷ 12
Try 10 12 × 10 = 120 too big
Try 5 12 × 5 = 60
Try 3 12 × 3 = 36
5 groups of 12 + 3 groups of 12 = 8 groups of 12
60 + 36 = 96
100 − 96 = 4
100 ÷ 12 = 8 with 4 left

b. Partitive division

Ian had 85 dimes. He wanted to share them equally among himself and 5 friends. How many dimes did each person get?

To solve this problem Koji counted out 8 tens and 5 ones, and made six circles to represent Ian and his five friends. He dealt out the tens first. Then, when he had 2 tens left, he traded the 2 tens for 20 ones and combined them with the 5 ones he already had. Then Koji dealt out the ones equally, so that 4 ones were placed in each circle, with 1 left over.

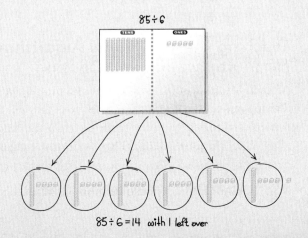

85 ÷ 6

85 ÷ 6 = 14 with 1 left over

When teaching the traditional algorithms, begin with word problems in familiar contexts and use models such as base-ten blocks, arrays, and place value mats to reinforce the idea of regrouping and connecting the concrete to the abstract. Have children record their work, and help them understand each step. The multiplication algorithm works from right to left, but the division algorithm works from left to right.

a. The traditional multiplication algorithm

Tanweer collected 15 aluminum cans for recycling each day for 14 days. How many cans did Tanweer collect altogether?

1. Represent both factors as an array on a hundreds grid. Also represent the problem on a place value mat.

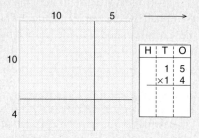

2. *Multiply 4 ones times 5 ones. How many ones are there altogether? (20) Do you need to regroup? (Yes) Trade 20 ones for 2 tens. Write your answer on the place value mat and locate the answer on the array.*

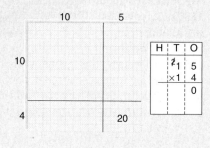

3. *Multiply 4 ones × 1 ten. How many tens are there altogether? (4) Do you need to regroup? (No) Write your answer on the place value mat, remembering to add 2 tens from the previous calculation. Locate the answer on the array.*

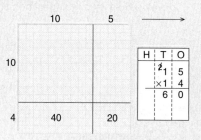

4. *Multiply 1 ten by 5 ones. How many tens are there altogether? (5) Do you need to regroup? (No) Write your answer on the place value mat and locate the answer on the array.*

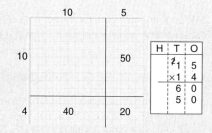

5. *Multiply 1 ten by 1 ten. How many tens are there altogether? (10) Do you need to regroup? (Yes) Trade 10 tens for 1 hundred. Write your answer on the place value mat and locate the answer on the array.*

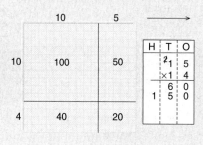

6. *Add the two rows of numbers to get the total. Add the four partial products on the array to get the total.*

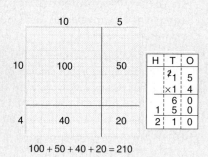

100 + 50 + 40 + 20 = 210

Teaching the Traditional Algorithms for Multiplication and Division

After children have created strategies for multiplication and division and have narrowed down the ones they use to a few reliable strategies, they are ready to learn the traditional algorithms (**Figure 10.13**). The traditional algorithm for division is demonstrated with a one-digit divisor (e.g., for the task 45 ÷ 7, 7 is the divisor). For two- and three-digit divisors, use estimation first and then a calculator to find an exact answer. In real life, we rarely use long division.

The traditional algorithms for multiplication and division present a number of difficulties for children. The multiplication algorithm works from right to left, even though children prefer to work from left to right. It

b. The traditional division algorithm

Jose has 212 crayons that he wants to share equally among himself and five friends. How many crayons will each child get?

1. Count out base-ten blocks: 2 hundreds, 1 ten, and 2 ones. Write the problem with the bring-down method, using the division symbol and drawing lines for place value.

2. *Can you share the 2 hundreds equally?* (No)

a. *Make a trade. Trade 2 hundreds for 20 tens. Combine the 20 tens with the ten you already have.*

b. *Deal out tens equally to each friend. Six ones times 3 tens equals 18 tens. How many tens does each person get?* (3) *How many tens are left?* (3)

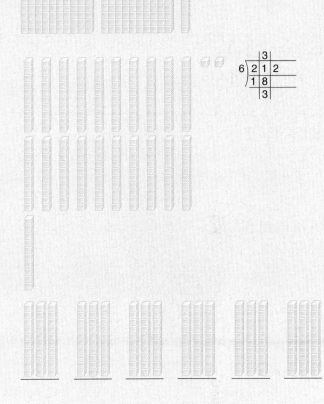

3. *Can you share the 3 tens left equally among 6 friends?* (No)

a. *Make a trade. Trade 3 tens for 30 ones. Combine the 30 ones with the 2 ones you already have.*

b. *Deal out ones equally to each friend. Six ones times 5 ones equals 30 ones. How many ones does each person get?* (5) *How many are left?* (2) *This is your remainder.*

requires children to multiply, add, and then multiply and add again. The division algorithm works from left to right, but it has two problems. It requires children to "determine the maximum copies of the divisor that they can take from the dividend" (Fuson, 2003, p. 86) and "creates no sense of the size of the answers that students are writing; in fact, they are always multiplying by single digits" (Fuson, 2003,

p. 86). For example, in **Figure 10.13b**, to find how many copies of 6 you can take from 212, you find how many sixes can go into 21, not 212.

Another algorithm for multiplication is lattice multiplication (see the *Lesson* on the next page). The standards are from the *Common Core State Standards* (NGA Center/CCSSO, 2010) for grades 3 and 4.

Strategies for Whole Number Multiplication and Division Computation   263

Lattice multiplication is an effective algorithm for multiplying larger numbers. The process shows digits that are being carried and breaks up the steps into reasonable parts. The lattice structure keeps the individual products more transparent.

GRADE LEVEL

3–4 (Intermediate)

OBJECTIVE

Students will use the array and area models of multiplication to learn lattice multiplication.

MATERIALS

- Paper and pencils

- 1 × 1, 1 × 2, 2 × 1, 2 × 2, 2 × 3 grids for children

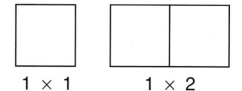

1 × 1   1 × 2

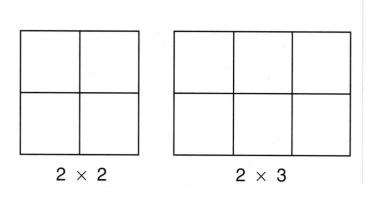

2 × 2   2 × 3

STANDARDS

Grade 3

Use multiplication and division within 100 to solve word problems in situations involving equal groups, arrays, and measurement quantities, e.g., by using drawings and equations with a symbol for the unknown number to represent the problem. (NGA Center/CCSSO, 2010)

Grade 4

Multiply a whole number of up to four digits by a one-digit whole number and multiply two two-digit whole numbers, using strategies based on place value and the properties of operations. Illustrate and explain the calculation by using equations, rectangular arrays, and/or area models. (NGA Center/CCSSO, 2010)

ASSESSMENT

Children will write a journal entry explaining lattice multiplication to someone who has never heard of it.

GROUPING

Whole class followed by individual work

Launch (5 minutes)

- Show children pictures of roses or ivy growing on a lattice. Ask: *What do you see in this picture?* Elicit from children that the structure that holds the roses or ivy up is called a lattice. Write the word *lattice* on the chalkboard or overhead, and pronounce it to make sure that all students understand the word.

- Say: *We are going to use a lattice for another kind of support. This lattice will show us a new way to write multiplication problems. This method of multiplication was introduced into Europe in the 1200s by a famous mathematician called Fibonacci.*

Instruct (30 minutes)

- Say: *Remember that when we use a place value mat, one column is for ones, one is for tens, and one is for hundreds. Now we are going to show place value using a grid.*

- Say: *You have several grids in front of you. Take the grid that has just one square and draw a diagonal line from the top right corner to the bottom left corner. We have just created a new kind of place value mat. The top half of the square holds the tens place and the bottom half of the square holds the ones place.*

- Say: *Now we are going to multiply 5 × 6 on this grid. Here is how we do it.*

- Say: *Let's try to multiply some larger numbers using this grid. Let's try to multiply 32 × 25. How many columns and how many rows will you need?* (2 rows and 2 columns) *Select the grid and draw the diagonals. Write 32 along the top of the grid and 25 vertically along the right side.*

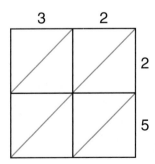

- Say: *Now let's multiply. Notice that when you multiply 2 × 2 = 4, you have to decide where to put the 4, in the top half or the bottom half of the square. Where do you think it should go?* (Put the 4 in the bottom and zero in the top because there are zero tens.)

- Say: *Continue to multiply each pair of numbers: 2 × 3, 5 × 2, and 5 × 3. Write all the products in their correct places.*

- Say: *Now we are ready to find the answer. First, extend the diagonal lines. Add the numbers in each diagonal column. The first diagonal column is 0. For the second diagonal column, add 4 + 1 + 5 = 10. Write 0 below the column, and carry 10 to the next diagonal column.*

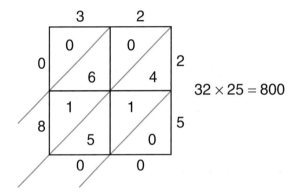

$$32 \times 25 = 800$$

- Say: *Try another one on your own: 54 × 36.*

- Have the children work on this problem individually. When they are finished, have them discuss their work.

- Say: *Now let's try this method with larger numbers: 125 × 67. How many rows and how many columns will you need?* (3 columns and 2 rows)

Summarize (5 minutes)

- Ask: *What are the advantages of the lattice method of multiplication?*

- Ask: *Is it easier or harder than the other strategies we have used?*

The partial products algorithm • Figure 10.14

The partial products algorithm helps children maintain their focus on the value of the digits.

```
  3 2
  2 4
    8      ← 4 × 2 = 8 or 4 ones × 2 ones = 8 ones
1 2 0      ← 4 × 30 = 120 or 4 ones × 3 tens = 12 tens = 1 hundred and 2 tens
  4 0      ← 20 × 2 = 40 or 2 tens × 2 ones = 4 tens
6 0 0      ← 20 × 30 = 600 or 2 tens × 3 tens = 6 hundreds
7 6 8
```

If you prefer to use the traditional algorithm for multiplication or if your school system requires you to teach it, the **partial products algorithm** can help minimize difficulties with the multiplication algorithm (**Figure 10.14**). Although it still works from right to left, it helps children focus on the value of the digits and not just the digits themselves.

> **partial products algorithm** A strategy that multiplies the digits in each place separately.

Multiplication problems with 2 or 3 digits are broken into smaller, more understandable steps. Similarly, the **partial quotients algorithm** can help minimize difficulties with the division algorithm by breaking down the division problem into a series of understandable steps (**Figure 10.15**).

> **partial quotients algorithm** A strategy that uses successive approximation to find the answer.

The partial quotients algorithm • Figure 10.15

To solve 1630 ÷ 12 using the partial quotients algorithm, use the following steps.

1. Find easy multiples of the divisor: 2 x 12 = 24, 5 x 12 = 60, 10 x 12 = 120.

2. Set up the problem as if you were using the traditional algorithm.

3. Try out different factors. Ask: *How many groups of 12 are in 1630?* Make an estimate— say, 100—then record the product of 100 x 12, subtract, and continue the same procedure.

```
12)1630
  -1200   100    100 × 12 = 1200
   430
  - 240    20     20 × 12 = 240
   190
   120    10     10 × 12 = 120
    70
    60     5      5 × 12 = 60
    10  |135

Answer: 135  Remainder 10
```

CONCEPT CHECK **STOP**

1. **Why** is it important for children to create their own strategies for multiplication and division?

2. **What** method of solving the multiplication problem does this figure illustrate? What are some advantages of using this method for multiplication and division computation?

3. **What** kinds of problems do you anticipate children will have with the traditional multiplication and division algorithms?

4. **How** can the partial products algorithm help children who have difficulty with the traditional multiplication algorithm?

```
            20    +    4
     ┌──────────────┬────────┐
  10 │              │ 10 × 4 │
     │ 10 × 20 = 200│ = 40   │
   + │              │        │
     ├──────────────┼────────┤
   2 │ 2 × 20 = 40  │ 2 × 4  │
     │              │ = 8    │
     └──────────────┴────────┘
```

Computational Estimation, Mental Computation, and Calculators

LEARNING OBJECTIVES

1. **Explain** the importance of computational estimation.
2. **Describe** strategies for computational estimation.
3. **Compare** and **contrast** computational estimation and mental computation.
4. **Explain** the importance of calculators in computation.

hildren spend a great deal of mathematics time in elementary school learning written computation. In real life, however, many tasks are better suited to computational estimation, mental computation, or calculators. For example, when counting your change to see whether you have enough money to buy a treat, you would probably use estimation or mental computation. When adding up how much your class spent on school supplies, you would probably use a calculator because of the large amount of data (NCTM, 2000). For children to have a complete understanding of whole number computation, they should be able to evaluate which computational tool is best suited to a given task and be proficient in using that tool. The rest of this chapter focuses on estimation, mental computation, and calculators.

Computational Estimation

Computational estimation is often underrepresented in elementary textbooks. Estimation "provides a tool for judging the reasonableness of calculator, mental, and paper-and-pencil computations" (NCTM, 2000, p. 155). Estimates are usually performed mentally and quickly. Sometimes, an estimate is more useful and efficient than exact computation. For example, on a trip to the grocery store, you might estimate how much money you are going to spend, how much food you need for a week, and how many reusable grocery bags to bring along with you.

Children find the concept of estimation quite difficult. They may have previously learned that in mathematics each problem has one right answer, but when they estimate, there can be a range of correct answers even though none of them is exact. Children also have difficulty understanding the difference between guessing and estimating and will sometimes substitute wild guesses for estimates. How can you teach children the difference between guessing and estimating? You can provide computational tasks with "easy" numbers and help children narrow the range of acceptable answers through questioning (**Activity 10.5**).

Activity 10.5 Over or under

Instructions

1. Provide students with a group of numbers to add: 25 + 30 + 20 + 40.
2. Ask: *Is the answer over 10 or under 10? Why?*
3. Ask: *Is the answer over 50 or under 50? Why?*
4. Ask: *Is the answer over 100 or under 100? Why?*
5. Ask: *Is the answer over 150 or under 150? Why?*

You can help children learn computational estimation skills by using language that encourages estimation. For younger children, use words such as *just over, just under, nearly, a little more than, a little less than,* and *close to.* For older children, use words such as *approximate* and *reasonable.* For all grades, provide familiar contexts in which estimation makes sense (**Activity 10.6**).

Activity 10.6 About how much

Instructions

1. Ask: *If you buy two pencils, one eraser, and one notebook, about how much money will you need? Will it be just over or just under $2.00?*
2. Ask: *If you buy two notebooks and one pencil, about how much money will you need? Will it be close to $3.00?*
3. Repeat the question with other quantities of pencils, erasers, and notebooks that use estimation language.

$1.49 each   10¢ each   45¢ each

CHILDREN'S LITERATURE

Estimating size and the reasonableness of results

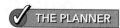 THE PLANNER

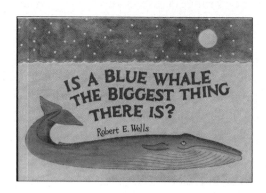

Is a Blue Whale the Biggest Thing There Is? • Figure 10.16a

Written and illustrated by Robert E. Wells

The reader learns that a blue whale can be 100 feet long and weigh as much as 150 tons. Although this story is about estimating size rather than computational estimation, it helps children develop the concept of estimation and meaning for words such as *almost as big as, about as big as,* and *close to.*

Strategy for the Classroom

- Ask children to make comparisons about things in their world. For example, a child might compare the size of her dog to a child, an adult, or another animal, using words such as *almost as big as, about as big as, not as big as,* and *close to.*

A Million Fish. . . More or Less • Figure 10.16b

Written by Patricia C. McKissack
Illustrated by Dena Schutzer

This is a fanciful tale about a boy who catches one million fish on the bayou. On his way home, he loses most of them to raccoons, cows, and a cat. Although the story does not explicitly deal with computational estimation, it provides a wonderful opportunity to discuss what is reasonable.

Strategy for the Classroom

- Ask questions such as: *How long do you think it would take to catch a million fish? Hugh was bringing the fish home in a little wagon. How many fish do you think would fit in his wagon?* Questions such as these help children begin to realize that in estimation several possible answers might be reasonable.

Hugh Thomas took a quick count, and saw he still had close to a half-million fish left. He followed the swamp path that was the quickest way to Papa-Daddy and Elder Abbajon's houseboat. Story had it that Jean Polet's pirate treasure was hidden somewhere 'mongst the cypress knees, but Hugh Thomas wasn't interested. "I've got my own treasure," he boasted.
The air grew thick, hovering over the swamp like a big smothering hand. Then the still came, a terrible kind of silence with its own sound. The boy hummed and quickened his step. Something was stalking him, closing in fast. The ghost of Jean Polet, maybe?

Children's literature is a wonderful way to introduce children to estimation (see *Children's Literature,* **Figure 10.16**).

Children should learn several computational estimation strategies. In addition to learning the strategies, children need to analyze each problem's context and operation and decide which strategy fits it best.

Front-end estimation In this strategy, the leading or front-end digit of each number is added to get a total. This is a good strategy when all numbers have the same number of digits. For example, when adding $239 + 426 + 394$, you would add $2 + 4 + 3 = 9$ or $200 + 400 + 300 = 900$, with an estimate of 900. When adding $39 + 426 + 394$, the front-end estimate adds $0 + 4 + 3$ or $0 + 400 + 300 = 700$.

The first number, 39, is ignored because it does not have a hundreds digit.

Front-end estimates can sometimes be far from the exact answer and require **adjustment**, which provides another look at the estimate to see whether you can get closer to the actual answer. For example, if you want to know whether you have enough money to purchase three items at a restaurant that cost $2.39, $4.26, and $3.94, the front-end estimate of $9.00 may not be exact enough. In this context, you might want to adjust your total by adding the digits next to the front-end digits, $3 + 2 + 9 = 14$ or $.30 + .20 + .90 = \$1.40$. A more reasonable estimate is $\$9.00 + \$1.40 = \$10.40$. These ideas are illustrated in **Activity 10.7.**

Compatible numbers When the **compatible numbers** strategy is used in addition, a few numbers are grouped together and adjusted to produce familiar benchmark numbers such as 10 and 100 (**Figure 10.17**).

Activity 10.7 Front-end estimates with adjustment

Instructions

Find the front-end estimate for the following numbers. Then adjust.

a.
245	200	40	
+ 387	+ 300	+ 80	1400
+ 984	+ 900	+ 80	+ 200
	= 1400	= 200	=1600
	Front-end estimate	Adjustment	Front-end with adjustment

b.
325	0	300	
+ 1297	+ 1000	+ 200	3000
+ 2309	+ 2000	+ 300	+ 800
	= 3000	= 800	=3800
	Front-end estimate	Adjustment	Front-end with adjustment

Using compatible numbers in addition • Figure 10.17

a. How can you use compatible numbers to estimate the cost of a chicken sandwich, salad, soft drink, and dessert at a fast-food restaurant?

~ *menu* ~

Chicken Sandwich...........................$6.29

Salad..$4.29

Soft Drink..$2.00

Dessert...$3.25

6 + 4 is 10 and 2 + 3 is 5...so, that's about 15 dollars

b. How can you use compatible numbers to estimate the number of cans collected by the third grade for the canned food drive?

Canned Food Drive – 3RD Grade

Class	Number of Cans of Food
Ms. Wilson	44
Mr. Hernandez	62
Ms. Chin	76
Mr. Lincoln	34
Mr. Durham	28

44 + 62 is about 100
76 + 34 is about 100
I didn't change the 28
so 100 + 100 + 28 = 228

The compatible numbers strategy can be used with other operations as well (**Activity 10.8** and **Activity 10.9**).

Rounding Rounding is a form of estimation. We often think of rounding as changing numbers to the nearest multiple of ten, but rounding is actually much more flexible. When we round numbers, we simply substitute numbers that are easier to work with. There are many ways to round numbers, and two children may round the same numbers differently but correctly. For example, 726 + 364 + 4240 can be rounded to 700 + 400 + 4200 = 5300 or 720 + 360 + 4240 = 5320. In addition and subtraction, round numbers to the same place value. In subtraction, it may be enough to round just the bottom number. Consider 4325 – 2216. If you round 2216 to 2200, it is easier to subtract: 4325 – 2200 = 2125.

Rounding in multiplication and division follows the same rules. Sometimes, rounding just one number makes the computation significantly easier. Consider the following problem.

Thirty-six children are going to the aquarium. If each child's ticket costs $9.00, about how much money will be needed for tickets?

If the first number, 36, is rounded to 40, the computation is much easier. The answer, 40 × 9 = $360, is high but a reasonable estimate. For a closer estimate, you might find 30 × 9 = $270, and then average the two different estimates: (270 + 360) ÷ 2 = 640 ÷ 2 = 320. This estimate is very close because 36 is about halfway between 30 and 40. Or you can round the second number to 10: 36 x 10 = 360.

Mental Computation

In both estimation and mental computation, you figure out the answer "in your head," but in estimation you do not find an exact answer. In mental computation, you always find an exact answer. Mental computation does not really have to be taught. When children are introduced to computations by creating their own strategies, they will naturally compute some of their answers mentally. The models described earlier, such as the open number line for addition and subtraction and the open array for multiplication and division, lend themselves to mental computation.

You can encourage children's mental computation skills with the tasks you select (**Activity 10.10**).

Students can use number sense and logic for mental computation (**Activity 10.11**).

Activity 10.11 Using number sense for mental computation

Instructions

1. Ask students to solve the following problem mentally:

   If 3 notebooks cost $2.40, how much would 12 notebooks cost?

2. Ask: *What answer did you get? How did you find your answer mentally?* (Some students realized that 3 × 4 = 12 so 4 × $2.40 = $9.60. Other students doubled $2.40 to find the cost of 6 notebooks and then doubled that amount to find the cost of 12 notebooks.)

3. Repeat with other problems.

Calculators

Calculators provide an alternative for written computation when computations become very tedious, as in three-digit by three-digit multiplication and division with two- or three-digit divisors. Calculators can also be used to check written and mental computations. Calculators and estimation go hand in hand. Estimation should always be used to check computations by calculator. It's very easy to hit a wrong key or add an extra zero and get an incorrect answer. When you estimate first, you will know whether your calculator-obtained answer is correct. **Activity 10.12** meaningfully links calculators and estimation. Students are given a "target" number in the bull's-eye and a starting number. Then by using addition or multiplication they are asked to hit the target (with addition) or come as close as possible (with multiplication).

Tech Tools

illuminations.nctm.org

The *NCTM Illuminations* Web site has a link to an electronic version of this game, called **Primary Krypto**. Users pick five number cards and one of the four arithmetic operations to create their target number.

Activity 10.12 Hit the bull's-eye

Instructions

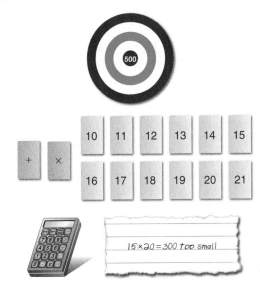

1. Place number cards in one bag and operation cards (+ or ×) in another bag. Each pair of students picks one card from each bag. (For example, one student picks the number 15 and the other student picks + for addition.)

2. Say: *The goal of the game is to hit the number in the bull's-eye by using either addition or multiplication.*

3. Say: *With the number and the operation picked, use the calculator to hit the bull's-eye. For example, if you picked 15 and the operation +, you will estimate 15 + what number is close to 500.*

4. *Try 450. Add 15 + 450 on your calculator. Is your number close to 500?* (Yes) *Can you still reach the target or get closer?*

5. *If you answered "yes" to the second question, pass the calculator to your partner. Start from the previous calculation. Keep going.*

6. *If you answered "no," pick a new number and operation and begin again.*

CONCEPT CHECK

1. **Why** is it important for children to understand and be able to use computational estimation and mental computation?

2. **What** are two strategies for estimation?

3. **How** are computational estimation and mental computation different? How are they the same?

4. **What** role do calculators play in estimation?

Summary

 Whole Number Computation in the Elementary Grades: An Overview 248

- **Algorithms** for whole number computation were invented in the ninth century by the great Persian mathematician Muhammad ibn Musa al-Khwarizmi. In the United States and Canada we still use these algorithms, although other algorithms are used in other parts of the world.

- Children should know and understand more than one algorithm for each operation. The goal is for children to deeply understand a small number of flexible and efficient algorithms and to be able to choose the algorithm that works best for a particular task. One algorithm for multiplication is shown here.

Figure 10.2

$$8 \times 24 = 8 \times (20 + 4) = 8 \times 20 + 8 \times 4$$
$$= 160 \times 32$$
$$= 192$$

- When teaching algorithms, begin with counting techniques, then make the transition to student-created algorithms. When these are well understood, make the transition to traditional algorithms. Encourage students to discuss their strategies and record their methods.

- Almost all textbooks teach the traditional algorithms. Delay teaching the traditional algorithms until children have created their own strategies. If you teach the tradition algorithms first, children will not create their own. Traditional algorithms usually work from right to left, even though children prefer to work from left to right. Traditional algorithms also lack flexibility.

 Strategies for Whole Number Addition and Subtraction Computation 252

- Children create many strategies for addition and subtraction. The **open number line** illustrated here is a useful tool that helps children record their work. Children also use place value language to split numbers into tens and ones.

Figure 10.4

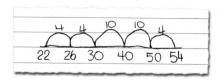

- In subtraction, children can count up, count down, and change the subtraction problem to an addition one.

- When teaching the traditional algorithm, use base-ten blocks and place value mats to model the operation. Teach the **partial sums algorithm** as a transition to or replacement for the traditional addition algorithm.

- For subtraction, the **equal sums algorithm** and the **partial differences algorithm** provide more accessible alternatives.

- Make sure to include **bridging** activities that help children add and subtract when moving from one decade to another.

 Strategies for Whole Number Multiplication and Division Computation 258

- Children create many strategies for multiplication and division. Many of these strategies involve splitting one or more factors into parts and using the distributive property, as shown here. The **open array** is an excellent model for understanding multiplication by one-digit and two-digit numbers, and it is a useful tool for recording children's work.

Figure 10.10

$$12 \times 24 =$$
$$12 \times (30 - 6)$$
$$12 \times 30 = 360 \qquad 12 \times 6 = 72$$
$$360 - 72 = 288$$

- When teaching the traditional algorithms, use arrays and place value mats as models. Use the **partial products algorithm** as a transition to or replacement for the traditional algorithm. In division, teach the traditional algorithm when dividing by a one-digit number. Discuss how the remainder should be handled. For two- or three-digit divisors, use calculators.

- There are many multiplication and division algorithms that have developed in different parts of the world. The Egyptian method of multiplication uses doubling and the distributive property. The lattice method is similar to the traditional algorithm but seems to be easier for children to understand. The partial quotients algorithm breaks division problems into a series of logical steps.

- Computational estimation is an important skill that receives little attention in elementary mathematics textbooks. There are a variety of methods of computational estimation, including front-end, front-end with adjustment, rounding, and compensation. Children should learn to use these methods and understand which method is best for a given task. This drawing illustrates the compatible numbers strategy.

Figure 10.17

- Mental computation requires exact answers that are "done in your head." It does not need to be explicitly taught if children are permitted to create their own strategies for the operations. It is an important skill that should be nurtured.

- Calculators and estimation skills go hand in hand. Children should always estimate when using calculators, because it is so easy to make mistakes on a calculator without realizing it.

Key Terms

- adjustment 269
- algorithm 248
- bridge 253
- chunking 256
- compatible numbers 269
- computational fluency 248

- equal additions algorithm 257
- front-end estimation 268
- lattice addition 256
- open array 259
- open number line 252

- partial differences algorithm 257
- partial products algorithm 266
- partial quotients algorithm 266
- partial sums algorithm 256
- rounding 270

Additional Children's Literature

- ***What's Faster Than a Speeding Cheetah?*** **written and illustrated by Robert E. Wells**
  This book uses approximations to find how fast a cheetah can run, how fast a peregrine can swoop, and many other interesting facts. Use this book to inspire your own students' estimates about their world.

- ***If You Hopped Like a Frog*** **written by David M. Schwartz and illustrated by James Warhola**
  This book makes many interesting comparisons about such topics as the strength of an ant, the brain of a dinosaur, and the growth rate of a baby. The book provides an excellent source for explorations using estimation, mental mathematics, and calculators.

Online Resources

- **National Library of Virtual Manipulatives** http://nlvm.usu.edu

  The activity **Number Line Arithmetic** allows the user to model the four operations on a virtual number line.

- **Math Forum** http://mathforum.org/

  This site is operated by Drexel University and offers activities for mathematics including the **Abacus International Math Challenge** and **Aritm**, which is a game that trains the user in mental calculation.

- **Shodor A National Resource for Computational Science Education** www.shodor.org/interactive/activities/ComparisonEstimator/

  This interactive activity shows the user two screens. The user must guess which screen has more starts. There are three different problem types and two different difficulty levels.

- **NCTM Illuminations** illuminations.nctm.org.

  The **Electronic Abacus** activity allows the user to add numbers up to four digits using an abacus.

Critical and Creative Thinking Questions

1. Compare and contrast student-created strategies and traditional algorithms. How are they different? How do students benefit from creating their own strategies?

2. Why is it important for students to model, discuss, and record strategies that they create?

3. Use two different strategies, an open array and the partial products algorithm, to find solutions for 26 × 75. Relate each area in the array to the appropriate product. Make up a story problem that can be solved by this multiplication task.

4. **Using visuals** Use two different strategies to solve the problem 357 − 148. Explain the strategies with words and drawings and write a story problem that can be solved with this subtraction task.

5. Why is it important for children to learn computational estimation? What factors should you keep in mind as you teach it to children?

6. **In the field** Ask an adult to solve a subtraction problem that involves more than one trade (for example, 2000 − 989). Did the person use the traditional algorithm? Ask her or him to explain why the chosen method works. Next, explain one of the alternative algorithms for subtraction discussed in this chapter. Ask the adult to compare both algorithms and see which one is easier to explain and which one makes more sense.

What is happening in this picture?

Think Critically

Look at these examples of children's computation in subtraction and multiplication.
1. What errors did Tammy make using the traditional subtraction algorithm? What misunderstandings do you think she had? How might you help Tammy to understand her errors and subtract correctly?
2. What errors did Scott make with the traditional multiplication algorithm? What misunderstandings do you think he had? How might you help Scott to understand his errors and multiply correctly?

Name _Tammy_

$$\begin{array}{r} \overset{3\;1}{2\cancel{4}5} \\ -1\,2\,3 \\ \hline 1\,1\,1\,2 \end{array} \qquad \begin{array}{r} \overset{6\;1}{3\cancel{7}6} \\ -\;\;\;3\,4 \\ \hline 3\,3\,1\,2 \end{array}$$

Name _Scott_

$$\begin{array}{r} \overset{1}{4}\,6 \\ \times\;\;\;3 \\ \hline 1\!\cdot\!5\,8 \end{array} \qquad \begin{array}{r} \overset{1}{7}\,3 \\ \times\;\;\;5 \\ \hline 4\,0\,5 \end{array}$$

Self-Test

(Check your answers in Appendix D.)

1. Solve 385 + 297 using the partial sums algorithm.

2. Solve 466 – 237 using the equal additions algorithm.

3. Solve 825 – 316 using the partial differences algorithm.

4. Solve 23 × 64 using the partial products algorithm.

5. True or False: Children should have lots of practice in creating their own algorithms before learning traditional algorithms.

6. True or False: Children prefer to work from right to left.

7. Describe the strategies used to solve these problems.

> Barbara
> 100 – 12 = 88
> 88 – 12 = 76
> 76 – 12 = 64
> 64 – 12 = 52
> 52 – 12 = 40
> 40 – 12 = 28
> 28 – 12 = 16
> 16 – 12 = 4
>
> 8 groups of 12 with 4 left
> 100 ÷ 12 = 8 with 4 left

> Ron
> 100 ÷ 12
> Try 10   12 × 10 = 120 too big
> Try 5   12 × 5 = 60
> Try 3   12 × 3 = 36
> 5 groups of 12 + 3 groups of 12 = 8 groups of 12
> 60 + 36 = 96
> 100 – 96 = 4
> 100 ÷ 12 = 8 with 4 left

8. Describe the strategy used by this child to solve the problem.

$$12 \times 24 =$$
$$12 \times (20 + 4) = 12 \times 20 + 12 \times 4$$
$$= 240 + 48$$
$$12 \times 24 = \quad = 288$$

9. Find the product of 15 × 36 using lattice multiplication.

10. Find the product of 9 × 26 using Egyptian multiplication.

11. Use the front-end strategy to estimate the sum of 335 + 318 + 598, then adjust the estimate.

12. Estimate the product of 225 × 23 in two different ways using rounding.

13. Use compatible numbers to estimate the sum of $48.93 + $34.00 + $54.08.

14. Describe two ways to find the following sum using mental computation: 36 + 84.

15. Describe two ways to find the following product using mental computation: 23 × 40.

THE PLANNER ✓

Review your Chapter Planner on the chapter opener and check off your completed work.

Understanding Fractions and Fraction Computation

Denise McSwain held up two equal-sized pizza boxes to her fifth-grade class and said, "Both of these boxes held pizzas of the same size. One box has $\frac{5}{8}$ of the pizza left and the other box has $\frac{2}{5}$ of the pizza left. Which box has more pizza?" Some children drew two fraction circles, others drew two rectangles, subdividing one into five equal pieces and the other into eight equal pieces. Still other children drew number lines to solve the problem. Ms. McSwain called on volunteers to provide answers and explain their thinking.

Cooper said, "I tried fraction circles first, but then I changed to rectangles. $8 \times 5 = 40$, so I divided both rectangles into 40 pieces. The box with $\frac{5}{8}$ of a pizza has more pizza." Nadia said, "I drew a number line with 0, $\frac{1}{2}$, and 1. I know that $\frac{2}{5}$ is a little less than $\frac{1}{2}$, because $2 \times 2 = 4$, and $\frac{5}{8}$ is a little more than $\frac{1}{2}$, because 4 is half of 8. So $\frac{5}{8}$ is bigger." Many of the children used solution strategies similar to the ones used by Cooper and Nadia.

Ms. McSwain was pleased at her students' ability to use different models and meanings to compare fractions. Their answers demonstrated understanding of fraction concepts and number sense about fractions. Cooper's explanation used equivalent fractions, whereas Nadia's explanation used familiar benchmarks on a number line.

Children need hands-on experience with concrete models and other representations to build a solid understanding of fractions.

CHAPTER OUTLINE

NCTM The NCTM Number and Operations Standard from *Principles and Standards for School Mathematics* (2000) includes several expectations for fraction concepts and computation.

In grades 3–5, all students should

- develop understanding of fractions as parts of unit wholes, as parts of a collection, as locations on number lines, and as divisions of whole numbers;
- use models, benchmarks, and equivalent forms to judge the size of fractions;
- recognize and generate equivalent forms of commonly used fractions, decimals, and percents;
- develop and use strategies to estimate computations involving fractions and decimals in situations relevant to students' experience;
- use visual models, benchmarks, and equivalent forms to add and subtract commonly used fractions and decimals.   (NCTM, 2000, p. 148)

In grades 6–8, all students should

- work flexibly with fractions, decimals, and percents, to solve problems;
- compare and order fractions, decimals, and percents efficiently and find their approximate locations on a number line;
- understand the meaning and effects of arithmetic operations with fractions, decimals, and integers.
                    (NCTM, 2000, p. 214)

Developing the Meaning of Fractions

LEARNING OBJECTIVES

1. **Explain** why children find it difficult to learn fractions.

2. **Compare** and **contrast** the four meanings of fractions.

3. **Compare** and **contrast** the three models for fractions.

F ractions are an important part of the elementary and middle school curriculum. Knowledge of fractions is necessary for learning measurement, ratio and proportion, probability, and algebra (Clarke, Roche, and Mitchell, 2008). *Curriculum Focal Points* (NCTM, 2006, p. 15) suggests that in grade 3, students "develop an understanding of the meanings and uses of fractions to represent parts of a whole, parts of a set, or points on a number line." This understanding is expanded and refined throughout the elementary and middle grades.

Why Do Children Have Difficulty Learning Fractions?

Many children and their teachers have difficulty understanding and using fractions. "Children are bound to find fraction computations arbitrary, confusing, and easy to mix up unless they receive help understanding what fractions and fraction operations mean" (Siebert and Gaskin, 2006, p. 394). There are many reasons why fractions are difficult to understand.

1. Fraction symbolism is very different from whole number symbolism. Fractional notation involves two numbers separated by a horizontal line, which represent one quantity. For children who understand whole numbers and place value, fractional notation at first makes no sense.

2. It is difficult to compare the size of fractions. After children learn to count meaningfully, they can compare whole numbers easily using a number line. However, as illustrated in the opening story of this chapter, comparing fractions such as $\frac{2}{5}$ and $\frac{5}{8}$ requires an understanding of complex models.

3. The rules for operations with fractions are different from the rules for operations with whole numbers. Children mistakenly use the rules for whole numbers with fractions. For example, a child might mistakenly write $\frac{1}{3} + \frac{2}{5} = \frac{3}{8}$.

4. There are more rules for operations with fractions than for operations with whole numbers, and the rules appear contradictory. In the previous example, when adding fractions, it is incorrect to add both the numerators and denominators. However, when multiplying fractions, it is correct to multiply the numerators and denominators—for example, $\frac{1}{3} \times \frac{2}{5} = \frac{2}{15}$.

5. Children mistakenly believe that parts do not have to be equal (**Figure 11.1**).

Children's mistakes with the size of parts • Figure 11.1

Which of these examples represent $\frac{3}{4}$? Children might think that $\frac{3}{4}$ means three parts of four but not three equal-sized parts of four.

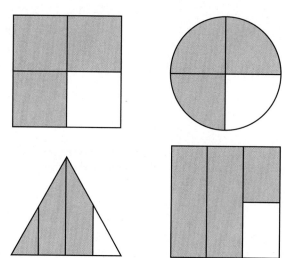

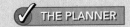
There are four meanings of fractions. Most of us are familiar with the part-whole meaning, but the other meanings are important to learn as well.

a. Part-Whole

A fraction can represent a quantity or set that is **partitioned** or divided into equal pieces. A pie might be partitioned into four equal pieces, with each piece representing $\frac{1}{4}$ of the pie. Three pieces of the pie is $\frac{3}{4}$. In the United States, this is considered to be the easiest meaning of fractions and is usually taught first.

b. Measure

A fraction can represent a comparison of lengths. A length is identified, and that length is used as the unit for comparison purposes. The fraction $\frac{3}{4}$ can be measured relative to the length of one whole or can be considered as three copies of the length $\frac{1}{4}$.

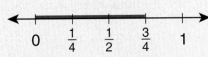

c. Quotient

A fraction can represent the division of two numbers. If three cookies are divided equally among four people, this can be written as $3 \div 4$, with each person getting $\frac{3}{4}$ of the cookie.

d. Ratio

A fraction can compare two sets or measurements. This interpretation of fractions is different from the other three because it does not include partitioning. If there are three girls and four boys in a group of children, then the ratio of girls to boys is 3:4, or $\frac{3}{4}$. This meaning of fractions is discussed extensively in Chapter 13.

Finding Meaning for Fractions

The part-whole meaning of fractions, which is the only meaning taught in many elementary mathematics textbooks, is just one of several meanings. Some researchers (Siebert and Gaskin, 2006) believe that children might learn to understand fractions more deeply if other meanings were taught as well. In Japan, fractions are introduced later than in the United States, in fourth grade rather than in third grade. Japanese textbooks initially explain fractions using measurement concepts and comparison, saving the part-whole meaning for fifth grade (Watanabe, 2006). Despite these differences, Japanese children perform better on fraction assessments than U.S. children.

The four meanings of fractions are illustrated in (**Figure 11.2**).

The three types of fraction models are *area, length,* and *set.* When children work with fractions, encourage them to use their models for as long as necessary. Eventually, they may be able to use mental models of fractions instead of pictorial or concrete ones. Use models before using symbols.

a. Area model

For the area model, the whole is portioned into parts that have equal area. The circle is considered to be the easiest example of the area model for children to learn.

Circular pieces

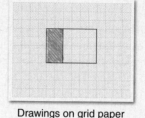

Drawings on grid paper

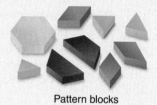

Pattern blocks

b. Length model

Lengths are compared to a unit length. Any one of the 10 *Cuisenaire rods* can be designated as the whole or unit. Children can make *fraction strips*. The *meter stick* is helpful as preparation for decimals because it is subdivided into 100 parts. The *number line* is more complex and should not be used until children have learned fraction number sense.

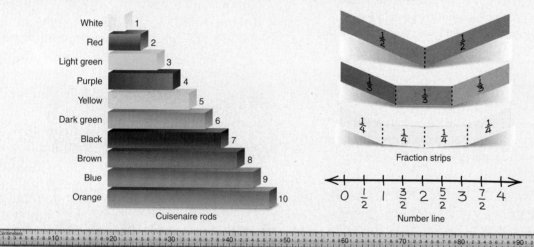

Cuisenaire rods

Fraction strips

Number line

Meter stick

c. Set model

The whole is a set of objects, and the parts of the set, or **subsets,** are fractional parts. Here, 3 of the 9 cookies are chocolate, so the chocolate cookies represent $\frac{1}{3}$ of the set; 5 of the 15 dots are red, so the 5 red dots also represent $\frac{1}{3}$ of the set. The set model is more complicated than the other two models and should not be taught until children develop an understanding of the first two models.

Models for Understanding Fractions

There are a wide variety of concrete and pictorial models that can help children understand fractions. Three types of fraction models are illustrated in **Figure 11.3**.

CONCEPT CHECK STOP

1. **How** might knowledge of whole number operations hamper understanding of fractions?

2. **Why** is it helpful for children to learn different meanings of fractions?

3. **Which** fraction model is more difficult to understand?

Developing Fraction Concepts

LEARNING OBJECTIVES

1. **Describe** how children learn how to find equal shares.

2. **Compare** and **contrast** partitioning and iterating.

3. **Explain** the importance of correct fraction language.

Curriculum Focal Points (NCTM, 2006) and the Common Core State Standards (NGA Center/CCSSO, 2010) recommend that children learn to understand the meanings of fractions and learn to represent fractions that are less than, equal to, or greater than one in grade 3. Partitioning and iterating are two processes that help children understand parts (Siebert and Gaskin, 2006). When children learn about fractions, they should have practice partitioning or finding equal shares, **iterating**, and using correct terminology. These concepts provide the focus for this section.

> **iterating** The process of copying the part over and over to get larger pieces of the whole.

Finding Equal Shares

Fractions were invented thousands of years ago for the purpose of finding equal shares (see *Multicultural Perspectives in Mathematics*).

Multicultural Perspectives in Mathematics

✓ THE PLANNER

Egyptian Unit Fractions

The Rhind Papyrus is a scroll made out of papyrus leaf. It contains hieroglyphics (picture writing) that describe the ancient Egyptians' method of working with fractions. This scroll was discovered by Henry Rhind in a tomb in Thebes, Egypt, in 1858.

The ancient Egyptians invented fractions for practical reasons. Because the Nile River overflowed annually, the pharaoh sent officials to determine the fraction of land that was washed away. Egyptians also used fractions to share food and supplies equally. No one knows why, but the Egyptians only worked with **unit fractions**, those whose numerators are 1, such as $\frac{1}{2}$ and $\frac{1}{3}$, with the exception of $\frac{2}{3}$. To express a fractional amount that was not a unit fraction, they used a combination of unit fractions. For $\frac{3}{4}$, they wrote $\frac{1}{2} + \frac{1}{4}$. They would never write $\frac{3}{4} = \frac{1}{4} + \frac{1}{4} + \frac{1}{4}$.

Let's see how the ancient Egyptians would solve the following:

Share three loaves of bread equally among five workers.

The Egyptians might divide each loaf in half, giving $\frac{1}{2}$ of a loaf to each of the five workers. This uses up $2\frac{1}{2}$ loaves. The remaining $\frac{1}{2}$ of

Global Locator

Thebes

NATIONAL GEOGRAPHIC

a loaf is divided equally into five pieces, giving each person $\frac{1}{5}$ of $\frac{1}{2}$ of a loaf or, $\frac{1}{10}$ of a loaf of bread. So, each person receives $\frac{1}{2} + \frac{1}{10}$ of a loaf.

$$\frac{3}{5} = \frac{1}{2} + \frac{1}{10}$$

Egyptian fractions can be used to compare fractional amounts. To compare $\frac{3}{4}$ and $\frac{4}{5}$, change each to sums of unit fractions:

$$\frac{3}{4} = \frac{1}{2} + \frac{1}{4}$$
$$\frac{4}{5} = \frac{1}{2} + \frac{1}{4} + \frac{1}{20}$$

- $\frac{4}{5}$ is the larger fraction.

(*Sources*: C. Fosnot and M. Dolk, 2002; K. D. Michaelowicz, 1996)

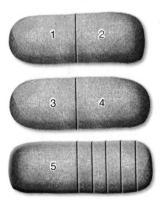

Strategies for the Classroom

- What are two advantages of Egyptian fractions?

- Why might you include information about ancient Egyptian fraction techniques in your own classroom?

- Ask your students to convert several fractions to unit fractions and then search the Internet to find an Egyptian fraction calculator for checking work.

Begin fraction instruction by teaching children about equal shares, or partitioning, using a method that is similar to the ancient Egyptians' method of calculating fractional parts. Start with story problems with familiar contexts to help children understand the concept of equally sharing the whole. Because children already have knowledge of halving and can do problems involving repeated halving without formal instruction, begin with problems that involve sharing numbers that are 2 or multiples of 2 (Empson, 2002). Consider the following problem:

Theresa baked two apple pies that she wants to share equally among four children. How many pieces of pie does each child get?

To solve this problem, a child might divide each pie in half and then give one piece (one half of the pie) to each of the four children. You can make the problem more complex by changing the number of pies or the number of children. Consider using five pies with four children, which requires repeated halving, and five pies with three children, which requires strategies beyond halving (**Figure 11.4**).

Help children recognize equal shares by providing activities such as **Activity 11.1**.

Activity 11.1 Are they thirds?

Instructions

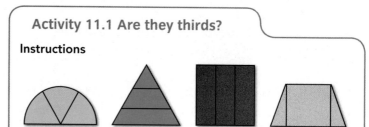

Say: *Look at the following diagrams. Which of these figures are partitioned into thirds? Which are not partitioned into thirds? Explain your answers.*

Sharing equally • Figure 11.4

a. Sharing five pies equally among four children

To share five pies among four children, Monica drew five fraction circles. She then partitioned each "pie" into two equal pieces and then distributed the pieces one at a time. The first four pies are distributed equally among the four children in this way. Then with two halves of one pie left to share among four children, Monica cuts each half of this pie in half again, and gives one piece to each child. Each child receives $\frac{1}{2} + \frac{1}{2} + \frac{1}{4}$ pieces of pie, or $\frac{5}{4}$ pieces of pie.

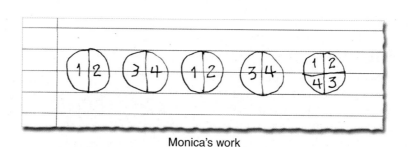

Monica's work

b. Sharing five pies equally among three children

To share five pies equally among three children, Joe drew five fraction circles. He drew a line down the center of each "pie" to halve it. Then he gave the pieces out one at a time, half a pie to each child and then another half pie to each child. The first $4\frac{1}{2}$ pies are distributed in this way. Now Joe has $\frac{1}{2}$ pie left. Joe partitions this $\frac{1}{2}$ pie into three equal pieces and gives $\frac{1}{6}$ of a pie to each child. Therefore, each child gets $\frac{1}{2} + \frac{1}{2} + \frac{1}{2} + \frac{1}{6}$ pieces of pie, or $\frac{10}{6}$ pieces of pie.

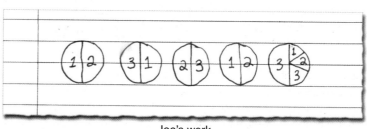

Joe's work

CHILDREN'S LITERATURE

Sharing equal parts

Eating Fractions • Figure 11.5a

Written and illustrated by Bruce McMillan
With colorful photographs of pies, cakes, pizza, and other foods that children like to eat, this book illustrates wholes and fractions such as halves, thirds, and fourths.

Strategy for the Classroom

- When reading the book with children, ask questions such as: *How many parts is the pizza separated into? Are all the parts equal size? Let's count parts. One slice of pizza is one-fourth of the whole pizza. Two slices of pizza is two-fourths. Three slices of pizza is three-fourths, and four slices of pizza is four-fourths, or one whole pizza.*

THIRDS

Fraction Action • Figure 11.5b

Written and illustrated by Loreen Leedy
Fractional parts are illustrated with fun illustrations that will appeal to children. Thirds are illustrated by the petals on a flower, the sections in a wallet, and a jester's hat. The book also illustrates the set model of fractions and includes questions about comparing fractions.

Strategy for the Classroom

- As you read the book with your class, examine each of the pictures and ask questions such as *How many examples of thirds can you find? What are other examples of thirds? Can you draw some pictures of thirds?*

Children's literature is a wonderful way to introduce equal sharing (see *Children's Literature*, **Figure 11.5**).

Iterating

Iterating means starting from the part and copying it over and over to get larger pieces of the whole. If a bar's length is $\frac{1}{6}$ of a whole, then five copies of the bar is $\frac{5}{6}$ of the whole and six copies of the bar is $\frac{6}{6}$ or one whole. Thinking of $\frac{5}{6}$ as five $\frac{1}{6}$s can help children understand that they are working with like-size units (Mack, 2004).

Iterating works very well with the length model (**Activity 11.2**).

Activity 11.2 Partitioning and iterating fractions

Instructions

1. Say: *Given this bar of length $\frac{1}{3}$, show pictures that represent bars of length $\frac{2}{3}$, 1, and $1\frac{1}{3}$. Explain your work.*

   $\frac{1}{3}$

2. *Given this bar of length $\frac{1}{4}$, show pictures that represent bars of length $\frac{3}{4}$, 1, $1\frac{1}{4}$, and $1\frac{1}{2}$.*

   $\frac{1}{4}$

3. *Given this bar of length 2, show pictures that represent bars of length $\frac{1}{4}$, $\frac{1}{2}$, 1, and 3.*

   2

4. *Given this bar of length $\frac{3}{4}$, show pictures that represent bars of length $\frac{1}{4}$, $\frac{1}{2}$, 1, and 3.*

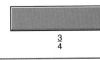

   $\frac{3}{4}$

Iterating is very useful in counting fractional parts, which in turn prepares children to learn about

<table>
<tr><td>

improper fraction
A fraction whose value is greater than one whole.

mixed number A number that has both a whole number and a fractional part.

</td><td>

improper fractions and mixed numbers. Improper fractions and mixed numbers are two different but equivalent ways of representing the same quantity. For example, $\frac{5}{4}$, an improper fraction, represents the same quantity as $1\frac{1}{4}$, a mixed number.

</td></tr>
</table>

Activity 11.3 illustrates how to introduce improper fractions and connect them to mixed numbers using the length model.

Activity 11.3 Mix it up

Instructions

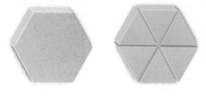

1. Show students a bar sectioned into fourths on a number line.
2. Count aloud: $\frac{1}{4}, \frac{2}{4}, \frac{3}{4}, \frac{4}{4}, \frac{5}{4}$.
3. Ask: *What is another name for $\frac{5}{4}$?* (Children should realize that $\frac{5}{4}$ is the same as $\frac{4}{4} + \frac{1}{4}$ or $1\frac{1}{4}$.)
4. Repeat with a new number line subdivided into thirds, then sixths or eighths.

Activity 11.4 illustrates how to represent improper fractions and mixed numbers with the area model.

Activity 11.4 Improper fractions with the area model

Instructions

1. Distribute pattern blocks to children.

2. Ask: *If the yellow hexagon is one whole, what shape represents $\frac{1}{6}$?* (Green triangle)

3. Say: *Show $\frac{7}{6}$ with seven pattern blocks.* (7 green triangles)

4. Say: *Show $\frac{7}{6}$ with two pattern blocks.* (1 yellow hexagon and 1 green triangle)

5. Ask: *What is another name for $\frac{7}{6}$?* ($1\frac{1}{6}$)

6. Say: *Again, using the yellow hexagon as one whole, show $\frac{3}{2}$ with three pattern blocks.* (3 red trapezoids) *Show $\frac{3}{2}$ with two pattern blocks.* (1 yellow hexagon and 1 red trapezoid)

7. Ask: *What is another name for $\frac{3}{2}$?* ($1\frac{1}{2}$)

8. Continue with other pattern block pieces.

Activity 11.5 demonstrates how iteration can be practiced with calculators such as the *TI-15*, which allows children to display fractions in their correct format. This type of calculator is commonly available in elementary schools.

Activity 11.5 Using a fraction calculator to practice iteration

Instructions

use

1. Use a TI-15 or another calculator capable of displaying fractions.

2. To iterate $\frac{1}{3}$ on the TI-15, press Op1 + 1 n + 3 d Op1

3. To initiate counting, press 0 and Op1 as many times as you like. Each time you press this key, the calculator will add another $\frac{1}{3}$ while keeping count on the left part of the screen of the number of thirds entered.

4. Ask: *How many times do I add $\frac{1}{3}$ to get $2\frac{1}{3}$?* (7 times) *How many times do I add $\frac{1}{3}$ to get $3\frac{2}{6}$?* (10 times)

Using Appropriate Fraction Language and Symbolism

The language used when talking about fractions is important. Avoid using the phrase "out of" as in "1 out of 4" when reading fractions because it implies taking one thing out of four things and gives the idea that the numbers are whole numbers rather than fractional parts. Help children understand that, for example, when a pizza is divided into four equal parts, the pizza is divided into fourths and each piece of pizza represents one fourth of the whole. Use the word *whole* or *one whole*. Make comparisons between the words *four* and *fourths*, *six* and *sixths*, and *eight* and *eighths*, because they sound similar. Write each pair of words on the chalkboard and help children pronounce them. This procedure is especially important for English-language learners and children with hearing impairments.

Although it is not necessary for children to know the terms **numerator** and **denominator**, they should be able to explain the meaning of the top and bottom numbers in fractions. The numerator is the counting number. The denominator tells what is being counted (fourths, fifths, sixths, etc.).

> **numerator** This part of the fraction counts how many equal shares you have.

> **denominator** This part of the fraction tells the number of equal parts the whole has been partitioned into.

CONCEPT CHECK 🛑 STOP

1. **When** teaching children to find equal shares, why is it easiest to begin with activities that share by multiples of 2?
2. **How** can the process of iteration prepare children to learn the meanings of improper fractions and mixed numbers?
3. **What** difficulties might children have with fractions if they learn to use expressions such as "5 out of 6"?

Fraction Comparison and Equivalence

LEARNING OBJECTIVES

1. **Compare** and **contrast** several methods for comparing and ordering fractions.
2. **Describe** the meaning of equivalent fractions.
3. **Identify** strategies for finding equivalent fractions.

Both the *Common Core State Standards* (NGA Center/CCSSO, 2010) and *Curriculum Focal Points* (NCTM, 2006, p. 15) recommend that in grade 3, children "solve problems that involve comparing and ordering fractions by using models, benchmark fractions, or common numerators or denominators. They understand and use models, including the number line, to identify **equivalent fractions**." In grade 4, they develop "techniques for generating equivalent fractions and simplifying fractions" (p. 16).

> **equivalent fractions** Fractions that represent the same quantity with different numbers.

Methods for Comparing and Ordering Fractions

When learning about fractions, the concept of the whole is very important. Children should understand that, when comparing and ordering fractions, they are always working with the same-size whole. Misunderstanding of this concept can lead to errors.

Virtual Classroom Observation

| Video | www.wiley.com/college/jones |

Click on **Student Companion Site.** Then click on:
- **Foundations of Effective Mathematics Teaching**
- **B. Focus on Teacher Content Knowledge**
- **3. Analyze Classroom Videos**

Scroll down and view:
- **The Magnitude of Fractions: Unequal wholes lead to unequal halves**

Notice how Miss Bradley helps the children understand that, in order to compare fractions, the wholes have to be the same size.

Making Fraction Strips to Compare Unit Fractions

GRADE LEVEL

3–4

OBJECTIVES

To compare the size of unit fractions with fraction strips

To recognize that $\frac{1}{1}, \frac{2}{2}, \frac{3}{3}$, etc. = 1 whole

STANDARDS

Grade 3

Understand a fraction $\frac{1}{b}$ as the quantity formed by 1 part when a whole is partitioned into b equal parts; understand a fraction $\frac{a}{b}$ as the quantity formed by a parts of size $\frac{1}{b}$. (NGA Center/CCSSO, 2010)

Explain equivalence of fractions in special cases, and compare fractions by reasoning about their size. (NGA Center/CCSSO, 2010)

Grade 4

Understand a fraction $\frac{a}{b}$ with $a > 1$ as a sum of fractions $\frac{1}{b}$. (NGA Center/CCSSO, 2010)

MATERIALS

- Scissors, ruler, pencil for each child

- Two pieces of large construction paper for each child about 18 inches long.

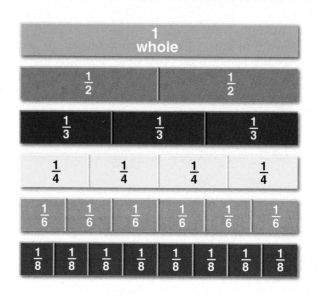

ASSESSMENT

- Choose three fraction strips. Identify three different unit fractions and order them from least to greatest. Explain how you ordered them.

- Write a journal entry that explains the meaning of unit fractions and how to compare unit fractions.

Begin ordering activities by comparing fractions to the benchmarks of $0, \frac{1}{2}$, and 1 and placing fractions on the number line (**Activity 11.6**).

2. Say: *For each of the following fractions, decide where to place it on the number line by deciding whether it is closest to $0, \frac{1}{2}$, or 1. If the fraction is closest to $\frac{1}{2}$, decide whether it is less than or greater than $\frac{1}{2}$. If the fraction is closest to 1, decide whether it is less than or greater than 1. Explain your thinking.*

$$\frac{26}{50}, \frac{102}{100}, \frac{37}{80}, \frac{42}{80}, \frac{99}{100}, \frac{1}{50}$$

> ### Activity 11.6 Using benchmarks of $0, \frac{1}{2}$, and 1 to order fractions
>
> **Instructions**
>
> 1. The first time you do this activity, use fractions that are easy for children to estimate because of their closeness to one of the benchmarks (such as $\frac{1}{5}, \frac{5}{8}, \frac{9}{10}$). Also include some fractions that are greater than 1.

3. Repeat with fractions that are more challenging, such as $\frac{1}{3}, \frac{3}{5}, \frac{1}{20}, \frac{55}{56}, \frac{72}{70}, \frac{2}{9}$.

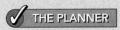

GROUPING

Whole class followed by small groups

Launch (5 to 10 minutes)

- Say: *We have been using many different kinds of fraction models. Can you name some that we have used?* (Pattern blocks, pie pieces, geoboards)

- Say: *Today you are going to make your very own fraction model. You can take this home with you and use it whenever you want to compare fractions.*

Instruct (30 minutes)

- Ask each child to cut six strips, each 2 inches wide and about 9 inches long, from construction paper.

- Ask each child to label one strip "one whole."

- Ask each child to fold the next strip into two equal parts. Draw a dark line along the fold mark. Label each part of the strip as "one half" and write "halves" on the back of the strip.

- Continue in the same way, folding other strips into 3, 4, 6, and 8 equal parts and labeling accordingly as thirds, fourths, sixths, and eighths.

- Ask children to lay out their fraction strips on their desks, with the strip representing one whole on top, the strip representing two halves below it, then thirds, fourths, sixths, and eighths.

- Say: *A unit fraction is a fraction that represents one part of a whole. It is written with a 1 as the top number. What are some unit fractions on your strips?* ($\frac{1}{2}, \frac{1}{3}, \frac{1}{4}, \frac{1}{6}, \frac{1}{8}$)

- Ask: *Which is larger, $\frac{1}{2}$ or $\frac{1}{3}$? How can you tell by looking at your strips? Which is larger, $\frac{1}{3}$ or $\frac{1}{4}$?* Continue until you have compared all the unit fractions on the strips.

- Ask: *Does anyone see a pattern? Which is the largest unit fraction on your strips? Which is the smallest unit fraction on your strips?*

- Say: *Now let's count along the fraction strips. On the second strip we count $\frac{1}{2}, \frac{2}{2}$. What is another name for $\frac{2}{2}$?* (1 whole) *On the third strip we count $\frac{1}{3}, \frac{2}{3}, \frac{3}{3}$. What is another name for $\frac{3}{3}$?* (1 whole) Continue in this way.

Summarize (5 minutes)

- Ask: *Are all of these fraction strips equal to the same-size whole?* (Yes)

- Ask: *Why is that important when comparing fractions?*

- Use these methods to compare $\frac{1}{8}$ and $\frac{1}{12}$.

Comparing unit fractions After children can order fractions by comparison to given benchmarks, help them to informally compare unit fractions. Instead of rushing to teach algorithms, help children develop fraction number sense, which they are less likely to forget.

Children tend to believe that the unit fraction with the largest denominator has the greatest value. This is a holdover from their work with whole numbers. Actually the inverse relationship holds. For unit fractions, the fraction with the largest number in the denominator has the smallest value, because the same-size whole is partitioned into more pieces. The process of actually making their own fraction strips can help children understand the size of unit fractions (see the *Lesson*). The fraction strips made in the lesson can be used later to learn about equivalent fractions. The standards are from the *Common Core State Standards* (NGS Center/CCSSO, 2010) for grades 3 and 4.

CHILDREN'S LITERATURE

Helping children compare unit fractions

To equal one loop by the inchworm,
the second worm had to loop twice.
For accuracy, the third worm looped three.
"I'm a one-third-inch fraction, how nice!"

Inchworm and a Half • Figure 11.6

Written by Elinor Pinczes
Illustrated by Randall Enos

The inchworm tries to measure all the vegetables in the garden by climbing on them. She goes about this task until she finds one vegetable that she cannot measure accurately. She measures 2 inches and a little more. Then along comes a half-inch worm to help with the measuring. They measure together until their measurements are a little bit off. Then along comes a quarter-inch worm.

Strategies for the Classroom

- Before reading this book with your class, create your own paper inchworms, half-inch worms, and quarter-inch worms. Bring objects for children to measure.

- Help children compare the lengths of the inchworm, half-inch worm, and quarter-inch worm and develop relationships such as two half-inch worms are the same length as one inchworm.

- When measuring different objects, ask: *Which kind of worm provides the most accurate measure for this?*

Children's literature offers a unique way to compare the unit fractions $\frac{1}{2}$ and $\frac{1}{4}$ with the length one whole (see *Children's Literature*, **Figure 11.6**).

Comparing other fractions Informal methods, based on number sense, can be used to compare other fractions.

Table 11.1 illustrates how to compare different types of fractions.

These informal strategies for comparing fractions will not work for all pairs of fractions, but when they do, they extend children's number sense. **Activity 11.7** illustrates how to order groups of fractions using informal strategies.

Strategies for comparing fractions   Table 11.1

Fractions	Reason
$\frac{2}{3}$ or $\frac{2}{5}$	**Same number of parts.** Both fractions have the same number of parts (numerators), but the parts are different sizes. $\frac{2}{3}$ is greater than $\frac{2}{5}$ because thirds are larger than fifths.
$\frac{3}{8}$ or $\frac{7}{8}$	**More of the same-size parts.** Both fractions have the same denominator (eighths). $\frac{7}{8}$ is greater than $\frac{3}{8}$.
$\frac{4}{9}$ or $\frac{5}{8}$	**More or less than** $\frac{1}{2}$. $\frac{4}{9}$ is less than $\frac{1}{2}$ and $\frac{5}{8}$ is more than $\frac{1}{2}$, so $\frac{5}{8}$ is greater than $\frac{4}{9}$.
$\frac{9}{10}$ or $\frac{4}{5}$	**Closer to one.** Both fractions are one part away from one whole. Because tenths are smaller than fifths, $\frac{9}{10}$ is closer to one and is greater than $\frac{4}{5}$.

Activity 11.7 One at a time

Instructions

1. Give students several fractions that can be compared using the rules explained in Table 11.1, such as $\frac{13}{12}, \frac{3}{8}, \frac{3}{5}, \frac{1}{4}, \frac{2}{4}, \frac{9}{10}$.

2. Ask students to order the fractions from least to greatest, place the fractions on a number line, and explain their reasoning.

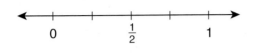

2. Fold the paper again the same way. Then fold it in half again in the other direction. Unfold so you can see the shaded portion. Ask again: *What fraction is the shaded part?* ($\frac{2}{4}$)

3. Continue this process one or two more times to get eight equal parts with a shaded part of $\frac{4}{8}$ and 16 equal parts with a shaded part of $\frac{8}{16}$.

4. Ask: *What can you tell me about the fractions $\frac{1}{2}, \frac{2}{4}, \frac{4}{8}, \frac{8}{16}$?* (They all represent the same shaded area.)

5. Say: *These fractions are called equivalent because they are different names for the same quantity.*

Children can also compare fractions by finding equivalent fractions. For example, to compare $\frac{7}{8}$ and $\frac{3}{5}$, rewrite both fractions so that they have a **common denominator**. These ideas will be explored in the next section.

In **Activity 11.9**, children use the fraction strips made in the lesson in this chapter and use the length model to find equivalent fractions.

Equivalent Fractions

The ability to find equivalent fractions is an important one. Children find equivalent fractions for comparison, to find common denominators for addition and subtraction, and to convert fractions to decimals and percents. Not surprisingly, children have difficulty understanding that two different numbers (for example, $\frac{1}{2}$ and $\frac{4}{8}$) or an infinite number of numbers can represent the same quantity. This is the first time they have been introduced to this idea. Start the development of equivalent fractions conceptually by having children use concrete or pictorial models to show the equivalence of two fractions. **Activity 11.8** provides an example of how to introduce equivalent fractions using the area model.

Activity 11.8 Shade me

Instructions

1. Ask each child to fold a piece of notebook paper in half. Unfold and shade one half. Ask: *What fraction is the shaded part?* ($\frac{1}{2}$)

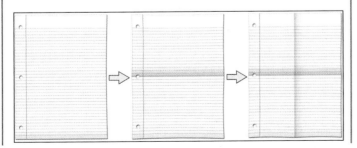

Activity 11.9 Who am I?

Instructions

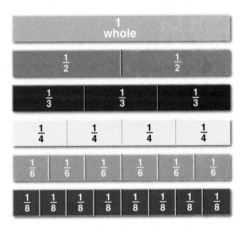

1. Use the fraction strips made in the lesson.

2. Ask children to line up their fraction strips end to end. Count along each strip, so that children identify $\frac{1}{2}, \frac{2}{2}, \frac{1}{3}, \frac{2}{3}, \frac{3}{3}$, and so on.

3. Ask children to use their fraction strips to identify fractions that are equivalent to $\frac{1}{2}$. ($\frac{2}{4}, \frac{3}{6}, \frac{4}{8}$) Ask: *Are there any other fractions that are equivalent to $\frac{1}{2}$? Do you see a pattern?* (All fractions equivalent to $\frac{1}{2}$ have a top number that is half of the bottom number.)

4. Ask children to use their fraction strips to identify fractions that are equivalent to $\frac{1}{3}$. ($\frac{2}{6}$) Ask: *Are there any other fractions that are equivalent to $\frac{1}{3}$? Do you see a pattern?*

5. Repeat and find fractions equivalent to $\frac{1}{4}, \frac{2}{3}$.

Let's take another look at the area model. It is very effective for finding equivalent fractions and will be used later with fraction operations. This model is illustrated in **Activity 11.10**.

Activity 11.10 Find another name

Instructions

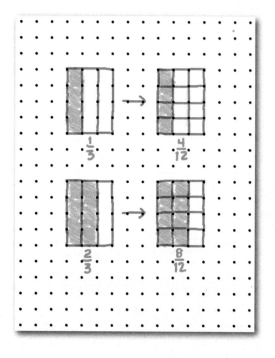

$$\frac{1}{3} \qquad \frac{4}{12}$$

$$\frac{2}{3} \qquad \frac{8}{12}$$

1. Ask students to draw a 4 × 3 rectangular grid on grid paper or dot paper, partition the rectangle into three equal columns, and shade the left-most column. Ask: *What fraction is represented by the shaded region?* $\left(\frac{1}{3}\right)$

2. Ask: *How can we find another name for this fraction?* If children do not suggest this, ask them to partition the grid into four equal rows. (The new name for the shaded region is $\frac{4}{12}$.)

3. Ask: *Do both of these fractions represent the same quantity? Do you notice any patterns?*

4. Tell students to shade the second column of the grid. Ask students to find two different names for the fraction represented by the shaded region. $\left(\frac{2}{3} \text{ or } \frac{8}{12}\right)$

5. Repeat with other grids: 3 × 6, 4 × 5, 4 × 6, and ask the same types of questions.

By completing activities of this type, children may recognize the pattern for finding equivalent fractions without being taught the algorithm. They may see that they can represent $\frac{1}{3}$ as the equivalent fraction $\frac{4}{12}$ by multiplying the numerator and denominator of $\frac{1}{3}$ by 4. In general, multiplying the numerator and denominator of any fraction by the same whole number creates an equivalent fraction. Any fraction can be represented by an infinite number of equivalent fractions. If children do not develop the algorithm on their own, provide activities such as the following (**Activity 11.11**).

Activity 11.11 Finding equivalent fractions

Instructions

1. Provide a series of problems in which each has an equation that shows an equivalence between two fractions, and one of the numbers is missing:

$$\frac{3}{4} = \frac{9}{\Box}$$

$$\frac{4}{5} = \frac{\Box}{25}$$

$$\frac{9}{4} = \frac{36}{\Box}$$

$$\frac{6}{8} = \frac{\Box}{40}$$

2. For each pair of fractions, find the missing number and draw a picture of the fractions.

Tech Tools _____

http://nlvm.usu.edu/en/nav/grade_g_2

The National Library of Virtual Manipulatives **Fractions Equivalent** applet is excellent. The screen shows a region model of a fraction alongside a symbolic representation. The user picks the number of pieces he or she wants the equivalent fraction to have and enters the new numerator and denominator.

Sometimes, when working with fractions, you may want to write a fraction in **simplest terms**. This is also a process of finding an equivalent fraction. To do this, divide the numerator and denominator of the fraction by the **greatest common factor (GCF)**. For example, the GCF of 24 and 36 is 12 and $\frac{2}{3}$ is equivalent to $\frac{24}{36}$ but is in simplest terms.

> **simplest terms** Form of a fraction whose numerator and denominator have no common whole-number factors.
>
> **greatest common factor (GCF)** The largest whole number that is a factor of both numbers.

$$\frac{24}{36} = \frac{24 \div 12}{36 \div 12} = \frac{2}{3}$$

Teaching Tip

Writing fractions in simplest terms

- You may have used the terminology "reducing" fractions when you meant "simplifying" fractions. Avoid this terminology, since it implies that you are changing the value of the fraction and thus it can be confusing to children.

- Children often ask whether they have to simplify their fractional answer. The answer is no! There is no need to simplify unless it is needed for the context of the problem and, in fact, simplifying provides more opportunities for errors.

CONCEPT CHECK

1. **Why** is it important for children to learn to compare fractions to benchmarks?
2. **Why** does each fraction have an infinite number of equivalent representations?
3. **How** can children use informal strategies to find equivalent fractions? Use these strategies to find two fractions equivalent to $\frac{5}{6}$.

Fraction Operations

LEARNING OBJECTIVES

1. **Describe** the four-step process for teaching fraction operations.
2. **Compare** and **contrast** the development of student-created and traditional algorithms for addition and subtraction of fractions.
3. **Compare** and **contrast** the development of student-created and traditional algorithms for multiplication and division of fractions.
4. **Describe** the differences between whole number and fraction computation algorithms.

B oth the *Curriculum Focal Points* (NCTM, 2006) and *Common Core State Standards* (NGA Center/CCSSO, 2010) recommend that by grade 5, students should be able to build on their understandings of fractions models to add and subtract fractions with unlike denominators by representing them as equivalent fractions with like denominators. Children in grade 6 "use the meanings of fractions, multiplication and division, and the inverse relationship between multiplication and division to make sense of procedures for multiplying and dividing fractions,

and explain why they work" (p. 18). This section explains how to teach fraction operations for fifth and sixth graders.

Fraction Operations: An Overview

Before learning fraction computation, children need to understand whole number operations, the meaning of fractions, how to use fraction models, and how to find equivalent representations for fractions. Even though addition, subtraction, multiplication, and division with

Learning fraction computation informally • Figure 11.7

When teachers help children learn fraction operations, they do so through a four-step process, beginning with story problems and using estimation, number sense, informal methods, and models to promote understanding. After children deeply understand the operations and can compute efficiently, traditional algorithms can be introduced.

1 Begin with story problems that have familiar contexts. Encourage children to develop their own strategies for solving the problems. Consider the following problem:

Jenna is baking cookies. She needs $\frac{2}{3}$ cup of chocolate chips for each batch of cookies. How many cups of chocolate chips does she need for five batches of cookies?

2 Use whole number computation to connect to fraction computation.

What is meant by 5 × 2?
What is meant by 5 × $\frac{2}{3}$?

3 Use estimation and informal methods.

$5 \times \frac{2}{3} = 5 \times \left(\frac{1}{3}\right) \times 2$

$5 \times \frac{1}{3} = \frac{5}{3}$ by counting or iteration.
Double $\frac{5}{3}$ is $\frac{10}{3}$.

OR

$5 \times \frac{2}{3} = 5 \times 2 \times \left(\frac{1}{3}\right) = 10 \times \frac{1}{3} = \frac{10}{3}$

"I know that $\frac{2}{3}$ is less than 1, so $5 \times \frac{2}{3}$ is less than 5"

4 Use models to illustrate each of the operations.

$5 \times \frac{2}{3} = \frac{2}{3} + \frac{2}{3} + \frac{2}{3} + \frac{2}{3} + \frac{2}{3} = \frac{10}{3}$

fractions are all very different, the approach to teaching fraction computation is similar for all four operations (**Figure 11.7**).

There are significant differences between whole number computation and fraction computation, especially in multiplication and division. For example, multiplication of two fractions cannot be modeled by repeated addition, and division of fractions cannot be modeled with repeated subtraction. Multiplication and division of fractions also bring unexpected results. When multiplying two fractions that are each less than 1 or a fraction less than 1 by a whole number, the answer is less than either of the factors. This concept is very difficult for children to understand. They expect multiplication to produce a larger answer. This confusion continues with division. When dividing a whole number by a fraction less than 1, the quotient is larger than either number.

Addition and Subtraction of Fractions

When children first learn addition and subtraction of fractions, encourage them to create their own strategies. Ask children to solve problems mentally or by drawing models. Children usually favor fraction circles; encourage them to use the length model as well. **Figure 11.8** illustrates two strategies for fraction addition created by children.

Teaching Tip _____

Adding and subtracting of fractions

- Begin with easy fractions that are familiar to children, such as halves, thirds, fourths, fifths, sixths, eighths, and tenths.

- Start by adding and subtracting fractions with the same denominator and fractions that will only require changing one fraction to an equivalent one (e.g., $\frac{1}{2} + \frac{3}{4}$).

Algorithms for addition and subtraction The traditional algorithm for addition and subtraction of fractions with the same denominator is similar to the one for addition and subtraction of whole numbers. If children understand the meaning of fractions, they should have no trouble with this algorithm. If the sum is greater than one whole, they may need to convert an improper fraction to a mixed number.

Addition of fractions with different denominators involves representing both fractions with the same common denominator. Begin with a task such as $\frac{1}{3} + \frac{1}{6}$, where only one denominator has to be changed. Let children try to solve this on their own. Some children will use their fraction strips to determine that $\frac{1}{3}$ is equivalent to $\frac{2}{6}$, while others will just know this. Next, provide an example in which both denominators have to be changed,

Using models to add fractions • Figure 11.8 _____

a. $\frac{1}{4} + \frac{2}{4}$

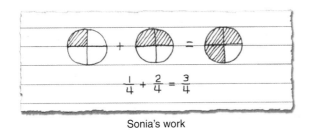

Sonia's work

Sonia adds the fractions by drawing fraction circles and adding the shaded parts.

b. $\frac{3}{8} + \frac{1}{4}$

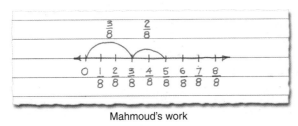

Mahmoud's work

Mahmoud draws a number line and counts $\frac{3}{8}$ along the line. Because he knows that $\frac{1}{4}$ is another name for $\frac{2}{8}$, he counts another $\frac{2}{8}$ on the number line.

such as $\frac{3}{4} + \frac{1}{3}$. Recommend that children find equivalent fractions, but do not force one method over another. After children have completed the task, ask them to share their strategies. One solution is illustrated in **Figure 11.9**.

Adding fractions with different denominators • Figure 11.9

Task: $\frac{3}{4} + \frac{1}{3}$

Becky drew two congruent rectangles, one to model $\frac{3}{4}$ and the other to model $\frac{1}{3}$. She found equivalent fractions with 12 as the common denominator. She subdivided each of the rectangles so that they now each had 12 parts. $\frac{3}{4} + \frac{1}{3}$ is the same as $\frac{9}{12} + \frac{4}{12}$. $\frac{9}{12} + \frac{4}{12} = \frac{13}{12} = 1\frac{1}{12}$.

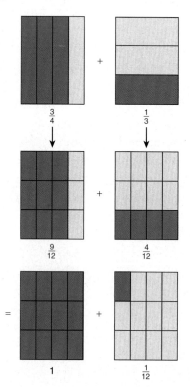

How can you help children who have difficulty finding common denominators? **Activity 11.12** illustrates one technique.

Addition and subtraction of improper fractions and mixed numbers It is much easier to add or subtract improper fractions than mixed numbers. With mixed numbers, children tend to deal with the whole numbers first and then work with the fractions, which creates problems if regrouping is necessary (**Figure 11.10**). One effective technique is to change all mixed numbers to improper fractions before attempting computation.

Children's errors in subtracting mixed numbers • Figure 11.10

a. If you subtract 4 – 2 first, then you are left with $\frac{1}{4} - \frac{3}{4}$ and need to regroup, which causes difficulties since you have already subtracted the whole numbers.

b. A common regrouping error is to regroup 1 ten as 10 ones instead of regrouping one whole as $\frac{4}{4}$, as illustrated here.

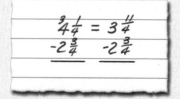

Multiplication of Fractions

Multiplication of fractions is taught in the fifth and sixth grades. Begin teaching this concept with word problems. Initially, focus on the multiplication of a whole number by a fraction. Consider the following problem:

Ricardo bought a box of 24 donuts. He and his friends ate $\frac{2}{3}$ of them. How many donuts did Ricardo and his friends eat?

To solve this problem, children must find $\frac{2}{3}$ of 24, written as $\frac{2}{3} \times 24$ (**Figure 11.11**).

Using an area model for multiplication of a whole number by a fraction • Figure 11.11

Children might draw an area model to represent 24 and partition it into three equal parts, with each part representing 8. Then, by counting, $\frac{1}{3}$ of 24 is 8, and $\frac{2}{3}$ of 24 is 16.

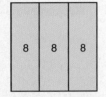

Next, provide examples in which the first number is a whole number. For example:

Dana filled six bowls with $\frac{3}{4}$ cup of ice cream in each. How many cups of ice cream did Dana use?

To solve this problem, children find six groups of $\frac{3}{4}$ or $6 \times \frac{3}{4}$, by repeated addition, an area model, or a length model. $6 \times \frac{3}{4} = \frac{18}{4}$ or $4\frac{1}{2}$ cups of ice cream.

Finally, give tasks that require multiplication of a fraction by a fraction. Consider the following problems (**Figure 11.12**).

Teaching Tip

Subdividing rectangular regions

When multiplying fractions by subdividing rectangular regions, use different colors to shade each region.

Multiplying a fraction by a fraction • Figure 11.12

The first problem, which requires no further subdividing, can be solved without multiplication. The second problem requires children to understand that taking one fractional part of another requires multiplication. There, further subdivision is required. Both solutions use the area model, which helps visualize the answer and connects to the array model used for whole number multiplication.

a.

Cindy had $\frac{3}{4}$ of a candy bar. She ate $\frac{1}{3}$ of it after lunch. What part of the candy bar did Cindy eat after lunch?

The part of the candy bar that is left is already divided into three equal pieces. To find $\frac{1}{3}$ of $\frac{3}{4}$, take one of the three equal pieces, and represent it as a part of the entire candy bar. Cindy ate one of the three equal pieces, which is $\frac{1}{4}$ of the candy bar.

b.

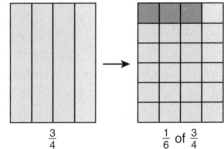

$\frac{3}{4}$ $\frac{1}{6}$ of $\frac{3}{4}$

Conan had $\frac{3}{4}$ of a carton of eggs. He used $\frac{1}{6}$ of the eggs to make cookies. What part of the original carton of eggs did he use?

To find $\frac{1}{6}$ of $\frac{3}{4}$, use the area model to represent $\frac{3}{4}$ by partitioning the whole into four equal parts and shading three of them. Then subdivide this shaded area into six equal parts and shade one of them. Conan used $\frac{3}{24}$ of the carton, or $\frac{1}{8}$ of the carton of eggs.

In the Classroom
Division of Fractions

Sixth-grade teacher John Baker brought a loaf of Italian bread to class and asked: *If I need $\frac{1}{3}$ of this loaf to make one sandwich, how many sandwiches can I make with this loaf of bread?* Terry answered: *You can make three sandwiches.*

Mr. Baker then drew two loaves of bread, and asked how many sandwiches he could make.

After several similar examples, the children found a pattern. They realized that $1 \times 3 = 3$, $2 \times 3 = 6$, and so on.

$$1 \div \tfrac{1}{3} = 3 \qquad\qquad 1 \times 3 = 3$$
$$2 \div \tfrac{1}{3} = 6 \qquad\qquad 2 \times 3 = 6$$
$$3 \div \tfrac{1}{3} = 9 \qquad\qquad 3 \times 3 = 9$$
$$3 \div \tfrac{2}{3} = \tfrac{9}{2} = 4\tfrac{1}{2} \qquad\qquad 3 \times \tfrac{3}{2} = \tfrac{9}{2}$$
$$4 \div \tfrac{2}{3} = \tfrac{12}{2} = 6 \qquad\qquad 4 \times 3 = 12; \tfrac{12}{2} = 6$$

Algorithm for multiplication of fractions After solving many problems by drawing models, children may develop the algorithm for themselves. Foster algorithm development by writing a list on the chalkboard of examples that were previously solved using models. For example, write

$$\frac{3}{5} \times \frac{2}{3} = \frac{6}{15}$$
$$\frac{1}{4} \times \frac{5}{7} = \frac{5}{28}$$
$$\frac{2}{9} \times \frac{1}{3} = \frac{2}{27}$$

Ask children whether they notice a pattern. They should realize that to multiply two fractions, multiply the numerators and multiply the denominators.

Multiplication of mixed numbers and improper fractions When multiplying mixed numbers, children tend to make errors by multiplying the whole number parts and the fraction parts separately. To avoid this, change mixed numbers to improper fractions. Simplify fractions before multiplying, and use calculators if the numbers are too large for easy computation.

Tech Tools_____

http://nlvm.usu.edu

The National Library of Virtual Manipulatives offers many excellent fraction activities, including the **Rectangle Multiplication** applet, which allows students to build virtual arrays for multiplication of fractions.

Division of Fractions

The algorithm for division of fractions is probably one of the least understood procedures in mathematics. Children

Next, Mr. Baker asked: *What if my loaves of bread are smaller and I need $\frac{2}{3}$ of a loaf to make a sandwich? How many sandwiches can I make with three loaves of bread?* Denzel said: *You can make four sandwiches and some left over.* Emma added: *You have four sandwiches and $\frac{1}{3}$ of a loaf left over, but the part left over makes $\frac{1}{2}$ of a sandwich, so the answer is $4\frac{1}{2}$.*

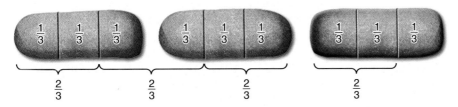

After students completed several similar tasks, Mr. Baker asked whether the pattern they found earlier still held true, and of course it did. For example, $4 \div \frac{2}{3} = 4 \times \frac{3}{2} = \frac{9}{2}$. Mr. Baker's class had invented the algorithm all on their own, through problem solving and observing patterns.

> **Think Critically**
>
> 1. How can these examples help children understand the division of fractions algorithm?
> 2. Why is Emma's answer correct? How would you explain this to children?

also are not sure when to multiply and when to divide. Consider the following problem:

> *Emanuel had eight baseballs and wanted to give $\frac{1}{4}$ of them to his cousin. How many baseballs did Emanuel give to his cousin?*

Although this is a multiplication problem, students' unease with fractions may lead them to believe it is a division problem.

To build understanding of division of fractions, begin with concrete models and build the algorithm through pattern recognition (see *In the Classroom*).

After children understand how to divide a whole number by a fraction, give them problems that require them to divide a fraction by a whole number and a fraction by a fraction. Although these types of problems are not easy to model, children can discover that the same algorithm works for these types of problems as well.

CONCEPT CHECK

1. **Why** is it important to teach fraction operations with contextual problems and informal strategies?

2. **How** could you add $\frac{1}{3} + \frac{2}{5}$ without using the traditional algorithm?

3. **What** are the advantages of using the area model to find the solution to the following problem?

   > *Eric has $\frac{1}{2}$ of a book left to read. After dinner he read $\frac{1}{3}$ of the remaining pages. What fraction of the book did Eric read?*

4. **What** are three differences between fraction computation and whole number computation? Why is it important for students to recognize these differences?

Summary

1 Developing the Meaning of Fractions 278

- Many children have difficulty learning fractions because the symbolism is strange to them after learning whole numbers. Fractions also behave differently from whole numbers. There are many more rules for operations with fractions than for operations with whole numbers.

- There are four meanings of fractions: part-whole, measure, quotient, and ratio. Many elementary mathematics textbooks focus entirely on the part-whole meaning, as shown in this drawing. This is usually considered the easiest to learn; however, the other meanings of fractions are also important.

Figure 11.2

- Three types of models are used for learning fractions: the area model, the length model, and the set model. In the set model, fractional parts are represented by **subsets.** This is the most complex model and should not be taught until children are comfortable using other models. In the area model, circles are the best-understood example.

2 Developing Fraction Concepts 281

- We begin to teach fractions by teaching children about **partitioning** into equal shares, as shown here. Usually, the area model is used first because it is easy to understand. Give children many opportunities to partition wholes into equal parts.

Figure 11.4

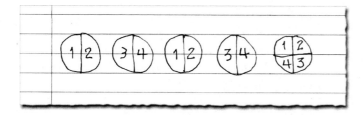

- **Iterating** is another important concept with fractions. It means taking a fractional part and copying it over and over. We can use iterating to start with a fraction, such as $\frac{1}{3}$, and find the whole or a larger fraction. Iterating is particularly helpful for learning the meaning of **mixed numbers** and **improper fractions.**

- It is important that children use correct terminology with fractions. You should never say "3 out of 4" when you read $\frac{3}{4}$. This can be confusing. Also be careful that words such as *fourths*, *thirds*, and *eighths* are distinguished from *fours*, *threes*, and *eights*.

3 Fraction Comparison and Equivalence 285

- Benchmarks are an effective way to order and compare fractions. Use a number line with hatch marks at 0, $\frac{1}{2}$, and 1, as illustrated here. Order fractions by comparing them to these three benchmarks.

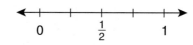

Activity 11.6

- Many times, fractions can be compared informally, if they have the same **numerator**, same **denominator**, are greater than or less than $\frac{1}{2}$, or are one part away from 1.

- **Equivalent fractions** provide another way to compare fractions. Sometimes when given a fraction, we want to put it in **simplest terms.** We can do this by finding the **greatest common factor** of the numerator and denominator and dividing by it.

4 Fraction Operations 291

- To add and subtract fractions with the same denominator, just add the numerators. To add and subtract fractions with different denominators, find a common denominator, and write both fractions as equivalent fractions with the same denominator. The open number line, as illustrated here, is a useful model.

Figure 11.8

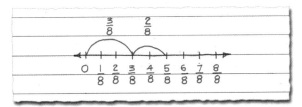

- To multiply fractions, multiply the numerators and the denominators. It is important for children to understand situations that require multiplication of fractions. When taking one fractional part of another fractional part, multiplication is required.

- Division of fractions is one of the least-understood algorithms in mathematics. Develop the algorithm by using easy-to-understand examples and recognizing patterns.

Key Terms

- common denominator 289
- denominator 285
- equivalent fractions 285
- greatest common factor (GCF) 291

- improper fraction 284
- iterating 281
- mixed number 284
- numerator 285

- simplest terms 291
- partitioned 279
- subset 280
- unit fractions 281

Additional Children's Literature

- ***The Doorbell Rang,*** **written and illustrated by Pat Hutchins**
  This book, originally discussed in Chapter 9, can also be used to learn about fractions. When Ma bakes 12 cookies for two children, they each get $\frac{1}{2}$ of the cookies. When there are four children, they each get $\frac{1}{3}$ of the cookies. Read the story and model it with real or paper cookies to help children understand equal sharing.

- ***Two Greedy Bears,*** **written by Mirra Ginsburg and illustrated by Jose Aruego and Ariane Dewey**
  This retelling of a Hungarian folktale offers many opportunities to discuss fractions. When a fox notices two bears fighting over a piece of cheese, he offers to help but breaks the cheese into two uneven pieces and eats some himself. Then the bears fight again over the leftover cheese and the fox offers to help again. This story is about equal sharing.

- ***Grandfather Tang's Story,*** **written by Ann Tompert**
  This book tells the story of two fox fairies, mythical figures from Chinese folklore. They change themselves into different animals that are described with tangrams. Children can use the tangram pieces as models of the area model of fractions. Let the large triangle represent one whole, and find the fractions of the whole that are represented by the other tangram pieces.

Online Resources

- **National Library of Virtual Manipulatives**
  http://nlvm.usu.edu

  This site offers numerous fraction activities, including representing fractions as parts of a whole, naming fractions, finding equivalent fractions, comparing fractions, and adding fractions.

- **PBS Cyberchase** www.pbs.org/cyberchase/parentsteachers/lessons/lessons.html

  Cyberchase is a television series that has some exciting mathematics. The site has a variety of video activities. A great one is **I'll Halve S'More Please,** which focuses on equal sharing.

- **PBS Teachers** www.pbs.org/teachers/mathline/concepts/farmingandgardening/

  This is an activity for grades K–5 in which students plan their own vegetable garden on a 10 × 10 grid, planting fractional sections of several vegetables. This activity provides a real-world example of fractions.

  www.pbs.org/teachers/mathline/concepts/movies/activity2.shtm

  In this activity for grades 6–8, students learn about making movies and use mathematics, including fractions, in the process.

Critical and Creative Thinking Questions

1. Children and adults tend to dislike fractions. They especially have difficulty finding the relative size of fractions. Why do you think this is true? How can the type of fraction instruction described in this chapter change your own students' opinions of fractions?

2. **Using visuals**   Both children and adults find it difficult to understand why multiplying a fraction by a fraction gives a result that is smaller than either of the original factors. How can you explain why this is true? Build a visual model to support your explanation.

3. What is iteration? Why is it important? Explain how you can use iteration to demonstrate the equivalence of $2\frac{3}{4}$ and $\frac{11}{4}$.

4. Children often have difficulty understanding that two fractions can be equivalent representations of the same quantity. Describe how you would help a child understand that $\frac{1}{2}$ and $\frac{15}{30}$ represent the same quantity. What models would you use to help a child understand this?

5. **In the field**   Examine two elementary mathematics textbook series for grades 3–5.

   - What meanings of fractions are used?
   - What models are used?
   - How do these textbooks teach comparison of fractions, ordering, and equivalence? Do they use algorithms to teach these concepts or include conceptual development?
   - Select one of the fraction units in one of the textbooks. If you were to teach this unit, how would you supplement it?

6. In the virtual classroom observation for this chapter, two fourth-grade children did not understand that to compare fractions, they have to have the same-size wholes. Building on what the teacher did in the video clip, what would you do next to help these children understand this concept?

What is happening in this picture?

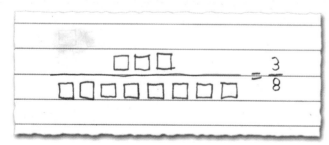

Think Critically

A student has drawn this picture to represent $\frac{3}{8}$.
1. What is wrong with this picture?
2. What misunderstandings does it show?
3. How might you help this student understand that the picture is incorrect, and how would you help the student to do this correctly?

Self-Test

(Check your answers in Appendix D.)

1. What is iteration? How can it be used to illustrate improper fractions?

2. Which of these figures do not illustrate thirds?

3. Which meaning of fractions is illustrated by this figure?

4. What are the three types of models used to illustrate fractions? Draw pictures to show the fraction $\frac{3}{4}$ with each of these models.

5. For each of the following fractions, decide which is larger. Use the techniques developed in this chapter to explain.
   a. $\frac{1}{5}$ or $\frac{1}{8}$
   b. $\frac{3}{4}$ or $\frac{3}{5}$
   c. $\frac{3}{7}$ or $\frac{5}{8}$
   d. $\frac{9}{10}$ or $\frac{11}{12}$

6. How can you build understanding of the equivalence between $1\frac{1}{5}$ and $\frac{6}{5}$? Draw pictures to explain.

7. Why are equivalent fractions important for children to know?

8. Use the techniques discussed in this chapter to find two equivalent representations for $\frac{3}{5}$. Use models, draw pictures, and explain your thinking.

9. What is the greatest common factor? How is it used to simplify fractions?

10. Use the techniques discussed in this chapter to put the fraction $\frac{48}{72}$ in simplest terms.

11. Explain your thinking and use models to show the following:
   a. $\frac{4}{7} + \frac{2}{7}$
   b. $\frac{1}{4} + \frac{1}{2}$
   c. $\frac{1}{5} + \frac{1}{6}$
   d. $\frac{3}{5} - \frac{1}{3}$

12. Explain your thinking and use models to show the following:
   a. $\frac{1}{3} \times 7$
   b. $5 \times \frac{1}{4}$
   c. $\frac{3}{8} \times \frac{4}{5}$

13. Illustrate $5 \div \frac{1}{3}$ with a model. Explain your thinking.

14. Explain the mistake made here, and show how the problem can be done correctly.

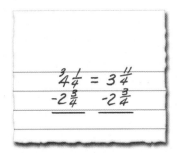

15. Solve the following problem:

   Rina was cutting ribbon to make bows. She had 2 feet of ribbon and needed $\frac{1}{3}$ foot for each bow. How many bows could Rina make?

THE PLANNER ✓

Review your Chapter Planner on the chapter opener and check off your completed work.

Decimals

In the sports world, the winner of an event can no longer be determined through observation. Racers are so fast and the margin between winning and losing is so small, sometimes in hundredths or thousandths of a second, that digital devices are used to measure finish times.

Consider track and field. Usain Bolt, a Jamaican sprinter, is a three-time Olympic gold medalist who holds the world record for the 100-meter and 200-meter races. Bolt set his first world record in May 2008, with a time of 9.72 seconds for the 100-meter race. He went on to set new world records in both the 100-meter and

200-meter events in the 2008 Beijing Summer Olympics. In the 100-meter race, he broke his previous record with a time of 9.69 seconds, and in the 200-meter race, he broke the previous world record with a time of 19.30 seconds. At the 2009 World Championships, Bolt surpassed his previous 100-meter and 200-meter world records to set new ones.

Sports statistics are just one of many examples of how decimals are used in real life. To really understand Bolt's achievements, one must have decimal sense: an understanding of what these numbers mean.

How much faster is 9.69 seconds than 9.72 seconds? Decimal number sense is an intuitive knowledge of decimals. This knowledge is necessary to understand Bolt's achievements.

CHAPTER PLANNER ✓

CHAPTER OUTLINE

Developing the Meaning of Decimals 304

Key Question: Why do students have difficulty learning decimals?

From Fractions to Decimals 305

Key Question: How can connecting decimals to their fraction equivalents and extending the place value system help students understand the meaning of decimals?

Decimal Number Sense 309

Key Question: How can teachers use models to help children understand how to compare and order decimals?

Decimal Operations 312

Key Question: How can teachers develop meaning for decimal operations using both student-created and traditional algorithms?

NCTM The NCTM Number and Operations Standard from *Principles and Standards for School Mathematics* (2000) includes several expectations for learning decimals and decimal operations.

In grades 3–5, all students should

• recognize and generate equivalent forms of commonly used fractions, decimals, and percents;

• develop and use strategies to estimate computations involving fractions and decimals in situations relevant to students' experience;

• use visual models, benchmarks, and equivalent forms to add and subtract commonly used fractions and decimals. (NCTM, 2000, p. 148)

In grades 6–8, all students should

• work flexibly with fractions, decimals, and percents, to solve problems;

• compare and order fractions, decimals, and percents efficiently and find their approximate locations on a number line;

• understand the meaning and effects of arithmetic operations with fractions, decimals, and integers.
 (NCTM, 2000, p. 214)

Developing the Meaning of Decimals

LEARNING OBJECTIVES

1. **Describe** why students have difficulty learning decimals.

2. **Distinguish** between the two approaches of learning decimals.

Decimals are used in all parts of our lives—from car odometers to the **Dewey Decimal System** (**Figure 12.1**). Decimals are used in many professions, such as medicine, finance, and engineering. For example, ball bearings used in wheels and guidance systems are engineered to a precision of less than one thousandth or one ten-thousandth of an inch. Despite the prevalence of decimals in our lives, both children and adults have difficulty understanding them and using them meaningfully. It is important that children understand how decimals are used in everyday life. This may help them to understand decimals and use them appropriately.

> **Dewey Decimal System** A method for organizing and categorizing library resources.

Decimals in everyday life • Figure 12.1

Decimals are used in many parts of our lives.

Why Do Students Have Difficulty Learning Decimals?

The Hindu-Arabic number system is a base-ten positional system—a decimal system. **Decimal fractions**, or decimals, are more difficult for students to learn than fractions. This difficulty may be due to how decimals are written. In a decimal the denominator is hidden. For example, in the mixed number $4\frac{1}{2}$, it is clear that the denominator is 2, but in the decimal 4.5, the value of the denominator is not immediately clear. Another problem is that the fraction and decimal symbolism for equivalent values look different: $4\frac{1}{2}$ does not look like 4.5, although it is equal in value. When teaching students about decimals, it is important that they recognize the connection between decimals and fractions and understand their equivalence. They should have many opportunities to represent fractions as decimals and vice versa. This chapter will show you how to make the connection between fractions and decimals for your own students.

How Should Students Learn About Decimals?

Curriculum Focal Points (2006) and the *Common Core State Standards* (NGA Center/CCSSO, 2010) suggest that decimal notation and decimal models be introduced in grade 4. In grade 5, students should "apply their understandings of decimal models, place value, and properties to add and subtract decimals" (NCTM, 2006, p. 17). In grade 6, they learn to multiply and divide decimals.

There are two approaches to introducing decimals. One approach is to extend the place value system and build decimal understanding in this way. Another approach is to build on students' knowledge of fractions and introduce decimals as an equivalent way to write **base-ten fractions** (Cramer et al., 2009). It is important for students to learn to extend the place value system, but they tend to be more successful if they first learn about decimals using their knowledge of fractions.

> **base-ten fractions** Fractions whose denominators are multiples of 10 (10, 100, 1000, etc.).

CONCEPT CHECK

1. **Why** do students have difficulty learning the meaning of decimals and decimal notation?

2. **What** are the two ways that students can learn about decimals?

From Fractions to Decimals

LEARNING OBJECTIVES

1. **Identify** base-ten fractions.
2. **Explain** methods for introducing decimal notation.
3. **Describe** how to extend the place value system.

By the fourth grade, students should have a good understanding of both the meaning and symbolism of fractions. For example, they should understand that for the fraction $\frac{3}{5}$, the whole is partitioned into five equal parts, three of which are counted, and that $\frac{3}{5}$ is greater than $\frac{1}{2}$ but less than 1. By this time, students should also understand place value and have had ample practice with base-ten blocks and arrays. This experience will be used to build an understanding of decimals.

Base-Ten Fractions

To teach students about decimal fractions, begin by modeling base-ten fractions (**Figure 12.2**).

Teaching Tip _____
Representing fractions on a 10 × 10 grid
When representing fractions on a 10 × 10 grid, color in the fractional parts. Color the columns in one color and the individual squares in a different color.

Education InSight

Modeling base-ten fractions • Figure 12.2  THE PLANNER

There are many excellent models for base-ten fractions. Most of these models will already be familiar to students from their experiences with whole number computation and measurement.

a. 10 x 10 grid

The 10 x 10 grid is an excellent model for visualizing fractions with denominators of 10, 100, or even 1000. Each row or column represents $\frac{1}{10}$, each small square represents $\frac{1}{100}$, and one section of a small square divided into 10 equal parts represents $\frac{1}{1000}$.

b. Meter stick

Because the metric system is a decimal system, the meter stick is another useful model for representing base-ten fractions. Each centimeter represents $\frac{1}{100}$ of the whole, and each millimeter represents $\frac{1}{1000}$ of the whole.

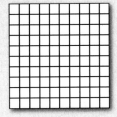
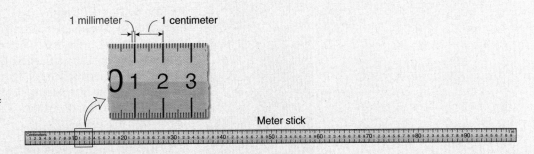

Meter stick

c. Number line

The number line is a linear model for base-ten fractions. Because it tends to be the most difficult for students to understand, it probably should not be used until students have some understanding of decimals.

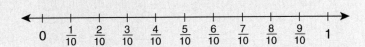

Provide students with many opportunities to work with base-ten fractions. Ask them to represent a variety of fractions with different models and to compare and order fractions. They should understand, for example, that $\frac{3}{10}$ is greater than $\frac{3}{100}$ but less than $\frac{35}{100}$. These ideas are illustrated in **Activity 12.1, Activity 12.2,** and **Activity 12.3.**

Activity 12.2 Say it! Write it!

Instructions

1. Ask students to represent a base-ten fraction such as $\frac{35}{100}$ with a model.

2. Ask them to write the fraction in words. (Thirty-five hundredths)

3. Ask students to write the fraction in two different ways. $\left(\frac{35}{100} \text{ and } \frac{3}{10} + \frac{5}{100}\right)$

Activity 12.1 Who am I?

Instructions

1. Show students a model of $\frac{25}{100}$ on a 10 × 10 grid. Ask them to identify the fraction, say it in words (25 hundredths), and write it as a fraction $\left(\frac{25}{100} \text{ or } \frac{2}{10} + \frac{5}{100}\right)$.

2. Continue with other base-ten fractions and other models, such as the meter stick and the number line.

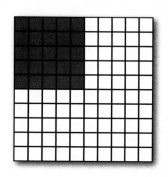

Activity 12.3 Where am I?

Instructions

1. Provide students with an example of a base-ten fraction such as $\frac{45}{100}$. Ask them to place the fraction on a number line.

2. Ask: *Is the fraction greater or less than $\frac{1}{2}$? How do you know? Is it greater or less than $\frac{2}{3}$? How do you know? Is it greater or less than $\frac{1}{4}$? How do you know?*

Children's literature is an excellent way to help students become familiar with base-ten fractions (see *Children's Literature,* **Figure 12.3**).

CHILDREN'S LITERATURE

Modeling base-ten fractions from real data

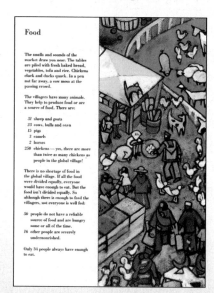

If the World Were a Village: A Book About the World's People • Figure 12.3

Written by David J. Smith
Illustrated by Shelagh Armstrong

If the world were a village of 100 people, it would be much easier to understand data about the languages people speak and other characteristics, such as their ages, religions, access to food, clean air, and water. This book tackles each of these issues and organizes these otherwise daunting statistics about the world in an understandable manner.

Strategies for the Classroom

- Read the book with your students, and ask them to express several of the statistics as fractions whose denominators are 100.

- Using a 10 x 10 grid, ask students to model the fractions. Express the fractions as decimals (and percents, when this topic is taught).

Introducing decimal notation • Figure 12.4

After students have knowledge of base-ten fractions and the models with which to represent them, they can build on this knowledge to learn decimal notation. In this way, decimals naturally connect to fractions and students see them as a different but equivalent representation of the same quantity.

1 Partition a square into 10 equal columns. Shade 4 of them. Ask students to identify the fraction.

2 Partition a square with 10 equal columns and 10 equal rows so that the square has 100 equal parts. Shade 4 columns and 7 small squares. Ask students to identify the fraction in two different ways.

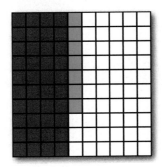

3 Explain that 0.47, read as "forty-seven hundredths" is another symbol for this fractional amount and that both the fraction $\frac{47}{100}$ and the decimal 0.47 express the same quantity.

$\frac{47}{100} = 0.47 = $ forty-seven hundredths

Introducing Decimal Notation

Decimals are another way to write fractions whose denominators are powers of 10, such as 10, 100, and 1000. The Rational Number Project (RNP) (Cramer et al., 2009) recommends introducing decimal notation in the following way (**Figure 12.4**).

The RNP (2009) maintains that the 10 × 10 grid is the most flexible model for decimals. Even thousandths can be represented by partitioning each small square into 10 equal parts. Other decimal models, such as base-ten blocks and money, can also be used. However, money should not be the first model used for decimals, because it only has two decimal places.

Extending the Place Value System

Before extending the place value system to decimals, review students' place value knowledge of whole numbers. Ask them to write a number such as 3245 in **expanded form**:

$$3245 = 3 \times 1000 + 2 \times 100 + 4 \times 10 + 5$$

Next, review the nature of place value. Students should know that each place is 10 times greater than the place to its right. Given that pattern, ask students: *What should be the value of the place to the right of the ones place?* This question should result in lively discussion. Ask students: *How would you write 23.76 in expanded form?* Help them understand that the place to the right of the ones place is the tenths place, to its right is the hundredths place, and so on.

$$23.76 = 2 \times 10 + 3 \times 1 + 7 \times \frac{1}{10} + 6 \times \frac{1}{100}$$

Explain that decimal numbers extend the place value system so that numbers less than 1 whole can be written with the digits 0 through 9, just as numbers greater than 1 can (**Figure 12.5**). The **decimal point** indicates the value of the digit (**Figure 12.6**).

Once the place value system has been extended to include decimals, they can be modeled with base-ten blocks (**Figure 12.7**). Note that in the first example, the whole is represented by a long, but in the second example the whole is represented by a flat. There is not one uniform way of representing decimals with base-ten blocks. Use the blocks in whatever way makes sense for the numbers.

The place value system • Figure 12.5_____

Each place to the left gets larger by a multiple of 10, and each place to the right gets smaller by a multiple of $\frac{1}{10}$.

1000	100	10	1	.	$\frac{1}{10}$	$\frac{1}{100}$	$\frac{1}{1000}$

The role of the decimal point • Figure 12.6_____

The decimal point is like a road sign that tells you in which direction to turn. The decimal point tells you that all the numbers to its left are greater than or equal to 1 and all the numbers to its right are less than 1.

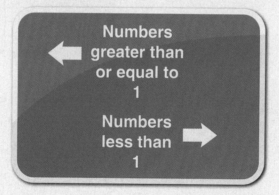

Using base-ten blocks to model decimals • Figure 12.7_____

a. 2.7 is represented by 2 longs (or rods) and 7 units. Each long represents 1 whole and each unit represents $\frac{1}{10}$.

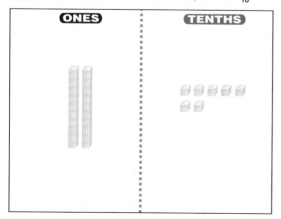

b. 1.75 is represented by 1 flat (square), 7 longs, and 5 units. Each flat represents 1 whole, each long represents $\frac{1}{10}$, and each unit represents $\frac{1}{100}$.

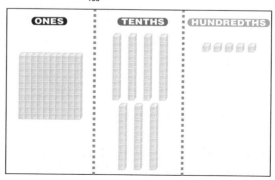

Extended place value mats can be used to model whole numbers and decimals (**Activity 12.4**).

Tech Tools

http://nlvm.usu.edu

Go to The National Library of Virtual Manipulatives Web site and select the **Base Block Decimals** applet. This shows decimal addition and subtraction problems on a place value mat using base-ten blocks. The user decides how many decimal places to put in each problem, and the place value mat and blocks are adjusted accordingly.

CONCEPT CHECK

1. **What** is a base-ten fraction? Give two examples.
2. **How** can you use 10 × 10 grids to introduce decimal notation?
3. **What** role does the decimal point play in extending the place value system?

Decimal Number Sense

LEARNING OBJECTIVES

1. **Describe** how to convert familiar fractions to decimals.
2. **Identify** techniques for ordering decimals.

R ecall the opening story of this chapter. Usain Bolt broke his own world record of running the 100-meter race in 9.69 seconds by running it in 9.58 seconds. In order to appreciate the significance of Bolt's achievements we need **decimal number sense**. Decimal number sense includes the ability to convert familiar fractions to decimals, compare and order decimals, and determine when two decimals are equivalent. These ideas form the foundation for this section.

> **decimal number sense** An understanding and intuition about the size and value of decimals.

Familiar Fractions and Decimals

Most fourth and fifth graders have attained number sense about the size of familiar fractions such as $\frac{1}{2}$, $\frac{1}{4}$, and $\frac{1}{5}$. However, they may not have a sense of their decimal equivalents. Teachers can help them achieve decimal number sense by learning to convert fractions to decimals.

Teaching Tip

Reviewing factors and multiples

Before teaching students to convert fractions to decimals, review factors and multiples of whole numbers. Ask students to find all the factors of 10, 100, and 1000 so that they will understand that fractions with any of these factors as denominators can be easily converted to decimals ($5 \times 2 = 10$, $10 \times 10 = 100$, $4 \times 25 = 100$, $8 \times 125 = 1000$).

Converting familiar fractions to decimals • Figure 12.8

Fractions can be converted to decimals by representing the fractions on 10 × 10 grids.

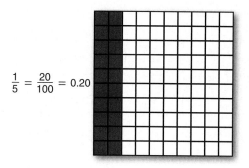

$$\frac{1}{5} = \frac{20}{100} = 0.20$$

Base-ten fractions are easily converted to decimals ($\frac{3}{10} = 0.3$, $\frac{14}{100} = 0.14$). Fractions whose denominators are not base ten but are **factors** of 10, 100, or 1000 are also easy to convert to decimals. To develop these ideas conceptually, use models and start with fractions with denominators of 2, 4, and 5 (**Figure 12.8**).

Ordering Decimals

Students have many misconceptions about the size of decimals. Some students think the decimal with a longer string of digits is greater. For example, they may think that 0.468 is greater than 0.5 because it has more digits (see *In the Classroom*). Although this would be true for whole numbers, it is not necessarily true for decimals. Conversely, some students think that the decimal with a shorter string of digits is always greater.

In the Classroom
Weighing Kittens

THE PLANNER

When fifth-grade teacher Barbara Boughen adopted two kittens from a shelter, she knew her students would be excited to hear about them. Ms. Boughen wrote two numbers on the chalkboard, 1.3 and 1.25, and told her students:

My kittens are named Thurber and Bijou. Thurber is the male and Bijou is the female. Thurber was 12 weeks old when I

adopted him and Bijou was 13 weeks old. These numbers represent their weights. Which one do you think is Thurber's weight and which one is Bijou's weight?

After some discussion the students decided that Thurber probably weighed more because he was a male, even though Bijou was a bit older. Their assumptions were correct, but the class members disagreed about which number was greater. Some students argued that 1.25 was the greater number because it had more digits. Others thought that 1.3 was the greater number. To help students determine the greater number, Ms. Boughen drew a number line from 0 to 2 and asked her students to place 1.3 and 1.25 on the number line. After much discussion, they realized that 1.3 is equivalent to 1.30 and is therefore greater than 1.25 and placed to its right on the number line.

Think Critically

1. How did the number line help students realize which decimal was greater?
2. What other models could have been used to find the greater decimal?
3. Why is it important to include real-life experiences in teaching decimals and other mathematics topics?

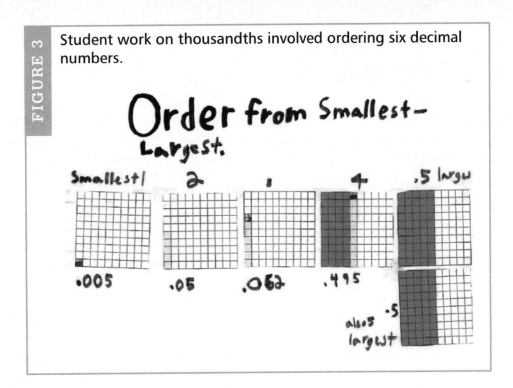

FIGURE 3

Student work on thousandths involved ordering six decimal numbers.

Ordering decimals using 10 × 10 grids • Figure 12.9

A sixth-grade student's work on ordering the decimals 0.005, 0.05, 0.062, 0.495, 0.5 from smallest to largest using successive 10 × 10 grids. Notice that the 10 × 10 grid representation for 0.062 uses two colors, and the representation for .495 uses three colors. The use of different colors makes it much easier to read the grid. (*Source:* Cramer et al., 2009)

Although ordering decimals such as 1.3 and 1.25 is not an easy task, it is much easier than ordering decimals such as 0.6 and 0.06. Martinie and Bay-Williams (2003) asked students to compare these decimals using a number line, a 10 × 10 grid, money, and place value. They found that the number line was the most difficult model for students to use. Whereas students had little trouble placing 0.6 on a number line, they had a lot of difficulty placing 0.06. Even though the number line is a difficult model to use, it is an excellent way to assess students' decimal sense.

Researchers (Cramer et al., 2009) suggest another way of ordering decimals using 10 × 10 grids (**Figure 12.9**).

The same models used to order decimals can be used to find decimal equivalence (**Activity 12.5**).

Activity 12.5 Finding an equivalent decimal

Instructions

1. Provide students with a decimal, and ask them to find an equivalent one by modeling the decimal on a 10 × 10 grid.

2. Begin with a decimal such as 0.5. Say: *Describe this decimal in terms of the model. What other decimal is it equivalent to?* (0.50)

3. Continue with other decimals such as 0.3, 0.8.

4. Ask: *Do you notice any patterns? Can you find an equivalent decimal without using the grid?*

CONCEPT CHECK

1. **How** might you use a model and not a calculator to convert the fraction $\frac{2}{5}$ to a decimal? How might you convert $\frac{3}{4}$ to a decimal without using a calculator?

2. **What** are two mistakes that students often make when ordering decimals?

Decimal Operations

LEARNING OBJECTIVES

1. **Describe** two methods for teaching addition and subtraction of decimals.

2. **Explain** the importance of estimation in learning decimal operations.

3. **Explain** how to use estimation when multiplying and dividing decimals.

Operations with decimals are very similar to operations with whole numbers and, therefore, much easier to learn than operations with fractions. Some curricular materials still emphasize learning rules for decimal computation, such as "carry" the decimal point for addition and subtraction of decimals and "add the number of decimal places in the factors" for decimal multiplication.

These rules are really not necessary to memorize or to learn. If students understand estimation with decimals and the relationship between decimals and fractions, then they can learn the four operations.

Addition and Subtraction of Decimals

There are different approaches to teaching addition and subtraction of decimals. One approach (Cramer et al., 2009) involves representing each decimal on a different 10 × 10 grid and then combining the decimals on a third grid (**Figure 12.10**). This technique works best when each of the decimals is less than 1. Another approach uses place value to add or subtract like units and regroup when necessary. This approach works well for numbers that have a combination of whole and decimal parts. Initially, it is helpful to place numbers on a place value chart (**Figure 12.11**).

Adding and subtracting decimals using the 10 × 10 grid • Figure 12.10

Students add or subtract two decimal numbers using a 10 × 10 grid.

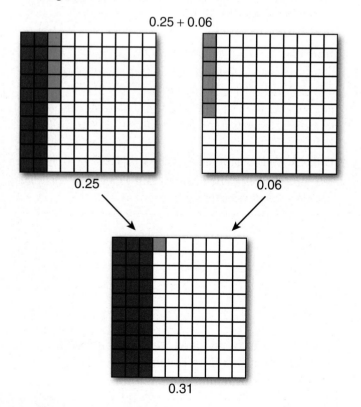

0.25 + 0.06

0.25   0.06

0.31

Adding and subtracting decimals using a place value chart • Figure 12.11

Students add or subtract two decimal numbers with a place value chart.

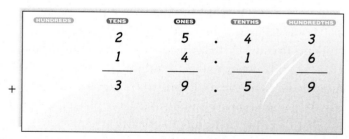

HUNDREDS	TENS	ONES	TENTHS	HUNDREDTHS
	2	5 .	4	3
	1	4 .	1	6
	3	9 .	5	9

+

HUNDREDS	TENS	ONES	TENTHS	HUNDREDTHS
3	2	6 .	4	3
1	1	5 .	2	2
2	1	1 .	2	1

−

Multicultural Perspectives in Mathematics

✓ THE PLANNER

The Russian Abacus

Many of us are familiar with the Chinese abacus or *suan pan*, but the Russian abacus is not as well known. Known as the *s'chyoty*, this abacus was used in Russian businesses until the mid-1990s. It is ideal for counting decimal quantities such as money.

The s'chyoty has 11 or 12 wires with beads. Beginning at the bottom, the first three wires have 10 beads each. The fourth wire has 4 beads, and wires 5 through 11 have 10 beads each. If there is a twelfth wire, it also has 10 beads. For the wires with 10 beads, the first four and last four are in one color, whereas the fifth and sixth bead are in a different color. This variety in color helps the user visually keep track of the beads counted. The fourth wire seems to function as a decimal point. Wires 5–11 are used to represent whole number amounts and wires 1–3 are used to represent decimal fractions.

Beginning in 1799, when Russians arrived in Sitka, Alaska, to colonize the area, they brought along many tools and instruments, including this abacus. During the 1800s, those who were educated in Russian schools in Alaska learned to use the s'chyoty.

(*Source:* www.nps.gov/sitk)

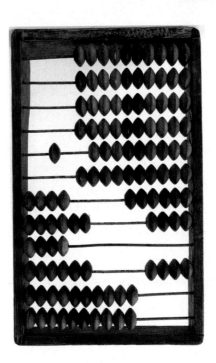

Strategies for the Classroom

- Have students create their own s'chyoty with pipe cleaners and beads. Ask them to solve several problems that involve addition and subtraction of money.

- Ask students to compare the s'chyoty to other models. Ask them to discuss advantages and disadvantages of the s'chyoty.

Teaching Tip

Adding and subtracting decimals

Whichever approach you take for teaching addition and subtraction of decimals, always estimate first by rounding the decimals to the nearest whole number. This will help you place the decimal point in the answer and check your work. It is also essential to use estimation when working with calculators.

We often use calculators for decimal operations. Before calculators, another instrument was designed to add and subtract decimals (see *Multicultural Perspectives in Mathematics*).

Multiplication and Division of Decimals

You probably learned algorithms for multiplying and dividing decimals. A more straightforward approach is to multiply and divide decimals as if they were whole numbers, round each number to the nearest whole number, estimate the size of the answer, and place the decimal point accordingly (see the *Lesson* on next page). The standards in the *Lesson* are from the *Common Core State Standards* (NGA Center/CCSSO, 2010).

The algorithm for decimal multiplication is: *Add the number of decimal places in each factor to get the number of decimal places in the answer.* Where did this rule come from? The answer lies in the meaning of decimals. Consider the following:

$$1.8 \times 3.4 = \frac{18}{10} \times \frac{34}{10}$$

Because decimals are equivalent to fractions, the denominator of the product is found by multiplying the two denominators: $10 \times 10 = 100$. This produces the same result as adding the decimal places in the factors.

LESSON Multiplying and Dividing Decimals

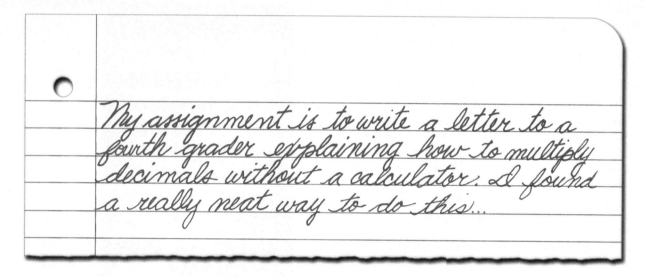

My assignment is to write a letter to a fourth grader explaining how to multiply decimals without a calculator. I found a really neat way to do this...

GRADE LEVEL

5

OBJECTIVE

Students use estimation and number sense to multiply and divide decimals.

MATERIALS

- Paper and pencil
- Worksheets (charts)

STANDARDS

Grade 5

Add, subtract, multiply, and divide decimals to hundredths, using concrete models or drawings and strategies based on place value, properties of operations, and/or the relationship between addition and subtraction; relate the strategy to a written method and explain the reasoning used. (NGA Center/CCSSO, 2010)

ASSESSMENT

Students will write a letter to children in a lower grade explaining how to multiply and divide decimals without a calculator.

GROUPING

Whole class and individual

Launch (5 minutes)

- Say: *A friend asked me: Why do you teach your students to multiply and divide decimals when they can use calculators? How would you answer that question?*

- Students discuss how easy it is to make mistakes with calculators. When you can do the mathematics without a calculator, it will help you estimate answers so that when you use a calculator you will know whether the answer is correct.

The algorithm for decimal division is: *Move the decimal point in the divisor enough places so the divisor is a whole number. Move the decimal point in the dividend the same number of places.* Where did this rule come from? Consider the following:

$$3.6 \div 0.6 = \frac{36}{10} \div \frac{6}{10}$$

Because decimals are equivalent to fractions, use the algorithm for fraction division, and invert the divisor and multiply. This yields

$$\frac{36}{10} \times \frac{10}{6}$$

The tenths cancel out, leaving $36 \div 6$, which effectively produced the same result as the decimal division algorithm would have.

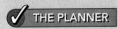
Instruct (30 minutes)

- Distribute the following chart. Say: *Fill in the chart. Find your answers without using a calculator. Look for patterns, and be prepared to explain your reasoning.*

Task	Answer
5 × 25	125
0.5 × 25	?
0.05 × 25	?
0.5 × 2.5	?

- Ask: *How did you find the answer to 0.5 × 25?* (Some students realize that 0.5 is equal to $\frac{1}{2}$ and $\frac{1}{2}$ of 25 is 12.5. Others realized that 0.5 is $\frac{1}{10}$ of 5, so the answer is $\frac{1}{10}$ of 5 × 25, which equals 12.5.)

- Ask: *How did you find the answer to 0.05 × 25?* (Some students realize that 0.05 is $\frac{1}{10}$ of 0.5, so the answer is $\frac{1}{10}$ of 0.5 × 25, which equals 1.25.)

- To find 0.5 × 2.5, most students realize that 0.5 is equal to $\frac{1}{2}$ and $\frac{1}{2}$ of 2.5 is 1.25.

- Say: *So it seems like you found the answer to the first problem and used that answer as a basis for the others, and then estimated where to place the decimal point.*

- Say: *Now try 0.3 × 27. Before working this problem, let's look at the answer to 3 × 27. Now, based on this answer, where should you place the decimal point for the answer to 0.3 × 27?* (3 × 27 = 81)

- *Should the answer be 81, 0.81, or 8.1?* (The answer is 8.1, because 0.3 is about $\frac{1}{3}$ and $\frac{1}{3}$ of 27 is 9.)

- Now distribute the next chart. Say: *Now let's look at division. Fill in this chart.*

Task	Answer
25 ÷ 5	5
25 ÷ 0.5	?
25 ÷ 0.05	?
2.5 ÷ 0.5	?

- Ask: *How did you get the answer to the second problem?* (Some students realize that 0.5 equals $\frac{1}{2}$ and $25 \div \frac{1}{2} = 25 \times 2 = 50$, from their work with fractions. Others realize that 0.5 is $\frac{1}{10}$ of 5, and given the inverse relationship of multiplication to division, dividing by a number that is $\frac{1}{10}$ as large is like multiplying by 10.)

- To find 25 ÷ 0.05, many students used the patterns in the previous problems. If 25 ÷ 0.5 = 50, then 25 ÷ 0.05 is 10 times as large, or 500.

- To find 2.5 ÷ 0.5, most students changed 0.5 to $\frac{1}{2}$ and divided 2.5 by $\frac{1}{2}$ to get 5.

Summarize (5 minutes)

- Say: *Wow! This is great! We have been able to multiply and divide decimals using these patterns.*

- Ask: *Who can summarize how we multiplied numbers that had decimals?*

- Ask: *Who can summarize how we divided numbers that had decimals?*

CONCEPT CHECK   STOP

1. **Why** is addition and subtraction of decimals easier than addition and subtraction of fractions?

2. **What** role does estimation play in decimal computation?

3. **Why** is it important for students to solve multiplication and division of decimals without using calculators?

Summary

1 Developing the Meaning of Decimals 304

- We use **decimal fractions** daily, as illustrated in this photo. Yet, they are more difficult to learn than fractions. Decimal notation does not make the size of the denominator clear.

Figure 12.1

- There are two approaches to teaching decimals: beginning with **base-ten fractions** and beginning by extending the place value system. Students have more success when their initial exposure to decimals is from base-ten fractions.

2 From Fractions to Decimals 305

- Model base-ten fractions with a 10 x 10 grid, meter stick, as shown here, or number line. Save the number line until children understand decimals because it is more complex.

Figure 12.2

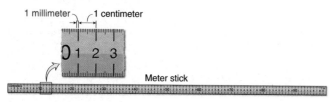

- Introduce decimal notation by modeling base-ten fractions on a 10 x 10 grid and showing students an equivalent way to write them.

- Extend the place value system to include values less than 1 whole. Define the **decimal point** as a symbol that separates values greater than or equal to one from values less than 1.

3 Decimal Number Sense 309

- Converting familiar fractions to decimals helps students develop **decimal number sense**. Review **factors** and multiples of 10, 100, and 1000 before converting fractions to decimals.

- Teach students to order and compare decimals by using models such as 10 x 10 grids, as shown in this example, or base-ten blocks and place value charts. Students often make the mistake of thinking that the decimal with a longer string of numbers is greater than one with a shorter string.

Figure 12.9

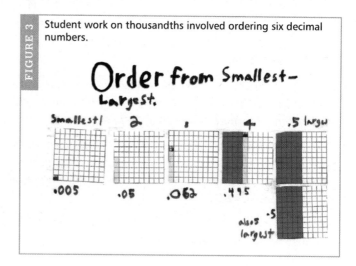

FIGURE 3

Student work on thousandths involved ordering six decimal numbers.

4 Decimal Operations 312

- Teach addition and subtraction of decimals by modeling decimals on 10 x 10 grids, place value charts, as illustrated here, or with base-ten blocks.

- Teach multiplication and division of decimals by using estimation to place the decimal point.

Figure 12.11

HUNDREDS	TENS	ONES		TENTHS	HUNDREDTHS
	2	5	.	4	3
	1	4	.	1	6
+					
	3	9	.	5	9

HUNDREDS	TENS	ONES		TENTHS	HUNDREDTHS
3	2	6	.	4	3
1	1	5	.	2	2
−					
2	1	1	.	2	1

Key Terms

- base-ten fraction 304
- decimal fraction 304
- decimal number sense 309

- decimal point 308
- Dewey Decimal System 304

- expanded form 307
- factors 310

Additional Children's Literature

- *Sam and the Lucky Money,* written by Karen Chinn and illustrated by Cornelius Van Wright and Ying-Hwa Hu
  A young Chinese-American boy has to decide how to spend his New Year's money. This lovely book creates a context for word problems that use money to practice decimal concepts.

- *If You Made a Million,* written by David M. Schwartz and illustrated by Steven Kellogg
  This book shows $1 in pennies, nickels, dimes, and quarters and $100 in $10 bills. It helps students understand the base-ten aspects of money and provides opportunities to express money in terms of decimals.

Online Resources

- **NCTM Illuminations**
  http://funbrain.com

  This is a Web link from the Illuminations Web site. It has activities for students, teachers, and parents. One activity, **Power Football**, uses a virtual football game to help students practice multiplication and division of decimals.

- **National Park Service**
  www.nps.gov/sitk

  This site includes a teacher's guide to using the Russian abacus, aligned with the state of Alaska's mathematics standards.

- **PBS Teachers**
  www.pbs.org/teachers/mathline/concepts/farmingandgardening/

  This is an activity for grades K–5 in which students plan their own vegetable garden on a 10 x 10 grid, planting fractional sections of several vegetables. This activity provides a real-world example of base-ten fractions.

Critical and Creative Thinking Questions

1. Children often have difficulty understanding that fractions and decimals can be equivalent representations of the same quantity. Describe how you would help a child understand that $\frac{23}{100}$ and 0.23 represent the same quantity. What models would you use to help the child understand?

2. What are some advantages of developing decimal notation and understanding with the 10 x 10 grid? What are some advantages of extending the place value system? What are some disadvantages of each model?

3. Given the prevalence of calculators today, why is it important for children to learn to estimate before calculation with decimals?

4. How can you use algorithms for adding or subtracting fractions to explain how to add or subtract decimals?

5. **In the field** Examine a fourth- or fifth-grade mathematics textbook. How are decimals introduced in the book? What models are used? Is any special attention paid to how decimals should be read (i.e., 24 hundredths instead of "point" 24)?

6. **Using visuals** Develop visual models to help children represent $\frac{6}{10}$, $\frac{2}{5}$, and $\frac{9}{20}$ as decimal fractions. Explain how you would use these models for teaching the meaning of decimal fractions.

What is happening in this picture?

Think Critically

Look at these examples of students' computation with decimals.
1. What errors did Latrice make when adding decimals? What misunderstandings do you think she had? How might you help her correct her errors?
2. What errors did Trevor make when multiplying decimals? What misunderstandings do you think he had? How might you help him correct his errors?

$$
\begin{array}{r}
.6 \\
+.6 \\
\hline
.12
\end{array}
\qquad
\begin{array}{r}
4.5 \\
+9.7 \\
\hline
13.12
\end{array}
$$

Latrice's work

$$
\begin{array}{r}
23.2 \\
\times\ .6 \\
\hline
139.2
\end{array}
\qquad
\begin{array}{r}
52.5 \\
\times\ .4 \\
\hline
210.0
\end{array}
$$

Trevor's work

Self-Test

(Check your answers in Appendix D.)

1. What are base-ten fractions? Give three examples of base-ten fractions.

2. Which model for representing base-ten fractions is illustrated by this figure?

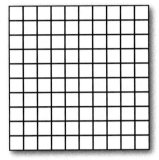

3. For the fraction $\frac{25}{100}$, illustrate with a model, find an equivalent way to write it as a fraction, and write it as a decimal.

4. Write each of the following fractions as decimals, without using a calculator:

   a. $\frac{4}{10}$ b. $\frac{3}{100}$ c. $\frac{55}{1000}$

5. What number is being modeled here?

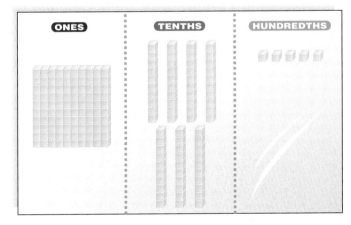

6. Write the number 1345.26 in expanded form.

7. Write the following number as a decimal: *3 and 25 thousandths*.

8. Illustrate the following decimal on a 10 × 10 grid: 0.6. Is it greater or less than $\frac{1}{2}$?

9. Order the following decimals from least to greatest and place them on a number line.

   0.25, 1.225, 0.22, 1.1, 0.02

10. Illustrate how to compare the following decimals with a place value mat.

    0.327, 0.301, 0.348, 0.35

11. Find an equivalent decimal representation for each of the following decimals.

    a. 0.5   b. 0.66

12. Illustrate how to add the following decimals using 10 x 10 grids.

    0.45 + 0.33

13. Add or subtract each of the following:

    a. 0.7 + 0.6
    b. 2.3 + 3.07
    c. 4.5 − 0.4
    d. 3.4 − 2.9

14. Given the following example: 3.4 × 12.7, show how estimation and whole number methods can be used to find the answer.

15. Given the following example: 5.6 ÷ 0.7, show how estimation and whole number methods can be used to find the answer.

THE PLANNER ✓

Review your Chapter Planner on the chapter opener and check off your completed work.

Ratio, Proportion, and Percent

Ms. Patel wanted to engage her fifth-grade class in developing number sense about percents. She said, "Yesterday, when I went to the mall with my friend, we saw an incredible sale. Everything that had previously been marked down 30% was marked down an additional 20%. My friend thought that meant everything was marked down a total of 50%. Do you agree?"

The students discussed this question in their groups but could not reach a conclusion. De Shawn said that he agreed with Ms. Patel's friend because 30% is equivalent to $\frac{3}{10}$, 20% is equivalent to $\frac{2}{10}$, and $\frac{3}{10} + \frac{2}{10} = \frac{5}{10}$, or 50%. Aisha said she disagreed because when you take 20% off, you are taking 20% from the part that's left, not of the whole amount.

Ms. Patel suggested the students test their opinions by solving a problem. She said, "Suppose I want to buy a DVD player that originally cost $100. How much would it cost after a 30% discount? (*$70*) How much would it cost after the sale price is discounted an additional 20%? (*$56*) Let's compare that to a 50% discount of the original price. (*$50*)"

The students agreed that a 50% discount was greater than a 30% discount followed by a 20% discount.

CHAPTER OUTLINE

What Is Proportional Reasoning?   322

Key Question: Why is proportional reasoning a focus for the middle grades?

Learning About Ratio   324

Key Questions: What are the different types of ratios? How are they used in mathematics?

Learning About Proportion   328

Key Question: How are proportions different from ratios?

Learning About Percents   333

Key Question: How can teachers help students develop the concept of percent?

NCTM The NCTM Number and Operations Standard includes several expectations for learning about ratios, proportions, and percents.

In grades 3–5, all students should

- recognize and generate equivalent forms of commonly used fractions, decimals, and percents.   (NCTM, 2000, p. 148)

In grades 6–8, all students should

- work flexibly with fractions, decimals, and percents to solve problems;
- develop meanings for percents greater than 100 and less than 1;
- understand and use ratios and proportions to represent quantitative relationships;
- develop, analyze, and explain methods for solving problems involving proportions, such as scaling and finding equivalent ratios.   (NCTM, 2000, p. 214)

In the upper elementary and middle grades, students develop number sense about percents.

What Is Proportional Reasoning?

LEARNING OBJECTIVES

1. **Compare** and **contrast** additive and proportional reasoning.

2. **Describe** the importance of teaching proportional reasoning in the middle grades.

3. **Identify** phases in the development of proportional reasoning.

C hildren begin to use **proportional reasoning** informally throughout their early schooling (Seeley and Schielack, 2007). In prekindergarten through grade 2, children study patterns and one-to-one correspondence. In grades 3–5, children begin to make the transition to **multiplicative reasoning** through their study of place value and other multiplicative relationships. For example, they understand that 245 is 2×100 plus 4×10 plus 5×1. In the middle grades, children formally study proportional reasoning.

> **proportional reasoning** A way of reasoning multiplicatively about relationships between quantities or measures.

Understanding Proportional Reasoning

"Proportional reasoning refers to a mathematical way of thinking in which students recognize proportional versus nonproportional situations and can use multiple approaches . . . for solving problems about proportional situations" (Lanius and Williams, 2003, p. 392). Proportional reasoning can be found in many areas of mathematics (place value, slope, functions, similarity) as well as other areas of life, such as adjusting recipes, making price comparisons, finding unit costs, saving money, paying taxes, and using scale drawings (**Figure 13.1**).

Children's development of proportional reasoning evolves through four phases (**Figure 13.2**).

It takes years for proportional reasoning to develop. In fact, by some estimates, about half of adults have never developed proportional reasoning (Lamon, 1999). It is a difficult concept that "requires significant time and attention to master" (Lanius and Williams, 2003, p. 395).

Why Is Proportional Reasoning Important?

Proportional reasoning is a prerequisite for the mathematics and science learned in secondary school and beyond. It has been called a "unifying theme of middle school mathematics" (Jamar and Wiest, 2003, p. 387). The study of ratio is a focal point for grade 6, and the study of proportionality is a focal point for grade 7 (NCTM, 2006). Proportional reasoning is an important focus in the middle grades for the following reasons:

- "Proportionality provides a framework for studying topics in algebra, geometry, measurement, and probability and statistics—all of which are important topics in the middle grades" (Lanius and Williams, 2003, p. 395).

- "Proportionality has many important connections outside of mathematics" (Lanius and Williams, 2003, p. 396).

Understanding distances on a map • Figure 13.1

To find distances on this map, use the scale of 1 inch = 100 miles to convert inches to miles. This is an example of proportional reasoning.

Children's development of proportional reasoning • Figure 13.2

Children's ability to use proportional reasoning is based on their ability to distinguish between additive and multiplicative relationships. As they develop proportional reasoning, they go through four phases. These phases are illustrated with solutions to the following problem.

Joe planted a pine tree and a spruce tree on the same day. The pine tree was 3 feet tall and the spruce tree was 4 feet tall. After one year, the pine tree had grown to 6 feet and the spruce tree had grown to 7 feet. Which tree grew at a greater rate?

Four phases of proportional reasoning

1 Nonproportional reasoning*

Very young students do not use proportional reasoning and would probably answer this question incorrectly by saying that both trees grew at the same rate because they each grew 3 feet. This incorrect answer demonstrates the result of applying **additive reasoning** to a multiplicative relationship.

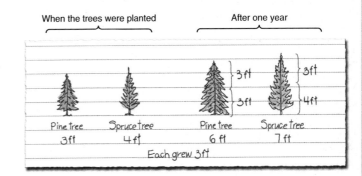

2 Informal reasoning about proportional situations*

In this stage, students solve proportional reasoning problems by using physical manipulatives and pictures. They use **multiplicative reasoning** but are not yet able to formally use numerical calculations to solve proportion problems.

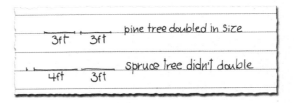

3 Quantitative reasoning*

Students still use drawings or physical manipulatives but also use calculations such as multiplication and division.

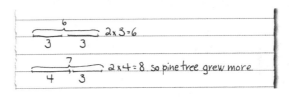

4 Formal proportional reasoning*

By this stage, students are able to set up and solve proportions, using mathematical algorithms such as cross multiplication.

(*Source: Langrall and Swafford, 2000, p. 256)

CONCEPT CHECK

1. **How** do additive and proportional reasoning differ? Provide an example.

2. **Why** is it important to teach proportional reasoning in the middle grades? What are some middle-grades mathematics topics that use proportional reasoning?

3. **How** might a student answer the following problem at each of the four phases of development of proportional reasoning?

Aunt Sara put money in two banks. She put $100 in Friendly Bank and at the end of one year she had $125. She put $200 in Neighborhood Bank and at the end of one year had $225. Which was the better deal?

Learning About Ratio

LEARNING OBJECTIVES

1. **Distinguish** among the three different types of ratios.

2. **Describe** examples of ratios used in mathematics and everyday experience.

 hen learning about proportional reasoning, children first learn about **ratio**. Prekindergarten children appear to have an intuitive idea of ratio. They are able to compare two objects to see which one is larger and are able to understand that "if one of two matched objects changes in size, the other must too" (Smith, 2002, p. 15). Students in elementary and middle school have many opportunities to use ratios in their everyday lives.

> **ratio** A comparison of two quantities or numbers.

- Ten dimes is equivalent to four quarters.

- Sales tax is 6%.
- The speed limit near the school is 35 miles per hour.
- The distance on a map uses a scale of 1 inch = 100 miles.
- The cost of two sodas is $2.89.
- The snow is falling at the rate of $\frac{1}{2}$ inch per hour.

Understanding Ratios

There are three types of ratios (**Figure 13.3**).

Children have difficulty understanding ratios because they have difficulty distinguishing situations that require additive reasoning from situations that require

---

Education InSight

Three types of ratios •
Figure 13.3

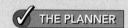 THE PLANNER

Ratios can appear in a variety of contexts. The ability to recognize ratios is an important component of the development of proportional reasoning. There are three types of ratios. The first two types compare the same kinds of quantities. The third type compares two different types of quantities or measures.

a. Part-to-whole ratios
The comparison of the number of blue chocolate candies to the total number of candies in the bowl is an example of a part-to-whole ratio because one part of the whole is compared to the whole. This is the most common type of ratio.

b. Part-to-part ratios
The comparison of the number of girls to the number of boys on a sports team is an example of a part-to-part ratio because one part of the whole is compared to another part of the whole.

c. Ratios with two different measures
The ratio 65 miles per hour is a comparison of two different kinds of units: miles and hours. Many ratios fall into this category, including money (four quarters per dollar), measurement (the river rising at 1 foot every 4 hours), and other measures (6 people per carload, 12 plants per flat).

multiplicative reasoning. Provide children with many opportunities to learn the difference between additive and multiplicative reasoning (**Activity 13.1**).

Activity 13.1 How many red?

Instructions

1. Show a group of marbles with 12 blue and 3 red marbles. Say: *What can you tell me about the number of red marbles and the number of blue marbles?*

2. Write all student responses on the board or overhead.

3. Sample responses: *There are 12 blue and 3 red. There are nine more blue marbles than red marbles. There are four times as many blue marbles as red marbles.*

4. Ask: *How would you write these answers with numbers and symbols?* (12 + 3 = 15; 12 − 3 = 9; 4 × 3 = 12)

5. Ask: *Which of these answers shows multiplication?*

6. Say: *So when we say there are four times as many blue marbles as red marbles, we are describing a multiplicative relationship.*

Teachers can ease children's transition to multiplicative reasoning by choosing contexts that are familiar to them (such as rates or distances) and using whole number ratios (twice as many or three times as much), which lend themselves to mental mathematics and intuitive thinking (**Activity 13.2**).

In teaching children about ratios, encourage them to organize information in a table (**Activity 13.3**). Tables are an excellent way to display information, look for patterns, and identify multiplicative relationships. They are used extensively in the seventh grade, when students learn about proportions and functions.

Activity 13.2 Where are the ratios?

Instructions

1. Provide children with several situations, and for each situation ask: *Is this a ratio? What is the ratio?*

---

2. Sample situations include the following:

   a. Justin, Tamika, and Ariel all ran a race.

      Justin ran the race at a rate of 3 miles per hour.

      Tamika ran the race twice as fast as Justin.

      Ariel ran 20 minutes longer than Justin.

   b. *The temperature is falling.*

      At noon, the temperature was three degrees lower than at 11 A.M.

      The temperature is falling three degrees every two hours.

      The temperature is below freezing.

3. Ask students to create other situations for which they can write ratios. Take all responses and decide as a class whether or not each situation represents a ratio.

Activity 13.3 Displaying ratios in tables

Instructions

1. Say: *We are going to make some punch. Here are some recipes I found for different quantities of punch.*

Cups of cranberry juice	3	6	9
Cups of water	2	4	6
Total cups of punch	5	10	15

2. Ask: *What is the ratio for the number of cups of cranberry juice to water in the recipe that makes 5 cups of punch?* (3 : 2)

3. *What is the ratio for the number of cups of cranberry juice to water for the recipes that make 10 cups and 15 cups of punch, respectively?* (6 : 4; 9 : 6)

4. *Do you notice any patterns?* (Each part of the ratio is multiplied by the same amount.)

5. *If I have 12 cups of cranberry juice, how many cups of water should I add to get punch with the same taste as the recipe above?* (8 cups of water)

Teaching Tip

Writing and saying ratios

There are several ways to write ratios. For example, in Activity 13.3, the ratio of cranberry juice to water can be written as $\frac{3}{2}$, 3 to 2, or 3 : 2. Although written differently, they all mean the same thing. There are also several ways to say ratios. For this ratio, you can say, "three halves" or "three to two."

LESSON | The Fibonacci Sequence and the Golden Ratio

GRADE LEVEL
6–8

OBJECTIVES
Students identify patterns in the Fibonacci sequence.

STANDARDS

Grades 6–8
All students should understand and use ratios and proportions to represent quantitative relationships. (NCTM, 2000, p. 214)

Grade 7
All students should recognize and represent proportional relationships between quantities. (NGA Center/CCSSO, 2010)

MATERIALS

- Photographs or Web pictures of sunflower, daisy, chambered nautilus (can be found through Internet search engines)

- Copies of each photo for each pair of students

- Scientific calculator for each student

- Blank chart for each student

ASSESSMENT

- Create another Fibonacci-like sequence, with different starting numbers. Find the first 12 terms and the ratios of each term to the one that comes before it. What patterns do you find?

- Using the photos provided in the lesson, find the number of clockwise and counterclockwise spirals in the yellow portion of the daisy. What patterns are revealed?

- Find the Fibonacci sequence in the chambered nautilus.

- Research the connection between Pascal's triangle and the Fibonacci sequence. Write a brief (one-page) report.

GROUPING
Whole class followed by pairs

Examples of Ratios

One of the most famous ratios of all time is the **golden ratio**. The **golden rectangle** is a rectangle whose length and width are in the golden ratio (**Figure 13.4**).

The golden ratio appears in many areas of mathematics, including the Fibonacci sequence, (see Chapter 1). The standards for the *Lesson* are from *Principles and Standards for School Mathematics* (NCTM, 2000) and the *Common Core State Standards* (NGA Center/CCSSO, 2010).

> **golden ratio** A ratio of two lengths that equals 1.61803 . . . .

Tech Tools

> http://math.rice.edu/~lanius/Lesson/

Mathematics educator Cynthia Lanius of Rice University has a Web site with examples of many types of mathematics activities, including ratios. The ratio examples engage elementary and middle-grades students in finding ratios that are the same and ratios that are different and problem-solving with ratios. Some of the activities on this Web site are available in English or Spanish.

Launch (5 to 10 minutes)

- Show pictures of sunflowers and daisies to the class. Ask: *What do you notice about the yellow area in the middle?* (There are two interlocking spirals coming from the center of the yellow area, one in a clockwise direction and one in a counterclockwise direction.)

- Say: *Let's try to count the number of spirals on the sunflower.* (The sunflower has 55 clockwise spirals and 89 counterclockwise spirals.)

- Ask: *What do you know about the numbers 55 and 89?* (They are part of the Fibonacci sequence.)

- Say: *We do not know why, but the Fibonacci sequence seems to appear quite frequently in nature.*

Instruct (30 minutes)

- Say: *Today we are going to find out more about the Fibonacci sequence. Let's write out the first 12 terms.*

    1, 1, 2, 3, 5, 8, 13, 21, 34, 55, 89, 144, . . .

- Ask: *Who can explain the pattern?* (Each term is equal to the sum of the previous two terms.)

- Say: *Now, working in pairs and using your calculators, please find the ratio of each term of the Fibonacci sequence to the term that comes before it. Carry out your calculations to six decimal places and then round to five decimal places. Place your findings in the chart.*

Ratio of Successive Terms	Decimal Equivalent
$\frac{1}{1}$	1.00000
$\frac{2}{1}$	2.00000
$\frac{3}{2}$	1.50000
$\frac{5}{3}$	1.66667
$\frac{8}{5}$	1.60000
$\frac{13}{8}$	1.62500
$\frac{21}{13}$	1.61538
$\frac{34}{21}$	1.61905
$\frac{55}{34}$	1.61765
$\frac{89}{55}$	1.61818
$\frac{144}{89}$	1.61798

- Ask: *What patterns have you discovered?* (The ratio of successive terms of the Fibonacci sequence is about 1.61, which is the golden ratio.)

- Say: *I wonder what would happen with another Fibonacci-like sequence. Let's try the sequence beginning with 1, 3. Generate the next 10 terms using the Fibonacci pattern of adding two terms to get the next one.*

    1, 3, 4, 7, 11, 18, 29, 47, 76, 123, 199, 322, . . .

- Say: *Let's see what happens if we divide each term of this sequence by the one that came before it. Try this with a partner, and let's discuss your results.*

- Ask: *What pattern did you discover?* (You still get the golden ratio.)

- Say: *Wow! That's really something!*

Summarize (5 minutes)

- Ask: *What did you learn about the Fibonacci sequence today?*

- Ask: *How would you describe the relationship of the Fibonacci sequence to the golden ratio?*

The golden rectangle • Figure 13.4

What do these pictures have in common? They both illustrate the golden rectangle. Mathematicians, artists, and architects have been fascinated by the golden ratio and the golden rectangle for more than 2500 years. What other examples can you find of the golden rectangle? Why do you think it is so popular?

CHILDREN'S LITERATURE

Learning about the ratio of the circumference of a circle to its diameter

Sir Cumference and the Dragon of Pi • **Figure 13.5**

Written by Cindy Neuschwander
Illustrated by Wayne Geehan

Radius's father, Sir Cumference, drinks the wrong potion and turns into a dragon. To reverse the potion, Radius searches for a magic number. For each of several circles, he finds its circumference and divides the circumference by its diameter, always obtaining the constant value pi.

Strategy for the Classroom

• After reading this book with your class, have them try similar experiments. Cut up circles or use the tops of cans and measure the circumference and diameter of each circle. Find the ratio of circumference to diameter, using calculators to carry out the answer to two or three decimal places. Ask students to draw conclusions about the ratio of the circumference to the diameter of a circle.

Another well-known ratio is pi, the ratio of the **circumference** of a circle to its diameter. Children's literature is an excellent way to introduce this ratio (see *Children's Literature*, **Figure 13.5**).

CONCEPT CHECK

1. **What** are the three types of ratios? Give a real-world example of each type.

2. **What** is the golden rectangle? Draw three rectangles that satisfy this definition.

Learning About Proportion

LEARNING OBJECTIVES

1. **Define** proportions.

2. **Explain** how proportions are used in mathematics.

3. **Compare** and **contrast** different ways of solving proportion problems.

Students begin their formal work with **proportion** in grade 7 by solving problems that involve proportionality. Students also use their knowledge of proportional relationships to solve problems

> **proportion** An expression of equality between two ratios.

about **similarity** of geometric figures, the **slope** of a line, and scaling problems.

Understanding Proportions

Most of us learned to solve proportions by using the cross-multiplication algorithm. Unfortunately, many students and adults who use this algorithm do not understand why or how it works. To help students understand proportions, begin by teaching them to solve proportion problems with intuitive approaches and introduce the algorithm only after students demonstrate an understanding of proportions.

> **slope** The ratio of the vertical change to the horizontal change in a line.
>
> **similarity** The quality of geometric shapes that have the same shape but not necessarily the same size.

Equivalent ratios Students who understand the concept of equivalent fractions already have some understanding of proportions, because a proportion represents a relationship between two **equivalent ratios,** which can also be viewed as equivalent fractions. This knowledge provides a foundation for learning about proportions. Teachers can begin teaching about proportions with activities similar to **Activity 13.4**, in which students are asked to find a ratio equivalent to a given one. When giving such activities, make sure that at least one of the incorrect choices shows additive reasoning. In this case, $\frac{2}{3}$ and $\frac{4}{5}$ are not equivalent ratios, but students might incorrectly think they are because $2 + 2 = 4$ and $3 + 2 = 5$. This type of activity helps assess whether students are reasoning additively or multiplicatively.

have a stronger chocolate taste: 4 tablespoons of hot cocoa mix to 8 ounces of milk or 5 tablespoons of mix to 9 ounces of milk? To solve this, students will have to compare the ratios of $4:8$ and $5:9$. Encourage them to rename the ratios as $\frac{4}{8}$ and $\frac{5}{9}$. Many students will reduce the first ratio to $\frac{1}{2}$ and then find equivalent ratios. They will find that $\frac{1}{2} = \frac{9}{18}$ and $\frac{5}{9} = \frac{10}{18}$, so the mixture with 5 tablespoons of hot cocoa mix is stronger. They may also reason informally that $\frac{5}{9}$ is greater than $\frac{1}{2}$, so the mixture with 5 tablespoons of hot cocoa mix is stronger.

Ratio tables Ratio tables are very effective for organizing information and showing how two quantities are related. The visual aspect of ratio tables is also helpful for visual learners and English-language learners. **Activity 13.6** can be solved with the table, drawings, or numerical computations and works well for students of all abilities.

Activity 13.4 Who am I?

Instructions

Present the ratio $\frac{2}{3}$ to the class. Then present several more ratios such as $\quad\frac{4}{5}\qquad\frac{6}{9}\qquad\frac{12}{18}\qquad\frac{4}{6}$

1. Ask: *Which of these ratios is equal to $\frac{2}{3}$? Please explain.* ($\frac{2}{3} = \frac{4}{6}$ because $2 \times 2 = 4$ and $3 \times 2 = 6$. $\frac{2}{3} = \frac{6}{9}$ and $\frac{2}{3} = \frac{12}{18}$.)

2. *What is a different ratio that is equivalent to $\frac{2}{3}$?* ($\frac{8}{12}$, $\frac{10}{15}$, etc.)

3. Repeat with other beginning ratios and choices for equivalency.

In **Activity 13.5,** students are again asked to find an equivalent ratio, but here the emphasis moves to finding a rate: the number of pieces of luggage for each person.

Students should also have the opportunity to compare unequal ratios. For example, which hot chocolate mix will

---

Activity 13.5 Which are the same?

Instructions

1. Prepare four pictures showing adults and luggage to display.

2. Say: *Many airlines have a limit on how many pieces of luggage you can carry onto the plane.*

3. Say: *Look at these four pictures of people getting ready to board a plane. Which of the pictures represents the same ratio of adults to luggage?*

Activity 13.6 Just the right amount

Instructions

1. Say: *We are going to make lemonade for the entire class. Let's take a look at this chart.*

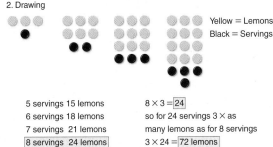

Number of lemons				?
Number of servings of lemonade	1	2	3...	24

2. Say: *Since there are 24 of us, how many lemons will we need to make 24 servings of lemonade? Explain your reasoning.* (We need 72 lemons, because the ratio of lemons to servings of lemonade is 3 to 1.)

1. Table

Number of lemons	3	6	9	12	15	18	21
Number of servings	1	2	3	4	5	6	7

3 lemons for each serving
24 servings and 3 lemons for each serving
$24 \times 3 = \boxed{72 \text{ lemons}}$

2. Drawing

Yellow = Lemons
Black = Servings

5 servings 15 lemons
6 servings 18 lemons
7 servings 21 lemons
8 servings 24 lemons

$8 \times 3 = \boxed{24}$
so for 24 servings 3 × as many lemons as for 8 servings
$3 \times 24 = \boxed{72 \text{ lemons}}$

3. Numerical computation
$1 \times 3 = 3$
$2 \times 3 = 6$
$3 \times 3 = 9$
$4 \times 3 = 12$
⋮
$24 \times 3 = \boxed{72}$

CHILDREN'S LITERATURE

Learning about rates and proportions

What's Faster than a Speeding Cheetah? • Figure 13.6a

Written and illustrated by Robert E. Wells
This well-illustrated book is filled with fun facts that students will enjoy learning about. Did you know that an ostrich can run at 45 miles per hour and that a cheetah can run at 70 miles per hour? Facts such as these are described throughout the book. The many facts provide excellent ideas for proportion problems that emphasize rates.

Strategies for the Classroom

• After reading the book with your class, ask questions such as: *If a cheetah can run at 70 miles per hour, how far can it run in 2 hours, 3 hours, $2\frac{1}{2}$ hours, $\frac{3}{4}$ of an hour?*

• Challenge your students to pose their own problems using the facts in this book.

If You Hopped Like a Frog • Figure 13.6b

Written by David M. Schwartz
Illustrated by James Warhola
How far could you jump if you hopped like a frog? How much could you lift if you had the strength of an ant? This book poses wonderful questions on topics that are appealing to middle-schoolers and illustrates the answers with terrific illustrations. At the back of the book, each of the comparisons is explained and questions are posed that can be solved with proportional reasoning.

Strategies for the Classroom

• Read the entire book with your class, or read one comparison at a time.

• Ask questions based on the explanations in the back of the book, such as: *An ant can lift 50 times its own weight. If this is also true for people, how much can a person weighing 100 lb lift? How much would you have to weigh to lift 2500 lb?*

Children's literature is an excellent way to develop understanding of proportions and provides a great source of problems (see *Children's Literature*, **Figure 13.6**).

Informal reasoning Students should have many opportunities to use informal reasoning to solve proportion problems before learning algorithms. This kind of reasoning encourages flexible thinking and deepens students' understanding. Consider the following problem:

Alex bought 50 blank CDs for $14.50. At the same price, how much would 60 CDs cost?

To solve this problem, you might first ask: *At this rate, how much does one CD cost?* To find the answer, use a calculator to divide $14.50 by 50. The answer is $0.29. Then to find the price of 60 CDs, multiply $0.29 × 60. For this problem, finding a **unit rate** provides an efficient solution. This is a powerful strategy for students to learn because unit rates are used in both science and mathematics.

Now, consider this problem:

Alex bought 50 blank CDs for $14.50. At the same price, how much would 100 CDs cost?

To solve this problem, you could find a unit rate. However, a more efficient method is to realize that 100 is twice 50, so the cost of 100 CDs would be twice the cost of 50 CDs, or 2 × $14.50.

Let's look at another problem:

Which is the better buy, six movie tickets for $15 or nine movie tickets for $20?

To solve this problem, you might use a **scaling strategy**, which means that you change both ratios so that they represent tickets for the same amount of money. Using this strategy, reason that 6 tickets for $15 is equivalent to 24 tickets for $60, because 4 × 6 = 24 and 4 × 15 = 60. Then 9 tickets for $20 is equivalent to 27 tickets for $60, because 3 × 9 = 27 and 3 × 20 = 60. Because 27 tickets is a greater number than 24 tickets, buying 9 movie tickets for $20 is the better deal.

Cross multiplication After students have had lots of practice with informal reasoning to solve proportion problems, introduce the cross-multiplication algorithm (**Activity 13.7**).

When students understand this algorithm, they can use it to solve many types of word problems. When setting up proportion problems, students often become confused about where to put the numbers. Using pictures as well as numbers can be very helpful (**Activity 13.8**).

Activity 13.8 Using pictures to set up proportions

Instructions

Ask students to solve the following problem by first drawing a picture and then setting up a proportion.

At the farmer's market, organic blueberries are on sale for two packages for $4.00. How much will five packages cost?

$$\frac{2}{4} = \frac{5}{?}$$

Activity 13.7 Introducing cross multiplication

Instructions

1. Give students several pairs of equal ratios:

   $\frac{3}{4} = \frac{6}{8}$

   $\frac{4}{10} = \frac{32}{80}$

   $\frac{2}{9} = \frac{10}{45}$

2. Ask: *What pattern do you notice in each pair of equal ratios?*

3. Students should notice that in each pair of equal ratios, the cross products of the fractions are equal. For example, 3 × 8 = 6 × 4.

4. Ask: *Why do you think this pattern is true?* (Equal ratios are like equivalent fractions. $\frac{4}{10} = \frac{32}{80}$, because when you multiply the numerator and denominator of $\frac{4}{10}$ by 8, you get $\frac{32}{80}$.)

Examples of Proportions in Mathematics

Proportional reasoning is used in algebra, geometry, and measurement.

Algebra Students learn about **functional relationships** in grades 3–5. In the seventh grade, students graph linear functions. They learn that when linear functions express proportional relationships, their graphs are lines that pass through the **origin** (the point where the horizontal and

> **linear function** A function whose graph is a straight line.

vertical axes intersect). In **Activity 13.9**, students graph the relationship using a rectangular grid before formally learning about functions.

Activity 13.9 Graphing proportional relationships

Instructions

1. Ask students to create a ratio table for the number of quarters in one, two, three, and four dollars and graph this on graph paper or a graphing calculator.

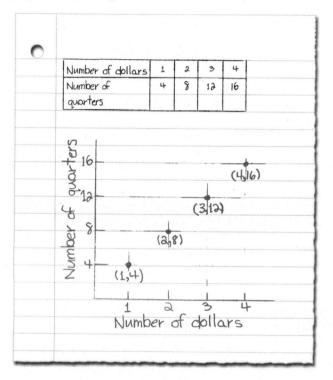

2. Ask: *What do you notice about the graph?* (The distance from one pair of points to the pair on its right is one unit horizontally to the right and four units vertically up.)

In **Activity 13.10**, students use their knowledge of functions to graph the relationship and generalize what they have found.

Tech Tools

Graphing calculators, such as the TI-73, are easy to use and appropriate for middle-grades students when graphing coordinates or linear functions.

Geometry and measurement Students use proportional reasoning to study similarity and to make **scale drawings**, which stretch or shrink figures without

Activity 13.10 Graphing linear functions with technology

Instructions

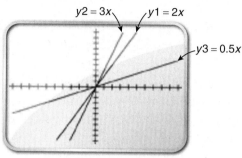

1. Say: *Using a graphing calculator, graph the functions y = 2x, y = 3x, and y = $\frac{1}{2}$x.*

2. Ask: *What patterns do you notice?* (All of these are lines that pass through the origin.)

3. Ask: *If you are given the function y = kx, with k = some integer, what can you say about the graph of this function?*

changing their shape. In **Activity 13.11** students stretch and shrink the same shape and discover that scale factors that are greater than 1 stretch a shape, whereas scale factors that are less than 1 shrink a shape. When students make scale drawings, encourage them to identify the ratios within and between figures.

Activity 13.11 Stretching and shrinking shapes

Instructions

1. Ask students to draw a shape with straight lines and **vertices** (corners) on the dots or corners of a grid.

2. Next, ask them to measure all sides of the shape and then choose a **scale factor** (a number by which they will multiply the lengths of all sides) to make the shape larger. Draw the new shape on the same grid. Identify the scale factor.

3. Say: *Choose one length from your original figure. What do you notice about that length when compared to the scaled figure? Repeat with other lengths. Are these shapes similar?*

4. Say: *Go back to your original shape and use a different scale factor to make the shape smaller. Draw the new shape on the same grid. Identify your scale factor.*

5. Say: *Now look at the same length you chose before (in #3). What do you notice about that length when compared to the scaled figure? Are these shapes similar?*

6. Ask: *Are all three shapes similar?*

Multicultural Perspectives in Mathematics

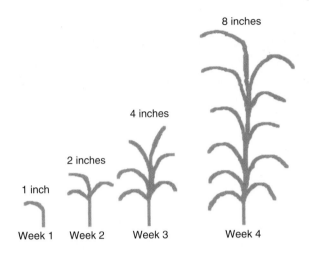

8 inches

4 inches

2 inches

1 inch

Week 1   Week 2   Week 3   Week 4

concept. To help American Indian students develop proportional reasoning skills, teachers at Grey Hills High School in Tuba City, Arizona (on the Navajo reservation), taught an alternative program to American Indian ninth and tenth graders. Most important was the use of language. Rather than using words such as "ratio" or "scale factor," they used the words "growing" and "shrinking," which are both important words in Navajo culture.

To help students understand ratio and proportion, teachers asked students to imagine the rate of growth of corn, a staple in the Navajo diet, from the time it first sprouts to the time it is ready to be picked. With careful questioning, students were able to understand the growth rate of the corn and express it as a ratio.

(*Source*: Giamati, 2002)

The Navajos' Understanding of Proportion

"**N**umerous studies and assessment tools have shown that Navajo students have great difficulty with ratio and proportion . . ." (Giamati, 2002, p. 201). The Navajos do not divide things into parts in their culture and have no words to express this

Strategies for the Classroom

- How can the use of language affect teaching mathematics, especially when teaching students who are English-language learners?
- What did you learn about using familiar contexts to teach mathematics? Why is this important?

Proportional reasoning, an important topic for the middle grades and beyond, is difficult for students to understand. Sometimes, difficulty with proportions can be cultural, based on students' use of language or cultural traditions (see *Multicultural Perspectives in Mathematics*).

| CONCEPT CHECK | STOP |

1. **What** is a proportion? Give an example.
2. **What** are three uses of proportions in mathematics?

3. **How** might you solve the following problem informally? How might you solve it with cross multiplication?

   If Kathie runs at a pace of two miles in 35 minutes, how long does it take her to run a five-mile race if she runs the whole race at the same pace?

Learning About Percents

LEARNING OBJECTIVES

1. **Define** percent.
2. **Explain** how to teach percents to elementary and middle school students.
3. **Describe** alternative methods for teaching percent problems.

"**P**ercent is a mathematical concept that permeates our lives" (Zambo, 2008, p. 419). Data about interest rates, sales, test grades, the chance of rain, or the probability that a favorite team will win the next game are all given in terms of percents. Students in grades 3–5 "should understand the meaning of a percent as part of a whole and use

Models for percents • Figure 13.7

10 × 10 grids, fraction circles, and fraction bars can all be used to model percents.

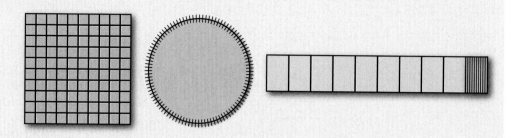

common percents such as 10 percent, $33\frac{1}{3}$ percent, or 50 percent as benchmarks in interpreting situations they encounter" (NCTM, 2000, pp. 150–151). Students in grades 6–8 should be able to use percents to solve problems and to convert percents to their fraction and decimal equivalents.

Understanding Percents

Percent comes from the Latin word *centum*, which means 100. Percent means "out of 100," or hundredths. Percents do not represent a new concept. They are just a different way of expressing something that students should already know: fractions with denominators of 100 or decimals. Therefore, 25 percent means 25 hundredths and can be written as $\frac{25}{100}$, 25%, or 0.25. All three symbols can be read "25 hundredths." Many fractions that are not already given in hundredths can be converted to hundredths and expressed as percents. Consider $\frac{4}{5}$. This is equivalent to 80 hundredths and can be written as $\frac{80}{100}$, 80%, or 0.80. Fractions that can be easily converted to hundredths, such as fourths, fifths, and tenths, can be modeled with 10 × 10 grids, fraction circles, fraction bars, or 100 pennies and converted to percents (**Figure 13.7**). Students should learn these familiar percents and be given lots of opportunities to recognize them visually (**Activity 13.12**).

Although this technique works well for fractions whose denominators are factors of 100, it does not work for fractions such as $\frac{1}{8}$, whose denominator is not a factor of 100. How can you convert a fraction such as $\frac{1}{8}$ to a percent and model it using a 10 × 10 grid? Zambo (2008) suggests an interesting counting technique for fractions such as $\frac{1}{8}$, which uses a 10 × 10 grid and depends on the set definition of fractions. To model $\frac{1}{8}$, he suggests shading one out of every eight squares (**Figure 13.8**).

Activity 13.12 Representing familiar percents on a 10 × 10 grid

Instructions

1. Say: *For each of the 10 × 10 grids given here, identify the fractional part shaded and convert it to a decimal and to a percent.*

2. Ask: *How did you convert each fraction to a percent? How did the 10 × 10 grid help you make this conversion?*

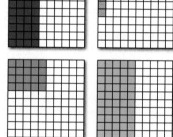

3. Reverse the activity by providing a percent (35%, 40%) and ask students to write it as a fraction and a decimal and illustrate on a 10 × 10 grid.

Showing $\frac{1}{8}$ on a 10 × 10 grid • Figure 13.8

To show $\frac{1}{8}$ as a percent, think of $\frac{1}{8}$ as 1 out of every 8 squares on the grid. In each row, shade the eighth square in that row. Next, shade the eighth square down in columns 9 and 10. You have shaded every eighth square or 12 squares in all with 4 left over. The 4 leftover squares are $\frac{1}{2}$ of a set of 8. $\frac{1}{8} = 12\frac{1}{2}$ small squares or $12\frac{1}{2}$%.

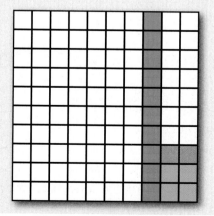

Fraction calculators convert fractions to percents and reinforce students' knowledge of common percents (**Activity 13.13**).

Activity 13.13 Using a calculator to find percents

Instructions

1. Distribute a fraction calculator to each pair of students.

2. Prepare cards with fractions written on them. Choose fractions such as $\frac{1}{4}, \frac{1}{2}, \frac{1}{3}, \frac{1}{5}, \frac{2}{5}, \frac{3}{5}, \frac{7}{10}, \frac{2}{25}, \frac{3}{50}$, or other fractions whose denominators are factors of 100.

3. For each pair of students, one student picks a fraction card and enters that fraction into the calculator. The other student gives the percent equivalent. They check their answer with the calculator. Then they switch roles and pick another fraction.

4. For the TI-15, use the following keystrokes to enter a fraction and convert to a percent:

$$1 \; \underline{n} \; 4 \; \overline{d} \; \% =$$

Teaching Tip

Connecting fractions, decimals, and percents

Take every opportunity to connect fractions, decimals, and percents. For example, if numbers in a problem are given as fractions, ask students to represent them also as decimals and percents. Use 10×10 grids to illustrate.

Teaching Percents

When should you teach percents? According to *Principles and Standards for School Mathematics* (NCTM, 2000) and *Curriculum Focal Points* (NCTM, 2006), students should become familiar with commonly used percents in grades 3–5 and learn to solve percent problems in grades 6–8. According to the *Common Core State Standards* (NGA Center/CCSSO, 2010), students should begin learning to solve percent problems in grade 6. Because percents are really fractions, the groundwork for learning about percents can be started as early as fourth grade, once students have a deep understanding of the meaning of fractions (see *In the Classroom*).

In the Classroom
Learning About Percents in the Fourth Grade

 THE PLANNER

Retail sales fell 5% in November!

Tuition increase of 10% expected!

Interest rates fall to a record low of '5%'

20% OFF all merchandise for the next 3 days

Unemployment rate for people under 30 is 15%!

Student teacher Mike Wilson wanted to introduce his fourth graders to percents. The children had heard the terms "unemployment rate," "mortgage rates," and "interest rates" in their discussion of current events and on television. Mr. Wilson wanted to relate these terms to mathematics. He brought a pile of newspapers and magazines to class and asked each child to

choose one. Then he asked the children to cut out as many examples as they could find that used percents. Maria found an ad that said, "Everything in the store has been reduced an additional 20%." Sean found an article that was titled, "Mortgage rates hit new low of 5%." Next, Mr. Wilson asked each student to make a percent scrapbook. Each student was to find at least four examples of percent, cut and paste that article, ad, or headline onto a page of construction paper, and illustrate the percent with a 10 x 10 grid or other visual representation. When they were finished, he showed the class members how to bind their books together.

Think Critically

1. What are the benefits of introducing percents to fourth graders?

2. How can children learn about percents before they learn about decimals?

3. What prior knowledge do children need in order to have a meaningful understanding of percents?

4. Why is it important to connect mathematics with other subjects in the curriculum?

a. Which of these pitchers is close to 0% full? Which pitcher is about 50% full? Which pitcher is close to 100% full?

b. Which of these jars of coins is about 25% full? Which is about 50% full? Which jar is about 75% full?

When beginning instruction on percents, make sure students have an intuitive understanding of some common percents. They should understand that 2% is practically nothing, 57% is about half, and 98% is close to one whole. They should become familiar with benchmark percents (0, 25, 50, 75, 100) and be able to estimate these benchmarks visually (**Figure 13.9**).

Students should have quick recall of some of the more common percents. You can help this process by connecting percents to their fraction equivalents. For example, if a student knows that $\frac{1}{2}$ is the same as 50% but cannot remember the percent equivalent of $\frac{1}{4}$, help them recognize that $\frac{1}{4}$ is $\frac{1}{2}$ of $\frac{1}{2}$, so the percent equivalent of $\frac{1}{4}$ must be $\frac{1}{2}$ of 50%, or 25% (Zambo, 2008).

Encourage students to use mental computation and estimation to find percents. Use easy percents, as illustrated by the following problems.

> 1. We spent $12.00 for lunch. If we want to leave a 20% tip, how much should the tip be?
>
> 2. The soccer team needs $3200 for new uniforms and equipment. If the team has already raised 90% of the money, how much has it raised?

To solve the first problem, you might change 20% to $\frac{1}{5}$ and find $\frac{1}{5}$ of $12.00, or you might realize that 20% is twice 10% and 10% of $12.00 is $1.20, so twice $1.20 is $2.40. The second problem may seem a bit more challenging at first. However, once you realize that 90% = 100% − 10%, you can find 10% of the total, or $320, and subtract that amount from $3200 to find the answer.

Solving Percent Problems

When you learned to solve percent problems in middle school you probably learned that there were three types of percent problems. These are illustrated in the following examples.

> 1. Find 20% of 80.
>
> 2. 20 is what percent of 80?
>
> 3. 80 is 20% of what number?

You were probably taught to change the percent to a decimal and then multiply, divide, or set up a proportion. When students learn to solve percent problems in this way, they usually have very little understanding of what they are doing and are prone to making mistakes. Because this approach is so dependent on interpreting the words of the problem, it is especially difficult for students who are English-language learners. Many students also have difficulty working with decimals, so asking them to convert percents to decimals can be problematic. A visual approach that makes use of fractions is illustrated in **Figure 13.10**.

Even though the approach explained in Figure 13.10 will not work for all numbers, it is a good way to initially approach percent problems because it helps students gain valuable experience with the different types of problems as well as opportunities to model the problems visually.

Problems that involve percent increase or decrease are often difficult for students. Parker (2004) suggests a three-part model that uses visualization and proportional reasoning to solve these problems. The model avoids the use of decimals, which can be confusing for students, and uses "a set of three rectangles that give a visual display

A visual approach to finding percents • Figure 13.10

a. Find 20% of 80. Draw a rectangle that represents the whole, or 80. Because 20% = $\frac{1}{5}$, subdivide this rectangle into five equal parts. Each part is $\frac{1}{5}$ of 80, or 16. Then 20% of 80 = 16.

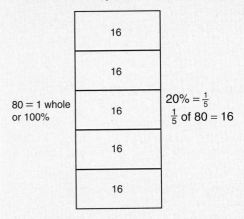

b. 20 is what percent of 80? Draw a rectangle that represents the whole, or 80. Because 20 is $\frac{1}{4}$ of 80, subdivide this rectangle into four equal parts. Then 20 is $\frac{1}{4}$, or 25%, of 80.

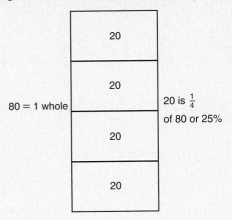

c. 80 is 20% of what number? Draw a rectangle that represents 80. Since this is 20%, or $\frac{1}{5}$, of the whole, scale the rectangle up. Make four more pieces that are each 80. Find the new whole.

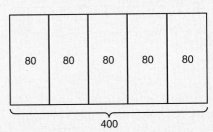

of the relative sizes of the three quantities in percent problems of part to whole, change, or comparison" (Parker, 2004, p. 327) (**Figure 13.11**).

Whenever you ask your students to solve percent problems, choose problems that have percents that convert to familiar fractions ($\frac{1}{2}$, $\frac{1}{3}$, $\frac{1}{4}$, $\frac{3}{5}$, etc.) and require students to use drawings and explain their work. Encourage students to use their own strategies and discuss these strategies as a class. When students learn to solve percent problems in this way, they will remember what they learned and not be thrown off if a problem is worded slightly differently.

A three-part model for solving percent increase and decrease problems • Figure 13.11

Hank's paper route had a 10% increase in customers. He now has 120 customers. How many customers did he have before the increase?

Draw a rectangle to represent the number of customers he has now. Call this the "final" rectangle. It represents 120 customers, or 110%. Draw a second rectangle to represent the percent increase of 10%. Draw a third rectangle. Call this the "original" rectangle, which represents 100%. This represents the number of customers before the increase. Start with the final rectangle and scale this down proportionally. Set up a proportion based on the drawing.

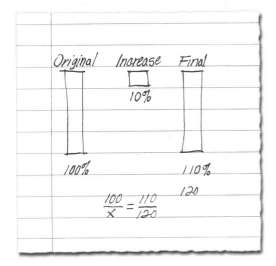

CONCEPT CHECK STOP

1. **How** might you use percents in everyday life?
2. **What** concrete models are helpful in teaching children about percents?
3. **How** might you help students to solve the following problem using mental mathematics?

   Jackie rode her bike 25% of the way to school before she had a flat tire. If the distance to school is two miles, how many miles did she ride her bike?

Summary

1 What Is Proportional Reasoning? 322

- Children use **proportional reasoning** informally in early elementary school when they use one-to-one correspondence to find out about counting. They use proportional reasoning later in elementary school when they learn place value and rates.

- Proportions are used in many parts of everyday life, for example, finding distances on maps, as shown here.

Figure 13.1

- Proportional reasoning is formally taught in the middle grades. Students learn ratio in sixth grade and proportions in seventh grade. Students often have great difficulty learning to reason proportionally and progress through four stages in their development of proportional reasoning. Some students and adults never learn it.

2 Learning About Ratio 324

- There are three types of **ratios**, but the part-whole definition is the most common, as illustrated in this photo. Students are often familiar with many real-world uses of ratio. It is helpful to teach ratio concepts with a ratio table. This helps organize information and makes it easy to identify patterns.

Figure 13.3

- In mathematics, there are famous ratios such as the **golden ratio** and pi, the ratio of the circumference to the diameter of a circle.

3 Learning About Proportion 328

- Students should learn to solve **proportions** using informal techniques before using cross multiplication. Teach students to use equivalent ratios, ratio tables, and other informal strategies.

- When teaching cross multiplication, require that students draw pictures so they know where to place the numerical amounts in the proportion.

Activity 13.11

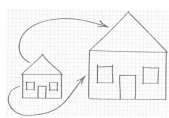

- Proportions are used in many other areas of mathematics, such as **slope, similarity,** and **linear functions,** as illustrated in this image.

4 Learning About Percents 333

- **Percent** means "out of one hundred." If students understand fractions, then they should understand percents. Expose students to many different percent models, as illustrated.

Figure 13.7

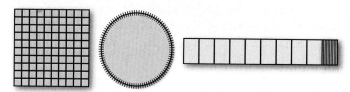

- When introducing percents, give students practice with percents in the real world, and teach them to use mental computation and estimation to solve percent problems.

- Encourage students to use informal techniques to solve percent problems. Ask them to draw pictures to explain their solutions.

Key Terms

- additive reasoning 323
- circumference 328
- equivalent ratios 329
- functional relationships 331
- golden ratio 326
- golden rectangle 326
- linear function 331
- multiplicative reasoning 322
- origin 331
- percent 334
- proportion 328
- proportional reasoning 322
- ratio 324
- scale drawings 332
- scale factor 332
- scaling strategy 331
- similarity 328
- slope 328
- unit rate 330
- vertices 332

Additional Children's Literature

- *Jim and the Beanstalk*, **written by Raymond Briggs**
  Jim helps out the giant Jack by taking measurements of his head and body and helping him get dentures, eyeglasses, and a wig. After reading the book, ask students to measure the circumference of their heads and the lengths of their arms. Ask them to scale the measurements and discuss the dimensions of their scaled figures.

- *Beanstalk: The Measure of a Giant,* **written by Ann McCallum and illustrated by James Balkovich**
  This is another extension of the Jack and the beanstalk story that uses clever illustrations and story to help children understand ratios when comparing a 4-foot boy to a 20-foot giant.

- *If the World Were a Village,* **written by David Smith and illustrated by Shelagh Armstrong**
  Imagine that the world is a village of 100 people. Because everything in the village is based on hundredths, we can find what percent of the people speak English or have electricity and running water. After reading the book, ask students to model some of the data with fractions, decimals, and percents.

Online Resources

- **National Library of Virtual Manipulatives**
  http://nlvm.usu.edu/

1. The **Fibonacci Sequence** activity computes the ratio of successive terms of the sequence, with content similar to the lesson in this chapter.

2. The **Golden Rectangle** activity begins with a golden rectangle and then draws a spiral that represents the Fibonacci sequence and shows iterations of the golden rectangle.

3. The **Percentages** activity shows three unknowns: the whole, the part, and the percentage. The user enters any two of those values and hits Compute.

- **NCTM Illuminations**
  www.figurethis.org/index40.htm

  This is a link from the Illuminations Web site. The **Grape Juice Jungle** activity asks questions about the strength of grape juice to reinforce learning about ratios and proportions.

- **Math Playground**
  www.mathplayground.com/visualpercent.html

  Use Math Playground's **Percent Equation** applet to explore part/whole relationships and percent.

Critical and Creative Thinking Questions

1. What is the difference between a ratio and a proportion? How would you describe that difference to students?

2. Describe how you use ratios and proportions in your own life. Provide at least three examples.

3. How can you help students learn to reason proportionally? Describe a situation that could be interpreted with additive reasoning or multiplicative reasoning. What kinds of questions would you ask students to help them see the difference between the two kinds of reasoning?

4. Describe two methods of solving the following problem. Both methods should use pictures.

   Tonya bought a coat that was marked down 30%. The sale price of the coat is $49. What was the original price?

5. **In the field** Create four word problems that use easy percents, have familiar contexts, and are meant to be solved using mental mathematics or estimation by students in grades 3–5. Ask a fourth or fifth grader to solve the problems. Reflect on their responses.

6. Consider the sample lesson in this section. If you were teaching this lesson to students, what prior knowledge would they need to understand first? What lessons might follow this one?

7. **Using visuals** This chapter illustrates several visual models for learning percents (Figures 13.7 through 13.11). Select one of these figures, and discuss its strengths and weakness. How would you use this model in your own classroom?

What is happening in this picture?

The American Horse (1998) by Nina Akamu is displayed at Frederik Meijer Gardens and Sculpture Park in Grand Rapids, Michigan. The sculptor made an 8-foot clay model before making the 24-foot bronze horse.

Think Critically

1. How might you use this picture to introduce the topics of ratio and proportion?
2. What questions might you ask about the scale of the horse?

Self-Test

(Check your answers in Appendix D.)

1. What are the four steps in children's development of proportional reasoning?

2. Identify two reasons why proportional reasoning is a major focus for the middle grades.

3. Which type of ratio is illustrated by this figure?

4. Write out the first 10 terms in the Fibonacci sequence. Explain how to get the next term.

5. Begin a Fibonacci-type sequence with the numbers 2, 4 as the first two terms. Write out the first 10 terms. Find the ratio of each term to the one that comes before. What do you notice?

6. What are the golden ratio and the golden rectangle? Measure a credit card. Are its dimensions in the golden ratio?

7. Given the ratio table, find the number of lemons needed for 15 servings. What is the ratio of lemons to servings?

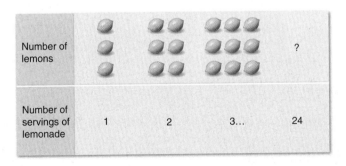

8. Solve the following problem without setting up a proportion or using cross multiplication:

   If two tubs of organic raspberries cost $5.00, how many can I buy for $15?

9. Describe how you could use ratios to solve the following problem:

   Which is the better buy, a 64-ounce container of lemonade for $3.50 or a 24-ounce container for $1.50?

10. Give a percent equivalent for each of the following fractions: $\frac{1}{2}, \frac{1}{4}, \frac{1}{3}, \frac{3}{5}$.

11. Using a 10 x 10 grid, illustrate how to represent 25%.

12. Using a 10 x 10 grid, illustrate how $\frac{1}{8} = 12\frac{1}{2}$ %.

13. John saw a bicycle on sale for 20% off. Then it was reduced an additional 30%. He expected to buy the bike for 50% off. Was he correct? Explain.

14. After Anne started working more hours at her job, her salary increased from $30,000 to $36,000. What is the percent increase for Anne's salary? Find the answer in at least two different ways.

15. Find the answer to the following question in at least two different ways: 18 is what percent of 72?

THE PLANNER ✓

Review your Chapter Planner on the chapter opener and check off your completed work.

Algebraic Reasoning

Ganasha Williams wondered, "How can I teach algebra to first-graders?" With the help of her methods instructor, Ganasha created an activity she thought the children would enjoy. She made construction-paper cutouts of one pair of jeans, one blue sweater, one white sweater, and one red sweater, and told her group of first-graders, "I'm going away for the weekend and I want to bring very few clothes with me. If I bring one pair of jeans and a blue sweater, how many outfits will I have?"

Ganasha taped the paper cutouts of the jeans and blue sweater to the chalkboard. After some discussion about the meaning of the word *outfit*, the children understood that the jeans and sweater made one outfit. Next, Ganasha said, "Now, suppose I also pack the white sweater. How many outfits will I have?" Then she said, "If I decide to bring the red sweater, too, how many outfits will I have?"

Next, she organized the information in a chart and asked, "Do you see a pattern?" After some discussion, children realized that each time Ganasha added a sweater, the number of outfits increased by one. Then Ganasha included a second pair of jeans and had children predict how many outfits she would have.

Ganasha helped the children identify patterns and make predictions about what happens when one quantity changes. This activity helped set the foundation for the formal algebra these children would learn later in middle and secondary school.

Introduce algebraic reasoning early. When children learn to identify patterns and make predictions, they are preparing to learn formal algebra later in their lives.

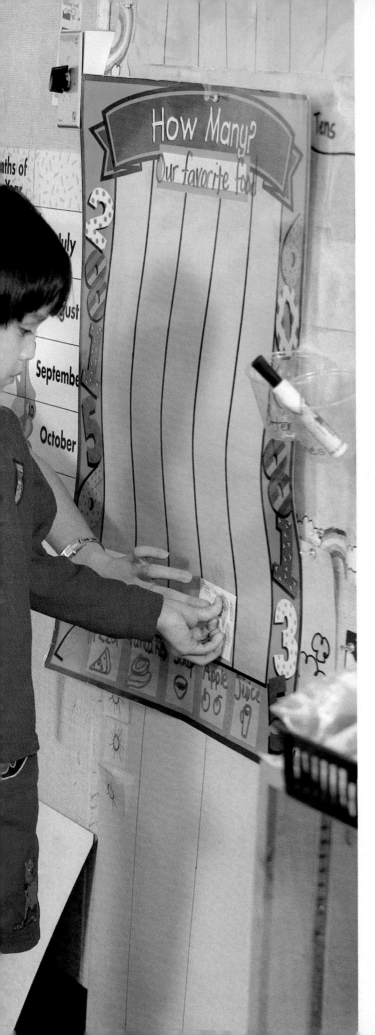

CHAPTER OUTLINE

What Is Algebra? 344

Key Question: What does algebraic reasoning mean for elementary and middle school students?

Algebraic Symbols 347

Key Question: What kinds of symbols are important to understand in algebraic reasoning?

Generalizing the Number System with Algebra 351

Key Question: How can teachers use properties of the number system to generate algebraic reasoning at the elementary and middle school levels?

Patterns and Functions 356

Key Question: How can teachers use patterns and functions to develop students' algebraic reasoning?

NCTM The NCTM Algebra Standard has four main objectives.

Instructional programs for prekindergarten through grade 12 should enable all students to

- understand patterns, relations, and functions;
- represent and analyze mathematical situations and structures using algebraic symbols;
- use mathematical models to represent and understand quantitative relationships;
- analyze change in various contexts.   (NCTM, 2000, p. 90)

Specific objectives for each grade-level band are listed within these four major categories and are in Appendix A.

CHAPTER PLANNER ✓

What Is Algebra?

LEARNING OBJECTIVES

1. **Identify** how algebraic reasoning develops across the grade levels.

2. **Describe** the importance of fostering algebraic thinking in the elementary grades.

"Many adults equate school algebra with symbol manipulation—solving complicated equations and simplifying algebraic expressions" (NCTM, 2000, p. 37). Although this is certainly an important part of algebra, computers and graphing calculators can perform many of the computational aspects of algebra that students used to figure out with paper and pencil. Today, educators think of algebra more broadly and are concerned with the development of algebraic reasoning at all grade levels, beginning in prekindergarten.

From concrete to abstract: The development of algebraic reasoning • Figure 14.1

✓ THE PLANNER

As children progress through the elementary and middle school mathematics curriculum, they revisit the same ideas with increasingly complex levels of algebraic reasoning. This process is illustrated through the development of even number concepts.

1 Prekindergarten–Grade 2

Young children skip count by twos, clapping their hands rhythmically as they call out in unison: *2, 4, 6, 8, 10, 12, 14, 16, 18, 20.*

2 Grades 3–5

Children examine, extend, and generalize patterns. They recognize that the sequence 0, 2, 4, 6, 8 . . . produces all even numbers. They understand that the next even number is two more than the previous even number. They may be able to express these numbers as *n* and *n* + 2.

1	2	3	4	5	6	7	8	9	10
11	12	13	14	15	16	17	18	19	20
21	22	23	24	25	26	27	28	29	30
31	32	33	34	35	36	37	38	39	40
41	42	43	44	45	46	47	48	49	50

3 Grades 6–8

Students make a **table of values**, which is a chart that lists values for *x* and the corresponding values for *y*, and they graph the function $y = 2x$. They understand that the graph of this function is a straight line that passes through the origin and illustrates proportionality. They investigate the slope of the line.

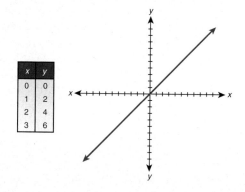

x	y
0	0
1	2
2	4
3	6

Developing Algebraic Reasoning Across the Grade Levels

Algebraic reasoning is more than a set of specific skills. It is "a process in which students build general mathematical relationships and express these relationships in increasingly sophisticated ways" (Soares, Blanton, and Kaput, 2006, p. 228). To emphasize its importance, the National Council of Teachers of Mathematics created an algebra standard for each of the grade-level bands in *Principles and Standards for School Mathematics* (2000). Algebra and the development of algebraic reasoning frame the goals of *Curriculum Focal Points for Prekindergarten through Grade 8 Mathematics* (NCTM, 2006) and the K–8 mathematics standards in *Common Core State Standards* (NGA Center/CCSSO, 2010).

Algebraic reasoning begins before children start school (Warren and Cooper, 2008). Young children observe patterns (who is facing forward or backward) and relationships (who has the bigger cookie). They represent relationships through physical modeling or drawing pictures and they analyze change (the puppy is getting bigger). This may not meet our traditional view of algebra, but it does represent the beginning of algebraic reasoning.

Throughout elementary and middle school, teachers can foster students' development of algebraic reasoning by infusing age-appropriate algebraic concepts into the curriculum. **Figure 14.1** traces how one algebraic pattern can be developed through the grade-level bands with increasing levels of sophistication, from counting and pattern recognition to functions.

> **function** A rule of correspondence between the elements of two sets such that members of the first set correspond to unique elements of the second set.

Teachers can encourage the development of children's algebraic reasoning by "algebrafying" (Blanton and Kaput, 2003, p. 71) the elementary curriculum. In other words, teachers can adapt the existing curriculum to algebra by varying the numbers in problems and looking for patterns and generalizations, in the same way that Ganasha Williams did in the opening of this chapter. Consider the following problem (adapted from Soares, Blanton, and Kaput, 2006):

Five families are going on a trip together. If each family talks on the phone to each of the other families once to make final plans, how many phone calls are made?

Adapting mathematics problems to develop algebraic reasoning • Figure 14.2

For each family to speak to each other, the first family calls the other 4, the second family calls the remaining 3, and so on. The fifth family does not have to make any calls because they have already been called by the other 4 families. So, 5 families make a total of 10 phone calls to one another. This is illustrated in the following chart with the families numbered 1, 2, 3, 4, and 5.

Family	Families they called	Number of calls they made
1	2, 3, 4, 5	4
2	3, 4, 5	3
3	4, 5	2
4	5	1
	Total	(10 Calls)

How many total calls will 6 families make? (15 phone calls) Do you see a pattern? Notice that 1 + 2 + 3 + 4 = 10 and 1 + 2 + 3 + 4 + 5 = 15. Can you generalize results? How many phone calls would 100 families make?

If you asked students in grades 3–5 to solve this problem, they might draw diagrams or charts to get the answer (**Figure 14.2**). To algebrafy the problem, you might change the number of families from 5 to 6, 7, or 8 and see whether children can find a pattern (Soares, Blanton, and Kaput, 2006). Increasing the number of families to 100 forces children to find a pattern they can generalize because drawing pictures or acting out the problem with 100 people is impractical.

Teaching Tip

Focusing on patterns with young children

For young children, develop algebraic reasoning by focusing on patterns. Find patterns in nature, in children's books, and in the classroom. Help children understand the patterns they find by asking questions such as:

- *Do you see a pattern?*
- *Can you explain what to do next?*
- *How is this number (picture, shape) related to the one that came before it and the one that comes after it?*

Multicultural Perspectives in Mathematics

✓ THE PLANNER

The Algebra Project: Engaging Children in Real-Life Experiences that Teach Algebra

The Algebra Project was created in the 1980s by voting-rights activist Robert P. Moses. Moses believes that mathematics literacy, especially knowledge of algebra, is a basic civil right and has been a barrier to educational opportunity and economic access for ethnically and culturally diverse people. He advocates teaching all children algebra, regardless of their mathematics background. Moses uses experiential learning as part of a five-step process that moves from concrete experiences to abstraction. For example, he took middle-grades students on trips back and forth on the subway in Cambridge, Massachusetts, to begin a unit on integers. He used African drumming to teach about ratio and proportion. The Algebra Project trains teachers and creates culturally sensitive materials for teaching algebra. Find out more at their Web site (www.algebra.org).

(*Source*: Moses and Cobb, 2001)

Strategies for the Classroom

- How can you make use of experiential learning to provide algebraic experiences for your own students?

- How can you use Moses' techniques of moving from the concrete to the abstract in other areas of the mathematics curriculum?

Why Is Algebraic Reasoning Important?

Children who have the opportunity to reason algebraically in elementary school have an easier transition to the more formal aspects of algebra they will study in the middle grades and secondary school. "[S]ystematic experience with patterns can build up to an understanding of the idea of function . . . and experience with numbers and their properties lays a foundation for later work with symbols and **algebraic expressions**" (NCTM, 2000, p. 37). Competence in algebra is a prerequisite for many college mathematics and science courses, and a lack of algebra skills often results in poor performance in courses such as calculus, physics, and statistics. Knowledge of algebra is often viewed as a gatekeeper to the more specialized courses needed for the highly technical needs of today's workplace (see *Multicultural Perspectives in Mathematics*).

> **algebraic expression**
> A statement that consists of a combination of numbers and variables with an arithmetic operation (such as $3x + 4$).

CONCEPT CHECK   STOP

1. **How** might a child in prekindergarten through grade 2 experience algebraic reasoning? In grades 3–5? In grades 6–8? Provide an example of an activity that could be used to foster algebraic reasoning for each grade-level range.

2. **Why** is algebra considered a gatekeeper to high-paying professions?

Algebraic Symbols

LEARNING OBJECTIVES

1. **Compare** and **contrast** different methods of teaching the meaning of the equals sign.
2. **Describe** the three different meanings of variable.
3. **Explain** how to introduce the concept of equations using balance scales.

A s adults, when we think of algebra we often think in terms of symbols such as x and y. Do you remember when you were first introduced to symbols in mathematics? Did they make sense to you then? Do you understand them now? Symbols are the foundation of algebra. However, many children and adults do not really understand their purpose or what they represent. In this section we discuss the meaning of two very important types of symbols used in algebraic reasoning: the equals sign and variables.

The Equals Sign

Although young children understand the concept of sharing equally, many elementary school children do not understand the meaning of the equals sign (Molina and Ambrose, 2006). They interpret the equals sign to mean "and the answer is" rather than recognize that "the equals sign is a symbol that indicates that a state of equality exists and that the two values on either side of the equals sign are the same" (Mann, 2004, p. 65). Consider the following problem, researched by Carpenter, Franke, and Levi (2003):

$$8 + 4 = \underline{} + 5$$

When given this task, children in grades 1–6 most often said that the blank should be filled in with 12 or 17. If they disregard the 5, their answer is 12. If they include the 5, their answer is 17. Of course, neither answer is correct. This problem is really asking what number when added to 5 gives the same answer as the sum of 8 and 4. The correct answer is 7.

How can teachers help children understand the equals sign? One technique is to use true/false statements. "Asking students to choose whether each number sentence is true or false can encourage them to challenge their assumptions about the equals sign" (Carpenter, Franke, and Levi, 2003, p.16). **Activity 14.1** has been adapted from their work. Notice that in each sequence of **number**

Activity 14.1 Using true/false statements to learn about the equals sign

Instructions

1. Give children a series of number sentences and ask them to discuss which are true and which are false. Include some number sentences with 0 because these are often easier for children to accept as true.

   $6 + 7 = 13$

   $6 + 7 = 13 + 0$

   $6 + 7 = 0 + 13$

   $6 + 7 = 12 + 1$

2. Give children additional series of number sentences and ask them to discuss which are true and which are false.

   $4 + 5 = 9$

   $9 = 4 + 5$

   $9 = 9$

   $4 + 5 = 5 + 4$

   $4 + 5 = 6 + 3$

3. Introduce the same type of examples but with open sentences, where some of the numbers are missing. Ask children what numbers can be put in the blank spaces to make the sentence true. These number sentences correlate to those in Step 2.

   $4 + 5 = \underline{}$

   $9 = 4 + \underline{}$

   $9 = \underline{}$

   $4 + 5 = \underline{} + 4$

   $4 + 5 = 6 + \underline{}$

---

sentences, the first number sentence is written in familiar form and the others progress in difficulty, with the last in each set as the most difficult.

This conceptualization of the equals sign helps students develop **relational thinking** about numbers and evaluate expressions without computation. Consider the following problem:

> **relational thinking**
> The ability to make connections between and among ideas and concepts.

Find the number that makes this sentence true without computation:

$$27 + 34 = 28 + \underline{}$$

If children understand the meaning of the equals sign, they will realize that, since 28 is one more than 27, the unknown quantity must be 33, which is one less than 34. Such understanding builds mathematical power.

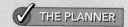
To encourage children's understanding of the equals sign, have them pretend that they are seesaws or balance scales by asking them to hold their arms out at their sides. Ask them to imagine they are holding things in each hand.

a. When both sides have equal weight, the balance scale is even.

b. When the bag of apples on one side is replaced by a bag of popcorn, that side of the balance scale is much lighter.

c. When the bag of popcorn is replaced by a watermelon, that side of the balance scale is much heavier.

The equals sign can also be conceptualized as a balance or a seesaw. In **Figure 14.3** (adapted from Mann, 2004), children physically act out situations illustrating equality or inequality by using their arms to simulate seesaws.

Many classrooms have balance scales that can be used to model equality for younger children and algebraic equivalence for older children. Balance problems can also be used as a prelude to solving simultaneous equations (Femiano, 2003), as illustrated in **Activity 14.2**.

Teaching Tip

Avoiding errors when using the equals sign

- Avoid long strings of numbers connected by equals signs, such as $70 + 30 = 100 + 20 = 120 + 45 = 165$. This is confusing and incorrect.

- Do not use the equals sign to equate pictures.

- Do not equate a name and a number, such as a child and his or her height or age (Paulo = 7; Tana = 4 ft).

Activity 14.2 Solving problems with a balance

Instructions

Show these drawings to students and ask them to find how many red weights are needed to balance the scale.

Variables

Variables are letters that represent quantities. Understanding and using variables is an important component of algebraic reasoning. There are three types of variables.

Variables as unknowns

The most common use of a variable is as an unknown. The variable represents one number that is missing. Children first experience variables as boxes or blanks in expressions, such as:

$$3 + 9 = \underline{\hspace{1em}} \qquad 120 \times \underline{\hspace{1em}} = 600 \qquad 52 - 48 = \underline{\hspace{1em}}$$

To familiarize children with variables, use a letter instead of a box or blank to represent the unknown. Write:

$$3 + 9 = s \qquad 120 \times p = 600 \qquad 52 - 48 = m$$

Use variables to represent unknowns in story problems. For example, present the following problem:

Mara had eight DVDs. Her mom gave her five more. How many DVDs does Mara have now?

Encourage children to write this problem with a variable, such as $8 + 5 = n$, where n represents the number of DVDs that Mara has now.

Variables in generalizations

Variables allow for the generalization of statements. For example, to illustrate the associative property of addition, rather than writing $4 + (3 + 9) = (4 + 3) + 9$, which only shows the property for these specific numbers, you can write $a + (b + c) = (a + b) + c$, where a, b, and c are whole numbers. This generalization shows that the property is true for all whole numbers.

Virtual Classroom Observation

| Video | www.wiley.com/college/jones |

Click on **Student Companion Site**. Then click on:

- **Foundations of Effective Mathematics Teaching**
- **B. Focus on Teacher Content Knowledge**
- **3. Analyze Classroom Videos**

Scroll down and view:

- **Pan Balance Equations: Constructing equations using a pan balance**

In this video, Ms. Soglin uses a pan balance to help her students understand how variables can be used to represent different quantities. How does Ms. Soglin help her students move from concrete representations to written representations of algebraic concepts?

Variables as unknowns that vary

Variables can also represent unknown quantities that vary. This is the form of variable that is used when graphing functions (**Activity 14.3** and **Activity 14.4**). In Activity 14.3, the value of b changes as the height of the ball changes. In Activity 14.4, q represents the number of quarters, d represents the number of dimes, and n represents the number of nickels. With each possible answer, the values of q, d, and n change.

Activity 14.3 Find the height of the ball

Instructions

Say: *I dropped some balls the other day from different heights. Each time a ball dropped, the first time it bounced back, it bounced back to half of its original height. Fill in the chart to find the height of the first bounce, letting* b *represent that height.*

Original height (in feet)	20	30	10	26	45	60
Height of first bounce b (in feet)	10	15	5	?	?	?

Activity 14.4 Find the number of ways to get $2.50 in quarters, dimes, and nickels

Instructions

Ask students to solve the following word problem:

I have $2.50 in quarters, dimes, and nickels. How many combinations of each coin can I have? Make a chart to display your answer (a partial chart is shown).

Number of quarters (q)	Number of dimes (d)	Number of nickels (n)
4	10	10
6	8	4
8	5	0
9	2	1
10	0	0

Expressions and Equations

Children in grades 3–5 solve **equations** using numbers and balance scales, as illustrated in **Activity 14.5** (adapted from Cuevas and Yeatts, 2001). These types of activities build on children's prior experience using balance scales to understand equality and prepare them for solving equations that use variables in middle school.

> **equation** Statement of equality between two expressions (such as $2x + 4 = 5x + 10$).

In grades 6–8, students simplify and solve expressions and equations with variables. In grade 6, "[s]tudents write mathematical expressions and equations that correspond to given situations, they evaluate expressions, and they use expressions and formulas to solve problems" (NCTM, 2006, p. 18). The balance scale is again an excellent representation to use because it builds on students' prior knowledge (**Activity 14.6**).

Activity 14.5 Balance or not?

Instructions

1. Say: *For the first two scales, decide whether the scale is balanced. If it is not balanced, what could you change to balance it?*

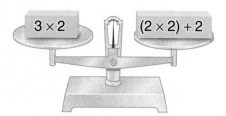

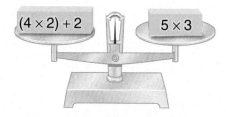

2. Ask: *For the third scale, is there more than one choice for each variable? List all solutions that you can find that will balance the scale.*

Activity 14.6 More balancing

Instructions

Say: *We are going to use a balance scale to solve this equation.*

1. Say: *To balance this scale, subtract 2 from both sides of the scale.*

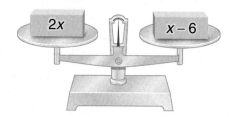

2. Say: *Now subtract x from both sides of the scale.*

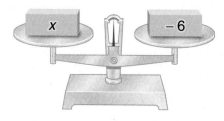

3. Now check your work. If $x = -6$, then both sides equal -10.

Teaching Tip _____

**Understanding the difference between
expressions and equations**

Sometimes students confuse equations and expressions and try to solve expressions. This error usually occurs when students do not understand the meaning of variables. To help students understand the difference between expressions and equations:

- Provide students with more practice on variables as unknowns.

- Say: *An expression is like an unfinished sentence. It can be simplified but it must equal something before it can be solved.*

Students tend to make mistakes when simplifying expressions and equations. To help students avoid simplification errors, provide them with simplifications of expressions and equations that already have errors and ask students to find the errors, correct them, and explain their reasoning. The insights gained from correcting others' errors can help students prevent these types of errors in their own work. For example, a common mistake occurs when students do not use the distributive property correctly. Consider the following equation:

$$3x + 5 - (2x + 3) = 7$$

Here is an incorrect simplification of this equation.

$$3x + 5 - 2x + 3 = 7$$

Students explaining the error would say that the error occurred because the negative in the expression $- (2x + 3)$ was not distributed. The correct simplification is

$$3x + 5 - 2x - 3 = 7$$

Tech Tools _____

http://nlvm.usu.edu/

The National Library of Virtual Manipulatives has an activity called **Algebra Balance Scales—Negatives**. To access the activity, select **Algebra** and **grades 6–8**. This activity uses virtual manipulatives to solve linear equations with a virtual balance beam. Click and drag on blocks representing units and blocks representing Xs to balance the beam.

CONCEPT CHECK	STOP

1. **How** might you help children understand that $9 = 5 + 4$ if they understand that $5 + 4 = 9$?

2. **How** do the three meanings of *variable* differ? Give an example of each one.

3. **How** can you use a balance scale to solve the equation $2 (x + 3) = 5x - 9$?

Generalizing the Number System with Algebra

LEARNING OBJECTIVES

1. **Explain** the importance of integrating algebraic reasoning with arithmetic.

2. **Identify** methods of using algebraic reasoning to generalize properties of the number system.

3. **Compare** and **contrast** different methods for learning integers.

When the elementary and middle school mathematics curriculum artificially separates arithmetic and algebra, students miss out on opportunities to connect these important areas of mathematics and tend to have more difficulty learning algebra later on (Carpenter, Franke, and Levi, 2003). As students learn the arithmetic that takes up much of the mathematics curriculum in the elementary grades, they can at the same time learn to think algebraically about the arithmetic properties and rules they are learning. Thinking algebraically about arithmetic is a process of **modeling** concepts concretely with physical objects or

Arithmetic properties   Table 14.1

Operation	Name of Property	Example	Generalization
+	Commutative property	$2 + 4 = 4 + 2$	$a + b = b + a$
+	Associative property	$2 + (3 + 4) = (2 + 3) + 4$	$a + (b + c) = (a + b) + c$
+, −	Additive identity	$5 + 0 = 5$	$a + 0 = a$
×	Commutative property	$2 \times 4 = 4 \times 2$	$a \times b = b \times a$
×	Associative property	$2 \times (3 \times 4) = (2 \times 3) \times 4$	$a \times (b \times c) = (a \times b) \times c$
×, +	Distributive property	$3 \times (4 + 5) = 3 \times 4 + 3 \times 5$	$a \times (b + c) = a \times b + a \times c$
×	Multiplicative identity	$4 \times 1 = 4$	$a \times 1 = a$
×	Zero property	$3 \times 0 = 0$	$a \times 0 = 0$

drawings in the primary grades and moving to abstract representations and generalizations of the same concepts with algebraic symbols, expressions, and equations in the upper elementary and middle grades. This section discusses three examples that move from concrete to abstract representations of the number system and help children integrate arithmetic and algebraic thinking.

Generalizing from Number Properties

Chapter 9 discussed arithmetic operations and their properties, summarized in **Table 14.1**. These properties can be used to help children develop algebraic thinking throughout the elementary grades. Consider the commutative property of addition. Children in the primary grades may recognize that $2 + 3 = 3 + 2$ because they can physically model this with counters by adding 2 counters and 3 counters to get 5 counters and then adding 3 counters and 2 counters to get 5 counters. Their concrete model tells them that $2 + 3 = 3 + 2$, but they are not sure whether, for example, $3 + 5 = 5 + 3$. They would have to physically model this, too.

In grades 3–5, children can begin generalizing this property by making verbal conjectures or using variables, which are abstract representations (**Activity 14.7**).

By the end of third or fourth grade, children should understand that this property is true for all pairs of numbers and be able to generalize verbally or by using variables. They may say something, such as *When I add two numbers I can turn them around and add them in a different order.* Similarly, in the primary grades, ask children to begin justifying other arithmetic properties concretely and build up to an abstract level of generalization in grades 3–5.

Generalizing the Properties of Odd and Even Numbers

Perhaps some of the most obvious properties of the number system are the properties of odd and even numbers. We know that numbers alternate: if a number is odd, then the next counting number is even, and so on. We also know that when adding two even numbers the sum is even, when adding an even and an odd number the sum is odd, and when adding two odd numbers the sum is even. Have you ever thought about why these rules are true? **Figure 14.4** illustrates how two children at different grade levels explain why the sum of two odd numbers is even.

Examining the properties of odd and even numbers gives children opportunities to make conjectures, generalize arithmetic properties, and justify their reasoning with concrete manipulatives, verbal arguments, or symbols.

Justifying why the sum of two odd numbers is even • Figure 14.4

a. First-graders are asked to show why the sum of 5 + 7 is an even number. Kara counted out 5 blocks and 7 blocks. She separated the 5 blocks into two groups of 2 with one left over and the 7 blocks into three groups of 2 with one left over. Then she put the leftover blocks from each group together to form another group of 2.

b. Fourth-graders are asked to show why the sum of any two odd numbers is an even number. Cheng-Yu says: *Any odd number can be written as an even number plus one. So if I have two odd numbers, each of them is an even number plus one, and then I add the two ones and that gives me two. 35 + 47 = 34 + 1 + 46 + 1. 34 + 46 is even and 1 + 1 is even, so the sum of 35 + 47 is even.*

To add 35 + 73, I know that 35 = 34 + 1 and 73 = 72 + 1. So, 35 + 73 = 34 + 1 + 72 + 1 = 34 + 72 + 1 + 1.

Generalizing Operations with Integers

Positive and negative integers provide a generalization of the number system that is relatively easy to learn and is an excellent way to introduce algebraic reasoning. Younger children are often exposed to the concept of negative numbers through their real-world experiences. For example, in areas with colder climates, children understand that when the temperature is below zero it is very cold, and –10 is colder than –5. Teachers can introduce all children to integers with concrete examples such as above and below sea level, profits and losses with money, and gains and losses on the football field. Children encounter negative integers when they use a calculator to find answers for expressions such as 5 – 7.

Teachers often introduce positive and negative integers as opposites of one another. They say –5 is the opposite of 5 and read –5 as "negative 5," not "minus 5." Children's literature is an excellent way to reinforce the concept of opposites (see *Children's Literature*, **Figure 14.5**).

CHILDREN'S LITERATURE

Teaching about opposites

✓ THE PLANNER

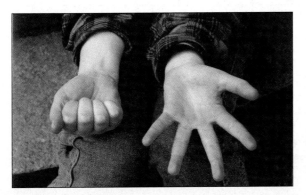

Exactly the Opposite • Figure 14.5

Written by Tana Hoban with photographs by the author
This book of photographs illustrates opposites from our everyday lives. For example, an open gate and a closed gate or an open fist and a closed fist are opposites. As you read the book to children, stress the word *opposite*. Say: *An open fist is the opposite of a closed fist.*

Strategy for the Classroom

- After reading the book, ask children to find their own examples of opposites.

When teaching operations with integers, first model the operations concretely and then generalize rules. Several models can be used, including number lines, thermometers, two-color chips, or electrical charges (**Figure 14.6**). Addition and subtraction of integers can be modeled quite effectively with a number line (see *In the Classroom*).

Using two-color chips to add and subtract integers • Figure 14.6

a. Adding integers

To add integers, line up all the black chips to represent the positive integers and below them line up all the red chips to represent the negative integers. Each pair of black and red chips cancels out. Count how many chips (black or red) remain to obtain the final answer.

● Black is positive ● Red is negative

Begin with whole numbers.

$3 + 2 = 5$

Add a positive integer and a negative integer.

$3 + (-2) = 1$

Add a negative integer and a positive integer.

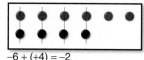

$-6 + (+4) = -2$

Add two negative integers.

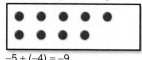

$-5 + (-4) = -9$

b. Subtracting integers

To subtract integers, begin by representing the first integer only with chips. Remove the amount to be subtracted. In some cases, this means you will have to add in the amount to be subtracted. For example, to find $4 - (-2)$, begin with 4 black chips. Since there are no red chips, put in 2 red chips to represent -2 and also put in 2 black chips, so that the value of the expression does not change.

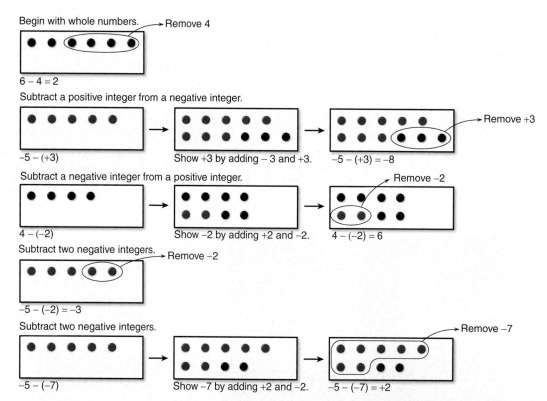

Begin with whole numbers. → Remove 4

$6 - 4 = 2$

Subtract a positive integer from a negative integer.

$-5 - (+3)$ → Show +3 by adding -3 and $+3$. → Remove +3 → $-5 - (+3) = -8$

Subtract a negative integer from a positive integer.

$4 - (-2)$ → Show -2 by adding $+2$ and -2. → Remove -2 → $4 - (-2) = 6$

Subtract two negative integers. → Remove -2

$-5 - (-2) = -3$

Subtract two negative integers. → Remove -7

$-5 - (-7)$ → Show -7 by adding $+2$ and -2. → $-5 - (-7) = +2$

In the Classroom

Using the Number Line to Add and Subtract Integers

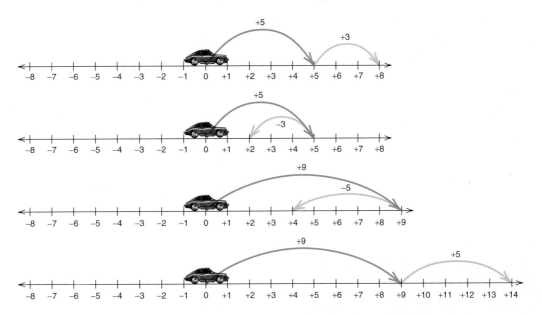

Student teacher Nick Kowalski used a number line to teach fifth-grade students operations with integers. He drew a number line, labeled it with positive and negative integers, and showed the class a model car. He said: *When the car goes forward we will call this positive, and when it backs up we will call this negative.* To model + 5 + (+ 3), he placed the car at 0, directed it and moved it forward 5 units to the right and then 3 more units. To model +5 + (−3), he started at 0, "drove" the car forward 5 units and backed up 3 units. Students practiced many different addition problems with their own number lines and model cars brought in by Mr. Kowalski.

Someone asked: *What about subtraction?* Drawing on their knowledge of inverse operations, students decided that for subtraction they should turn the car around. To model +9 − (+5), Mr. Kowalski drove the car forward 9 units to the right, turned it around and drove it forward another 5 units to the left, to +4. After much discussion, students decided that this must be correct. To model +9 − (−5), a student volunteered to "drive." She moved the car to the right and forward 9 units and then turned the car around. To move −5 units, she had to back up. This meant backing up to the right 5 units to +14.

Think Critically

1. In what ways does this integer example illustrate algebraic reasoning?
2. How did children's understanding of the inverse relationship between addition and subtraction help them understand subtraction with integers?

CONCEPT CHECK

1. **How** might children in prekindergarten to grade 2 explain why the sum of an odd number and an even number is odd? How might children in grades 3–5 explain and generalize the same idea?

2. **How** might children in prekindergarten to grade 2 explain the additive identity? How might children in grades 3–5 explain and generalize the same idea?

3. **How** could you explain the problem 3 + (−2) with the number line model and the colored chip model?

Patterns and Functions

LEARNING OBJECTIVES

1. **Distinguish** between repeating patterns and growing patterns.
2. **Compare** and **contrast** several ways of representing patterns.
3. **Describe** functional relationships.

Chapter 1 defined mathematics as the study of patterns and examined patterns in the natural world as well as patterns that have been designed by people from ancient times to the present. Patterns form the foundation of algebra and many other branches of mathematics. Learning the rules for extending and growing patterns in the elementary grades helps children transition to learning about functions, an important concept used in advanced mathematics in the middle grades and beyond.

Patterns

The study of patterns extends throughout the elementary curriculum. In prekindergarten, children learn to "recognize and duplicate simple sequential patterns" (NCTM, 2006, p. 11). In kindergarten, children continue their study of patterns and learn to "extend simple number patterns and sequential and growing patterns" (NCTM, 2006, p. 12). In grade 1 they apply number patterns to learn about properties of numbers and basic facts (NCTM, 2006). In grade 2, "[c]hildren use number

Education InSight

The two types of patterns • Figure 14.7

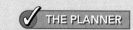 THE PLANNER

The two types of patterns are repeating, or sequential, patterns and growing patterns. Children in the primary grades should learn to identify and extend repeating patterns. Children in the upper elementary grades should learn to identify and extend both numeric and nonnumeric repeating and growing patterns.

a. Repeating patterns

All repeating patterns have a **core**, which represents two complete repetitions of the pattern. Here, the same repeating pattern is illustrated in three different ways. By recognizing these as different representations of the same pattern, children are making a generalization.

b. Growing patterns

Some growing patterns grow by a constant amount, and others grow by a varying amount. In the first pattern, made with color tiles, each successive design has two more tiles. In the second pattern, each successive design has another row of dots. Children should be able to extend these patterns and explain the rules, verbally or with written symbolism.

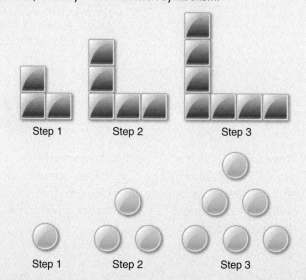

CHILDREN'S LITERATURE

Teaching about repeating patterns

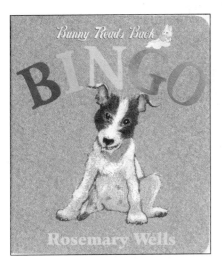

Bingo • Figure 14.8a

Written and illustrated by Rosemary Wells
Read and sing the familiar song illustrated in this children's book with young children.

Strategies for the Classroom

- After the first reading, read it again. In this second reading, replace one letter of the name either with a handclap or silence. For example, you might sing *[clap]-i-n-g-o, every time "Bingo" appears in the song.*
- *The third time you sing the song, take away another letter (that is, substitute a clap for "b" and "i"), and so on.* Children are learning a repeating pattern through a fun activity.

There Was an Old Lady Who Swallowed a Fly • Figure 14.8b

Written and illustrated by Simms Taback
In this retelling of the classic children's poem, illustrations make the story come alive. Technically, the story represents a growing pattern, because with each verse the old lady swallows one more animal and the refrain becomes longer. Even so, the level of this book is appropriate for young children.

Strategies for the Classroom

Emphasize the repetitive nature of the pattern.
- When reading the book to children, with each new page you might say, *"There was an old lady who swallowed a _____."* (Let children fill in the word for the animal.)
- Use a magnetic board and shapes to create the pattern as you read the book.

---

patterns to extend their knowledge of properties of numbers and operations" (NCTM, 2006, p. 14). In grade 3, they analyze patterns that relate to multiplication and division of whole numbers. In grade 4, they "continue identifying, describing, and extending numeric patterns involving all operations and nonnumeric growing or repeating patterns" (NCTM, 2006, p. 16). In grade 5, "[s]tudents use patterns, models, and relationships as contexts for writing and solving simple equations and inequalities" (NCTM, 2006, p. 17).

There are two types of patterns, as illustrated in **Figure 14.7**.

Repeating patterns Young children find patterns everywhere. They "can be found in the rhythm and words of songs, the days of the week, and the increase or decrease in a set of stairs" (Mattone, 2007, p. 202). Teachers can help children discover more patterns by using hand clapping, drum beating, and children's literature (see *Children's Literature*, **Figure 14.8**).

http://nctm.org/

Go to the NCTM Web site. Select **Standards and Focal Points** and then **E-Examples.** Select **4.1 Creating, Describing, and Analyzing Patterns**. This applet has an interactive figure that allows the user to make different kinds of repeating patterns and to analyze them.

Provide children with many opportunities to work with repeating patterns. Create patterns by using concrete manipulatives, such as pattern blocks, color tiles, and stacking cubes. For each pattern, encourage children to identify the core of the pattern, explain the core verbally, and extend the pattern. Challenge children to create their own repeating patterns (**Activities 14.8** and **14.9**).

Activity 14.8 Calculator patterns

Instructions

1. Make repeating patterns using a calculator. Select a starting number, enter it, and then press ⊞, and ⑤, and ⊜ sequentially. Press ⊜ again several times.

2. Ask: *What are some other repeating patterns you can make with your calculator?*

Activity 14.9 Make one too!

Instructions

1. Give each student or pair of students at least two sets of manipulatives. Choose from pattern blocks, color tiles, beads, and connecting cubes.

2. Make a pattern with one manipulative. Ask the children to make the same pattern using one of their manipulatives.

3. Ask the children to describe the pattern verbally.

4. Continue in this way, using a different kind of manipulative each time you create a pattern.

5. Create a pattern using the letters of the alphabet, such as A B B A B B A. Ask the children to make the same pattern with manipulatives.

Illustrating growing patterns with geometric designs • Figure 14.9

Geometric patterns can be made with concrete manipulatives or on grid paper.

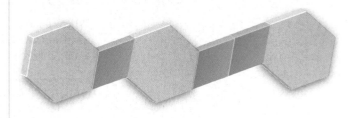

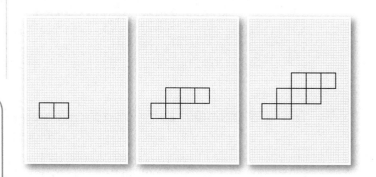

Growing patterns These are patterns that change. Geometric designs are a good way to introduce growing patterns, because the designs make it easier to distinguish the patterns. Geometric representations of patterns are especially helpful for visual learners and English-language learners (**Figure 14.9**).

Children's literature is a great way to help children learn about growing patterns. Recall that in Chapter 1, the children's book *A Grain of Rice* by Helena Clare Pittman was used in the chapter's *Lesson.* In the story, when a grain of rice was doubled each day for 100 days, the amount of rice grew very quickly, producing the sequence 1, 2, 4, 8, 16, 32, . . . Many other books also describe growing patterns (see *Children's Literature,* **Figure 14.10**).

CHILDREN'S LITERATURE

Teaching growing patterns

Anno's Magic Seeds • Figure 14.10

Written and illustrated by Mitsumasa Anno
Jack is given two magic seeds. He eats one and plants the other. The next year, two seeds are sprouted, and he continues this pattern of eating one and planting the other. This continues for several years until he decides to plant both seeds. The next year, four seeds are sprouted. He eats one and plants the remaining three. Several events occur that change the number of seeds Jack eats and plants, and several different growing patterns can be traced.

Strategies for the Classroom

• Read the book through once with your class. Then read it again.

• Have students make a chart to keep track of the year, number of seeds eaten, planted, and produced. Ask: *How many patterns can you find?*

Using real-world contexts is a good way to develop children's thinking about growing patterns. On a typical school day there are many things to compare (**Activity 14.10**). A T-chart is an effective tool for recording data and identifying patterns.

Activity 14.10 The number of wheels on the car

Instructions

1. Say: *Let's compare the number of cars in the parking lot to the number of wheels. Write down your data in a T-chart.*

2. Ask: *What's the rule? Can you identify how the number of wheels is growing? Can you write this symbolically?* (W = 4 x C)

C Number of cars	W Number of wheels
1	4
2	8
3	12
4	16

Number patterns	Table 14.2
Patterns	**Explanation**
3, 5, 3, 5, . . .	Alternating the numbers 3 and 5.
2, 4, 6, 8, . . .	Even numbers. Add 2 to a number to get the next number.
1, 1, 2, 3, 5, 8, . . .	Fibonacci sequence. Add two numbers to get the next number.
1, 4, 9, 16, 25, . . .	Each number is the square of a counting number: $1^2, 2^2, 3^2 \ldots$
3, 8, 18, 38, . . .	Double a number and add 2 to get the next number.
3, 5, 9, 17, . . .	Double the previous number and subtract 1 to get the next number.
1, 8, 27, 64, . . .	Each number is the cube of a counting number: $1^3, 2^3, 3^3, \ldots$

Sequences Patterns with numbers are called sequences. Students investigate number patterns to learn how to use a rule to describe a sequence of numbers. Sequences can vary in complexity from easy to very challenging, so that all students can be successful in solving some of them. **Table 14.2** illustrates some number patterns.

> **recursive** Refers to an expression that describes how to find the value of a term from the value of the previous term.

When working with numeric patterns, students often look for the **recursive** relationship (Bezuszka and Kenney, 2008). They find the value of a term based on the patterns they notice from term to term. For example, consider the triangular numbers

$$1, 3, 6, 10, 15, 21, 28 \ldots$$

which were illustrated in Figure 14.7. By finding the differences between terms, you may notice that the difference increases by one with each successive pair of terms ($3 - 1 = 2; 6 - 3 = 3$, etc.). Following this reasoning, the next term is 15 and the one after that is 21.

> **explicit** Refers to an expression that describes how to find the value of a term from the step or term number.

Sometimes it is helpful to find an **explicit** expression for the pattern in a sequence of numbers. This procedure allows you to find the 20th term without knowing the value of the 19 terms that precede it and the nth term to generalize the pattern. To find the explicit pattern for the triangular numbers, see **Table 14.3**. The explicit formula tells you that, to find the number of dots in the nth term, find $n(n + 1)/2$. If you test this formula for each pair of numbers (the term number and number of dots), you will see that it works. There is no sure-fire way to teach students how to find explicit formulas. It

comes easily to some students and is very difficult for others. Practice helps a lot. When students are trying to find explicit patterns, encourage them to make charts and focus, not only on the sequence of numbers in the bottom row, but also on the relationship between the step or term number in the top row and the value of that term.

Triangular numbers	Table 14.3						
Term Number n	1	2	3	4	5...	10...	20
Number of Dots	1	3	6	10	15...	55...	210

Functions

The work students do with patterns in elementary school provides excellent preparation for learning about functions. Students study functions in middle school, secondary school, and beyond. In grade 8 they "use linear functions, linear equations, and systems of linear equations to represent, analyze, and solve a variety of problems" (NCTM, 2006, p. 20).

Recall from earlier in the chapter that a function is a relationship between two sets of values where the value of one quantity (the dependent variable) depends on the value of the other quantity (the independent variable). For example, the rate at which snow melts depends on how sunny it is. The function rule determines the relationship between the sets of values. The **domain** of the function is the set of values for the independent variable. The **range** of the function is the set of values for the dependent variable. When students are introduced to functions, explain how functions are part of everyday life. For example, the faster you pedal on a bicycle, the farther you will go. The distance traveled

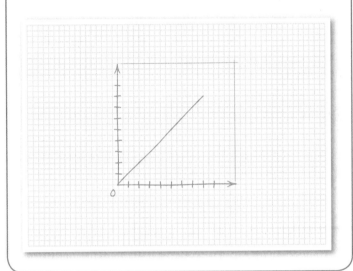
is a function of the speed of the bicycle. Ask students to provide other examples of functions in everyday life (**Activity 14.11**).

Tech Tools

www.mathplayground.com/functionmachine.html

Math Playground's function applet provides a fun way for students to guess a function rule. To play, choose **Beginner** and then select **You Decide the Input**.

In the middle grades, students should have many opportunities to graph functions and interpret graphs, because the visuals provide an excellent means of investigating how patterns grow. A frequent mistake made by middle-grades students when interpreting graphs is to interpret the graph literally rather than symbolically (You, 2009). For students to interpret a graph symbolically they must understand the mathematical relationship that the graph represents.

Provide students with opportunities to interpret and create graphs based on real situations (**Activity 14.12**).

In the *Lesson* on the next page, students investigate a function that is based on a typical context, determine the relationship between the two variables in two different ways, and graph the function. This lesson is accessible to students of different ability levels because the rule for the function can be stated in different ways. For students

who need additional support, provide the table of values rather than asking them to create one. Focus on the graph of the function rather than the symbolic function. For other students, ask them to determine the table of values and the symbolic function using the more abstract idea of intervals of time. Note that the problem discussed in this lesson has a context: a plausible, real-life experience that students can relate to. The data are represented with a table or by an equation. If an equation is used, symbols are used to represent the unknown variables in the problem. The equation is graphed, and the results can be discussed verbally. In this lesson, students use **multiple representations** and choose the one that works best (NCTM, 2000). The standards are from *Curriculum Focal Points for Prekindergarten through Grade 8 Mathematics* (NCTM, 2006) and the *Common Core State Standards* (NGA Center/CCSSO, 2010).

Ryan's Dog-Walking Business: Graphing Functions

GRADE LEVEL

6–7

OBJECTIVES

- Describe the function rule verbally and symbolically.

- Graph the function.

STANDARDS

Grade 6

Students write mathematical expressions and equations that correspond to given situations, they evaluate expressions, and they use expressions and formulas to solve problems. (NCTM, 2006, p. 18)

Grade 6

Evaluate expressions at specific values of their variables. Include expressions that arise from formulas used in real-world problems. (NGA Center/CCSSO, 2010)

Grade 7

Use variables to represent quantities in a real-world mathematical problem, and construct simple equations and inequalities to solve problems by reasoning about the quantities. (NGA Center/CCSSO, 2010)

MATERIALS

- Graphing calculator for each student

- Copy of Ryan's dog-walking flyer to display for class

ASSESSMENT

- Write a journal entry to explain the rule for Ryan's dog-walking rates.

- Design your own flyer for walking dogs, feeding cats, or some other chore that you can do.

- Create your own rate for the chore.

- Research on the Internet how much dog walkers make per hour.

GROUPING

Whole class followed by pairs

Launch (5 to 10 minutes)

- Ask: *How many of you have dogs?*

- Ask: *What kinds of dogs do you have?*

- Ask: *Have you ever walked someone else's dog for them or asked someone else to walk your dog when you were busy?*

- Say: *My neighbor Ryan is 10 years old. He has decided to start a dog-walking business. He made this flyer. He has figured out the rates for his dog-walking fees but needs help to figure*

Are you too busy to walk your dog? Let me do it for you.

I will walk your dog for $10 for a 15-minute walk. Each additional 15 minutes costs $5.

Linear functions The function graphed in the *Lesson* is an example of a **linear function**. Students study linear functions extensively in the middle grades, specifically the eighth grade (NCTM, 2006). They should have ample practice in graphing linear functions by creating a table of values for each function and then graphing the function by hand and with a graphing calculator (**Activity 14.13**).

> **linear function** A function whose graph is a straight line.

Activity 14.13 Graphing functions

Instructions

1. Say: *Create tables of values for the following functions: y = 2x + 4, y = 3x, y = x + 7.*

2. Say: *Graph each function on graph paper and then on a graphing calculator.*

3. Ask: *What do you notice?* (All the graphs are straight lines.)

out the actual amount of money he can make. I thought that our class could work on this together. Here is Ryan's flyer.

- Say: *We are going to figure out how much Ryan will make when he walks dogs for different lengths of time.*

Instruct (30 minutes)

Say: *Take a graphing calculator from the bin, and with your partner, do the following: Create a table that shows how much Ryan will charge for a 15-minute walk, a 30-minute walk, a 45-minute walk, and a 60-minute walk. Graph your results, and describe a rule for the amount of money Ryan will make in terms of the time he spends walking the dogs.*

- Students discuss the problem while the teacher walks around and observes and offers suggestions or answers questions.

- Student tables look like the following:

Number of Minutes	15	30	45	60
Cost of Walk in Dollars	10	15	20	25

- Student graphs look like the following:

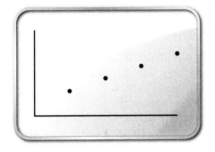

- Say: *Use the graph or extend the table of values to determine how much money Ryan will make if he walks a dog for 2 hours. (2 hours = 120 minutes. Ryan makes $45.)*

- Say: *Now let's look at this information in a different way. Instead of using the total number of minutes Ryan walks the dog, let's look at the number of additional 15-minute intervals and find out how much money he makes based on the intervals.*

- Ask: *Can anyone tell what the rule is for how much money Ryan earns? (He earns $10 for a 15-minute walk and an extra $5 for each additional 15-minute interval. For 30 minutes he is paid for 1 additional interval; for 45 minutes he is paid for 2 additional intervals. Ryan is paid $10 + $5 x [the number of additional 15-minute intervals].)*

- Ask: *Who can write this as a function? ($y = 10 + 5x$, where y is the amount of money Ryan is paid and x is the number of additional 15-minute intervals.)*

Summarize (5 minutes)

- Say: *We have represented the money Ryan will make with a table, with a verbal explanation, with variables, and with a graph. Which representation made it easier for you to find the answer?*

- Ask: *Could you say that the amount of money Ryan earns depends on how long he walks the dog?*

You can determine whether a function is linear before graphing it by looking at the recursive relationship expressed in the table of values. In the function graphed in the lesson, the rate of change from one step to the next is + 5, a constant rate of change. Note that for each of the functions graphed in Activity 14.13, the rate of change is also constant. This means that each of the functions is linear. In contrast, look again at the table of values for the triangular numbers (in Table 14.3). There the rate of change from one step to the next is not constant, so this is not a linear relationship.

The rate of change of a function is also called its **slope**. This can be defined as the change in y for each increase in x. In Activity 14.13, each of the functions has a slope. For $y = 2x + 4$, the slope is 2. This means that y increases by 2 each time x increases by 1. For $y = 3x$, the slope is 3, and for $y = x + 7$, the slope is 1. The slope of a line determines whether it increases or decreases as you view it from left to right and

Activity 14.14 Finding slopes

Instructions

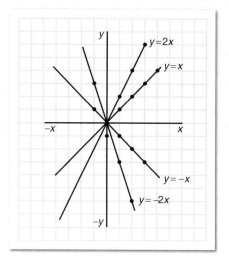

1. Say: *Graph the following functions:* y = x, y = 2x, y = − x, y = −2x.

2. Say: *Determine the slope of each function. What patterns do you notice?* (When the slope is positive, the line increases from left to right. When the slope is negative, the line decreases from left to right. The larger the slope, the steeper the line.)

3. Say: *Without graphing, tell everything you know about the graphs of the following functions:*

   y = 3x + 4   y = −8x + 9

CONCEPT CHECK

1. **What** is the difference between repeating patterns and growing patterns? Provide an example of each.

2. **How** should young children be introduced to patterns? Provide several examples.

3. **How** can you determine whether a function is linear without graphing it?

Summary

1 What Is Algebra? 344

Figure 14.1

- Algebraic reasoning develops across the grade levels and begins before children start school. Teachers should provide children with opportunities to identify and extend repeating patterns and make conjectures in the early grades, as shown in this photo. In later elementary school, children should extend both repeating and growing patterns using both **recursive** and **explicit** reasoning.

- Children who develop algebraic reasoning early on have an easier time making the transition to the formal algebra they will learn in middle and secondary school. Algebraic reasoning is important in advanced mathematics and science courses.

2 Algebraic Symbols 347

Figure 14.3

- Children often misunderstand the equals sign. The meaning of the equals sign should be introduced early because it is very important. Use a variety of activities to help children understand the equals sign, as shown in this image. Children use the equals sign to solve both simple and complex **equations**.

- Children should learn about **variables**, learn the three meanings of *variable*, and have opportunities to use variables to solve **number sentences**, word problems, and make generalizations. Also give children problems that highlight how a variable might change.

3 Generalizing the Number System with Algebra 351

- Children should have opportunities to use algebraic reasoning to understand the number system. They can generalize rules, such as the commutative property, and understand the properties of odd and even numbers.

- Extending the number system by learning about integers is a great way to foster the development of algebraic reasoning. The rules for integers can be derived from several different physical models and are easily accessible to elementary and middle school students. A good way of introducing integers is through the concept of opposites, as in the closed fist and open hand illustrated here.

Figure 14.5

4 Patterns and Functions 356

- There are two types of patterns: repeating patterns and growing patterns. From prekindergarten to grade 4, children can identify, extend, and create repeating patterns with pictures, geometric shapes, and, later, numbers. They learn to identify the **core** of a repeating pattern. This image shows the same repeating pattern with different objects. From fourth grade on, children can identify, extend, and create growing patterns. Numeric growing patterns are called sequences.

Figure 14.7

- Children encounter the concept of **function** early on. In middle school, students learn the vocabulary of functions, such as **domain** and **range**. They learn to identify **linear functions** and find the **slope** of a linear function. They graph functions by creating a **table of values**.

Key Terms

- algebraic expression 346
- core 356
- domain 360
- equation 350
- explicit 360
- function 345

- linear function 362
- modeling 351
- multiple representations 361
- number sentences 347
- range 360

- recursive 360
- relational thinking 347
- slope 363
- table of values 344
- variables 349

Additional Children's Literature

- *Rooster's Off to See the World,* written and illustrated by Eric Carle
  Although this is meant as a counting book, it also can be used to illustrate growing patterns. Each time a group of animals joins the rooster, there is one more set than before; for example, there is one rooster, two cats, three frogs.

- *One Grain of Rice: A Mathematical Folktale,* written by Demi
  A young woman tricks the raja into giving her a grain of rice, doubled each day, for 30 days. The pattern of doubling the rice makes the amount grow very quickly. This is a great book for examining growing patterns and also touches on sociocultural themes of poverty and hunger.

- *A Grain of Rice,* written and illustrated by Helena Clare Pittman
  A humble servant saves the life of the emperor's daughter and, for his reward, asks for one grain of rice, to be doubled each day for 100 days.

- *Two of Everything,* written by Lily Toy Hong
  This folktale from ancient China is about a magic pot that doubles everything that is put into it. The story can be used to encourage early reasoning about functions.

- *Patterns in Peru,* written by Cindy Neuschwander and illustrated by Bryan Langdo
  This entertaining book tells the story of two young children who go to Peru with their parents. While there, they become intrigued by an ancient Incan tunic and decipher the patterns on the tunic to find a lost city.

Online Resources

- **National Library of Virtual Manipulatives**
  http://nlvm.usu.edu/

  1. The **Color Patterns** activity for grades K–2 and 3–5 presents beads in different colors, illustrating repeating patterns. Students identify the pattern and fill in the unknown bead colors.

  2. The **Graph Functions** activity for grades 3–5 graphs functions on the coordinate plane.

- **NCTM Illuminations**
  Illuminations.nctm.org/

  1. The **Pan Balance–Expressions** applet allows students to enter what they think are equivalent algebraic expressions. If the expressions are equivalent, the pan will balance.

  2. The **Pan Balance–Numbers** applet does the same thing with numerical expressions.

Critical and Creative Thinking Questions

1. Describe what is meant by algebraic reasoning. What aspects of algebraic reasoning should teachers focus on in each of the grade-level bands: pre-K–grade 2, grades 3–5, and grades 6–8?

2. What are students' misunderstandings about the equals sign? Describe an activity that can help students understand the equals sign.

3. **In the field** Interview a student in third to fifth grade about the equals sign. Present the student with a problem similar to the following: $5 + 9 = \_\_ + 6$. Ask the student to explain his or her thinking.

4. What are some advantages of using a pan balance to solve algebraic equations? Illustrate how you might use a pan balance to solve $3x + 7 = 4x - 9$.

5. Given the following table, how would you find the recursive relationship? What is it? How would you find the explicit relationship? What is it? Why is it important to be able to find explicit relationships?

1	2	3	4	5	6	7
2	5	8	11	14	17	20

6. How can you tell whether a function is linear without graphing it? Give examples of two linear functions and two nonlinear functions.

7. **Using visuals** This chapter illustrates repeating and growing patterns with interesting visuals. Develop a visual display that might appear on a bulletin board in your own classroom to illustrate examples of repeating and growing patterns.

What is happening in this picture?

Think Critically

Look closely at this photograph. How might you use this photograph to introduce the concept of integers with elementary school students?

Self-Test

(Check your answers in Appendix D.)

1. What other topics within mathematics use algebra extensively?

2. What concepts were being introduced by taking students on the train in the Algebra Project?

3. What incorrect answers might children give for the following statement? $6 + 9 = \underline{\quad} + 5$
   What is the correct answer?

4. Solve the following without computation: $373 + 29 = \underline{\quad} + 32$. Explain your solution.

5. What are the three different meanings of *variable*? Provide an example of each meaning.

6. Solve the following: $2x + 3 = 6x - 9$.

7. What kinds of patterns are shown in this figure?

8. What are the two types of patterns? Give a nonnumerical example of each type.

9. Explain how to find the 20th triangular number and the *n*th triangular number.

Triangular numbers	Table 14.3						
Term Number *n*	1	2	3	4	5…	10…	20
Number of Dots	1	3	6	10	15…	55…	210

10. Explain the difference between an explicit and a recursive formula.

11. Solve each of the following:

    a. $(+3) + (-5)$

    b. $(-9) + (-4)$

    c. $(+12) - (-3)$

    d. $(-10) - (+5)$

12. Give the next three terms for each of the following sequences.

    a. 2, 2, 4, 6, 10, __, __, __

    b. 1, 4, 9, 16, __, __, __

    c. 2, 6, 12, 20, __, __, __

    d. 4, 8, 16, 32, __, __, __

13. Given the following table:

1	2	3	4	5
5	7	9	11	13

    a. Find the sixth term.

    b. Find the *n*th term.

14. Is the rule illustrated by the table of values illustrated in question 13 a function? How can you tell? If so, list the domain and the range.

15. Is the rule illustrated by the table of values in question 13 a linear function? How can you tell?

THE PLANNER ✓

Review your Chapter Planner on the chapter opener and check off your completed work.

Geometry

Throughout history, events such as births, deaths, and marriages were recorded with textiles including quilts. In the United States, women made quilts as early as the 1700s. Quilting gained in popularity in the mid-1800s, after fabrics became widely available. During the 1800s and early 1900s, quilting remained a way to record important family events but also evolved into a social and creative outlet for women. Quilting circles or quilting bees were organized to share patterns and help friends finish their projects.

Although distinctive quilt designs have emerged in different geographic regions and through diverse cultural traditions, quilts share many geometric properties. Children in the primary grades can examine the shapes, patterns, and symmetry in quilts and even design their own quilt squares with construction paper. Children in the upper elementary and middle grades can analyze the polygonal shapes, symmetry, and transformations often displayed in quilts. By studying the geometric characteristics of quilts, children can learn that geometry is a tool that has been used by people for centuries to help them understand and interpret their physical environment.

Quilting is one real-world use of geometry that provides a concrete way for children to begin to understand the subject. Most quilts are made from square blocks of patterns and display polygonal shapes as well as symmetry and transformations.

CHAPTER OUTLINE

Learning About Geometry   370

Key Question: How do the van Hiele levels influence the geometry curriculum in the elementary and middle grades?

Learning About Shapes and Properties   372

Key Question: What should students in the elementary and middle grades know about shapes and properties?

Learning About Location   384

Key Question: What types of knowledge should students in the elementary and middle grades learn about location?

Learning About Transformations   388

Key Question: How does the study of transformations connect to art and culture?

Learning About Visualization   393

Key Question: What types of experiences help students in the elementary and middle grades develop visualization skills?

NCTM The NCTM Geometry Standard has four main objectives.

Instructional programs from prekindergarten through grade 12 should enable all students to

- analyze characteristics and properties of two- and three-dimensional geometric shapes and develop mathematical arguments about geometric relationships;
- specify locations and describe spatial relationships using coordinate geometry and other representational systems;
- apply transformations and use symmetry to analyze mathematical situations;
- use visualization, spatial reasoning, and geometric modeling to solve problems. (NCTM, 2000, p. 96)

Specific objectives for each grade-level band are listed within these four major categories and can be found in Appendix A.

Learning About Geometry

LEARNING OBJECTIVES

1. **Describe** the van Hiele levels of geometric thought.

2. **Discuss** why learning geometry is important at every grade level.

Geometry can be a fascinating topic for children. Just as children spend hours building models and solving puzzles for play, they can spend hours engaged with physical or virtual manipulatives for learning geometry. Geometry is a practical, engaging, and important topic that is often ignored or underrepresented in the elementary and middle school curriculum. Geometry should receive a great deal more attention than it does. This section examines the theory of how children learn geometry and explains why geometric knowledge is crucial to children's mathematical development.

The van Hiele Levels of Geometric Thought

In 1959, two Dutch researchers, Pierre van Hiele and Dina van Hiele-Geldof, developed a theory of how children learn geometry that is still widely accepted today. The van Hiele theory influenced how geometry curriculum was developed. As you read about the van Hiele levels of geometric thought, try to determine your own level of geometric thought. Clements and Battista (1992) and Battista (2009, 2007) have studied this model extensively and made some modifications (**Figure 15.1**).

Most children in prekindergarten through grade 2 perform at level 1. Some children in the upper elementary and middle grades are also at level 1. Strive to move children from level 1 to level 2 in the elementary grades and to level 3 in the middle grades (Battista, 2009).

The van Hiele model will not tell you how to teach geometry, but it can help you diagnose the level at which your students are working. This knowledge can help you adapt activities to meet the level of each of your students.

Why Is It Important for Children to Learn Geometry?

"Geometry enables us to describe, analyze, and understand our physical world, so there is little wonder that it holds a central place in mathematics or that it should be a focus throughout the school mathematics curriculum" (Findell et al., 2001, p. 1). Through the study of geometry, teachers can help children understand both the artistic and the logical components of mathematics and can provide them with opportunities to test their conjectures and actually prove them. Through the study of geometry, children will

- learn to reason logically, make justifications, and build connections between ideas. They can use these skills to study other topics in mathematics and science.

- learn to make sense of their physical environment and develop spatial and location skills. This can help children develop awareness of their physical space as well as practical skills such as map reading.

- learn to understand geometric representations. These can be applied to topics such as fractions, area, whole number multiplication, and data analysis.

- increase their spatial ability and the ability to visualize how objects look from different perspectives.

CONCEPT CHECK **STOP**

1. **How** might children at level 1 describe a triangle? How might children at level 2 describe a triangle?

2. **How** can learning geometry help students succeed in other academic areas? Provide two examples.

The van Hiele model of geometric thought (as modified by Clements and Battista) • Figure 15.1

The van Hiele model describes how children's geometric reasoning develops. Although their theory applies to all areas of geometry, it is explained here using properties of shapes. Three features of the model are as follows:

1. Children move through all the levels sequentially.
2. Children's advancement through the levels is influenced by instruction rather than maturity.
3. Children cannot learn geometry if they are instructed at a higher level than they have attained.

Level 1: Visual-Holistic Reasoning (Battista, 2009, p. 92)

At this level, children sort objects holistically. They may think that a shape is a rectangle because it is long and narrow. Orientation is very important for them. For example, children may not think a square is a square if it is rotated.

Level 2: Descriptive-Analytic Reasoning (Battista, 2009, p. 92)

At this level, children use a combination of informal and formal language to describe geometric shapes. They begin to focus on the properties of specific figures, such as what makes a shape a square, and ignore irrelevant features such as size, color, and orientation.

Level 3: Relational-Inferential Reasoning (Battista, 2009, p. 93)

At this level, children make inferences about geometric properties and understand abstract definitions. For example, a child might say, "If it is a square then it is also a rectangle, because a square has all the properties of a rectangle." They begin to understand the minimum characteristics necessary to define each type of shape.

Level 4: Formal Deductive Proof (Battista, 2009, p. 94)

At this level, students construct formal proofs. This is the type of geometry that is often taught in secondary school in the United States.

Level 5: Rigor (Battista, 2009, p. 94)

At this level, students are able to work with alternative systems of geometry. College-level geometry courses often discuss these systems.

PROCESS DIAGRAM

Learning About Shapes and Properties

LEARNING OBJECTIVES

1. **Describe** how children learn about shapes and properties in prekindergarten through grade 2.

2. **Describe** how children learn about shapes and properties in grades 3–5.

3. **Describe** how children learn about shapes and properties in grades 6–8.

Much of the elementary geometry curriculum is devoted to the study of shapes and their properties. According to *Curriculum Focal Points* (2006) and the *Common Core State Standards* (NGS Center/CCSSO, 2010), children begin their study of shapes in the primary grades (prekindergarten through grade 2) and continue to study shapes and their properties in the upper elementary grades (3–5) and middle school. As children progress through school, their knowledge of shapes becomes more formalized. They come to understand both two- and three-dimensional shapes, develop more precise vocabulary, and build generalizations about classes of geometric shapes.

Shapes and Properties for Prekindergarten Through Grade 2

Children in prekindergarten through grade 2 usually perform at van Hiele level 1 (visual-holistic reasoning), although many of the activities presented here also can be adapted to level 2. In prekindergarten, "they find shapes in their environment and describe them in their own words" (NCTM, 2006, p. 11). In kindergarten, they focus on shape orientation, learn to identify shapes by name, and begin to observe what makes shapes alike and different (NCTM, 2006). In grade 1, children begin to **compose** and **decompose** geometric shapes. In grade 2, children continue to compose and decompose shapes, "intentionally substituting arrangements of smaller shapes for larger shapes or substituting larger shapes for many smaller shapes" (NCTM, 2006, p. 14).

Sorting and classifying In the primary grades, children need many opportunities to sort and classify both two- and three-dimensional shapes. Ask children to work with three-dimensional shapes first because they are more realistic reflections of their environment. Two-dimensional shapes are really just very thin three-dimensional shapes

and initially can be confusing for children. **Activity 15.1** and **Activity 15.2** illustrate some beginning activities for classifying three-dimensional shapes. In these activities, focus on children's ability to identify shapes holistically, recognize their characteristics, and identify what is alike and different, rather than focusing on the formal names or properties of the shapes. Help children focus on what distinguishes one shape from another, such as the number of sides, the number of **vertices** (corners), and the number of **faces** (flat surfaces for three-dimensional shapes). Gradually include formal vocabulary, so that, by the end of grade 2, children are able to identify shapes by their names and properties (*it is a cube and it has six faces*).

Activity 15.1 Alike and different (van Hiele level 1)

Instructions

1. Show a cube, rectangular prism, and cylinder. It is not necessary for students to identify these shapes by name. Say: *Two of these shapes belong together and one does not. Which shape does not belong with the others? Why?* (Many explanations are possible, but the cylinder does not belong. It has no corners.)

2. Repeat with other examples in which two of the figures are alike in some way and the other is different, such as (1) a tall cylinder, a short and wide cylinder, and a cone or (2) a triangular pyramid, a square pyramid, and a sphere.

After the children have had many opportunities to sort and classify three-dimensional shapes, introduce two-dimensional shapes. Ask the children to sort

Activity 15.2 Find my shape
(van Hiele levels 1 and 2)

Instructions

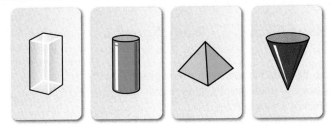

1. Children work in groups of four. Give each group the same set of four three-dimensional shapes. Make up a card with an accurate drawing for each of the shapes (four cards). Place the cards face-down with each group.

2. Designate one child in each group to select a card so that the other children cannot see what is drawn on it. Each of the other children in the group guess which shape is on the card by asking questions about it. Sample questions are: *Is it curved? Does it have a point on top?*

3. After the shape is correctly identified, another child in the group selects a new card and becomes the card holder. Then they play the game again.

4. Continue playing until all four cards have been used.

and classify two-dimensional shapes using Activities 15.1 and 15.2. Focus on the number of sides and vertices. Rather than giving formal definitions of two-dimensional shapes, have children select examples and non-examples of individual shapes (**Activity 15.3**). Templates for geoboards and dot paper can be found in Appendix E.

The **circle** is a two-dimensional shape that does not have sides or vertices. It is a shape that young children learn easily because it is already a part of their everyday experiences. Teachers often ask children to make a circle when playing games, learning dances, or sitting on the floor for reading time. Let the activities of the classroom help children identify the properties of a circle. **Activity 15.4** offers a kinesthetic approach and differentiates instruction for those students who learn in this way. It also introduces the **center** of a circle.

circle A set of points that are equally distant from a fixed point.

center A point inside the circle that is equally distant from all points on the circle.

Activity 15.3 Am I a triangle?
(van Hiele levels 1 and 2)

Instructions

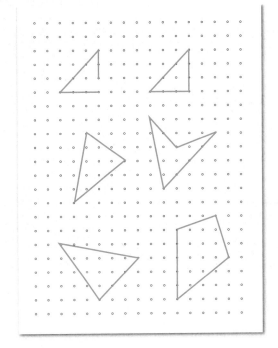

1. Show children examples of triangles and non-triangles. Ask them to decide which of these are triangles and why.

2. Ask children to create examples of non-triangles and triangles on geoboards and record on dot paper.

3. Ask: *What makes a shape a triangle?*

4. Repeat with other two-dimensional shapes.

Activity 15.4 Make a circle
(van Hiele levels 1 and 2)

Instructions

1. Select 12 or 15 children for each group, depending on the size of your class.

2. Give each child in each group a colorful sheet of paper. Have many colors available.

3. Ask each group of children to form a circle, put their sheet of paper down at their feet, and step outside of the circle.

4. As a class, look at each circle formed by the sheets of paper. Ask children to walk around and through their circle. Identify the inside and the outside of the circle.

5. Ask: *Is there a point from inside the circle where you can see all the pieces of paper clearly?* (Identify the center of the circle.)

CHILDREN'S LITERATURE

Identifying circles and squares in everyday life

So Many Circles, So Many Squares •
Figure 15.2

Written by Tana Hoban, with photographs by the author
In this book of photographs, Tana Hoban finds two- and three-dimensional circles and squares in her everyday world. Circles and spheres are found in buttons, bicycle wheels, onions, and tomatoes. Squares and cubes are found in grids, pipes, exhaust fans, luggage, and boxes.

Strategies for the Classroom

- Show your class each picture and ask them to identify all the shapes they see.

- For each shape, ask: *Can you think of another example of this shape?*

After introducing circles, ask children to find real-world examples of them. Compare circles to other shapes, and describe how they are different or alike. Children's literature provides a great way to help children sort and classify both two- and three-dimensional shapes and recognize that they are part of our physical environment (see *Children's Literature,* **Figure 15.2**).

Composing and decomposing shapes Children need many opportunities to play with two- and three-dimensional shapes, to build with them and see how things fit together and come apart. Pierre M. van Hiele (1999) believes that, for children, geometry should begin with free play. He uses a seven-piece mosaic puzzle as the source of his activities (**Activity 15.5**). Van Hiele suggests that children be given the opportunity to play with the pieces of the puzzle. In this way, they will discover on their own how to compose and decompose the shapes of the puzzle and build new shapes.

Activity 15.5 Van Hiele's mosaic puzzle (van Hiele levels 1 and 2)

Instructions

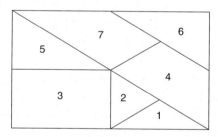

1. Create the mosaic puzzle on cardstock for your students. Number each piece as in the figure.

2. Ask the children to find all the triangles and all the quadrilaterals by number.

3. Say: *Use some or all of these pieces to create your own designs.* Give the children time to play and explore with the pieces of the puzzle.

4. Ask: *Which of these pieces can be made from others?* (One example: 5 and 6 can make 3.)

5. Ask: *Are there any pieces that cannot be made by combining others?* (1 and 2)

Pattern blocks and geoboards are popular tools for composing and decomposing shapes (**Activities 15.6** and **15.7**). Find templates for these manipulatives in Appendix E.

Activity 15.6 Making designs with pattern blocks (van Hiele levels 1 and 2)

Instructions

1. Distribute to each group of four students one set of pattern blocks, consisting of 2 yellow hexagons, 4 red trapezoids, 6 blue rhombuses, and 12 green triangles.

2. Ask the children to make designs using 3, 4, 5, or 6 green triangles. For each design, ask: *Can you make this design with other pieces too?* Questions such as these encourage children to discover the relationships between the different pieces (*6 green make a yellow, 2 red make a yellow, 3 green make a red, etc.*).

3. After the children have had many opportunities to make designs that start with triangles, have them begin with other combinations such as triangles and rhombuses. In each case, ask how they can substitute one shape for another.

Activity 15.7 Making designs with a geoboard (van Hiele levels 1 and 2)

Instructions

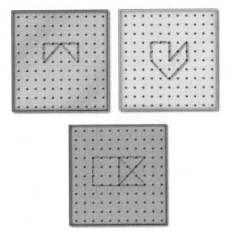

1. Distribute geoboard and rubber bands to each child. Have a transparent geoboard for your projection system.

2. Make shapes on the transparent geoboard, beginning with simpler shapes that require one band and progressing to more complex shapes that require two or more bands. Ask the children to reproduce each shape on their own geoboards.

3. Ask: *Who can draw a house on the geoboard?* Invite a child or pair of children to illustrate for the class. Ask: *Who can draw the letter* L? *Who can draw the letter* X?

4. Challenge children to create their own representations on the geoboards.

Tech Tools

www.nctm.org

Go to the NCTM Web site. Select **Standards and Focal Points** and then **e–Examples**. Under pre-K to grade 2, select example 4.2, **Investigating the Concept of a Triangle.** This applet uses an interactive geoboard to allow the user to make triangles and other figures.

CHILDREN'S LITERATURE

Composing and decomposing geometric shapes

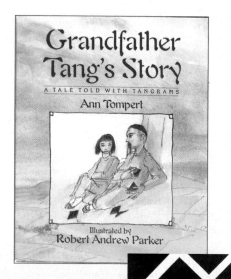

Grandfather Tang's Story: A Tale Told with Tangrams • Figure 15.3

Written by Ann Tompert
Illustrated by Robert Andrew Parker

In this charming tale from Chinese folklore, two fox fairies change themselves into different creatures as part of a game. Each time they change form, their new form is described with tangrams. Even though their game began as fun, it soon becomes competitive and even dangerous.

Strategies for the Classroom

- Before you read the story with children, provide each child with a set of tangram pieces and time to explore them.

- While reading the story, ask the children to make each of the figures described. It can be helpful to make transparencies of the figures so that the children can refer to them easily.

- After reading the story, challenge the children to use some or all of the shapes to make animals or objects from their everyday lives.

- Challenge the children to make a square from two shapes (easy) and a square from four shapes (difficult).

- Ask the children to make a rectangle from three shapes (easy) and a rectangle from all seven shapes (difficult).

Tangrams are another popular manipulative for composing and decomposing shapes. This ancient Chinese puzzle is made out of a square that is subdivided into seven pieces: five triangles and two quadrilaterals (see *Children's Literature*, **Figure 15.3**). Find a template for making your own tangram in Appendix E.

Teaching Tip

Helping children learn the names of geometric shapes

- Add the names of geometric shapes to weekly spelling lists. Give children the opportunity to spell, say, and write the names of shapes as well as to pair the name of a shape with its picture.

- Post pictures of shapes along with their names around the classroom or make a chart with shapes and their names.

By the end of grade 2, children should know the names of geometric shapes. This can be very difficult for some children. Sometimes, the vocabulary words are problematic (Casa and Gavin, 2009). Some terms, such as *rhombus*, are completely new and are not spelled the way they sound. Other words can have more than one meaning. For example, "right" has a geometric meaning and more than one meaning in everyday life. This is especially challenging for English-language learners. Casa and Gavin suggest modeling appropriate language, encouraging children to use precise vocabulary, and asking them to justify their reasoning in writing.

Shapes and Properties for Grades 3–5

In grades 3–5, children continue their exploration of shapes but in a more focused and formal way. In grade 3, "students describe, analyze, and compare two-dimensional shapes by their sides and angles and connect these attributes to the definitions of shapes" (NCTM, 2006, p. 15). In grade 4, they focus on areas of two-dimensional shapes (discussed in Chapter 16). In grade 5, they analyze the properties of three-dimensional shapes. Some children may still be at van Hiele level 1, while others may be making the transition from level 1 to level 2.

Simple closed curves and polygons • Figure 15.4

  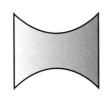

a. Which of these figures represent simple closed curves?

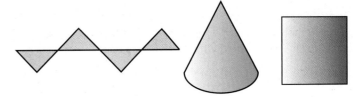

b. Which of these figures represent polygons?

> **simple closed curve**
> A curve that can be traced from starting point to ending point without crossing over the curve or retracing any part of it.
>
> **polygon** A simple closed curve whose sides are straight.

Two-dimensional shapes

As children formalize their knowledge of two-dimensional shapes, explain the definitions of **simple closed curve** and **polygon** (**Figure 15.4**). Most of the two-dimensional shapes discussed are polygons.

Children often learn to identify **angles** and **sides** for two-dimensional shapes first. In order to classify polygons and identify their properties, children must understand angle measure (**Figure 15.5**). This concept is more completely discussed in Chapter 16.

> **congruence** Quality of geometric figures by which they have the same size and shape.

To classify polygons, children need to understand **congruence** for shapes, sides, and angles. In **Activity 15.8** children are asked to make congruent shapes that match the shape made by their teacher. This activity assesses not only children's understanding of congruence but also their van Hiele level of geometric thought. If children have difficulty recognizing that two shapes may be congruent even when they are colored or rotated differently, they are still at van Hiele level 1.

Activity 15.8 Making congruent shapes (van Hiele levels 1 and 2)

Instructions

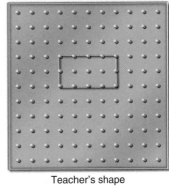 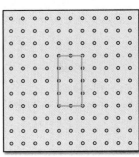

Teacher's shape   Students' shape

1. Make a shape on a geoboard that all class members can see. This works best if you have a transparent geoboard that can be used at an overhead projector or a virtual geoboard.

2. Ask the students to make a congruent shape on their geoboards and then make and color the shape on dot paper.

3. Discuss student responses by asking individual students to bring their drawn shapes to the front of the class to compare with the teacher's.

The different types of angles • Figure 15.5

Angles are measured in degrees.

 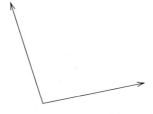 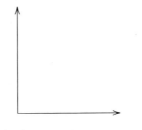

a. An **acute angle** measures less than 90 degrees.

b. An **obtuse angle** measures more than 90 degrees and less than 180 degrees.

c. A **right angle** measures exactly 90 degrees.

d. A **straight angle** measures exactly 180 degrees.

Education InSight

Classifying two-dimensional shapes • Figure 15.6

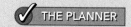
In grades 3–5, children classify triangles and quadrilaterals. Triangles are classified by their sides or their angles. Quadrilaterals are classified by the lengths of their sides, by the size of their angles, or by whether their sides are parallel.

a. Triangles

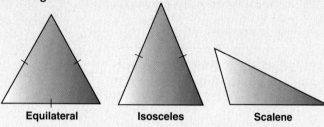
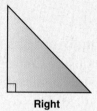
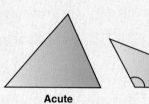
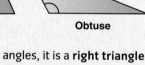

Equilateral Isosceles Scalene Right Acute Obtuse

1. When a triangle is classified by its sides, it is an **equilateral triangle** if all sides are equal, an **isosceles triangle** if at least two sides are equal, and a **scalene triangle** if no sides are equal.

2. When a triangle is classified by its angles, it is a **right triangle** if one angle is a right angle, an **acute triangle** if each angle is an acute angle, and an **obtuse triangle** if one angle is obtuse.

b. Quadrilaterals

Three types of quadrilaterals are classified: kites, parallelograms, and trapezoids.

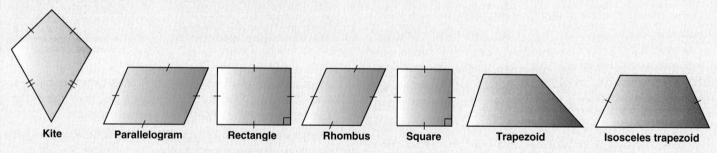

Kite Parallelogram Rectangle Rhombus Square Trapezoid Isosceles trapezoid

1. A quadrilateral with two pairs of adjacent congruent sides is a kite.

2. A quadrilateral that has opposite sides congruent and parallel is a **parallelogram**. A parallelogram with four right angles is a **rectangle**. A parallelogram with all sides congruent is a **rhombus**. A parallelogram with four sides equal and a right angle is a **square**.

3. A quadrilateral with one pair of parallel sides is a **trapezoid**. A trapezoid whose nonparallel sides are congruent is an **isosceles trapezoid**.

c. Circles

All circles have the same shape, whether they are large or small. The center of the circle is the point inside the circle that is equally distant from all points on the circle. The **radius** is the line segment drawn from the center to a point on the circle.

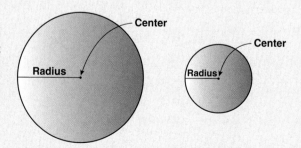

Center
Center
Radius
Radius

Classifying quadrilaterals • Figure 15.7

How can this diagram help you to classify quadrilaterals?

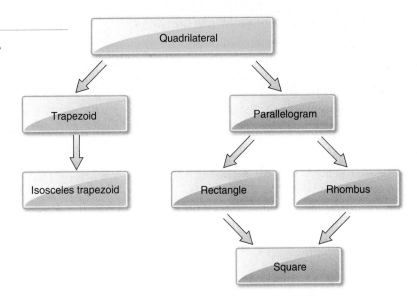

parallel Term describing two lines or line segments that never intersect.

perpendicular Term describing two lines or line segments that intersect in a 90-degree angle.

Children also need an understanding of **parallel** and **perpendicular** lines or line segments. They should have an informal understanding of these concepts from their everyday lives.

After children learn the meaning of these geometric concepts they are ready to learn to classify two-dimensional shapes (**Figure 15.6**).

Children may become confused when some shapes are classified by more than one name. For example, a square is also a rectangle, a rhombus, and a parallelogram. You can help them understand these multiple classifications by asking them how they would describe themselves. A girl might describe herself as daughter, sister, granddaughter, and Girl Scout. There are many different classifications for one child, just as there may be many classifications for one figure. **Figure 15.7** provides a helpful visual method for remembering the classifications of quadrilaterals. The *Virtual Classroom Observation* highlights how you might talk to children about squares and rectangles.

Virtual Classroom Observation

Video www.wiley.com/college/jones

Click on **Student Companion Site**. Then Click on:

• **Foundations of Effective Mathematics Teaching**

• **B. Focus on Teacher Content Knowledge**

• **3. Analyze Classroom Videos**

View:

• **2D and 3D Figures: Is a square a rectangle?**

In this video, Ms. Airesman questions her students about rectangles and squares and helps them understand that all squares are rectangles but not all rectangles are squares. She emphasizes the use of appropriate mathematical language.

Geometry software can help children understand quadrilaterals. Many commercial products are available, such as *Shape Makers*, an add-on to *Geometer's Sketchpad*. With the Parallelogram Maker applet from this software, children can click and drag on parallelograms to change their shape and size but retain their identity (Yu, Barrett, and Presmeg, 2009). There are also many free applets available.

Tech Tools

www.nctm.org

Go to the NCTM Web site. Select **Standards and Focal Points**, then select **e–Examples**. Under grades 3–5, select applet 5.3, **Exploring Properties of Rectangles and Parallelograms: Using Dynamic Software**. These types of explorations can help move children from van Hiele level 1 to level 2.

The sum of the angles of a triangle •
Figure 15.8

Draw a triangle. Imagine that you have torn off each corner to represent each of the angles. Now take these corners and arrange them around a point. Together they form a straight line or a straight angle, which measures 180 degrees. The sum of the angles of any triangle is 180 degrees. Because any quadrilateral is composed of two triangles, the sum of the angles of any quadrilateral is 360 degrees.

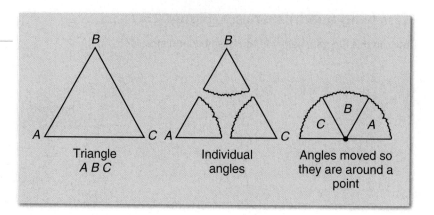

Triangle ABC

Individual angles

Angles moved so they are around a point

The sum of the angles in a triangle It is relatively easy to have children prove for themselves that the sum of the angles in a triangle is 180 degrees. This is a helpful fact for them to know and applies to other concepts in geometry (**Figure 15.8**).

Three-dimensional shapes

In grades 3–5, children learn more formal definitions of three-dimensional figures. Many of these shapes are **polyhedra**. **Table 15.1** provides a list of some commonly used shapes.

> **polyhedra** Three-dimensional shapes made up of polygonal regions that have no more than one side in common.

Once students learn the different types of three-dimensional solids, they learn to distinguish **right** prisms, cylinders, pyramids, or cones and the different types of prisms and pyramids (**Figure 15.9**). Prisms and pyramids are classified by

> **right** A type of prism, pyramid, cylinder, or cone whose base is perpendicular to its height.

Prisms, cylinders, pyramids, and cones •
Figure 15.9

Can you find the right cylinder, the square pyramid, the triangular pyramid, and the right cone?

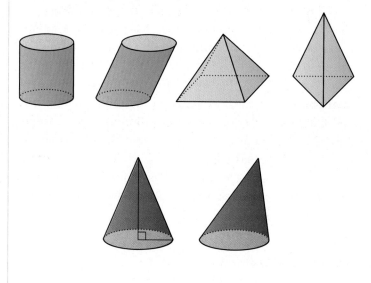

Three-dimensional shapes		Table 15.1
Name	**Shape**	**Definition**
Prism		A polyhedron with two opposite faces that are congruent and parallel.
Pyramid		A polyhedron that has a polygon for its base with triangular sides that meet at a point not on the base, called the **apex**.
Cylinder		A curved solid that has opposite, simple, closed-curve bases. The lines joining the bases are parallel.
Cone		A curved solid that has one simple, closed-curve base and one vertex that is not part of the base.

the shapes of their bases. Thus a square pyramid has a square base and a rectangular prism has rectangular bases.

Children can build their own three-dimensional shapes using toothpicks and marshmallows, straws and pipe cleaners, or newspapers and tape. When children construct three-dimensional objects themselves, they develop insights into the object's component parts (**Activity 15.9**).

Geometry has many definitions that can be stressful for children to learn, especially for English-language learners. Teachers can create games and other fun activities to help children learn the meaning of geometric terms (see *In the Classroom*).

Activity 15.9 Constructing polyhedra from newspaper and tape (van Hiele levels 2 and 3)

Instructions

1. Pairs of students work with several sheets of newspaper and tape.

2. Each pair of students rolls at least three sheets of newspaper tightly together from corner to opposite corner and secures with tape.

3. Repeat until six rolls have been completed. Assemble them as a pyramid.

4. Ask: *What geometric shapes make up this pyramid?* (Triangles) *How many triangles make up this pyramid?* (4)

5. Ask the children to identify the faces, vertices, and edges.

6. Ask them to construct other polygonal solids with rolled-up newspaper.

In the Classroom

Learning Geometric Terms with "Geometry Simon Says"

 THE PLANNER

Third-grade teacher Katie Wilson plays a game with her students during geometry. As each new geometric term is introduced, Ms. Wilson demonstrates a body position for the term and then has her students model it. Here are some examples.

Term	Body Position
Line	Arms straight out at sides with fingers pointing out
Line segment	Arms straight out at sides with hands in fists
Ray	Arms straight out at sides, one hand pointing out and other in fist
Right angle	One arm straight out to side, other hand straight up
Parallel lines	Arms straight out in front or straight up

After all the terms are introduced, Ms. Wilson calls out terms at random and the children use their bodies to illustrate each term. Playing the game is fun for students, and it helps them to visualize what the terms mean by making the motion with their bodies. The children take turns being the caller, so that Ms. Wilson can play, too!

Think Critically

1. How might children represent a triangle with their bodies?
2. Why do you think using a technique such as the one demonstrated by Ms. Wilson might help children learn shapes?

Shapes and Properties for Grades 6–8

In the middle grades, students use logical reasoning to examine properties of shapes more formally, considering, for example, the minimum characteristics necessary to define a rhombus. They also investigate the properties of **similarity** and congruence, topics that are addressed informally in the lower grades. In **Activity 15.10**, students construct a **Sierpinski triangle** to study similarity and congruence in triangles. In **Activity 15.11**, students answer questions that test their understanding of geometric shapes and similarity.

> **similarity** The quality of geometric shapes that have the same shape but not necessarily the same size.
>
> **Sierpinski triangle** A fractal design that is constructed from iterations of an equilateral triangle.

Activity 15.10 Finding similarity and congruence in the Sierpinski triangle (van Hiele levels 2 and 3)

Instructions

1. Ask students to draw an equilateral triangle (all sides equal) with a horizontal base and each side measuring 2 inches. Imagine that this triangle is solid.

2. Ask students to find the midpoint of each side and connect those points. Imagine that this inverted triangle has been removed.

3. Ask: *How many small triangles remain?* (3)

4. Ask: *Which of the triangles are congruent?* (The three small triangles)

5. Ask: *Are the small triangles similar to the large triangle? Why?* (The small triangles are also equilateral, so they are similar to the larger triangle.)

Activity 15.11 Which shapes are similar? (van Hiele levels 2 and 3)

Instructions

1. Ask: *Are all squares similar? Why or why not?* (Yes, they all have the same shape.)

2. Ask: *Are all rectangles similar? Why or why not?* (No, rectangles can have different shapes.)

3. Say: *Draw a pair of rectangles that are similar and a pair that are not similar.*

4. Ask: *What other shapes are always similar to one another?* (Circles)

Students in the middle grades formally explore the **Pythagorean relationship** (**Activity 15.12**). This is an important relationship and one that is fairly easy to prove. Students extend their knowledge of the Pythagorean relationship in **Activity 15.13**.

> **Pythagorean relationship** In a right triangle, the square of the side opposite the right angle is equal to the sum of the squares of the other two sides.

Activity 15.12 The Pythagorean relationship (van Hiele levels 2 and 3)

Instructions

1. Ask students to draw a right triangle on grid paper so that one leg is horizontal and one leg is vertical.

2. Next, draw a square on each leg of the triangle and on the leg opposite the **hypotenuse** (the side opposite the right angle).

3. Find the area of each square.

4. The sum of the areas of the smaller squares is equal to the area of the large square.

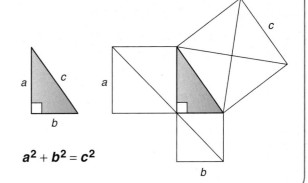

$$a^2 + b^2 = c^2$$

Activity 15.13 Finding Pythagorean triples (van Hiele levels 2 and 3)

Instructions

1. Ask students to construct a right triangle on grid paper, with perpendicular sides of length 3 and 4 units long on the grid.

2. Say: *Use the Pythagorean relationship to find the length of the hypotenuse.* (5 units)

3. Next ask students to construct a new right triangle on the same sheet of grid paper with the same orientation and sides of length 6 and 8 units.

4. Ask: *Can anyone guess the length of the hypotenuse without using the Pythagorean relationship? Support your guess with reasoning.* (Because these triangles are similar, their sides are proportional. Since 2 x 3 = 6 and 2 x 4 = 8, 2 x 5 = 10 and the length of the hypotenuse = 10 units.)

5. Ask: *How could you describe these two triangles?* (They are similar.)

6. Ask: *Now suppose you had a right triangle with perpendicular sides of length 12 and 16 units. What is the length of the hypotenuse?* (20 units)

7. Say: *Numbers such as 3, 4, and 5 form what is called a **Pythagorean triple**. All multiples of these numbers can also be the sides of a right triangle. Would all such triangles be similar?* (Yes)

8. Say: *There are other Pythagorean triples. Can you find one set?* (5, 12, 13)

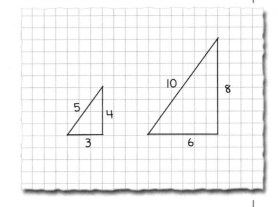

CONCEPT CHECK   **STOP**

1. **What** are two types of activities that are important for children to experience in prekindergarten through grade 2 when learning about shapes and properties?

2. **What** are three types of shapes that children learn to classify in grades 3–5?

3. **What** concepts about shapes and their properties are studied in more depth in grades 6–8?

Learning About Location

LEARNING OBJECTIVES

1. **Describe** how to teach location to children in prekindergarten through grade 2.

2. **Describe** how to teach location to children in grades 3–5.

3. **Explain** how to use the Pythagorean relationship to learn how to find the distance between two points.

Do you remember how you learned the meaning of words such as *in front*, *in back*, and *between*? Children in the primary grades learn the meanings of these terms as part of their beginning work on location. In the upper elementary grades, children's understanding of location becomes more complex. In the middle grades, they apply what they learned about location to coordinate geometry. This section discusses how to teach children about location and spatial relationships at different grade levels.

Location for Prekindergarten Through Grade 2

In the primary grades, children learn to answer the questions, "Where is it?" and "Which way is it?" (Findell et al., 2001, p. 4). At first, they learn to place an object in relation to other objects. For example, when asked, "Where is the teddy bear?" a child might say, "It's on the bed." Later, through acting out stories and other activities based in play, children learn the meaning of "above, below, in front, behind, between, to the left, to the right, next to, and other relative positions" (p. 4). Young children can also learn to use simple grids and to construct basic maps (**Activities 15.14** and **15.15**).

Activity 15.14 Follow directions (van Hiele level 1)

Instructions

1. Working with a small group of children, set out the same number of chairs as there are children in a semicircle and place an object that will not roll off on each chair (a book or stuffed toy works well).

2. Ask each child to stand in front of a chair.

3. Ask each child to stand behind the chair.

4. Ask them to hold the object that was placed on the chair above the chair.

5. Ask them to place the object under the chair.

6. Ask them to put the object between their chair and the next chair.

Activity 15.15 Find my place (van Hiele level 1)

Instructions

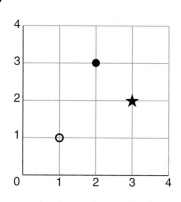

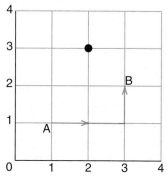

1. Give each child a 4 x 4 grid.

2. Show children how to number the grid. Explain that the numbers along the bottom, or horizontal line, tell how far to move to the right and the numbers along the side, or vertical line, tell how far to move up.

3. Select a point and describe that point for children. For example, say, *This point is 2 right and 3 up.*

4. Point to other locations and ask children to identify them with **coordinates**.

5. Identify two points on the grid. Label one with a circle and one with a star. Ask: *How can I get from the circle to the star by traveling along the lines of the grid?*

6. Repeat with other pairs of points.

7. Replace circle and star with A and B. Explain that these letters help us name the points.

Tech Tools

www.nctm.org

Go to the NCTM Web site. Select **Standards and Focal Points** and then **e–Examples**. Under **pre-K to grade 2**, select example 4.3, **Learning Geometry and Measurement Concepts by Creating Paths and Navigating Mazes**. Select the **Hiding Ladybug** applet. To play, children must choose a path for a ladybug who is trying to hide under a leaf.

Location for Grades 3–5

In grades 3–5, children's understanding of directions becomes more sophisticated. They replace the directional terms with more accurate terms, such as *north* and *south*. Children also learn that there may be more than one route between two places and that one may be better (shorter)

Activity 15.16 Where did I go? (van Hiele level 1)

Instructions

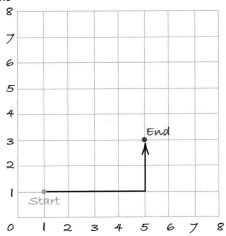

1. Provide each student with a grid, at least 8 x 8 in size. Have one copy for projection.

2. Ask the students to number their grids. Mark a spot in the lower left side of the projected grid.

3. Say: *The other day my friend started out at her house, here* (show marked spot on grid).

4. Say: *She was talking to me on her cell phone as she walked, and she told me that she walked four blocks east and then two blocks north. Where did she go?*

5. Say: *Please identify my friend's final location.*

6. Say: *If you started out from my friend's house, could you get to where she is now by taking another path (only walking along the lines of the grid)?*

than the other. In these grades, children also understand that some directions are relational (such as left or right) or subjective, whereas others, such as north, south, east, and west, are fixed. Children also become more adept at using coordinate grids and learn the terms *x axis* and *y axis*. They come to understand that the first coordinate is *x* and the second coordinate is *y*. These ideas are illustrated in **Activities 15.16** and **15.17**.

Activity 15.17 What's the same? (van Hiele level 1)

Instructions

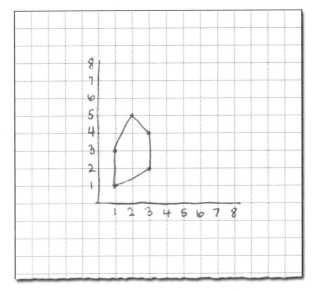

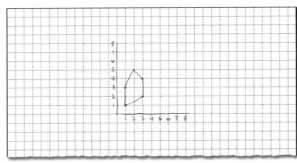

1. Provide each child with two sheets of grid paper: $\frac{1}{2}$-centimeter grid paper and 1-centimeter grid paper.

2. Challenge the children to design a shape, graph it on the 1-centimeter grid paper, and record all the coordinates of the shape.

3. Ask the children to graph the same coordinates on the $\frac{1}{2}$-centimeter grid paper.

4. Ask: *What do you notice?* (The shapes have the same set of coordinates, but the second shape is smaller because the grid is smaller. Both shapes are similar, but the corresponding sides of the shape on the smaller grid are one-half the length of those of the larger grid.)

LESSON Finding the Distance Between Two Points

GRADE LEVEL
8

OBJECTIVES
Find the distance between any two points.
Express the distance between any two points with variables.

STANDARDS

Grade 8
They apply the Pythagorean theorem to find distances between points in the Cartesian coordinate plane to measure lengths and analyze polygons and polyhedra. (NCTM, 2006, p. 20)

Apply the Pythagorean Theorem to find the distance between two points in a coordinate system. (NGA Center/CCSSO, 2010)

MATERIALS
- Graph paper or a graphing calculator for each student
- Coordinate map to show class

ASSESSMENT
- Students will find the distance between several pairs of points, without graphing.
- Students will write in their journals how to find the distance between two points. They will explain how this method is based on the Pythagorean relationship.

GROUPING
Whole group followed by small groups of three or four students

Launch (5 to 10 minutes)
Show the class a coordinate grid, with two points identified in the first quadrant. Say: *Here is a map with the locations of my home (1, 3) and school (5, 6) drawn on a coordinate grid. I am going to name my home with the letter* A *and school with the letter* B. *I want to find out how far apart these two locations are, if I were to travel between them in a straight line.*

Location for Grades 6–8
In the middle grades, students learn about location by extending their knowledge of coordinate geometry. If they have not done so before, they learn about the four quadrants in the coordinate **plane** and plot points and lines. They may be introduced to the distance formula, which is based on the Pythagorean relationship (see the *Lesson*). The standards are from *Curriculum Focal Points for Prekindergarten through Grade 8* (NCTM, 2006) and the *Common Core State Standards* (NGA Center/CCSSO, 2010).

In the middle grades, students use their knowledge of **slope**, similarity, and coordinate geometry to create triangles from the change in *y* and the change in *x* when given a line in the coordinate plane (NCTM, 2006) (**Activity 15.18**).

> **slope** The ratio of the vertical change to the horizontal change in a line.

| CONCEPT CHECK | |

1. **What** types of spatial relationships are important for children in prekindergarten through grade 2 to learn?
2. **How** can teachers in grades 3–5 use coordinate grids to teach children about location?
3. **How** can teachers in grades 6–8 use students' knowledge of coordinate geometry and the Pythagorean relationship to teach the distance formula?

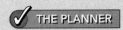
Instruct (30 to 35 minutes)

- Ask: *Does anyone have any ideas about how we can do this? Do you think the Pythagorean relationship can help us find the answer?*

- As students discuss possible solutions, elicit the idea of drawing a triangle by drawing a horizontal line from point *A* to the point directly below point *B* and a vertical line from point *B* down to that horizontal line. Connect points *A* and *B* to complete the triangle.

- Ask: *What kind of triangle is this?* (A right triangle)

- Ask: *What part of the triangle is the distance from* A *to* B? (The hypotenuse)

- Say: *I would like you to work in your groups to find the lengths of the legs of this triangle and decide how we can use the Pythagorean relationship to find the distance from* A *to* B.

- As the students work in their groups, circulate and offer help if necessary. Students should be able to find the length of the horizontal and vertical legs by subtracting. Then they should apply the Pythagorean relationship to determine that the distance from *A* to *B* is 5.

- Ask: *Will this work all the time? Let's try it with some other coordinates.*

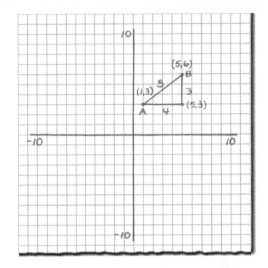

- After students have tried several examples, ask them to find the distance between two points without drawing pictures.

Summarize (5 to 10 minutes)

- Ask: *Who can explain how we used the Pythagorean relationship to find the distance between two points?*

- Ask: *Who can summarize how to find the distance between any two points in the coordinate plane?*

Activity 15.18 Finding slopes (van Hiele levels 2 and 3)

Instructions

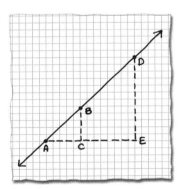

1. Say: *Find the vertical distance from point* A *to point* B. *Find the horizontal distance. Find the slope of line* AB.

2. Say: *Find the vertical distance from point* A *to point* D. *Find the horizontal distance. Find the slope of line* AD. *What do you notice?* (The slopes of *AB* and *AD* are the same because they are the same line.)

3. Ask: *What is true about triangles* ABC *and* ADE? (They are similar triangles.)

Learning About Transformations

LEARNING OBJECTIVES

1. **Describe** how to teach transformations in pre-kindergarten through grade 2.
2. **Describe** how to teach transformations in grades 3–5.
3. **Describe** how to teach transformations in grades 6–8.

I f you have ever looked at wallpaper or tile patterns, then you have seen transformations. Transformations are probably the most artistic part of geometry. Cultures from all over the world have used transformations to decorate their textiles, dwellings, and pottery. When children in the primary grades discover transformations, they find that they can move, flip, or turn shapes without changing their size or shape. Children in the upper elementary grades learn the formal language of transformations. In middle school, students use transformational geometry to explore spatial relationships. This section discusses how to teach children about transformations at different grade levels.

Transformations for Prekindergarten Through Grade 2

Children in prekindergarten through grade 2 learn **line symmetry** and **rotation symmetry**. By the second grade they should have been introduced to these concepts. Children's early experiences with shape may cause them to believe that all shapes are symmetrical. They have probably worked with squares, rectangles, and circles, all of which are symmetrical. It is important to introduce them to shapes that are symmetrical and nonsymmetrical so they can understand the difference. Children's earliest experiences with symmetry can be accomplished with a mirror. Ask the children to stand in front of a full-length mirror and describe what they see. They have one eye, one eyebrow, and one ear on either side of an imaginary vertical line that runs from the top of their head down through the middle of their body. Other activities such as those described in **Activities 15.19, 15.20**, and **15.21** can help young children learn the language of symmetry.

Activity 15.19 Do I have symmetry? (van Hiele level 1)

Instructions

1. Cut out a large square. Show how the square can be folded in half by folding a line down the middle vertically. Ask: *Do both sides of the square show the same shape?*
2. Show how the square can be folded in half horizontally. Ask similar questions.
3. Say: *When a shape has a mirror image on either side of a line, we say it has* **line symmetry.**
4. Rotate the square 90 degrees clockwise. Ask: *Is this the same shape?*
5. Continue rotating the square in 90-degree intervals. With each rotation, ask: *Is this the same shape?*
6. Say: *When a shape is turned and still looks the same, we say it has* **rotation symmetry.**
7. Say: *Look at these drawings. Can you pick out the figures that do not have symmetry? Let's cross those out. Now look at the figures that do have symmetry. What type of symmetry do they have?*

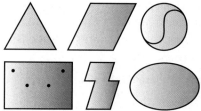

Activity 15.20 Symmetry with the alphabet (van Hiele levels 1 and 2)

Instructions

1. Write or post large versions of the alphabet, capitalized. A good method is to draw the letters on card stock, cut them out, and tape them to a surface so they can be moved around.

2. Ask: *Which of the letters have symmetry? For those that do, what type of symmetry do they have?* (A, H, I, M, O, T, X, U, V, Y have vertical line symmetry. E, H, I, O have horizontal line symmetry.)
3. Ask: *Are there any letters that have both line and rotational symmetry?* (O and I have both line and rotational symmetry; so may H and X, depending on how they are written.)

Activity 15.21 Kooky grids (van Hiele levels 1 and 2)

Instructions

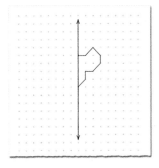

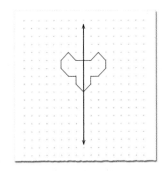

1. Distribute dot or grid paper to pairs of students.

2. Ask the students to draw vertical lines down the paper.

3. Ask one student in each pair to create a design on one half of the page that extends to the vertical line.

4. Ask the other student to find the mirror image of the design on the other side of the vertical line.

5. Exchange roles.

6. Repeat with horizontal lines and diagonal lines. All designs should touch the lines of symmetry.

Young children should have lots of practice working with transformations. Initially, they use the informal language of *slide*, *flip*, and *turn*. These are important concepts for children to understand because they form the foundation for later work on congruence of shapes. The easiest transformation is the flip, because all other transformations can be derived from it (**Activity 15.22**).

After children have had a number of experiences with flips, introduce slides and rotations. Start with the same figure that was used in Activity 15.22, and ask the children to slide their figure horizontally or diagonally, keeping the same orientation. Then ask them to rotate the figure by making $\frac{1}{4}$ and $\frac{1}{2}$ turns in the clockwise direction (**Figure 15.10**).

Activity 15.22 Easy flips (van Hiele levels 1 and 2)

Instructions

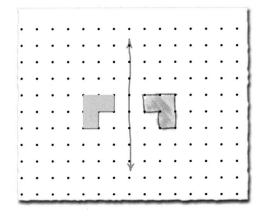

1. Cut out a basic figure on card stock for each child, and give each child a piece of paper and the card-stock figure.

2. Ask the children to draw a vertical line down the middle of the paper, trace the figure on one side of the paper, and then flip it to the other side of the paper and trace the resulting figure.

3. Ask: *What do you notice?*

Flips, slides, and turns • Figure 15.10

Young children can learn about flips, slides, and turns by practicing with a nonsymmetrical cut-out figure. Can you identify the flips, slides, and turns?

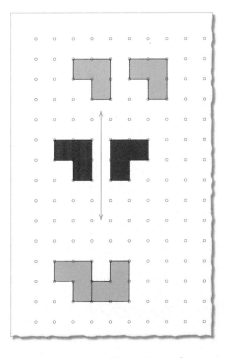

Activity 15.23 Can you guess my moves? (van Hiele level 2)

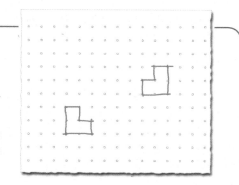

Instructions

1. Give the children dot paper or grid paper.

2. Working in pairs, ask one child to draw a nonsymmetrical figure and then use two or more transformations on the figure.

3. The other child sees only the original figure and the final figure after transformations and is asked to guess what transformations were used to get to the final figure. There will be more than one correct answer.

4. Switch roles and continue the activity.

Transformations for Grades 3–5

In grades 3–5, children learn the correct terminology for transformations. They learn that a flip is a **reflection**, a slide is a **translation**, and a turn is a **rotation**. Children also learn how to compose transformations or do a

> **tessellations** Pattern in which a shape is repeated over and over again, covering a plane without any gaps or overlaps. Another word for a tessellation is a tiling.

combination of more than one transformation and predict the outcome of a transformation without actually doing it (**Activity 15.23**).

Children in grades 3–5 enjoy working with **tessellations**. Introduce the concept of tessellations with children's literature (see *Children's Literature*, **Figure 15.11**).

Frieze patterns are a natural extension of transformations and are fun to investigate (Schattschneider, 2009) (see *Multicultural Perspectives in Mathematics*).

> **frieze patterns** Also known as border patterns, they repeat along a line, a strip, or between two parallel lines.

Tech Tools

www.coolmath.com/lesson-tessellations-1.htm

The Coolmath site uses excellent visuals to illustrate which polygons tessellate.

CHILDREN'S LITERATURE

Learning about shapes that tessellate

✓ THE PLANNER

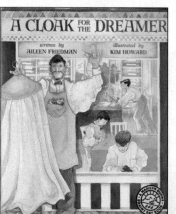

A Cloak for the Dreamer • Figure 15.11

Written by Aileen Friedman
Illustrated by Kim Howard

A tailor asks his sons to help make cloaks for the archduke. One son sews together colored squares of fabric. The second son sews together equilateral triangles of fabric. The youngest son makes a cloak out of circles of fabric, which leave gaps when they are sewn together. The tailor and his two oldest sons repair the cloak by cutting each circle into a hexagon and sewing them together. They give this cloak to the youngest son for his sea journey.

Strategies for the Classroom

- Read the book with your class. Then give the children construction paper, tape, and scissors and ask them to design their own tessellation pattern using one of the shapes in the book.

- Ask why the author chose the shapes used in the book. What is special about these shapes?

Multicultural Perspectives in Mathematics

Using Frieze Patterns to Learn About Transformations

A frieze pattern is a design that repeats infinitely in both directions, such as a wallpaper border. It is often used ornamentally in architecture along the eaves of a building. Frieze patterns are abundant in many cultures, used as decorative borders on textiles, doorways, and pottery. Here are some examples:

In Europe, Australia, and American cities such as New Orleans, ironwork on balconies is decorative and ornate. It also displays frieze patterns.

Many different tribes of American Indians have used frieze patterns to decorate their clothing and pottery. It is evident on Navajo rugs, Pueblo pottery, and the beadwork of Wisconsin Woodland Indians, as well as on wampum belts and the border patterns on Yup'ik (Eskimo) parkas.

There are exactly seven different types of frieze patterns. Each pattern is composed by creating a basic shape and then translating, reflecting, rotating, or using a combination of these transformations to create a horizontal repeating pattern.

- Give each child a long strip of grid paper and ask the children to create their own frieze pattern with one or two designs. They begin by drawing the design and then extending it horizontally through flips, slides, or turns.

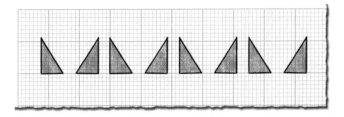

- Investigate the seven types of frieze patterns by clicking on illuminations.nctm.org and selecting the frieze pattern activity.

- Ask the children to research the frieze patterns of different cultures.

Regular polygons tessellate the plane • Figure 15.12

The measures of the vertex angles of an equilateral triangle, square, and regular hexagon are all factors of 360 degrees. These shapes tessellate because, when their vertices meet at a point, they make a circle (360 degrees).

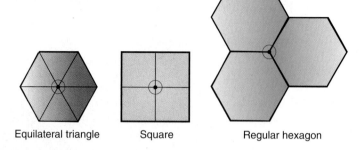

Equilateral triangle   Square   Regular hexagon

regular hexagon A six-sided polygon with all sides congruent to each other and all vertex angles congruent to each other.

regular polygon A polygon with all sides congruent to each other and all vertex angles congruent to each other.

Children will learn that an equilateral triangle, square, and **regular hexagon** are the only **regular polygons** that tessellate the plane (**Figure 15.12**).

Tessellations are a wonderful way to integrate mathematics and art (**Figure 15.13**). By teaching children to create Escher-like tessellations you can ease their anxiety about mathematics, broaden their view of the subject, and teach them about translations, rotations, reflections, and symmetry (**Activity 15.24**).

Activity 15.24 Creating translation tessellations (van Hiele level 2)

Instructions

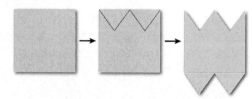

1. Show students examples of Escher tessellations.
2. Say: *You are going to create your own tessellations.*
3. Give each student a sheet of paper. Ask the students to draw and cut out a square.
4. Ask them to draw a design on one side of the square.
5. Ask them to cut out the design and slide it to the opposite side of the square and tape it there.
6. Say: *This represents one tile of the tessellation.*
7. Say: *Use this tile as a template and trace it repeatedly on a large sheet of paper to create the tessellation. Color creatively.*
8. Say: *Find vertical or horizontal symmetry in your finished design.*

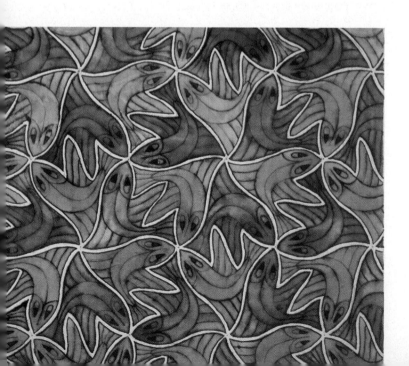

M. C. Escher tessellations • Figure 15.13

Tessellations are often composed of geometric shapes but can also be created from other shapes. The artist M. C. Escher is known as the "father of tessellations." Children may enjoy looking at one of Escher's books and discussing the tessellations.

Teaching Tip

Creating tessellations

- Begin making tessellations with geometric shapes drawn on dot paper because this method is easiest.

- Once a template has been created, make translation tessellations first.

- Next create translation tessellations using drawings of animals or other figures.

- Then create rotation tessellations.

Transformations for Grades 6–8

In grades 6–8, students understand that objects that have been translated, rotated, or reflected maintain their size and shape. They use their previously gained knowledge of transformations to understand how two shapes may be similar or congruent even though at first they may not appear that way. For students in this grade range, dynamic geometry software is an excellent way to approach transformations.

CONCEPT CHECK

1. **How** might you introduce line and rotational symmetry to children in prekindergarten through grade 2?

Tech Tools

www.nctm.org

Go to the NCTM Web site. Select **Standards and Focal Points** and **e-examples**. Example 6.4, **Understanding Congruence and Similarity and Symmetry Using Transformations and Interactive Figures,** provides four excellent activities. In the first activity, students choose a transformation and apply it to a figure. In the second activity, they are asked to guess which transformation was applied. In the third activity, students reflect a shape repeatedly through two different lines, and in the fourth activity they compose two or more transformations in two different ways.

illuminations.nctm.org

Go to the *NCTM Illuminations* Web site. Select **lessons for grades 6–8** and select **What's Regular About Tessellations?** Use the tessellation creator to make your own tessellations.

2. **How** does *A Cloak for the Dreamer* show that circles do not tessellate?

3. **How** might students use transformations to show that two shapes are congruent?

Learning About Visualization

LEARNING OBJECTIVES

1. Describe how to teach visualization in prekindergarten through grade 2.

2. Describe how to teach visualization in grades 3–5.

3. Describe how to teach visualization in grades 6–8.

The ability to create mental images and manipulate two- and three-dimensional objects is one of the most important aspects of geometry and provides practical preparation for many careers (Sack and van Niekerk, 2009). "Beginning in the early years of schooling, students should develop visualization skills through hands-on experiences with a variety of geometric objects and through the use of technology..." (NCTM, 2000, p. 43). This section discusses how to teach children visualization at different grade levels.

Visualization for Prekindergarten Through Grade 2

Young children should be given the opportunity to develop spatial reasoning by working with two- and three-dimensional representations. Encourage children to create models and to describe them using geometric language. Begin with activities that ask children to recreate three-dimensional figures (**Activity 15.25**). As children describe the block structures, they will display different levels of geometric knowledge. For example, some children might say, "It looks like an upside-down T." Others will be able to describe the positions of the blocks more accurately: "There are three blocks on the bottom row and another one in the next row." Children's visualization skills will improve with practice.

Activity 15.25 Just alike
(van Hiele level 1)

Instructions

1. Provide each child with several blocks, all the same color and size.
2. Create a solid by putting four of the blocks together in some way.
3. Ask the children to recreate the same solid with their own blocks.
4. Ask them to explain what the block structure looks like.
5. Repeat with other block formations.
6. To extend the activity, show a top view of a block construction and ask the children to create the structure that matches the top view.

Activity 15.26 Find my twin
(van Hiele level 1)

Instructions

1. Bring to class several models of three-dimensional objects: prisms, cylinders, pyramids. Whenever possible, bring examples of everyday objects such as cereal boxes and soup cans.
2. Hold up each object. Ask: *Have you ever seen one of these before? Do you know its name?* Examine each object carefully with the class, pass it around, and ask: *How many faces, vertices, and edges does it have?*
3. Show the children two-dimensional drawings of the same objects.
4. Ask the children to match the two-dimensional drawing to the real object.

Children need to learn to move between two- and three-dimensional representations of the same object, as illustrated in **Activity 15.26**.

Teaching Tip

Developing spatial visualization skills

Spatial visualization skills vary quite a bit with children, and they develop these skills at different rates. Let children use physical models of cubes and other three-dimensional shapes for as long as necessary.

Visualization for Grades 3–5

Children's visualization skills improve with practice. In grades 3–5, use children's prior knowledge to extend their ability to create two-dimensional representations of three-dimensional shapes. Have children create **nets** for a cube and other three-dimensional shapes, as demonstrated in **Activity 15.27**, adapted from Jeon, 2009.

> **net** Two-dimensional representation of a three-dimensional object.

Activity 15.27 Nets for a cube (van Hiele levels 1 and 2)

Instructions

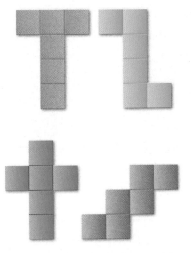

1. Give children several possible nets for a cube. Ask them to cut out each net and test whether it works.

2. Ask them to draw the remaining nets for a cube. This will take some experimentation. (There are 11 in all.) Cut out each net to make sure it works.

3. Ask: *What do you notice?* (All nets for a cube are made up of six congruent squares, although all the nets are not congruent to each other.)

Children also need practice visualizing what happens when two-dimensional shapes intersect. **Activity 15.28** has been adapted from Tayeh (2005). Children may be

Activity 15.28 Square overlap

Instructions

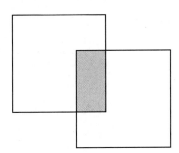

1. Draw two squares that overlap. The squares do not have to be congruent.

2. Ask: *What is the shape of the overlap?*

3. Ask children to draw two squares that overlap differently from the model and to find the shape of the resulting overlap.

4. Continue by overlapping other figures, such as two right triangles.

surprised to find out that there are many different ways to overlap two squares and many possible shapes that result.

Visualization for Grades 6–8

In grades 6–8, students use their spatial visualization skills to determine surface area and volume of solids, which are discussed more completely in Chapter 16. They also expand upon their visualization skills to study cross sections of three-dimensional shapes. They learn what happens when a plane intersects a solid (**Figure 15.14**).

Cross sections of solids • Figure 15.14

A cross section of a cube is a square, and a cross section of a cylinder is a circle. Finding cross sections helps students visualize the intersection of two- and three-dimensional shapes.

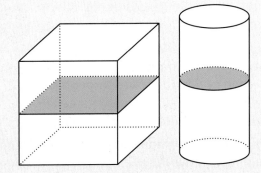

The Platonic solids • Figure 15.15

Although there are an infinite number of regular polygons in the plane, there are only five Platonic, or regular, solids in space. Each of them looks identical from every view.

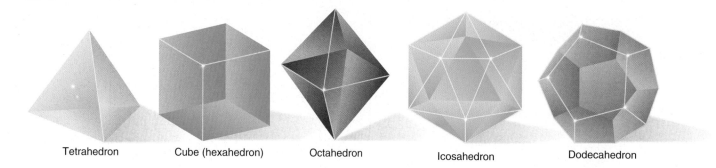

Tetrahedron   Cube (hexahedron)   Octahedron   Icosahedron   Dodecahedron

---

> **Platonic solids** Three-dimensional shapes whose faces are all regular polygons.

In the middle grades, students learn about the Platonic solids (**Figure 15.15**). As is apparent from their name, mathematicians have been interested in these solids for thousands of years. "For centuries, the Platonic solids were associated with mystical powers" (Burger and Starbird, 2000, p. 273). Students in the middle grades should learn the names of the Platonic solids and build them by making nets (**Activity 15.29**).

CONCEPT CHECK   **STOP**

1. **What** is a major goal of teaching visualization to children in prekindergarten through grade 2?

2. **What** are nets? How can they be used to improve children's visualization skills?

3. **What** is meant by finding the cross section of a three-dimensional shape?

Activity 15.29 Building Platonic solids (van Hiele levels 2 and 3)

Instructions

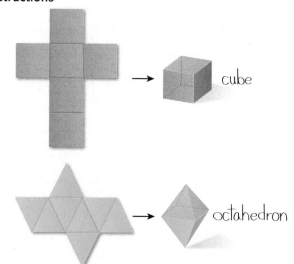

cube

octahedron

1. Ask the students to build the simplest of the Platonic solids, the cube, or **hexahedron**.

2. Ask them to draw a net for a cube on construction paper, cut out the net, and fold and tape it together.

3. Ask students to make the **octahedron**, an eight-sided Platonic solid, by constructing eight congruent equilateral triangles and taping them together or by drawing a net for the octahedron, cutting out the net and folding it and taping it together.

Summary

1 Learning About Geometry 370

- Children learn geometry by passing through several levels, called the van Hiele levels of geometric thought. These levels are determined by instruction rather than maturity, and if a child is taught at one level but is functioning at a level below that, the child will not benefit from instruction. The child in this image is functioning at van Hiele level 1.

Figure 15.1

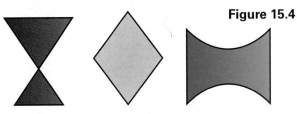

- Geometry is an important topic in mathematics and should be included at every grade level. We generally believe that children learn logical thinking skills in geometry. Geometric models are also applied in many other areas of mathematics.

2 Learning About Shapes and Properties 372

- When we think of geometry, we tend to think of shapes and their properties. This takes up a large part of the geometry curriculum. In prekindergarten through grade 2, children learn to sort and classify two- and three-dimensional shapes. They learn to identify **faces, edges,** and **vertices**.

- In grades 3–5, children learn the meaning of **simple closed curve, polygon, congruence,** and **similarity**. They learn

to identify shapes more formally. For example, they learn whether the shapes illustrated here are simple closed curves. For **quadrilaterals**, they learn the meaning of **parallel** and **perpendicular** sides. They learn to identify **parallelograms, rectangles, rhombuses, squares,** and **trapezoids**.

Figure 15.4

- In grades 6–8, students learn the minimum qualifying characteristics for different quadrilaterals. They learn to prove the **Pythagorean relationship.**

3 Learning About Location 384

- In prekindergarten through grade 2, children learn the meaning of terms such as *in front of, behind,* and *between.* They learn to draw maps and understand simple grids.

- In grades 3–5, children learn directional terms such as *north, south, east,* and *west.* They learn to number coordinate grids and to find points on a grid identified by two coordinates, as in this drawing.

Activity 15.16

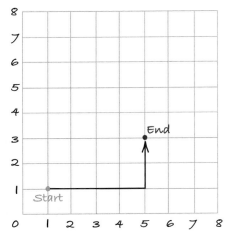

- In grades 6–8, students learn to identify the four quadrants and graph points in all four quadrants. They use their knowledge of the **Pythagorean relationship** to derive the formula for the distance between two points.

4 Learning About Transformations 388

- In prekindergarten through grade 2, children learn the meaning of **line** and **rotational symmetry**. They learn about transformations using words such as *flips*, *slides*, and *turns*.

- In grades 3–5, children begin to use correct terminology for transformations. They learn about **translations, rotations**, and **reflections**. They learn how to combine two or more transformations and learn about **tessellations**. The tessellation shown, drawn by M. C. Escher, does not use familiar geometric shapes. Children at this grade level also learn to understand why only three **regular polygons** tessellate the plane.

Figure 15.13

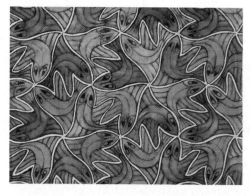

- In grades 6–8, students use their knowledge of transformations to determine whether polygons display **congruence** or **similarity**.

5 Learning About Visualization 393

- In prekindergarten through grade 2, children make three-dimensional representations using blocks and learn to recognize two-dimensional representations of three-dimensional figures.

- In grades 3–5, children learn to make the **nets** of a cube, as shown here, and other three-dimensional shapes. They can practice visualization by determining the results of intersecting two squares or two **right triangles**.

Activity 15.27

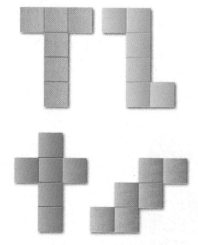

- In grades 6–8, students extend their visualization skills by finding cross sections of three-dimensional shapes and constructing nets for the **Platonic solids**.

Key Terms

Additional Children's Literature

- *The Quiltmaker's Gift*, written by Jeff Brumbeau and illustrated by Gail de Marcken
  This beautifully illustrated book has an engaging story and many quilt patterns to inspire children. Read the story and ask children to analyze the patterns for symmetry and transformations.

- *The Fly on the Ceiling*, written by Julie Glass and illustrated by Richard Walz
  This story is a mythical interpretation of the creation of coordinate geometry by the mathematician Rene Descartes. The book provides an excellent introduction to coordinates and graphing.

- *Mapping Penny's World*, written and illustrated by Loreen Leedy
  This book is filled with information about location and maps for children in grades 3–5. This book is charmingly illustrated and extremely useful for helping children learn about maps.

- *Mummy Math: An Adventure in Geometry*, written by Cindy Neuschwander and illustrated by Bryan Langdo
  Two children are lost in an Egyptian tomb and have to decode a secret message written with three-dimensional shapes to find their way out. This is a great book for learning to identify three-dimensional shapes.

- *What's Your Angle, Pythagorus? A Math Adventure*, written by Julie Ellis and illustrated by Phyllis Hornung
  This is a fictional and highly entertaining account of how Pythagorus, as a young boy in ancient Greece, discovered the theorem that bears his name. The book provides a proof for the theorem that children in the upper elementary or middle grades can readily understand.

Online Resources

- **NCTM Illuminations**
  illuminations.nctm.org/

  1. **Geometric Solids:** An activity for grades K–12 that allows children to manipulate and color shapes in order to find the relationship between the number of vertices, faces, and edges for any polyhedron.
  2. **Cube Nets:** An activity that examines two-dimensional nets that can be folded into a cube. For grades 3–5.
  3. **Frieze Patterns:** An activity that allows the user to experiment with the seven different types of frieze patterns. For grades 3–5.

- **Mathforum**
  http://www.mathforum.org/

  This site provides an explanation on tessellations and illustrations of the regular polygons that tessellate. It also explains semiregular tessellations with examples.

- **National Library of Virtual Manipulatives**
  http://nlvm.usu.edu/

  1. **Attribute Blocks:** Sort blocks to learn color and shape. For pre-K through grade 2.
  2. **Pentominoes:** Build two congruent figures from two pentomino shapes. For grades K–12.
  3. **Koch and Sierpinski Fractals:** Make fractal designs and pause at any time. For grades 3–5.
  4. **Geoboard–Coordinate:** Make figures on a geoboard and play the game "Battleship." For grades 3–5.
  5. **Congruent Triangles:** Build congruent triangles from combinations of sides and angles. For grades 6–8.

Critical and Creative Thinking Questions

1. Why is it important for children to learn geometry at every grade level? Examine each of the four areas of geometry discussed in this chapter and summarize why each is important.

2. **In the field** Design an activity that asks children to classify triangles or quadrilaterals. Your activity should be open-ended enough so that children can classify the figures holistically or formally by properties. Ask two students to complete the activity, one in the primary grades and one in the upper elementary grades. From their responses, determine the students' level of geometric thought, using the van Hiele levels for classification. Justify your conclusions.

3. According to the van Hiele theory, why is it important to know each child's level of geometric thought? How can you realistically accomplish this in the classroom?

4. You may have children at more than one level of geometric thought in your classroom. What can you do if children are at different van Hiele levels?

5. Take one of the level 2 activities from this chapter and modify it to meet the needs of children at level 1. Take one of the level 1 activities and modify it to meet the needs of children at level 2.

6. What are the advantages of using computer applets to learn geometry? Examine one of the applets listed in this chapter and describe its strengths and weaknesses. How would you use this applet to supplement instruction on geometry?

7. **Using visuals** Figure 15.1 illustrates the process of moving from concrete to abstract when learning about shapes and their properties. Create your own process diagram to explain how children learn about location, from prekindergarten to grade 8, with examples and illustrations for each step.

What is happening in this picture?

Look closely at this picture of a Navajo rug.
1. How might you use this picture to teach children about the prevalence of patterns and shapes in the world?
2. How might you use this picture to teach children about symmetry, tessellations, congruence, and similarity?

Self-Test

(Check your answers in Appendix D.)

1. What are the five van Hiele levels of geometric thought?

2. At what van Hiele level are most children in prekindergarten through grade 2?

3. What van Hiele level should students attain by the time they reach middle school?

4. Look at the images in Activity 15.3, shown here. What makes a shape a triangle? Why do you think each of these images was included?

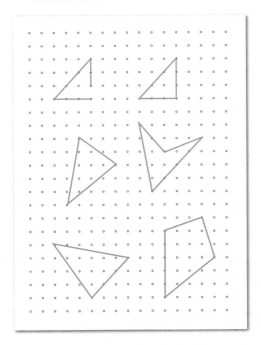

5. How do parallelograms, kites, and trapezoids differ?

6. What makes a shape a rhombus?

7. Is every rectangle a rhombus? Is every rhombus a square? Explain.

8. Identify each of these three-dimensional shapes as specifically as possible.

 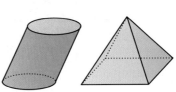 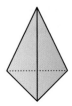

9. Which of the following sets of numbers exhibit the Pythagorean relationship?
   a. 3, 4, 5   b. 6, 8, 10   c. 8, 16, 17   d. 4, 9, 13

10. Find all the uppercase letters in the alphabet that display horizontal and/or vertical line symmetry.

11. What are the three types of transformations that leave a shape's size unchanged?

12. Which transformations change the orientation of a shape?

13. What is the result of reflecting a shape across a vertical line and then reflecting it back across that same line?

14. Why are equilateral triangles, squares, and regular hexagons the only regular polygons that tessellate? What is one nonregular polygon that tessellates?

15. Use the distance formula to find the distance between (3, 5) and (7, 4).

THE PLANNER ✓

Review your Chapter Planner on the chapter opener and check off your completed work.

Measurement

Rita Johnson's fifth-grade class was creating their school's first vegetable garden. The children worked together to plant an organic garden on the school's grounds. They planned their garden by staking out the border, deciding on the dimensions of individual beds, and figuring out how much soil and materials they would need. They created raised beds and planted their garden with donated materials and volunteer labor.

Ms. Johnson was excited about the educational benefits of the garden project. In addition to teaching her students about nutrition, she planned related science and social studies lessons about George Washington Carver, the Lewis and Clark Expedition, and the victory gardens of World War II. Ms. Johnson also knew that the garden project contained many valuable mathematics ideas. Children learned about length, perimeter, and area as they staked the boundary of the garden and decided where to place their beds. When deciding how much soil to place in each bed, they estimated capacity. Of course, they also estimated how much produce their garden would yield.

The garden project involved children in a real-world investigation that integrated measurement with other subject areas. Because many of the children's families had their own small vegetable gardens, this project also bridged the gap between the mathematics children learn in school and the everyday mathematics we use in our lives.

CHAPTER OUTLINE

 The NCTM Measurement Standard has two main objectives.

Instructional programs from prekindergarten through grade 12 should enable all students to

- understand measurable attributes of objects and the units, systems, and processes of measurement;
- apply appropriate techniques, tools, and formulas to determine measurements. (NCTM, 2000, p. 102)

Specific objectives for each grade-level band are listed within these two major categories and can be found in Appendix A.

What mathematical questions might arise as students work in a vegetable garden?

Learning About Measurement

LEARNING OBJECTIVES

1. **Describe** the meaning of measurement.
2. **Identify** why it is important for children to learn measurement.
3. **Distinguish** between standard and nonstandard units of measure.
4. **Discuss** the importance of estimation in measurement.

When you decide whether to wear a coat based on the outside temperature, use a tire pressure gauge, or check the time schedule for a movie, you are using measurement. Despite these everyday uses of measurement, children's achievement in this area lags behind their achievement in other areas of mathematics. This section discusses the meaning of measurement, the differences between standard and nonstandard units of measurement, the role of estimation in measurement, and the importance of measurement in the mathematics curriculum.

What Is Measurement?

"Measurement is the assignment of a numerical value to an **attribute** of an object, such as the length of a pencil" (NCTM, 2000, p. 44). There are many different kinds of attributes, including length, area, volume, capacity, temperature, time, and angle measure. Each of these attributes is discussed in this chapter.

Technically, all measurement is comparison. Children often begin the measurement process using **direct comparison**—comparing two crayons to see which is longer or two backpacks to see which is heavier. At other times, they use **indirect comparison**—comparing the areas of two shapes by covering them with lima beans to see which shape is covered by more beans. Next, children measure through comparison to a unit of measure. Children often begin by using **nonstandard units** of measure—finding the length of a desk by placing pencils end to end across the desk or finding out how many small paper cups worth of lemonade are in a pitcher.

> **nonstandard unit** A unit of measure that is not universally accepted.

Children gradually make the transition to using **standard units**, using a ruler and designating the length of the desk by the

> **standard unit** A unit of measure that is universally accepted, such as inches or centimeters.

units of the ruler or finding out how many eight-ounce cups of lemonade are in a pitcher. Here, it is crucial that children choose the appropriate unit of measure for the particular attribute. For example, the amount of lemonade in the pitcher should be measured with ounces or liters and not with inches or centimeters. The measurement process is illustrated in **Figure 16.1**.

Why Is Measurement Important?

Measurement "can develop in the earliest years from children's experience, and it readily lends itself to real-world application. Further, it spans and connects mathematics and other sciences and thus can ideally integrate subject matter areas" (Clements, 2003, p. xi).

More than any other area of mathematics, measurement connects to our everyday lives. These connections can spark children's interest in mathematics and motivate children who might otherwise think that mathematics has nothing to do with their lives outside of school.

Measurement is also used in many other parts of mathematics. For example, children use measurement when they learn about fractions, decimals, algebra, integers, and statistics. The concrete and pictorial models used in measurement, such as rulers, arrays, protractors, and thermometers, are useful in learning other areas of mathematics.

Knowledge of measurement is important in many disciplines, including science, physical education, and art. For example, a scientist might heat a solution to a given temperature, races are timed, and artists mix paints to obtain desired colors. A solid understanding of measurement helps children succeed in other areas of the curriculum.

Standard and Nonstandard Units

When young children first learn to measure, they use nonstandard units and counting. Nonstandard units have many advantages.

The measurement process • Figure 16.1

Measurement is a process that is independent of the attribute or the unit. Length is one of the first attributes that children learn and will be used here, although the measurement process is the same with any attribute and any unit. With each new attribute, children cycle through the same steps. To measure an attribute of an object, follow the steps in this diagram.

1 Identify the attribute to be measured.

2 Select an appropriate unit to measure the attribute. This may be a standard or nonstandard unit.

3 Compare the units of the object you wish to measure to the units of the measuring instrument.

- The units of measure can be tailored to the attribute. You can use small units such as paper clips to measure the length of a crayon and large units such as pencils to measure the length of a desk.
- Nonstandard units may be easier and more engaging for small hands to handle and understand. For example, snap-together cubes are easier to use than rulers.
- Using nonstandard units keeps the focus of the investigation on measuring rather than understanding the units of measure or the measuring instrument. For example, children often have difficulty using rulers and need knowledge of fractions to read rulers accurately, but they do not need detailed knowledge of fractions to measure the length of their desks with pencils.

After children have many experiences with nonstandard units, they gradually progress to standard units and

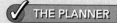

It is important for children to have experience with both standard and nonstandard units of measure. Instruction always begins with nonstandard units and moves gradually to the use of standard units and sometimes formulas.

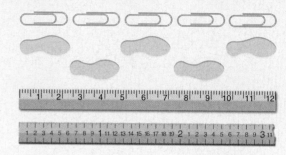

a. Standard and nonstandard units of length
Nonstandard units of length include paper clips and footprints. Standard units of length include rulers and meter sticks.

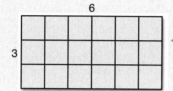

b. Standard and nonstandard units of area
Nonstandard units of area include beans or chips to cover shapes. Standard units of area include arrays indicating base and height, measured in inches, feet, centimeters, and meters.

c. Standard and nonstandard units of weight
Nonstandard units of weight are perceptual. We decide which feels heavier. A scale is a standard unit of weight.

d. Standard and nonstandard units of temperature
Nonstandard units of temperature are perceptual. We feel what is hot or cold. A thermometer is a standard unit of temperature.

counting, and finally, depending on the attribute, they may also use formulas (**Figure 16.2**).

Nonstandard units bring up important questions about measurement. In **Activity 16.1**, children learn that the smaller the unit (a paper clip instead of a pencil), the more accurate the measure. You want them to discover that as the measuring unit becomes smaller, the number of units needed to measure the object increases. (It will require more paper clips than pencils to measure the length of your friend's arm.) In **Activity 16.2,** children learn some drawbacks of nonstandard units of measure. They discover that using different units to measure the same object provides different measurements.

Activity 16.1 How wide is your chair?

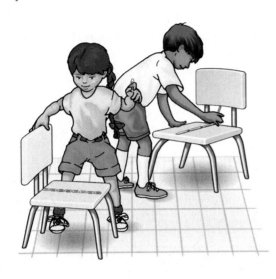

Instructions

1. Ask: *How wide is your chair? How can you find out?*

2. Ask the children to measure the width of their chair with paper clips and again with pencils.

3. Record the answers.

4. Measuring with paper clips requires less estimation than measuring with pencils, although the children may make more mistakes in counting the paper clips because there are more of them.

5. Ask: *Which is better for measuring the width of your chair?* (Discuss the benefits of each tool.)

6. Repeat by measuring other objects in the classroom, such as the length of the stapler or calculator, using pencils and paper clips.

7. Ask: *Which is the better way to measure?* (Through discussion, draw the conclusion that the smaller the unit of measure, the more accurate the measurement.)

Activity 16.2 Measure the classroom

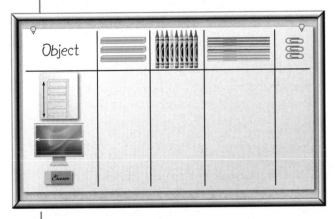

Instructions

1. Measure different objects in the classroom, such as the height of the bookshelves or the width of the computer screen, using different measuring tools, such as Cuisenaire rods, crayons, straws, and paper clips.

2. Record all answers for each object measured on a chart.

3. Ask: *Why do we get different answers?* (The children use different objects with which to measure.)

4. Ask: *Could there be any problems with getting different answers? How could we all get the same answer?* (Use the same unit.)

5. Say: *So that everyone gets the same answer, we learn to measure with standard units.*

6. Ask: *Is there a measuring tool that we seem to use the most often?* (The tool depends on what is being measured.)

In **Activity 16.3,** children learn that the relative lengths of the units to one another affect the length of the measurement. If one unit is half the size of another unit, you will need twice as many units to measure an object when using the smaller unit of measure.

Activity 16.3 How long is your math book?

Instructions

1. Distribute to each child several straws of the same length and straws that are cut in half.

2. Ask each child to measure the length of their math book with the whole straw. Record the length. Some approximation will be necessary.

3. Ask each child to measure the length of their math book again with the half straw. Record the length.

4. Ask: *Do you have to use more or less units when you use the smaller straw?* (More) *Why do you think that is?* (That straw is smaller, so it takes more of them.)

5. Ask: *What else do you notice?* (You need about twice as many small straws as big ones to measure the length of the math book.)

6. Say: *Now measure the length of your desk with the small straws. Can you predict how many big straws you will need to measure the desk?* (Twice as many)

7. Repeat with other tools.

Nonstandard units of measure have been used throughout history and are still used by some people (see *Multicultural Perspectives in Mathematics*).

Children's literature is an excellent way to help children understand the difference between standard and nonstandard units of measure (see *Children's Literature*, **Figure 16.3**). In *Measuring Penny*, different types of measurement are examined within the familiar context of owning a dog.

Multicultural Perspectives in Mathematics

✓ THE PLANNER

Yup'ik Ways of Measuring

The Yup'ik Eskimo people of Alaska created a unique system of measurement that uses their bodies for nonstandard measurement. One measure is the *yagneg*, the distance from fingertip to fingertip when the arms are outstretched at one's sides. This provides a close approximation of a person's height. The measurement from the middle of the chest to the tip of an outstretched hand and arm is called *taluyaeq*. The distance from the armpit to an outstretched arm making a fist is called *tallinin*.

Measuring in this way allows for the making of kayaks that custom fit the owner. Each kayak is designed so that it is exactly "two yagneg, one taluyaneg, and one tallinin in length" (Lipka, Shockey, and Adams, 2003, p. 184), or approximately three times the owner's height.

In mainstream American culture, we see this kind of personalized design as well, although with standard measures.

For example, bicycle racers have bikes made to fit their bodies, professional tennis players have special rackets designed for them, and racers sometimes wear custom-designed running shoes.

(*Source:* Lipka, Shockey, and Adams, 2003)

Strategies for the Classroom

- Ask the children what nonstandard measures they and their families use.

- Ask the children to find on their bodies the three Yu'pik measures discussed. Does the yagneg actually approximate their height? What is the relationship between the yagneg and the taluyaneg?

- Ask the children why they think using a nonstandard unit works better for the Eskimos.

CHILDREN'S LITERATURE

Using standard and nonstandard units of measure

 THE PLANNER

Measuring Penny • Figure 16.3

Written and illustrated by Loreen Leedy

Lisa's mathematics homework is to measure something in as many ways as possible using both standard and nonstandard units. Lisa decides to measure her dog Penny. She measures the length of Penny's nose with a ruler and the length of her tail with dog biscuits. She measures the length of her ears with cotton swabs and the width of her pads with centimeters. Lisa measures many different attributes of Penny, such as how much money and time it takes to care for her. This wonderful book offers many imaginative ideas that you can try out with your own class.

Strategy for the Classroom

- Measure the same attributes Lisa did with your class. If it is not feasible to bring a real dog to class, use a stuffed dog, or perhaps the classroom pet.

Customary and Metric Units

Two sets of standard units are used in the United States: the customary, or English, system and the metric system. Your students will be expected to use both of these in their mathematics and science classes throughout their education. Some of the units are rarely used, whereas others are used quite often. Consult your state's standards or curriculum guide to decide which specific units you need to reinforce.

When introducing children to standard units, help them become familiar with each unit through visual cues and practice. For example, ask them to estimate the capacity of familiar objects with liters or ounces. Next, help children learn to select the appropriate unit for measuring a given attribute. For example, a paper clip would be weighed in grams but a puppy would be weighed in kilograms. Finally, help children understand the relationship between different units that measure the same attribute. This is easily done with the metric system but not as easily done with the customary system because relationships are different for each type of measure (12 inches = 1 foot, but 16 ounces = 1 pound).

In the elementary grades, students do not convert from one system to the other but should be able to convert to equivalent measures within one system. For example, for the customary system they should know that 12 inches = 1 foot, 16 ounces = 1 pound, and 60 minutes = 1 hour. For the metric system they should know that 100 centimeters = 1 meter, 1000 grams = 1 kilogram, and 1 liter = 1000 milliliters.

Converting in the metric system is easier because it is a base-ten system and the prefixes of the terms indicate their place value. Teach children all six prefixes:

kilo	hecto	deka	deci	centi	milli
1000	100	10	$\frac{1}{10}$	$\frac{1}{100}$	$\frac{1}{1000}$

Metric measurement reinforces place value knowledge and understanding of base-ten fractions and decimals.

Although elementary school children do not formally convert between the customary and metric systems, they should know some rough equivalents. Use metric and customary rulers to discover some relationships. For example, one centimeter is about half an inch and one meter is a little longer than one yard. The metric measure that is most familiar in this country is the liter. Using quart and liter bottles, compare these measurements and discover that a liter is a little more than a quart.

Teaching Tip

Converting between Fahrenheit and Celsius

Students in the middle grades can find the formula for this conversion by finding the equation of the line through two points (212, 100) and (32, 0), which represent the boiling and freezing temperatures in Fahrenheit and Celsius. The conversion formula will express Celsius as a function of Fahrenheit. To express Fahrenheit as a function of Celsius, reverse the x- and y-coordinates. Use (100, 212) and (0, 32).

Estimation in Measurement

By asking children to estimate before they measure, they will come to realize that all measurements are approximate. For example, if you were to measure the length of a pencil with a 12-inch ruler, you would probably find that the pencil is about 6 inches long. You could give a more precise measure, but a standard ruler would probably not be able to give you the exact length of the pencil. To help children understand that measurements are approximations, use words such as *about* six inches long or *just over* six inches to describe the length of the pencil.

When children use standard units, estimation helps them focus on the unit itself. For example, to estimate the area of a room in square feet, they need to understand about how much space is taken up by one square foot.

Estimation is a skill that is used in everyday life. You probably estimate how long it will take to complete your homework, drive to school, or shop for groceries. You may estimate ingredients when cooking. Many of us have had the experience of asking for a recipe from a friend, only to find terms such as *add a pinch of salt* or *salt to taste* in the recipe. These are all examples of estimation in measurement.

Teaching Tip

Estimating measurements

- When estimating measurements, use benchmarks, such as more or less than one foot or heavier or lighter than one pound.

- Teach children to "chunk" the attribute by mentally subdividing it into equal, more manageable pieces, such as measuring the length of a room by counting the number of floor tiles or counting every pair of floor tiles.

CONCEPT CHECK

1. **What** is an attribute of an object? Select two everyday objects and describe two or more attributes for each object.

2. **What** other curricular areas use measurement? Describe one.

3. **Why** is it important for children to use both nonstandard and standard units of measure?

4. **How** does estimation enhance the accuracy of measurement?

Length and Area

LEARNING OBJECTIVES

1. **Describe** how children learn length and perimeter.

2. **Describe** how children learn area.

Length and **area** are both important attributes. Length is often the first attribute taught. Although length seems easy for adults to understand, it is often difficult for children to understand. By grade 3, children "form an understanding of **perimeter** as a measurable attribute and select appropriate

> **area** The space inside a region.
> **perimeter** The length around a region or object.

units, strategies, and tools to solve problems involving perimeter" (NCTM, 2006, p. 15). In grade 4 "[s]tudents recognize area as an attribute of two-dimensional regions" (NCTM, 2006, p. 16). Throughout elementary and into middle school, children often confuse perimeter and area, especially if formulas are introduced too early.

Length

Children first learn about length in prekindergarten through second grade (Kamii, 2006). Begin with nonstandard units, and do not introduce a ruler until at least second grade (NCTM, 2006; NGA Center/CCSSO, 2010). At that time, introduce a ruler that has only inches or centimeters, with no additional subdivisions of units (**Activity 16.4**). In order to understand further subdivisions on rulers, children need an understanding of fractional parts, and they will not have this experience by second grade. The standard ruler can be introduced in third or fourth grade.

Children form many misconceptions about length. Words that are used for mathematical length are also used in other ways. "And in many contexts, time and length are interconnected" (Battista, 2006, p. 140). For example, you might ask, "Will it take longer to walk up the stairs or wait for the elevator?" This example is not really about length but about time. However, the word *longer* is used, which can be confusing to children trying to understand the attribute of length. Another difficulty is that the mathematical meaning of length differs from the conventional meaning. Some of children's difficulties with the concept of length are illustrated in **Figure 16.4**.

When children learn about length, first they usually use "nonmeasurement reasoning" (Battista, 2006, p. 141). This means that their knowledge of length is based on perception—the blue crayon looks longer than the red crayon. Their reasoning is usually vague and imprecise. Next, children gradually develop "measurement reasoning" (Battista, 2006, p. 141), which means that they find "the number of unit lengths that fit end to end along an object, with no gaps or overlaps" (Battista, 2006, p. 141). They do this first with nonstandard units and later with standard units. Eventually, children integrate these two types of reasoning about length to develop a more accurate and sophisticated understanding.

The *Common Core State Standards* (NGA Center/CCSSO, 2010) specify that children learn iteration in grade 1. According to *Curriculum Focal Points* (NCTM, 2006), by second grade, children should understand the following concepts about measuring length:

- **Partitioning** or dividing up the whole into equal-sized parts

- **Transitivity**, the concept that if length *A* is longer than length *B* and length *B* is longer than length *C*, then length *A* is longer than length *C*

- **Iteration**, the process of repeating the unit along an object to measure its length

Different meanings of length • Figure 16.4

In everyday use, length means a straight-line distance, but in mathematical terms length means the total distance traveled. This dual meaning can be especially difficult for English-language learners.

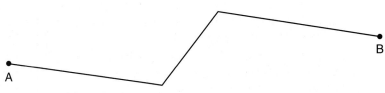

Comparison activities for length • Figure 16.5

a. To compare two lengths directly, line up the two objects and observe which is longer.

b. To compare lengths indirectly, compare them to a third object, such as a piece of string.

Which is wider, my desk or the doorway?

Comparison activities are very important for developing the concept of length. Children should have opportunities for both direct comparison and indirect comparison of length (**Figure 16.5**). Provide children with opportunities to measure the length of objects that are not long and straight, such as the length around trees or columns, in preparation for learning about perimeter.

Children often have difficulty measuring length because they do not know how to use units. Whether their units are paper clips, macaroni, footprints, inches, or centimeters, they should learn to line up the unit with the object and iterate the unit along the object, from end to end, without leaving gaps or overlapping. Demonstrate this technique for children and reinforce it with activities (**Activity 16.5**). As children complete measurement activities, they should discover the inverse relationship between the size of a unit and the length of the object being measured (**Activity 16.6**).

Perimeter is the length around something. Introduce perimeter in grade 3 (NCTM, 2006). Give children many opportunities to solve perimeter problems, but do not provide formulas for the perimeters of geometric shapes (**Activity 16.7**). When children learn formulas too early, they tend to ignore the conceptual meaning of perimeter.

Introduce children to the perimeter around a circle by grade 3 and use the term **circumference**, but do not use formulas until the upper elementary grades or middle school. The relationship between the **diameter** of a circle and its circumference is exciting for children in the upper elementary grades to discover (**Activity 16.8**).

> **circumference** The perimeter of a circle.
>
> **diameter** A line segment that passes through the center of a circle from one side of a circle to the other.

Reinforce elementary and middle school children's understanding of circles with children's literature (see *Children's Literature*, **Figure 16.6**).

Activity 16.5 First steps

Instructions

1. Provide the children with construction paper and scissors.

2. Group the children in pairs and ask them to make an outline of their partner's foot (shoe on) on the construction paper and cut it out.

3. Ask them to use their individual footprint unit to measure several objects in the classroom, such as the length or height of the teacher's desk or the length of the chalkboard.

4. Assess the children's measuring. Do they leave gaps or overlap their unit? Do they line up their unit of measurement at the beginning of the object they wish to measure and iterate until the end? Do they start counting before they move their footprint unit, or do they move and then count?

Activity 16.6 My own unit

Instructions

1. Create paper strips that are one inch, two inches, and three inches long. Each strip should be about two inches wide. All strips of the same length should be the same color. Use a different color for each length.

2. Ask each child to select one of the paper strips for his or her unit. Each child measures several items in the classroom with that unit.

3. Be sure to have objects to measure that are not exactly whole inches so that the children will have to decide how to handle fractional measures.

4. Compare measurements of the same object with strips of different lengths. Ask: *What is the length of the eraser in one-inch strips? In two-inch strips? Which measure used more units? Why?*

5. Ask: *Which unit is easier to measure with?*

Activity 16.7 Finding perimeters

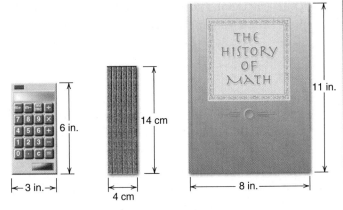

Instructions

1. Ask the students to find the perimeter of objects in the class-room using a ruler in inches or centimeters.

2. Record the dimensions and find the perimeters without using formulas.

3. Ask the students whether they notice any patterns. (They should notice that the perimeter of a figure is the sum of its dimensions. For a rectangular shape, the perimeter is the sum of twice the width plus twice the length.)

Activity 16.8 The relationship of the diameter of a circle to its circumference

Instructions

1. Show the children several cans of different sizes. Ask: *What shape is the top of each can?* (A circle)

2. Provide the children with measuring tapes and ask them to measure the circumference of the top of each can as well as its diameter.

3. Ask the children to use scientific calculators to divide the circumference of each can by its diameter. Their answers should approach 3.14, which is an approximation for pi.

4. Ask: *Can you write an equation that represents the relationship between the circumference of a circle and its diameter?* (The circumference is equal to the product of pi and the diameter of the circle.)

CHILDREN'S LITERATURE

Learning the parts of a circle

THE PLANNER

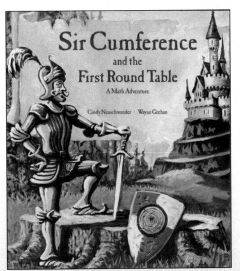

Sir Cumference and the First Round Table: A Math Adventure • Figure 16.6

Written by Cindy Neuschwander
Illustrated by Wayne Geehan

The kingdom was in danger of being attacked and all the knights wanted to meet to find a peaceful solution, but they could not agree on the shape of table to sit around. Finally, they decided on a round table, because it would give everyone an equal position. They named the distance from the center of the table to the edge *radius*, after Sir Cumference's son, and they named the distance across the table *diameter*, because it was equal to Lady Di of Ameter's reach.

Strategies for the Classroom

• Read the book with children as you identify the parts of the circle.

• Ask: *What are some of the advantages of sitting at a circular table?*

Area

Adults often "understand area as a formula rather than as a concept—the amount of space covered by the inside boundaries of a two-dimensional figure" (Casa, Spinelli, and Gavin, 2006, p. 168). Children in the primary grades should develop a conceptual understanding of the meaning of area by learning to compose and decompose two-dimensional shapes. This will provide a foundation for their work on area in the upper elementary and middle grades (NCTM, 2006). Early area activities focus on covering shapes with nonstandard units. At this stage, it is not important that the units fit the shape exactly. What is important is that children understand that area means finding the number of units that will cover the space and that an irregular shape can be covered by breaking the shape into pieces (**Activity 16.9**).

Activity 16.9 Areas of footprints

Instructions

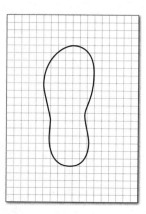

1. Use the same footprint unit described in Activity 16.5.

2. Ask the children to cover their footprint with triangular pattern blocks and count how many blocks it takes to cover the region.

3. Ask them to cover the same footprint with another nonstandard unit, such as small beads.

4. Ask: *What do you find?* (The smaller the unit, the more that are needed to cover the footprint.)

5. Ask the children to trace their footprint on grid paper and count the number of squares it takes to cover their shape. In many cases, because the footprint is an irregular shape, children will have to break up the footprint into pieces and count partial squares.

6. Discuss children's methods for counting partial squares.

7. Ask: *Is it easier to find the area of a footprint with units such as beads or with grid-paper squares?*

Tech Tools

http://nlvm.usu.edu/

Go to the **National Library of Virtual Manipulatives** and select **Measurement** and **Grades 3–5**. The Geoboard activity presents polygons with irregular areas on a virtual geoboard.

The development of area concepts closely parallels the development of length. Children must once again understand the concept of partitioning and iteration, this time with two-dimensional space. They must also understand **conservation of area** and **structuring an array** (McDuffie and Eve, 2009). Conservation of area means that when a region is broken up or rearranged, its area remains constant. It is an important concept but one that is often overlooked in area instruction. Children in the primary grades do not usually understand conservation of area, but children in the upper elementary grades should understand this concept. **Activity 16.10**, adapted from McDuffie and Eve (2009, p. 23), illustrates how to teach conservation of area.

Activity 16.10 Conservation of area

Instructions

1. Show the children drawings of the letter *A* made from pattern blocks. Use all triangles.

2. Ask: *How many triangles make up the letter* A? (13) *If each triangle is one unit, what is the area of the triangle?* (13)

3. Say: *Now see how many different ways you can make the letter* A *by substituting other pattern blocks for triangles. Find the area.*

4. Ask: *What did you find?* (The area always adds up to the equivalent of 13 triangles.)

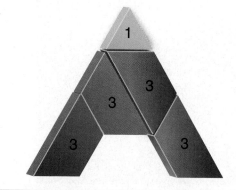

In grade 4, students "learn that they can quantify areas by finding the total number of same-sized units of area that cover the shape without gaps or overlaps" (NCTM, 2006, p. 16). They also learn to use the tools of whole number multiplication, specifically arrays, with area and to connect the area of a rectangle with multiplication. To find the areas of regions, children learn to create arrays of square units that fit within the boundaries of the regions, do not overlap, and do not have gaps. Arrays are probably the most difficult measurement concept for children to learn. They have difficulty visualizing the array and partitioning the space without using physical manipulatives. In **Activity 16.11**, the concept of array is developed by asking children to fill in rectangular shapes with square units. In **Activity 16.12**, parts of an array are given and children fill in the rest of the array. This connects the number of rows and columns of a rectangular array with its dimensions and sets the groundwork for area formulas.

Activity 16.11 Developing arrays

Instructions

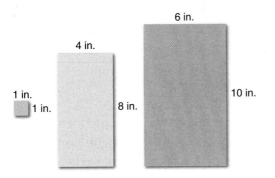

1. Distribute two different-size construction-paper rectangles to children: 4 inches × 8 inches and 6 inches × 10 inches.

2. Distribute one-inch-square units to the children.

3. Ask the children to cover each rectangle with one-inch squares. Make sure there are no overlaps or gaps. For each rectangle, ask: *How many rows and how many columns are there in your array? How many squares did you use in all? What is the area of the rectangle?*

4. Ask: *If I cover a rectangle with three rows and four columns of one-inch squares, how many squares will it take to cover the entire rectangle? What is its area?*

5. Repeat, asking similar questions with different dimensions.

6. Discuss square inches, or in.², and square centimeters, or cm², as units of area.

7. To extend the activity, say: *I have a rectangle that I covered with 16 square inches. What array can you make for the rectangle?* (There are several correct answers.)

Activity 16.12 Structuring arrays

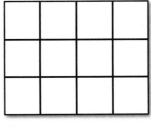

A.

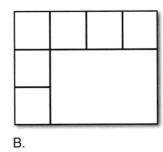

B.

Instructions

1. Show drawing A. Ask: *How many rows and columns does this array have?*

2. Show drawing B. Ask: *How many rows and columns does this array have?*

3. Ask: *What are the lengths of each side of the rectangle in A and B? What do you notice?* (The length of the sides corresponds to the number of square units in each row or the number of square units in each column.)

4. Ask: *How can you find the area of the rectangle if you know the lengths of its sides?* (Multiply them.)

Teaching Tip

Learning area formulas

Although it is tempting to move quickly to area formulas and children may even know formulas from parents or older siblings, resist the temptation to move to formulas too quickly. When children are given time to develop the concept of area, there will be less chance of them mixing it up with perimeter later on.

Area formulas Children learn area formulas in the upper elementary grades. According to the *Common Core State Standards* (NGA Center/CCSSO, 2010), perimeter and area formulas should be introduced in grade 4. Build on children's experiences with building arrays to develop the formula for the area of a rectangle. Notice how this connects to the conceptual development of multiplication discussed in Chapter 10. Rather than using the conventional terms *length* and *width*, use *base* and *height* to achieve consistency with formulas for three-dimensional shapes. The formulas for the areas of squares, parallelograms, and triangles can be derived from the formula for the area of a rectangle (Area = base × height), as illustrated in **Activities 16.13** and **16.14**. Both activities use the concept of conservation of area.

Activity 16.13 The area of a parallelogram

Instructions

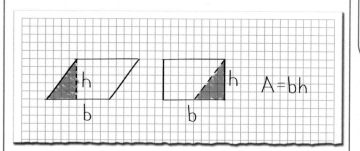

1. Provide the children with a parallelogram drawn on grid paper.
2. Ask them to draw the height of the parallelogram (the vertical line from one vertex to the opposite side).
3. Slice off the triangle formed and attach it to the other side of the parallelogram.
4. Ask: *What kind of shape have you created?* (A rectangle) *What is its area? What is the area of the original parallelogram?*

Activity 16.14 The area of a triangle

Instructions

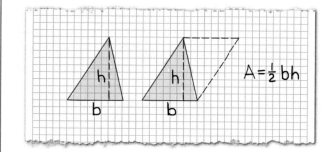

1. Provide the children with a triangle drawn on grid paper.
2. Ask them to extend the triangle to make a parallelogram.
3. Ask: *What is the relationship between the original triangle and the parallelogram?* (The triangle covers half the area of the parallelogram.)
4. Ask them to find the area of the parallelogram, using the technique from Activity 16.13 and the area of the triangle.

The formula for the area of a rectangle can also be used to find the area of a square. Since a square is a rectangle with all sides congruent, its base is equal to its height, so the area is equal to the square of the length of the side (base or height).

Use the area of a parallelogram to find the area of a trapezoid (**Figure 16.7**).

The relationship between perimeter and area

Children's literature can help students distinguish between perimeter and area and learn the relationship between these two important attributes. The book described in *Children's Literature*, **Figure 16.8**, illustrates how area can

The area of a trapezoid • Figure 16.7

To find the area of a trapezoid, make a copy of the trapezoid, flip it, and place it next to the original trapezoid. These two trapezoids form a parallelogram. Find the area, using the formula for the area of a parallelogram and then find half of the area.

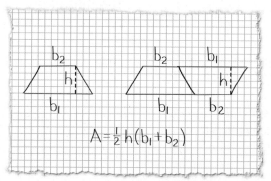

CHILDREN'S LITERATURE

Understanding the relationship between perimeter and area

Spaghetti and Meatballs for All! A Mathematical Story • Figure 16.8

Written by Marilyn Burns
Illustrated by Debbie Tilley

Mr. and Mrs. Comfort decided to have a party and invited 32 people. Mrs. Comfort rented tables and chairs and set up eight tables with four chairs at each table. However, as her guests arrived they decided to push the tables together. Each time they pushed tables together, more seats were lost. Eventually, they discovered their error and rearranged the tables.

Strategies for the Classroom

- Read this book with your students. As you read, have them draw each configuration of eight tables or make the configurations using one-inch-square color tiles.

- Each time the tables are moved, ask: *How many seats are there now? How many were lost?*

- After your class has modeled each configuration of tables and chairs, explain that the tables represent the area with each table representing one square unit, and the chairs represent the perimeter.

- Ask: *When they rearrange the tables in the story, does the area change? Does the perimeter change?* (The area does not change, but the perimeter does.)

---

remain constant but perimeter may vary when a shape is decomposed and rearranged.

To reinforce this concept, follow up with an activity that shows the relationship between perimeter and area, adapted from *Principles and Standards for School Mathematics* (NCTM, 2000, p. 173) (**Activity 16.15**).

Formulas for the perimeter and area of polygons are often presented at the same time. This can cause confusion. Children who have memorized formulas but do not understand the distinction between perimeter and area often do not know whether to write an answer in units or square units, because they are not sure whether they

---

Activity 16.15 The relationship between perimeter and area

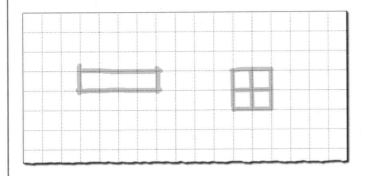

Instructions

1. Distribute grid paper to each student.

2. Ask the students to draw a line around a rectangle of four squares arranged horizontally in one row on the grid paper.

3. Ask: *What is the area of this rectangle?* (4) *What is the perimeter?* (10)

4. Say: *Find different arrangements of these four squares. All squares must be connected to at least one other square at a side.*

5. Say: *Find the area and perimeter of each arrangement of squares. What do you notice?* (The area is always 4, but the perimeter varies.)

are measuring perimeter or area (Moyer, 2001). **Activity 16.16**, adapted from Moyer, helps children distinguish between perimeter and area by using irregularly shaped polygons that do not lend themselves to formulas.

Chapter 15 discussed similarity for geometric figures. Recall that similar figures are the same shape but not necessarily the same size. This means that the lengths of corresponding sides are proportional. Similarity also affects perimeters and areas of polygons. **Activity 16.17**, which is appropriate for students in upper elementary or middle grades, connects the concepts of similarity to perimeter and area.

Tech Tools

www.nctm.org

Select **Standards and Focal Points** and then **e-Examples**. Select e-Example 6.3 **Learning About Length, Perimeter, Area, and Volume of Similar Objects Using Interactive Figures**. Next, select **Side Length and Area of Similar Figures**. This interactive site allows the user to discover the relationships of perimeters and areas that were discussed in Activity 16.17.

Activity 16.16 Finding the areas of irregular shapes

Instructions

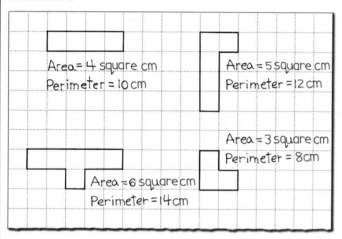

1. Provide the children with several irregular polygons on centimeter grid paper.

2. Ask the children to find the perimeter and the area for each polygon.

3. They will find the perimeter by counting the number of sides and the area by counting the number of one-centimeter squares.

4. Alternately, create irregular polygons using one-inch sides. Ask the students to cover the interior with one-inch-square color tiles to find the area and count the number of exposed sides of the color tiles to find the perimeter.

Activity 16.17 Perimeters and areas of similar figures

Instructions

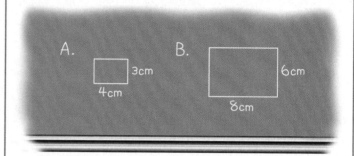

1. Say: *This diagram shows two similar rectangles. The base of rectangle A is 4 cm and its height is 3 cm. The base of rectangle B is 8 cm and its height is 6 cm. What is the ratio of corresponding sides?* (1:2)

2. Say: *Find the perimeters of rectangle A and rectangle B.* (For rectangle A, P = 14 cm. For rectangle B, P = 28 cm.)

3. Ask: *What do you notice?* (The perimeters are in the ratio of 1:2, the same as the sides.)

4. Ask: *Do you think the areas of the polygons will have the same ratio? Let's find out.*

5. Students find out that the area of rectangle A is 12 cm² and the area of rectangle B is 48 cm², in the ratio of 1:4.

6. Ask: *Why is the ratio for the areas 1:4 instead of 1:2?* (Through discussion, students should realize that area is two-dimensional, so the ratio of the areas is the square of the ratio for the sides and the perimeter.)

CONCEPT CHECK   STOP

1. **How** do children use the concepts of partitioning, iteration, and transitivity when they learn length? Why are these concepts important for children to understand?

2. **What** is conservation of area? Why is this important for children to know?

Volume, Capacity, Mass, and Weight

LEARNING OBJECTIVES

1. **Distinguish** between capacity and volume.

2. **Describe** the attribute of weight and how children learn weight.

Volume, capacity, mass, and weight are attributes of three-dimensional objects. When we think of capacity, we think of how much something can hold. Capacity is measured in liters, milliliters, gallons, quarts, and cups. Volume also refers to capacity but also can be used to determine the size of solid objects. Volume is measured in cubic units of length. Mass measures the amount of matter in an object, and weight is technically the pull of gravity on an object. In outer space, weight and matter will differ because the pull of gravity is different. On earth, however, weight and mass mean the same thing. Adults and children are more familiar with the term *weight*, which is measured in ounces, pounds, grams, and kilograms.

Volume and Capacity

It is very difficult to compare the volumes of two solids. Even adults can be easily misled about which solid has greater volume. For example, a tall narrow jar may appear to hold less than a short wide one but may actually have greater volume. For children in the primary grades, focus instead on activities that compare capacity, and save volume for the upper elementary grades. Capacity can be introduced to children through direct comparison activities. Give children many opportunities to compare the capacities of different solids, using fillers such as birdseed, sand, or dried beans (**Activity 16.18**).

According to *Curriculum Focal Points* (NCTM, 2006) and the *Common Core State Standards* (NGA Center/CCSSO, 2010), volume should be introduced in grade 5. At this grade level, students should understand, for example, that they can measure the volume of a cube by filling it with unit cubes and counting how many unit cubes are necessary to completely fill it. They should also be able to estimate or measure volume using appropriate units.

Before this formal introduction to volume, ask children to fill open solids (for example, an open box) with small wooden cubes. Such activities, which are measures

of capacity, prepare children to learn about volume. It is also important for children to build towers and other structures using wooden cubes and then take them apart again. Ask children to count the layers both horizontally and vertically and to describe how they count the parts that are hidden.

Activity 16.18 Which holds more?

Instructions

1. Show your class two birdfeeders. Say: *I can only hang one of these outside our classroom window. How should we decide which one to hang?* (The one that holds more birdseed)

2. *Which one do you think holds more seed? How can we find out?*

3. Discuss with the children different options for finding out how much seed each birdfeeder holds. Elicit the idea of filling each feeder with seed, using a small cup to measure out the seed, and counting the number of cups it takes to fill each feeder.

4. Discuss the results.

5. Repeat with other objects to compare, such as two empty different-size cans or boxes of cereal.

The volume of a rectangular prism and a right circular cylinder • Figure 16.9

a. Fill the base of this box with three rows of 4 cubes each. The base holds 12 cubes. Five layers of 12 cubes fill the box. The box has volume 3 × 4 × 5 = 60 cubic units.

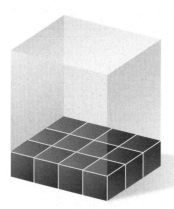

b. Fill the base of this cylinder with a circular chip whose top has a radius of 3 units. The base of this cylinder is a circle with radius 3. The area of the top of this circular chip is 9 pi. Six layers of circular chips fill this cylinder. The cylinder has volume 9 pi × 6 = 54 pi cubic units.

Formulas for volume Perhaps the easiest volume formulas for children to understand are the volumes of a rectangular prism (a box) and a right circular cylinder (a can) (**Figure 16.9**).

Teaching Tip

Modeling the volumes of prisms and cylinders

- To model the volume of a prism, distribute square tiles. Ask the children to find the area of each tile and then pile several same-sized tiles one on the other, noting how many tiles have been stacked and referring to this as the height of the prism.

- Repeat with triangular-shaped tiles, such as green pattern blocks.

- To model the volume of a cylinder, stack pennies, nickels, or quarters one at a time, one on top of the other. Find the area of one of the coins and note how many have been stacked.

Weight

Weight cannot be measured directly. To begin instruction on weight, use comparison activities. Give children in primary grades two bags of unequal weight, and ask them to hold one bag in each hand and decide which feels heavier or weighs more. These types of activities prepare children for using two-pan balance scales or spring scales to compare weight. Demonstrate

how a two-pan balance scale or spring scale works by putting objects of equal weight on both sides of the scale and then putting heavier objects on one side. Make sure children understand how the scale looks when it is "even." Ask them to describe what happens when heavier objects are placed on one side of the scale. Small washers that can be purchased at the hardware store or centimeter cubes are great tools for these types of activities (**Activity 16.19**).

Activity 16.19 Using a balance scale

Instructions

1. Use a balance scale for a whole class activity or distribute balance scales to each pair of children.
2. Choose two objects, one of which is heavier than the other.
3. Ask the students to guess which one is heavier.
4. Place the objects on the balance scale, one on each side to decide which is heavier.
5. Ask: *Was your guess correct?*
6. Repeat with other pairs of objects.

Children can use balance scales to order the weights of several objects. **Activity 16.20,** adapted from Mailley and Moyer (2004), explains how this can be done.

The standard unit for mass in the metric system is one kilogram. To help children understand about how much this weighs, use a one-kilogram weight and place it on one side of the scale. Place other objects, one at a time, on the other side and compare. Decide whether each item is heavier or lighter than one kilogram. Create a list of objects that are heavier than one kilogram and objects that are lighter than one kilogram.

Activity 16.20 Which candy weighs the most?

Instructions

1. To prepare for this activity, select several types of candy and put equal numbers of each type in plastic bags, with a different bag for each type of candy.

2. Ask children whether they have ever gone to a candy store or the candy counter in a grocery store and picked out some candy. Discuss the procedure of choosing candy and having the clerk weigh the candy, assuming that the cost of different kinds of candy depends only on its weight.

3. Say: *Here are four types of candy. Which type do you think weighs the most?*

4. Gather the students around a balance scale. Place one bag of one type of candy on one side of the balance scale and centimeter cubes or washers of uniform size on the other side of the scale until the scale balances.

5. Record with your class how many cubes or washers were needed to balance the scale.

6. Begin again with a second type of candy and cubes or washers.

7. After all the candy has been measured, ask the students to list the candy from most expensive to least expensive, based on its weight.

CONCEPT CHECK

1. **Why** should young children be taught about capacity rather than volume?

2. **What** makes weight an attribute that can be easily studied?

Time, Money, Temperature, and Angle Measure

LEARNING OBJECTIVES

1. **Explain** children's difficulties in learning the attribute of time.
2. **Describe** how children learn to use money.
3. **Explain** how children learn about temperature.
4. **Identify** the attribute of angle measure.

In order to function effectively in our society, it is necessary to understand and use the attributes of time, money, and temperature. Children often begin learning about these concepts as early as prekindergarten and often have some experience with them before they begin school. Angles are a more subtle topic that children probably will not experience outside of school.

Time

The concept of time is elusive for many children because they cannot see or feel it. Adults tend to think that learning about time means clock reading or telling time, but this is only one part of understanding time. To understand the concept of time, children also must understand sequencing and elapsed time. They should be familiar with the standard units of time (the second, the minute, and the hour), develop an intuitive understanding of each, and be able to convert between these units.

Sequencing time Do you remember what you ate for dinner yesterday or where you are planning to go tomorrow? To answer these questions, you must understand the concept of sequencing of time. Although this is easy for adults, children in the primary grades often have difficulty with sequencing. Help them understand this concept by using sequencing vocabulary such as *before, after, earlier,* and *later,* and *yesterday, today,* and *tomorrow.* Engage children in discussions that use these terms. You might say: *Do you remember that yesterday we had a visitor in class? The visitor came before lunch. Today we are not having a visitor before lunch but we are going to read a special book after lunch.* **Activity 16.21** demonstrates an effective way to teach sequencing.

Activity 16.21 What happened today?

Instructions

1. Say: *We are going to draw some pictures about what you did in school today. Remember, in the morning we painted and later we had story time.*

2. *First draw a picture of what you did earlier today. Next, draw a picture of what you did later today.*

3. Create a bulletin board with two columns: **Earlier** and **Later**.

4. Ask the children to place their drawings on the bulletin board in the correct order.

5. Expand this activity by asking each child to create a timeline of several things he or she did in one school day by creating illustrations for each part of the timeline and placing them in order from earliest to latest.

Telling time You may wonder why children need to learn to read a dial clock when digital clocks are commonly used. One reason is that digital clocks require advanced knowledge that children in primary grades do not possess. Digital clocks provide the exact time, such as 3:27, but do not indicate how close that time is to 3:00, 3:30, or 4:00. To understand this, a child must understand that there are 60 minutes in an hour and that 27 is about halfway between 0 and 60. Children in the primary grades do not yet have this knowledge.

Begin teaching children to tell time in the first grade by using dial clocks, either real ones or ones that you make from paper plates. **Activity 16.22** illustrates how to begin telling time with a clock that has one hand. In **Activity 16.23**, children use a two-handed clock to learn how the little hand changes position as the big hand goes around the clock. In **Activity 16.24**, children learn to read the clock in five-minute intervals after the hour and learn to use the language of time.

Activity 16.22 Telling time by the hour

Instructions

1. Show the children a clock that has one hand. Such a clock can be made out of heavy construction paper, cut into a circle, or a paper plate, with a hole in the center and a brass fastener attaching a construction-paper hand to the center.

2. Ask: *What number is the hand pointed to?* (2) *We call that 2 o'clock.*

3. Say: *Now let's count together as the hand goes around the clock.* (Move the hand to 3, 4, 5, etc.)

Activity 16.23 The hands of the clock

Instructions

1. Show the children a clock with two hands.

2. Say: *Watch what happens as the big hand moves around the clock.* Move it yourself.

3. Ask: *What do you notice?* (As the big hand moves, the little hand moves gradually to the next number.)

4. Ask: *What happens when the big hand moves all the way around?* (The little hand moves to the next number.)

Activity 16.24 The language of time

Instructions

1. Show the children a clock with two hands.

2. Position the clock so that it is 5 minutes after the hour. Ask: *What time is it?*

3. Encourage the children to say *5 after 7* instead of *7:05* to help them understand that this time is later than 7.

4. Reposition the clock in five-minute intervals and ask: *What time is it?*

Children need a variety of skills to tell time. First, they need to be able to count and understand the magnitude of numbers. That is, they need to understand that 10 minutes past 7 is later than 5 minutes past 7. Because children often learn to tell time in five-minute intervals, they should know how to skip count by fives. Practice this by moving the long hand around the clock and simultaneously chanting "5, 10, 15, 20, . . . 60." This will provide a good model for multiplication in later grades. Children also need to know that one hour is 60 minutes, one quarter of an hour is 15 minutes, and half an hour is 30 minutes.

Children develop misconceptions about telling time. When using the terms *a quarter to* the hour or *a quarter past* the hour, they often associate this with the number 25, because 25 cents is equal to one quarter. **Figure 16.10** illustrates how to overcome this difficulty.

Tech Tools

http://nlvm.usu.edu/

Go to the **National Library of Virtual Manipulatives.**

1. Select **Measurement** and **Grades K–2**. The **Time-Match Clocks** applet presents the faces of an analog and digital clock and lets the user match the times. This activity provides children with practice reading both analog and digital clocks and develops their ability to move from one representation of time to the other.

2. Select the **What Time Will It Be?** applet. The screen presents two dial clocks that show the same time and asks the user to move the dials on the second clock to answer questions showing a new time earlier or later than the given time. This provides children with practice reading an analog clock and understanding the terminology of time, such as **later than, after,** and **earlier than.**

Children's misconceptions about time • Figure 16.10

Ask the children to fold paper clock faces into four equal parts. This will help them to recognize the location on the clock that means *quarter after the hour or half past the hour.* If they understand that 60 minutes is one hour, they will recognize that a *quarter after the hour* is 15 minutes after the hour and *half past the hour* is 30 minutes after the hour.

LESSON Learning Elapsed Time with an Open Number Line

GRADE LEVEL

3

OBJECTIVES

Find the elapsed time when a starting time and ending time are given.

Find the end time when the starting time and elapsed time are given.

Find the starting time when the end time and elapsed time are given.

STANDARDS

Grade 3

Tell and write time to the nearest minute and measure time in intervals of minutes. Solve word problems involving addition and subtraction of time intervals in minutes, e.g., by representing the problem on a number line diagram. (NGA Center/CCSSO, 2010)

MATERIALS

- Paper and pencils
- Word problems
- Template with open number lines

ASSESSMENT

- Provide the children with open number lines that indicate elapsed time. Ask them to provide the starting and ending time. There are many ways to get a correct answer.
- Ask the children to write elapsed-time problems.

- Ask the children to create illustrated timelines about events in a day in their life that illustrate elapsed time.

GROUPING

Whole class followed by small group

Launch (10 to 15 minutes)

- Say: *Solve the following problem: Lynette found 30 strawberries in her garden and then found an extra 14 strawberries. How many strawberries did she have in all?*

- Discuss several ways of solving the problem. If no one suggests using the open number line, then suggest it to the class.

- Say: *If we use the open number line, we can start at 30 and count up 10 more and then 4 more. Or we can start at 30 and count up 20 and go back 6.*

- Say: *We are going to use a similar strategy to learn about time.*

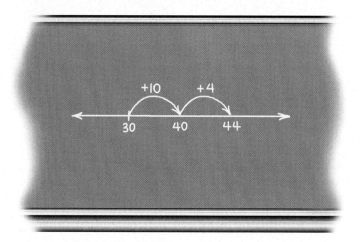

Benchmarks for time Children need benchmarks for time (McMillan and Ortiz, 2008). Help them understand how long a minute is by conducting experiments. While timing them with a stopwatch, ask children how many times they can write their name, jump rope, or clap their hands together in a minute. According to McMillan and Ortiz, children often believe there will be the same number of repetitions for each of the activities they try in a minute. They do not understand, for example, that

writing their name will take longer than clapping their hands, so there will be fewer repetitions of writing their name in one minute than clapping their hands together.

After children understand the benchmark of one minute, help them to discover how many seconds are in a minute (McMillan and Ortiz, 2008). Using a large clock, count the movement of the second hand all around the clock. Do this several times, starting at different positions on the clock.

Instruct (30 to 35 minutes)

- Say: *How can you use the open number line to solve the following problem?*

    Kristina started playing on the computer at 10:15 and finished at 11:45. How long did Kristina play on the computer?

- Ask the children to work in pairs to model the problem on an open number line and find their solution. Ask different pairs of children to display their answers and explain their work. Children might count up 1 hour to 11:15 and then another 30 minutes to 11:45. Next, they add 1 hour and 30 minutes to get the final answer.

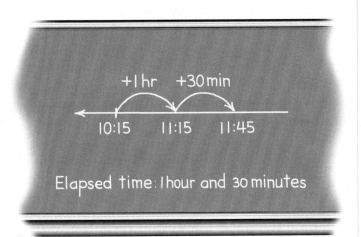

- Say: *Now let's try another problem:*

    Mohammed played ball with his friends. He started at 3:00 and played for 2 hours and 15 minutes. What time did Mohammed finish playing ball?

- Ask the children: *Can you use a number line to solve this problem, as well? Work in pairs again and try this one.*

- Children might draw an open number line and count up by 2 hours to 5:00 and then another 15 minutes to 5:15. Other solution methods are possible.

- Say: *Now let's try one more problem:*

    Dina practiced piano for 1 hour and 10 minutes. She finished her practice at 6:30. When did she start?

- Say: *This one is a little harder because you might have to use a different strategy.*

- Walk around and observe pairs of children as they work on this problem. One method is to start at 6:30 and count back 1 hour to 5:30 and another 10 minutes to 5:20. Some children may guess a start number and see whether it works in the problem using a guess-and-check strategy.

Summarize (5 minutes)

- Ask: *Who can explain how to use an open number line to describe the amount of time that has elapsed?*

- Ask: *How is this similar to the way we used the number line with addition and subtraction?*

Elapsed time How long was your drive to school today? Was it longer or shorter than your friend's drive? These questions relate to understanding elapsed time, or how long something takes. Begin teaching children about elapsed time in the primary grades with comparison activities, such as the following:

Both Arielle and Diego started working on the computer at the same time. Arielle worked on the computer for 20 minutes and Diego worked on the computer for 35 minutes. Who worked on the computer longer?

Consider using open number lines, the same models used by children to develop algorithms for addition and subtraction of whole numbers in Chapter 10, to illustrate elapsed-time problems (Dixon, 2008) (see the *Lesson*). The standards for this lesson are from the *Common Core State Standards* (NGA Center/CCSSO, 2010).

Money

Money is an important part of our culture. In the primary grades, children learn to identify coins by their appearance, their names, and their value. They often have misconceptions about money—for example, a nickel is worth more than a dime because of its size. Children will not discover the value of money through discovery or guided activities. You will have to tell them the value of each coin. Consider making a chart with the picture of each coin, its name, and its value.

Children in the second grade should learn to count the value of groups of coins, make exchanges between equivalent collections of different coins, and make change. Give children lots of practice playing with and evaluating make-believe money through games and activities. In **Activity 16.25** children put together different coins to make a given amount. In **Activity 16.26** they make exchanges for equivalent coins. In **Activity 16.27** they learn to make change. When teaching children to make change, show them how to count up. It is easier than subtraction and helps develop number sense for whole number computation.

Activity 16.25 Find the coins that make 45 cents

Instructions

1. Give the children make-believe money. Write an amount less than one dollar on the board or overhead and ask: *Can you find three coins that sum to 45 cents? What are they? Can you find five coins that sum to 45 cents? What are they?*

2. Repeat with other amounts.

3. Extend the activity by naming the amount of money and asking for coins that add to that amount without giving the number of coins needed.

Activity 16.26 Making equal exchanges

Instructions

1. Give the children make-believe coins for nickels, dimes, and quarters.

2. Say: *I have 2 quarters. Who can show an equal amount in dimes?* (5 dimes) *In nickels?* (10 nickels)

3. Say: *I have 12 nickels. Who can show an equal amount in dimes?* (6 dimes) *In quarters?* (Impossible)

4. Say: *I have 11 nickels. Who can show an equal amount in dimes?* (Impossible) *In quarters?* (Impossible)

5. Say: *I have 2 dimes. Who can show an equal amount in nickels?* (4 nickels)

6. Continue by exchanging coins of one type for a mixture of more than one type of coin, such as 2 quarters for 3 dimes and 4 nickels.

Activity 16.27 Making change

Instructions

1. Give the children make-believe money. Begin making change with coins only and then move to dollars.

2. Say: *I want to spend 35 cents on gum. I have 2 quarters. How much change should I get? Show your work by making exchanges.* (Exchange 1 quarter for 2 dimes and 1 nickel. Give 1 dime and 1 nickel as change.)

3. Say: *I want to spend 80 cents but I only have a one-dollar bill. How much change should I get? Show your work by making exchanges.* (Exchange 1 dollar for 10 dimes. Give 2 dimes as change.)

4. Continue with problems of this type, asking children to make the actual exchanges with make-believe money.

Read about how one second-grade teacher taught her students about the value of money by engaging them in a real-life activity (see *In the Classroom*).

In the Classroom
At the Mathematics Auction

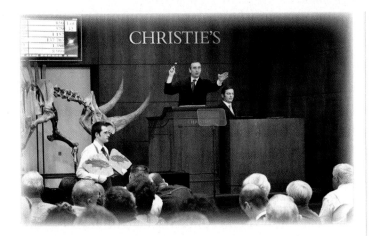

At Timonium Elementary School in Baltimore, Maryland, second-grade teacher Betty McCue taught her students about money by "paying" them in make-believe money for doing good work in class. Each student had a bank book and at the end of each day, the students tallied up their "earnings." The students knew that they would be able to use their make-believe money to bid for used items at an auction to be held at the end of their two-month money unit. The used items for the auction came from the class itself. Ms. McCue sent a letter home to parents asking them to donate used toys and other items.

When the big day arrived, a professional auctioneer who was a friend of Ms. McCue volunteered to help. The auctioneer demonstrated how he usually spoke at auctions but spoke more slowly for the students. They bid on many different items, including a karaoke machine. The auctioneer even showed children how they could pool their money to buy something that one individual could not afford alone. The auction was a great success.

(*Source:* www.bcps.org/news/2006/Timonium/Elementary)

Think Critically

1. How did Ms. McCue's money unit teach children about the value of different denominations of money?
2. In what ways did the auction serve to extend children's concepts of money?
3. What are some other real-life activities you can think of for teaching about money in your own classroom?
4. What other lessons about using and saving money might children have learned from this activity?

Temperature

Temperature is measured in degrees Fahrenheit in the customary system and degrees Celsius in the metric system. Unlike time, temperature is an attribute that can be perceived by children. Help children in the primary grades understand words such as *warm*, *hot*, *cool*, and *cold* before introducing a thermometer (**Activity 16.28**).

Activity 16.28 Knowing what's cool

Instructions

1. Ask the children: *What does it mean for something to be warm, hot, cool, or cold?* Write their responses in columns on the board or overhead. Discuss each response to see whether the whole class agrees on each example.

2. Show pictures similar to the ones illustrated in this activity and ask: *Would you use the word warm, hot, cool, or cold to describe this scene? Why?*

3. Ask the children to arrange the pictures from coldest to warmest or from warmest to coldest.

4. Continue with other examples.

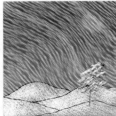

Reading a thermometer •
Figure 16.11

Thermometers are an excellent way to introduce negative integers. When the temperature falls below zero, it is denoted with a negative sign. The thermometer serves as a vertical number line. As students become familiar with reading a thermometer, they should learn the benchmarks for boiling (212 degrees Fahrenheit or 100 degrees Celsius) and freezing (32 degrees Fahrenheit or 0 degrees Celsius).

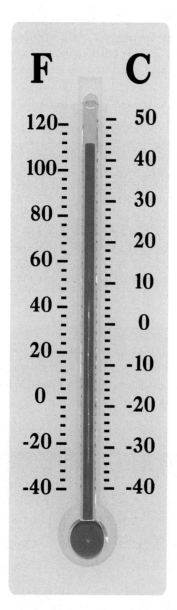

Introduce a thermometer and teach children in grades 3–5 how to read it (**Figure 16.11**). Explain that the liquid in the thermometer expands when the temperature is warmer, forcing the liquid up the tube, and contracts when the temperature is cooler. Demonstrate by placing a real thermometer in several cups of water at different

temperatures. To help children gain familiarity with the units of temperature, make a point of talking about the temperature outside each day. Show children photos of people skiing or swimming and ask: *I wonder what the temperature was when this picture was taken?*

Angle Measure

Angles are technically part of geometry and were discussed in Chapter 15, but the measure of angles is part of measurement. Children often have a misconception about angle measure. They tend to think that angle measure means the length of the sides of the angle rather than the openness of the angle. Help them understand the meaning of angle measure by making several angles with straws or pencils and then filling in the inside of the angle with beans or some other filler to show that angle measure is an attribute that is similar to area.

By grade 5 or 6, children can measure angles with a **protractor**, an instrument that measures angles in units called **degrees** (**Figure 16.12**). Before children learn to use this instrument, they should learn to informally assess the size of angles using the benchmark of 90 degrees. Initially, children can learn to compare angles to see whether they are greater than, equal to, or less than 90 degrees (**Activity 16.29**).

> **protractor** A semicircular tool for measuring angles.

Using a protractor • Figure 16.12

Protractors are used to measure angles up to 180 degrees. Because most protractors have two scales on them, children have difficulty using them to measure angles unless they know how to estimate whether the angle is less than or greater than 90 degrees. Make certain that children can estimate different-size angles by their appearance before using a protractor.

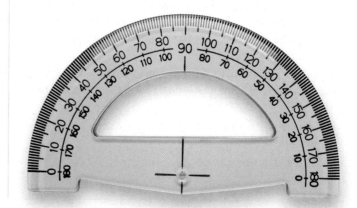

Activity 16.29 Comparing angles to a benchmark

Instructions

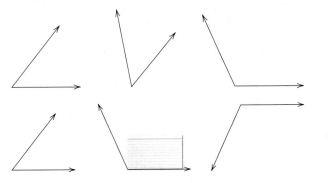

1. Give each child a handout with different-size angles and an index card.

2. Explain that the corner of the card shows a 90-degree angle.

3. Ask students to place this corner, or vertex, in the vertex of each angle on the handout to determine whether it is greater than, less than, or equal to 90 degrees.

CONCEPT CHECK

1. **What** is elapsed time? How can an open number line be helpful in teaching children about elapsed time?

2. **What** should children learn about money by the second grade?

3. **Why** is temperature an attribute that can be perceived by children?

4. **What** misconceptions do children often have about angle measure?

THE PLANNER ✓

Summary

1 Learning About Measurement 404

- Children go through the same process of selecting an attribute to measure, choosing the unit of measurement, and comparing the object with the unit, for all attributes.

- When children first learn to measure, they use **nonstandard units**, as illustrated in this figure. In later elementary grades they use **standard units**.

Figure 16.2

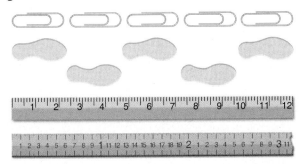

- It is important for children to estimate before measuring. Estimating helps focus attention on the **attribute** and the unit of measure.

- Measurement is an important area of the curriculum. It has connections to many other topics in mathematics as well as to other curricular areas.

2 Length and Area 410

- Length is usually the first attribute to be taught. Children can begin to learn about length through direct or indirect comparisons without the use of units. This image illustrates direct comparison. In the later elementary grades, they learn about a special kind of length, called **perimeter**, as well as the length around a circle, or the **circumference**.

Figure 16.5

- **Area** measures how much space a two-dimensional shape takes. Early area activities involve covering irregular shapes with beans or other counters. Children gradually begin to associate area with square units and the array. In the upper elementary grades children can learn about area formulas.

3 Volume, Capacity, Mass, and Weight 419

- Children often confuse capacity and volume. Capacity refers to how much something can hold. Volume refers to the same thing but can also refer to the size of solid objects. Capacity is much easier to compare than volume. This can be done by filling two containers with a filler, such as sand or birdseed, and determining which container holds more of the filler.

- Weight is an attribute that children can perceive, as shown here. If they hold up two objects they will know which is heavier. Balance scales can also be used to compare the weight of two objects or shapes.

Figure 16.2

4 Time, Money, Temperature, and Angle Measure 421

- Reading a clock is one aspect of learning about time, but it is not the only aspect. Children also need to understand sequencing and determining elapsed time.

- Money is an important attribute and one that is studied in early elementary grades. Give children make-believe money and many opportunities to learn each denomination and to make change.

- Temperature is an easier attribute to learn than time because it can be perceived. Before teaching children units of temperature, give them many opportunities to experience temperature and develop vocabulary such as *warm, hot, cool,* and *cold.*

- Angle measure can be taught through comparison activities. Give children opportunities to use 90 degrees as a benchmark and to compare the size of other angles to this benchmark before they learn to use a **protractor**, shown here.

Figure 16.12

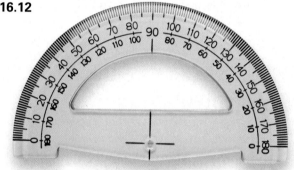

Key Terms

- area 410
- attribute 404
- circumference 412
- conservation of area 414
- degrees 428
- diameter 412

- direct comparison 404
- indirect comparison 404
- iteration 411
- nonstandard unit 404
- partitioning 411
- perimeter 410

- protractor 428
- standard unit 404
- structuring an array 414
- transitivity 411

Additional Children's Literature

- *Pigs on a Blanket: Fun with Math and Time,* written by Amy Axelrod and illustrated by Sharon McGinley-Nally
  It's 11:30 in the morning, and Mr. and Mrs. Pig and their children decide to go to the beach. The trip to the beach should take one and a half hours, but there are many delays. Will they arrive in time to enjoy the beach before it closes at 5:30 pm?

- *Everybody Cooks Rice,* written by Nora Dooley and illustrated by Peter J. Thornton

  A young girl visits her neighbors and finds that they all are cooking rice in different ways, based on their cultural traditions. An excellent book for learning about units of measure and conversions.

- *A Toad for Tuesday,* written by Russell E. Erickson and illustrated by Larry Di Fiori

  A toad goes off on a dangerous mission and encounters mischief. This is a fun way to teach about the days of the week and the sequencing of activities.

- *Is It Larger? Is It Smaller?* written by Tana Hoban

  In this book of photographs, the author uses pictures from everyday life to help children understand size and space. This helps children understand capacity.

- *The Snowy Day,* written and illustrated by Ezra Jack Keats
  This tells the story of a boy who wakes up to snow and has several adventures playing in it. Even though it does not discuss specific degrees or temperature measurement, it is a great book for introducing a unit on temperature to children in the primary grades.

- *The Librarian Who Measured the Earth,* written by Kathryn Lasky and illustrated by Kevin Hawkes
  This imaginative book tells the story of Eratosthenes and how he figured out how to measure the Earth. This is more appropriate for students in the upper elementary or middle grades.

- *How Big Is a Foot?* written and illustrated by Rolf Myller
  This wonderful book describes what happens when a king wants a bed made for his queen and uses his own foot to supply the dimensions to the carpenter. The mistake that occurs explains the need for standard units.

- *Just a Little Bit,* written by Ann Tompert and illustrated by Lynn Munsinger
  Two friends, an elephant and a mouse, sit on different ends of a seesaw. To balance, they invite more animal friends to sit with the mouse. This book provides a wonderful introduction to weight for young children.

- *Chimp Math: Learning About Time from a Baby Chimpanzee,* written by Ann Whitehead Nagda and Cindy Bickel
  This book tells the true story of the early life of a baby chimpanzee, Jiggs, who was rejected by his mother. Through text and graphs, Jiggs's weight and growth are tracked over weeks and months.

- *Inchworm and a Half,* written by Elinor Pinczes and illustrated by Randall Enos
  The inchworm moves around the garden measuring vegetables until it finds a vegetable it cannot measure. It then recruits the aid of a half-inchworm and then a quarter-inchworm. This book helps children conceptualize measuring length with nonstandard units.

Online Resources

- **National Library of Virtual Manipulatives**
  http://nlvm.usu.edu

  1. **Money:** These three activities ask you to count how much money you have, pay an exact amount, and make one dollar.

  2. **Time:** Three activities ask you to compare time on analog and digital clocks, illustrate elapsed time on the face of a clock, and match times on an analog and digital clock.

  3. **Geoboard:** Create shapes on a virtual geoboard and find their perimeter and area.

- **NCTM Illuminations**
  illuminations.nctm.org/

  1. **Chairs:** A restaurant pushes tables together and rearranges chairs to accommodate friends who want to eat together. Examines perimeter and area.

  2. **Pan Balance—Shapes:** A virtual pan balance enables the user to compare the weight of shapes.

- **Shodor, A National Resource for Computational Science Education**
  www.shodor.org

  1. **Image tool:** Measure angles, areas, and distances from a selection of several types of images.

  2. **Perimeter Explorer:** Select a fixed number of square units. The applet then creates a shape and you find the perimeter of the shape.

Critical and Creative Thinking Questions

1. Explain why it is important for children to experience both nonstandard and standard units of measure.

2. Discuss the three steps involved in the measurement process. Think about how you use measurement in your everyday life, and recognize and describe how you have applied these three steps to these measures.

3. Why is measurement an important part of the elementary curriculum? Find three connections to measurement within mathematics and three connections to measurement in other curricular areas. Explain each of these connections.

4. **In the field**   Textbooks often address time by teaching children how to read time on a clock. Examine a recent second-grade elementary-level mathematics textbook and discuss how this textbook teaches time. Does it address

sequencing and elapsed time as well as clock reading? If so, describe the methods used. Many public libraries have elementary textbooks that are in use in their school district.

5. This chapter describes four concepts that children need to understand in order to learn area. What are these four concepts? Explain why each is important to children's understanding of the attribute of area. How do children use these four concepts when decomposing and composing this figure with different pattern blocks?

6. **Using visuals**   Figure 16.1 illustrates the process of learning to measure. Create your own process diagram to illustrate how children learn to tell time.

What is happening in this picture?

Look closely at this picture of a typical occurrence from everyday life.

1. How might you use this picture to teach children about the importance of standard units in measurement?

2. How might you use this picture to teach children about the importance of estimation in measurement?

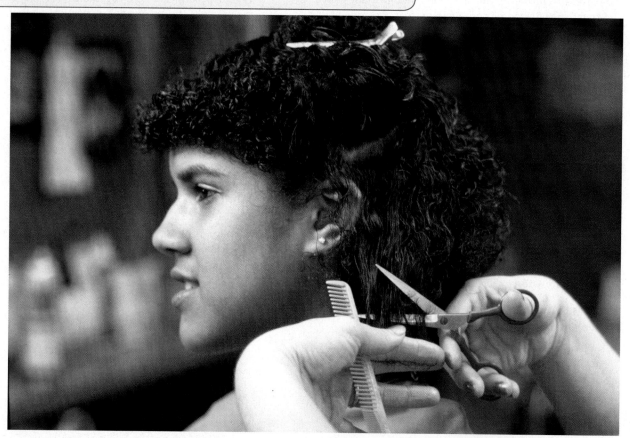

Self-Test

(Check your answers in Appendix D.)

1. What is an attribute? Identify at least three attributes of the birdfeeders in this figure that could be measured.

2. Which of the attributes discussed in question 1 could be evaluated through direct comparison?

3. What three concepts about measuring length should children understand by the second grade?

4. Identify the dimensions for the arrays. What is the area?

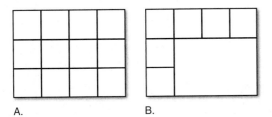

A.   B.

5. If the circumference of a circle is 15 cm, find the diameter, using pi = 3.14.

6. If the diameter of a circle is 6 inches, find the circumference, using pi = 3.14.

7. Find the area of a parallelogram with a base of 7 cm and a height of 4 cm.

8. Draw three different shapes that have the same area and perimeter.

9. If you know that a container of milk is one gallon, what attribute is being described?

10. Name two units that can be used to measure weight.

11. True or False: Time is an easy attribute for children to understand.

12. True or False: Temperature is a difficult attribute for children to understand.

13. Draw an open number line to solve the following elapsed time problem: *Martin spent 3½ hours doing homework. If he finished his homework at 10:00, what time did he start?*

14. Find the volume of a rectangular prism with base dimensions 5 inches × 3 inches and whose height is 7 inches. Sketch the prism and explain your work.

15. Find the volume of a right circular cylinder whose base is a circle with a circumference of 12 cm and whose height is 5 cm. Round your answer to the nearest hundredth place, using pi = 3.14. Sketch the cylinder and explain your work.

THE PLANNER ✓

Review your Chapter Planner on the chapter opener and check off your completed work.

Data Analysis and Probability

Student teacher Anh Nguyen asked her class of 25 fifth-graders, "What do you think the chances are that two people in this room have their birthdays on the same day in the same month?" After some discussion, the students did not think this was very likely, because there are 365 days in a typical year and just 26 people in their classroom (including Ms. Nguyen). Ms. Nguyen was engaging students in learning about probability—without them even realizing it.

Next Ms. Nguyen asked, "How many people's birthdays do you think we will need to check to have a 50% chance of getting a birthday match?" Most children reasoned that you would need about 182 people, because this is almost half of 365. Ms. Nguyen responded, "Actually, if there are 23 people, then there is about a 50% chance that two of them have the same birthday." This stunned the students, who immediately wanted to see whether they had a birthday match in their class. As each student called out his or her birthday month and day, Ms. Nguyen wrote the date on the chalkboard. After listing 18 dates, they found a match: May 21.

Ms. Nguyen's activity not only interested her students in probability, but it also helped them understand that the likelihood of events is sometimes difficult to predict.

CHAPTER PLANNER ✓

- ❏ Study the picture and read the opening story.
- ❏ Scan the Learning Objectives in each section:
  p. 436 ❏   p. 438 ❏   p. 439 ❏
  p. 442 ❏   p. 449 ❏   p. 453 ❏
- ❏ Read the text and study all visuals and Activities.
  Answer any questions.

Analyze key features

- ❏ Process Diagram, p. 437
- ❏ In the Classroom, p. 439
- ❏ Multicultural Perspectives in Mathematics, p. 441
- ❏ Education InSight, p. 443
- ❏ Children's Literature, p. 447 ❏   p. 455 ❏
- ❏ Lesson, p. 456
- ❏ Stop: Answer the Concept Checks before you go on:
  p. 437 ❏   p. 439 ❏   p. 442 ❏
  p. 449 ❏   p. 453 ❏   p. 460 ❏

End of chapter

- ❏ Review the Summary and Key Terms.
- ❏ Answer the Critical and Creative Thinking Questions.
- ❏ Answer What is happening in this picture?
- ❏ Complete the Self-Test and check your answers.

Sunday

Monday

Tuesday

Wednesday

CHAPTER OUTLINE

What Is Data Analysis?   436

Key Questions: How is statistics different from mathematics? What is the process of doing statistics?

Formulating Statistics Questions   438

Key Questions: How do students formulate questions for statistics? How is this process different for lower elementary and upper elementary and middle school students?

Collecting Data   439

Key Question: What processes do children in elementary and middle school use for collecting data?

Analyzing Data Using Graphs   442

Key Questions: How can graphs be used to analyze data? What types of graphs are best for certain types of data?

Analyzing Data Using Descriptive Statistics   449

Key Questions: What is the difference between the mean, mode, and median? When should each of these be used?

Probability   453

Key Questions: How is probability used in our everyday lives? How do children learn about probability?

NCTM The NCTM Data Analysis and Probability Standard has four main objectives.

Instructional programs from prekindergarten through grade 12 should enable all students to

- formulate questions that can be addressed with data and collect, organize, and display relevant data to answer them;
- select and use appropriate statistical methods to analyze data;
- develop and evaluate inferences and predictions that are based on data;
- understand and apply basic concepts of probability.
  (NCTM, 2000, p. 48)

Specific objectives for each grade-level band are listed within these four major categories and are in Appendix A.

In grades 3–5, children learn that probability is about chance and randomness and that the probability of an event is often counterintuitive.

What Is Data Analysis?

Data analysis and probability is a standard in *Principles and Standards for School Mathematics* (2000) and figures prominently in *Curriculum Focal Points* (NCTM, 2006) and the *Common Core State Standards* (NGA Center/CCSSO, 2010) for most grade levels from prekindergarten through grade 8. Its increased emphasis in the prekindergarten through grade 12 mathematics curriculum reflects its importance in modern society **(Figure 17.1)**. Today, we are required to make countless decisions in every part of our lives and have access to more data than ever before—for example, deciding what kind of car to buy, how to vote, and what kind of cereal to have for breakfast. Understanding data analysis—or statistics, as it is sometimes called—helps students make sense of data and navigate their way successfully through life.

How Do Statistics and Mathematics Differ?

"Mathematics is about numbers and their operations, generalizations, and abstractions; it is about spatial configurations and their measurement, transformations, and abstractions" (Shaeffer, 2006, p. 310). Statisticians call numbers **data**. They are interested in the **context** of data and its **variability**, which can be measured in several ways, some of which will be discussed later in this chapter.

> **variability** A measure of the change or spread of the data.

Statisticians collect data to make decisions. Suppose you collect data on the number of letters in your students' last names. The mathematician might look for patterns such as the number of last names that have odd or even numbers of letters or the number of last names that have more than five letters. The statistician would use the same data to answer a question or solve a problem, such as, "How wide should I make the column in my spreadsheet to accommodate each class member's last name?"

In mathematics, how the numbers are collected is not usually relevant. However, in statistics, how the data are collected is crucially important (Rossman, Chance, and Medina, 2006). For example, if you conduct a survey of people's favorite football team, it would make a difference where you collect your data. If you ask people from Pennsylvania you will probably get very different data than if you ask people from Arizona.

Another important difference between statistics and mathematics is that in mathematics it is often possible to obtain one correct answer, but in statistics there are often many ways to interpret the data. In fact, different statisticians may reach different conclusions using the same data. In statistics, you are more likely to hear "The data strongly suggest that . . ." (Rossman, Chance, and Medina, 2006, p. 329) rather than "The answer is . . ."

The Process of Doing Statistics

A statistical investigation is composed of four main steps. The steps outlined in **Figure 17.2** are based on *Guidelines for Assessment and Instruction in Statistics Education (GAISE) Report: A Pre-K-12 Curriculum Framework* (Franklin et al., 2007, pp. 11–12).

**Statistics in everyday life •
Figure 17.1**

Grocery stores collect data on customers' preferences and buying patterns and use their data analysis to make future marketing decisions.

Conducting a statistical investigation • Figure 17.2

Students should be involved in the process of doing statistics. In the lower elementary grades, teachers can formulate questions or help students formulate questions. In the upper elementary and middle grades, students should be able to formulate their own questions. All students should be able to complete the four steps of the entire process.

Should our family have unlimited texting? What is the average number of text messages our family sends each day?

1 "**Formulate Questions**
- clarify the problem at hand
- formulate one (or more) questions that can be answered with data"

I will have everyone in my family count the number of text messages they make each day for a week.

2 "**Collect Data**
- design a plan to collect appropriate data
- employ the plan to collect the data"

3 "**Analyze Data**
- select appropriate graphical and numerical methods
- use these methods to analyze the data"

Day	Number of Text Messages I sent
Monday	8
Tuesday	5
Wednesday	13
Thursday	4
Friday	12
Saturday	3
Sunday	2

I sent 47 text messeges this week
Our family sent 854 text messages this week
$854 \div 7 = 122$

Our family sends an average of 122 text messages each day. Maybe we should get a phone plan with unlimited text messaging.

4 "**Interpret Results**
- interpret the analysis
- relate the interpretation to the original question"

(*Source*: Franklin et al. 2007)

CONCEPT CHECK STOP

1. **Why** is the way in which numbers are collected important in statistics but not in mathematics?

2. **What** are the four steps in conducting a statistical investigation? Why are they important?

What Is Data Analysis? **437**

Formulating Statistics Questions

LEARNING OBJECTIVES

1. **Describe** how to help children formulate statistical questions.

2. **Compare** and **contrast** the kinds of questions children might ask in the primary grades and upper elementary or middle school.

Every statistical investigation begins with a question or multiple questions. The purpose of the investigation is to find answers to those questions. It is important to distinguish between questions that will have mathematical answers and questions that will have statistical answers. For example, the question "How old am I?" is not a statistical question because there is one definitive answer, but the question "How old are the students in my school?" is a statistical question because the answer will have variability. "The anticipation of variability is the basis for understanding the statistics question distinction" (Franklin et al., 2007, p. 11).

Formulating Questions with Students in the Primary Grades

Teachers can help elementary school students formulate questions that can be answered through statistical investigations. Children in the primary grades are interested in themselves, their families, their classmates, and their surroundings, so these are good topics for questions.

In elementary school, students often ask questions that can be answered through surveys. Here are some examples of typical questions:

- What time do you go to bed?
- How much allowance do you get?
- How many siblings do you have?
- How many states did you visit last year?
- What do you do after school?
- What is your favorite pizza topping?

Creating meaningful questions is difficult for primary school children. Help students generate and refine questions so that the responses will tell them what they really want to know (Russell, 2006). For example, if children are wondering how their classmates spend their free time after school, will the question "What do you do after school?" provide meaningful data? Perhaps the question should be changed to "What do you do after school before you do your homework?" or "What do you do after school before dinner time?" Always have children try out their questions before beginning to collect data.

Teaching Tip

Asking good questions

Help children evaluate their questions by using the following criteria.

- Does this question make sense? Would anyone be confused by it?
- Will people understand the words you use?
- Will your question require additional explanation or directions?

Provide parameters for questions. For example, suppose your class is planning to order pizza. If you ask, "What is your favorite pizza topping?" you may receive many different responses. Instead, ask, "What is your favorite pizza topping? Choose from cheese, pepperoni, or beef." The responses you receive are more likely to help you decide what kind of pizza to order.

Children in the primary grades can formulate questions with the help of their teachers (see *In the Classroom*).

Formulating Questions with Students in Upper Elementary and Middle Grades

Students in the upper elementary or middle grades should formulate their own questions and expand their interests beyond themselves and their own class. They might ask questions of their friends or compare data collected about more than one class or group. In middle school, students compare two or more sets of data to determine whether

In the Classroom

Kindergartners Asking Statistical Questions ✓ THE PLANNER

Carolyn Cook's kindergarten class had already graphed data on many different topics. To help them formulate their own questions, Ms. Cook asked her students to generate questions for data collection. The students generated 17 questions, and then by a show of hands they eliminated question after question until they found their favorite: *"What is your favorite flavor of ice cream?"* (Cook, 2008, p. 539). After they decided on this question, they selected six flavors from which to choose. Next, the children had to decide how to collect their data. Ms. Cook typed a list of children's names and distributed it to each child. Then each child asked every other child to identify his or her favorite flavor of ice cream. Because some children could not read or write, they drew pictures of the flavors.

After collecting data, each child represented their data with a bar graph or tally marks. Together the class analyzed both the most popular and least popular flavors.

(*Source*: C. D. Cook, 2008, pp. 538–546)

Think Critically

1. How did generating and then eliminating questions help children learn how to ask good questions for statistical analysis?
2. What other statistical techniques did children learn through this activity?

---

a relationship exists between the variables. For example, they might investigate whether there is a relationship between students' ages and the number of hours they spend per week using the Internet. In this grade range, students can learn how statistics are used in sports, science, current events, and social studies and how statistical data can be used to make **inferences** or draw conclusions. This is an excellent opportunity to integrate mathematics and statistics with other curriculum areas, especially social studies and science.

CONCEPT CHECK STOP

1. **What** ambiguities can be found in the question, "How many states have you visited?" How might a student improve this question to make it more meaningful?
2. **What** are some questions that students might investigate using statistics in the lower elementary grades, upper elementary grades, and middle grades?

Collecting Data

LEARNING OBJECTIVES

1. **Identify** two different ways of collecting data.
2. **Explain** the importance of recording data in meaningful ways.

Once a question is formulated, the next step is collecting and recording data. The process used for data collection depends on the nature of the question asked and the age of the children collecting the data. Children in the primary grades usually collect a single set of data. Students in the upper elementary or middle grades may collect two or more sets of data and compare them. Both elementary and middle school students use surveys and experiments to collect data.

The U.S. Census • Figure 17.3

The U.S. Census Bureau has taken a count of everyone living in the United States every 10 years since 1790. Its actions are mandated by the Constitution. The Census provides many types of data. The Census Bureau also collects other types of data monthly, quarterly, and yearly. For example, it conducts a survey to predict monthly changes in sales for retail and food services.

Surveys

Most of us have completed surveys at one time or another. They can be an effective method of collecting information (**Figure 17.3**).

Before children collect data, help them refine their questions so that the data collected are meaningful. Help children decide not only what questions to ask, but whom to ask and when to ask questions. Children should understand that the results of surveys are variable. For example, consider the question, "How do you spend your free time after school?" Young children will probably answer this question differently than older children. Children in lower socioeconomic groups may answer this question differently than children in higher socioeconomic groups. Children who live in warmer climates will answer differently than children who live in colder climates.

Teachers can help children organize and record their data. Organizing data so that they can be easily retrieved and understood is a formidable task. When the children described in Ms. Cook's class (*In the Classroom*) conducted their survey, they had difficulty keeping track of whom they had already asked, so they developed a recording procedure that included crossing off each student's name on their list after that student answered their survey. Even students who could not yet read were able to recognize their written name.

Recording data in a way that is meaningful and easy to understand is an age-old problem. When large amounts of data are collected, it is important to record the data so that they can be easily retrieved. Today we often use spreadsheets to record large amounts of data. Ancient civilizations also dealt with the problem of record keeping (see *Multicultural Perspectives in Mathematics*).

Activity 17.1 shows children how to make their own quipus to record data. Real quipus also had a summation cord, but this has been eliminated to simplify the activity.

Activity 17.1 Making a quipu to record data

Instructions

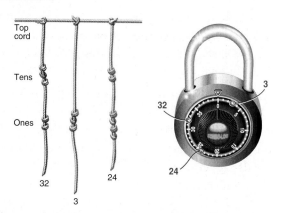

1. Distribute one piece of heavy cord about 12 inches long and three pieces of yarn (each 12 to 15 inches long) in three different colors to each child.

2. Say: *We are each going to make a quipu to keep track of the three numbers on a combination lock. Each number is one or two digits.*

3. Say: *Here's how to make this quipu. First you need about 12 inches of cord for the top cord. Lay this horizontally on your desk.*

4. Say: *Attach each of the three pieces of yarn to the top cord with a knot. Each piece of yarn represents one number of the combination. The top row of knots is for hundreds, the second row is for tens, and the bottom row is for ones.*

5. Say: *If my combination is 32 – 3 – 24, on the first piece of yarn I will tie three knots on the tens row and two knots on the ones row. On the second piece of yarn I will tie three knots on the*

Multicultural Perspectives in Mathematics

Quipu: The First Spreadsheets

Global Locator

PERU

NATIONAL GEOGRAPHIC

The Incan empire was located in what is now known as Peru. The Incas thrived for hundreds of years before they were conquered by the Spanish in 1535. During their heyday, they had a sophisticated society characterized by a highway system and extensive record keeping.

The Incas kept food and other important provisions in large warehouses spread across their vast empire. They needed a method of keeping track of the provisions in each warehouse so they could be moved to other parts of the empire as needed. Today, we would use spreadsheets and e-mail to record and communicate this information. The Incas' information was sent by runners who traveled throughout the empire.

The Incas had no writing system. Because there was too much information for the runners to memorize and pass on to the next runner, the Incas developed an intricate system of record keeping by tying knots on a string. This collection of knots is known as a *quipu*. Each runner would pass on the quipu to the next runner and, in this way, communicate information accurately.

Quipu makers held high positions in Incan society. Each quipu maker developed his own method of tying the knots, and quipus were buried with their maker. Few quipus remain, and it has taken hundreds of years to understand their structure.

(*Source*: M. Bazin and M. Tamez, 2002, pp. 36–45)

Strategies for the Classroom

- Ask children why the quipu was important for maintaining the Incan empire.
- Ask children what kind of information they would like to keep track of with a quipu.

---

ones row. On the third piece of yarn I will tie two knots on the tens row and four knots on the ones row.

6. Say: *Work in pairs. Each of you pick out a secret combination that has three numbers and make a quipu to represent the combination, and see whether your partner can guess the combination. Do not use the actual combination of your lock.*

7. Ask: *What other things can you keep track of with a quipu?* (Phone numbers, birthdays, allowance) *You will need different numbers of cords for each of these quipus.*

8. Ask: *How many pieces of yarn will you have to attach to the top cord to represent your phone number?* (7; 10 with the area code)

When collecting data from a large number of people, you may choose a representative **sample**, if collecting data from the entire **population** is not feasible. This technique is used often with political polling. If your students are collecting data in this way, discuss the importance of choosing a

fair sample so that the data collected are **unbiased**. For example, if your school is choosing a new name for its baseball team, ask for input from the same number of children in each grade rather than just sampling one grade level, because the team represents the entire school.

Tech Tools

www.census.gov

Students in the upper elementary grades and middle school can collect data from Web sites and newspapers and other print material. The U.S. Census Bureau's Web site contains great quantities of data organized by state, county, or district.

http://www.cia.gov

The Central Intelligence Agency maintains a very useful Web site with information about every nation in the world.

Experiments

Experiments are more complex than surveys, require additional planning, and often use the **scientific method**. Many experiments can be simulated with computer technology. When simulating an experiment with computer applets, more data can be collected very quickly. Computer simulations have the added advantage of consistency. For example, each time a coin is tossed in a simulation it is tossed in exactly the same way.

Tech Tools

| http://nlvm.usu.edu |

The **Coin Tossing** Activity at the National Library of Virtual Manipulatives Web site simulates the tossing of a coin 100 times, records the number of heads and tails, and then records the results in a bar graph.

CONCEPT CHECK STOP

1. **Why** is it important to get a representative sample when collecting survey data?
2. **What** are two ways of recording data?

Analyzing Data Using Graphs

LEARNING OBJECTIVES

1. **Compare** and **contrast** the different types of graphs.
2. **Describe** how tally marks, bar graphs, and circle graphs are used.
3. **Describe** how line plots, stem-and-leaf plots, and line graphs are used.
4. **Describe** how scatter plots can identify relationships between data.

A fundamental idea in prekindergarten through grade 2 is that data can be organized or ordered and that this 'picture' of the data provides information about the phenomenon or question. In grades 3–5, students should develop skill in representing their data, often using bar graphs, tables, or line plots . . . Students in grades 6–8 should begin to compare the effectiveness of various types of displays in organizing the data for further analysis" (NCTM, 2000, p. 49). This section discusses various methods of analyzing data using graphs.

Tally Marks and Bar Graphs

Tally marks, or hatch marks, have been used for several thousand years to keep track of data. According to *Curriculum Focal Points* (NCTM, 2006), children in prekindergarten through grade 2 should use these basic graphs to collect data (**Figure 17.4**).

Meatball sub	卌 卌 卌 I
Veggie sub	卌
Milk only	IIII

Using tally marks for the lunch count • Figure 17.4

Tally marks are often used to keep track of simple counts. Here, the teacher keeps track of the lunch orders for her students.

Bar graphs are effective for students of all ages. They are useful for representing data that are collected in categories. Children in the primary grades can also make bar graphs (**Figure 17.5**).

Teaching Tip

Creating real bar graphs

Give children many opportunities to create real bar graphs. Use their favorite type of cookie, crayon, or colored tile as a basis for the graph.

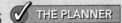
Children often have trouble reading and interpreting bar graphs. Help them to understand bar graphs by beginning with concrete or "real graphs," then moving to semiconcrete, and finally to symbolic or abstract bar graphs. Here, three representations of a bar graph illustrate the same data collected in response to the following question:

Which is your favorite kind of shoes—sneakers or sandals?

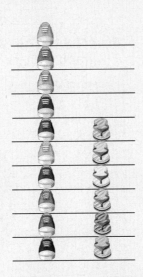

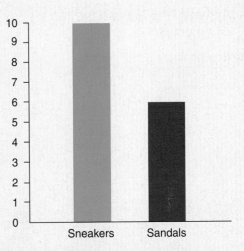

a. Concrete representation
A "real" graph arranges real objects in rows and columns. Here, 10 sneakers and 6 sandals are arranged in two columns.

b. Semiconcrete representation
A semiconcrete bar graph shows pictures of the objects arranged in rows and columns.

c. Abstract representation
An abstract bar graph shows the same information symbolically. The blue bar represents the number of sneakers and the red bar represents the number of sandals.

Provide children with many opportunities to draw and interpret bar graphs. To make graphs easily accessible, begin with sticky notes, paper with a large grid pattern, or graphs created with paper clips, as illustrated in **Activity 17.2**. Gradually move to drawing symbolic graphs on paper. Ask the children to explain what their graphs represent.

Activity 17.2 Making an easy bar graph

Instructions

1. Say: *Please raise your hand if you have a dog. Please raise your hand if you have a cat. Please raise your hand if you have any other kinds of pets (fish, rabbits, guinea pigs).* Record the information as the students have their hands raised.

2. Say: *The data we collected show that 15 of you have dogs, 10 have cats, and 5 of you have other kinds of pets.*

3. Give each child four different-color pieces of paper, each about 12 inches in length and 2 inches wide, and a set of paper clips.

4. Ask: *Can you make a bar graph illustrating our data with the paper and paper clips? Lay the paper out vertically on your desktop. Attach the paper clips to show the data.*

5. Ask: *What do you notice?* (More children have dogs than any other kind of pet.)

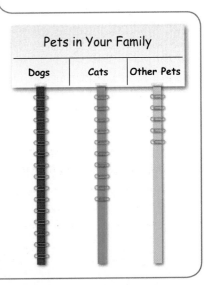

Circle Graphs

Circle graphs or pie charts are excellent for comparing the parts of a whole. They are not usually taught in the elementary grades because they use percentages, proportional reasoning, and degrees, but they can be used by children in the elementary grades with modifications (**Activity 17.3**).

Children in grades 3–5 can analyze simplified circle graphs to find the number of degrees of each colored slice or **sector**. They should understand that the number of degrees in all parts of the circle must sum to 360. Begin with a circle partitioned into 10 equal parts. Next, partition a circle into 100 parts (**Activity 17.4**).

Activity 17.3 Make a human circle graph

Instructions

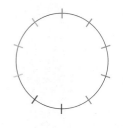

1. Each child receives four large cards (8 inches x 11 inches), one in each of the following colors: blue, red, yellow, green.

2. Ask each child to pick his or her favorite color and hold the card of that color in front of him- or herself.

3. Form a circle with the children, with all the children with like-colored cards next to one another.

4. Draw the circle on the chalkboard or overhead to illustrate how the circle graph looks.

5. Say: *This is called a circle graph or a pie chart.*

6. Ask: *What do you notice about the circle graph?*

7. Ask: *How many blue cards are there? How many red cards are there? How many yellow cards? How many green cards?*

Activity 17.4 Analyzing a circle graph with fractional parts

Instructions

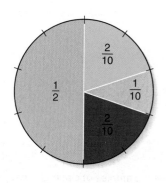

1. Ask: *Into how many equal parts is this circle partitioned?* (10)

2. Ask: *If the entire circle is 360 degrees, how many degrees is each of the equal parts?* (36)

3. Say: *So each $\frac{1}{10}$ of the circle is 36 degrees.*

4. Ask: *How can we find the number of degrees in the blue slice or sector?* (The blue sector is $\frac{5}{10}$ of the circle or 5 x 36. The blue sector is 180 degrees.)

5. Ask: *How many degrees is the red sector?* (The red sector is $\frac{2}{10}$ of the circle or 2 x 36. The red sector is 72 degrees.)

6. Ask: *How many degrees is the yellow sector?* (The yellow sector is $\frac{1}{10}$ of the circle or 36 degrees.)

7. Ask: *How many degrees is the green sector?* (The green sector is $\frac{2}{10}$ of the circle or 2 x 36. The green sector is 72 degrees.)

8. Ask: *What is the sum of the degrees of all the sectors?* (180 + 72 + 36 + 72 = 360)

9. Repeat with a circle partitioned into 100 equal parts.

It is not always practical to convert the parts of a circle to fractional parts. Students in grades 6–8 can analyze a circle graph using a more general approach, by finding the percent of the circle represented by each slice and converting that to degrees (**Activity 17.5**).

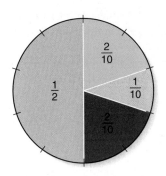
For children in grades 3–5 and 6–8, circle graphs are an excellent way to analyze data that fall into distinct categories (**Figure 17.6**).

Graphs with Continuous Data

Bar graphs and circle graphs are excellent for illustrating data in categories, such as a favorite color, snack, sport, movie, or flavor of ice cream. However, they are not good for illustrating numerical data or **continuous data** that may change over time, such as salaries, test scores, or temperatures. These types of data can be illustrated with stem-and-leaf plots, line plots, histograms, and line graphs.

Stem-and-leaf plots display and organize numerical data in an easy-to-read format. Children in grade 4 should be able to make them (NCTM, 2006). If the data are organized by tens, then the tens form the "stems" and are listed in a column on the left, and the ones are the "leaves" and are listed on the right. If the data are organized by hundreds, the hundreds and tens digits are the stems and the ones digits are the leaves. Stem-and-leaf plots can display whole number or decimal quantities. They can organize one set of data or compare two sets of

Using a circle graph to display favorite movies • Figure 17.6

The Nickelodeon Kids' Choice Awards of 2009 favorite movies are displayed in this circle graph. Notice that the sum of the percentages is 100%.

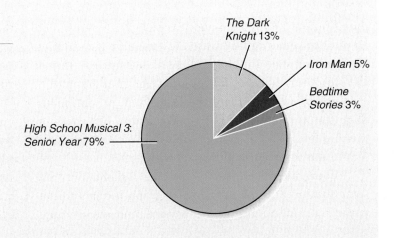

The Dark Knight 13%

Iron Man 5%

Bedtime Stories 3%

High School Musical 3: Senior Year 79%

The stem-and-leaf plot • Figure 17.7

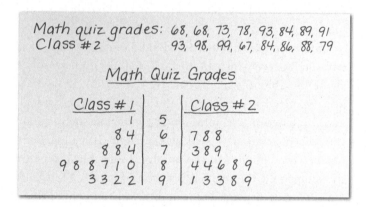

Math quiz grades: 64, 92, 87, 89, 74, 78, 81, 92
Class #1   93, 68, 78, 88, 88, 93, 51, 80

Stems	Leaves
5	1
6	4 8
7	4 8 8
8	0 1 7 8 8 9
9	2 2 3 3

a. A stem-and-leaf plot for one set of grades on a math quiz

The stem-and-leaf plot shows all data values. When making this graph, write in the stems first and then add the leaves. When a value in the data set occurs more than once, record it in the stem-and-leaf plot as many times as it occurs in the data.

Math quiz grades: 68, 68, 73, 78, 93, 84, 89, 91
Class #2   93, 98, 99, 67, 84, 86, 88, 79

Math Quiz Grades

Class #1		Class #2
1	5	
8 4	6	7 8 8
8 8 4	7	3 8 9
9 8 8 7 1 0	8	4 4 6 8 9
3 3 2 2	9	1 3 3 8 9

b. A stem-and-leaf plot comparing two sets of grades on a math quiz

The stem-and-leaf plot can be used to compare two sets of grades. Write the stem in the middle and extend the leaves out to either side.

96, 108, 109, 110, 112, 119, 121, 122, 125, 130

Stems	Leaves
9	6
10	8 9
11	0 2 9
12	1 2 5
13	0

c. A stem-and-leaf plot using data above 100

Ms. Markus measured the heights of her students in centimeters and recorded the heights on a stem-and-leaf plot.

data (**Figure 17.7**). Stem-and-leaf plots are a convenient way of displaying data because they preserve the order of the data and show the shape of the data. Note, too, that if the plot is turned on its side, it looks like a bar graph.

Line plots are perhaps the easiest type of continuous data plot (**Figure 17.8**). To make a line plot, draw a number line with the appropriate values for the data, and mark each occurrence of the data with an X.

Histograms look similar to bar graphs but are somewhat more complicated. In a bar graph, the bars are not connected, but in a histogram they are connected because the bars represent consecutive intervals along a numeric scale. This can make them difficult to construct. According to the *Common Core State Standards* (NGA Center/CCSSO, 2010), by grade 6, students should be able to construct and interpret histograms. **Figure 17.9** shows a histogram of the same data that were used for the line plot in Figure 17.8. Note that, for the histogram, the number of people living in a home is organized by intervals, such as 0–3, 4–6, 7–10, and the height of the bar represents the **frequency**.

> **frequency** The number of occurrences of the data within an interval.

A line plot of the number of people living in your household • Figure 17.8

Mr. Denton's third-grade class collected data on the number of people living in each student's home. The students made a line plot to illustrate their data.

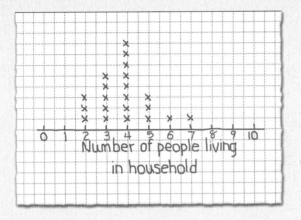

Tech Tools

illuminations.nctm.org

The *NCTM Illuminations* Web site has a histogram tool applet that allows the user to input information for a virtual histogram.

A histogram of the number of people living in your household • Figure 17.9

Mr. Shepard's seventh-grade class reorganized the data collected by Ms. Denton's class into a histogram that shows the number of people living in a home for each interval. The class decided on the intervals to use. Different intervals would produce a different histogram with the same data.

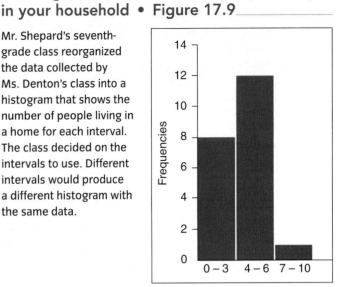

Line graphs are helpful for plotting data over time to identify trends. Students can learn about line graphs and other types of graphs through children's literature (see *Children's Literature*, **Figure 17.10**).

CHILDREN'S LITERATURE

✓ THE PLANNER

Learning about graphs

Tiger Math: Learning to Graph from a Baby Tiger • Figure 17.10

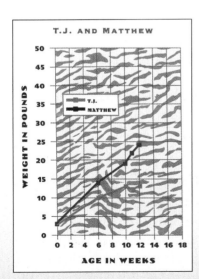

Written by Ann Whitehead Nagda and Cindy Bickel
T. J., a baby tiger born at the Denver Zoo, was orphaned when he was a few weeks old. The staff at the zoo raised T. J. themselves. Despite many setbacks, T. J. grew to be a large, healthy tiger. This heartwarming, true story tells the story of T. J.'s development, using many types of graphs, including picture graphs, bar graphs, circle graphs, and line graphs. The line graphs are particularly effective in illustrating the change in T. J.'s weight over time and comparing it to his father's weight as a baby.

Strategies for the Classroom

- Read the book with your class, and for each graph, ask: *What do you notice? What does this tell us about T. J.'s weight?*

- After reading the book, encourage your class to choose a characteristic, collect data about its change over time, and graph the data using one or more of the graphs discussed in this book.

A scatter plot showing the relationship of age vs. computer usage • Figure 17.11_____

This scatter plot indicates that a possible relationship exists between age and computer usage because the data are close to a line. In general, a scatter plot that does show a relationship can be used to predict data that have not been collected. From this graph, you might predict that a 15-year-old would probably use the computer about 14 hours per week.

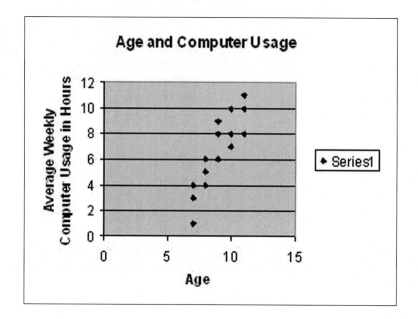

Scatter Plots

Scatter plots are used to determine whether there is a relationship between two variables and is a very useful tool in research of all kinds. According to *Curriculum Focal Points* (NCTM, 2006) and the *Common Core State Standards* (NGA Center/CCSSO, 2010), in grade 8, students create scatter plots to display data, determine **regression lines** or **lines of best fit**, and test conjectures. For example, if you want to determine whether there is a relationship between students' age and the number of hours they spend using a computer each week, you might collect data on this question and graph the data using a scatter plot. This type of data is collected in pairs. Each person who provides data would give their age and the average number of hours they spend on the computer each week. The data are then graphed on a coordinate plane. Each axis represents one of the variables (age or hours of computer use) and each data point is identified by a dot or pixel. If there is a relationship between the data, then the data will appear in an approximate line of best fit, either increasing or decreasing from left to right. If there is no relationship, then the data appear to be

randomly scattered. Scatter plots are most appropriate for students in the middle grades and can be created with graphing calculators or spreadsheets. The scatter plot illustrated in **Figure 17.11** was created using Microsoft Excel.

Teaching Tip _____

Finding a line of best fit

To help students identify whether there is a relationship between the data on a scatter plot, distribute straws or toothpicks and have them lay the straws or toothpicks along the data to see whether the data points roughly form a line.

Interpreting Results for Graphical Data

To complete the process of doing statistics, students must interpret their results. With graphical data, this means that they should understand what the graph is illustrating and be able to identify trends, **clusters** or bunches of data that are close together, as well as the overall shape of the data. Ask children to interpret graphs that they make as well as graphs of real-world data from print resources such as newspapers and Internet sources such as government reports. Discuss the graphs, asking questions such as:

What is this graph telling us?
What conclusions can you draw from the graph?
How are the data changing?

Where are they concentrated?
How widely are they distributed?

For example, the graph in Figure 17.11 does show a relationship between the age of a student and the hours of computer usage. As the student's age increases, the hours of computer usage also increases. The data are not concentrated in any one area. They increase at an almost steady rate.

CONCEPT CHECK

1. **What** types of graphs are useful for illustrating data that are collected in categories? What types are useful for illustrating continuous or numerical data?

2. **What** type of graph might you use to illustrate the following?

   Ms. Winowski surveyed her students and found out that 10 walk to school, 15 take the bus, and 5 are driven to school by their parents.

3. **What** kind of graph might be useful for displaying the daily high temperatures during the month of January in your hometown?

4. **What** kind of graph can help determine whether two variables are related?

Analyzing Data Using Descriptive Statistics

LEARNING OBJECTIVES

1. **Distinguish** among different measures of central tendency.

2. **Describe** how to create box-and-whisker plots.

Graphs are a powerful way of analyzing data. Other powerful methods use numerical processes to analyze data. Beginning in grades 3–5, students learn to analyze data by informally finding measures of center with a focus on the median. In grade 6, students learn the meaning of measures of center and recognize that a measure of center uses one number to summarize a set of data (NGA Center/CCSSO, 2010). In grade 7, they use descriptive statistics to calculate the mean, mode, and median and investigate how these measures are influenced by changes in data values (NCTM, 2006; NGA Center/CCSSO, 2010). They also learn to graphically depict measures of center with box-and-whisker plots.

Measures of Central Tendency

Both children and adults are familiar with the term *average*. For example, you may have read about average salaries for a given profession, the average home price in your area, or the average height or weight of children at a certain age. You have probably calculated your average test grade in a college course. In terms of data analysis, there are three different types of averages: **mode**, **median**, and **mean**.

> **mode** A measure of the data that occurs most often. There can be more than one mode for a given set of data.
>
> **median** The middle of an ordered data set.
>
> **mean** A measure that is computed by adding all the numbers in the data set and dividing by the number of items.

Mode This is probably the easiest measure of center to learn and is very accessible to children in the primary grades. It is very popular for finding trends. For example, if a shoe store is reordering shoes, they will most likely order more shoes in the size that is sold most frequently. They are using the mode to make their decision. **Activity 17.6** illustrates how you might introduce the concept of mode to children in the primary grades.

Activity 17.6 How old are you?

Instructions

Age	# of students
6	₥ ₥ ||
7	₥ ₥ |||
8					

1. Say: *Let's collect data on everyone's age. I'm going to ask each of you your age and write it on the chalkboard.*

2. Say: *Is there one age that appears the most often? We call this the mode.*

---

find their average by adding them together and dividing by 2 (**Activity 17.7**).

Activity 17.7 How many DVDs do you own?

Instructions

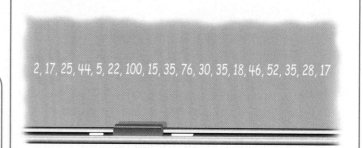

2, 17, 25, 44, 5, 22, 100, 15, 35, 76, 30, 35, 18, 46, 52, 35, 28, 17

1. Say: *We are going to collect data on the number of DVDs each of you owns.*

2. Collect data from each student and write the data on the chalkboard or overhead.

3. Say: *First arrange the numbers from least to greatest. If a value is written more than once, record it as many times as it occurs* (2, 5, 15, 17, 17, 18, 22, 25, 28, 30, 35, 35, 35, 44, 46, 52, 76, 100)

4. Say: *Because there are 18 values, there is no middle number. Select the two middle numbers, 28 and 30, and find their average by adding them together and dividing by 2. The median is 29.*

Median Some researchers recommend teaching median in the elementary school and teaching the mean later, in middle school (Russell, 2006). *Principles and Standards for School Mathematics* (NCTM, 2000), *Curriculum Focal Points for Prekindergarten through Grade 8 Mathematics* (NCTM, 2006), and the *Common Core State Standards* (NGA Center/ CCSSO, 2010) all recommend that the median and the mean be taught in middle school. Even though the median is an easier concept to understand than the mean, it is still quite difficult because it involves choosing one value to represent an entire set of data. To find the median of a set of numerical data, order the entries from least to greatest and pick the middle number. If the set of data has an even number of entries, there will be no middle number. In that case, pick the two middle numbers and

Mean The mean is perhaps the least understood measure of central tendency. Even though most people know how to compute the mean, or average, of a set of numbers, they do not know what it represents. The following activity investigates the leveling approach to understanding the mean. Students also find that two different sets of data can have the same mean (**Activity 17.8**).

Comparing the mean, mode, and median By grade 8, students should understand how to find the mean, mode, and median and when it is appropriate to use each one. The mode is used when you are looking for trends or the most popular item. The median is a reliable measure of center and is probably more appropriate for

the data set by adding an extreme value, and ask the students to calculate the mean and median again (**Activity 17.9**).

describing average home prices or salaries because it is not affected by **extreme values** (those much larger or smaller than other data). The mean evens out the data and is affected by extreme values in the data set (Martinie, 2006). Suppose, for example, that you are comparing the salaries of former students at your middle school. If a famous movie star or rock musician went to the school, his or her salary would be so much higher than the rest of the data that it would skew the results. In this case the median would be a more appropriate measure than the mean.

Students tend to use the mean because they are most familiar with it even though there are many situations in which the median is more appropriate. To help students understand how sensitive the mean is to extreme values, ask them to calculate the mean and median for a set of data for which the mean and median are close to one another in value. Then adjust

Box-and-Whisker Plots

Box-and-whisker plots, also called box plots, provide a graphical means of organizing and displaying data using the median. They also supply information about the **range** and **distribution** of the data. Each box plot consists of a box that shows the center of the data, or the middle 50%, with a vertical line inside the box indicating placement of the median and a line from each side of the box to the highest and lowest values. The sides of the box are the **lower quartile** and the **upper quartile**. The data to the left of the lower quartile fall in the lowest 25% of the data. The data to the right of the upper quartile fall in the highest 25% of the data. In a box plot, to find the distribution of the data compute the **interquartile range**.

> **range** The difference between the highest and lowest data values.

> **lower quartile** The median of the lower half of the data. This represents the bottom quarter of the data.
>
> **upper quartile** The median of the upper half of the data. This represents the top quarter of the data.
>
> **interquartile range** The numeric difference of the upper quartile and the lower quartile.

Activity **17.10** illustrates how to construct a box-and-whisker plot, using the data that were first discussed in Figure 17.7.

Activity 17.10 A box-and-whisker plot

Instructions

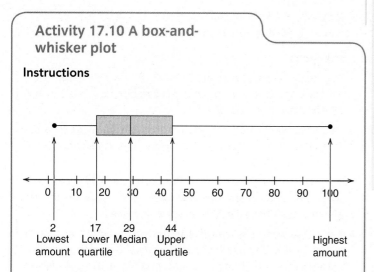

1. Say: *We are going to make a box-and-whisker plot of the following data, which represent the number of DVDs owned by each student in a class:*

    2, 17, 25, 44, 5, 22, 100, 15, 35, 76,
    30, 35, 18, 46, 52, 35, 28, 17

2. Say: *First, put the data in order from least to greatest:*

    2, 5, 15, 17, 17, 18, 22, 25, 28, 30,
    35, 35, 35, 44, 46, 52, 76, 100

3. *Now find the median. It is 29. The median is the middle of the data. Half of the data is greater than the median and half of the data is less than the median.*

4. *Find the range.* (The highest score is 100. The lowest score is 2. The range is 100 − 2 = 98.)

5. *Find the lower quartile. This means that you will find the median of the lower half of the data: 2, 5, 15, 17, 17, 18, 22, 25, 28.* (The lower quartile is 17.)

6. *Find the upper quartile. This means that you will find the median of the upper half of the data: 30, 35, 35, 35, 44, 46, 52, 76, 100.* (The upper quartile is 44.)

7. *Find the interquartile range.* (44 − 17 = 27)

8. Ask: *What do you notice about the data?* (Answers will vary. Students should notice that the top half of the data is much more spread out than the bottom half of the data and that 75% of the data is between 2 and 44.)

Comparing data with box-and-whisker plots • Figure 17.12

These box-and-whisker plots show test scores for two fourth-grade classes. The plots indicate that the scores for class 1 are much more widely spread. The distance to the highest and lowest scores is greater for class 1 than for class 2. The scores for class 2 are closer together and the median score is higher than for class 1.

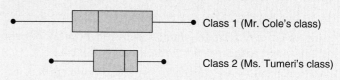

Class 1 (Mr. Cole's class)

Class 2 (Ms. Tumeri's class)

Box-and-whisker plots communicate a great deal of information about data sets, such as how widely spread the data is and how close the data is to the median. They are especially helpful for comparison of two or more sets of data (**Figure 17.12**).

Teaching Tip

Addressing students' errors with box-and-whisker plots

When making box-and-whisker plots, a common mistake made by students is to use the mean instead of the median. Students sometimes need to be reminded that box-and-whisker plots can only be used to represent the median of a set of data. Another common mistake is to try to find the median without first putting the data into ascending order.

Interpreting Results for Descriptive Statistics

Descriptive statistics can be misleading, so it is important to discuss the reasonableness of results with your class. For example, suppose you see a commercial that claims that 75% of dentists recommend a particular brand of toothpaste. How would you evaluate this statement? Ask questions such as: *Does this represent an average value for these* data? What does this value tell us? How can we use it to make decisions? Find examples of descriptive statistics in the media. There are many advertisements on television, radio, and the Internet that recommend certain products or services. Discuss and evaluate them with students so that they understand exactly what information the statistics are providing.

CONCEPT CHECK

1. **When** is it most appropriate to use the mean, mode, and median? Give an example of each.
2. **What** are box-and-whisker plots? How are they helpful?

Probability

LEARNING OBJECTIVES

1. **Describe** the concept of probability.
2. **Distinguish** between theoretical and experimental probability.
3. **Distinguish** between independent and dependent events.
4. **Describe** simulations.

When meteorologists predict a 40% chance of thunderstorms, they are using probability. When you take a certain route to work because it is less likely to have traffic, you are using probability. Because probability is so prevalent in our lives, it has become increasingly important in the mathematics curriculum, from prekindergarten through grade 12. This section discusses the meaning of probability and how to teach it to students in prekindergarten through grade 8.

What Is Probability?

Probability is closely related to data analysis. It is a "measurement of the likelihood of an event" (Chapin et al., 2002, p. 7). Children enter school with some informal ideas about probability. For example, a young child may say "I never get to go first" or "We usually go out to play" (Tarr, 2002). Teachers should expand on these ideas by discussing the likelihood of events with children in the primary grades. Children should learn to distinguish between events that are certain to happen, events that are impossible, and events that are more or less likely (**Activity 17.11**).

Activity 17.11 Is it likely?

Instructions

1. Provide children with a list of statements (either written or verbal for nonreaders and ELLs).
2. Sample statements are: "It is going to be sunny tomorrow." "I'm going to play after school." "I will have homework tonight." "My allowance will be one million dollars."
3. For each statement, ask the children to classify it as impossible, certain, or uncertain.
4. For uncertain statements, ask the children to classify them as more or less likely.
5. Ask the students to generate their own lists and discuss.

Teaching Tip

Learning about the likelihood of events

Have children place events on a "likelihood line" (Tarr, 2002, p. 483) with the categories *Impossible, Unlikely, Likely,* and *Certain* written on the line. For children who cannot yet read, the word *impossible* can be replaced by an image of two thumbs down, and *certain* can be replaced by an image of two thumbs up.

Begin teaching probability to children in grades 3–5 with easy experiments that use coins, colored chips, or cubes. Before conducting each experiment, ask the children what they expect to happen. You may find that children have many misconceptions about probability. For example, although most adults assume that children know a coin is equally likely to land on heads or tails, many children do not know this (Nicolson, 2005). Discuss the children's ideas prior to conducting experiments. **Activity 17.12** and **Activity 17.13** are examples of the kinds of activities that work well with children.

Activity 17.12 Flip a coin

Instructions

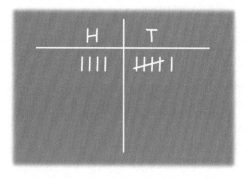

1. With the whole class, hold up a coin, either a quarter or half-dollar so that it is large enough for everyone to see.

2. Ask: *If I flip this coin, how do you think it will land—on heads or tails?* (Children give various answers.)

3. Say: *Let's do an experiment. I need a helper to flip the coin 10 times. Each time it lands we are going to record whether it landed on heads or tails.*

4. Say: *The coin landed on heads four times and on tails six times. What do you think will happen next?* (Children will provide various answers. There is not really a right answer. It could land on heads or tails.)

5. Ask: *Do you think it is equally likely that the coin will land on heads or tails?*

Spinners are an excellent tool for probability activities in grades 3–5 (**Activity 17.14**). You can make a spinner by cutting a circle out of an index card and twirling a paper clip around the point of a pencil through the center of the circle (Nicolson, 2005). Begin with an easy spinner that is divided into three parts, with each part a different color.

Activity 17.13 Tossing a bag of chips

Instructions

1. Place 20 colored chips in a bag. Chips should be two different colors (such as red and blue). Do not tell the children how many of each color are in the bag.

2. Make a T-chart with headings **Red** and **Blue**.

3. Walk around the class and have various children pull a chip out of the bag without looking first.

4. Record the color of each chip pulled out of the bag.

5. After about five tries, ask: *What color do you think the next chip will be? Why?*

6. Ask: *Do you think there are more red chips or blue chips in the bag? Why?* (If on several tries, more red chips were chosen than blue, then the children might predict there are more red chips. This may or may not be true.)

7. After discussion, show the children the number of red and blue chips.

8. Play again with a different number of red and blue chips but a total of 20 chips in all.

Activity 17.14 Spinning for colors

Instructions

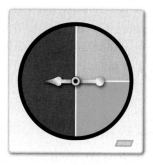

1. Distribute spinners to each pair of children.

2. Ask: *Which color is the spinner most likely to land on?* (The spinner is most likely to land on red, but children may not realize this.)

3. Say: *With a partner, spin the spinner and record what color it lands on. Have one person spin and the other record. Do this ten times.*

4. Combine all the results as a class and discuss the results.

5. Ask: *Do you expect the spinner to land on red more than it lands on the other colors? Why? Did your results turn out the way you expected them to?*

Children's misconceptions about spinners • Figure 17.13

Children may not realize that the probability of the spinner landing on green is the same in spinners **a.** and **b.**

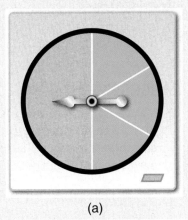 

(a)   (b)

One part should equal half the area of the spinner and the other two parts should each equal one-fourth of the spinner. First predict where the spinner will land and then spin it many times to collect data. Discuss the results with your class.

Children also harbor many misconceptions about spinners (Nicolson, 2005) (**Figure 17.13**).

Children's literature is an excellent way to introduce children to the language of probability (see *Children's Literature*, **Figure 17.14**).

CHILDREN'S LITERATURE

Using the language of probability

 THE PLANNER

It's Probably Penny • Figure 17.14

Written and illustrated by Loreen Leedy

Lisa's mathematics assignment is to make predictions about things that might happen, things that are certain to happen, things that are impossible to happen, and things that have an equal chance of happening or not happening and then to find out which of her predictions are correct. Lisa decides to use her dog Penny for the experiment. Lisa predicts, for example, that Penny will want a walk and might get to chase a squirrel. This excellent book is beautifully illustrated and cleverly written. It uses the language of probability in an engaging story that children will enjoy.

Strategy for the Classroom

• After reading the book with your class, give them the same assignment that Lisa had. Make sure that children make predictions about things they can measure.

LESSON How Likely Is It?

GRADE LEVEL
6–8

OBJECTIVES
Students will identify the likelihood of an event.
Students will learn the meaning of the probability of an event.
Students will measure the probability of an event on a number line.

STANDARDS

Grade 7
Understand that the probability of a chance event is a number between 0 and 1 that expresses the likelihood of the event occurring. Larger numbers indicate greater likelihood. A probability near 0 indicates an unlikely event, a probability around $\frac{1}{2}$ indicates an event that is neither unlikely nor likely, and a probability near 1 indicates a likely event. (NGA Center/CCSSO, 2010)

MATERIALS
- A sheet of paper for each student with a number line drawn on it and endpoints at 0 and 1

ASSESSMENT
- Make a list of three events that are impossible, three events that are certain, three events that are unlikely to happen, and three events that are likely to happen. Place these events on a number line.

- Write a journal entry explaining what probability means.

- Make a pictorial number line, with a picture of something impossible, a picture of something that might happen, and a picture of something certain.

GROUPING
Whole group

Launch (10 minutes)
- Ask: *Have you ever been to a boardwalk or county or state fair and played the games? Which games do you like to play?* (The children discuss their favorite games.)

- Ask: *How many of you have played the spinner game? How many times did you win?*

- The children discuss and make comments such as "I never win" or "I played eight times and only won once."

- Write the children's responses on the board.

In middle school, students begin to translate their earlier notions of probability and words such as *likely* or *unlikely* into numeric measurement and realize that an impossible event has probability 0, a certain event has probability 1, and all other likelihoods have values that fall somewhere on the number line between 0 and 1 (see the *Lesson*). The standards in the *Lesson* are from the *Common Core State Standards* (NGA Center/CCSSO, 2010).

Games are an excellent way for children in the upper elementary grades and middle school to learn the concepts and language of probability. As they play a wide variety of games, ask them to decide whether each game is "fair" and whether the results are random.

- Ask: *Do you think it is likely or not likely that you will win the spinner game?*

- The children discuss and decide it is not very likely.

Instruct (25 to 30 minutes)

- Say: *When you assign a number to the likelihood of an event, such as winning the spinner game, this is called probability.*

- Ask: *How can you use a number line to show probability?*

- Through discussion, guide the children to create a number line with endpoints at 0 and 1, with 0 representing events that are impossible and 1 representing events that are certain.

- Ask: *What are some events that are impossible?* (Sample replies: rain falling up, red elephants) *All these events are placed at 0. We say that they have probability 0.*

- Ask: *What are some events that are certain?* (Having dinner tonight, taking the school bus home) *All of these events are placed at 1. We say that they have probability 1.*

- Ask: *Where should we put the probability of winning the spinner game on our number line?*

- Discuss. Elicit that $\frac{1}{2}$ is halfway between 0 and 1, so an unlikely event should be less than $\frac{1}{2}$.

- Ask: *Let's make a list of some other events and place them on the number line. What are some events that are unlikely?* (Having a snow day tomorrow)

- Ask: *What are some events that are likely to happen?* (Having homework tonight)

- Say: *Place these events on your number line.*

- Ask: *What kinds of events would be placed at the $\frac{1}{2}$ point on the number line?* (Something that has an equal chance to happen or not happen) *For example, if there was an equal chance that it would rain or not rain today, this would have a probability of $\frac{1}{2}$.*

Summarize (5 minutes)

- Say: *Let's go back to the spinner game again. You said that it was unlikely you would win. What does that tell you about the probability of winning the spinner game? What kind of number will that be?* (A fraction less than $\frac{1}{2}$)

- Ask: *What about the probabilities of other games you play at the boardwalk or the county or state fair? Do you think their probabilities of winning are high or low? Why?*

Virtual Classroom Observation

Video | www.wiley.com/college/jones

Click on **Student Companion Site**. Then click on:
- **Foundations of Effective Mathematics Teaching**
- **B. Focus on Teacher Content Knowledge**
- **3. Analyze Classroom Videos**

Scroll down and view:
- **Using Data to Make Predictions: Sampling from a bag of colored tiles**

Read the commentary. Students in this fifth-grade class are playing the game "First to 21." At this grade level they are very concerned with the concept of fairness. Why is the game unfair? What reasoning do the students use to come to this conclusion?

Theoretical and Experimental Probability

In grades 6–8 students refine their understanding of probability and relate it to proportional reasoning. They understand the relationship between the likelihood of an event occurring and the likelihood of it not occurring (the **complement**).

There are two types of probability: **theoretical probability** and **experimental probability**. Both of these probabilities have values between 0 and 1 and represent the chance of an event occurring. They can be represented as fractions, decimals, or percents. The theoretical probability of an event is

$$\frac{\text{The number of ways the event can occur}}{\text{The number of possible outcomes}}$$

For example, for a fair six-sided die, the probability of the die landing on a 5 is $\frac{1}{6}$ because there is one way of landing on 5 out of six possible outcomes.

Whereas the theoretical probability is a measure of what should happen under ideal circumstances, the experimental probability computes what actually occurs when an experiment is repeated. The experimental probability of an event is

$$\frac{\text{The number of times the event has occurred}}{\text{The number of possible outcomes}}$$

Using the die example, even though the theoretical probability of landing on 5 is $\frac{1}{6}$, you might repeat this experiment 100 times and not land on 5 at all or land on 5 several times (**Activity 17.15**).

According to the **law of large numbers**, the experimental probability of an event is closer to the theoretical probability when there is a large amount of data. In other words, if you were to toss a die several thousands of times, the experimental probability of it landing on 5 would approach $\frac{1}{6}$. Although both the theoretical probability and experimental probability are important concepts, experimental probability is more meaningful to students because it measures what can be observed and recorded. Virtual manipulatives are very helpful for finding experimental probabilities because the virtual tool can, for example, toss a coin many more times than a child can, allowing the child to focus on the data rather than on the physical tossing of coins (Beck and Huse, 2007).

The **sample space** of an experiment is the list of all possible outcomes. For more complicated experiments, it is helpful to list the sample space before computing probabilities. **Activity 17.16** illustrates the sample space for tossing two coins simultaneously.

Activity 17.16 Tossing coins

Instructions

1. Say: *Sometimes we want to list all the possible outcomes of an experiment without actually conducting it.*

2. Say: *Let's work together to list all the possible outcomes of tossing two coins simultaneously, writing H for heads and T for tails. When we do this we create a sample space for the experiment.*

3. Ask: *How many possible outcomes are there for tossing two coins?*

4. Say: *Now suppose you tossed three coins simultaneously. Can you list the sample space?* (HHH, HHT, HTH, THH, TTH, THT, HTT, TTT)

Activity 17.15 Tossing a die

Instructions

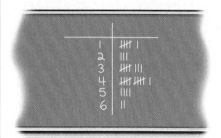

1. Give each pair of children one die and a recording sheet.

2. Ask one child in each pair to toss the die ten times while the other child in the pair records. Switch roles.

3. As a class, list all outcomes and compute experimental probabilities for tossing 1, 2, 3, 4, 5, or 6.

Understanding choices for a sample space

Students invariably ask why HT is a different outcome than TH. To help them understand the distinction, ask them to imagine that the first coin is blue and the second coin is black. Then HT means heads on the blue coin and tails on the black coin, whereas TH means tails on the blue coin and heads on the black coin.

The coin toss experiment brings up an interesting pattern that students in the middle grades will enjoy exploring (**Activity 17.17**).

Activity 17.17 Exponential patterns in the coin toss

Instructions

1. Ask students to fill in the chart, either by conducting the experiments or listing all possibilities in a systematic way.

2. Ask: *Do you see any patterns? If there were five coins being tossed, how many elements would be in the sample space?* (32)

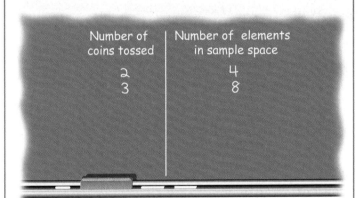

Number of coins tossed	Number of elements in sample space
2	4
3	8

3. Continue in this way until the students recognize the pattern. (The number of elements in the sample space is 2^n, where *n* is the number of coins tossed.)

When an experiment involves two events, such as the tossing of two coins or the removal of two socks one at a time from a drawer, you need to consider the nature of the events, as explained in the following section.

Independent and Dependent Events

The concept of independence of events is important for students in the middle grades to understand, although it does not develop intuitively. Two events are **independent events** if the occurrence of one event does not influence the occurrence of the second event. For example, if a coin is tossed three times, the probability of getting a head on the first toss of the coin does not affect the probability of getting a head on the second or third toss. Two events are **dependent events** if the occurrence of the first event does influence the occurrence of the second event. This becomes important in problems that have sampling and replacement. In **Activity 17.18,** both situations are presented. When you pick a sock, replace it, and pick a sock again, both events are independent. When you pick a sock and do not replace it before picking a second sock, the result of the second event is dependent on the result of the first because there are fewer socks in the drawer after the first event.

Activity 17.18 Pick a sock

Instructions

1. Say: *Suppose you have six single socks in a drawer. Four are blue and two are white. What is the probability of putting your hand in the drawer without looking and picking a blue sock?* $\left(\frac{4}{6}\right)$

2. Say: *Now suppose you replace the sock in the drawer. What is the probability of picking a blue sock again?* $\left(\frac{4}{6}\right)$

3. Say: *Suppose you do not replace the sock in the drawer. What is the probability of picking a blue sock on this second try?* (It depends on whether or not you got a blue sock on the first try.)

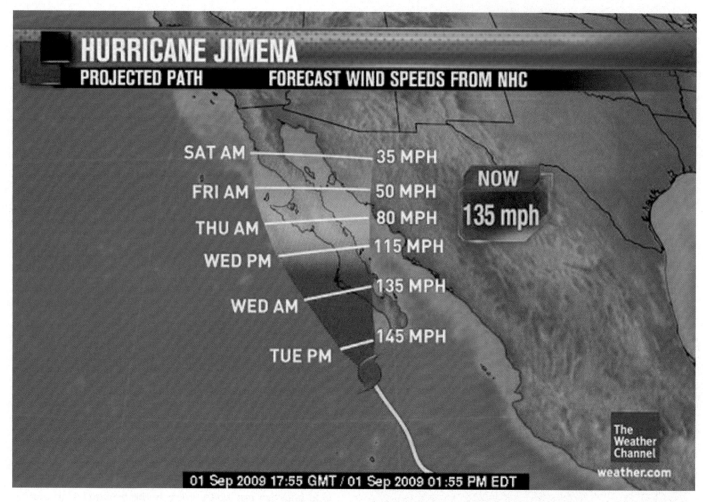

HURRICANE JIMENA
PROJECTED PATH   FORECAST WIND SPEEDS FROM NHC

NOW
135 mph

SAT AM ———————— 35 MPH
FRI AM ——————— 50 MPH
————— 80 MPH
THU AM ————— 115 MPH
WED PM —————
————— 135 MPH
WED AM ————
————— 145 MPH
TUE PM

The Weather Channel
weather.com

01 Sep 2009 17:55 GMT / 01 Sep 2009 01:55 PM EDT

Simulating the path of a hurricane • Figure 17.15

Through computer simulation, meteorologists predict the path of Hurricane Jimena, September 2009.

Simulations

Students in the middle grades should have opportunities to do **simulations**. A simulation is an imitation of something real. It is a way to conduct an experiment for something that is not easily measured, is impossible to measure, or is dangerous to measure. Simulations are used in a variety of contexts (**Figure 17.15**). For example, pilots are trained with flight simulators, readiness to respond to terror attacks and natural disasters are evaluated with simulation, and medical personnel are trained to perform procedures through simulation. Here is an example of a simulation you can do in the classroom: If you assume that the chance of giving birth to a male child or female child is equally likely, you can simulate this by flipping a fair coin, which is equally likely to land on heads or tails.

CONCEPT CHECK   STOP

1. **What** do young children understand about probability? What terms do they use to describe the probability of events?

2. **What** is the difference between theoretical and experimental probability? Provide an example of each.

3. **How** can you adapt the following situation so it is a probability problem that uses repeated sampling of independent events and a probability problem with repeated sampling of dependent events?

   Josie has a bucket with five balls. Three of them are blue and two are red.

4. **What** is the purpose of simulations?

Summary

1 What Is Data Analysis? 436

- Mathematics and statistics are related but different subjects. Statisticians call numbers **data**. They are interested in the **variability** or change in data. In mathematics it is sometimes possible to obtain one correct answer, but that is usually not possible in statistics.

- Statistics is used in everyday life, as shown in this photo.

Figure 17.1

- Every statistical investigation is composed of four main steps: formulating questions, collecting data, analyzing data, and interpreting results.

2 Formulating Statistics Questions 438

- All children can carry out the four main steps of a statistical investigation. Younger children are interested in themselves, their friends, and things that happen in their classroom. Teachers should help them formulate questions that make sense and will provide them with the data they need to answer their questions. In this photo, a teacher is helping her students write questions for a statistical investigation.

In the Classroom

- Students in the upper elementary and middle grades can formulate their own questions. They can extend their interest to questions beyond the classroom and formulate questions that integrate other subject areas. At this point, students can also compare more than one set of data.

3 Collecting Data 439

- Surveys are a popular way of collecting data in elementary school, and in real life, the U.S. Census is one example of a survey, as shown here.

Figure 17.3

- Experiments are another way of collecting data but are not used as frequently in elementary school because they are more complex than surveys.

4 Analyzing Data Using Graphs 442

- **Bar graphs** are a popular way of graphing data and can be used at all grade levels. The bar graph in this image compares the number of children wearing sneakers to the number wearing sandals.

Figure 17.5

- **Circle graphs** are another way of graphing data that fall into categories but are not usually introduced until upper elementary school because they use percentages.

- **Stem-and-leaf plots** organize numerical data. **Line plots** and **histograms** graph **continuous data**. **Line graphs** are helpful for identifying trends over time.

- **Scatter plots** graph two variables and determine whether a relationship exists between the variables.

- To interpret graphical results, look at the overall shape of the graph to find patterns, **clusters**, and variability.

5 Analyzing Data Using Descriptive Statistics 449

- The **mean, mode,** and **median** are measures of central tendency. Each should be used where appropriate to the data set.

- A **box-and-whisker plot** is a graphical method of displaying the median of a set of data. This plot also shows the **lower quartile,** or median of the lower half of the data, and the **upper quartile,** or median of the upper half of the data. The **interquartile range** is the difference between the two quartiles. The box plot illustrated here compares test scores in two classes.

Figure 17.12

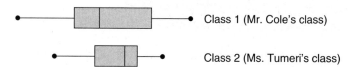

Class 1 (Mr. Cole's class)

Class 2 (Ms. Tumeri's class)

- When interpreting results for descriptive statistics, make sure that the answer makes sense. This is especially important with measures of central tendency, because using the wrong measure will provide an answer but not one that is representative of the data.

6 Probability 453

- Probability measures the likelihood of an event. Young children entering school have an intuitive idea of probability. This should be encouraged in the early grades with formal instruction in the upper elementary and middle grades.

- There are two types of probability: **theoretical probability** and **experimental probability.** Theoretical probability tells your chances in ideal circumstances. Experimental probability measures what actually occurs over a number of trials of an experiment.

    This illustration shows the results of tossing a die repeatedly and can be used to find the experimental probability of each outcome.

Activity 17.15

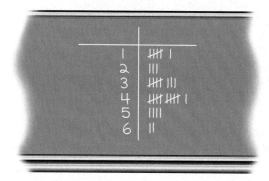

- Two events are **independent events** if the probability of one does not affect the probability of the other. They are **dependent events** if the probability of one does affect the probability of the other.

- When it is too difficult or dangerous to conduct an actual experiment, a **simulation** can be conducted. Simulations are done in the real world, often using computer software.

Key Terms

- bar graph 442
- box-and-whisker plot 451
- circle graph 444
- cluster 448
- complement 458
- context 436
- continuous data 445
- data 436
- dependent events 459
- distribution 451
- experimental probability 458
- extreme values 451
- frequency 446
- histogram 446

- independent events 459
- inferences 439
- interquartile range 451
- law of large numbers 458
- line graph 447
- line of best fit 448
- line plot 446
- lower quartile 451
- mean 449
- median 449
- mode 449
- population 441
- range 451
- regression line 448

- sample 441
- sample space 458
- scatter plot 448
- scientific method 442
- sector 444
- simulation 460
- stem-and-leaf plot 445
- tally marks 442
- theoretical probability 458
- unbiased 441
- upper quartile 451
- variability 436

Additional Children's Literature

- ***If the World Were a Village: A Book about the World's People,* written by David J. Smith and illustrated by Shelagh Armstrong**
  This wonderful book imagines the world as a village of 100 people to make it easier to relate data about many different aspects of life.

- ***The Secret Life of Math: Discover How (and Why) Numbers Have Survived from the Cave Dwellers to Us!* written by Ann McCallum and illustrated by Carolyn McIntyre Norton**
  This nonfiction book is filled with stories and activities. Read about tally marks and quipus, with directions for making your own quipu.

- ***Do You Wanna Bet?: Your Chance to Find Out About Probability,* written by Jean Cushman and illustrated by Martha Weston**
  Through interesting vignettes, this book examines many examples of probability and odds for children in the upper elementary grades.

- ***Pigs at Odds: Fun with Math and Games,* written by Amy Axelrod and illustrated by Sharon McGinley-Nally**
  The pigs are off to the county fair, where they have many opportunities to compute probability and odds.

Online Resources

- **Math Playground** www.mathplayground.com/probability/html
  Includes a spinner activity that can be used to generate data. Students can record data and use them for probability.

- **NCTM Illuminations** illuminations.nctm.org
  Go to **Weblinks**. Find a number of **Direct to web** activities that use data analysis and probability, such as **Water Measurement**, an activity that collects data on the evaporation of water, and **Hand Squeeze**, an activity that collects data as different people try a hand squeeze.

- **National Library of Virtual Manipulatives** http://nlvm.usu.edu
  Choose the **Spinners** activity. This gives users the opportunity to spin the spinner, change the size and color of the regions, and record the results. They can predict what will occur with various spinners and compare their predictions to actual results.

- **National Council of Teachers of Mathematics** www.nctm.org
  Go to **Standards and Focal Points** and select **e-Examples**.

  1. **Accessing and Investigating Data Using the World Wide Web (Activity 5.4)** for grades 3–5: Students use data sets on the Internet, such as census data, to answer questions.

  2. **Collecting, Representing, and Interpreting Data using Spreadsheets and Graphing Software (Activity 5.5)** for grades 3–5: This activity demonstrates how weather data are collected and evaluated.

  3. **Comparing Properties of the Mean and the Median through the Use of Technology (Activity 6.5)** for grades 6–8: This illustrates how a change in the data set affects the median and the mean.

Critical and Creative Thinking Questions

1. The purpose of data analysis or statistics is to answer questions. Give some examples of questions that children in the lower elementary grades might want to answer by collecting data. Also give some examples for the upper elementary grades.

2. The best uses of the median and the mean are sometimes unclear. Give two real-world examples in which it would be best to use the mean and two real-world examples in which it would be best to use the median. Explain your choices.

3. How do theoretical probability and experimental probability differ? What is the law of large numbers, and how does it apply to these concepts?

4. **In the field** Develop a survey on a topic that would be interesting to students in the elementary or middle grades (e.g., how often do you text or play games on the computer?). Give your survey to a few students, and determine whether your questions were formulated to give you the data you needed. Discuss how you might improve your questions.

5. What conclusions can you draw from this scatter plot about students' ages and their computer usage? What is an example of another question that can be answered with a scatter plot?

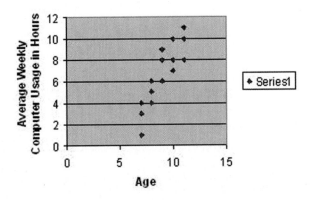

Age and Computer Usage

What is happening in this picture?

Look at this screen image of an online weather forecast.

1. Identify which data analysis and probability concepts are used in these data.
2. How might you use this image to teach children about the uses of probability and data analysis in our daily lives?

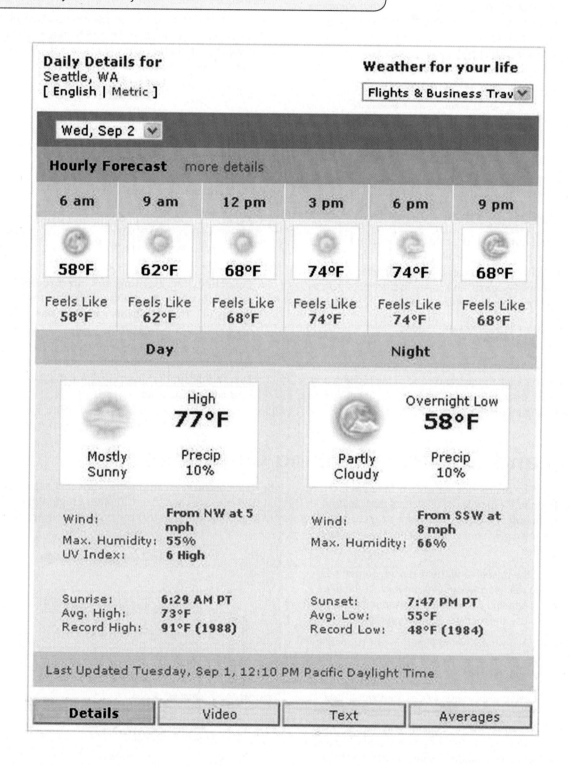

Self-Test

(Check your answers in Appendix D.)

1. Create a bar graph for the following data: Brooke Middle School has 125 students in sixth grade, 194 students in seventh grade, and 208 students in eighth grade.

2. Create a circle graph for the following data: Ms. Simon's students voted on their favorite color. Twenty-five percent of the students liked blue, 50% of the students liked red, 20% of the students liked yellow, and 5% of the students liked green.

3. Compare the two classes represented by these stem-and-leaf plots. Did one class perform better than the other on the quiz? Explain your answer.

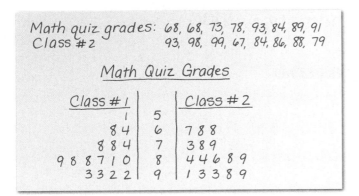

4. Make a stem-and-leaf plot for the following data. Mr. Wilson's science class earned the following grades on their quiz.

   45, 45, 57, 82, 65, 77, 89, 76, 78, 99, 88, 91, 85, 86, 67

5. How would you interpret these data?

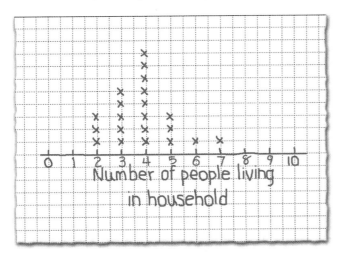

6. On five tests, Erin earned 75, 83, 75, 94, 86, and 95. Compute the mean, mode, and median for Erin's test grades. Which of these measures has the most meaning?

7. The owners of Best Cupcakes Bakery sold 75 peanut butter cupcakes, 102 chocolate nut cupcakes, and 84 banana cupcakes. Which kind of cupcakes should they make the most of? Which measure of central tendency are you using to make your decision?

8. The students in Ms. Nichols's class were weighed. Their average weight was 65 pounds and their total weight was 1300 pounds. How many students were in Ms. Nichols's class?

9. Acme Printing is a small company with an owner and four employees. Here are their salaries:

Position	Yearly Salary
Owner	$80,000
Manager	$40,000
Salesperson	$25,000
Clerk	$15,000
Clerk	$15,000

What is the average salary at their company? Which measure of central tendency did you use and why?

10. Ms. Dalal's fifth-grade class earned the following scores on their mathematics quiz:

    48, 57, 87, 66, 62, 75, 80, 81, 73, 84, 99, 67, 87, 92, 86

    Make a box-and-whisker plot of the data. Identify the median, lower quartile, upper quartile, and interquartile range.

11. Mr. Johnston's fifth-grade class earned the following scores on the same quiz as in question 10:

    45, 55, 90, 60, 75, 75, 80, 65, 62, 72, 100, 67, 80, 73, 74

    Make a box-and-whisker plot of these data using the same set of axes as in question 10. Identify the median, lower quartile, upper quartile, and interquartile range. Which class did better?

12. Identify each of the following as impossible, might happen, or certain to happen.

    a. It's going to rain tomorrow.
    b. The sun will set in the evening.
    c. The United States is going to have 112 senators.
    d. I'm going to meet my favorite movie star.

13. What do you think your chances are of winning a state lottery?

14. If a fair coin is flipped, what is the probability of getting a head?

15. If a fair six-sided die is tossed, what is the probability of it landing on 3? What is the probability of it landing on an even number?

THE PLANNER

Review your Chapter Planner on the chapter opener and check off your completed work.

Appendix A

Standards and Expectations,
National Council of Teachers of Mathematics, 2000

Number and Operations

Standard	Pre-K–2	Grades 3–5	Grades 6–8
Instructional programs from prekindergarten through grade 12 should enable all students to—	*EXPECTATIONS* In prekindergarten through grade 2 all students should—	*EXPECTATIONS* In grades 3–5 all students should—	*EXPECTATIONS* In grades 6–8 all students should—
Understand numbers, ways of representing numbers, relationships among numbers, and number systems	• count with understanding and recognize "how many" in sets of objects; • use multiple models to develop initial understandings of place value and the base-ten number system; • develop understanding of the relative position and magnitude of whole numbers and of ordinal and cardinal numbers and their connections; • develop a sense of whole numbers and represent and use them in flexible ways, including relating, composing, and decomposing numbers; • connect number words and numerals to the quantities they represent, using various physical models and representations; • understand and represent commonly used fractions, such as $\frac{1}{4}$, $\frac{1}{3}$, and $\frac{1}{2}$.	• understand the place-value structure of the base-ten number system and be able to represent and compare whole numbers and decimals; • recognize equivalent representations for the same number and generate them by decomposing and composing numbers; • develop understanding of fractions as parts of unit wholes, as parts of a collection, as locations on number lines, and as divisions of whole numbers; • use models, benchmarks, and equivalent forms to judge the size of fractions; • recognize and generate equivalent forms of commonly used fractions, decimals, and percents; • explore numbers less than 0 by extending the number line and through familiar applications; • describe classes of numbers according to characteristics such as the nature of their factors.	• work flexibly with fractions, decimals, and percents to solve problems; • compare and order fractions, decimals, and percents efficiently and find their approximate locations on a number line; • develop meaning for percents greater than 100 and less than 1; • understand and use ratios and proportions to represent quantitative relationships; • develop an understanding of large numbers and recognize and appropriately use exponential, scientific, and calculator notation; • use factors, multiples, prime factorization, and relatively prime numbers to solve problems; • develop meaning for integers and represent and compare quantities with them.
Understand meanings of operations and how they relate to one another	• understand various meanings of addition and subtraction of whole numbers and the relationship between the two operations; • understand the effects of adding and subtracting whole numbers; • understand situations that entail multiplication and division, such as equal groupings of objects and sharing equally.	• understand various meanings of multiplication and division; • understand the effects of multiplying and dividing whole numbers; • identify and use relationships between operations, such as division as the inverse of multiplication, to solve problems; • understand and use properties of operations, such as the distributivity of multiplication over addition.	• understand the meaning and effects of arithmetic operations with fractions, decimals, and integers; • use the associative and commutative properties of addition and multiplication and the distributive property of multiplication over addition to simplify computations with integers, fractions, and decimals; • understand and use the inverse relationships of addition and subtraction, multiplication and division, and squaring and finding square roots to simplify computations and solve problems.
Compute fluently and make reasonable estimates	• develop and use strategies for whole-number computations, with a focus on addition and subtraction; • develop fluency with basic number combinations for addition and subtraction; • use a variety of methods and tools to compute, including objects, mental computation, estimation, paper and pencil, and calculators.	• develop fluency with basic number combinations for multiplication and division and use these combinations to mentally compute related problems, such as 30 × 50; • develop fluency in adding, subtracting, multiplying, and dividing whole numbers; • develop and use strategies to estimate the results of whole-number computations and to judge the reasonableness of such results; • develop and use strategies to estimate computations involving fractions and decimals in situations relevant to students' experience; • use visual models, benchmarks, and equivalent forms to add and subtract commonly used fractions and decimals; • select appropriate methods and tools for computing with whole numbers from among mental computation, estimation, calculators, and paper and pencil according to the context and nature of the computation and use the selected method or tool.	• select appropriate methods and tools for computing with fractions and decimals from among mental computation, estimation, calculators or computers, and paper and pencil, depending on the situation, and apply the selected methods; • develop and analyze algorithms for computing with fractions, decimals, and integers and develop fluency in their use; • develop and use strategies to estimate the results of rational-number computations and judge the reasonableness of the results; • develop, analyze, and explain methods for solving problems involving proportions, such as scaling and finding equivalent ratios.

Algebra

Standard	Pre-K–2	Grades 3–5	Grades 6–8
Instructional programs from prekindergarten through grade 12 should enable all students to—	*EXPECTATIONS* In prekindergarten through grade 2 all students should—	*EXPECTATIONS* In grades 3–5 all students should—	*EXPECTATIONS* In grades 6–8 all students should—
Understand patterns, relations, and functions	• sort, classify, and order objects by size, number, and other properties; • recognize, describe, and extend patterns such as sequences of sounds and shapes or simple numeric patterns and translate from one representation to another; • analyze how both repeating and growing patterns are generated.	• describe, extend, and make generalizations about geometric and numeric patterns; • represent and analyze patterns and functions, using words, tables, and graphs.	• represent, analyze, and generalize a variety of patterns with tables, graphs, words, and, when possible, symbolic rules; • relate and compare different forms of representation for a relationship; • identify functions as linear or nonlinear and contrast their properties from tables, graphs, or equations.
Represent and analyze mathematical situations and structures using algebraic symbols	• illustrate general principles and properties of operations, such as commutativity, using specific numbers; • use concrete, pictorial, and verbal representations to develop an understanding of invented and conventional symbolic notations.	• identify such properties as commutativity, associativity, and distributivity and use them to compute with whole numbers; • represent the idea of a variable as an unknown quantity using a letter or symbol; • express mathematical relationships using equations.	• develop an initial conceptual understanding of different uses of variables; • explore relationships between symbolic expressions and graphs of lines, paying particular attention to the meaning of intercept and slope; • use symbolic algebra to represent situations and to solve problems, especially those that involve linear relationships; • recognize and generate equivalent forms for simple algebraic expressions and solve linear equations.
Use mathematical models to represent and understand quantitative relationships	• model situations that involve the addition and subtraction of whole numbers, using objects, pictures, and symbols.	• model problem situations with objects and use representations such as graphs, tables, and equations to draw conclusions.	• model and solve contextualized problems using various representations, such as graphs, tables, and equations.
Analyze change in various contexts	• describe qualitative change, such as a student's growing taller; • describe quantitative change, such as a student's growing two inches in one year.	• investigate how a change in one variable relates to a change in a second variable; • identify and describe situations with constant or varying rates of change and compare them.	• use graphs to analyze the nature of changes in quantities in linear relationships.

Geometry

Standard	Pre-K–2	Grades 3–5	Grades 6–8
Instructional programs from prekindergarten through grade 12 should enable all students to—	*EXPECTATIONS* In prekindergarten through grade 2 all students should—	*EXPECTATIONS* In grades 3–5 all students should—	*EXPECTATIONS* In grades 6–8 all students should—
Analyze characteristics and properties of two- and three-dimensional geometric shapes and develop mathematical arguments about geometric relationships	• recognize, name, build, draw, compare, and sort two- and three-dimensional shapes; • describe attributes and parts of two- and three-dimensional shapes; • investigate and predict the results of putting together and taking apart two- and three-dimensional shapes.	• identify, compare, and analyze attributes of two- and three-dimensional shapes and develop vocabulary to describe the attributes; • classify two- and three-dimensional shapes according to their properties and develop definitions of classes of shapes such as triangles and pyramids; • investigate, describe, and reason about the results of subdividing, combining, and transforming shapes; • explore congruence and similarity; • make and test conjectures about geometric properties and relationships and develop logical arguments to justify conclusions.	• precisely describe, classify, and understand relationships among types of two- and three-dimensional objects using their defining properties; • understand relationships among the angles, side lengths, perimeters, areas, and volumes of similar objects; • create and critique inductive and deductive arguments concerning geometric ideas and relationships, such as congruence, similarity, and the Pythagorean relationship.
Specify locations and describe spatial relationships using coordinate geometry and other representational systems	• describe, name, and interpret relative positions in space and apply ideas about relative position; • describe, name, and interpret direction and distance in navigating space and apply ideas about direction and distance; • find and name locations with simple relationships such as "near to" and in coordinate systems such as maps.	• describe location and movement using common language and geometric vocabulary; • make and use coordinate systems to specify locations and to describe paths; • find the distance between points along horizontal and vertical lines of a coordinate system.	• use coordinate geometry to represent and examine the properties of geometric shapes; • use coordinate geometry to examine special geometric shapes, such as regular polygons or those with pairs of parallel or perpendicular sides.
Apply transformations and use symmetry to analyze mathematical situations	• recognize and apply slides, flips, and turns; • recognize and create shapes that have symmetry.	• predict and describe the results of sliding, flipping, and turning two-dimensional shapes; • describe a motion or a series of motions that will show that two shapes are congruent; • identify and describe line and rotational symmetry in two- and three-dimensional shapes and designs.	• describe sizes, positions, and orientations of shapes under informal transformations such as flips, turns, slides, and scaling; • examine the congruence, similarity, and line or rotational symmetry of objects using transformations.
Use visualization, spatial reasoning, and geometric modeling to solve problems	• create mental images of geometric shapes using spatial memory and spatial visualization; • recognize and represent shapes from different perspectives; • relate ideas in geometry to ideas in number and measurement; • recognize geometric shapes and structures in the environment and specify their location.	• build and draw geometric objects; • create and describe mental images of objects, patterns, and paths; • identify and build a three-dimensional object from two-dimensional representations of that object; • identify and build a two-dimensional representation of a three-dimensional object; • use geometric models to solve problems in other areas of mathematics, such as number and measurement; • recognize geometric ideas and relationships and apply them to other disciplines and to problems that arise in the classroom or in everyday life.	• draw geometric objects with specified properties, such as side lengths or angle measures; • use two-dimensional representations of three-dimensional objects to visualize and solve problems such as those involving surface area and volume; • use visual tools such as networks to represent and solve problems; • use geometric models to represent and explain numerical and algebraic relationships; • recognize and apply geometric ideas and relationships in areas outside the mathematical classroom, such as art, science, and everyday life.

Measurement

Standard	Pre-K-2	Grades 3-5	Grades 6-8
Instructional programs from prekindergarten through grade 12 should enable all students to—	*EXPECTATIONS* In prekindergarten through grade 2 all students should—	*EXPECTATIONS* In grades 3-5 all students should—	*EXPECTATIONS* In grades 6-8 all students should—
Understand measurable attributes of objects and the units, systems, and processes of measurement	• recognize the attributes of length, volume, weight, area, and time; • compare and order objects according to these attributes; • understand how to measure using nonstandard and standard units; • select an appropriate unit and tool for the attribute being measured.	• understand such attributes as length, area, weight, volume, and size of angle and select the appropriate type of unit for measuring each attribute; • understand the need for measuring with standard units and become familiar with standard units in the customary and metric systems; • carry out simple unit conversions, such as from centimeters to meters, within a system of measurement; • understand that measurements are approximations and understand how differences in units affect precision; • explore what happens to measurements of a two-dimensional shape such as its perimeter and area when the shape is changed in some way.	• understand both metric and customary systems of measurement; • understand relationships among units and convert from one unit to another within the same system; • understand, select, and use units of appropriate size and type to measure angles, perimeter, area, surface area, and volume.
Apply appropriate techniques, tools, and formulas to determine measurements	• measure with multiple copies of units of the same size, such as paper clips laid end to end; • use repetition of a single unit to measure something larger than the unit, for instance, measuring the length of a room with a single meterstick; • use tools to measure; • develop common referents for measures to make comparisons and estimates.	• develop strategies for estimating the perimeters, areas, and volumes of irregular shapes; • select and apply appropriate standard units and tools to measure length, area, volume, weight, time, temperature, and the size of angles; • select and use benchmarks to estimate measurements; • develop, understand, and use formulas to find the area of rectangles and related triangles and parallelograms; • develop strategies to determine the surface areas and volumes of rectangular solids.	• use common benchmarks to select appropriate methods for estimating measurements; • select and apply techniques and tools to accurately find length, area, volume, and angle measures to appropriate levels of precision; • develop and use formulas to determine the circumference of circles and the area of triangles, parallelograms, trapezoids, and circles and develop strategies to find the areas of more complex shapes; • develop strategies to determine the surface area and volume of selected prisms, pyramids, and cylinders; • solve problems involving scale factors, using ratio and proportion; • solve simple problems involving rates and derived measurements for such attributes as velocity and density.

Data Analysis and Probability

Standard	Pre-K–2	Grades 3–5	Grades 6–8
Instructional programs from prekindergarten through grade 12 should enable all students to—	*EXPECTATIONS* In prekindergarten through grade 2 all students should—	*EXPECTATIONS* In grades 3–5 all students should—	*EXPECTATIONS* In grades 6–8 all students should—
Formulate questions that can be addressed with data and collect, organize, and display relevant data to answer them	• pose questions and gather data about themselves and their surroundings; • sort and classify objects according to their attributes and organize data about the objects; • represent data using concrete objects, pictures, and graphs.	• design investigations to address a question and consider how data-collection methods affect the nature of the data set; • collect data using observations, surveys, and experiments; • represent data using tables and graphs such as line plots, bar graphs, and line graphs; • recognize the differences in representing categorical and numerical data.	• formulate questions, design studies, and collect data about a characteristic shared by two populations or different characteristics within one population; • select, create, and use appropriate graphical representations of data, including histograms, box plots, and scatterplots.
Select and use appropriate statistical methods to analyze data	• describe parts of the data and the set of data as a whole to determine what the data show.	• describe the shape and important features of a set of data and compare related data sets, with an emphasis on how the data are distributed; • use measures of center, focusing on the median, and understand what each does and does not indicate about the data set; • compare different representations of the same data and evaluate how well each representation shows important aspects of the data.	• find, use, and interpret measures of center and spread, including mean and interquartile range; • discuss and understand the correspondence between data sets and their graphical representations, especially histograms, stem-and-leaf plots, box plots, and scatterplots.
Develop and evaluate inferences and predictions that are based on data	• discuss events related to students' experiences as likely or unlikely.	• propose and justify conclusions and predictions that are based on data and design studies to further investigate the conclusions or predictions.	• use observations about differences between two or more samples to make conjectures about the populations from which the samples were taken; • make conjectures about possible relationships between two characteristics of a sample on the basis of scatterplots of the data and approximate lines of fit; • use conjectures to formulate new questions and plan new studies to answer them.
Understand and apply basic concepts of probability		• describe events as likely or unlikely and discuss the degree of likelihood using such words as *certain, equally likely,* and *impossible;* • predict the probability of outcomes of simple experiments and test the predictions; • understand that the measure of the likelihood of an event can be represented by a number from 0 to 1.	• understand and use appropriate terminology to describe complementary and mutually exclusive events; • use proportionality and a basic understanding of probability to make and test conjectures about the results of experiments and simulations; • compute probabilities for simple compound events, using such methods as organized lists, tree diagrams, and area methods.

Problem Solving

Standard

Instructional programs from prekindergarten through grade 12 should enable all students to—

- Build new mathematical knowledge through problem solving
- Solve problems that arise in mathematics and in other contexts
- Apply and adapt a variety of appropriate strategies to solve problems
- Monitor and reflect on the process of mathematical problem solving

Reasoning and Proof

Standard

Instructional programs from prekindergarten through grade 12 should enable all students to—

- Recognize reasoning and proof as fundamental aspects of mathematics
- Make and investigate mathematical conjectures
- Develop and evaluate mathematical arguments and proofs
- Select and use various types of reasoning and methods of proof

Communication

Standard

Instructional programs from prekindergarten through grade 12 should enable all students to—

- Organize and consolidate their mathematical thinking through communication
- Communicate their mathematical thinking coherently and clearly to peers, teachers, and others
- Analyze and evaluate the mathematical thinking and strategies of others
- Use the language of mathematics to express mathematical ideas precisely

Connections

Standard

Instructional programs from prekindergarten through grade 12 should enable all students to—

- Recognize and use connections among mathematical ideas
- Understand how mathematical ideas interconnect and build on one another to produce a coherent whole
- Recognize and apply mathematics in contexts outside of mathematics

Representation

Standard

Instructional programs from prekindergarten through grade 12 should enable all students to—

- Create and use representations to organize, record, and communicate mathematical ideas
- Select, apply, and translate among mathematical representations to solve problems
- Use representations to model and interpret physical, social, and mathematical phenomena

Curriculum Focal Points,
National Council of Teachers
of Mathematics, 2006

5

Curriculum Focal Points for Mathematics in Prekindergarten through Grade 8

Three curriculum focal points are identified and described for each grade level, pre-K–8, along with connections to guide integration of the focal points at that grade level and across grade levels, to form a comprehensive mathematics curriculum. To build students' strength in the use of mathematical processes, instruction in these content areas should incorporate—

- the use of the mathematics to solve problems;
- an application of logical reasoning to justify procedures and solutions; and
- an involvement in the design and analysis of multiple representations to learn, make connections among, and communicate about the ideas within and outside of mathematics.

The purpose of identifying these grade-level curriculum focal points and connections is to enable students to learn the content in the context of a focused and cohesive curriculum that implements problem solving, reasoning, and critical thinking.

These curriculum focal points should be considered as major instructional goals and desirable learning expectations, not as a list of objectives for students to master. They should be implemented with the intention of building mathematical competency for all students, bolstered by the pedagogical understanding that not every student learns at the same rate or acquires concepts and skills at the same time.

Those who are involved in curriculum planning for grades 6–8 should note that this set of curriculum focal points has been designed with the intention of providing a three-year middle school program that includes a full year of general mathematics in each of grades 6, 7, and 8. Those whose programs offer an algebra course in grade 8 (or earlier) should consider including the curriculum focal points that this framework calls for in grade 8 in grade 6 or grade 7. Alternatively, these topics could be incorporated into the high school program. Either way, curricula would not omit the important content that the grade 7 and grade 8 focal points offer students in preparation for algebra and for their long-term mathematical knowledge.

Curriculum Focal Points and Connections for Prekindergarten

The set of three curriculum focal points and related connections for mathematics in prekindergarten follow. These topics are the recommended content emphases for this grade level. It is essential that these focal points be addressed in contexts that promote problem solving, reasoning, communication, making connections, and designing and analyzing representations.

Prekindergarten Curriculum Focal Points	Connections to the Focal Points
Number and Operations: **Developing an understanding of whole numbers, including concepts of correspondence, counting, cardinality, and comparison** Children develop an understanding of the meanings of whole numbers and recognize the number of objects in small groups without counting and by counting—the first and most basic mathematical algorithm. They understand that number words refer to quantity. They use one-to-one correspondence to solve problems by matching sets and comparing number amounts and in counting objects to 10 and beyond. They understand that the last word that they state in counting tells "how many," they count to determine number amounts and compare quantities (using language such as "more than" and "less than"), and they order sets by the number of objects in them.	*Data Analysis:* Children learn the foundations of data analysis by using objects' attributes that they have identified in relation to geometry and measurement (e.g., size, quantity, orientation, number of sides or vertices, color) for various purposes, such as describing, sorting, or comparing. For example, children sort geometric figures by shape, compare objects by weight ("heavier," "lighter"), or describe sets of objects by the number of objects in each set. *Number and Operations:* Children use meanings of numbers to create strategies for solving problems and responding to practical situations, such as getting just enough napkins for a group, or mathematical situations, such as determining that any shape is a triangle if it has exactly three straight sides and is closed. *Algebra:* Children recognize and duplicate simple sequential patterns (e.g., square, circle, square, circle, square, circle, . . .).
Geometry: **Identifying shapes and describing spatial relationships** Children develop spatial reasoning by working from two perspectives on space as they examine the shapes of objects and inspect their relative positions. They find shapes in their environments and describe them in their own words. They build pictures and designs by combining two- and three-dimensional shapes, and they solve such problems as deciding which piece will fit into a space in a puzzle. They discuss the relative positions of objects with vocabulary such as "above," "below," and "next to."	
Measurement: **Identifying measurable attributes and comparing objects by using these attributes** Children identify objects as "the same" or "different," and then "more" or "less," on the basis of attributes that they can measure. They identify measurable attributes such as length and weight and solve problems by making direct comparisons of objects on the basis of those attributes.	

Reprinted with permission from *Curriculum Focal Points for Prekindergarten through Grade 8 Mathematics: A Quest for Coherence*, copyright 2006 by the National Council of Teachers of Mathematics. All rights reserved.
The Curriculum Focal Points identify key mathematical ideas for these grades. They are not discrete topics or a checklist to be mastered; rather, they provide a framework for the majority of instruction at a particular grade level and the foundation for future mathematics study.

Curriculum Focal Points and Connections for Kindergarten

The set of three curriculum focal points and related connections for mathematics in kindergarten follow. These topics are the recommended content emphases for this grade level. It is essential that these focal points be addressed in contexts that promote problem solving, reasoning, communication, making connections, and designing and analyzing representations.

Kindergarten Curriculum Focal Points	Connections to the Focal Points
Number and Operations: **Representing, comparing, and ordering whole numbers and joining and separating sets** Children use numbers, including written numerals, to represent quantities and to solve quantitative problems, such as counting objects in a set, creating a set with a given number of objects, comparing and ordering sets or numerals by using both cardinal and ordinal meanings, and modeling simple joining and separating situations with objects. They choose, combine, and apply effective strategies for answering quantitative questions, including quickly recognizing the number in a small set, counting and producing sets of given sizes, counting the number in combined sets, and counting backward.	*Data Analysis:* Children sort objects and use one or more attributes to solve problems. For example, they might sort solids that roll easily from those that do not. Or they might sort solids that roll easily from those that do not. Or they might collect data and use counting to answer such questions as, "What is our favorite snack?" They re-sort objects by using new attributes (e.g., after sorting solids according to which ones roll, they might re-sort the solids according to which ones stack easily).
Geometry: **Describing shapes and space** Children interpret the physical world with geometric ideas (e.g., shape, orientation, spatial relations) and describe it with corresponding vocabulary. They identify, name, and describe a variety of shapes, such as squares, triangles, circles, rectangles, (regular) hexagons, and (isosceles) trapezoids presented in a variety of ways (e.g., with different sizes or orientations), as well as such three-dimensional shapes as spheres, cubes, and cylinders. They use basic shapes and spatial reasoning to model objects in their environment and to construct more complex shapes.	*Geometry:* Children integrate their understandings of geometry, measurement, and number. For example, they understand, discuss, and create simple navigational directions (e.g., "Walk forward 10 steps, turn right, and walk forward 5 steps"). *Algebra:* Children identify, duplicate, and extend simple number patterns and sequential and growing patterns (e.g., patterns made with shapes) as preparation for creating rules that describe relationships.
Measurement: **Ordering objects by measurable attributes** Children use measurable attributes, such as length or weight, to solve problems by comparing and ordering objects. They compare the lengths of two objects both directly (by comparing them with each other) and indirectly (by comparing both with a third object), and they order several objects according to length.	

Curriculum Focal Points and Connections for Grade 1

The set of three curriculum focal points and related connections for mathematics in grade 1 follow. These topics are the recommended content emphases for this grade level. It is essential that these focal points be addressed in contexts that promote problem solving, reasoning, communication, making connections, and designing and analyzing representations.

Grade 1 Curriculum Focal Points

Number and Operations and Algebra: Developing understandings of addition and subtraction and strategies for basic addition facts and related subtraction facts

Children develop strategies for adding and subtracting whole numbers on the basis of their earlier work with small numbers. They use a variety of models, including discrete objects, length-based models (e.g., lengths of connecting cubes), and number lines, to model "part-whole," "adding to," "taking away from," and "comparing" situations to develop an understanding of the meanings of addition and subtraction and strategies to solve such arithmetic problems. Children understand the connections between counting and the operations of addition and subtraction (e.g., adding two is the same as "counting on" two). They use properties of addition (commutativity and associativity) to add whole numbers, and they create and use increasingly sophisticated strategies based on these properties (e.g., "making tens") to solve addition and subtraction problems involving basic facts. By comparing a variety of solution strategies, children relate addition and subtraction as inverse operations.

Number and Operations: Developing an understanding of whole number relationships, including grouping in tens and ones

Children compare and order whole numbers (at least to 100) to develop an understanding of and solve problems involving the relative sizes of these numbers. They think of whole numbers between 10 and 100 in terms of groups of tens and ones (especially recognizing the numbers 11 to 19 as 1 group of ten and particular numbers of ones). They understand the sequential order of the counting numbers and their relative magnitudes and represent numbers on a number line.

Geometry: Composing and decomposing geometric shapes

Children compose and decompose plane and solid figures (e.g., by putting two congruent isosceles triangles together to make a rhombus), thus building an understanding of part-whole relationships as well as the properties of the original and composite shapes. As they combine figures, they recognize them from different perspectives and orientations, describe their geometric attributes and properties, and determine how they are alike and different, in the process developing a background for measurement and initial understandings of such properties as congruence and symmetry.

Connections to the Focal Points

Number and Operations and Algebra: Children use mathematical reasoning, including ideas such as commutativity and associativity and beginning ideas of tens and ones, to solve two-digit addition and subtraction problems with strategies that they understand and can explain. They solve both routine and nonroutine problems.

Measurement and Data Analysis: Children strengthen their sense of number by solving problems involving measurements and data. Measuring by laying multiple copies of a unit end to end and then counting the units by using groups of tens and ones supports children's understanding of number lines and number relationships. Representing measurements and discrete data in picture and bar graphs involves counting and comparisons that provide another meaningful connection to number relationships.

Algebra: Through identifying, describing, and applying number patterns and properties in developing strategies for basic facts, children learn about other properties of numbers and operations, such as odd and even (e.g., "Even numbers of objects can be paired, with none left over"), and 0 as the identity element for addition.

Reprinted with permission from *Curriculum Focal Points for Prekindergarten through Grade 8 Mathematics: A Quest for Coherence*, copyright 2006 by the National Council of Teachers of Mathematics. All rights reserved.
The Curriculum Focal Points identify key mathematical ideas for these grades. They are not discrete topics or a checklist to be mastered; rather, they provide a framework for the majority of instruction at a particular grade level and the foundation for future mathematics study.

476

Curriculum Focal Points and Connections for Grade 2

The set of three curriculum focal points and related connections for mathematics in grade 2 follow. These topics are the recommended content emphases for this grade level. It is essential that these focal points be addressed in contexts that promote problem solving, reasoning, communication, making connections, and designing and analyzing representations.

Grade 2 Curriculum Focal Points	Connections to the Focal Points
Number and Operations: **Developing an understanding of the base-ten numeration system and place-value concepts** Children develop an understanding of the base-ten numeration system and place-value concepts (at least to 1000). Their understanding of base-ten numeration includes ideas of counting in units and multiples of hundreds, tens, and ones, as well as a grasp of number relationships, which they demonstrate in a variety of ways, including comparing and ordering numbers. They understand multidigit numbers in terms of place value, recognizing that place-value notation is a shorthand for the sums of multiples of powers of 10 (e.g., 853 as 8 hundreds + 5 tens + 3 ones). *Number and Operations and Algebra:* **Developing quick recall of addition facts and related subtraction facts and fluency with multidigit addition and subtraction** Children use their understanding of addition to develop quick recall of basic addition facts and related subtraction facts. They solve arithmetic problems by applying their understanding of models of addition and subtraction (such as combining or separating sets or using number lines), relationships and properties of number (such as place value), and properties of addition (commutativity and associativity). Children develop, discuss, and use efficient, accurate, and generalizable methods to add and subtract multidigit whole numbers. They select and apply appropriate methods to estimate sums and differences or calculate them mentally, depending on the context and numbers involved. They develop fluency with efficient procedures, including standard algorithms, for adding and subtracting whole numbers, understand why the procedures work (on the basis of place value and properties of operations), and use them to solve problems. *Measurement:* **Developing an understanding of linear measurement and facility in measuring lengths** Children develop an understanding of the meaning and processes of measurement, including such underlying concepts as partitioning (the mental activity of slicing the length of an object into equal-sized units) and transitivity (e.g., if object A is longer than object B and object B is longer than object C, then object A is longer than object C). They understand linear measure as an iteration of units and use rulers and other measurement tools with that understanding. They understand the need for equal-length units, the use of standard units of measure (centimeter and inch), and the inverse relationship between the size of a unit and the number of units used in a particular measurement (i.e., children recognize that the smaller the unit, the more iterations they need to cover a given length).	*Number and Operations:* Children use place value and properties of operations to create equivalent representations of given numbers (such as 35 represented by 35 ones, 3 tens and 5 ones, or 2 tens and 15 ones) and to write, compare, and order multidigit numbers. They use these ideas to compose and decompose multidigit numbers. Children add and subtract to solve a variety of problems, including applications involving measurement, geometry, and data, as well as nonroutine problems. In preparation for grade 3, they solve problems involving multiplicative situations, developing initial understandings of multiplication as repeated addition. *Geometry and Measurement:* Children estimate, measure, and compute lengths as they solve problems involving data, space, and movement through space. By composing and decomposing two-dimensional shapes (intentionally substituting arrangements of smaller shapes for larger shapes or substituting larger shapes for many smaller shapes), they use geometric knowledge and spatial reasoning to develop foundations for understanding area, fractions, and proportions. *Algebra:* Children use number patterns to extend their knowledge of properties of numbers and operations. For example, when skip counting, they build foundations for understanding multiples and factors.

Curriculum Focal Points and Connections for Grade 3

The set of three curriculum focal points and related connections for mathematics in grade 3 follow. These topics are the recommended content emphases for this grade level. It is essential that these focal points be addressed in contexts that promote problem solving, reasoning, communication, making connections, and designing and analyzing representations.

Grade 3 Curriculum Focal Points	Connections to the Focal Points
Number and Operations and Algebra: **Developing understandings of multiplication and division and strategies for basic multiplication facts and related division facts** Students understand the meanings of multiplication and division of whole numbers through the use of representations (e.g., equal-sized groups, arrays, area models, and equal "jumps" on number lines for multiplication, and successive subtraction, partitioning, and sharing for division). They use properties of addition and multiplication (e.g., commutativity, associativity, and the distributive property) to multiply whole numbers and apply increasingly sophisticated strategies based on these properties to solve multiplication and division problems involving basic facts. By comparing a variety of solution strategies, students relate multiplication and division as inverse operations.	*Algebra:* Understanding properties of multiplication and the relationship between multiplication and division is a part of algebra readiness that develops at grade 3. The creation and analysis of patterns and relationships involving multiplication and division should occur at this grade level. Students build a foundation for later understanding of functional relationships by describing relationships in context with such statements as, "The number of legs is 4 times the number of chairs."
Number and Operations: **Developing an understanding of fractions and fraction equivalence** Students develop an understanding of the meanings and uses of fractions to represent parts of a whole, parts of a set, or points or distances on a number line. They understand that the size of a fractional part is relative to the size of the whole, and they use fractions to represent numbers that are equal to, less than, or greater than 1. They solve problems that involve comparing and ordering fractions by using models, benchmark fractions, or common numerators or denominators. They understand and use models, including the number line, to identify equivalent fractions.	*Measurement:* Students in grade 3 strengthen their understanding of fractions as they confront problems in linear measurement that call for more precision than the whole unit allowed them in their work in grade 2. They develop their facility in measuring with fractional parts of linear units. Students develop measurement concepts and skills through experiences in analyzing attributes and properties of two-dimensional objects. They form an understanding of perimeter as a measurable attribute and select appropriate units, strategies, and tools to solve problems involving perimeter. *Data Analysis:* Addition, subtraction, multiplication, and division of whole numbers come into play as students construct and analyze frequency tables, bar graphs, picture graphs, and line plots and use them to solve problems.
Geometry: **Describing and analyzing properties of two-dimensional shapes** Students describe, analyze, compare, and classify two-dimensional shapes by their sides and angles and connect these attributes to definitions of shapes. Students investigate, describe, and reason about decomposing, combining, and transforming polygons to make other polygons. Through building, drawing, and analyzing two-dimensional shapes, students understand attributes and properties of two-dimensional space and the use of those attributes and properties in solving problems, including applications involving congruence and symmetry.	*Number and Operations:* Building on their work in grade 2, students extend their understanding of place value to numbers up to 10,000 in various contexts. Students also apply this understanding to the task of representing numbers in different equivalent forms (e.g., expanded notation). They develop their understanding of numbers by building their facility with mental computation (addition and subtraction in special cases, such as $2,500 + 6,000$ and $9,000 - 5,000$), by using computational estimation, and by performing paper-and-pencil computations.

Reprinted with permission from *Curriculum Focal Points for Prekindergarten through Grade 8 Mathematics: A Quest for Coherence*, copyright 2006 by the National Council of Teachers of Mathematics. All rights reserved.

The Curriculum Focal Points identify key mathematical ideas for these grades. They are not discrete topics or a checklist to be mastered; rather, they provide a framework for the majority of instruction at a particular grade level and the foundation for future mathematics study.

Curriculum Focal Points and Connections for Grade 4

The set of three curriculum focal points and related connections for mathematics in grade 4 follow. These topics are the recommended content emphases for this grade level. It is essential that these focal points be addressed in contexts that promote problem solving, reasoning, communication, making connections, and designing and analyzing representations.

Grade 4 Curriculum Focal Points	Connections to the Focal Points
***Number and Operations and Algebra:* Developing quick recall of multiplication facts and related division facts and fluency with whole number multiplication** Students use understandings of multiplication to develop quick recall of the basic multiplication facts and related division facts. They apply their understanding of models for multiplication (i.e., equal-sized groups, arrays, area models, equal intervals on the number line), place value, and properties of operations (in particular, the distributive property) as they develop, discuss, and use efficient, accurate, and generalizable methods to multiply multidigit whole numbers. They select appropriate methods and apply them accurately to estimate products or calculate them mentally, depending on the context and numbers involved. They develop fluency with efficient procedures, including the standard algorithm, for multiplying whole numbers, understand why the procedures work (on the basis of place value and properties of operations), and use them to solve problems.	***Algebra:*** Students continue identifying, describing, and extending numeric patterns involving all operations and nonnumeric growing or repeating patterns. Through these experiences, they develop an understanding of the use of a rule to describe a sequence of numbers or objects. ***Geometry:*** Students extend their understanding of properties of two-dimensional shapes as they find the areas of polygons. They build on their earlier work with symmetry and congruence in grade 3 to encompass transformations, including those that produce line and rotational symmetry. By using transformations to design and analyze simple tilings and tessellations, students deepen their understanding of two-dimensional space. ***Measurement:*** As part of understanding two-dimensional shapes, students measure and classify angles. ***Data Analysis:*** Students continue to use tools from grade 3, solving problems by making frequency tables, bar graphs, picture graphs, and line plots. They apply their understanding of place value to develop and use stem-and-leaf plots. ***Number and Operations:*** Building on their work in grade 3, students extend their understanding of place value and ways of representing numbers to 100,000 in various contexts. They use estimation in determining the relative sizes of amounts or distances. Students develop understandings of strategies for multidigit division by using models that represent division as the inverse of multiplication, as partitioning, or as successive subtraction. By working with decimals, students extend their ability to recognize equivalent fractions. Students' earlier work in grade 3 with models of fractions and multiplication and division facts supports their understanding of techniques for generating equivalent fractions and simplifying fractions.
***Number and Operations:* Developing an understanding of decimals, including the connections between fractions and decimals** Students understand decimal notation as an extension of the base-ten system of writing whole numbers that is useful for representing more numbers, including numbers between 0 and 1, between 1 and 2, and so on. Students relate their understanding of fractions to reading and writing decimals that are greater than or less than 1, identifying equivalent decimals, comparing and ordering decimals, and estimating decimal or fractional amounts in problem solving. They connect equivalent fractions and decimals by comparing models to symbols and locating equivalent symbols on the number line.	
***Measurement:* Developing an understanding of area and determining the areas of two-dimensional shapes** Students recognize area as an attribute of two-dimensional regions. They learn that they can quantify area by finding the total number of same-sized units of area that cover the shape without gaps or overlaps. They understand that a square that is 1 unit on a side is the standard unit for measuring area. They select appropriate units, strategies (e.g., decomposing shapes), and tools for solving problems that involve estimating or measuring area. Students connect area measure to the area model that they have used to represent multiplication, and they use this connection to justify the formula for the area of a rectangle.	

Curriculum Focal Points and Connections for Grade 5

The set of three curriculum focal points and related connections for mathematics in grade 5 follow. These topics are the recommended content emphases for this grade level. It is essential that these focal points be addressed in contexts that promote problem solving, reasoning, communication, making connections, and designing and analyzing representations.

Grade 5 Curriculum Focal Points	Connections to the Focal Points
Number and Operations and Algebra: Developing an understanding of and fluency with division of whole numbers	*Algebra:* Students use patterns, models, and relationships as contexts for writing and solving simple equations and inequalities. They create graphs of simple equations. They explore prime and composite numbers and discover concepts related to the addition and subtraction of fractions as they use factors and multiples, including applications of common factors and common multiples. They develop an understanding of the order of operations and use it for all operations.
Students apply their understanding of models for division, place value, properties, and the relationship of division to multiplication as they develop, discuss, and use efficient, accurate, and generalizable procedures to find quotients involving multidigit dividends. They select appropriate methods and apply them accurately to estimate quotients or calculate them mentally, depending on the context and numbers involved. They develop fluency with efficient procedures, including the standard algorithm, for dividing whole numbers, understand why the procedures work (on the basis of place value and properties of operations), and use them to solve problems. They consider the context in which a problem is situated to select the most useful form of the quotient for the solution, and they interpret it appropriately.	*Measurement:* Students' experiences connect their work with solids and volume to their earlier work with capacity and weight or mass. They solve problems that require attention to both approximation and precision of measurement.
Number and Operations: Developing an understanding of and fluency with addition and subtraction of fractions and decimals	*Data Analysis:* Students apply their understanding of whole numbers, fractions, and decimals as they construct and analyze double-bar and line graphs and use ordered pairs on coordinate grids.
Students apply their understandings of fractions and fraction models to represent the addition and subtraction of fractions with unlike denominators as equivalent calculations with like denominators. They apply their understandings of decimal models, place value, and properties to add and subtract decimals. They develop fluency with standard procedures for adding and subtracting fractions and decimals. They make reasonable estimates of fraction and decimal sums and differences. Students add and subtract fractions and decimals to solve problems, including problems involving measurement.	*Number and Operations:* Building on their work in grade 4, students extend their understanding of place value to numbers through millions and millionths in various contexts. They apply what they know about multiplication of whole numbers to larger numbers. Students also explore contexts that they can describe with negative numbers (e.g., situations of owing money or measuring elevations above and below sea level).
Geometry and Measurement and Algebra: Describing three-dimensional shapes and analyzing their properties, including volume and surface area	
Students relate two-dimensional shapes to three-dimensional shapes and analyze properties of polyhedral solids, describing them by the number of edges, faces, or vertices as well as the types of faces. Students recognize volume as an attribute of three-dimensional space. They understand that they can quantify volume by finding the total number of same-sized units of volume that they need to fill the space without gaps or overlaps. They understand that a cube that is 1 unit on an edge is the standard unit for measuring volume. They select appropriate units, strategies, and tools for solving problems that involve estimating or measuring volume. They decompose three-dimensional shapes and find surface areas and volumes of prisms. As they work with surface area, they find and justify relationships among the formulas for the areas of different polygons. They measure necessary attributes of shapes to use area formulas to solve problems.	

Reprinted with permission from *Curriculum Focal Points for Prekindergarten through Grade 8 Mathematics: A Quest for Coherence,* copyright 2006 by the National Council of Teachers of Mathematics. All rights reserved.

The Curriculum Focal Points identify key mathematical ideas for these grades. They are not discrete topics or a checklist to be mastered; rather, they provide a framework for the majority of instruction at a particular grade level and the foundation for future mathematics study.

Curriculum Focal Points and Connections for Grade 6

The set of three curriculum focal points and related connections for mathematics in grade 6 follow. These topics are the recommended content emphases for this grade level. It is essential that these focal points be addressed in contexts that promote problem solving, reasoning, communication, making connections, and designing and analyzing representations.

Grade 6 Curriculum Focal Points	Connections to the Focal Points
Number and Operations: Developing an understanding of and fluency with multiplication and division of fractions and decimals	**Number and Operations:** Students' work in dividing fractions shows them that they can express the result of dividing two whole numbers as a fraction (viewed as parts of a whole). Students then extend their work in grade 5 with division of whole numbers to give mixed number and decimal solutions to division problems with whole numbers. They recognize that ratio tables not only derive from rows in the multiplication table but also connect with equivalent fractions. Students distinguish multiplicative comparisons from additive comparisons.
Students use the meanings of fractions, multiplication and division, and the inverse relationship between multiplication and division to make sense of procedures for multiplying and dividing fractions and explain why they work. They use the relationship between decimals and fractions, as well as the relationship between finite decimals and whole numbers (i.e., a finite decimal multiplied by an appropriate power of 10 is a whole number), to understand and explain the procedures for multiplying and dividing decimals. Students use common procedures to multiply and divide fractions and decimals efficiently and accurately. They multiply and divide fractions and decimals to solve problems, including multistep problems and problems involving measurement.	
Number and Operations: Connecting ratio and rate to multiplication and division	**Algebra:** Students use the commutative, associative, and distributive properties to show that two expressions are equivalent. They also illustrate properties of operations by showing that two expressions are equivalent in a given context (e.g., determining the area in two different ways for a rectangle whose dimensions are $x + 3$ by 5). Sequences, including those that arise in the context of finding possible rules for patterns of figures or stacks of objects, provide opportunities for students to develop formulas.
Students use simple reasoning about multiplication and division to solve ratio and rate problems (e.g., "If 5 items cost $3.75 and all items are the same price, then I can find the cost of 12 items by first dividing $3.75 by 5 to find out how much one item costs and then multiplying the cost of a single item by 12"). By viewing equivalent ratios and rates as deriving from, and by analyzing simple drawings that indicate the relative sizes of quantities, students extend whole number multiplication and division to ratios and rates. Thus, they expand the repertoire of problems that they can solve by using multiplication and division, and they build on their understanding of fractions to understand ratios. Students solve a wide variety of problems involving ratios and rates.	**Measurement and Geometry:** Problems that involve areas and volumes, calling on students to find areas or volumes from lengths or to find lengths from volumes or areas and lengths, are especially appropriate. These problems extend the students' work in grade 5 on area and volume and provide a context for applying new work with equations.
Algebra: Writing, interpreting, and using mathematical expressions and equations	
Students write mathematical expressions and equations that correspond to given situations, they evaluate expressions, and they use expressions and formulas to solve problems. They understand that variables represent numbers whose exact values are not yet specified, and they use variables appropriately. Students understand that expressions in different forms can be equivalent, and they can rewrite an expression to represent a quantity in a different way (e.g., to make it more compact or to feature different information). Students know that the solutions of an equation are the values of the variables that make the equation true. They solve simple one-step equations by using number sense, properties of operations, and the idea of maintaining equality on both sides of an equation. They construct and analyze tables (e.g., to show quantities that are in equivalent ratios), and they use equations to describe simple relationships (such as $3x = y$) shown in a table.	

Reprinted with permission from *Curriculum Focal Points for Prekindergarten through Grade 8 Mathematics: A Quest for Coherence*, copyright 2006 by the National Council of Teachers of Mathematics. All rights reserved.
The Curriculum Focal Points identify key mathematical ideas for these grades. They are not discrete topics or a checklist to be mastered; rather, they provide a framework for the majority of instruction at a particular grade level and the foundation for future mathematics study.

Curriculum Focal Points and Connections for Grade 7

The set of three curriculum focal points and related connections for mathematics in grade 7 follow. These topics are the recommended content emphases for this grade level. It is essential that these focal points be addressed in contexts that promote problem solving, reasoning, communication, making connections, and designing and analyzing representations.

Grade 7 Curriculum Focal Points	Connections to the Focal Points
Number and Operations and Algebra and Geometry: Developing an understanding of and applying proportionality, including similarity Students extend their work with ratios to develop an understanding of proportionality that they apply to solve single and multistep problems in numerous contexts. They use ratio and proportionality to solve a wide variety of percent problems, including problems involving discounts, interest, taxes, tips, and percent increase or decrease. They also solve problems about similar objects (including figures) by using scale factors that relate corresponding lengths of the objects or by using the fact that relationships of lengths within an object are preserved in similar objects. Students graph proportional relationships and identify the unit rate as the slope of the related line. They distinguish proportional relationships ($y/x = k$, or $y = kx$) from other relationships, including inverse proportionality ($xy = k$, or $y = k/x$).	***Measurement and Geometry:*** Students connect their work on proportionality with their work on area and volume by investigating similar objects. They understand that if a scale factor describes how corresponding lengths in two similar objects are related, then the square of the scale factor describes how corresponding areas are related, and the cube of the scale factor describes how corresponding volumes are related. Students apply their work on proportionality to measurement in different contexts, including converting among different units of measurement to solve problems involving rates such as motion at a constant speed. They also apply proportionality when they work with the circumference, radius, and diameter of a circle; when they find the area of a sector of a circle; and when they make scale drawings.
Measurement and Geometry and Algebra: Developing an understanding of and using formulas to determine surface areas and volumes of three-dimensional shapes By decomposing two- and three-dimensional shapes into smaller, component shapes, students find surface areas and develop and justify formulas for the surface areas and volumes of prisms and cylinders. As students decompose prisms and cylinders by slicing them, they develop and understand formulas for their volumes (Volume = Area of base × Height). They apply these formulas in problem solving to determine volumes of prisms and cylinders. Students see that the formula for the area of a circle is plausible by decomposing a circle into a number of wedges and rearranging them into a shape that approximates a parallelogram. They select appropriate two- and three-dimensional shapes to model real-world situations and solve a variety of problems (including multistep problems) involving surface areas, areas and circumferences of circles, and volumes of prisms and cylinders.	***Number and Operations:*** In grade 4, students used equivalent fractions to determine the decimal representations of fractions that they could represent with terminating decimals. Students now use division to express any fraction as a decimal, including fractions that they must represent with infinite decimals. They find this method useful when working with proportions, especially those involving percents. Students connect their work with dividing fractions to solving equations of the form $ax = b$, where a and b are fractions. Students continue to develop their understanding of multiplication and division and the structure of numbers by determining if a counting number greater than 1 is a prime, and if it is not, by factoring it into a product of primes. ***Data Analysis:*** Students use proportions to make estimates relating to a population on the basis of a sample. They apply percentages to make and interpret histograms and circle graphs. ***Probability:*** Students understand that when all outcomes of an experiment are equally likely, the theoretical probability of an event is the fraction of outcomes in which the event occurs. Students use theoretical probability and proportions to make approximate predictions.
Number and Operations and Algebra: Developing an understanding of operations on all rational numbers and solving linear equations Students extend understandings of addition, subtraction, multiplication, and division, together with their properties, to all rational numbers, including negative integers. By applying properties of arithmetic and considering negative numbers in everyday contexts (e.g., situations of owing money or measuring elevations above and below sea level), students explain why the rules for adding, subtracting, multiplying, and dividing with negative numbers make sense. They use the arithmetic of rational numbers as they formulate and solve linear equations in one variable and use these equations to solve problems. Students make strategic choices of procedures to solve linear equations in one variable and implement them efficiently, understanding that when they use the properties of equality to express an equation in a new way, solutions that they obtain for the new equation also solve the original equation.	

Reprinted with permission from *Curriculum Focal Points for Prekindergarten through Grade 8 Mathematics: A Quest for Coherence,* copyright 2006 by the National Council of Teachers of Mathematics. All rights reserved.
The Curriculum Focal Points identify key mathematical ideas for these grades. They are not discrete topics or a checklist to be mastered; rather, they provide a framework for the majority of instruction at a particular grade level and the foundation for future mathematics study.

Curriculum Focal Points and Connections for Grade 8

The set of three curriculum focal points and related connections for mathematics in grade 8 follow. These topics are the recommended content emphases for this grade level. It is essential that these focal points be addressed in contexts that promote problem solving, reasoning, communication, making connections, and designing and analyzing representations.

Grade 8 Curriculum Focal Points	Connections to the Focal Points
Algebra: Analyzing and representing linear functions and solving linear equations and systems of linear equations	*Algebra:* Students encounter some nonlinear functions (such as the inverse proportions that they studied in grade 7 as well as basic quadratic and exponential functions) whose rates of change contrast with the constant rate of change of linear functions. They view arithmetic sequences, including those arising from patterns or problems, as linear functions whose inputs are counting numbers. They apply ideas about linear functions to solve problems involving rates such as motion at a constant speed.
Students use linear functions, linear equations, and systems of linear equations to represent, analyze, and solve a variety of problems. They recognize a proportion ($y/x = k$, or $y = kx$) as a special case of a linear equation of the form $y = mx + b$, understanding that the constant of proportionality (k) is the slope and the resulting graph is a line through the origin. Students understand that the slope (m) of a line is a constant rate of change, so if the input, or x-coordinate, changes by a specific amount, a, the output, or y-coordinate, changes by the amount ma. Students translate among verbal, tabular, graphical, and algebraic representations of functions (recognizing that tabular and graphical representations are usually only partial representations), and they describe how such aspects of a function as slope and y-intercept appear in different representations. Students solve systems of two linear equations in two variables and relate the systems to pairs of lines that intersect, are parallel, or are the same line, in the plane. Students use linear equations, systems of linear equations, linear functions, and their understanding of the slope of a line to analyze situations and solve problems.	*Geometry:* Given a line in a coordinate plane, students understand that all "slope triangles"—triangles created by a vertical "rise" line segment (showing the change in y), a horizontal "run" line segment (showing the change in x), and a segment of the line itself—are similar. They also understand the relationship of these similar triangles to the constant slope of a line.
Geometry and Measurement: Analyzing two- and three-dimensional space and figures by using distance and angle	*Data Analysis:* Building on their work in previous grades to organize and display data to pose and answer questions, students now see numerical data as an aggregate, which they can often summarize with one or several numbers. In addition to the median, students determine the 25th and 75th percentiles (1st and 3rd quartiles) to obtain information about the spread of data. They may use box-and-whisker plots to convey this information.
Students use fundamental facts about distance and angles to describe and analyze figures and situations in two- and three-dimensional space and to solve problems, including those with multiple steps. They prove that particular configurations of lines give rise to similar triangles because of the congruent angles created when a transversal cuts parallel lines. Students apply this reasoning about similar triangles to solve a variety of problems, including those that ask them to find heights and distances. They use facts about the angles that are created when a transversal cuts parallel lines to explain why the sum of the measures of the angles in a triangle is 180 degrees, and they apply this fact about triangles to find unknown measures of angles. Students explain why the Pythagorean theorem is valid by using a variety of methods—for example, by decomposing a square in two different ways. They apply the Pythagorean theorem to find distances between points in the Cartesian coordinate plane to measure lengths and analyze polygons and polyhedra.	Students make scatterplots to display bivariate data, and they informally estimate lines of best fit to make and test conjectures.

Number and Operations: Students use exponents and scientific notation to describe very large and very small numbers. They use square roots when they apply the Pythagorean theorem. |
| **Data Analysis and Number and Operations and Algebra: Analyzing and summarizing data sets** | |
| Students use descriptive statistics, including mean, median, and range, to summarize and compare data sets, and they organize and display data to pose and answer questions. They compare the information provided by the mean and the median and investigate the different effects that changes in data values have on these measures of center. They understand that a measure of center alone does not thoroughly describe a data set because very different data sets can share the same measure of center. Students select the mean or the median as the appropriate measure of center for a given purpose. | |

These standards, developed by The National Governor's Association Center for Best Practices and The Council of Chief State School Officers (NGA Center/CCSSO, 2010), were released on June 2, 2010. They may be viewed or downloaded at www.corestandards.org. More than 40 states have pledged to adopt the standards. Each state either adopts the standards completely or adopts the standards and then aligns them with their existing state standards by adding up to 15% of additional material.

The Common Core State Standards for Mathematics have two components: Standards for Mathematical Practice and Standards for Mathematical Content. The content standards for grades K–8 are organized by grade-level, domain, cluster, and standard. Domains represent major themes, standards describe learning objectives for students, and clusters are sets of related standards. For each grade level, K–8, the overview provides easy access to both the content and practice standards.

Grade K Overview

Counting and Cardinality
- Know number names and the count sequence.
- Count to tell the number of objects.
- Compare numbers.

Operations and Algebraic Thinking
- Understand addition as putting together and adding to, and understand subtraction as taking apart and taking from.

Number and Operations in Base Ten
- Work with numbers 11–19 to gain foundations for place value.

Measurement and Data
- Describe and compare measurable attributes.
- Classify objects and count the number of objects in categories.

Geometry
- Identify and describe shapes.
- Analyze, compare, create, and compose shapes.

Mathematical Practices
1. Make sense of problems and persevere in solving them.
2. Reason abstractly and quantitatively.
3. Construct viable arguments and critique the reasoning of others.
4. Model with mathematics.
5. Use appropriate tools strategically.
6. Attend to precision.
7. Look for and make use of structure.
8. Look for and express regularity in repeated reasoning.

Grade 1 Overview

Operations and Algebraic Thinking

- Represent and solve problems involving addition and subtraction.
- Understand and apply properties of operations and the relationship between addition and subtraction.
- Add and subtract within 20.
- Work with addition and subtraction equations.

Number and Operations in Base Ten

- Extend the counting sequence.
- Understand place value.
- Use place value understanding and properties of operations to add and subtract.

Measurement and Data

- Measure lengths indirectly and by iterating length units.
- Tell and write time.
- Represent and interpret data.

Geometry

- Reason with shapes and their attributes.

Mathematical Practices

1. Make sense of problems and persevere in solving them.
2. Reason abstractly and quantitatively.
3. Construct viable arguments and critique the reasoning of others.
4. Model with mathematics.
5. Use appropriate tools strategically.
6. Attend to precision.
7. Look for and make use of structure.
8. Look for and express regularity in repeated reasoning.

Grade 2 Overview

Operations and Algebraic Thinking

- Represent and solve problems involving addition and subtraction.
- Add and subtract within 20.
- Work with equal groups of objects to gain foundations for multiplication.

Number and Operations in Base Ten

- Understand place value.
- Use place value understanding and properties of operations to add and subtract.

Measurement and Data

- Measure and estimate lengths in standard units.
- Relate addition and subtraction to length.
- Work with time and money.
- Represent and interpret data.

Geometry

- Reason with shapes and their attributes.

Mathematical Practices

1. Make sense of problems and persevere in solving them.
2. Reason abstractly and quantitatively.
3. Construct viable arguments and critique the reasoning of others.
4. Model with mathematics.
5. Use appropriate tools strategically.
6. Attend to precision.
7. Look for and make use of structure.
8. Look for and express regularity in repeated reasoning.

Grade 3 Overview

Operations and Algebraic Thinking
- Represent and solve problems involving multiplication and division.
- Understand properties of multiplication and the relationship between multiplication and division.
- Multiply and divide within 100.
- Solve problems involving the four operations, and identify and explain patterns in arithmetic.

Number and Operations in Base Ten
- Use place value understanding and properties of operations to perform multi-digit arithmetic.

Number and Operations—Fractions
- Develop understanding of fractions as numbers.

Measurement and Data
- Solve problems involving measurement and estimation of intervals of time, liquid volumes, and masses of objects.
- Represent and interpret data.

- Geometric measurement: understand concepts of area and relate area to multiplication and to addition.
- Geometric measurement: recognize perimeter as an attribute of plane figures and distinguish between linear and area measures.

Geometry
- Reason with shapes and their attributes.tes.

Mathematical Practices
1. Make sense of problems and persevere in solving them.
2. Reason abstractly and quantitatively.
3. Construct viable arguments and critique the reasoning of others.
4. Model with mathematics.
5. Use appropriate tools strategically.
6. Attend to precision.
7. Look for and make use of structure.
8. Look for and express regularity in repeated reasoning.

Grade 4 Overview

Operations and Algebraic Thinking
- Use the four operations with whole numbers to solve problems.
- Gain familiarity with factors and multiples.
- Generate and analyze patterns.

Number and Operations in Base Ten
- Generalize place value understanding for multidigit whole numbers.
- Use place value understanding and properties of operations to perform multi-digit arithmetic.

Number and Operations—Fractions
- Extend understanding of fraction equivalence and ordering.
- Build fractions from unit fractions by applying and extending previous understandings of operations on whole numbers.
- Understand decimal notation for fractions, and compare decimal fractions.

Measurement and Data
- Solve problems involving measurement and conversion of measurements from a larger unit to a smaller unit.

- Represent and interpret data.
- Geometric measurement: understand concepts of angle and measure angles.

Geometry
- Draw and identify lines and angles, and classify shapes by properties of their lines and angles.

Mathematical Practices
1. Make sense of problems and persevere in solving them.
2. Reason abstractly and quantitatively.
3. Construct viable arguments and critique the reasoning of others.
4. Model with mathematics.
5. Use appropriate tools strategically.
6. Attend to precision.
7. Look for and make use of structure.
8. Look for and express regularity in repeated reasoning

Grade 5 Overview

Operations and Algebraic Thinking
- Write and interpret numerical expressions.
- Analyze patterns and relationships.

Number and Operations in Base Ten
- Understand the place value system.
- Perform operations with multi-digit whole numbers and with decimals to hundredths.

Number and Operations—Fractions
- Use equivalent fractions as a strategy to add and subtract fractions.
- Apply and extend previous understandings of multiplication and division to multiply and divide fractions.

Measurement and Data
- Convert like measurement units within a given measurement system.
- Represent and interpret data.
- Geometric measurement: understand concepts of volume and relate volume to multiplication and to addition.

Geometry
- Graph points on the coordinate plane to solve real-world and mathematical problems.
- Classify two-dimensional figures into categories based on their properties.

Mathematical Practices
1. Make sense of problems and persevere in solving them.
2. Reason abstractly and quantitatively.
3. Construct viable arguments and critique the reasoning of others.
4. Model with mathematics.
5. Use appropriate tools strategically.
6. Attend to precision.
7. Look for and make use of structure.
8. Look for and express regularity in repeated reasoning

Grade 6 Overview

Ratios and Proportional Relationships
- Understand ratio concepts and use ratio reasoning to solve problems.

The Number System
- Apply and extend previous understandings of multiplication and division to divide fractions by fractions.
- Compute fluently with multi-digit numbers and find common factors and multiples.
- Apply and extend previous understandings of numbers to the system of rational numbers.

Expressions and Equations
- Apply and extend previous understandings of arithmetic to algebraic expressions.
- Reason about and solve one-variable equations and inequalities.
- Represent and analyze quantitative relationships between dependent and independent variables.

Geometry
- Solve real-world and mathematical problem involving area, surface area, and volume.

Statistics and Probability
- Develop understanding of statistical variability.
- Summarize and describe distributions.

Mathematical Practices
1. Make sense of problems and persevere in solving them.
2. Reason abstractly and quantitatively.
3. Construct viable arguments and critique the reasoning of others.
4. Model with mathematics.
5. Use appropriate tools strategically.
6. Attend to precision.
7. Look for and make use of structure.
8. Look for and express regularity in repeated reasoning

Grade 7 Overview

Ratios and Proportional Relationships
- Analyze proportional relationships and use them to solve real-world and mathematical problems.

The Number System
- Apply and extend previous understandings of operations with fractions to add, subtract, multiply, and divide rational numbers.

Expressions and Equations
- Use properties of operations to generate equivalent expressions.
- Solve real-life and mathematical problems using numerical and algebraic expressions and equations.

Geometry
- Draw, construct and describe geometrical figures and describe the relationships between them.
- Solve real-life and mathematical problems involving angle measure, area, surface area, and volume.

Statistics and Probability
- Use random sampling to draw inferences about a population.
- Draw informal comparative inferences about two populations.
- Investigate chance processes and develop, use, and evaluate probability models.

Mathematical Practices
1. Make sense of problems and persevere in solving them.
2. Reason abstractly and quantitatively.
3. Construct viable arguments and critique the reasoning of others.
4. Model with mathematics.
5. Use appropriate tools strategically.
6. Attend to precision.
7. Look for and make use of structure.
8. Look for and express regularity in repeated reasoning.

Grade 8 Overview

The Number System
- Know that there are numbers that are not rational, and approximate them by rational numbers.

Expressions and Equations
- Work with radicals and integer exponents.
- Understand the connections between proportional relationships, lines, and linear equations.
- Analyze and solve linear equations and pairs of simultaneous linear equations.

Functions
- Define, evaluate, and compare functions.
- Use functions to model relationships between quantities.

Geometry
- Understand congruence and similarity using physical models, transparencies, or geometry software.
- Understand and apply the Pythagorean Theorem.
- Solve real-world and mathematical problems involving volume of cylinders, cones and spheres.

Statistics and Probability
- Investigate patterns of association in bivariate data.

Mathematical Practices
1. Make sense of problems and persevere in solving them.
2. Reason abstractly and quantitatively.
3. Construct viable arguments and critique the reasoning of others.
4. Model with mathematics.
5. Use appropriate tools strategically.
6. Attend to precision.
7. Look for and make use of structure.
8. Look for and express regularity in repeated reasoning.

Excerpts from *Common Core State Standards* used by permission. © Copyright 2010, National Governors Association Center for Best Practices and Council of Chief State School Officers. All rights reserved. Available on line at http://www.corestandards.org.

Appendix D   Answers to Self-Tests

Chapter 1

1. Seedhead of sunflower, chambered nautilus, family trees of bees. **2.** Laying tiles in bathroom, swinging golf club, planting garden. **3.** Mathematics is active. Children investigate problems and develop solution strategies. **4.** *The New Math: Advantage*—conceptual learning. *Disadvantage*—parents not informed and teachers not trained. *Back to Basics: Advantage*—children learn basic facts. *Disadvantage*—not enough conceptual learning or problem solving. **5.** We teach what is needed in the workplace. In the industrial age only basic arithmetic was needed. In the space age, we need more advanced mathematics to understand technology. **6.** Number and Operations, Algebra, Geometry, Measurement, Data Analysis and Probability. **7.** a **8.** b **9.** a **10.** b **11.** NCLB **12.** Representations include graphs, equations, charts, pictures, tables. The lesson used a table. **13.** Assessment tells us what children already know, how they know it, and what they still need to learn. **14.** Portfolios, self-assessment, tests, quizzes. **15.** *Advantages*: Clearly organized objectives; coherent curriculum. *Disadvantages*: State objectives not uniform across country; some topics may not be covered in textbooks.

Chapter 2

1. Someone who has relational understanding in mathematics can be flexible in how he or she solves a problem. Someone who has instrumental understanding must solve a problem in one set way, by following a set of rules. **2.** Factual knowledge: 1 foot is 12 inches long. In Fahrenheit temperature, 32 degrees is freezing and 212 degrees is boiling. **3. (a)** *Whole numbers: Procedural knowledge*: When adding $28 + 34$, $8 + 4 = 12$ so regroup the 10 ones into 1 ten. *Conceptual knowledge*: 28 means two tens and eight ones. **(b)** *Fractions, decimals, and percents: Procedural knowledge*: To convert 5/25 to a percent, multiply numerator and denominator by 4 so $5/25 = 20/100$ and $20/100 = 20\%$. *Conceptual knowledge:* 20% means 20 out of 100 equal parts. **(c)** *Geometry: Procedural knowledge*: If you know the measure of two angles of a triangle, to find the measure of the third, add the two known angle measures and subtract from 180 degrees. *Conceptual knowledge*: A parallelogram is a quadrilateral with both pairs of opposite sides parallel. **(d)** *Measurement: Procedural knowledge*: The perimeter of a rectangle $= 2L + 2W$. *Conceptual knowledge*: The perimeter of a rectangle is the length around the rectangle. **4.** Understanding brings new knowledge, helps with remembering, means less to memorize, shapes our ideas about nature of mathematics, and builds confidence. **5.** Behaviorism has clear learning objectives and outcomes; learning is a series of steps and happens with stimulus and response. Constructivism means constructing our own knowledge; the input of the learner is important; it is not time-driven. **6.** The child is finger counting. Finger counting shows cognitive variability because children are using multiple strategies to add. **7.** Adaptive choice means adapting the strategy to the problem. For example, if solving 6000×20, we might do this in our heads rather than writing it out because it lends itself to mental math. **8.** Timed tests are not consistent with a supportive learning environment because they put children under pressure and do not give them the time to reason about mathematics and connect what they know to the task at hand. **9.** Foster communication: Ask questions, restate what the student said, ask another student to restate what the student said. **10.** Wait time is the time you wait after you ask a question of a student and before you answer the question yourself or ask another student to answer it. It is important because not all students think at the same rate and some students, especially English-language learners, may be thinking in one language and speaking in another, so it takes them longer. **11.** They discuss how decimals look like whole numbers and through reflection realize that is why

the mistake was made. Questions to foster this include: *Does this remind you of something else we learned? Have you done something like this before? Why do you think this works? Did anyone do this differently?* **12.** Cooperative group learning: Explain rules ahead of time; choose challenging tasks and explain to whole class as a launch; create group accountability. **13.** Additional techniques for collaboration: Think-pair-share is done with a partner; in peer tutoring one student helps another; in peer collaboration students are paired to solve a problem that neither could solve alone. **14.** Selecting word problems: The problem should have a real-world situation that can be modeled with mathematics. The situation should allow children to use concrete models. The situation should be one in which children can ask questions and identify patterns. **15.** Concrete learning tools: pattern blocks, base-ten blocks, unifix cubes, counters.

Chapter 3

1. (a) The two knowledge standards are (1) knowledge of mathematics and general pedagogy and (2) knowledge of student learning. These mean understanding of mathematics concepts and procedures, knowledge of how to teach specific mathematics topics, and knowledge of how students learn. **(b)** The three implementation standards are (1) the learning environment, (2) discourse, and (3) worthwhile mathematical tasks. It is the teacher's responsibility to create a supportive learning environment, choose or create worthwhile tasks for students to investigate, and manage discourse to push for understanding. **(c)** The two analysis standards are (1) reflection on practice and (2) reflection on student learning. When we reflect on practice we analyze what went well, what we would like to change, and how to make our practice better. When we reflect on student learning we analyze what students understand and how they understand it as well as how to improve their understanding. **2.** tiering **3.** revoicing **4.** scaffolding **5.** filtering **6.** c **7.** Children's literature (1) provides rich contexts for understanding mathematical ideas, (2) shows children how to view the world mathematically, and (3) illustrates how mathematics has been used throughout history. **8.** (1) Select children's books that have mathematical integrity. (2) Select books that are aesthetically pleasing. (3) Select books that appeal to multiple grade levels. **9.** False **10.** Calculators, computer software, applets. **11.** Share mouse and keyboard with your partner if you are working with one; look up and pay attention when the teacher is speaking or another student is addressing the entire class; keep focused on the task you have been given; do not hang around the computer or talk to computer users when it is not your turn. **12.** A driver's test has validity because it measures what it is supposed to—whether someone can drive. Validity refers to the appropriateness of the data collected. Tests need to measure what they are supposed to because many decisions are based on these tests. **13.** Reliability refers to the extent to which the data are free of errors. In high-stakes tests different users need to come to the same diagnostic conclusions with the same results. **14.** a **15.** b

Chapter 4

1. Yearly planning, unit planning, and daily planning **2.** Every unit plan should have prior knowledge, vocabulary, formative and summative assessments, daily plans, and pacing. Planning is important because it gives a unified view of what you want to accomplish and keeps a record of what you have done. **3.** Check that the student understands the meaning of multiplication and division, multiplication basic facts, when to use division, and what to do with remainders. **4.** Launch (about 5 to 10 minutes), Instruct or Explore (about 25 to 30 minutes), Summarize (about 5 to 10 minutes). **5.** Students can take the resource boxes and use one, then move on to the next.

This way, each student uses the boxes that are appropriate for him or her. Mini-lessons help individualize instruction to the needs of the learner.   **6.** Differentiated instruction means that instruction is adapted to the needs of the individual student. It is important because no two students are alike; special-needs students are included in the classroom, and ELL students have special needs as well.   **7.** An accommodation is a different learning environment or circumstance. A modification is a change in the task. Three examples of accommodations are to give the students more time, to have the students work in a quiet place, and to redesign charts. Modifications include tasks with multiple entry points, several versions of the same task, and the problem broken down into smaller parts.   **8.** The teacher writes the task on the board.   **9.** Students with dyslexia reverse digits or letters, so someone may read 83 as 38. Because we are asking students to reverse digits, this can be very confusing. To accommodate, have students write digits on index cards so they physically reverse them, color-code them so they can see that the colors are reversing, or write out the numbers: 83 = 8 tens and 3, 38 = 3 tens and 8. In the palindrome *Lesson*, each word is written on the board and pronounced. The meaning of the word is also explained.   **11.** Formative.   **12.** A rubric is a scoring tool that allows you to grade all papers according to a pre-designed scale. An analytic rubric assigns points to different parts of a task. A holistic rubric scores the entire task, usually with a four- or five-point scale. It is easier to use than an analytic rubric but may not provide as much detail.   **13.** Observation   **14.** Self-assessment with journal   **15.** Homework gives children opportunities to practice what they learned and apply it to new situations.

Chapter 5

1. Culture refers to our traditions, the way things are done based on our backgrounds. Three obvious cultural examples are type of jewelry and piercings, foods, and religious celebrations. Three not so obvious examples are how loudly or softly we speak, whether we value independence or interdependence, and how family-oriented we are.   **2.** Sonia Sotomayor represents the value that anything can be achieved through hard work. Two other examples are (1) the election of President Barack Obama and (2) Horatio Alger.   **3.** Examples of individualism: (1) people often move away from home and live far from parents; (2) older parents and grandparents do not live with adult children; (3) each person tries to succeed on his or her own. Examples of individual opportunity: (1) home loans have been readily available; (2) many people are small-business owners; (3) Americans are entrepreneurs who think of ideas and get rich—Henry Ford and his Model T, Amazon, and Apple computers are examples. **4.** A field-dependent culture is more interested in the well-being of the group than in the well-being of the individual. Traditional classrooms favor individualism and individual responsibility, whereas field-dependent classrooms favor the success of the group.   **5.** Benjamin Banneker is at the additive level. The four levels of content integration are social action, transformational, additive, and contributions. At the social action level students might investigate the emissions from a plant and take action to stop excess emissions. At the transformational level, students might investigate the fractal patterns in Adinkra cloth. At the additive level, students might investigate the life of a famous mathematician or scientist from a diverse cultural background. At the contributions level, students might learn about foods or words in other languages.   **6.** The achievement gap is the gap in mathematics achievement between white males and students from diverse ethnic and cultural backgrounds. The graph tells us that the gap is narrowing but white males still outperform other groups. **7.** Use small-group instruction, encourage students to use their native language and gestures or pictures, and push for details.   **8.** RTI is

Response to Intervention, a three-tiered system to support students with disabilities.   **9.** Think-alouds, where students verbalize their thinking during problem solving, and systematic and explicit teaching.   **10.** IDEA, in 2004.   **11.** Newsletters, letters home, emails, and activities that parents and children can do together.   **12.** The gender gap is the gap in achievement in mathematics between white male students and all female students. In the past 30 years the gender gap has almost disappeared in K–12 and in undergraduate achievement in mathematics.   **13.** The four factors are attitudinal differences, support from significant others, classroom atmosphere, and out-of-school learning.   **14.** Women have reached parity in the field of medicine (in certain specialties) but have not reached parity in science and engineering.   **15.** Five strategies for achieving gender-fair classrooms: have sign-up sheets for computer and other technology use to ensure equal access; track your own questioning techniques to make sure you call on equal numbers of males and females and give equal wait time; invite speakers who challenge stereotypes; make children aware of the interesting career opportunities in mathematics and science; encourage peer tutoring and cooperative learning.

Chapter 6

1. Routine problems use words to build stories around computation practice and can have one or more steps. Nonroutine problems may have extraneous information, there are usually several approaches to solving them, and there can often be more than one correct answer.   **2.** Four stages: understand the problem, devise a plan, carry out the plan, look back.   **3.** Enhances skill development, encourages connections between concepts and skills.   **4.** Model confidence, perseverance, the flexibility to try different strategies, and a willingness to be wrong.   **5.** Students collaborate with one another, respect each others' thinking, and really listen to each other so they can understand and evaluate what their classmates are saying while giving everyone a chance to participate.   **6.** Cooperative groups or pairs work well.   **7.** Multiply 1 billion by 4 feet. Divide by 5,280 feet to find the number of miles of children. Divide this figure by 239.000 miles.   **8.** Problem-posing involves modifying a previously existing problem.   **9.** Possible response: Is there a relationship between a student's height and age?   **10.** Knowledge, beliefs and affect, self-regulation, sociocultural factors.   **11.** Change context, structure, or difficulty of mathematics.   **12.** She made $10.   **13.** Used the Make a List strategy.   **14.** Possible response: Five children came to a candy exchange and each brought 6 candies for each of the other children. How many candies were at the candy exchange all together? The answer: 120. Each of the five children brings 6 candies for the four other children. So each child brings 6 × 4 = 24 candies and 5 × 24 = 120.   **15.** Explain vocabulary with words and pictures in the context of the problem; pair students with others who speak their language but have better English skills; allow students to discuss the problem in their groups either in English or in their native language so everyone understands what is asked.

Chapter 7

1. d   **2.** Conceptual subitizing. It helps to make them more efficient counters, which helps with addition and subtraction.   **3.** One-to-one correspondence means there is a unique pairing between each object counted and the word that represents the number counted.   **4.** A rote counter does not do at least one of the following: count in proper sequence, display one-to-one correspondence, or know how many are counted. A rational counter does all three.   **5.** Cardinal number: How many cookies. Ordinal number: Third in line. Nominal number: Football player with #17 on jersey.   **6.** Counting on and counting back are efficient ways to add and subtract.   **7.** They can learn that 4 is 1 less than 5. Place chips on a five-frame, say *3 chips* and say *3 and 2 more is 5.* Do similar with a ten-frame.   **8.** The English words do not mean what they represent, whereas the Chinese words do.   **9.** Find patterns. Link two to twenty, three to thirty, and so on.   **10.** Examples from other cultures give children more examples of how to represent numbers. Finger counting gives a physical, concrete representation of number.   **11.** Using a hundreds chart, start anywhere (12) and count down the column.   **12.** Show a jar of candy. Ask: *Are there more or less than 30 in the jar?*

13.

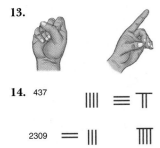

14. 437

2309

15. Are there more or less than 20? Are there more or less than 30?

Chapter 8

1. 375

2. The Egyptian numeration system did not have place value and did not specify the order in which symbols were to be written.

3. 90

4. All place value systems have explicit trading, in which you must trade up for the next place when you get the maximum number in a place and all systems have rules for ordering the digits.   **5.** The Hindu-Arabic system has zero, place value, additive property, and is a decimal system with base-ten.

6. 325

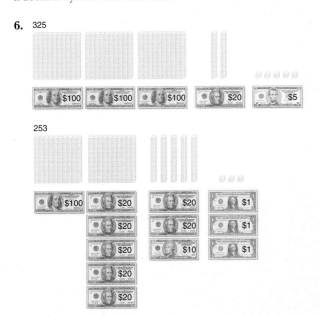

253

7. In proportional models, the pieces representing tens are ten times as large as the piece representing ones, and so on. An example is snap-together cubes. Nonproportional models are not based on size. An example is money.   **8.** Groupable models can be put together and taken apart, such as beans and cups. Pregrouped models are already put together and cannot be taken apart, such as base-ten blocks.   **9.** Composing and decomposing numbers are skills used all the time with adding and subtraction. When children trade, they do so by composing and decomposing.   **10.** Children have difficulty writing numbers with zero as a placeholder. For example, when writing three thousand four, they might write 30004.   **11.** The numbers from 11 to 19 don't have a pattern. The word "eleven" does not literally mean ten and one, so children have to learn a new naming convention in which the word does not relate to its numerical meaning.   **12.** When children reverse the digits, ask them to express the number using concrete and semiconcrete models. For example, if a student writes 27 instead of 72, help the student realize that 27 is two tens and seven and 72 is seven tens and two. With concrete models they can see that these are not the same.

13.

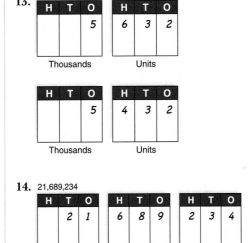

14. 21,689,234

H	T	O		H	T	O		H	T	O
	2	1		6	8	9		2	3	4

Millions   Thousands   Units

15. (a) 830 **(b)** 800 **(c)** 3600 **(d)** 4000

Chapter 9

1. (1) Textbooks often give only the easiest types of problems. (2) When problems are at the end of a section, children know which operation to use without thinking. (3) Children need the experience of seeing problem situations before learning the operations.   **2.** False.   **3.** False.   **4.** In join and separate problems, start unknown are the most difficult because children don't know how to begin. Part-part whole and compare problems are difficult because they don't involve action.   **5.** True.   **6.** The commutative property, named that way because the numbers literally turn around the addition sign.   **7.** Additive identity.   **8.** Multiplicative identity.   **9.** (*Various answers*) Darcy has six candies. Four of them are chocolate and the rest are caramel. How many candies are caramel?   **10.** (*Various answers*) Etan brought 12 dog biscuits to the park. He wanted to give 4 dog biscuits to each dog. How many dogs got dog biscuits?   **11.** (*Various answers*) Sanjay bought 15 strawberries, equally divided into 3 boxes. How many strawberries were in each box?   **12.** (*Various answers*) Sarah has eight candies. Three are chocolate and the rest are peppermint. How many candies are peppermint? $8 - 3 = 5$ **13.** The child is solving

$6 \times 8 = 6 \times 6 + 6 \times 2$, using the distributive property. **14.** William is counting up to and changing the subtraction problem to think addition. **15.** The problem is $7 + 8$. The strategy is make ten.

Chapter 10

1. $385 + 297$: $5 + 7 = 12$; $80 + 90 = 170$; $300 + 200 = 500$; $500 + 170 + 12 = 682$. **2.** $466 - 237$: $466 + 10$ ones $= 4$ hundreds $+ 6$ tens $+ 16$ ones; $237 + 1$ ten $= 2$ hundreds $+ 4$ tens $+ 7$ ones; the difference is 229. **3.** $825 - 316$: $800 - 300 = 500$; $20 - 10 = 10$; $5 - 6 = -1$: $510 - 1 = 509$. **4.** 23×64: $3 \times 4 = 12$; $3 \times 60 = 180$; $20 \times 4 = 80$; $20 \times 60 = 1200$; $1200 + 180 + 80 + 12 = 1472$. **5.** True. **6.** False. **7.** In part a, Barbara uses repeated subtraction, seeing how many copies of 12 can be removed from 100. Ron changes the problem to multiplication and uses guess and check to see $12 \times$ what number $= 100$. **8.** The 24 is split into 20 and 4. Each part is multiplied by 12.

9.

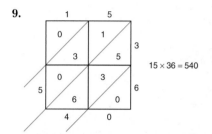

$15 \times 36 = 540$

10. 9×26:

$$1 \times 26 = 26$$
$$2 \times 26 = 52$$
$$4 \times 26 = 104$$
$$8 \times 26 = 208$$
$$9 \times 26 = (8 + 1) \times 26 = 208 + 26 = 234$$

11. $300 + 300 + 500 = 1100$ without adjustment. With adjustment, it is 1230. **12.** $200 \times 20 = 4000$; $225 \times 20 = 4500$ **13.** $\$50 + \$50 + \$34 = \$134$ **14.** $36 + 84$: $36 + 4 = 40$; $40 + 80 = 120$ or $30 + 80 = 110$ and $6 + 4 = 10$, so the sum $= 120$. **15.** 23×40: $20 \times 40 = 800$ and $3 \times 40 = 120$; $800 + 120 = 920$ or $25 \times 4 = 100$ so $25 \times 40 = 1000$; $2 \times 40 = 80$ so $1000 - 80 = 920$.

Chapter 11

1. Iteration means repeating something over and over. If you take a unit fraction, such as $\frac{1}{4}$, and iterate it on the number line, you can generate improper fractions such as $\frac{5}{4}$, $\frac{6}{4}$, and so on. **2.** The triangle is not thirds because the parts are not equal. For the same reason, the trapezoid does not represent thirds. **3.** The quotient meaning of fractions; 3 cookies divided equally among 4 people.

4. The three models are region, length, and set.

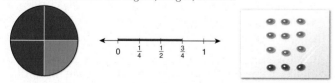

5. **(a)** $\frac{1}{5}$ is larger because fifths are larger than eighths. **(b)** $\frac{3}{4}$ is larger because fourths are larger than fifths. **(c)** $\frac{5}{8}$ is larger because it is greater than $\frac{1}{2}$. **(d)** $\frac{11}{12}$ is larger because it is closer to 1. **6.** Use a number line, start at $\frac{1}{5}$, and iterate until you have six copies. **7.** Equivalent fractions are important for ordering, comparison, addition and subtraction, decimals and percents.

8. $\frac{3}{5} = \frac{6}{10} = \frac{9}{15}$

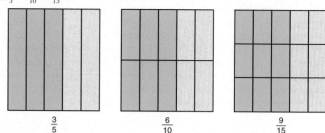

| $\frac{3}{5}$ | $\frac{6}{10}$ | $\frac{9}{15}$ |

9. The greatest common factor is the greatest whole number that is a factor of both the numerator and denominator. It is used for simplifying fractions. **10.** $\frac{48}{72}$: 24 is the greatest common factor. $\frac{48}{72} = \frac{2}{3}$. **11.** **(a)** $\frac{4}{7} + \frac{2}{7} = \frac{6}{7}$ **(b)** $\frac{1}{4} + \frac{1}{2} = \frac{1}{4} + \frac{2}{4} = \frac{3}{4}$ **(c)** $\frac{1}{5} + \frac{1}{6} = \frac{6}{30} + \frac{5}{30} = \frac{11}{30}$ **(d)** $\frac{3}{5} - \frac{1}{3} = \frac{9}{15} - \frac{5}{15} = \frac{4}{15}$ **12.** **(a)** $\frac{1}{3} \times 7 = \frac{7}{3}$ **(b)** $5 \times \frac{1}{4} = \frac{5}{4}$ **(c)** $\frac{3}{8} \times \frac{4}{5} = \frac{12}{40}$

13. $5 \div \frac{1}{3} = 5 \times 3 = 15$

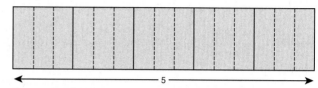

14. The child borrowed 1 ten and made it 10 ones instead of borrowing 1 whole and changing it to $\frac{4}{4}$. To do this correctly, $4\frac{1}{4} = 3$ and $\frac{5}{4}$. Then $\frac{5}{4} - \frac{3}{4} = \frac{2}{4}$ and $4 - 3 = 1$. **15.** Six ribbons.

Chapter 12

1. Fractions that have a power of 10 in the denominator, such as $\frac{1}{10}$, $\frac{20}{100}$. **2.** 10×10 grid.

3. 0.25, $\frac{2}{10} + \frac{5}{100}$

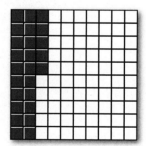

4. $0.4, 0.03, 0.055$ **5.** 1.75 **6.** $1 \times 1000 + 3 \times 100 + 4 \times 10 + 5 \times 1 + 2 \times \frac{1}{10} + 6 \times \frac{1}{100}$ **7.** 3.025

8. Greater than $\frac{1}{2}$.

9.

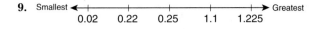

Smallest ◄—|———|———|————|————► Greatest
    0.02   0.22   0.25   1.1   1.225

10.

TENTHS	HUNDREDTHS	THOUSANDTHS	
3	5		Greatest
3	4	8	↑
3	2	7	↓
3	0	1	Smallest

11. (a) 0.50 **(b)** 0.660

12.

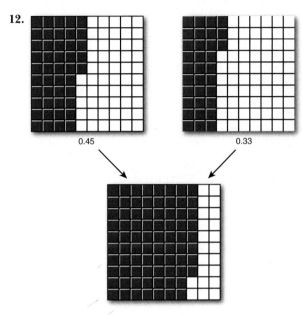

0.45   0.33

13. (a) 1.3 **(b)** 5.37 **(c)** 4.1 **(d)** 0.5 **14.** 43.18; 3 × 12 = 36 and 3 × 13 = 39, so the answer should be close to 40. **15.** 8; 56 divided by 7 = 8; 5.6 divided by 0.7 = 8 because 0.7 is a little less than 1.

Chapter 13

1. (1) Using additive reasoning; (2) using multiplicative reasoning but drawing pictures; (3) drawing pictures and using multiplication and division; (4) setting up a proportion and solving it. **2.** Many middle-grade mathematics topics utilize proportional reasoning; proportional reasoning connects to many topics outside of mathematics. **3.** This is a part-to-part ratio. **4.** 1, 1, 2, 3, 5, 8, 13, 21, 34, 55. Add the previous two terms to get the next. **5.** 2, 4, 6, 10, 16, 26, 42, 68, 110. The ratios are 2, 1.5, 1.667, 1.6, 1.625, 1.615, 1.619, 1.617. The ratios approach the golden ratio. **6.** The golden ratio is 1.61. The golden rectangle is a rectangle whose lengths and widths are in the golden ratio. Yes, a credit card is a golden rectangle. **7.** 45 lemons. The ratio is 3 to 1. **8.** 6 tubs **9.** Find a unit rate. The 64-ounce container costs about .054 cents per ounce and the 24-ounce container costs about .0625 cents per ounce. **10.** 50%, 25%, 33 1/3%, 60%.

11.

25%

12.

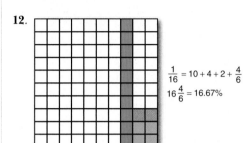

$\frac{1}{16} = 10 + 4 + 2 + \frac{4}{6}$

$16\frac{4}{6} = 16.67\%$

13. No. Suppose the bike was originally $100. At 20% off it is $80. At another 30% off he saves $24, which brings the price to $56. If he saved 50% it would be $50. **14.** 6/30 = $\frac{1}{5}$ or 20%. **15.** $\frac{18}{72} = \frac{1}{4}$ = 25% or scale up: 4 × 18 = 72.

Chapter 14

1. Algebra is used in calculus and statistics. **2.** Integers **3.** 15 or 20. The correct answer is 10. **4.** 370. 32 is 3 more than 29, so the blank must be 3 less than 373. **5.** First, an unknown, as in 5 + 8 = w. Second, for generalizations, as in a + b = b + a. Third, as a value that varies, as in q + d = $1.00, where q = number of quarters and d = number of dimes. **6.** x = 3 **7.** Repeating patterns **8.** Repeating patterns and growing patterns. An example of a repeating pattern is ABABAB. An example of a growing pattern is ABABBABBB. **9.** To find the 20th term, find [(20 × 21)/2]. To find the nth term, find [(n × (n + 1)/2)] **10.** A recursive formula tells you the next term, whereas an explicit formula tells you the nth term. **11. (a)** –2 **(b)** –13 **(c)** +15 **(d)** –15 **12. (a)** 16, 26, 42 **(b)** 25, 36, 49 **(c)** 30, 42, 56 **(d)** 64, 128, 256 **13. (a)** Sixth term = 15 **(b)** nth term = 2n + 3 **14.** Yes, this is a function because each member of the first set (the domain) corresponds with only one member of the second set (the range). Domain = {1, 2, 3, 4, 5, . . .}; range = {5, 7, 9, 11, 13, . . .}. **15.** It is linear because it has a constant rate of change.

Chapter 15

1. Visual-holistic, descriptive-analytic, relational-inferential, formal deductive proof, rigor. **2.** Level 1 **3.** Level 3 **4.** A shape is a triangle when it is composed of three intersecting line segments. **5.** Kites have adjacent sides equal, parallelograms have opposite sides equal and parallel, and trapezoids have just one pair of opposite sides parallel. **6.** A rhombus is a parallelogram with all sides equal. **7.** Every rectangle is not a rhombus because rectangles do not have to have all sides equal. Every rhombus is not a square because rhombi do not necessarily have right angles and squares do. **8.** Right cylinder, oblique cylinder, right pyramid with square base and right pyramid with triangular base, right cone and oblique cone **9.** a and b **10.** Horizontal symmetry: E, H, O, I, X, possibly B, K, S, depending on how they are written. Vertical symmetry: A, H, I, M, O, T, U, V, X. **11.** Translations, rotations, and reflections. **12.** Rotations and possibly reflections. **13.** Return to original position of shape. **14.** Each vertex angle of a triangle is 60 degrees, a factor of 360. Each vertex angle of a square is 90 degrees, also a factor of 360. Each vertex angle of a regular hexagon is 120, also a factor of 360. A rectangle tessellates because its vertex angle is 90 degrees, but it is not regular. **15.** $\sqrt{17}$ or the square root of 17.

Chapter 16

1. An attribute is a measurable property of an object. The birdfeeders have volume, capacity, and weight. **2.** The capacity of the birdfeeders can be compared directly by filling them from a uniform cup size. Their weight can be compared directly. **3.** Partitioning, transitivity, and iteration. **4.** Dimensions are 3 × 4. Area is 12 square units. **5.** 4.78 cm **6.** 18.84 inches **7.** 28 cm²

8.

9. Capacity **10.** Grams and kilograms **11.** False **12.** False

13.

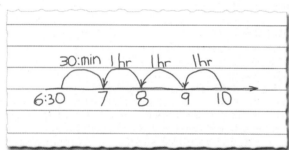

14. 105 cubic inches

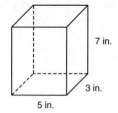

15. 57.29 cubic centimeters

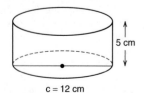

Chapter 17

1.

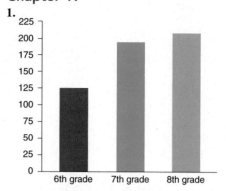

2.

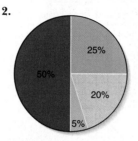

3. Both did about the same.

4.

4	5 5
5	7
6	5 7
7	6 7 8
8	2 5 6 8 9
9	1 9

5. More households had four people than any other number. **6.** No mode; median is 86; mean is 86.6 **7.** Chocolate nut cupcakes, using the mode. **8.** 20 students **9.** The median is $25,000 and the mean is $35,000. The median is a better average for this. **10.** Median is 80; lower quartile is 66; upper quartile is 87.

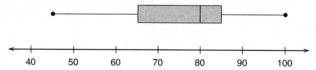

11. Median is 73; lower quartile is 61; upper quartile is 80. Ms. Dalal's class did better.

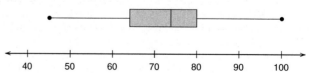

12. **(a)** Might happen **(b)** Certain **(c)** Impossible **(d)** Might happen **13.** Very low **14.** $\frac{1}{2}$ or 50% **15.** $\frac{1}{6}$; $\frac{3}{6}$

Altman, L. J. 1993. *Amelia's Road.* New York: Lee and Low.

Anno, M. 1977. *Anno's Counting Book.* New York: Harper Collins.

Anno, M. 1982. *Anno's Counting House.* New York: Philomel.

Anno, M. 1995. *Anno's Magic Seeds.* New York: Penguin.

Axelrod, A. 1996. *Pigs on a Blanket: Fun with Math and Time.* New York: Simon & Schuster.

Axelrod, A. 2003. *Pigs at Odds.* New York: Aladdin.

Birch, D. 1988. *The King's Chessboard.* New York: Puffin Pied Piper.

Briggs, R. 1997. *Jim and the Beanstalk.* New York: Putnam.

Brown, T. 1986. *Hello Amigos.* New York: Henry Holt.

Burns, M. 1997. *Spaghetti and Meatballs for All: A Mathematical Story.* New York: Scholastic.

Calmenson, S. 1991. *Dinner at the Panda Palace.* New York: Harper Trophy.

Carle, E. 1972. *Rooster's Off to See the World.* New York: Aladdin.

Chinn, K. 1995. *Sam and the Lucky Money.* New York: Lee and Low.

Christelow, E. 1989. *Five Little Monkeys Jumping on the Bed.* New York: Harper Collins.

Clement, R. 1991. *Counting on Frank.* Milwaukee, WI: Gareth Stevens.

Coerr, E. 1993. *Sadako and the Thousand Paper Cranes.* New York: Dell Yearling.

Cushman, J. 1991. *Do You Wanna Bet?* New York: Houghton Mifflin.

Dee, R. 1988. *Two Ways to Count to Ten.* New York: Henry Holt.

Demi. 1997. *One Grain of Rice: A Mathematical Folktale.* New York: Scholastic.

Dodds, D. A. 2004. *The Great Divide.* Cambridge, MA: Candlewick Press.

Dooley, N. 1991. *Everybody Cooks Rice.* Minneapolis, MN: Carolrhoda.

Dooley, N. 1996. *Everybody Bakes Bread.* Minneapolis, MN: Carolrhoda.

Ellis, J. 2004. *What's Your Angle, Pythagoras? A Math Adventure.* Watertown, MA: Charlesbridge.

Erickson, R. E. 1974. *A Toad for Tuesday.* New York: Lothrop, Lee, & Shepard.

Feelings, M. 1971. *Moja Means One.* New York. Dial.

Friedman A. 1994. *The King's Commissioners.* New York: Scholastic.

Friedman, A. 1994. *A Cloak for the Dreamer.* New York: Scholastic.

Ginsburg, M. 1998. *Two Greedy Bears.* New York: Aladdin.

Goble, P. 1988. *Her Seven Brothers.* New York: Aladdin.

Grifalconi, A. 1986. *The Village of Round and Square Houses.* New York: Little, Brown.

Hoban, T. 1990. *Exactly the Opposite.* New York: Mulberry.

Hoban, T. 1985. *Is It Larger? Is It Smaller?* New York: Harper Collins.

Hoban, T. 1998. *So Many Circles, So Many Squares.* New York: Greenwillow.

Hong, L. T. 1993. *Two of Everything.* Morton Grove, IL: Albert Whitman.

Hutchins, P. 1986. *The Doorbell Rang.* New York: Greenwillow.

Keats, E. J. 1962. *The Snowy Day.* New York: Viking.

Lasky, K. 1994. *The Librarian Who Measured the Earth.* New York: Little, Brown.

Leedy, L. 1994. *Fraction Action.* New York: Holiday House.

Leedy, L. 1997. *Measuring Penny.* New York: Henry Holt.

Leedy, L. 2005. *The Great Graph Contest.* New York: Holiday House.

Leedy, L. 2007. *It's Probably Penny.* New York: Henry Holt.

McCallum, A. 2006. *Beanstalk: The Measure of a Giant.* Boston: Charlesbridge.

McKissack, P. C. 1992. *A Million Fish . . . More or Less.* New York: Dragonfly.

McMillan, B. 1992. *Eating Fractions.* New York: Scholastic.

Mendez, P. 1989. *The Black Snowman.* New York: Scholastic.

Merriam, E. 1996. *12 Ways to Get to 11.* New York: Aladdin.

Myller, R. 1990. *How Big Is a Foot?* New York: Dell Young Yearling.

Nagda, A. W., and C. Bickel. 2000. *Tiger Math: Learning to Graph from a Baby Tiger.* New York: Henry Holt.

Nagda A. W., and C. Bickel. 2002. *Chimp Math: Learning about Time from a Baby Chimpanzee.* New York: Henry Holt.

Neuschwander, C. 1997. *Sir Cumference and the First Round Table: A Math Adventure.* Watertown, MA: Charlesbridge.

Neuschwander, C. 1998. *Amanda Bean's Amazing Dream: A Mathematical Story.* New York: Scholastic.

Neuschwander, C. 1999. *Sir Cumference and the Dragon of Pi.* Watertown, MA: Charlesbridge.

Neuschwander, C. 2007. *Patterns in Peru.* New York: Henry Holt.

Pinczes, E. 1993. *One Hundred Hungry Ants.* Boston: Houghton Mifflin.

Pinczes, E. 1995. *A Remainder of One.* Boston: Houghton Mifflin.

Pinczes, E. 2001, *Inchworm and a Half.* Boston: Houghton Mifflin.

Pittman, H. C. 1986. *A Grain of Rice.* New York: Bantam Doubleday Dell.

Schmandt-Besserat, D. 1999. *The History of Counting.* New York: Morrow.

Schwartz, D. M. 1985. *How Much Is a Million?* New York: Lothrop, Lee, & Shepard.

Schwartz, D. M. 1989. *If You Made a Million.* New York: Lothrop, Lee, & Shepard.

Schwartz, D. M. 1999. *If You Hopped Like a Frog.* New York: Scholastic.

Schwartz, D. M. 2001. *On Beyond a Million: An Amazing Math Journey.* New York: Dragonfly.

Scieszke, J. 1995. *Math Curse.* New York: Viking.

Smith, D. J. 2002. *If the World Were a Village: A Book about the World's People.* Toronto: Kids Can Press.

Taback, S. 1997. *There Was an Old Lady Who Swallowed a Fly.* New York: Viking.

Tang, G. 2001. *The Grapes of Math.* New York: Scholastic.

Tang, G. 2002. *Math for All Seasons.* New York: Scholastic.

Thimmesh, C. 2000. *Girls Think of Everything: Stories of Ingenious Inventions by Women.* Boston: Houghton Mifflin.

Tompert, A. 1990. *Grandfather Tang's Story: A Tale Told with Tangrams.* New York: Crown.

Tompert, A. 1993. *Just a Little Bit.* Boston: Houghton Mifflin.

Wells, R. 1999. *Bingo.* New York: Scholastic.

Wells, R. B. 1993. *Is a Blue Whale the Biggest Thing There Is?* Morton, Grove, IL: Albert Whitman.

Wells, R. B. 1997. *What's Faster than a Speeding Cheetah?* Morton, Grove, IL: Albert Whitman.

Zaslavsky, C. 2000. *Counting on Your Fingers African Style.* New York: Black Butterfly Children's Books.

This appendix contains thumbnails of 24 blackline masters that can be downloaded from the companion Web site, www.wiley.com/college/jones. The manipulative materials that can be created from these blackline masters are used extensively in the activities throughout the text and provide a good foundation for concrete mathematics activities you can do with your own students. A good way to make use of them is to print the materials on heavy-duty paper, laminate, and then cut out individual shapes. Children can write on the laminated materials with crayon and then wipe them clean for reuse. Store individual sets of materials in clear, zip-top plastic bags or manila folders and write the type of material and quantity on each bag or folder, e.g., *Five Frames (25)*.

When you create your materials, choose light-colored paper for materials that show subdivisions, such as five-frames and ten-frames. Use the same colored paper for multiple parts of one manipulative. For example, all tangram pieces that are part of one set should be the same color. Also, respect existing color traditions. For pattern blocks, triangles are always green, rhombuses are red, trapezoids are blue, and hexagons are yellow. You also may want to color-code certain manipulatives.

Some of the blackline masters are paper versions of commercially available materials. If your school has classroom sets of these manipulatives, consider allowing children to take home the make-your-own variety for homework and individual exploration.

Some teachers create math kits for their students to take home at the beginning of the year. A kit can be made from a paper bag or shoe box. Consider stocking the kit with any of the manipulatives your students will be using, along with some interesting problems or worksheets. This is a great way to get parents involved in what their children are learning at school.

Blackline Masters

E1 Cuisenaire Rods
E2 Isometric Paper
E3 Centimeter Dot Paper
E4 Centimeter Grid Paper
E5 Geometric Design paper
E6 Half-Inch Grid Paper
E7 Inch Grid Paper
E8 Two-Centimeter Grid Paper
E9 Base-Ten Blocks
E10 Decimal or Percent Paper
E11 Five- and Ten-Frames
E12 Fraction Strips
E13a Fraction Models and Spinners
E13b Fraction Models and Spinners
E14 Geoboard Recording Paper
E15 Geoboard Template
E16 Hundreds Chart
E17 Hundreds Chart
E18 Magic Square 3 × 3 Grid
E19 Pattern Blocks
E20 Place Value Mat
E21 Tangram Puzzle
E22 Rulers
E23 Compass

E1 Cuisenaire Rods

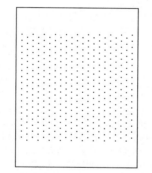

E2 Isometric Paper

E3 Centimeter Dot Paper

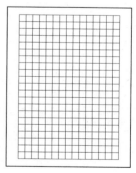

E4 Centimeter Grid Paper

E5 Geometric Design paper

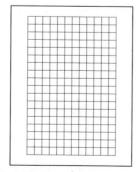

E6 Half-Inch Grid Paper

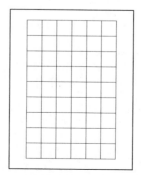

E7 Inch Grid Paper

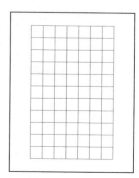

E8 Two-Centimeter Grid Paper

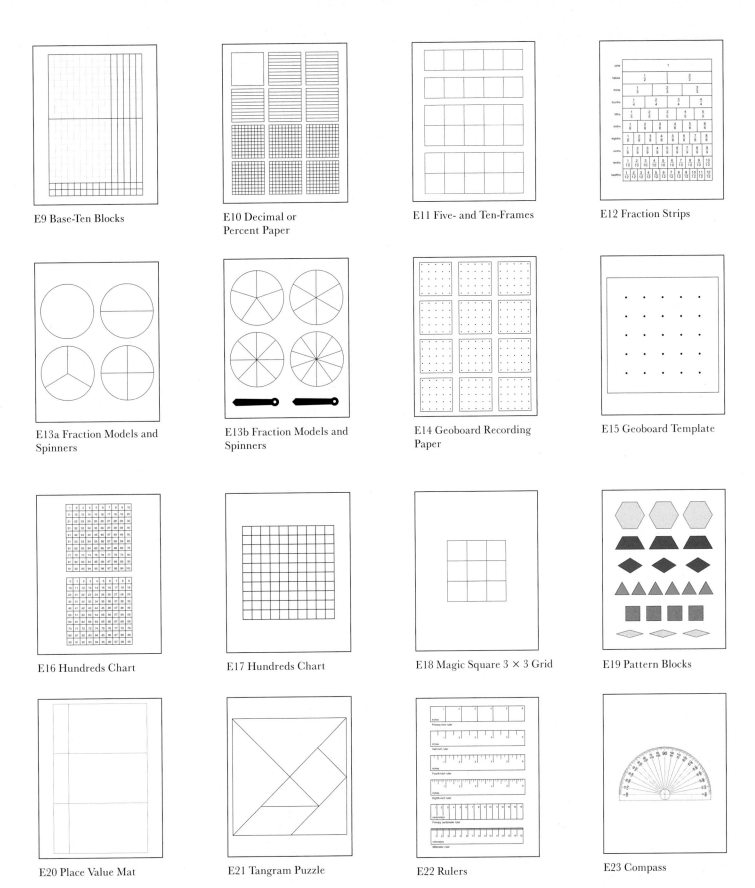

E9 Base-Ten Blocks

E10 Decimal or Percent Paper

E11 Five- and Ten-Frames

E12 Fraction Strips

E13a Fraction Models and Spinners

E13b Fraction Models and Spinners

E14 Geoboard Recording Paper

E15 Geoboard Template

E16 Hundreds Chart

E17 Hundreds Chart

E18 Magic Square 3 × 3 Grid

E19 Pattern Blocks

E20 Place Value Mat

E21 Tangram Puzzle

E22 Rulers

E23 Compass

Glossary

accommodation A different environment or circumstance made with a particular student or students in mind.

achievement gap The observed disparity on a number of educational assessments between the performance of certain groups, especially groups defined by gender, race/ethnicity, and socioeconomic status.

adaptive choice Selecting or adjusting the choice of strategy based on the characteristics of the problem.

additive identity A number that, when added to or subtracted from another number, does not change its value.

algebraic expression A statement that consists of a combination of numbers and variables with an arithmetic operation (such as $3x + 4$).

algorithm A procedure or formula for solving a mathematical problem.

area The space inside a region.

automaticity The use of thinking strategies to retrieve the basic facts.

base The size of the group being counted.

base-ten fractions Fractions whose denominators are multiples of 10 (10, 100, 1000, etc.).

behaviorism A theory of learning that asserts that learning occurs when bonds are created between stimuli (events in the environment) and responses (reactions to the stimuli).

center A point inside the circle that is equally distant from all points on the circle.

circle A set of points that are equally distant from a fixed point.

circumference The perimeter of a circle.

classroom discourse The language that teachers and students use to communicate with each other in the classroom.

cognitive psychology A branch of psychology that examines internal processes, such as problem solving, memory, and the acquisition of language.

cognitive variability The use of multiple strategies when solving the same type of problem.

composite wholes A group of objects, such as oranges in a bag, keys on a key ring, or houses on a street.

concrete operational stage of development The stage in which children gain the ability to think logically about concrete concepts such as mathematics.

congruence Quality of geometric figures by which they have the same size and shape.

conservation of number A principle that states that the number of objects remains the same even when they are rearranged.

constructivism A theory of learning that asserts that humans construct their own knowledge.

control In self-regulation, to be able to make changes in strategies and approaches.

culture The values or beliefs we think are important, what we think is true, and the way we believe things are done.

decimal number sense An understanding and intuition about the size and value of decimals.

denominator This part of the fraction tells the number of equal parts the whole has been partitioned into.

Dewey decimal system A method for organizing and categorizing library resources.

diagnostic assessment Informs teachers about what students already know, what they need to learn, and what misconceptions they may have.

diameter A line segment that passes through the center of a circle from one side of a circle to the other.

differentiate instruction Create different but equal methods of teaching students based on their individual preferences, abilities, and learning styles.

efficacy The ability to produce a desired effect.

equal sums algorithm A strategy that adds one ten, one hundred, or one thousand to the top and bottom numbers so that trading is not necessary.

equation Statement of equality between two expressions (such as $2x + 4 = 5x + 10$).

equivalent fractions Fractions that represent the same quantity with different numbers.

equivalent representations A method of grouping that uses fewer than the maximum number of tens.

ethnomathematics The study of the mathematics of different cultural groups.

explicit Refers to an expression that describes how to find the value of a term from the step or term number.

Fibonacci sequence A sequence of numbers whose first two terms are 1 and 1 and whose subsequent terms are derived from the sum of the previous two terms (1, 1, 2, 3, 5, 8, 13, . . .).

formative assessment Tells teachers what students are learning during a lesson or activity.

frequency The number of occurrences of the data within an interval.

frieze patterns Also know as border patterns, they repeat along a line, a strip, or between two parallel lines.

function A rule of correspondence between the elements of two sets such that members of the first set correspond to unique elements of the second set.

golden ratio A ratio of two lengths that equals 1.61803 . . .

grade-level learning expectations (GLEs) Specific academic content standards for mathematics, developed at the state level in response to NCLB.

greatest common factor The largest whole number that is a factor of both numbers.

heterogeneous grouping A relatively even distribution of students with different abilities, backgrounds, and cultural experiences.

heuristics Methods of problem solving that involve trial and error.

high-stakes tests Tests characterized by a single standardized assessment.

Hindu-Arabic numeration system A positional decimal numeral system.

hypothesize To suggest an explanation for facts or observations.

improper fraction A fraction whose value is greater than one whole.

individual opportunity The idea that each person has the opportunity to achieve success through hard work and that failure to achieve success is the person's own fault.

individualism A social outlook that stresses independence and self-reliance.

instrumental understanding Type of understanding that is characterized by the possession of a rule and the ability to use it.

interquartile range The numeric difference of the upper quartile and the lower quartile.

iterating The process of copying the part over and over to get larger pieces of the whole.

KWL chart Chart that determines what students know, what they want to know, and what they learned.

linear function A function whose graph is a straight line.

lower quartile The median of the lower half of the data. This represents the bottom quarter of the data.

mean A measure that is computed by adding all the numbers in the data set and dividing by the number of items.

median The middle of an ordered data set.

mixed number A number that has both a whole number and a fractional part.

mode A measure of the data that occurs most often. There can be more than one mode for a given set of data.

modification A change in the task or problem.

monitor In self-regulation, to keep track of one's own thinking.

multiplicative identity A number whose product when multiplied with any other number is the other number.

net Two-dimensional representation of a three-dimensional object.

New Math A mathematics curriculum that emphasized understanding of mathematical concepts through inquiry and discovery.

nonproportional models Models in which there is no size relationship between the representation for one and the representation for ten.

nonstandard unit A unit of measure that is not universally accepted.

number base A number base tells you how many digits you have. Base ten uses the digits 0 through 9. Computers often use base two, called binary systems.

numerals Mathematical notations for representing numbers of a given set by symbols in some sort of consistent manner.

numerator This part of the fraction counts how many equal shares you have.

one-to-one correspondence A unique matching of pairs of items from two sets where each item from one set is paired with one and only one item from the other set.

parallel Term describing two lines or line segments that never intersect.

partial differences algorithm A strategy that subtracts the bottom digit from the top digit in each place, regardless of size, and requires no trades.

partial products algorithm A strategy that multiplies the digits in each place separately.

partial quotients algorithm A strategy that uses successive approximation to find the answer.

partial sums algorithm A strategy that adds the digits in each place separately.

pedagogy Strategies or methodologies for teaching.

perimeter The length around a region or object.

perpendicular Term describing two lines or line segments that intersect in a 90-degree angle.

place value The position of a digit to represent its value.

Platonic solids Three-dimensional shapes whose faces are all regular polygons.

polygon A simple closed curve whose sides are straight.

polyhedra Three-dimensional shapes made up of polygonal regions that have no more than one side in common.

problem posing A strategy in which a learner looks at an existing mathematical problem and either extends or modifies it.

problems Tasks or activities for which the solution method is not immediately obvious.

proportion An expression of equality between two ratios.

proportional models Models in which ten is represented as ten times as large as one, and so on.

proportional reasoning A way of reasoning multiplicatively about relationships between quantities or measures.

protractor A semicircular tool for measuring angles.

Pythagorean relationship In a right triangle, the square of the side opposite the right angle is equal to the sum of the squares of the other two sides.

Pythagorean theorem This theorem states that the sum of the squares of the sides of a right triangle is equal to the square of the hypotenuse of the right triangle (the side opposite the right angle).

range The difference between the highest and lowest data values.

ratio A comparison of two quantities or numbers.

recursive Refers to an expression that describes how to find the value of a term from the value of the previous term.

regular hexagon A six-sided polygon with all sides congruent to each other and all vertex angles congruent to each other.

regular polygon A polygon with all sides congruent to each other and all vertex angles congruent to each other.

relational thinking The ability to make connections between and among ideas and concepts.

relational understanding Type of understanding that is characterized by knowing what to do and why.

reliability The extent to which the data are free of errors.

remainders The amounts left over in division problems.

right A type of prism, pyramid, cylinder, or cone whose base is perpendicular to its height.

rubric A scoring tool that allows for standardized evaluation according to specified criteria.

self-regulation Resource allocation during problem-solving activity.

set theory A branch of mathematics that studies collections of objects known as sets.

Sierpinski triangle A fractal design that is constructed from iterations of an equilateral triangle.

similarity The quality of geometric shapes that have the same shape but not necessarily the same size.

simple closed curve A curve that can be traced from starting point to ending point without crossing over the curve or retracing any part of it.

simplest terms Form of a fraction whose numerator and denominator have no common whole-number factors.

slope The ratio of the vertical change to the horizontal change in a line.

standard unit A unit of measure that is universally accepted, such as inches or centimeters.

student-centered lessons Lessons that involve students in inquiry-based explorations and practice.

subitizing Looking at a set and instantly seeing how many objects are in the set, without counting.

summative assessment Tells teachers what students have learned.

symbolic numeration system An abstract system in which symbols represent quantities.

teacher-directed lessons Lessons in which the teacher plays a central role in disseminating information, communicating ideas, and asking questions. Also called *direct instruction*.

tessellations Pattern in which a shape is repeated over and over again, covering a plane without any gaps or overlaps. Another word for a tessellation is a tiling.

upper quartile The median of the upper half of the data. This represents the top quarter of the data.

validity The meaningfulness, usefulness, and appropriateness of the data collected from the test.

variability A measure of the change or spread of the data.

virtual manipulatives Web-based representations of physical objects that are stand-alone applications on the Internet and can be manipulated by children using a computer mouse.

References

Altman, L. J. 1993. *Amelia's Road*. New York: Lee and Low.

Anno, M. 1977. *Anno's Counting Book*. New York: Harper Collins.

Anno, M. 1982. *Anno's Counting House*. New York: Philomel.

Anno, M. 1995. *Anno's Magic Seeds*. New York: Penguin.

Ascher, M. 2002. *Mathematics Elsewhere*. Princeton, NJ: Princeton University Press.

Auriemma, S. 1999. "How huge is a hundred." *Teaching Children Mathematics* 6 (4), November, pp. 154–159. Reston, VA: NCTM.

Axelrod, A. 1996. *Pigs on a Blanket: Fun with Math and Time*. New York: Simon & Schuster.

Axelrod, A. 2003. *Pigs at Odds*. New York: Aladdin.

Banks, J. A. 2007a. "Multicultural education: Characteristics and goals." In *Multicultural Education: Issues and Perspectives*, 6th ed., ed. J. A. Banks and C. A. M. Banks, pp. 3–26. New York: John Wiley & Sons.

Banks, J. A. 2007b. "Approaches to multicultural curriculum reform." In *Multicultural Education: Issues and Perspectives*, 6th ed., ed. J. A. Banks and C. A. M. Banks, pp. 247–267. New York: John Wiley & Sons.

Banks, J. A., and C. A. M. Banks. 2007. "Exceptionality." In *Multicultural Education: Issues and Perspectives*, 6th ed., ed. J. A. Banks and C. A. M. Banks, p. 327. New York: John Wiley & Sons.

Barger, R. H. 2009. "Gifted, talented, and high achieving." *Teaching Children Mathematics* 16 (3), October, pp. 154–161. Reston, VA: NCTM.

Baroody, A. J. 2006. "Why children have difficulties mastering the basic number combinations and how to help them." *Teaching Children Mathematics*, 13 (1), August, pp. 22–31. Reston, VA: NCTM.

Battista, M. T. 2006. "Understanding the development of students' thinking about length." *Teaching Children Mathematics* 13 (3), October, pp. 140–147. Reston, VA: NCTM.

Battista, M. T. 2007. "The development of geometric and spatial thinking." In *Second Handbook of Research on Mathematics Teaching and Learning*, ed. F. K. Lester, pp. 843–908. Greenwich, CT: Information Age.

Battista, M. T. 2009. "Highlights of research on learning school geometry." In *Understanding Geometry for a Changing World: 71st NCTM Yearbook*, ed. T. V. Craine and R. Rubenstein, pp. 91–105. Reston, VA: NCTM.

Bazin, M., and M. Tamez. 2002. "Quipus: The Inca counting system." In *Math and Science Across Cultures: Activities and Investigations from the Exploratorium*, pp. 36–45. San Francisco: The New Press.

Bazin, M., M. Tamez, and The Exploratorium Teacher Institute. 2002. "Counting like an Egyptian: Math in ancient Egypt." In *Math and Science Across Cultures: Activities and Investigations from the Exploratorium*. New York: The New Press.

Beck, S. A., and V. E. Huse. 2007. "A virtual spin on the teaching of probability." *Teaching Children Mathematics* 13 (9), May, pp. 482–486. Reston, VA: NCTM.

Bezuszka, S. J., and M. J. Kenney. 2008. "The three R's: Recursive thinking, recursion, and recursive formulas. In *Algebra and Algebraic Thinking in School Mathematics: 70th NCTM Yearbook*, ed. C. E. Greenes and R. Rubenstein, pp. 81–97. Reston, VA: NCTM.

Birch, D. 1988. *The King's Chessboard*. New York: Puffin Pied Piper.

Blanton, M. L., and J. J. Kaput. 2003. "Developing elementary teachers' algebra eyes and ears." *Teaching Children Mathematics* 10 (2), October, pp. 70–77. Reston, VA: NCTM.

Bresser, R. 2003. "Helping English-language learners develop computational fluency." *Teaching Children Mathematics* 9 (6), February, pp. 294–299. Reston, VA: NCTM.

Brown, T. 1986. *Hello Amigos*. New York: Henry Holt.

Burger, E. B., and M. Starbird. 2000. *The Heart of Mathematics*. Emeryville, CA: Key College.

Burns, M. 1997. *Spaghetti and Meatballs for All: A Mathematical Story*. New York: Scholastic.

Burns, M. 2000. *About Teaching Mathematics*, 2d ed. Sausalito, CA: Math Solutions.

Calmenson, S. 1991. *Dinner at the Panda Palace*. New York: Harper Trophy.

Carle, E. 1972. *Rooster's Off to See the World*. New York: Aladdin.

Carpenter, T. P., E. Fennema, M. L. Franke, L. Levi, and S. B. Empson. 1999. *Children's Mathematics: Cognitively Guided Instruction*. Portsmouth, NH: Heinemann.

Carpenter, T. P., M. L. Franke, and L. Levi. 2003. *Thinking Mathematically: Integrating Arithmetic and Algebra in Elementary School*. Portsmouth, NH: Heinemann.

Casa, T. M., A. M. Spinelli, and M. K. Gavin. 2006. "This about covers it! Strategies for finding area." *Teaching Children Mathematics* 13 (3), October, pp. 168–173. Reston, VA: NCTM.

Casa, T. M., and M. K. Gavin. 2009. "Advancing students' understanding of quadrilaterals." In *Understanding Geometry for a Changing World: 71st NCTM Yearbook*, ed. T.V. Craine and R. Rubenstein, pp. 205–220. Reston, VA: NCTM.

Cavanagh, M., L. Dacey, C. R. Findell, C. E. Greenes, L. J. Sheffield, and M. Small. 2004. *Navigating through Number and Operations in Prekindergarten–Grade 2*. Reston, VA: NCTM.

Chapin, S. H., and C. O'Connor. 2007. "Academically productive talk: Supporting students' learning in mathematics." In *The Learning of Mathematics: Sixty-Ninth Yearbook*, ed. W. G. Martin and M. E. Strutchens, pp. 113–128. Reston, VA: NCTM.

Chapin, S., A. Koziol, J. MacPherson, and C. Rezba. 2002. *Navigating through Data Analysis and Probability in Grades 3–5*. Reston, VA: NCTM.

Chinn, K. 1995. *Sam and the Lucky Money*. New York: Lee and Low.

Christelow, E. 1989. *Five Little Monkeys Jumping on the Bed*. New York: Harper Collins.

Clarke, D. M., A. Roche, and A. Mitchell. 2008. "Ten practical tips for making fractions come alive and make sense." *Mathematics Teaching in the Middle School* (13) 7, January, pp. 372–381. Reston, VA: NCTM.

Clement, R. 1985. *Counting on Frank*. Milwaukee, WI: Gareth Williams.

Clements, D. H. 1999. "Subitizing: What is it? Why teach it?" *Teaching Children Mathematics* 5 (7), March, pp. 400–405. Reston, VA: NCTM.

Clements, D. H. 2003. "Preface." In *Learning and Teaching Measurement: 65th NCTM Yearbook*, ed. D. H. Clements, pp. xi–xiii. Reston, VA: NCTM.

Clements, D. H., and J. Sarama. 2005. "Young children and technology: What's appropriate?" In *Technology-Supported Mathematics Learning Environments, 67th Yearbook*, ed. W. J. Masalski, 51–74. Reston, VA: NCTM.

Clements, D. H., and M. T. Battista. 1992. "Geometry and spatial reasoning." In *Handbook of Research on Mathematics Teaching and Learning*, ed. D. A. Grouws, pp. 420–464. Reston, VA: National Council of Teachers of Mathematics.

Coburn, T. G., B. J. Bushy, L. C. Holton, D. Latinas, D. Mortimer, and D. Shotwell. 1993. *Curriculum and Evaluation Standards for School Mathematics Addenda Series, Grades K–6: Patterns*. Reston, VA: NCTM.

Coerr, E. 1993. *Sadako and the Thousand Paper Cranes*. New York: Dell Yearling.

Cook, C. D. 2008. "I scream, you scream: Data analysis with kindergartners." *Teaching Children Mathematics*, 14 (9), May, pp. 538–546. Reston, VA: NCTM.

Cramer, K. A., D. S. Monson, T. Wyberg, S. Leavitt, and S. B. Whitney. 2009. "Models for initial decimal ideas." *Teaching Children Mathematics* 16 (2), September, pp. 106–117. Reston, VA: NCTM.

Crown, W. D. 2003. "Using technology to enhance a problem-based approach to teaching: What will and will not work." In *Teaching Mathematics through Problem Solving*, ed. F. K. Lester and R. I. Charles, pp. 217–228. Reston, VA: NCTM.

Cueves, G. J., and K. Yeatts. 2001. *Navigating through Algebra in Grades 3–5*. Reston, VA: NCTM.

Cushman, J. 1991. *Do You Wanna Bet?* New York: Houghton Mifflin.

Davidson, E., and L. Kramer. 1997. "Integrating with integrity: Curriculum, instruction, and culture in the mathematics classroom." In *Multicultural and Gender Equity in the*

Mathematics Classroom: The Gift of Diversity (1997 Yearbook), ed. J. Trentacosta, pp. 131–141. Reston, VA: NCTM.

Dee, R. 1988. *Two Ways to Count to Ten*. New York: Henry Holt.

Demi. 1997. *One Grain of Rice: A Mathematical Folktale*. New York: Scholastic.

Devlin, K. 1994. *Mathematics: The Science of Patterns*. New York: Scientific American Library.

Dixon, J. K. 2008. "Tracking time: Representing elapsed time on an open timeline." *Teaching Children Mathematics* 15 (1), August, pp. 18–24. Reston, VA: NCTM.

Dodds, D. A. 2004. *The Great Divide*. Cambridge, MA: Candlewick.

Dooley, N. 1991. *Everybody Cooks Rice*. Minneapolis, MN: Carolrhoda.

Dooley, N. 1996. *Everybody Bakes Bread*. Minneapolis, MN: Carolrhoda.

Ellis, J. 2004. *What's Your Angle, Pythagoras? A Math Adventure*. Watertown, MA: Charlesbridge.

Empson, S. B. 2002. "Organizing diversity in early fraction thinking." In *Making Sense of Fractions, Ratios, and Proportions, 64th NCTM Yearbook*, ed. Bonnie Litwiller, pp. 29–40. Reston, VA: NCTM.

Erickson, R. E. 1974. *A Toad for Tuesday*. New York: Lothrop, Lee, & Shepard.

Feelings, M. 1971. *Moja Means One*. New York. Dial.

Femiano, R. B. 2003. "Algebraic problem solving in the primary grades." *Teaching Children Mathematics* 9 (8), April, pp. 444–449. Reston, VA: NCTM.

Findell, C. R., M. Small, M. Cavanaugh, L. Dacey, C. E. Greenes, and L. J. Sheffield. 2001. *Navigating through Geometry in Prekindergarten–Grade 2*. Reston, VA: National Council of Teachers of Mathematics.

Flores, A. 2002. "Learning and teaching mathematics with technology." In *Teaching Children Mathematics* 8 (6), February, pp. 308–310. Reston, VA: NCTM.

Fosnot, C. T. 2005. "Constructivism: A psychological theory of learning." In *Constructivism: Theory, Perspectives, and Practice*. 2d ed., ed. C. T. Fosnot, pp. 8–38. New York: Teachers College Press.

Fosnot, C. T., and M. Dolk. 2001a. *Young Mathematicians at Work: Constructing Number Sense, Addition and Subtraction*. Portsmouth, NH: Heinemann.

Fosnot, C. T., and M. Dolk. 2001b. *Young Mathematicians at Work: Constructing Multiplication and Division*. Portsmouth, NH: Heinemann.

Fosnot, C. T., and M. Dolk. 2002. *Young Mathematicians at Work: Constructing Fractions, Decimals, and Percents*. Portsmouth, NH: Heinemann.

Franke, M. L., G. Kazemi, and D. Battey. 2007. "Understanding teaching and classroom practice in mathematics." In *Second Handbook of Research on Mathematics Teaching and Learning*, ed. F. K. Lester, Jr., pp. 225–256. Charlotte, NC: Information Age.

Franklin, C., G. Kader, J. Mewborn, J. Moreno, R. Peck, M. Perry, and R. Scheaffer. 2007. *Guidelines for Assessment and Instruction in Statistics Education (GAISE) Report: A Pre-K–12 Curriculum Framework*. Alexandria, VA: American Statistical Association.

Friedman A. 1994. *The King's Commissioners*. New York: Scholastic.

Friedman, A. 1994. *A Cloak for the Dreamer*. New York: Scholastic.

Fuson, K. C. 1992. "Research on whole number addition and subtraction." In *Handbook of Research on Mathematics Teaching and Learning*, ed. Douglas A. Grows, pp. 243–275. New York: Macmillan.

Fuson, K. C. 2003. "Developing mathematical power in whole number operations." In *A Research Companion to Principles and Standards for School Mathematics*, ed. J. Kilpatrick, W. G. Martin, and D. Schifter, pp. 68–94. Reston, VA: NCTM.

Fuson, K. C., L. Grandeur, and P. A. Sugiyama. 2001. "Achievable numerical understandings for all young children. *Teaching Children Mathematics* 7 (9), May, pp. 522–526. Reston, VA: NCTM.

Georgia Department of Education. (2006) *3–5 Mathematics Georgia Performance Standards*. Atlanta: Author.

Giamati, C. 2002. "Ratio, proportion, similarity, and Navajo students." In *Changing the Faces of Mathematics: Perspectives on Indigenous People of North America*, ed. J. E. Hankes and G. R. Fast. Reston, VA: NCTM.

Giganti, P. 1988. *Each Orange Had 8 Slices*. New York: Greenwillow.

Ginsburg, M. 1998. *Two Greedy Bears*. New York: Aladdin.

Goble, P. 1988. *Her Seven Brothers*. New York: Aladdin.

Goodrow, A. M., and K. Kidd. 2008. "We all have something that has to do with tens: Counting school days." *Teaching Children Mathematics* 15 (2), September, pp. 74–79. Reston, VA: NCTM.

Grifalconi, Ann. 1986. *The Village of Round and Square Houses*. New York: Little, Brown.

Gutstein, E., and T. A. Romberg. 1995. "Teaching children to add and subtract." *Journal of Mathematical Behavior*, 14 (3), pp. 283–324. Cambridge: Cambridge University Press.

Hankes, J. E., and G. R. Fast. 2002. "Investigating the correspondence between Native American pedagogy and constructivist-based instruction." In *Changing the Faces of Mathematics: Perspectives on Indigenous People of North America*, ed. J. E. Hankes and G. R. Fast, pp. 37–47. Reston, VA: NCTM.

Hartweg, K., and M. Heisler. 2007. "No tears here! Third-grade problem solvers." *Teaching Children Mathematics* 13 (7), pp. 362–368. Reston, VA: NCTM.

Hiebert, J. 2003. "Signposts for teaching mathematics through problem solving." *Teaching Mathematics through Problem Solving*, ed. F. K. Lester and R. I. Charles, pp. 53–62. Reston, VA: NCTM.

Hiebert, J. 2003. "What research says about the standards." In *A Research Companion to Principles and Standards for School Mathematics*, ed. J. Kilpatrick, W. G. Martin, and D. Shifter, pp. 5–24. Reston, VA: NCTM.

Hiebert, J., and T. C. Carpenter. 1992. "Learning and teaching with understanding." In *Handbook of Research on Mathematics Teaching and Learning*, ed. D. A. Grouws, pp. 65–100. Reston, VA: NCTM.

Hiebert, J., T. C. Carpenter, E. Fennema, K. C. Fuson, D. Wearne, H. Murray, A. Olivier, and P. Human. 1997. *Making Sense: Teaching and Learning Mathematics with Understanding*. Portsmouth, NH: Heinemann.

Hoban, T. 1985. *Is It Larger? Is It Smaller?* New York: Harper Collins.

Hoban, T. 1990. *Exactly the Opposite*. New York: Mulberry.

Hoban, T. 1998. *So Many Circles, So Many Squares*. New York: Greenwillow.

Hong, L. T. 1993. *Two of Everything*. Morton Grove, IL: Albert Whitman.

Hopkinson, D. 2003. *Sweet Clara and the Freedom Quilt*. New York: Dragonfly.

Huinker, D. 2002. "Calculators as learning tools for young children's explorations of number." In *Teaching Children Mathematics* 8 (6), pp. 316–321. Reston, VA: NCTM.

Hume, J. N. 1991. *Sea Squares*. New York: Hyperion.

Hutchins, P. 1986. *The Doorbell Rang*. New York: Greenwillow.

Jamar, I., and L. Wiest. 2003. "By way of introduction: A unifying theme." *Mathematics Teaching in the Middle School*, 8 (8) April, pp. 387–391. Reston, VA: NCTM.

Jeon, K. 2009. "Mathematics hiding in the nets of a cube." *Teaching Children Mathematics* 15 (7) March, pp. 394–399. Reston, VA: NCTM.

Jeon, K., and J. Bishop. 2007. "Problem solvers: Nine jumping numbers." 13 (6), p. 330. Reston, VA: NCTM.

Joseph, G. C. 2000. *The Crest of the Peacock: Non-European Roots of Mathematics*. Princeton, NJ: Princeton University Press.

Kamii, C. 2006. "Measurement of length: How can we teach it better? *Teaching Children Mathematics* 13 (3), October pp. 154–158. Reston, VA: NCTM.

Kamii, C., and L. Joseph. 1988. "Teaching place value and double-column addition." *The Arithmetic Teacher* 35 (6), pp. 48–52. Reston, VA: NCTM.

Karp, K., and P. Howell. 2004. "Building responsibility for learning in students with special needs." *Teaching Children Mathematics* 11 (3), October, pp. 118–125. Reston, VA: NCTM.

Keats, E. J. 1962. *The Snowy Day*. New York: Viking.

Kempf, S. 1997. *Finding Solutions to Hunger*. New York: World Hunger Year.

Kendall/Hunt. 2008. *Math Trailblazers Third Edition Grade Two*. Dubuque, IA: Author.

Kerrigan, J. 2002. "Powerful software to enhance the elementary school mathematics program." *Teaching Children Mathematics* 8 (6), February, pp. 364–371. Reston, VA: NCTM.

Killian, K., L. P. Steffe. 2002. "Children's mathematics." In *Putting Research into Practice in the Elementary Grades*, ed. D. L. Chambers, pp. 90–92. Reston, VA: NCTM.

Kilmann, R. H., M. J. Saxton, and R. Serba. 1985. "Introduction: Five key issues in understanding and changing culture." In *Handbook of Research in Multicultural Education*, ed. J. A. Banks and C. A. M. Banks. New York: Macmillan.

Lambdin, D. V. 2003. "Benefits of teaching through problem solving." In *Teaching Mathematics through Problem Solving*, ed. F. K. Lester and R. I. Charles, pp. 3–14. Reston, VA: NCTM.

Lambdin, D. V., and C. Walcott. 2007. "Changes through the years: Connections between psychological learning theories and the school mathematics curriculum." In *The Learning of Mathematics: Sixty-Ninth Yearbook*, ed. W. G. Martin and M. E. Strutchens, pp. 3–26. Reston, VA: NCTM.

Lambdin, D. V., S. J. Russell, J. Van de Walle, F. K. Lester, and R. I. Charles. 2003. "Preface." In *Teaching Mathematics through Problem Solving*, ed. F. K. Lester and R. I. Charles, xi–xvi. Reston, VA: NCTM.

Lamon, S. 1999. *Teaching Fractions and Ratios for Understanding: Essential Content Knowledge and Instructional Strategies for Teachers*. Mahwah, NJ: Lawrence Erlbaum.

Langrall, C. W., and J. Swafford. 2000. "Three balloons for two dollars: Developing proportional reasoning." *Mathematics Teaching in the Middle School*, 6 (4) December, pp. 254–261. Reston, VA: NCTM.

Lanius, C. S., and S. E. Williams. 2003. "Proportionality: A unifying theme for the middle grades." *Mathematics Teaching in the Middle School*, 8 (8), April, pp. 392–397. Reston, VA: NCTM.

Lasky, K. 1994. *The Librarian Who Measured the Earth*. New York: Little Brown.

Leedy, L. 1994. *Fraction Action*. New York: Holiday House.

Leedy, L. 1997. *Measuring Penny*. New York: Henry Holt.

Leedy, L. 2005. *The Great Graph Contest*. New York: Holiday House.

Leedy, L. 2007. *It's Probably Penny*. New York: Henry Holt.

Leff, R. 2004. "Vive La difference! Gifted kindergartners and mathematics." *Teaching Children Mathematics* 11 (3), October, pp. 155–157. Reston, VA: NCTM.

Lesh, R., and J. Zawojewski. 2007. "Problem Solving and Modeling." In *Second Handbook of Research on Mathematics Teaching and Learning*, ed. F. K. Lester. Charlotte, NC: Information Age.

Lester, F. K., Jr., and D. L. Kroll. 1996. "Evaluation: A new vision." In *Emphasis on Assessment: Readings from NCTM's School-Based Journals*, pp. 3–8. Reston, VA: NCTM.

Lewis, C. C. 2002. *Lesson Study: A Handbook of Teacher-Led Instructional Change*. Philadelphia: Research for Better Schools.

Lipka, J., T. Shockey, and B. Adams. 2003. "Bridging Yu'pik ways of measuring to western mathematics." In *Learning and Teaching Measurement: 65th NCTM Yearbook*, ed. D. H. Clements, pp. 181–194. Reston, VA: NCTM.

Losq, C. S. 2005. "Number concepts and special needs students: The power of ten-frame tiles." *Teaching Children Mathematics* 11 (6), February, pp. 310–315. Reston, VA: NCTM.

Mack, N. K. 2004. "Connecting to develop computational fluency with fractions." *Teaching Children Mathematics*, 11 (4), November, pp. 226–232. Reston, VA: NCTM.

Macmillan McGraw-Hill. 2009. *Math Connects Teacher's Edition Grade 1 Volume 2*. Columbus, OH: Author.

Mailley, E., and P. S. Moyer. 2004. "The mathematical candy store: Eight matters." *Teaching Children Mathematics* 10 (8), April, pp. 388–391. Reston, VA: NCTM.

Maldonado, L. A., E. E. Turner, H. Dominguez, and S. B. Empson. 2009. "English-language learners learning from, and contributing to, mathematical discussions." In *Mathematics for Every Student: Responding to Diversity. Grades Pre-K–5*, ed. D. Y. White and J. S. Spitzer, pp. 7–22. Reston, VA: NCTM.

Mann, R. L. 2004. "Balancing act: The truth behind the equals sign." *Teaching Children Mathematics* 11 (2), September, pp. 65–69. Reston, VA: NCTM.

Martine, S. 2006. "Data analysis and statistics in the middle school." *Mathematics Teaching in the Middle School*, 12 (1), August, pp. 48–49. Reston, VA: NCTM.

Martinie, S. L., and J. Bay-Williams. 2003. "Investigating students' conceptual understanding of decimal fractions using multiple representations." *Mathematics Teaching in the Middle School*, 8 (5), January, pp. 244–247. Reston, VA: NCTM.

Mattone, L. 2007. "I know an old lady: Using children's literature to explore patterns." *Teaching Children Mathematics* 14 (4), November, pp. 202–205. Reston, VA: NCTM.

McCallum, A. 2005. *The Secret Life of Math*. Nashville, TN: Williamson.

McCallum, A. 2006. *Beanstalk: The Measure of a Giant*. Boston: Charlesbridge.

McDuffie, A. M., and N. Eve. 2009. "Break the area boundaries." *Teaching Children Mathematics* 16 (1), August, pp. 18–27. Reston, VA: NCTM.

McKissack, P. C. 1992. *A Million Fish . . . More or Less*. New York: Knopf.

McMillan, B. 1992. *Eating Fractions*. New York: Scholastic.

McMillen, S., and B. Ortiz. 2008. "Taking time to understand telling time." *Teaching Children Mathematics* 15 (4), November, pp. 248–256. Reston, VA: NCTM.

Mendez, P. 1989. *The Black Snowman*. New York: Scholastic.

Merriam, E. 1996. *12 Ways to Get to 11*, New York: Aladdin.

Michaelowicz, K. D. 1996. "Fractions of ancient Egypt in the contemporary classroom." *Mathematics Teaching in the Middle School* (1) 10, pp. 786–789. Reston, VA: NCTM.

Molina, M., and R. C. Ambrose. 2006. "Fostering relational thinking while negotiating the meaning of the equals sign." *Teaching Children Mathematics*, 13 (2), September, pp. 111–117. Reston, VA: NCTM.

Mora, P. 1996. *Uno, Dos, Tres: One, Two, Three*. New York: Clarion.

Moses, R. P., and C. E. Cobb. 2001. *Radical Equations: Civil Rights from Mississippi to the Algebra Project*. Boston: Beacon Press.

Moyer, P. S. 2001. "Using representations to explore perimeter and area." *Teaching Children Mathematics* 8 (1), September, pp. 52–59. Reston, VA: NCTM.

Moyer, P., D. Niezgoda, and J. Stanley. 2005. "Young children's use of virtual manipulatives and other forms of mathematical representations." In *Technology-Supported Mathematics Learning Environments, 67th Yearbook*, ed. W. J. Masalski, pp. 17–34. Reston, VA: NCTM.

Murata, A., N. Otani, N. Hattori, and K. C. Fuson. 2004. "The NCTM Standards in a Japanese primary school classroom: Valuing students' diverse ideas and learning paths." In *Perspectives on the Teaching of Mathematics: 66th Yearbook*, ed. R. N. Rubenstein, pp. 82–95. Reston, VA: NCTM.

Murrey, D. L. 2008. "Differentiating instruction in mathematics for the English language learner." *Mathematics Teaching in the Middle School* 14 (3), October, pp. 146–153. Reston, VA: NCTM.

Myller, Rolf. 1990. *How Big Is a Foot?* New York: Dell Young Yearling.

Nagda, A. W., and C. Bickel. 2000. *Tiger Math: Learning to Graph from a Baby Tiger*. New York: Henry Holt.

Nagda, A. W., and C. Bickel. 2002. *Chimp Math: Learning about Time from a Baby Chimpanzee*. New York: Henry Holt.

National Assessment of Educational Progress. http://nces.ed.gov/nationsreportcard/pdf/main2007/2007494-2.pdf.

National Council of Teachers of Mathematics. 1980. *An Agenda for Action.* Reston, VA: NCTM.

National Council of Teachers of Mathematics. 1989. *Curriculum and Evaluation Standards for School Mathematics.* Reston, VA: NCTM.

National Council of Teachers of Mathematics. 1991. *Professional Standards for Teaching Mathematics.* Reston, VA: NCTM.

National Council of Teachers of Mathematics. 1995. *Assessment Standards for School Mathematics.* Reston, VA: NCTM.

National Council of Teachers of Mathematics. 2000. *Principles and Standards for School Mathematics.* Reston, VA: NCTM.

National Council of Teachers of Mathematics. 2006. *Curriculum Focal Points for Prekindergarten through Grade 8 Mathematics.* Reston, VA: NCTM.

National Council of Teachers of Mathematics. 2007. *Mathematics Teaching Today.* 2nd ed. Reston, VA: NCTM.

National Council of Teachers of Mathematics. 2007. *Research Brief: Effective Strategies for Teaching Students with Disabilities in Mathematics, 2007.* Retrieved September 26, 2009, from www.nctm.org/news/content.aspix?id=8452.

National Governors Association for Best Practices and Council of Chief State School Officers. 2010. *Common Core State Standards: Mathematics Standards.* Retrieved from www.corestandards.org.

Neuschwander, C. 1997. *Sir Cumference and the First Round Table: A Math Adventure.* Watertown, MA: Charlesbridge.

Neuschwander, C. 1998. *Amanda Bean's Amazing Dream: A Mathematical Story.* New York: Scholastic.

Neuschwander, C. 1999. *Sir Cumference and the Dragon of Pi.* Watertown, MA: Charlesbridge.

Neuschwander, C. 2007. *Patterns in Peru.* New York: Henry Holt.

Nicolson, C. P. 2005. "Is chance fair? One student's thoughts on probability." *Teaching Children Mathematics* 12 (2), September, pp. 83–89. Reston, VA: NCTM.

Novakowski, J. 2007. "Developing 'Five-ness' in kindergarten." *Teaching Children Mathematics* 14 (4), November, pp. 228–231. Reston, VA: NCTM.

O'Connell, S. R., C. Beamon, J. Beyea, S. S. Denvir, L. A. Dowdall, N. G. Friedland, and J. D. Ward. 2005. "Aiming for understanding: Lessons learned about writing in mathematics." *Teaching Children Mathematics,* 12 (4), November, pp. 192–199. Reston, VA: NCTM.

Parker, M. 2004. "Reasoning and working proportionally with percent." *Mathematics Teaching in the Middle School,* 9 (6), February, pp. 326–330. Reston, VA: NCTM.

Payne, J. M. 2002. "Place value for tens and ones." In *Putting Research into Practice in the Elementary Grades,* pp. 105–108. Reston, VA: NCTM.

Pearson Scott Foresman. 2008. *Investigations in Number, Data, and Space Second Edition: Student Activities Book Grade 3.* Glenview, IL: Author.

Pearson. 2009. *Connected Mathematics 2.* Glenview, IL: Author.

Phillips, V. J., W. H. Leonard, R. M. Horton, R. J. Wright, and A. K. Stafford. 2003. "Can math recovery save children before they fail?" *Teaching Children Mathematics* 10 (2), October, pp. 107–111. Reston, VA: NCTM.

Piccone-Zocchia, J., and G. O. Martin-Kniep. 2008. *Supporting Mathematical Learning.* San Francisco: Jossey-Bass.

Pinczes, E. 1993. *One Hundred Hungry Ants.* Boston: Houghton Mifflin.

Pinczes, E. 1995. *A Remainder of One.* Boston: Houghton Mifflin.

Pinczes, E. 2001. *Inchworm and a Half.* Boston: Houghton Mifflin.

Pittman, H. C. 1986. *A Grain of Rice.* New York: Bantam Doubleday Dell.

Polya, G. 1948. *How to Solve It.* Princeton, NJ: Princeton University Press.

Reed, K. M. 2000. "How many spots does a cheetah have?" *Teaching Children Mathematics* 6 (6), February, pp. 346–349. Reston, VA: NCTM.

Reys, B. J., K. Chval, S. Dingman, M. McNaught, T. P. Regis, and J. Togashi. 2007. "Grade-level learning expectations: A new challenge for elementary mathematics teachers." *Teaching Children Mathematics* 14 (1), August, pp. 6–11. Reston, VA: NCTM.

Rohm, K. and Spencer, D. L. 2006. *Timonium Elementary Second Graders Bid on Math Success.* Retrieved February 21, 2009 from www.bcps.org/news/2006/Timonium_Elementary.

Rossman, A., B. Chance, and E. Medina. 2006. "Some important comparisons between statistics and mathematics, and why teachers should care." In *Thinking and Reasoning with Data and Chance: 68th NCTM Yearbook,* ed. G. F. Burrill and P. C. Elliott, pp. 323–334. Reston, VA: NCTM.

Russell, S. J. 2006. "What does it mean that '5 has a lot'? From the world to data and back." In *Thinking and Reasoning with Data and Chance: 68th NCTM Yearbook,* ed. G. F. Burrill and P. C. Elliott, pp. 17–30. Reston, VA: NCTM.

Sack, J. and van Niekerk, R. 2009. "Developing the spatial operational capacity of young children using wooden cubes and dynamic simulation software." In *Understanding Geometry for a Changing World: 71st NCTM Yearbook,* ed. T.V. Craine and R. Rubenstein, pp. 141–154. Reston, VA: NCTM.

Sadker, D., and K. Zittleman. 2007. "Gender bias: From colonial America to today's classrooms." In *Multicultural Education: Issues and Perspectives,* 6th ed., ed. J. A. Banks and C. A. M. Banks, pp. 133–164. New York: John Wiley & Sons.

Schaeffer, R. L. 2006. "Statistics and mathematics: On making a happy marriage." In *Thinking and Reasoning with Data and Chance: 68th NCTM Yearbook,* ed. G. F. Burrill and P. C. Elliott, pp. 309–322. Reston, VA: NCTM.

Schattschneider, D. 2009. "Enumerating symmetry types of rectangle and frieze patterns: How Sherlock might have done it." In *Understanding Geometry for a Changing World: 71st NCTM Yearbook,* ed. T.V. Craine and R. Rubenstein, pp. 17–32. Reston, VA: NCTM.

Schifter, D. 2001. "Perspectives from a mathematics educator." In *Center for Education, Knowing and Learning Mathematics for Teaching,* pp. 69–71. Washington, D.C.: National Academies Press.

Schmandt-Besserat, D. 1999. *The History of Counting.* New York: Morrow.

Schwartz, D. M. 1985. *How Much Is a Million?* New York: Lothrop, Lee, and Shepard.

Schwartz, D. M. 1989. *If You Made a Million.* New York: Lothrop, Lee, and Shepard.

Schwartz, D. M. 1999. *If You Hopped Like a Frog.* New York: Scholastic.

Schwartz, D. M. 2001. *On Beyond a Million: An Amazing Math Journey.* New York: Dragonfly.

Schwerdtfeger, J. K., and A. Chan. 2007. "Counting collections." *Teaching Children Mathematics,* 13(7), March, pp. 356–358. Reston, VA: NCTM.

Scieszke, J. 1995. *Math Curse.* New York: Viking.

Seeley, C., and J. F. Schielack. 2007. "A look at the development of rates and proportionality." *Mathematics Teaching in the Middle School,* 13 (3), March, pp. 140–142. Reston, VA: NCTM.

Siebert, D., and N. Gaskin. 2006. "Creating, naming, and justifying fractions." *Teaching Children Mathematics,* 12 (8), April, pp. 394–400. Reston, VA: NCTM.

Siegler, R. S. 2003. "Implications of cognitive science research for mathematics education. In *A Research Companion to Principles and Standards for School Mathematics,* ed. J. Kilpatrick, W. G. Martin, and D. Schifter, pp. 289–303. Reston, VA: NCTM.

Sleeter, C. E., and C. A. Grant. 2009. *Making Choices for Multicultural Education: Five Approaches to Race, Class, and Gender,* 6th ed. New York: John Wiley & Sons.

Smith, D. J. 2002. *If the World Were a Village: A Book about the World's People.* Toronto: Kids Can Press.

Smith, J. P. 2002. "The development of student's knowledge of fractions and ratios." In *Making Sense of Fractions, Ratios, and Proportions, 64th NCTM Yearbook,* ed. Bonnie Litwiller, pp. 3–17. Reston, VA: NCTM.

Soares, J., M. L. Blanton, and J. J. Kaput. 2005–2006. "Thinking algebraically across the elementary school curriculum." *Teaching Children Mathematics* 12 (5), December/January, pp. 228–241. Reston, VA: NCTM.

Stephan, M., and D. H. Clements. 2003. "Linear, area, and time measurement in prekindergarten to grade 2." In *Learning and Teaching Measurement: 65th NCTM Yearbook,* ed. D. H. Clements, pp. 3–16. Reston, VA: NCTM.

Stephan, M., and J. Whitenack. 2003. "Establishing social and sociomathematical norms for problem solving." In *Teaching Mathematics through Problem Solving,* ed. F. K. Lester and R. I. Charles, 149–162. Reston, VA: NCTM.

Strutchens, M. E. 2002. "Multicultural literature as a context for problem solving: Children and parents learning together." *Teaching Children Mathematics,* 8 (8), April, pp. 448–454. Reston, VA: NCTM.

Sun, W., and J. Y. Zhang. 2001. "Teaching addition and subtraction facts: A Chinese perspective." *Teaching Children Mathematics,* September, 8 (1), September, pp. 28–31. Reston, VA: NCTM.

Sweeney, L. 2003. "Listening to one another: Ears open, mouths closed. In *Teaching Mathematics through Problem Solving,* ed. F. K. Lester and R. I. Charles, 123–126. Reston, VA: NCTM.

Taback, S. 1997. *There Was an Old Lady Who Swallowed a Fly.* New York: Viking.

Tang, G. 2001. *The Grapes of Math.* New York: Scholastic.

Tang, G. 2002. *Math for All Seasons.* New York: Scholastic.

Tarr, J. 2002. "Providing opportunities to learn probability concepts." *Teaching Children Mathematics,* 8 (8) April, pp. 482–487. Reston, VA: NCTM.

Tayeh, C. 2005. "What's the overlap?" *Teaching Children Mathematics* 12(1), August, pp. 41–46. Reston, VA: NCTM.

The Mathematics Association of America. 1996. *101 Careers in Mathematics,* ed. A. Sterret. Washington, D.C.: MAA.

Thimmesh, C. 2000. *Girls Think of Everything: Stories of Ingenious Inventions by Women.* Boston: Houghton Mifflin.

Thomas, C. S. 2000. "100 activities for the 100th day." *Teaching Children Mathematics,* 6 (5), January, pp. 276–280. Reston VA: NCTM.

Tompert, A. 1990. *Grandfather Tang's Story: A Tale Told with Tangrams.* New York: Crown.

Tompert, A. 1993. *Just a Little Bit.* Boston: Houghton Mifflin.

Turner, E. E., Celedon-Pattichis, S., Marshall, M., Tennison, A. *"Figense amorcitos, les voy a contra una historia":* The power of story to support solving and discussing mathematical problems among Latino and Latina kindergarten students." In *Mathematics for Every Student: Responding to Diversity. Grades Pre-K–5,* ed. D. Y. White and J. S. Spitzer, pp. 23–42. Reston, VA: NCTM.

van Hiele, P. M. 1999. "Developing geometric thinking through activities that begin with play." *Teaching Children Mathematics* 5 (6), February, pp. 310–316. Reston, VA: NCTM.

Viadero, D. 2004. *In Lesson Study Teachers Polish Their Craft* (February 11). Retrieved from http://www.edweek.org/login. html?source=http://www.edweek.org/ew/articles/2004/02/11/22lesson.h23. html&destination=http://www.edweek.org/ew/articles/2004/02/11/22lesson.h23. html&levelId=2100.

Wallenstein, N. 2004. "Creative discovery through classification." *Teaching Children Mathematics,* 11 (2), September, pp. 103–108. Reston, VA: NCTM.

Warren, E., and T. J. Cooper. 2008. "Patterns that support early algebraic thinking in elementary school." In *Algebra and Algebraic Thinking in School Mathematics: 70th NCTM Yearbook,* ed. C. E. Greenes and R. Rubenstein, pp. 113–126. Reston, VA: NCTM.

Watanabe, T. 2006. "The teaching and learning of fractions: A Japanese perspective." *Teaching Children Mathematics,* March, pp. 368–374. Reston, VA: NCTM.

Weiland, L. 2007. "Experiences to help children learn to count on." *Teaching Children Mathematics* 14 (3), October, pp. 188–192. Reston, VA: NCTM.

Weinglass, J. 2000. "No compromise on equity in mathematics education: Developing an infrastructure." In *Changing the Faces of Mathematics: Perspectives on Multiculturalism and Gender Equity,* ed. W. G. Secada, pp. 5–24. Reston, VA: NCTM.

Wells, R. 1999. *Bingo.* New York: Scholastic.

Wells, R. B. 1993. *Is a Blue Whale the Biggest Thing There Is?* Morton Grove, IL: Albert Whitman.

Wells, R. B. 1997. *What's Faster than a Speeding Cheetah?* Morton Grove, IL: Albert Whitman.

Wheeler, M. M. 2002. "Children's understanding of zero and infinity." In *Putting Research into Practice in the Elementary Grades.* Reston, VA: NCTM.

White, D. Y. 2000. "Reaching all students mathematically through questioning." In *Changing the Faces of Mathematics: Perspectives on African Americans,* ed. M. E. Strutchens, M. L. Johnson, and W. F. Tate, pp. 21–32. Reston, VA: NCTM.

White, D. Y. 2001. "Kenta, kilts, and kimonos: Exploring cultures and mathematics through fabrics." *Teaching Children Mathematics* 7 (6), February, pp. 354–359. Reston, VA: NCTM.

Whitin, D. J. 2004. "Building a mathematical community through problem-posing. In *Perspectives on the Teaching of Mathematics* (66th Yearbook), ed. R. N. Rubinstein, 129–140. Reston: VA: NCTM.

Whitin, D. J., and P. Whitin. 2001. "Linking literature and mathematics in meaningful ways." NCTM Central Regional Conference, Madison, WI.

Whitin, D. J., and P. Whitin. 2004. *New Visions for Linking Literature and Mathematics.* Reston, VA: NCTM.

Wiest, L. R. 2008. "Problem solving support for English language learners." *Teaching Children Mathematics,* 14 (8), pp. 479–484. Reston, VA: NCTM.

Wilkins, M. M., J. L. M. Wilkins, and T. Oliver. 2006. "Differentiating the curriculum for elementary gifted mathematics students." *Teaching Children Mathematics,* 13 (1), August, pp. 6–13. Reston, VA: NCTM.

Willoughby, S. S. 2000. "Perspectives on mathematics education." In *Learning Mathematics for a New Century 2000 Yearbook,* ed. M. J. Burke, pp. 1–15. Reston, VA: NCTM.

Wilson, L. D. 2007. "High-stakes testing in mathematics." In *Second Handbook of Research in Mathematics Teaching and Learning,* ed. F. K. Lester, Jr., pp. 1099–1110. Charlotte, NC: Information Age.

You, Z. 2009. "How students interpret graphs." *Teaching Children Mathematics* 15 (4), pp. 188–190, November. Reston, VA: NCTM.

Yu, P., J. Barrett, and N. Presmeg. 2009. "Prototypes and categorical reasoning: A perspective to explain how children learn about interactive geometry objects." In *Understanding Geometry for a Changing World: 71st Yearbook,* ed. T.V. Craine and R. Rubenstein, pp. 109–126. Reston, VA: NCTM.

Zambo, R. 2008. "Percents can make sense." *Mathematics Teaching in the Middle School,* 13 (7), March, pp. 418–422. Reston, VA: NCTM.

Zaslavsky, C. 1999. *Africa Counts: Number and Pattern in African Cultures.* 3rd ed. Chicago: Lawrence Hill.

Zaslavsky, C. 2000. *Counting on Your Fingers African Style.* New York: Black Butterfly Children's Books.

Zaslavsky, C. 2001. "Developing number sense: What other cultures can tell us." *Teaching Children Mathematics* 7 (6), February, pp. 312–319. Reston, VA: NCTM.

Credits

TEXT, TABLE, AND LINE ART CREDITS

Excerpts from *Common Core State Standards* used by permission. ©Copyright 2010, National Governors Association Center for Best Practices and Council of Chief State School Officers. All rights reserved. Available on line at http://www.corestandards.org.

Excerpts from *Principles and Standards for School Mathematics* used by permission. ©Copyright 2000 by the National Council of Teachers of Mathematics. NCTM does not endorse the content or the validity of these alignments.

Excerpts from *Curriculum Focal Points for Prekindergarten through Grade 8 Mathematics: A Quest for Coherence* used by permission. ©Copyright 2006 by the National Council of Teachers of Mathematics. All rights reserved.

The Curriculum Focal Points identify key mathematical ideas for these grades. They are not discrete topics or a checklist to be mastered; rather, they provide a framework for the majority of instruction at a particular grade level and the foundation for future mathematics study.

Chapter 1

Figure 1.12: Reprinted with permission from *Principles and Standards for School Mathematics*, p. 30, by NCTM. ©Copyright 2000 by the National Council of Teachers of Mathematics. Reproduced with permission of National Council of Teachers of Mathematics.

Chapter 3

Table 3.1: From *Mathematics Teaching Today* by NCTM. ©Copyright 2007 by the National Council of Teachers of Mathematics. Reproduced with permission of the National Council of Teachers of Mathematics. Figure 3.3: Adapted with permission from *Mathematics Teaching Today* by NCTM. ©Copyright 2007 by the National Council of Teachers of Mathematics. Reproduced with permission of the National Council of Teachers of Mathematics. Page 59: Excerpts from *Mathematics Teaching Today* by NCTM. ©Copyright 2007 by the National Council of Teachers of Mathematics. Reproduced with permission of the National Council of Teachers of Mathematics. Figure 3.10: From CONNECTED MATH PROGRAM GRADE 6 PRIME TIME STUDENT EDITION. ©1998 by Michigan State University, Glenda Lappan, James T. Fey, William M. Fitzgerald, Susan N. Friel, and Elizabeth D. Phillips. Used by permission of Pearson Education, Inc. All Rights Reserved. Figure 3.11: Reprinted

with permission from *Navigating through Geometry in Grades 3–5 (Principles and Standards for School Mathematics Navigation Series)* by Gavin, Belkin, Spinelli, St. Marie. ©Copyright 2001 by the National Council of Teachers of Mathematics. Reproduced with permission of the National Council of Teachers of Mathematics.

Chapter 4

Page 91: Excerpt from Karp, K., and P. Howell. Building responsibility for learning in students with special needs. *Teaching Children Mathematics* (October 2004). ©Copyright 2004 by the National Council of Teachers of Mathematics. Reproduced with permission of the National Council of Teachers of Mathematics. Figure 4.7a: From *Math Trailblazers*, 3rd Edition by the TIMS PROJECT. ©Copyright 2008 by Kendall Hunt Publishing Company. Reprinted with permission. Figure 4.7b: From INVESTIGATIONS STUDENT ACTIVITY BOOK GRADE 3. ©Copyright 2008 Pearson Education, Inc., or its affiliates. Used by permission. All Rights Reserved. Figure 4.8: From MathConnects 1. ©Copyright 2009 Macmillan/McGraw Hill. Used by permission of The McGraw-Hill Companies.

Chapter 5

Pages 113 and 114: Excerpts from Multicultural education: Characteristics and goals. In *Multicultural Education: Issues and Perspectives.* 6th ed. Eds. Banks, J. A. and Banks, C. A. M. 2007. New York: John Wiley & Sons. Reprinted with permission of John Wiley & Sons, Inc. Page 122: Lesson, three sand drawings: Adapted from Zaslavsky, C. African Networks and African American Students. In *Changing the Faces of Mathematics: Perspectives on African Americans.* Eds. Strutchens, M. E., M. L. Johnson, W. F. Tate. p. 158. ©Copyright 2000 by the National Council of Teachers of Mathematics. Adapted with permission of the National Council of Teachers of Mathematics.

Chapter 6

Page 146: Lesson, drawing of Loh-Shu: Adapted with permission of the artist, Linda Braatz-Brown, University of California, Riverside. Figure 6.7: TinkerPlots®, Key Curriculum Press, 1150 65th Street, Emeryville, CA 94608, 1–800–995–MATH, www.keypress.com. Page 153: Excerpt from Wiest, L. R. Problem-Solving Support for English Language Learners. *Teaching Children Mathematics* 14 (8) (April 2008). ©Copyright 2008 by the National Council of Teachers of Mathematics. Reproduced

with permission of the National Council of Teachers of Mathematics.

Chapter 8

Page 193: Multicultural Perspectives in Mathematics, Egyptian numerals chart: Adapted from Heddens, Speer, and Brahler. 2009. *Today's Mathematics: Concepts, Methods, and Classroom Activities* 12th ed., p. 131. Reprinted with permission of John Wiley & Sons, Inc.

Chapter 12

Figure 12.9: From *Teaching Children Mathematics* by Cramer, Monson, Wyberg, Leavitt, and Whitney. ©Copyright 2009 by the National Council of Teachers of Mathematics. Reproduced with permission of the National Council of Teachers of Mathematics.

Chapter 13

Page 322: Excerpts from Lanius, C. S. and Williams, S. E. Proportionality: A unifying theme for the middle grades. In *Mathematics Teaching in the Middle School* 8 (8) April 2003. ©Copyright 2003 by the National Council of Teachers of Mathematics. Reproduced with permission of the National Council of Teachers of Mathematics. Page 333: Multicultural Perspectives in Mathematics, drawing: Adapted from Giamati, C. Ratio. 2002. Proportion, Similarity, and Navajo Students. In *Changing the Faces of Mathematics: Perspectives on Indigenous People of North America*. Eds. Hankes, J. E., and Fast, G. R. ©Copyright 2002 by the National Council of Teachers of Mathematics. Reproduced with permission of the National Council of Teachers of Mathematics. Figure 13.8: Adapted from Zambo, R. Percents can make sense. *Mathematics Teaching in the Middle School* 13 (7) March 2008, pp. 418–422. ©Copyright 2008 by the National Council of Teachers of Mathematics. Reproduced with permission of the National Council of Teachers of Mathematics.

Chapter 15

Activity 15.5, drawing: From Developing Geometric Thinking Through Activities That Begin With Play. In *Teaching Children Mathematics*. February 1999, p. 312. ©Copyright 1999 by the National Council of Teachers of Mathematics. Reproduced with permission of the National Council of Teachers of Mathematics.

Chapter 16

Activity 16.10, drawing: Adapted from McDuffie, A. R. and Eve, N. Breaking the Area

Boundaries. *In Teaching Children Mathematics.* August 2009, p. 23. ©Copyright 2009 by the National Council of Teachers of Mathematics. Reproduced with permission of the National Council of Teachers of Mathematics.

Chapter 17

Figure 17.15: ©Copyright 1995–2010, The Weather Channel Interactive, Inc. weather. com®. Page 464: What is happening in this picture?: ©Copyright 1995–2010, The Weather Channel Interactive, Inc. weather. com®.

PHOTO CREDITS

Chapter 1

Page 2: Eddy Lund/iStockphoto; Page 4 (left): SuperStock; Page 4 (center): Cultura Limited/SuperStock; Page 4 (right): Radius/SuperStock; Page 5 (left): Lowe Art Museum/SuperStock; Page 5 (right): Glow Images /SuperStock; Page 5 (bottom): Image Asset Management, Ltd./SuperStock; Page 6: COUNTING ON FRANK by Rod Clement. Reproduced with permission from Rosen Publishing, NY.; Page 8 (top): Photononstop/SuperStock; Page 8 (bottom): Glow Images /SuperStock; Page 9 (top left): Museum of Natural Sciences, Brussels, Belgium.; Page 9 (bottom left): Ingram Publishing /SuperStock; Page 9 (right): Erich Lessing/Art Resource; Page 10: age fotostock/SuperStock; Page 11 (left): Courtesy IUCAA, Pune; Page 11 (center): Galleria dell 'Accademia, Venice/Bridgeman Art Library/SuperStock; Page 11 (top right): Pixtal/SuperStock; Page 11 (bottom right): Science and Society/SuperStock; Page 11 (bottom): ∏ Vicente Barcelo Varona/iStockphoto; Page 13: Library of Congress; Page 16: Bob Daemmrich/PhotoEdit Page 20: Jacket Cover from A GRAIN OF RICE by Helena Pittman. Used by permission of Yearling, an imprint of Random House Children s Books, a division of Random House, Inc.; Page 22: Jim West/Alamy; Page 23: Radius /SuperStock; Page 24: Library of Congress; Page 25: Jim West/Alamy; Page 26: Museum of Natural Sciences, Brussels, Belgium.; Page 26: Paul Conklin /PhotoEdit; Page 27 (top): Bob Daemmrich/PhotoEdit; Page 27 (bottom): Jim West/Alamy

Chapter 2

Page 28: William A. Bake/∏Corbis; Page 36 (left): Steven L. Raymer/NG Image Collection; Page 36 (right): Bryan & Cherry Alexander Photography/Alamy; Page 37: Jiang Jin/SuperStock; Page 38 (left):

Science and Society/SuperStock; Page 38 (right): Bruce McGowan/Alamy; Page 39 (left): Jim West/PhotoEdit; Page 39 (right): Olivier Ribardiere/Getty Images, Inc.; Page 39 (bottom): Photo of Paul Erdîs by George Csicsery from his documentary film N is a Number: A Portrait of Paul Erdîs© 1993 All Rights Reserved.; Page 40 (top right): Radius/SuperStock; Page 40 (bottom left): Andersen Ross/Blend Images/Getty Images, Inc.; Page 40 (bottom right): Image Source/SuperStock; Page 42: Mark Edward Atkinson/Blend Images/Getty Images, Inc.; Page 43: SuperStock; Page 45 (bottom left): THE MATH CURSE by Jon Scieszka, illustrated by Lane Smith. Reproduced with permission from Penguin Group USA, Inc.; Page 46 (top left): Will Hart/PhotoEdit; Page 46 (top right): Avril O'Reilly/Alamy; Page 46 (bottom left): Ellen Senisi/The Image Works; Page 46 (bottom right): Monika Graff/The Image Works; Page 49 (top left): Jim West/PhotoEdit; Page 49 (bottom left): Radius/SuperStock; Page 49 (bottom right): Ellen Senisi/The Image Works; Page 50: Richard Hutchings/PhotoEdit; Page 51 (left): Jiang Jin/SuperStock; Page 51 (right): Mark Edward Atkinson/Blend Images/Getty Images, Inc.

Chapter 3

Page 53 (top right): Library of Congress; Page 53: Exactostock/SuperStock; Page 54: SOMOS/SuperStock; Page 55: Justin Guariglia/NG Image Collection; Page 56: David Butow/∏Corbis; Page 57: SOMOS/SuperStock; Page 61 (left): SuperStock; Page 61 (right): Couretsy MathCounts; Page 62 (left): image100/SuperStock; Page 62 (right): SuperStock; Page 64: Blend Images/SuperStock; Page 65: Michael Newman/PhotoEdit; Page 66: Jose Luis Pelaez Inc/Getty Images, Inc.; Page 67 (top left): Jacket Cover from ON BEYOND A MILLION by David M. Schwartz. Used by permission of Doubleday, an imprint of Random House Children s Books, a division of Random House, Inc.; Page 67 (center): DINNER AT THE PANDA PALACE by Stephanie Calmenson. Illustrated by Nadine Bernard Westcott. Used by permission of Harper-Collins Publishers.; Page 67 (bottom left): THE DOORBELL RANG by Pat Hutchins. Copyright© 1986 by Pat Hutchins. Used by permission of HarperCollins Publishers.; Page 71: Ellen B. Senisi/The Image Works; Page 72: Cusp/SuperStock; Page 74: Blend Images/SuperStock; Page 75 (top): SOMOS/SuperStock; Page 75 (bottom left): SuperStock; Page 75 (bottom left): SuperStock; Page 75 (bottom right): Jacket Cover from ON BEYOND A MILLION by

David M. Schwartz. Used by permission of Doubleday, an imprint of Random House Children s Books, a division of Random House, Inc.; Page 76: Blend Images/SuperStock; Page 78: Bill Aron/PhotoEdit; Page 79: Blend Images/SuperStock

Chapter 4

Page 80: Al Bello/Staff/Getty Images, Inc.; Page 80: Ezra Shaw /Getty Images, Inc.; Page 82: Spencer Grant/PhotoEdit; Page 83: Michael Newman/PhotoEdit; Page 88: Exactostock/SuperStock; Page 89 (left): Radius/SuperStock; Page 89 (right): Blend Images/SuperStock; Page 90: Kamin Bonnie/Index Stock/Alamy; Page 93: Cindy Charles/Photoedit; Page 93 (top left): Alex Mares-Manton /Asia Images/Getty Images, Inc.; Page 93 (bottom right): Cindy Charles/Photoedit; Page 93 (bottom right): Lenscap/Alamy; Page 93 (bottom left): IndexStock/SuperStock; Page 93 (top right): Michael Newman/PhotoEdit; Page 99 (left): Ellen B. Senisi/The Image Works; Page 99 (right): Bob Daemmrich/Photedit; Page 105 (left): Spencer Grant/PhotoEdit; Page 105 (right): Blend Images/SuperStock: Page 108: Richard Hutchings/PhotoEdit; Page 109: Exactostock /SuperStock

Chapter 5

Page 110: Courtesy Joan Jones; Page 113 (right): Image Source/SuperStock; Page 113 (left): Gabe Palmer/∏Corbis; Page 113 (left): Jeremy Edwards/iStockphoto; Page 113 (top right): AFP PHOTO/Mike Clark/NewsCom; Page 113 (bottom right): Alex Wong /Getty Images, Inc.; Page 115 (top): IndexStock/SuperStock; Page 115 (center): Robert Harding Picture Library/SuperStock; Page 115 (bottom): Alamy; Page 114: Alex Wong/Getty Images, Inc.; Page 117: Will & Deni McIntyre/∏Corbis; Page 120 (left): NewsCom; Page 120 (top right): ∏AP/Wide World Photos; Page 120 (bottom right): Robert Harding Picture Library/SuperStock; Page 121 (top right): Book cover from THE BLACK SNOWMAN by Phil Mendez, illustrations by Carole Byard. Illustration copyright© 1989 by Carole Byard. Reprinted by permission of Scholastic Inc.; Page 121 (center): From MOJA MEANS ONE: SWAHILI COUNTING BOOK by Muriel Feelings, copyright© 1971 by Muriel Feelings. Used by permission of Dial Books for Young Readers, A Division of Penguin Young Readers Group, A Member of Penguin Group USA, Inc. 345 Hudson St. New York, NY 10014. All rights reserved.; Page 121 (bottom right): EVERYBODY BAKES BREAD by Norah Dooley with illustrations by Peter J. Thornton. Illustrations copyright

From A MILLION FISH...MORE OR LESS by Patricia McKissack, copyright© 1992 by Patricia C. McKissack. Illustrations copyright© 1992 by Dena Schutzer. Used by permission of Alfred A. Knopf, an imprint of Random House Children s Books, a division of Random House, Inc.

Chapter 11

Page 277: Myrleen Ferguson Cate/PhotoEdit; Page 281: NG Maps; Page 283 (top): Illustration from EATING FRACTIONS by Bruce McMillan. Copyright© 1991 by Bruce McMillan. Reprinted by permission of Scholastic Inc.; Page 283 (bottom): Copyright© 1994 by Loreen Leedy. Reprinted from FRACTION ACTION by permission of Holiday House.; Page 288: Illustration from INCHWORM AND A HALF by Elinor J. Pinczes, illustrated by Randall Enos. Illustrations copyright© 2001 by Randall Enos. Reprinted by permission of Houghton Mifflin Harcourt Publishing Company. All rights reserved.

Chapter 12

Page 303: AFP/Staff/Getty Images, Inc.; Page 304: Natalia Bratslavsky/iStockphoto; Page 306: Material from IF THE WORLD WERE A VILLAGE is used by permission of Kids Can Press Ltd., Toronto, Canada. Text© 2002 David J. Smith. Illustrations© 2002 Shelagh Armstrong.; Page 310: Florence Delva/Getty Images, Inc.; Page 313: Alf Ertsland/iStockphoto; Page 316: Natalia Bratslavsky/iStockphoto

Chapter 13

Page 321: Michael Neelon/Alamy; Page 324 (left): Ann Cutting/Getty Images, Inc.; Page 324 (center): Ronnie Kaufman/Getty Images, Inc.; Page 324 (right): Wonderlust Industries/Getty Images, Inc.; Page 327 (left): TODD GIPSTEIN/NG Images; Page 327 (right): Jeremy Edwards/iStockphoto; Page 236 (left): Jozsef L. Szentpeteri/NG Images; Page 326 (center): Clare Hooper/Alamy; Page 326 (right): Ryan Lane/iStockphoto; Page 328: SIR CUMFERENCE AND THE DRAGON OF PI. Text copyright© 1999 by Cindy Neuschwander. Illustrations copyright© 1999 Wayne Geehan. Used with permission by Charlesbridge Publishing, Inc. All rights reserved.; Page 330 (top): Cover of WHAT'S FASTER THAN A SPEEDING CHEETAH? by Robert E. Wells. Published by Albert Whitman & Company.; Page 330 (bottom): Book cover from IF YOU HOPPED LIKE A FROG by David Schwartz, illustrated by James Warhola. Cover illustration copyright© 1999 by James Warhola.

Reprinted by permission of Scholastic Inc.; Page 340: Joel Zatz/Alamy; Page 341: Ronnie Kaufman/Getty Images, Inc.

Chapter 14

Page 342: Michael Newman/PhotoEdit; Page 344: SuperStock; Page 346: Rogelio Solis/∏AP/Wide World Photos; Page 353: EXACTLY THE OPPOSITE by Tana Hoban. Used by permission of HarperCollins Publishers.; Page 357 (top): Book cover from BINGO by Rosemary Wells. Copyright© 1999 by Rosemary Wells. Reprinted by permission of Scholastic Inc.; Page 357 (bottom): THE WAS AN OLD LADY WHO SWALLOWED A FLY by Simms Taback. Reproduced with permission from Penguin Group USA, Inc.; Page 359: ANNO S MAGIC SEEDS by Mitsumas Anno. Reprinted with permission from Penguin Group USA, Inc.; Page 364: SuperStock; Page 365: EXACTLY THE OPPOSITE by Tana Hoban. Used by permission of HarperCollins Publishers.; Page 367: Justin Guariglia/NG Images

Chapter 15

Page 368: Loren Rye/Alamy; Page 374: SO MANY CIRCLES, SO MANY SQUARES by Tana Hoban. Copyright© 1998 Tana Hoban. Used by permission of Harper Collins Publishers.; Page 376 (left): Book Cover, copyright© 1990 by Crown Publishers, from GRANDFATHER TANG S STORY by Ann Tompert, illustrated by Robert Andrew Parker. Used by permission of Crown Publishers, an imprint of Random House Children s Books, a division of Random House, Inc.; Page 376 (right): Book Cover, copyright© 1990 by Crown Publishers, from GRANDFATHER TANG S STORY by Ann Tompert, illustrated by Robert Andrew Parker. Used by permission of Crown Publishers, an imprint of Random House Children s Books, a division of Random House, Inc.; Page 381: Mary Kate Denny/PhotoEdit; Page 391 (center): Pattie Steib/iStockphoto; Page 391 (top right): Pattie Steib/iStockphoto; Page 390: Illustration from A CLOAK FOR THE DREAMER by Aileen Friedman. Copyright© 1995 by Marilyn Burns Associates. Reprinted by permission of Scholastic Inc.; Page 392: M.C. Escher Company, The; Page 398: M.C. Escher Company, The; Page 400: Lowe Art Museum /SuperStock

Chapter 16

Page 402: NewsCom; Page 408 (left): Edward S. Curtis/∏Corbis; Page 408 (right): RICH REID/NG Imges; Page 413: Used with permission by Charlesbridge

Publishing, Inc. All rights reserved.; Page 409: Cover of MEASURING PENNY by Loreen Leedy. Cover illustration copyright© 1998 by Loreen Leedy. Reprinted by arrangement with Henry Holt and Company.; Page 417: Book cover from SPAGHETTI AND MEATBALLS FOR ALL by Marilyn Burns, illustrations by Debbie Tilley. Copyright© 1997 by Marilyn Burns Associates. Reprinted by permission of Scholastic Inc.; Page 427: Arne Hodalic/∏Corbis; Page 428 (left): Martin McCarthy/iStockphoto; Page 428 (right): Claudio Baldini/iStockphoto; Page 430: Claudio Baldini/iStockphoto; Page 432: Richard Hutchings/PhotoEdit

Chapter 17

Page 434: Bill Aron/PhotoEdit; Page 436: Radius Images/SuperStock; Page 439: David Young-Wolff /PhotoEdit; Page 440 (left): Spencer Platt/Getty Images, Inc.; Page 441: NG Maps; Page 441: Library of Congress; Page 447: Graph from TIGER MATH by Ann Whitehead Nagda and Cindy Bickel. Graph copyright© 2000 by Ann Whitehead Nagda. Reprinted by arrangement with Henry Holt and Company.; Page 456: Michael Newman/PhotoEdit; Page 455: Cover of IT S PROBABLY PENNY by Loreen Leedy. Cover illustration copyright© 2007 by Loreen Leedy. Reprinted by arrangement with Henry Holt and Company.; Page 461 (top left): Radius Images/SuperStock; Page 461 (bottom left): David Young-Wolff/PhotoEdit; Page 461 (top right): Spencer Platt/Getty Images, Inc.

Appendix A

Reprinted with permission from *Principles and Standards for School Mathematics*. ©Copyright 2000 by the National Council of Teachers of Mathematics. NCTM does not endorse the content or the validity of these alignments.

Appendix B

Reprinted with permission from *Curriculum Focal Points for Prekindergarten through Grade 8 Mathematics: A Quest for Coherence*. ©Copyright 2006 by the National Council of Teachers of Mathematics. All rights reserved. The Curriculum Focal Points identify key mathematical ideas for these grades. They are not discrete topics or a checklist to be mastered; rather, they provide a framework for the majority of instruction at a particular grade level and the foundation for future mathematics study.

Index

Explicit trading, 192
Explorations, 84
Expressions, algebraic, 350–351
Extreme values, 451

F

Fabrics, use of, 124
Faces, 372
Fact families, 238, 239
Factors, 18t, 58, 59, 70f, 87, 226f, 228, 230,
    233, 239–241, 258f, 260–261, 261f,
    262f, 266f, 270, 293, 310, 312, 313,
    334, 335
common factors, 120f, 291
factors and multiples, 309
sociocultural, 151
Factual knowledge, 32, 32f
Fahrenheit conversions, 409
Fairness, 457
Familiar fractions and decimals,
    309–310, 310f
Family members, engaging in education,
    126–127
Fibonacci, Leonard, 264
Fibonacci sequence, 4, 326–327
Field dependence, 113–114
Filtering, 63f
Finger counting in Africa, 178–179
Five-frames, 181, 187, 196f
Five Little Monkeys Jumping on the Bed, 175
"Five-ness", 177
Fleming, Alexander, 38f
Flips, 389–390, 389f
Formal proportional reasoning, 323
Formative assessment, 98–99
Formulas, area, 415–416
Four-point holistic rubric, 104
Fractal geometry, 11, 11f
Fraction Action, 283
Fraction strips, 58, 286–287
Fractions
    addition and subtraction and,
        293–294, 293f
    base-ten fractions, 304–306, 305f
    comparing and ordering of, 285–286
    comparing unit fractions, 287–288
    connecting with decimals and
        percents, 335
    denominator, 285, 287, 288t, 289, 291,
        293, 294f, 304, 313, 331, 334
    difficulty learning and, 278
    division of, 296–297
    equivalent fractions, 285, 289–291
    familiar fractions and decimals,
        309–310, 310f
    finding equal shares and, 281–283
    finding meaning for, 279, 279f
    fraction operations, 291–292
    greatest common factor and, 291
    improper fractions, 284, 294, 294f
    iterating fractions, 283–284

language and symbolism, 184–185
learning computation informally, 292f
making fraction strips, 286–287
mistakes with size of parts, 278f
mixed numbers, 284
models for understanding, 280, 280f
multiplication of, 295–296, 295f
numerator, 285
ordering, 285–286
sharing equally, 282f, 283
simplest terms and, 291
strategies for comparing, 288t
tools for addition of, 47f
unit fractions, comparing, 287–288
Franklin, Benjamin, 147
Frieze patterns, 390–391
Front-end estimation, 268–269
Functional relationships, 331
Functions
    algebraic reasoning and, 345
    domain of, 360
    in everyday life, 361
    graphing functions, 362–363
    linear functions, 362–364
    multiple representations and, 361
    range of, 360

G

Gardner, Howard, 34
Gender equity
    elementary and middle-grade classroom
        strategies and, 130–131
    evolution of, 128f–129f
    twenty-first century and, 130, 130t
Generalizations, variables as, 349
Geoboards, 46f, 375
Geometer's Sketchpad, 379
Geometric thought, 370, 371f, 377
Geometry
    distance between two points,
        386–387
    finding slopes, 386–387
    hexagons, 392, 392f
    illustrating patterns with, 358f
    importance of, 370
    location (grades 3-5), 385
    location (grades 6-8), 386
    location (prekindergarten through
        grade 2), 384
    multicultural connections and, 120f
    obtuse angle, 377f
    platonic solids, 396, 396f
    polygons, 377, 377f, 381
    proportional reasoning and, 332–333
    shapes and properties (grades 3-5),
        376–381
    shapes and properties (grades 6-8),
        382–383
    shapes and properties (prekindergarten
        through grade 2), 372–376
software, 379

Standard (NCTM), 122
    transformations (grades 3-5), 390–392
    transformations (grades 6-8), 393
    transformations (prekindergarten
        through grade 2), 388–389
    using problem solving in, 141f
    van Hiele's mosaic puzzle and,
        370, 371f
    visualization (grades 3-5), 394–395
    visualization (grades 6-8), 395–396
    visualization (prekindergarten through
        grade 2), 393–394
Geometry Simon Says, 381
Gifted students, 92, 118–119
Golden ratio, 326
Golden rectangle, 326–327, 327f
Goodman, Nelson, 34
Grade-level learning expectations
    (GLEs), 22
*Grandfather Tang's Story: A Tale Told with
    Tangrams*, 376
Graphics, interpretation of, 448–449
Graphing calculators, 69, 332, 344, 448
Graphs
    circle graphs, 444–445, 445f
    with continuous data, 445–447
    creating and interpreting, 361
    graphing functions, 362–363
    histograms, 446, 447f
    line plots, 446, 447f
    literature and, 447
    proportional relationships and, 332
    scatter plots, 448, 448f
    stem-and-leaf plots, 445–446, 446f
    tally marks and bar graphs, 442–443,
        442f, 443f
Great Divide: A Mathematical Marathon, 145
Greatest common factor (GCF), 291
Group accountability, 89, 89f
Groupable base-ten models, 200, 200f
Grouping facts activity, 161
Grouping
    for instruction, 88–89
    in learning place value, 192
Growing patterns, 356f, 358–359
Guess and Check strategy, 154

H

Heuristics, 140
Hexagons, 392, 392f
High-stakes testing, 74–75
Hindu-Arabic numeration system,
    192–193
Histograms, 446, 447f
Hit the bull's-eye activity, 271
Holistic rubrics, 104–105, 104f
Homework, 103
Hundreds chart, 60, 191, 197,
    204–205, 254
Hurricane simulations, 460, 461f
Hypotheses, 34, 167

Part-to-whole ratios, 324f
Partial differences algorithm, 257, 257f
Partial products algorithm, 266, 266f
Partial quotients algorithm, 266, 266f
Partial sums algorithm for addition,
    256, 256f
Partitioning, 411
Partitioning fractions, 283
Partitive division, 225, 261f
Patterns
    characteristics of, 169–170
    geometric designs and, 358f
    growing patterns, 358–359
    literature and, 357
    multiplication and division facts and, 239
    with numbers, 175
    pattern blocks, 46f, 375
    in real world, 5, 5f
    repeating patterns, 357–358
    sequences, 360, 360t
    types of, 356–357, 356f
Peer collaboration, 39
Peer tutoring, 39, 72
Percents
    connecting with fractions and
        decimals, 335
    estimating visually, 336f
    learning in fourth grade, 335
    models for, 334f
    representing on 10 x 10 grid, 334
    solving percent problems, 336–337, 337f
    teaching, 335–336
    understanding, 334–335
    using calculator to find, 335
    visual approach to, 337f
Perceptual subitizing, 166
Perimeter
    area relationship and, 416–418
    definition of, 410
    finding of, 412–413
    similar figures and, 418
Perpendicular lines, 379
Pi, 9, 32f, 328, 413, 420f
Piaget, Jean, 34
Place value
    base-ten notation and, 198, 198f
    characteristics of, 192
    charts, 312f
    children's difficulties with, 205–206
    comparing magnitude of numbers, 207
    concrete place value models,
        198–201, 199f
    decomposing and composing numbers
        using models, 196, 196f
    early place value ideas, 195–198
    equivalent representations and, 195–196
    extending, 307–309, 308f
    Hindu-Arabic system and, 192–193
    hundreds chart and, 204–205
    learning about thousands, 207–208
    mats, 203, 207, 207f, 208, 213, 255f, 256,
        262f, 309
    millions and billions, 208, 210–211

modeling large numbers, 207f
models for, 198–201, 199f
nonproportional models, 198, 199f
pre-base-ten ideas and, 194–195, 194f
pregrouped base-ten models, 200, 201f
proportional models, 198–199, 199f
regrouping and trading and, 197
reversing digits and, 2095
rounding and, 209, 209t
special needs children and, 201
teaching, 202–203, 202f
technology use and, 200
teen numbers and, 206
thousands chart, 208
using base-ten blocks and, 209
Place value mats, 203, 207f
Planning
    daily planning, 83
    diversity and, 90–93
    lesson planning, 84–90
    unit planning, 82
    yearly planning, 82, 82f
Platonic solids, 396, 396f
Polygons, 377, 377f, 381
    regular hexagon, 392, 392f
    regular polygon, 392
    rhombus, 382
Populations, data, 441
Portfolios, 103, 103f
Positive attitudes, 62
Pre-base-ten ideas, 194–195, 194f
Pre-number concepts
    classification, 167–168, 167f
    more, less, and the same, 168–169, 168f
    patterns, 169–170
    subitizing, 166–167, 166f
Pregrouped base-ten models, 200, 201f
Primary Krypto, 271
Prime factorization, 18
Prime numbers, 44, 60–61
*Principles and Standards for School
    Mathematics*, 14–19
    Assessment Principle, 17
    Communication Standard, 19
    Connections Standard, 19
    Content Standards, 17–18, 17f, 18t
    Curriculum Principle, 16
    Equity Principle, 16
    Learning Principle, 17
    Problem Solving Standard, 18
    Process Standards, 18–19
    Reasoning and Proof Standard, 19
    Representation Standard, 19
    Teaching Principle, 16
    Technology Principle, 17
Prior knowledge, student's, 16
Prism, 380, 380f, 380t
Prism volumes, 420, 420f
Probability
    characteristics of, 453–457
    children's misconceptions about, 455f
    flipping a coin and, 454
    independent and dependent events, 459

likelihood of events, 453, 456–457
literature and, 455
simulations, 460, 461f
spinning for colors and, 454
theoretical and experimental, 458–459
Problem posing, 144–145
Problem solving
    addressing difficulties in, 152
    beliefs and affect and, 151
    benefits of, 140–141
    changing context in, 152
    changing mathematics in, 152
    choosing effective problems, 144, 144f
    developing lessons and, 145
    English-language learners and, 152–153
    factors influencing success in, 151
    geometry and, 141f
    heuristics, 140
    how much to explain in, 150
    nonroutine problems, 140
    planning for, 143
    prior knowledge and, 151
    problem posing, 144–145
    problems defined, 138–140
    process of, 142–143, 142f
    in real world, 138f, 139–140
    routine problems, 140
    self-regulation and, 151
    sociocultural factors and, 151
    Standard (NCTM), 18
    story problems, 140
    teaching mathematics through, 140
    using multiple strategies in,
        158–159, 158f
    using technology in, 148–149
Problem solving strategies
    Act It Out strategy and, 154
    Draw a Diagram strategy, 157
    Guess and Check strategy, 154
    Look for a Pattern strategy, 157
    Make a Table strategy, 156
    Solve a Simpler Problem strategy, 155
    Work Backwards strategy, 156
Procedural knowledge, 32–33, 32f
Professional development, 83, 116, 144
Proficiency areas, teacher, 56t
Project IMPACT, 64
Proof, 19
Proportional models, 198–199, 199f
Proportional reasoning
    children's development of, 323
    distances on map, 322f
    formal proportional reasoning, 323
    importance of, 322
    informal reasoning about proportional
        situations, 323
    understanding of, 322
Proportions
    algebra and, 331–332
    cross multiplication and, 331
    equivalent ratios, 329
    geometry and measurement and,
        332–333

9 780470 450314